PRINCIPLES OF REAL ESTATE PRACTICE IN OKLAHOMA

First Edition

Stephen Mettling
David Cusic
Ryan Mettling

PERFORMANCE PROGRAMS COMPANY

Material in this book is not intended to represent legal advice and should not be so construed. Readers should consult legal counsel for advice regarding points of law.

6810 190th Street East, Bradenton, FL
www.performanceprogramscompany.com

ISBN: 978-1965482650

Table of Contents

Section I: National Principles, Practices and Laws

1 **The Real Estate Business** **7**
Real Estate Professions 7
Real Estate Brokerage 10
Professional Organizations 12
Regulation And Licensing 14

2 **Rights In Real Estate** **16**
Real Estate As Property 16
Real Versus Personal Property 23
Regulation Of Real Property Interests 25

3 **Interests And Estates** **29**
Interests And Estates In Land 29
Freehold Estates 31
Leasehold Estates 36

4 **Ownership** **39**
Sole Ownership 39
Co-Ownership 39
Estates In Trust 45
Ownership By Business Entities 47
Condominiums 48
Cooperatives 51
Time-Shares 53

5 **Encumbrances And Liens** **55**
Encumbrances 55
Easements 56
Encroachments 61
Licenses 61
Deed Restrictions 61
Liens 62
Foreclosure 68

6 **Transferring & Recording Title To Real Estate** **73**
Title To Real Estate 73
Deeds Of Conveyance 75
Wills 80
Involuntary Title Transfer 83
Title Records 84

7 **Leasing Essentials** **90**
The Lease Contract 90
Types of Lease 94
Default And Termination 96
Uniform Residential Landlord And Tenant Act (Urlta) 98
Real Estate Planning 101
Public Land Use Control 104
Private Land Use Control 111
Environmental Controls 112

9 **Legal Descriptions** **120**
Methods of Legal Description 120
Metes And Bounds 121
The Rectangular Survey System 123
Recorded Plat Method 126
Describing Elevation 127

10 **Fundamentals Of Contract Law** **130**
Contract Validity And Enforceability 130
Contract Creation 135
Classifications Of Contracts 138
Contract Termination 139

11 **National Agency** **142**
The Agency Relationship 142
Fiduciary Duties 144
Forms of Real Estate Agency 148
Agency Disclosure Rules 153

12 **Listing Agreements: An Overview** **157**
Review of Legal Foundations 157
Types of Listing Agreement 159
Fulfillment and Termination 162
Listing Agreement Clauses 166

13 **General Brokerage Practices** **175**
Function And Organization 175
The Broker-Salesperson Relationship 181
Operating a Real Estate Brokerage 185
Business Brokerage 193

14 **Overview Of Conveyance Contracts** **199**
Contract For Sale 199
Sale Contract Provisions 202
Option-To-Buy Contract 206
Contract For Deed 208

15 **Real Estate Market Economics** **212**
The Market System 212
Real Estate Market Dynamics 216

16 **Appraising And Estimating Market Value** **224**
Real Estate Value 224
Appraising Market Value 228
The Sales Comparison Approach 231
The Cost Approach 238
The Income Capitalization Approach 242
Regulation of Appraisal Practice 247

17 **Real Estate Finance** **250**
Anatomy of Mortgage Lending 250
Initiating a Mortgage Loan 256
Qualifying For a Mortgage Loan 258
Closing a Loan 266
Laws Affecting Mortgage Lending 266
The Mortgage Market 268
Types of Real Estate Loans 273

18 **Real Estate Investment** **282**
Investment Fundamentals 282
Real Estate as an Investment 285
Real Estate Investment Entities 286
Taxation of Real Estate Investments 287
Investment Analysis of a Residence 289
Investment Analysis of an Income Property 292

19 **Real Estate Taxation** **298**
Taxing Entities 298
Ad Valorem Taxation 299
Special Assessments 302
Tax Lien Enforcement 303

20 **Professional Practices** **306**
Fair Housing Laws 306
Property Disclosures 312
Other Professional Practices 324

21 **Closings** **330**
The Closing Event 330
Real Estate Settlement Procedures Act (Respa) 333
Financial Settlement Of The Transaction 335
Computing Prorations 339
Taxes Due At Closing 341
Closing Cost Itemization: Case Illustration 342
Tila/Respa Integrated Disclosure Rule 345

22 **Risk Management** **359**
Risk Management Strategies 359
Risk Management Procedures 361
Primary Areas of Risk 365

23 **Property Management** **381**
Management Functions 381
The Management Agreement 389
Leasing Considerations 393
The Management Business 398

24 **Real Estate Mathematics** **402**
Real Estate Mathematics: Answer Key 428

Section II: Oklahoma Principles, Practices and Laws

25 **The Oklahoma Regulatory Environment** **429**
Authority of The Real Estate Commission 429
Licensed Activities: Acts of The Associates 429
Prohibited Activities And Causes For Discipline 429
The Complaint And Disciplinary Process 429
The Oklahoma Real Estate Education And Recovery Fund 429
Orec Notification Requirements 429
Authority of The Real Estate Commission 429
The Commission and Its Members 429
Powers and Duties 429
Two Bodies Of Law: Code And Rules 429
Licensed Activities: Acts of the Associates 430
Prohibited Activities And Causes For Discipline 432
The Complaint And Disciplinary Process 433
The Oklahoma Real Estate 434
Education And Recovery Fund 434
OREC Notification Requirements 436

26 **Oklahoma Licensing** **439**
Who Must Hold a License 439
Salesperson License Requirements 441
Broker and Broker Associate Requirements 442
Business Entity Licensing 444
Licensing Nonresidents 445
License Renewals and Continuing Education 446
License Transfer to a New Broker 448
License Types and Statuses 449

27 **The Oklahoma Broker Relationships Act** **453**
Definitions 453
Brokerage Service Agreements 454
Services Provided To The Parties 456
Duties Owed To All Parties 457
Duties Owed To The Party Served 458
Disclosure of Duties And Services 460
Disclosure of The Licensee's 461
Status and Interest 461
Broker-Salesperson Relationship 462
And Compensation 462

28 **Regulation of Brokerage Practices** **467**
Advertising Regulation 467
Unlicensed Assistants and Licensed Activity 469
The Line Between Licensed and Unlicensed Activity 469
What Unlicensed Assistants May And May Not Do 469
The Broker Remains Responsible 469
Broker Supervision 470
The Duty To Supervise 470
Ensuring Associates are Licensed and Supervised 470
Practical Supervision 470
Env Place of Business Requirements 471
Maintaining a Place of Business 471
Office Identification and The Home Office 471
Branch Offices 471
Change of Address 471
Trade Names 472
What A Trade Name Is 472
Registering Trade Names 472
Name Changes 472
Teams 473
What a Team Is and Why it is Registered 473
Team Name Standards 473
Team Advertising 473
Cessation of Brokerage Activities 474
Voluntarily Ceasing Real Estate Activities 474
Death Or Disability of the Broker 474
Branch Office Closing 474
Impact of Broker Suspension or Cessation 475
When a Broker Can No Longer Act 475
Effect On Associates and Branch Offices 475
Listings, Advertising, and Funds 475
Wholesaling 476
The Licensing Line for Equitable Interests 476
The 2025 Wholesaler Disclosure Law 476
Consequences of Noncompliance 476
Trust Accounts 477
Handling Trust Funds 477
Commingling Prohibited 477
Account Registration 477
Earnest Money, Disbursements, and Disputes 477

29 **Oklahoma Disclosures and Hazards** **482**
Residential Property Disclosure Statement 482
Residential Property Disclaimer Statement 484
When A Disclaimer may be Used 484
How The Disclaimer Differs 484
Exemptions From The Act 484
The Licensee's Disclosure Responsibilities 485

Psychologically Impacted Property 486
Oklahoma Environmental Hazards 487

30 **Oklahoma Property Management** **491**
License Requirements 491
Broker Relationships Act Requirements 492
The Management Agreement Is A Brokerage Agreement 492
Duties To The Owner And The Tenant 492
Property Management Agreements 493
The Landlord And Tenant Act 495

31 **Other Oklahoma Laws and Practices** **499**
Fair Housing and Anti-Discrimination 499
Antitrust Issues 501
Price Fixing and Collusion 501
Market Allocation and Boycotts 501
Blockbusting and Steering as Related Wrongs 501
The Statute of Frauds 502
Lien Theory and Title Theory 503
Adverse Possession 504
Native American Lands 505
Property Ownership by Foreign Nationals 505
The Oklahoma Mineral Estate 506

Chapter Tests **510**

Chapter Tests Answer Key **552**

Practice Examination **559**

Practice Examination Answer Key **569**

Glossary of General Real Estate Terms **571**

Index **581**

PREFACE

About the text

Principles of Real Estate Practice in Oklahoma contains the essentials of the national and Oklahoma real estate law, principles, and practices necessary for basic competence as a real estate professional and as mandated by Oklahoma license law. It is based on our highly successful and popular national publication, **Principles of Real Estate Practice**, which is in use in real estate schools nationwide.

The text is tailored to the needs of the pre-license student. It is designed to

- make it easy for students to learn the material
- prepare students for numerous career applications
- stress practical, as well as theoretical, skills and knowledge.

It is streamlined, direct and to-the-point. It includes multiple learning reinforcements. It has a student-oriented organization, both within each chapter and from chapter to chapter. Its examples and exercises are grounded in the authors' many years in real estate education.

Inside the cover

Each chapter begins with an overview of the main section heads covered in the chapter. As each of these heads is expanded, the subheads are displayed in the margin. Key terms are printed in bold type the first time they are used and defined. The chapters conclude with a study aid called the "Snapshot Review," which compresses the main points of the chapter into one or two pages. At the end of the chapter section are tests on each chapter. The answer key following the tests refers to the page in the text that explains the correct answer.

About the authors

For over forty years, Stephen Mettling and David Cusic have operated one of the nation's most successful custom training organizations specializing in real estate program development. Mr. Mettling has also served as vice president and author for a major real estate training and publishing organization. Under various capacities, he has managed the acquisition, development, and sale of national real estate textbooks and publications, as well as directed the country's largest affiliated group of real estate schools.

Mr. Cusic, an author and educator with international real estate training experience, has been engaged in vocation-oriented education since 1966. Specializing in real estate training since 1983, he has developed numerous real estate training programs for corporate and institutional clients around the country.

Ryan Mettling, partner and publisher of Performance Programs, is an experienced online curriculum designer, author, and course developer.

1 The Real Estate Business

Real Estate Professions
Real Estate Brokerage
Professional Organizations
Regulation and Licensing

REAL ESTATE PROFESSIONS

Real estate activities
Professional specialties
Property type specialization

In its broadest sense, the real estate industry is the largest single industry in the American economy. Within it one might include the construction industry, itself often considered our country's largest business. In addition, the real estate industry may be said to include the creation, management, and demolition of every residence and business facility in the nation: offices, warehouses, factories, stores, and special purpose buildings such as hospitals and government facilities. The real estate business would include as well the managing of all the undeveloped land in the country: national parks, forests, and the vast quantity of unused federal property.

Real estate professionals are individuals and business organizations whose *sole enterprise is performing a real estate-related service or function.* A wide range of professions is available to persons wishing to enter the real estate business.

Real estate activities

Real estate professionals perform the following property-related functions:

- creation and improvement
- management and maintenance
- demolition
- investment ownership
- regulation
- transfer

Creation and improvement. Creating real properties from raw land involves capital formation, financing, construction contracting, and regulatory approvals. The key parties involved in this aspect of the business are generally the developer, the landowner, and the mortgage lender. Also involved are market analysts, architects, engineers, space planners, interior designers, and construction subcontractors.

Experts who manage the legal aspects of the development project include real estate attorneys, title companies, surveyors, property insurance companies, and government regulatory officials. The brokerage community, with the assistance of professional appraisers, usually handles the ownership and leasing transactions that occur over the many phases of development.

Management and maintenance. All real estate, whether raw land or improved property, must be managed and maintained. The two principal types of managers are property managers and asset managers. Property managers and their staff oversee specific properties on behalf of the owners, making sure the condition of the property and its financial performance meet specific standards.

Asset managers oversee groups of properties, or portfolios. Their role is to achieve the investment objectives of the owners as opposed to managing day-to-day operations.

Maintenance personnel include engineers, systems technicians, janitorial staff, and other employees needed to maintain the property's condition.

Demolition. Demolition experts in conjunction with excavation and debris removal experts serve to remove properties that are no longer economically viable from the market.

Investment ownership. A specialized niche in the real estate business is the real estate investor who risks capital in order to buy, hold, and sell real properties. In contrast to property owners whose primary interest is in some other business, the real estate investor focuses on identifying and exploiting real estate investment opportunities for profit. The real estate investor provides capital and liquidity to the real estate market.

Regulation. All real estate is to some degree regulated by government. The principal areas of regulation are usage, taxation, and housing administration. Professional regulatory functions include public planners, zoning administrators, building inspectors, assessors, and administrators of specific federal statutes such as Federal Fair Housing Laws.

Transfer. Rights and interests in real estate can be bought, sold, assigned, leased, exchanged, inherited, or otherwise transferred from one owner to another. Real estate brokers and the brokers' salespeople are generally centrally involved in such transfers. Other professional participants are mortgage brokers, mortgage bankers, appraisers, insurers, and title companies.

Professional specialties

In summary, the six primary functional areas are populated by professionals with the following specialties.

Exhibit 1.1 Professions in Real Estate

Creating	developers public and private planners architects building contractors space planners mortgage lenders and bankers title and escrow companies insurers real estate brokers and agents	market analysts surveyors engineers public and private inspectors mortgage brokers securities companies attorneys appraisers
Managing & Maintaining	property managers maintenance engineers technicians corporate managers	asset managers maintenance
Destroying	demolition contractors	excavators
Holding	investors	corporate managers
Regulating	assessors zoning administrators	public planners building inspectors
Transferring	brokers and agents lenders and bankers title and escrow companies insurers	appraisers mortgage brokers attorneys surveyors

Property type specialization

In addition to specializing by function, many professionals also specialize in the type of property they work with. According to the purpose of ownership, properties are classified as residential, commercial, or investment properties.

Residential property refers to property that is owned and used for habitation. Such properties may be further classified in terms of how many families they are designed to house, whether they are attached to other units or detached, and so forth.

Commercial property generally refers to retail and office properties, but may also include industrial real estate. The term "commercial" relates to the fact that the property can potentially generate income from a business's usage.

Investment property refers to any property that is held by its owners for investment purposes. All classifications of property may be investment properties. Generally, however, the term does not refer to owner-occupied residences, even though such properties constitute an investment. Apartments, condominiums, cooperatives, and single-family homes may be considered as investment property if non-occupants own the property for investment purposes. These properties are also referred to as residential income properties.

According to use, the following classifications of real properties are commonly accepted.

Exhibit 1.2 Classifications of Real Estate by Use

residential	industrial
residential income	farm and ranch
office	special purpose
retail	land

These categories are not absolute, since properties often have overlapping uses. A bank, for example, may have retail as well as office operations. An industrial distribution facility may include extensive office space. A retail center may contain offices.

Special purpose properties include publicly or privately owned recreational facilities, government buildings, churches and schools, and so on.

REAL ESTATE BROKERAGE

Forms of specialization
Skills and knowledge

Most newly licensed practitioners choose to begin their real estate careers in residential brokerage.

Primary real estate brokerage activities involve performance of one or more of the following tasks:

- locating a buyer for a seller
- locating a seller for a buyer
- locating a tenant for a landlord
- locating a landlord for a tenant

A seller, buyer, landlord or tenant hires a broker to procure the opposite party to the sale or lease transaction. To help get the job done, the broker hires licensed agents as assistants. The brokerage company, in its simplest form, consists of a broker and the broker's agents, who together work to locate buyers, sellers, tenants and landlords for the broker's clients.

Forms of specialization

In the modern brokerage environment, brokers and agents specialize along the following lines:

- property type
- geographical area
- type of transaction
- type of client
- type of relationship

One's choice of specialization is influenced by competitive factors in the market and by perceived opportunities.

Property type. Since different properties have different features and potential buyers, brokers commonly choose to specialize in a property type. Thus there are:

- residential agents
- commercial agents (office, retail)
- industrial agents
- land agents

Geographical area. Brokers and agents must maintain current, accurate data on properties. It is not possible to keep track of every property in larger markets. Therefore, one must create an area of geographical specialization. One's area may be defined by natural barriers; by streets and highways; or by a certain set of subdivisions.

Type of transaction. The principal types of transaction are sales, leases and subleases, exchanges, and options.

Each form of transaction involves particular legal documents and considerations. As a result, many agents, particularly commercial agents, specialize in a type of transaction. For example, in an urban commercial property market, agents generally specialize in either leases or sales.

Type of client. Brokers increasingly represent buyers and tenants as well as sellers and landlords. Since conflicts of interest may be involved, many brokers restrict their business to representing either buyers and tenants or sellers and landlords exclusively.

Some brokers and agents also specialize according to the type of business their clients are in or their motivations for the transaction. Thus one finds brokers who focus exclusively on hospitals, or fast food chains, or executive relocations.

Type of relationship. In recent years, many brokers have specialized in providing advisory services to clients instead of the traditional transaction-based, commission-compensated services. In the advisory relationship, the broker works on identified real estate tasks or projects in exchange for a fee, salary, or retainer. The fee advisor may or may not focus on completing a transaction.

Some of the individual brokerage services that one might perform for a pre-set fee are:

- comparative price analysis
- database search
- prospect screening
- site analysis

Skills and knowledge

Professionals in the brokerage business must have a broad range of real estate knowledge and skills. Agents must develop a thorough awareness of their local market and the properties within it. In addition, agents must develop a proficiency with the economics of real estate: prices, financing, closing costs, and so forth. Equally important are "people" skills: communicating with clients and responding to their needs.

Exhibit 1.3 Skills and Knowledge in Real Estate Brokerage

Knowledge	Skills
local market conditions	financial qualification
local properties	market analysis
real estate principles	marketing practices
real estate law	ethical practices
value estimation	liability management
real estate financing	data management
investment principles	selling
license laws	time management
related math calculations	communication
closing procedures	writing
	basic computer operation

PROFESSIONAL ORGANIZATIONS

There are trade organizations within the real estate industry that support and promote virtually every form of business specialization. Benefits of membership include training programs, professional designations, and communication channels for keeping abreast of events and laws. Trade organization membership also generally enhances one's business image in the eyes of clients and the public at large.

Some of the major trade organizations, institutes and related professional designations are listed below.

Exhibit 1.4 Real Estate Trade Organizations and Designations

American Society of Appraisers
www.appraisers.org

American Society of Home Inspectors
www.ashi.com

Association of Real Estate License Law Officials (ARELLO)
https://www.arello.org/

Building Owners and Managers Association
www.boma.org

CCIM Institute
www.ccim.com

Certified Commercial-Investment Member (CCIM)

Corenet Global
www.corenetglobal.org

Master of Corporate Real Estate (MCR)

Counselors of Real Estate
www.cre.org

Counselor of Real Estate (CRE)

Institute of Real Estate Management
www.irem.org

Certified Property Manager (CPM)

International Association of Assessing Officers
www.iaao.org

International Council of Shopping Centers
www.icsc.org

Mortgage Bankers Association of America
www.mba.org

Certified Mortgage Banker (CMB)

National Association of Exclusive Buyer's Agents
www.naeba.org

National Association of Home Builders
www.nahb.org

NAIOP Commercial Real Estate Development Association
www.naiop.org

National Association of Real Estate Brokers
www.nareb.com

National Association of Realtors
www.nar.realtor

Graduate, Realtors Institute (GRI)
Certified International Property Specialist (CIPS)

Real Estate Educators Association
www.reea.org

Realtors Land Institute
www.rliland.com

Accredited Land Consultant (ALC)

Society of Industrial and Office Realtors

www.sior.com

The Appraisal Institute
www.appraisalinstitute.org

Member, Appraisal Institute (MAI)
Senior Residential Appraiser (SRA)

Women's Council of Realtors
www.wcr.org

Performance Management Network (PMN)

REGULATION AND LICENSING

Regulation of business practices
Real estate license laws

Regulation of business practices

The real estate industry is regulated by every level of government. Federal and state statutes, as well as a large body of court decisions, generally referred to as common law, circumscribe how real estate can be developed, managed, and transferred.

Among the laws most relevant to agents and brokers are those relating to:

- agency
- contracts
- disclosure
- environmental impact
- fair housing

In addition to federal, state, and local laws and regulations, the real estate industry is, to a degree, self-regulated by the codes of ethical conduct propounded by the industry's many trade organizations. For example, the National Association of Realtors® Code of Ethics not only reflects the law but sets an even higher standard of performance for member brokers and agents.

It is imperative for new practitioners to understand and abide by the many laws which regulate the industry.

Real estate license laws

State real estate license laws comprise the primary body of laws and regulations governing real estate brokerage practice. License laws in each state specify who must obtain a license to practice real estate and set the requirements for obtaining and maintaining the license. License laws also define critical aspects of real estate brokerage, including

- procedures for handling escrow deposits and fees
- procedures for advertising
- guidelines for dealing with clients and customers

State license laws are administered in each state by a **real estate commission**. The commission is charged with administering and enforcing license laws. In addition, the commission may pass regulations that further refine or clarify state statutes.

1 The Real Estate Business Snapshot Review

REAL ESTATE PROFESSIONS		
Real estate activities	•	create, improve, manage, maintain, demolish, own, regulate, and transfer real properties
Property type specializations	•	residential; residential income; office; retail; industrial; farm and ranch; special purpose; land
REAL ESTATE BROKERAGE	•	procure a buyer or tenant for an owner or landlord, or vice versa
Forms of specialization	•	by property type; geographical area; type of transaction; type of client; by form of business organization; or by form of client relationship
Skills and knowledge	•	market conditions; law; financing; marketing; ethics; selling; communications; computer basics; and other skills
PROFESSIONAL ORGANIZATIONS	•	promote interests of practitioners and enhance their professional standing
REGULATION AND LICENSING		
Regulation of business practices	•	all facets of the industry are regulated by federal, state, and local laws; agents must understand relevant laws and adapt business practices accordingly
Real estate license laws	•	the primary body of laws and regulations governing the licensure and conduct of real estate brokers and agents
	•	license laws are administered and enforced under the jurisdiction of the state real estate commission

2 Rights in Real Estate

Real Estate as Property
Real Versus Personal Property
Regulation of Real Property Interests

REAL ESTATE AS PROPERTY

Land
Real estate
Property
Real property rights
Water rights

A simple definition of real estate is that it is air, water, land, and everything affixed to the land. Real estate in the United States may be owned privately by individuals and private entities or publicly by government entities. Private ownership rights in this country are not absolute. The government can impose taxes and restrictions on private ownership rights, and it can take private property away altogether. In addition, other private parties can exert their rights and interests on one's real property. A bank, for example, can take a property if the owner fails to pay a mortgage. A neighbor can claim the right to walk across one's property whether the owner likes it or not, provided he or she has done so for a certain number of years.

In attempting to define real estate, it is essential to understand *what rights and interests parties have in a parcel of real estate*. And to understand real estate rights and interests, one must first recognize the distinctions between:

- land and real estate
- real estate and property
- real property and personal property

Land

The legal concept of land encompasses

- the surface area of the earth
- everything beneath the surface of the earth extending downward to its center
- all *natural* things permanently attached to the earth
- the air above the surface of the earth extending outward to infinity.

Land, therefore, includes minerals beneath the earth's surface, water on or below the earth's surface, and the air above the surface. In addition, land includes all plants attached to the ground or in the ground, such as trees and grass. A **parcel**, or **tract**, of land is a portion of land delineated by boundaries.

Physical characteristics. Land has three unique physical characteristics: *immobility, indestructibility, and heterogeneity.*

Land is immobile, since a parcel of land cannot be moved from one site to another. In other words, the geographical location of a tract of land is fixed and cannot be changed. One can transport portions of the land such as mined coal, dirt, or cut plants. However, as soon as such elements are detached from the land, they are no longer considered land.

Land is indestructible in the sense that one would have to remove a segment of the planet all the way to the core in order to destroy it. Even then, the portion extending upward to infinity would remain. For the same reason, land is considered to be permanent.

Land is non-homogeneous, since no two parcels of land are exactly the same. Admittedly, two adjacent parcels may be very similar and have the same economic value. However, they are inherently different because each parcel has a unique location.

Real estate

The legal concept of real estate encompasses:

- land
- all *man-made structures* that are "permanently" attached to the land

Real estate therefore includes, in addition to land, such things as fences, streets, buildings, wells, sewers, sidewalks and piers. Such man-made structures attached to the land are called **improvements**. The phrase "permanently attached" refers primarily to one's intention in attaching the item. Obviously, very few if any manmade structures can be permanently attached to the land in the literal sense. But if a person constructs a house with the intention of creating a permanent dwelling, the house is considered real estate. By contrast, if a camper affixes a tent to the land with the intention of moving it to another camp in a week, the tent would not be considered real estate.

Exhibit 2.1 The Legal Concept of Land and Real Estate

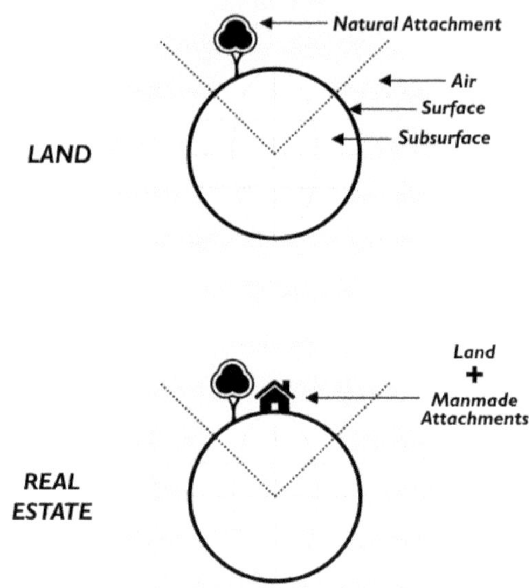

Property

In common understanding, property is something that is owned by someone. A car is the property of Bill Brown if Bill Brown owns the car. If the item is not owned, it is not property. For example, if a car is abandoned and left to rust in the desert, the car is no longer property, since no one claims ownership. Similarly, the planet Jupiter is not property, since no one owns it.

From a more technical standpoint, property is not only the item that is owned but also a *set of rights to the item enjoyed by the owner*. These rights are commonly known as the "bundle of rights."

Exhibit 2.2 The Bundle of Rights

In owning property, one has the right to possess and use it as the law allows. The owner has the right to transfer ownership of the item (sell, rent, donate, assign, or bequeath). The owner may also encumber the item by mortgaging it as collateral for debt. Finally, the owner has the right to exclude others from use of the item. In the example of the car, when Bill Brown bought the car, the car became his property: he owned the car itself. At the same time, he also acquired the legal rights to transfer, use, encumber, exclude, and possess the car.

Classifications of property. Our legal system recognizes two classifications of property: *real property* and *personal property*. **Real property** is ownership of real estate and the bundle of rights associated with owning the real estate. **Personal property** is ownership of anything which is not real estate, and the rights associated with owning the personal property item. Items of personal property are also called **chattels** or **personalty**.

Note: since all real estate in the United States is owned by some person, private organization, or government entity, all real estate in the country *is* real property. Given that fact, this text will follow the customary practice of using the two terms interchangeably and synonymously.

Tangible versus intangible property. Real and personal property may be further categorized as **tangible** or **intangible** property. Tangible property is physical, visible, and material. Intangible property is abstract, having no physical existence in itself, other than as evidence of one's ownership interest.

Exhibit 2.3 Tangible vs. Intangible Property

	Tangible	**Intangible**
Real Property	all types	
Personal Property	boat, car, jewelry	stock certificate, contract, patent

All real estate, by its physical nature, is tangible property. Personal property may be tangible or intangible. Boats, jewelry, coins, appliances, computers, and art work are examples of tangible personal property. Stocks, copyrights, bonds, trademarks, patents, franchises, and listing agreements are examples of intangible personal property.

Real property rights

Real property rights consist of the bundle of rights associated with owning a parcel of real estate. Foremost of these rights is the right of possession.

The *right to use* a property refers to the right to use it in certain ways, such as mining, cultivating, landscaping, razing, and building on the property. The right is subject to the limitations of local zoning and the legality of the use. One's right to use may not infringe on the rights of others to use and enjoy their property. For example, an owner may be restricted from constructing a large pond on her property if in fact the pond would pose flooding and drainage hazards to the next door neighbor.

The *right to transfer* interests in the property includes the right to sell, bequeath, lease, donate, or assign ownership interests. An owner may transfer certain individual rights to the property without transferring total ownership. Also, one may transfer ownership while retaining individual interests. For example, a person may sell mineral rights without selling the right of possession. On the other hand, the owner may convey all rights to the property except the mineral rights.

While all rights are transferrable, the owner can only transfer what the owner in fact possesses. A property seller, for example, cannot sell water rights if there are no water rights attached to the property.

The *right to encumber* the property essentially means the right to mortgage the property as collateral for debt. There may be restrictions to this right, such as a spouse's right to limit the degree to which a homestead may be mortgaged.

The *right to exclude* gives the property owner the legal right to keep others off the property and to prosecute trespassers.

The bundle of real property rights also applies separately to the individual components of real estate: the air, the surface, and the subsurface. An owner can, for example, transfer subsurface rights without transferring air rights. Similarly, an owner can rent air space without encumbering surface or subsurface rights. This might occur in a city where adjoining building owners want to construct a walkway over a third owner's lot. Such owners would have to acquire the air rights for the walkway. If the city wants to construct a subway through the owner's subsurface, the city has to obtain the subsurface rights to do so.

An ordinary lease is a common example of the transfer of a portion of one's bundle of rights. The owner relinquishes the right to possess portions of the surface, perhaps a building, in return for rent. The tenant enjoys the rights to possess and use the building over the term of the lease, after which these rights revert to the landlord. During the lease term, the tenant has no rights to the property's subsurface or airspace other than what the building occupies. Further, the tenant does not enjoy any of the other rights in the bundle of rights: he cannot encumber the property or transfer it. To a limited degree, the tenant may exclude persons from the property, but he may not exclude the legal owner.

Surface rights. Surface rights apply to the real estate contained within the surface boundaries of the parcel. This includes the ground, all natural things affixed to the ground, and all improvements. Surface rights also include water rights.

Air rights. Air rights apply to the space above the surface boundaries of the parcel, as delineated by imaginary vertical lines extended to infinity. Since the advent of aviation, air rights have been curtailed to allow aircraft to fly over one's property, provided the overflights do not interfere with the owner's use and enjoyment of the property. The issue of violation of air rights for the benefit of air transportation is an ongoing battle between airlines, airports, and nearby property owners.

Subsurface rights. Subsurface rights apply to land beneath the surface of the real estate parcel extending from its surface boundaries downward to the center of the earth. Notable subsurface rights are the rights to extract mineral and gas deposits and subsurface water from the water table.

Water rights

Water rights basically concern the rights to own and use water found in lakes, streams, rivers, and the ocean. In addition, they determine where parcel boundaries can be fixed with respect to adjoining bodies of water. What water rights does an owner of a property that contains or adjoins a body of water enjoy? The answer depends on three variables:

- whether the state controls the water
- whether the water is moving
- whether the water is navigable

Doctrine of Prior Appropriation. Since water is a resource necessary for survival, some states -- particularly those where water is scarce -- have taken the legal position that the state owns and controls all bodies of water. Called the Doctrine of Prior Appropriation, this position requires that property owners obtain permits for use of water. If a proposed usage is reasonable and beneficial, the state will grant a permit which, over time, can attach to the property of the permit holder. If a state does not operate under prior appropriation, it operates under the common law doctrines of *littoral rights* and *riparian rights*.

Littoral rights. Littoral rights concern properties abutting bodies of water that are not moving, such as lakes and seas. Owners of properties abutting a navigable, non-moving body of water enjoy the littoral right of use, but do not own the water nor the land beneath the water. Ownership extends to the high-water mark of the body of water.

Exhibit 2.4 Littoral Rights

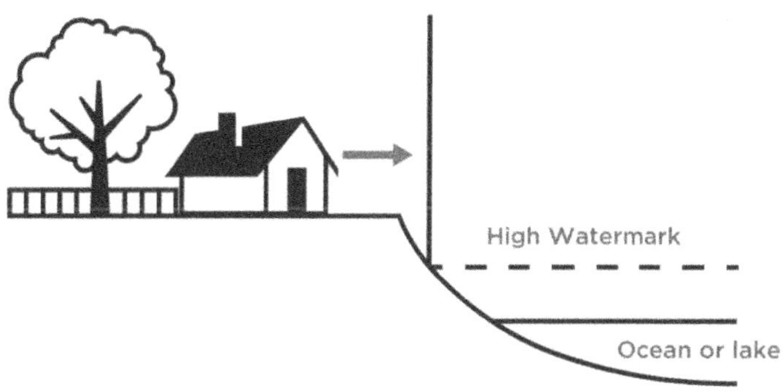

Oceans, Seas and Lakes

The legal premise underlying the definition of littoral rights is that a lake or sea is a *navigable body of water, therefore, public property* owned by the state. By contrast, a body of water entirely contained within the boundaries of an owner's property is not navigable. In such a case, the owner would own the water as well as unrestricted rights of usage.

Littoral rights attach to the property. When the property is sold, the littoral rights transfer with the property to the new owner.

Riparian rights. Riparian rights concern properties abutting moving water such as streams and rivers. If a property abuts a stream or river, the owner's riparian rights are determined by whether the water *is navigable or not navigable*. If the property abuts a non-navigable stream, the owner enjoys unrestricted use of the water and *owns the land beneath the stream to the stream's midpoint*. If the waterway in question is navigable, the waterway is considered to be a public easement. In such a case, the owner's property extends *to the water's edge* as opposed to the midpoint of the waterway. The state owns the land beneath the water.

Exhibit 2.5 Riparian Rights

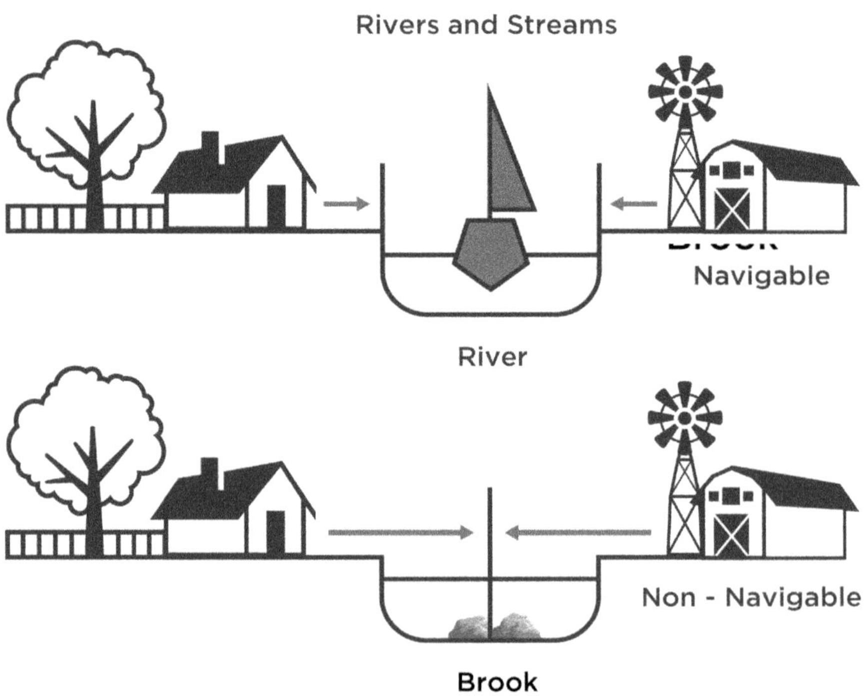

One's riparian rights to use flowing water are subject to the conditions that:

- the usage is reasonable and does not infringe on the riparian rights of other owners downstream
- the usage does not pollute the water
- the usage does not impede or alter the course of the water flow.

Like littoral rights, riparian rights attach to the property.

REAL VERSUS PERSONAL PROPERTY

Fixtures
Differentiation criteria
Trade fixtures
Emblements
Factory-built housing
Conversion

In conveying real property, it is vitally important to recognize the distinctions between personal property and the real property that is to be conveyed. Confusion can arise because items of property *may be either personal property or real property, depending on circumstances.*

The primary criterion for distinguishing real from personal property is whether the item is permanently attached to the land or to structures attached to the land. For example, a tree growing in one's yard is an item of real property. However, when the owner cuts the tree down, it becomes personal property. Similarly, a swimming pool pump on a shelf in the owner's garage is personal property. When it is installed with the rest of the pool, it becomes real property.

While the "attachment" criterion is pivotal in distinguishing between real and personal property, there are other tests to be applied. In addition, the attachment rule is subject to exceptions.

Fixtures

A personal property item that has been converted to real property by attachment to real estate is called a fixture. Typical examples are chandeliers, toilets, water pumps, septic tanks, and window shutters.

The owner of real property inherently owns all fixtures belonging to the real property. When the owner sells the real property, the buyer acquires rights to all fixtures. Fixtures not included in the sale must be itemized and excluded in the sale contract.

Differentiation criteria

In the event that the attachment criterion is insufficient to determine whether an article of property is real or personal, a court may apply one or more of the following additional criteria.

Intention. One's original intention can override the test of movability in determining whether an item is a fixture or not. If someone attached an item to real property, yet intended to remove it after a period of time, the article may be deemed personal property. If a person intended an article to be a fixture, even though the item is easily removable, the article may be deemed a fixture.

For example, an apartment renter installs an alarm system, fully intending to remove the system upon lease expiration. Here, the alarm system would be considered personal property.

Adaptation. If an item is uniquely adapted to the property, or the property is custom-designed to accommodate the item, it may be deemed real property whether the item is easily removable or not. House keys, a garbage compactor, and a removable door screen are examples.

Functionality. If an item is vital to the operation of the building, it may be deemed a fixture, even though perhaps easily removable. Window-unit air conditioners and detachable solar panels are possible examples.

Relationship of parties. If a tenant installs a fixture in order to conduct business, the fixture may be considered a trade fixture, which is the tenant's personal property.

Sale or lease contract provisions. In a sale or lease transaction, the listing of an item in the contract as a personal property item or a fixture overrides all other considerations. Unless otherwise stated as exceptions, all fixtures are included in the sale. For example, if a sale contract stipulates that the carpeting is not included in the sale, it becomes a personal property item. If the carpeting is not mentioned, it goes with the property, since it is attached to the floor of the building.

Trade fixtures

Trade fixtures, or **chattel fixtures,** are items of a tenant's *personal property* that the tenant has temporarily affixed to a landlord's real property in order to conduct business. Trade fixtures may be detached and removed before or upon surrender of the leased premises. Should the tenant fail to remove a trade fixture, it may become the property of the landlord through *accession*. Thereafter, the fixture is considered real property.

Examples of trade fixtures include a grocer's food freezers, a merchant's clothes racks, a tavern owner's bar, a dairy's milking machines, and a printer's printing press.

Emblements

Growing plants, including agricultural crops, may be either real property or personal property. Plants and crops that grow naturally without requiring anyone's labor or machinery are considered real property.

Plants and crops requiring human intervention and labor are called **emblements**. Emblements, despite their attachment to land, are considered personal property. If an emblement is owned by a tenant farmer, the tenant has the right to the harvested crop whether the tenant's lease is active or expired. If the tenant grew the crop, it is his or her personal property, and the landlord cannot take it.

Factory-built housing

Factory-built housing consists of dwelling units constructed off-site and transported to and assembled on a building site. The category also includes readily moveable housing of the type that can be relocated from place to place, once known by the term **mobile home.** The National Manufactured Housing Construction and Safety Standards Act of 1976 defined the types of factory-built housing and retired the mobile home designation. **Manufactured housing** is factory-built housing that conforms to HUD standards. Factory-built housing may be considered real property or personal property, depending on whether it is permanently affixed to the ground, and according to state law. Real estate practitioners should understand the local laws before selling any kind of factory-built housing.

Conversion

The classification of an item of property as real or personal is not necessarily fixed. The classification may be changed by the process of conversion. **Severance** is the conversion of real property to personal property by detaching it from the real estate, such as by cutting down a tree, detaching a door from a shed, or removing an antenna from a roof. **Affixing**, or attachment, is the act of converting personal property to real property by attaching it to the real estate, such as by assembling a pile of bricks into a barbecue pit, or constructing a boat dock from wood planks.

Exhibit 2.6 Real Property vs. Personal Property

Real Property	Personal Property
land fixtures attachments conversions by affixing	trade fixtures emblements conversions by severance

---

REGULATION OF REAL PROPERTY INTERESTS

Areas of regulation
Federal regulation
State regulation
Local regulation
Judicial regulation

Although the Constitution guarantees private ownership of real estate, laws and regulations at every level of government qualify and limit individual real property ownership and the bundle of rights associated with it.

Areas of regulation

Government entities regulate the following aspects of real property interests:

- the bundle of rights: possession, usage, transfer, encumbering and exclusion
- legal descriptions
- financing
- insurance
- inheritance
- taxation

Regulation takes the form of federal and state laws and regulations; county and local ordinances and codes; and court decisions in the judicial system.

Federal regulation

In regulating real property rights, the federal government is primarily concerned with broad standards of real property usage, natural disaster, land description, and discrimination.

Federal agencies such as the Federal Housing Administration promote and regulate home ownership. The Environmental Protection Agency establishes protective usage restrictions and guidelines for dealing with hazardous materials and other environmental concerns. Federal flood insurance legislation requires certain homeowners to obtain flood insurance policies. Federal laws such as the Federal Fair Housing Act of 1968 prohibit discrimination in housing based on race, religion, color, or national origin. Such laws as the Americans with Disabilities Act prescribe design and accessibility standards.

The federal government does not levy real estate taxes.

State regulation

State governments are the primary regulatory entities of the real estate business. State governments establish real estate license laws and qualifications. In addition, state governments have established real estate commissions to administer license laws and oversee activities of licensees.

State governments also exert regional influence in the usage and environmental control of real estate within the state. Relevant state laws might include laws relating to flood zones, waste disposal, drainage control, shore preservation, and pollution standards.

States also play a role in defining how real property may be owned, transferred, encumbered, and inherited. For example, in some states a mortgaged property becomes the legal property of the lender until the mortgage loan is paid.

States have the power to levy real estate taxes but generally pass this power to local government.

Local regulation

County and local government regulation focuses on land use control, control of improvements, and taxation. Land use regulations and ordinances control how all property within the jurisdiction may be developed, improved, demolished, and managed. County and local governments have the power to zone land, take over land for the public good, issue building permits, and establish the rules for all development projects.

County and local governments, along with school districts and other local jurisdictions, have the power to levy real estate taxes.

Judicial regulation

The judicial system exerts an influence on real estate ownership and use through decisions based on case law and common law, as distinguished from statutory law. Case law consists of decisions based on judicial precedent. Common law is the collective body of law deriving from custom and generally accepted practice in society.

Exhibit 2.7 Regulation of Real Property Interests

Federal	Constitution	Establishes absolute right of private ownership of real estate Prohibits federal government from levying real property taxes
	Laws	Create, regulate real estate-related agencies Prohibit discrimination Create standards for legal descriptions of real estate Establish environmental standards for all property Establish standards for protecting interests of handicapped people
	Agencies	Establish mortgage lending standards Establish housing construction standards Establish environmental standards
State	Constitution	May establish right to levy tax; or may delegate right to counties and municipalities
	Laws	Regulate real estate licensing Establish broad usage standards Define, qualify ownership rights
	Agencies	Regulate practitioners, administer real estate license laws
Local	Laws	Create and enforce real estate taxation Control land usage over specific parcels of land
Courts	Common law	Regulates real estate ownership and usage according to customary and accepted practices
	Case law	Regulates real estate ownership and usage according to prior court decisions

2 Rights and Interests in Real Estate Snapshot Review

REAL ESTATE AS PROPERTY	•	Constitution guarantees private ownership of real estate; ownership rights not absolute; others may exert claims against one's property
Land	•	surface, all natural things attached to it, subsurface, and air above the surface; unique aspects: immobile, indestructible, heterogeneous
Real estate	•	land plus all permanently attached man-made structures, called improvements
Property	•	something that is owned by someone and the associated rights of ownership
	•	the bundle of rights: possession, use, transfer, exclusion, and encumbrance
	•	property is real or personal, tangible or intangible
Real property rights	•	any of the bundle of rights, applied to airspace (air rights), surface (surface rights), and subsurface (subsurface rights)
Water rights	•	Doctrine of Prior Appropriation: state controls water usage; grants usage permits
	•	littoral rights: abutting property owners own land to high water mark; may use, but state owns underlying land
	•	riparian rights: if navigable, abutting property owners own land to water's edge; may use, but state owns underlying land; if not navigable, owner owns land to midpoint of waterway
REAL VS PERSONAL PROPERTY	•	an item may be real or personal property depending on the "attachment" criterion and other circumstances
Fixtures	•	real property converted from personal property by attachment to real estate
Differentiation criteria	•	intention; adaptation; functionality; relationship of parties; contract provisions
Trade fixtures	•	personal property items temporarily attached to real estate in order to conduct business; to be removed at some point
Emblements	•	plants or crops considered personal property since human intervention is necessary for planting, harvesting
Factory-built housing	•	housing pre-built off-site; includes mobile homes; real or personal depending on attachment to land
Conversion	•	transforming real to personal property through severance, or personal to real property through affixing
REGULATION OF REAL PROPERTY INTERESTS		
Federal regulation	•	grants overall rights of ownership; controls broad usage standards, discrimination
State regulation	•	governs the real estate business; sets regional usage standards
Local regulation	•	levies real estate taxes; controls specific usage
Judicial regulation	•	applies case law and common law to disputes

3 Interests and Estates

Interests and Estates in Land
Freehold Estates
Leasehold Estates

INTERESTS AND ESTATES IN LAND

Interests
Estates in land

Interests

An interest in real estate is *ownership of any combination of the bundle of rights* to real property, including the rights to

- possess
- use
- transfer
- encumber
- exclude

Undivided interest. An undivided interest is an owner's interest in a property in which two or more parties share ownership. The terms "undivided" and "indivisible" signify that the owner's interest is in a fractional part of the entire estate, not in a physical portion of the real property itself. If two co-owners have an undivided equal interest, one owner may not lay claim to the northern half of the property for his or her exclusive use.

Examples of interests include:

- an owner who enjoys the complete bundle of rights
- a tenant who temporarily enjoys the right to use and exclude
- a lender who enjoys the right to encumber the property over the life of a mortgage loan
- a repairman who encumbers the property when the owner fails to pay for services
- a buyer who prevents an owner from selling the property to another party under the terms of the sale contract
- a mining company which temporarily owns the right to extract minerals from the property's subsurface
- a local municipality which has the right to control how an owner uses the property
- a utility company which claims access to the property in accordance with an easement

Interests differ according to

- how long a person may enjoy the interest
- what portion of the land, air, or subsurface the interest applies to
- whether the interest is public or private
- whether the interest includes legal ownership of the property

Exhibit 3.1 Interests in Real Estate

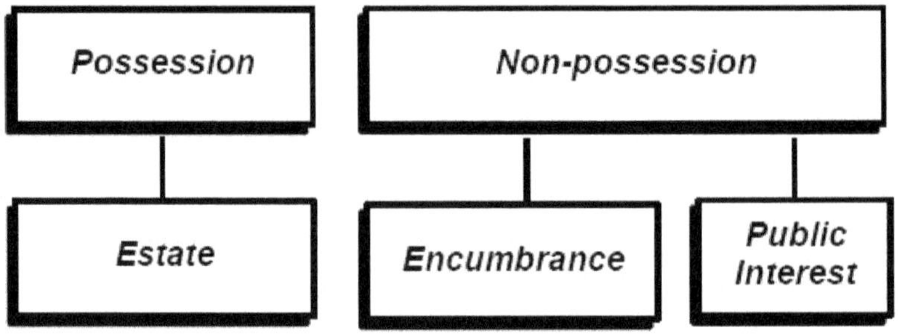

Interests are principally distinguished by whether they include possession. If the interest-holder enjoys the right of possession, the party is considered to have an **estate in land**, or, familiarly an estate. If a private interest-holder does not have the right to possess, the interest is an **encumbrance.** If the interest-holder is not private, such as a government entity, and does not have the right to possess, the interest is some form of *public interest*.

An encumbrance enables a non-owning party to restrict the owner's bundle of rights. Tax liens, mortgages, easements, and encroachments are examples.

Public entities may own or lease real estate, in which case they enjoy an estate in land. However, government entities also have non-possessory interests in real estate which act to control land use for the public good within the entity's jurisdiction. The prime example of public interest is **police power**, or the right of the local or county government to **zone**. Another example of public interest is the right to acquire ownership through the power of eminent domain.

Estates in land

An estate in land is an interest that includes the right of possession. Depending on the length of time one may enjoy the right to possess the estate, the relationships of the parties owning the estate, and specific interests held in the estate, an estate is a freehold or a leasehold estate.

Exhibit 3.2 Estates in Land

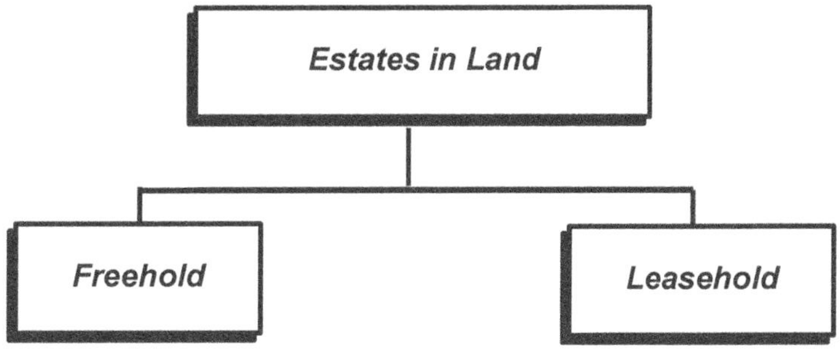

In a **freehold estate**, the duration of the owner's rights cannot be determined: the rights may endure for a lifetime, for less than a lifetime, or for generations beyond the owner's lifetime.

A **leasehold estate** is distinguished by its specific duration, as represented by the lease term.

Ownership of a freehold estate is commonly equated with ownership of the property, whereas ownership of a leasehold estate is not so considered because the leaseholder's rights are temporary.

Both leasehold and freehold estates are referred to as **tenancies**. The owner of the freehold estate is the **freehold tenant**, and the renter, or lessee, is the **leasehold tenant**.

FREEHOLD ESTATES

Fee simple estate
Life estate
Conventional life estate
Legal life estate

Freehold estates differ primarily according to the duration of the estate and what happens to the estate when the owner dies. A freehold estate of potentially unlimited duration is a fee simple estate: an estate limited to the life of the owner is a life estate.

Exhibit 3.3 Freehold Estates

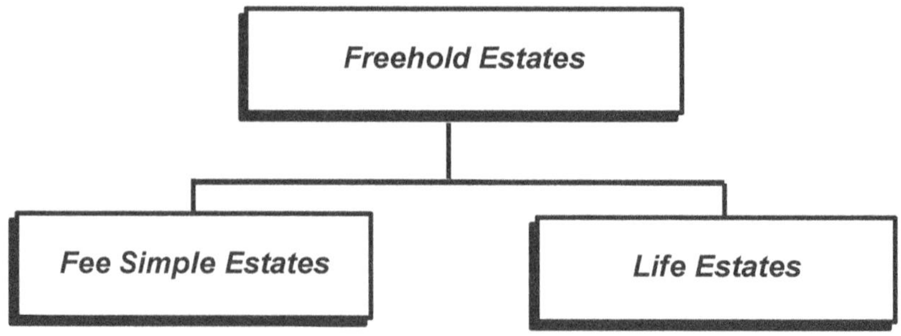

Fee simple estate

The **fee simple** freehold estate is the *highest form of ownership interest* one can acquire in real estate. It includes the complete bundle of rights, and the tenancy is unlimited, with certain exceptions indicated below. The fee simple interest is also called the "fee interest," or simply, the "fee." The owner of the fee simple interest is called the **fee tenant**.

Fee simple estates, like all estates, remain subject to government restrictions and private interests.

There are two forms of fee simple estate: **absolute** and **defeasible**.

Exhibit 3.4 Fee Simple Estates

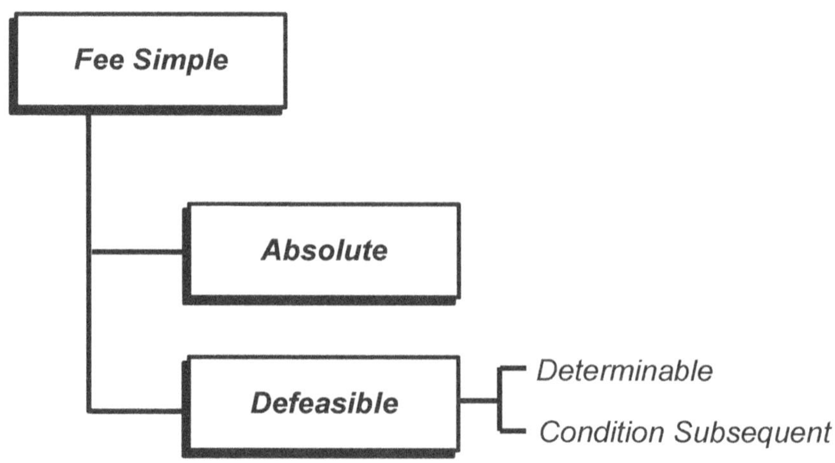

Fee Simple Absolute. The fee simple absolute estate is a perpetual estate that is *not conditioned by stipulated or restricted uses.* It may also be freely passed on to heirs. For these reasons, the fee simple absolute estate is the most desirable estate that can be obtained in residential real estate. It is also the most common.

Fee Simple Defeasible. The defeasible fee estate is perpetual, provided the usage *conforms to stated conditions.* Essential characteristics are:

- the property must be used for a certain purpose or under certain conditions
- if the use changes or if prohibited conditions are present, the estate reverts to the previous grantor of the estate.

The two types of fee simple defeasible are **determinable** and **condition subsequent**.

Determinable. The deed to the determinable estate states usage limitations. If the restrictions are violated, the estate automatically reverts to the grantor or heirs.

Condition subsequent. If any condition is violated, the previous owner may repossess the property. However, reversion of the estate is not automatic: the grantor must re-take physical possession within a certain time frame.

Life estate

A life estate is a freehold estate that is limited in duration to the life of the owner or other named person. Upon the death of the owner or other named individual, *the estate passes to the original owner or another named party*. The holder of a life estate is called the **life tenant**.

The distinguishing characteristics of the life estate are:

- the owner enjoys full ownership rights during the estate period
- holders of the future interest own either a reversionary or a remainder interest
- the estate may be created by agreement between private parties, or it may be created by law under prescribed circumstances.

Remainder. If a life estate names a third party to receive title to the property upon termination of the life estate, the party enjoys a future interest called a remainder interest or a remainder estate. The holder of a remainder interest is called a **remainderman**.

Reversion. If no remainder estate is established, the estate reverts to the original owner or the owner's heirs. In this situation, the original owner retains a reversionary interest or estate.

The two types of life estates are the **conventional** and the **legal** life estate.

Exhibit 3.5 Life Estates

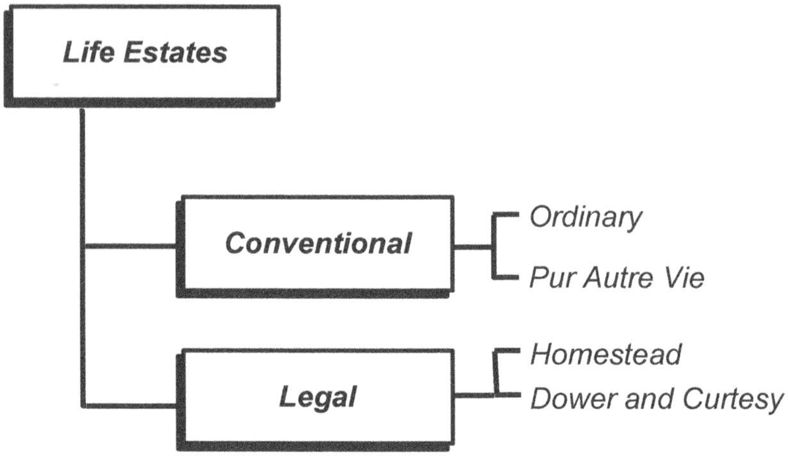

Conventional life estate

A conventional life estate is created by grant from a fee simple property owner to the grantee, the life tenant. Following the termination of the estate, rights pass to a remainderman or revert to the previous owner.

During the life estate period, the owner enjoys all ownership rights, provided he or she does not infringe on the rights of the remainder or reversion interest holders, such as by damaging the property or jeopardizing its value. Should such actions occur, holders of the future interest may take legal action against the property owners.

The two types of conventional life estate are the **ordinary** and the **pur autre vie** life estate.

Exhibit 3.6 Conventional Life Estates

	Ordinary Life Estate	Pur Autre Vie
With reversion	duration: owner's life reverts to grantor	duration: another's life reverts to grantor
With remainder	duration: owner's life reverts to another	duration: another's life reverts to another

Ordinary life estate. An ordinary life estate *ends with the death of the life estate owner* and may pass back to the original owners or their heirs (reversion) or to a named third party (remainder).

For example, John King grants a life estate in a property to Mary Brown, to endure over Mary's lifetime. John establishes that when Mary dies, the property will revert to himself.

Pur autre vie. A pur autre vie life estate endures over the lifetime of a third person, after which the property passes from the tenant holder to the original grantor (reversion) or a third party (remainderman).

For example, Yvonne grants a life estate to Ryan, to endure over the lifetime of Yvonne's husband Steve. Upon Steve's death, Yvonne establishes that her mother, Rose, will receive the property.

Legal life estate

A legal life estate is *created by state law* as opposed to being created by a property owner's agreement. Provisions vary from state to state. The focus of a legal life estate is defining and protecting the property rights of surviving family members upon the death of the husband or wife.

The major forms of legal life estate are the **homestead**, **dower and curtesy.**

Homestead. A homestead is one's principal residence. Homestead laws protect family members against losing their homes to general creditors attempting to collect on debts.

Homestead laws generally provide that:

- all or portions of one's homestead *are exempt* from a forced sale executed for the collection of general debts (judgment liens). The various states place different limits on this exemption.
- tax debts, seller financing debt, debts for home improvement, and mortgage debt are *not exempt*
- the family *must occupy* the homestead
- the homestead interest *cannot be conveyed by one spouse*; both spouses must sign the deed conveying homestead property
- the homestead exemption and restrictions *endure over the life* of the head of the household, and pass on to children under legal age. State laws define specifically how the interest transfers upon the death of the household head
- homestead interests in a property *are extinguished* if the property is sold or abandoned
- in some states the exemption is automatic; in others, homeowners must file for the exemption.

The homestead exemption from certain debts should not be confused with the *homestead tax* exemption, which exempts a portion of the property's value from taxation.

Dower and curtesy. Dower is a wife's life estate interest in the husband's property. When the husband dies, the wife can make a claim to portions of the decedent's property. Curtesy is the identical right enjoyed by the husband in a deceased wife's property. Property acquired under dower laws is owned by the surviving spouse for the duration of his or her lifetime.

LEASEHOLD ESTATES

Estate for years
Estate from period-to-period
Estate at will
Estate at sufferance

A leasehold estate, or **leasehold**, arises from the execution of a lease by a fee owner- the **lessor,** or **landlord**-- to a **lessee**, or **tenant**. Since tenants do not own the fee interest, a leasehold estate is technically an item of personal property for the tenant.

Leasehold tenants are entitled to possess and use the leased premises during the lease term in the manner prescribed in the lease. They also have restricted rights to exclusion.

Estate for years

The estate for years is a leasehold estate for a definite period of time, with a beginning date and an ending date. The estate for years may endure for any length of term. At the end of the term, the estate automatically terminates, without any requirement of notice.

For example, a landlord grants a tenant a three-year lease. After the three years, the leasehold terminates, and the landlord may re-possess the premises, renew the lease, or lease to someone else.

If a tenant with a leasehold estate for years remains in possession of the leased premises after lease expiration, a **holdover lease** is created. In the absence of a new lease agreement stating otherwise, the **holdover tenancy** becomes a periodic tenancy.

Estate from period-to-period

In an estate from period-to-period, also called a **periodic tenancy**, the tenancy period automatically renews for an indefinite period of time, subject to timely payment of rent. At the end of a tenancy period, if the landlord accepts another regular payment of rent, the leasehold is considered to be renewed for another period.

For example, a two-year lease expires, and the landlord grants a six-month lease that is automatically renewable, provided the monthly rent is received on time. At the end of the six months, the tenant pays, and the landlord accepts another monthly rent payment. The acceptance of the rent automatically extends the leasehold for another six months.

The most common form of periodic tenancy is the month-to-month lease, which may exist without any written agreement.

Either party may terminate a periodic tenancy by giving proper notice to the other party. Proper notice is defined by state law.

Estate at will

The estate at will, also called a **tenancy at will**, has no definite expiration date and hence no "renewal" cycle. The landlord and tenant agree that the tenancy will have no specified termination date, provided rent is paid on time and other lease conditions are met.

For example, a son leases a house to his father and mother "forever," or until they want to move.

The estate at will is terminated by proper notice, or by the death of either party.

Estate at sufferance

In an estate at sufferance, a tenant occupies the premises without consent of the landlord or other legal agreement with the landlord. Usually such an estate involves a tenant who fails to vacate at the expiration of the lease, continuing occupancy without any right to do so.

For example, a tenant violates the provisions of a lease and is evicted. The tenant protests and refuses to leave despite the eviction order.

3 Interests and Estates Snapshot Review

INTERESTS AND ESTATES IN LAND	
Interests	• any combination of bundle of rights
	• estates, encumbrances, police powers
Estates in land	• include right of possession; also called tenancies
	• leaseholds: of limited duration
	• freeholds: duration is not necessarily limited
FREEHOLD ESTATES	• implies "ownership" in contrast to leasehold
Fee simple estate	• also "fee"; most common form of estate; not limited by one's lifetime
	• fee simple absolute: highest form of ownership interest
	• defeasible: can revert to previous owner for violation of conditions
Life estate	• fee estate passes to another upon death of a named party
	• remainder: interest of a named party to receive estate after holder's death
	• reversion: interest of previous owner to receive estate after holder's death
Conventional life estate	• full ownership interest, limited to lifetime of life tenant or another named party
	• created by agreements between parties
	• ordinary: on death of life tenant, passes to remainderman or previous owner
	• pur autre vie: on death of another; passes to remainderman or previous owner
Legal life estate	• automatic creation of estate through operation of law
	• designed to protect family survivors
	• homestead: rights to one's principal residence
	• laws protect homestead from certain creditors
	• dower and curtesy: a life estate interest of a widow(er) in the real property
LEASEHOLD ESTATES	• non-ownership possessory estates of limited duration
Estate for years	• specific, stated duration, per lease
Estate from period-to-period	• lease term renews automatically upon acceptance of monthly or periodic rent
Estate at will	• tenancy for indefinite period subject to rent payment; cancelable with notice
Estate at sufferance	• tenancy against landlord's will and without an agreement

4 Ownership

Sole Ownership
Co-Ownership
Estates in Trust
Ownership by Business Entities
Condominiums
Cooperatives
Time-Shares

There are numerous ways of holding ownership of a freehold estate according to how many parties (tenants) share the ownership and how they share it. The primary distinction is between ownership by a single party, and ownership by multiple parties. Various trust structures enable an owner to employ a trustee to hold and manage an estate. Condominiums, cooperatives and time-shares are hybrids that combine several forms of ownership.

SOLE OWNERSHIP

Tenancy in severalty

Tenancy in severalty If *a single party owns* the fee or life estate, the ownership is a **tenancy in severalty**. Synonyms are **sole ownership**, **ownership in severalty**, and **estate in severalty**. When the would-be sole owner is a husband or wife, state laws may require homestead, dower or elective share rights to be released to allow ownership free and clear of any marriage-related claims.

The estate of a deceased tenant in severalty passes to heirs by probate.

CO-OWNERSHIP

Tenancy in common
Joint tenancy
Tenancy by the entireties
Community property
Tenancy in partnership

If more than one person, or a legal entity such as a corporation, owns an estate in land, the estate is held in some form of co-ownership. Co-owners are also called **cotenants**.

Tenancy in common

The tenancy in common, also known as the **estate in common,** is the most common form of co-ownership when the owners are not married. The defining characteristics are:

- two or more owners
- identical rights
- interests individually owned
- electable ownership shares
- no survivorship
- no unity of time

Two or more owners. Any number of people may be co-tenants in a single property.

Identical rights. Co-tenants share an indivisible interest in the estate, i.e., all have equal rights to possess and use the property subject to the rights of the other cotenants. No co-tenant may claim to own any physical portion of the property exclusively. They share what is called undivided possession or unity of possession.

Interests individually owned. All tenants in common have distinct and separable ownership of their respective interests. Co-tenants may sell, encumber, or transfer their interests without obstruction or consent from the other owners. (A co-tenant may not, however, encumber the entire property.)

Electable ownership shares. Tenants in common determine among themselves what share of the estate each party will own. For example, three co-tenants may own 40%, 35%, and 25% interests in a property, respectively. In the absence of stated ownership shares, it is assumed that each has a share equal to that of the others.

No survivorship. A deceased co-tenant's estate passes by probate to the decedent's heirs and devisees rather than to the other tenants in common. Any number of heirs can share in the ownership of the willed tenancy.

No unity of time. It is not necessary for tenants in common to acquire their interests at the same time. A new co-tenant may enter into a pre-existing tenancy in common.

The following exhibit illustrates how tenants in common may transfer ownership interests to other parties by sale or will.

Exhibit 4.1 Tenancy in Common

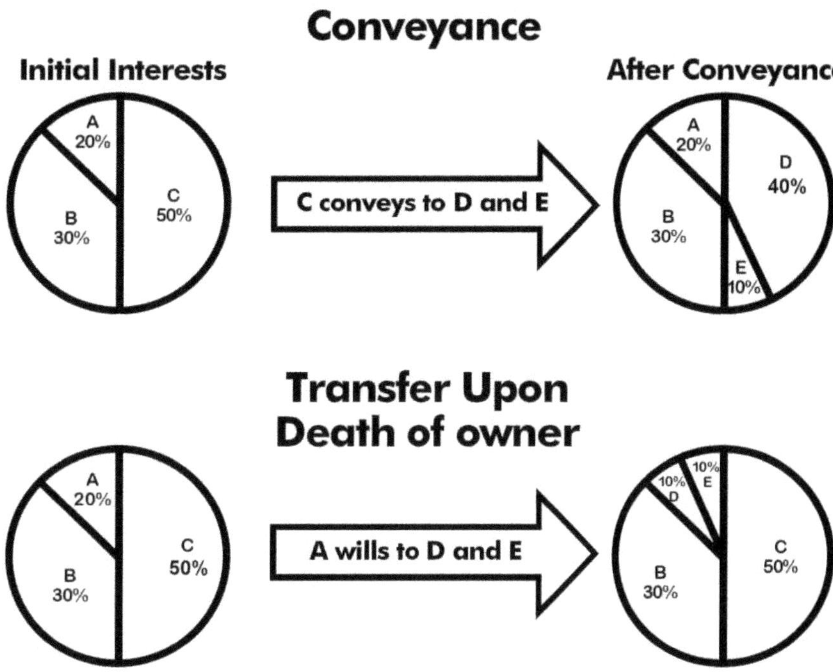

The exhibit shows three owners of a property as tenants in common: A owns 20%, B owns 30%, and C owns 50%. C decides to sell 4/5 of his interest to D and 1/5 to E. D's interest in the estate will be 40% (4/5 times 50%), and E's will be 10% (1/5 times 50%). Both new tenants are tenants in common with A and B. Note that any owner may sell any portion of his or her interest to other owners or outside parties.

The second part of the exhibit shows how, when co-owner A dies, she might bequeath her 20% share of the ownership to heirs D and E equally. In such a case, the heirs would each acquire a 10% share of ownership as tenants in common with B and C.

Joint tenancy

In a joint tenancy, two or more persons collectively own a property as if they were a single person. Rights and interests are indivisible and equal: each has a shared interest in the whole property which cannot be divided up. Joint tenants may only convey their interests to outside parties as tenant-in-common interests. One cannot convey a joint tenant interest.

The defining characteristics and requirements of joint tenancy are:

- unity of ownership
- equal ownership
- transfer of interest
- survivorship

Unity of ownership. Whereas tenants in common hold separate title to their individual interests, joint tenants together hold a single title to the property.

Equal ownership. Joint tenants own equal shares in the property, without exception. If there are four co-tenants, each owns 25% of the property. If there are ten co-tenants, each owns 10%.

Transfer of interest. A joint tenant may transfer his or her interest in the property to an outside party, but only as a tenancy in common interest. Whoever acquires the interest co-owns the property as a tenant in common with the other joint tenants. The remaining joint tenants continue to own an undivided interest in the property, less the new cotenant's share.

Survivorship. In most states, joint tenants enjoy rights of survivorship: if a joint tenant dies, all interests and rights pass to the surviving joint tenants free from any claims of creditors or heirs.

In other states, joint tenancy does not inherently include survivorship; survivorship must be expressly stated to be effected on transfer.

When only one joint tenant survives, the survivor's interest becomes an estate in severalty, and the joint tenancy is terminated. The estate will be then probated upon the severalty owner's death.

The survivorship feature of joint tenancy presents an advantage to tenancy in common, in that interests pass without probate proceedings. On the other hand, joint tenants relinquish any ability to will their interest to parties outside of the tenancy.

Exhibit 4.2 Joint Tenancy

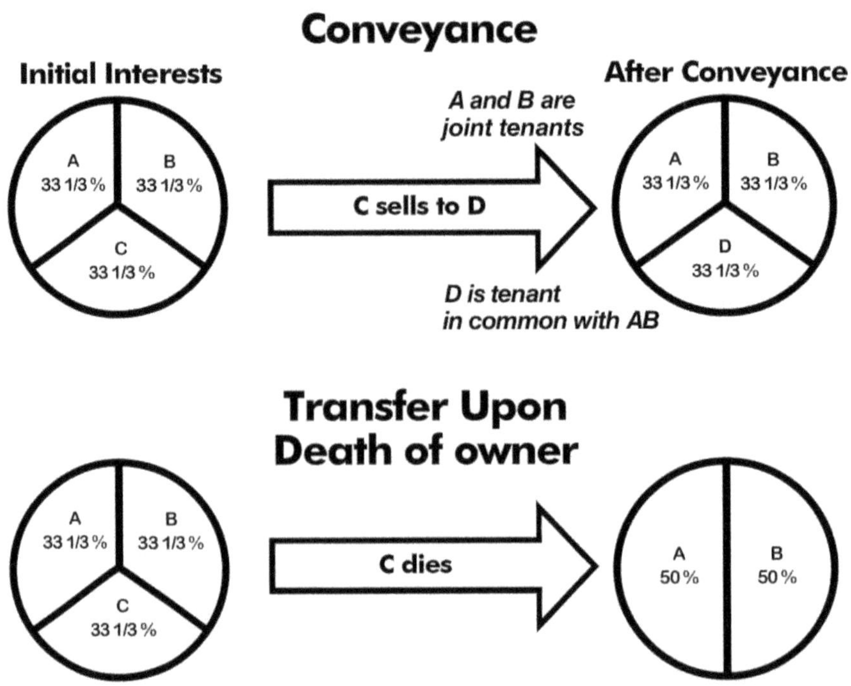

The exhibit shows three parties, A, B and C, who acquired a property as joint tenants. By definition, each owns a one-third share. If C sells to D, A and B automatically become joint tenants of two-thirds of the property. D becomes a tenant in common with A and B. D's interest will pass to her heirs upon her death.

If C dies, A and B receive equal shares of C's estate, making the remaining shares an equal 50%. If B then dies, A acquires the whole estate and becomes the sole owner. This event terminates the joint tenancy estate, and it becomes an estate in severalty.

Creation of joint tenancy. To create a joint tenancy, all owners must acquire the property at the same time, use the same deed, acquire equal interests, and share in equal rights of possession. These are referred to as the **four unities**.

- **unity of time**

  all parties must acquire the joint interest at the same time

- **unity of title**

  all parties must acquire the property in the same deed of conveyance

- **unity of interest**

  all parties must receive equal undivided interests

- **unity of possession**

  all parties must receive the same rights of possession

In most states, the conveyance must name the parties as joint tenants with rights of survivorship. Otherwise, and in the absence of clear intent of the parties, the estate will be considered a tenancy in common. In addition, a joint tenancy can only be created by agreement between parties, and not by operation of law.

In some states, a severalty owner may create a joint tenancy with other parties without the presence of the four unities by deeding the property to himself or herself and other parties as joint tenants.

Termination by partition suit. A partition suit can terminate a joint tenancy or a tenancy in common. Foreclosure and bankruptcy can also terminate these estates.

A partition suit is a legal avenue for an owner who wants to dispose of his or her interest against the wishes of other co-owners. The suit petitions the court to divide, or **partition**, the property physically, according to the owner's respective rights and interests. If this is not reasonably feasible, the court may order the property sold, whereupon the interests are liquidated and distributed proportionately.

Tenancy by the entireties

Tenancy by the entireties is a form of ownership traditionally reserved for **husband and wife,** though now available for same-sex spouses in some states. It features survivorship, equal interests, and limited exposure to foreclosure.

Survivorship. On the death of husband or wife, the decedent's interest passes automatically to the other spouse.

Equal, undivided interest. Each spouse owns the estate as if there were only one owner. Fractional interests cannot be transferred to outside parties. The entire interest may be conveyed, but only with the consent and signatures of both parties.

No foreclosure for individual debts. The estate is subject to foreclosure only for jointly incurred debts.

Termination. The estate may be terminated by divorce, death, mutual agreement, and judgments for joint debt.

Community property

Some states have established a community property form of ownership. This type of ownership defines property rights of legal spouses before, during, and after their marriage, as well as after the death of either spouse.

Community property law distinguishes real and personal property into categories of **separate** and **community** property. Separate property belongs to one spouse; community property belongs to both spouses equally.

Separate property consists of:

- property owned by either spouse at the time of the marriage
- property acquired by either spouse through inheritance or gift during the marriage
- property acquired with separate-property funds
- income from separate property

Community property consists of:

- all other property earned or acquired by either party during the marriage

For instance, John owns a car and a motorcycle, and Mary owns a car. They marry and buy a house. A year later, Mary's father dies and leaves her $10,000, which she uses to buy furniture. John, meanwhile, sells the motorcycle and buys a computer. John rents the computer to a programmer for $50 a month. The ownership of these properties is as follows:

John	Mary	Community
car 1	car 2	house
motorcycle	$10,000	
computer	furniture	
$50 income		

A spouse owns separate property free and clear of claims by the other spouse. He or she can transfer it without the other spouse's signature. Upon the death of the separate property owner, the property passes to heirs by will or laws of descent. Community property cannot be transferred or encumbered without the signatures of both spouses. Upon the death of either spouse, half of the deceased's community property passes to the surviving spouse, and the other half passes to the decedent's heirs.

Tenancy in partnership

Tenancy in partnership is a form of ownership held by business partners, as provided by the **Uniform Partnership Act**. The partnership tenancy grants equal rights to all partners, but the property must be used in connection with the partnership's business. Individual rights are not assignable.

ESTATES IN TRUST

Living trust
Land trust

In an estate in trust, a fee owner-- the **grantor** or **trustor**-- transfers legal title to a fiduciary-- the **trustee**-- who holds and manages the estate for the benefit of another party, the **beneficiary**. The trust may be created by a deed, will, or trust agreement.

The trustee has fiduciary duties to the trustor and the beneficiary to maintain the condition and value of the property. The specific responsibilities and authorities are set forth in the trust agreement.

Exhibit 4.3 Estate in Trust

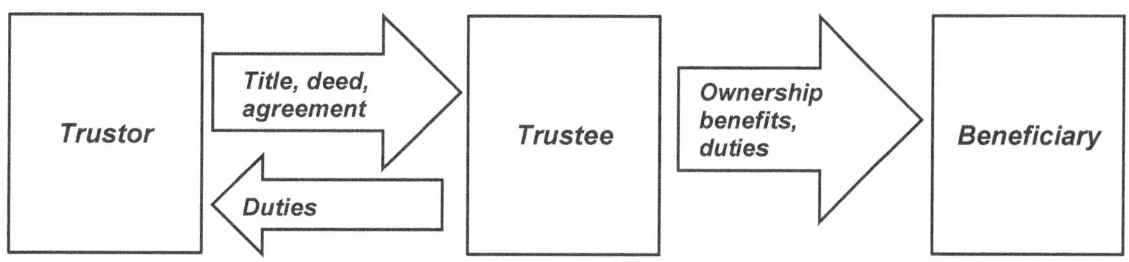

Living trust

A living trust allows the trustor, during his or her lifetime, to convey title to a trustee for the benefit of a third party. The trustor charges the trustee with all necessary responsibilities for managing the property, protecting its value, and securing whatever income it may produce. The trustee may also be ordered to sell the property at a given point. The beneficiary receives all income and sales proceeds, net of the trustee's fees.

Testamentary trust. A testamentary trust is structurally and mechanically the same as a living trust, except that it takes effect only when the trustor dies. Provisions of the decedent's will establish the trust.

Living and testamentary trusts may involve personal property as well as real property.

Land trust

A land trust allows the trustor to convey the fee estate to the trustee and *to name himself or herself the beneficiary*. The land trust applies only to real property, not to personal property. The agreement, or **deed in trust**, grants the beneficiary the rights to possess and use the property, and to exercise control over the actions of the trustee.

Conventional trust structure. The trustee holds legal title and has conventional fiduciary duties. The trustor must be a living person, but the beneficiary may be a corporation.

The distinguishing features of the land trust are:

- **beneficiary controls property**

  this includes occupancy and control of rents and sale proceeds

- **beneficiary controls trustee**

  the trustee is empowered to sell or encumber the property, but generally only with the beneficiary's approval

- **beneficiary identity not on record**

  public records do not identify the beneficiary; the beneficiary owns and enjoys the property in secrecy

- **limited term**

  the term of the land trust is limited and must be renewed or else the trustee is obligated to sell the property and distribute the proceeds

Beneficial interest. The beneficiary's interest in a land trust is *personal property*, not real property. This distinction offers certain advantages in transferring, encumbering, and probating the beneficiary's interest:

- **transferring**

  the beneficiary may transfer the interest by assignment instead of by deed

- **encumbering**

  the beneficiary may pledge the property as security for debt by collateral assignment rather than by recorded mortgage

- **probating**

  the property interests are probated in the state where the beneficiary resided at the time of death rather than the state where the property is located

---

OWNERSHIP BY BUSINESS ENTITIES

Corporation
Partnership
Limited liability company

Corporation

A corporation is a legal entity owned by stockholders. An elected board of directors oversees the business. Officers and managers conduct day-to-day activities. Officers and directors may be held fully liable for the corporation's actions, while shareholders are liable only to the extent of the value of their shares. Corporations, like individuals, may own real estate in severalty or as tenants in common.

Partnership

In a partnership, two or more persons agree to work together and share profits. A general partnership is not a distinct legal entity like a corporation. All the partners bear full liability for debts and obligations. A limited partnership has two or more partners, one or more being general partners and the others limited partners. The general partners run the business and are liable for debts and obligations. The limited partners are liable only to the extent of their investment in the partnership. Both general and limited partnerships may own real estate.

Limited liability company

A limited liability company (LLC) combines features of the corporation and the limited partnership. The LLC offers its members limited liability like a corporation, but income is passed directly to the members and is taxed to them as individual income. The management structure is flexible. Like a corporation or a partnership, an LLC may own real estate.

CONDOMINIUMS

Airspace and common elements
Interests and rights
Condominium creation
Organization and management
Owner responsibilities

A condominium is a hybrid form of ownership of multi-unit residential or commercial properties. It combines ownership of a fee simple interest in the **airspace** within a unit with ownership of an undivided share, as a tenant in common, of the entire property's **common elements,** such as lobbies, swimming pools, and hallways.

A condominium **unit** is one airspace unit together with the associated interest in the common elements.

Airspace and common elements

The unique aspect of the condominium is its fee simple interest in the airspace contained within the outer walls, floors, and ceiling of the building unit. This airspace may include internal walls which are not essential to the structural support of the building.

Common elements are all portions of the property that are necessary for the existence, operation, and maintenance of the condominium units. Common elements include:

- the land (if not leased)
- structural components of the building, such as exterior windows, roof, and foundation
- physical operating systems supporting all units, such as plumbing, power, communications installations, and central air conditioning
- recreational facilities
- building and ground areas used non-exclusively, such as stairways, elevators, hallways, and laundry rooms

Exhibit 4.4 The Condominium

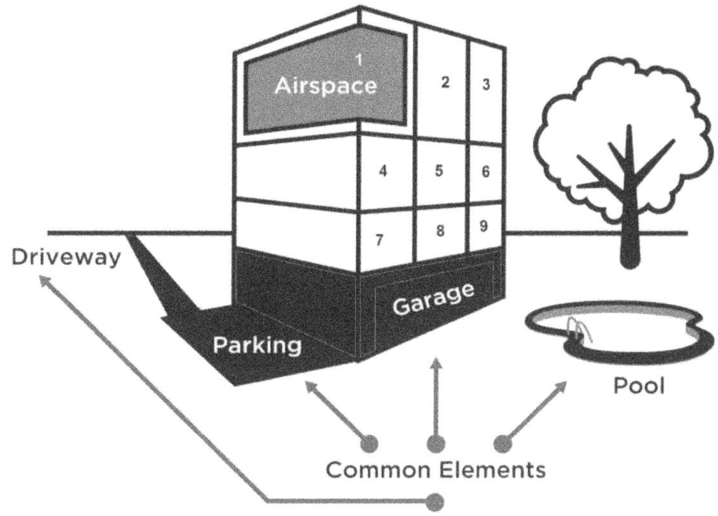

A buyer who purchases Unit #1 of the condominium illustrated obtains a fee simple interest in the airspace of apartment 1 and a tenancy in common interest in her pro rata share of the common elements. If all units in the building have the same ownership interest, the buyer would own an indivisible one-ninth interest in the common elements-- pool, parking lot, garage, pool, building structure, tree, etc.

Interests and rights

The condominium unit can be owned jointly, in severalty, in trust, or in any other manner allowed by state law. Unit owners hold an exclusive interest in their individual apartments, and co-own common elements with other unit owners as tenants in common.

Possession, use, and exclusion. Unit owners exclusively possess their apartment space, but must share common areas with other owners. The property's legal documents may create exceptions. For example, unit owners may be required to join and pay fees for use of a health club.

Unit owners as a group may exclude non-owners from portions of the common area, for instance, excluding uninvited parties from entering the building itself.

Transfer and encumbrance. Condominium units can be individually sold, mortgaged, or otherwise encumbered without interference from other unit owners. As a distinct entity, the condominium unit may also be foreclosed and liquidated. An owner may not sell interests in the apartment separately from the interest in the common elements.

Resale of a unit interest may entail limitations, such as the condominium association's prior approval of a buyer.

Condominium units are individually assessed and taxed. The assessment pertains to the value of the exclusive interest in the apartment as well as the unit's pro rata share of common elements.

Condominium creation

Condominium properties are created by executing and recording a condominium declaration and a **master deed**. The declaration must be legally correct in form and substance according to local laws. The party creating the declaration is referred to as the **developer**. The condominium may include ownership of the land or exclude it if the land is leased.

Declaration provisions. The condominium declaration may be required to include:

- a legal description and/or name of the property
- a survey of land, common elements, and all units
- plat maps of land and building, and floor plans with identifiers for all condominium units
- provisions for common area easements
- an identification of each unit's share of ownership in the overall property
- organization plans for creation of the condominium association, including its bylaws
- voting rights, membership status, and liability for expenses of individual owners
- covenants and restrictions regarding use and transfer of units

Organization and management

Organization. Condominium declarations typically provide for the creation of an **owner's association** to enforce the bylaws and manage the overall property. The association is often headed by a board of directors. The association board organizes how the property will be managed and by whom. It may appoint management agents, hire resident managers, and create supervisory committees. The board also oversees the property's finances and policy administration.

Management. Condominium properties have extensive management requirements, including maintenance, sales and leasing, accounting, owner services, sanitation, security, trash removal, etc. The association engages professional management companies, resident managers, sales and rental agents, specialized maintenance personnel, and outside service contractors to fulfill these functions.

Owner responsibilities

Individual units. Owner responsibilities relating to the apartment include:

- maintaining internal systems
- maintaining the property condition
- insuring contents of the unit

Common area assessments. Unit owners bear the costs of all other property expenses, such as maintenance, insurance, management fees, supplies, legal fees, and repairs. An annual operating budget totals these expenses and passes them through as **assessments** to unit owners, usually on a monthly basis.

Should an owner fail to pay periodic assessments, the condominium board can initiate court action to foreclose the property to pay the amounts owed.

The unit's pro rata share of the property's ownership as defined in the declaration determines the amount of a unit owner's assessment. For example, if a unit represents a 2% share of the property value, that unit owner's assessment will be 2% of the property's common area expenses.

COOPERATIVES

Interests, rights, and obligations
Organization and management

In a cooperative, or co-op, one owns **shares** in a non-profit corporation or cooperative association, which in turn acquires and owns an apartment building as its principal asset. Along with this stock, the shareholder acquires a **proprietary lease** to occupy one of the apartment units.

The number of shares purchased reflects the value of the apartment unit in relation to the property's total value. The ratio of the unit's value to total value also establishes what portions of the property's expenses the owner must pay.

Exhibit 4.5 The Cooperative

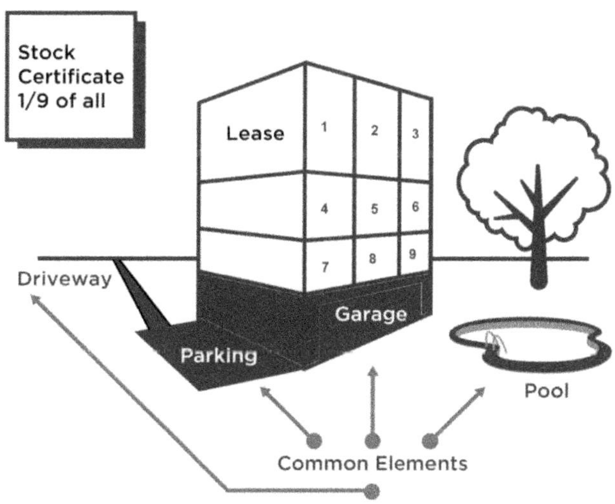

The exhibit shows a nine-unit apartment building. A cooperative corporation buys the building for $900,000. All nine units are of equal size, so the corporation decides that each apartment represents a value of $100,000, or 1/9 of the total. The co-op buyer pays the corporation $100,000 and receives 1/9 of the corporation's stock. The shareholder also receives a proprietary lease for apartment 1. The shareholder is now responsible for the apartment unit's pro rata share of the corporation's expenses, or 11.11%.

Interests, rights and obligations

Cooperative association's interest. The corporate entity of the cooperative association is the only party in the cooperative with a real property interest. The association's interest is an undivided interest in the entire property. There is no ownership interest in individual units, as with a condominium.

Shareholder's interest. In owning stock and a lease, a co-op unit owner's interest is *personal property* that is subject to control by the corporation. Unlike condominium ownership, the co-op owner owns neither a unit nor an undivided interest in the common elements.

Proprietary lease. The co-op lease is called a proprietary lease because the tenant is an owner (proprietor) of the corporation that owns the property. The lease has no stated or fixed rent. Instead, the proprietor-tenant is responsible for the unit's pro rata share of the corporation's expenses in supporting the cooperative. Unit owners pay monthly assessments. The proprietary lease has no stated term and remains in effect over the owner's period of ownership. When the unit is sold, the lease is assigned to the new owner.

Expense liability. The failure of individual shareholders to pay monthly expense assessments can destroy the investment of all the other co-op owners if the co-op cannot pay the bills by other means.

Since the corporation owns an undivided interest in the property, debts and financial obligations apply to the property as a whole, not to individual units. Should the corporation fail to meet its obligations, creditors and mortgagees may foreclose *on the entire property.* A completed foreclosure would terminate the shareholders' proprietary lease, and bankrupt the owning corporation. Compare this situation with that of a condominium, in which an individual's failure to pay endangers only that individual's unit, not the entire property.

Transfers. The co-op interest is transferred by assigning both the stock certificates and lease to the buyer.

Organization and management

A developer creates a cooperative by forming the cooperative association, which subsequently buys the cooperative property. The association's articles of incorporation, bylaws, and other legal documents establish operating policies, rules, and restrictions.

The shareholders elect a board of directors. The board assumes the responsibility for maintaining and operating the cooperative, much like a condominium board. Cooperative associations, however, also control the use and ownership of individual apartment units, since they are the legal owners. A shareholder's voting power is proportional to the number of shares owned.

TIME-SHARES

Time-share lease
Time-share freehold
Regulation

Time-share ownership is a fee or leasehold interest in a property whose owners or tenants agree to use the property on a periodic, non-overlapping basis. This type of ownership commonly concerns vacation and resort properties. Time-share arrangements provide for equal sharing of the property's expenses among the owners.

Time-share lease

In a leasehold time-share, the tenant agrees to rent the property on a scheduled basis or under any pre-arranged system of reservation, according to the terms of the lease. Generally, the scheduled use is denominated in weeks or months over the duration of the lease, a specified number of years.

Time-share freehold

In a freehold time-share, or **interval ownership estate**, tenants in common own undivided interests in the property. Expense prorations and rules governing interval usage are established by separate agreement when the estate is acquired.

For instance, the Blackburns want a monthly vacation in Colorado once a year. They find a time-share condominium that needs a twelfth buyer. The available month is May, which suits the Blackburns. The total price of the condominium is $240,000, and annual expenses are estimated to be $9,600. The Blackburns buy a one-twelfth interest with the other tenants in common by paying their share of the price, $20,000. They are also obligated to pay one-twelfth of the expenses every year, or $800. They have use of the property for one-twelfth of the year, in the month of May.

Interval owners must usually waive the right of partition, which would enable an owner to force the sale of the entire property.

Regulation

The development and sale of time-share properties has come under increased regulation in recent years. Developers and brokers in many states face more stringent disclosure requirements regarding ownership costs and risks. Other laws provide for a cooling-off period after the signing of a time-share sales contract, and require registration of advertising.

4 Ownership Snapshot Review

SOLE OWNERSHIP	
Tenancy in severalty	• sole ownership of a freehold estate
CO-OWNERSHIP	• ownership by two or more owners
Tenancy in common	• co-tenants enjoy an individually owned, undivided interest; any ownership share possible; no survivorship
Joint tenancy	• equal, undivided interest jointly owned, with survivorship
	• requires four unities to create: time, title, interest, possession
Tenancy by the entireties	• equal, undivided interest jointly owned by husband and wife
Community property	• per state law, joint ownership of property by spouses as opposed to separate property
	• separate: acquired before marriage or by gift or inheritance
Tenancy in partnership	• ownership by business partners
TRUSTS	• property granted by trustor to fiduciary trustee for benefit of beneficiary
Living trust	• personal and real property ownership created to take effect during one's lifetime (living trust) or after one's lifetime (testamentary)
Land trust	• real property ownership where grantor and beneficiary are same party; beneficiary uses, controls property, does not appear on public records
OWNERSHIP BY BUSINESS ENTITIES	
Corporation	• owned by stockholders; board of directors, officers, directors run business; liability of shareholders limited to value of shares; may own real estate in severalty or tenant in common
Partnership	• two or more partners; in general partnership, all partners run business and share liability; in limited partnership, general partners run business and are liable, limited partners liable only to the extent of their investment; both types may own real estate
Limited liability company	• members liability limited like in corporation, management flexible, income passed through and taxed as personal income; may own real estate
CONDOMINIUMS	• freehold ownership of a unit of airspace plus an undivided interest in the common elements as tenant in common with other owners
	• may be sold, encumbered or foreclosed without affecting other unit owners
	• creation: by developer's declaration
COOPERATIVES	• ownership of shares in owning corporation, plus proprietary lease in a unit; corporation has sole, undivided ownership
TIME SHARES	• a lease or ownership interest in a property for the purpose of periodic use by the owners or tenants on a scheduled basis

5 Encumbrances and Liens

Encumbrances
Easements
Encroachments
Licenses
Deed Restrictions
Liens
Foreclosure

ENCUMBRANCES

An encumbrance is an interest in and right to real property that limits the legal owner's freehold interest. In effect, an encumbrance is another's right to use or take possession of a legal owner's property, or to prevent the legal owner from enjoying the full bundle of rights in the estate.

An encumbrance does not include the right of possession and is therefore a lesser interest than the owner's freehold interest. For that reason, encumbrances are not considered estates. However, an encumbrance can lead to the owner's loss of ownership of the property.

Easements and liens are the most common types of encumbrance. An easement, such as a utility easement, enables others to use the property, regardless of the owner's desires. A lien, such as a tax lien, can be placed on the property's title, thereby restricting the owner's ability to transfer clear title to another party.

The two general types of encumbrance are those that affect the property's use and those that affect legal ownership, value and transfer.

Exhibit 5.1 General Types of Encumbrance

Restrictions on Owner's Use by Others' Rights to Use	Restrictions on Ownership, Value and Transfer
easements encroachments licenses deed restrictions	liens deed conditions

EASEMENTS

Easement appurtenant
Easement in gross
Easement creation
Easement termination

An **easement** is an interest in real property that gives the holder the right to use portions of the legal owner's real property in a defined way. Easement rights may apply to a property's surface, subsurface, or airspace, but the affected area must be defined.

The receiver of the easement right is the **benefited party**; the giver of the easement right is the **burdened party**.

Essential characteristics of easements include the following:

- An easement must involve the owner of the land over which the easement runs, and another, non-owning party. *One cannot own an easement over one's own property.*
- an easement pertains to a specified physical area within the property boundaries
- an easement may be **affirmative**, allowing a use, such as a right-of-way, or **negative**, *prohibiting a use*, such as an airspace easement that prohibits one property owner from obstructing another's ocean view

The two basic types of easement are appurtenant and gross.

Easement appurtenant

An easement appurtenant gives a property owner a right of usage to portions of an *adjoining property* owned by another party. The property enjoying the usage right is called the **dominant tenement**, or **dominant estate**. The property containing the physical easement itself is the **servient tenement**, since it must serve the easement use.

The term appurtenant means "attaching to." An easement appurtenant attaches to the estate and transfers with it unless specifically stated otherwise in the transaction documents. More specifically, the easement attaches as a beneficial interest to the dominant estate, and as an encumbrance to the servient estate. The easement appurtenant then becomes part of the dominant estate's bundle of rights and the servient estate's obligation, or encumbrance.

Transfer. Easement appurtenant rights and obligations automatically transfer with the property upon transfer of either the dominant or servient estate, whether mentioned in the deed or not. For example, John grants Mary the right to share his driveway at any time over a five-year period, and the grant is duly recorded. If Mary sells her property in two years, the easement right transfers to the buyer as part of the estate.

Non-exclusive use. The servient tenement, as well as the dominant tenement, may use the easement area, provided the use does not unreasonably obstruct the dominant use.

Exhibit 5.2 Easements appurtenant

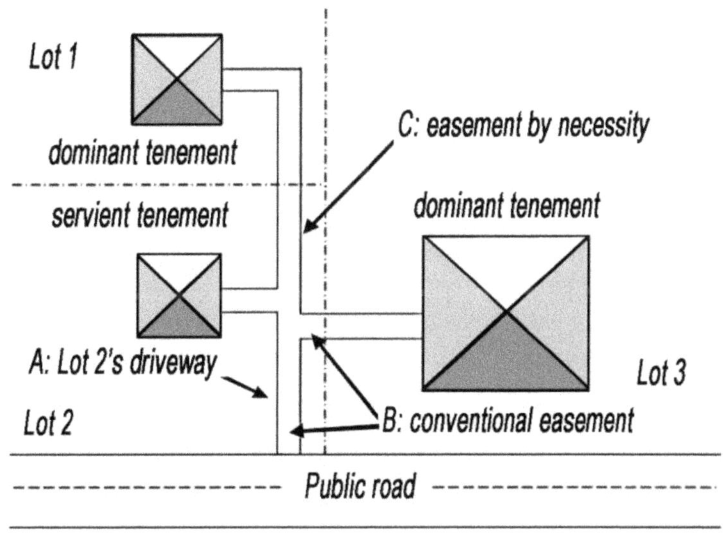

The exhibit shows a conventional easement appurtenant. The driveway marked A belongs to parcel #2. An easement appurtenant, marked B, allows parcel #3 to use #2's driveway. Parcel #3 is the dominant tenement, and #2 is the servient tenement.

Easement by necessity. An easement by necessity is an easement appurtenant granted by a court of law to a property owner because of a circumstance of necessity, most commonly the need for access to a property. Since property cannot be legally **landlocked**, or *without legal access to a public thoroughfare*, a court will grant an owner of a landlocked property an easement by necessity over an adjoining property that has access to a thoroughfare. The landlocked party becomes the dominant tenement, and the property containing the easement is the servient tenement.

In the exhibit, parcel #1, which is landlocked, owns an easement by necessity, marked C, across parcel #2.

Party wall easement. A party wall is a common wall shared by two separate structures along a property boundary.

Party wall agreements generally provide for severalty ownership of half of the wall by each owner, or at least some fraction of the width of the wall. In addition, the agreement grants a *negative* easement appurtenant to each owner in the other's wall. This is to prevent unlimited use of the wall, in particular a destructive use that would jeopardize the adjacent property owner's building. The agreement also establishes responsibilities and obligations for maintenance and repair of the wall.

For example, Helen and Troy are adjacent neighbors in an urban housing complex having party walls on property lines. They both agree that they separately own the portion of the party wall on their property. They also grant each other an easement appurtenant in their owned portion of the wall. The easement restricts any use of the wall that would impair its condition. They also agree to split any repairs or maintenance evenly.

Other structures that are subject to party agreements are common fences, driveways, and walkways.

Easement in gross

An easement in gross is a *personal right* that one party grants to another to use the grantor's real property. The right *does not attach* to the grantor's estate. It involves only one property, and, consequently, does not benefit any property owned by the easement owner. *There are no dominant or servient estates in an easement in gross*. An easement in gross may be personal or commercial.

Exhibit 5.3 Easements in Gross

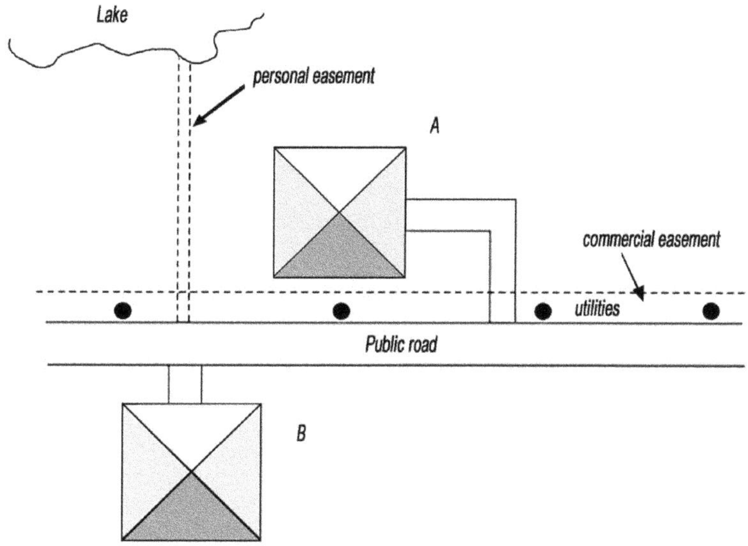

Personal. A personal easement in gross is granted for the grantee's lifetime. The right is irrevocable during this period, but terminates on the grantee's death. It may not be sold, assigned, transferred, or willed. A personal gross easement differs from a license in that the grantor of a license may revoke the usage right.

The exhibit shows that a beachfront property owner (A) has granted a neighbor (B) across the street the right to cross A's property to reach the beach.

Commercial. A commercial easement in gross is granted to a business entity rather than a private party. The duration of the commercial easement is not tied to anyone's
lifetime. The right may by assigned, transferred, or willed.

Examples of commercial gross easements include:

- a marina's right-of-way to a boat ramp
- a utility company's right-of-way across a lot owners' property to install and maintain telephone lines (as illustrated in the exhibit).

Easement creation

An easement may be created by *voluntary action, by necessary or prescriptive operation of law,* and *by government power of eminent domain.*

Voluntary. A property owner may create a voluntary easement by express grant in a sale contract, or as a reserved right expressed in a deed.

Necessity. A court decree creates an easement by necessity to provide access to a landlocked property. **Easement by prescription.** If someone uses another's property as an easement without permission for a statutory period of time and under certain conditions, a court order may give the user the easement right by **prescription**, *regardless of the owner's desires.*

For a prescriptive easement order to be granted, the following circumstances must be true:

- **Adverse and hostile use**

  the use has been occurring without permission or license

- **Open and notorious use**

  the owner knows or is presumed to have known of the use

- **Continuous use**

  the use has been generally uninterrupted over the statutory prescriptive period

For example, a subdivision owns an access road, which is also used by other neighborhoods to access a grocery store. One day, the subdivision blocks off the road, claiming it has never granted the neighbors permission to use the road. If the neighbors have been using the road for the prescribed period, they may sue for an easement by prescription, since the subdivision owners can be assumed to have known of the usage.

Eminent domain. Government entities can create easements through the exercise of eminent domain, wherein they condemn a portion of a property and cause it to be sold "for the greater good." A typical example is a town's condemnation of private land to create a new municipal sewer system.

Easement termination

Easements terminate by:

- *express release of the right* by the easement holder
- *merger*, as when a dominant tenement acquires the servient property, or vice versa
- *purposeful abandonment* by the dominant tenement
- *condemnation* through eminent domain
- *change or cessation of the purpose* for the easement
- *destruction* of an easement structure, such as a party fence
- *non-use* of an easement by prescription

ENCROACHMENTS

An encroachment is the unauthorized, physical intrusion of one owner's real property into that of another.

Examples of encroachments are:

- a tree limb extending into the neighbor's property, violating his or her airspace
- a driveway extending beyond the lot line onto the neighbor's land
- a fence built beyond the property line

Encroachments cause infringements on the rights of the trespassed owner, and may diminish the property's value, particularly when the property is to be sold.

Encroachments often do not appear on a property's title records. A survey may be required to detect or demonstrate the existence of an encroachment.

An owner may sue for removal of an encroachment or for compensation for damages. If an encroached owner takes no remedial action over a prescribed number of years, the encroachment may become an easement by prescription.

LICENSES

A license, much like a personal easement in gross, is a personal right that a property owner grants to another to use the property for a specific purpose. Licenses are not transferrable and do not attach to the land. They cease on the death of either party, or on the sale of the property.

Unlike a personal easement in gross, a license is revocable at any time. Licenses are often granted informally, as a verbal statement of permission.

A farmer granting a neighbor permission to cross his land to reach and fish in his pond is an example of a license.

DEED RESTRICTIONS

A deed restriction is a limitation imposed on a buyer's use of a property by stipulation in the deed of conveyance or recorded subdivision plat.

A deed restriction may apply to a single property or to an entire subdivision. A developer may place restrictions on all properties within a recorded **subdivision plat**. Subsequent re-sales of properties within the subdivision are thereby subject to the plat's covenants and conditions.

A private party who wants to control the quality and standards of a property can establish a deed restriction. Deed restrictions take precedence over zoning ordinances if they are more restrictive.

Deed restrictions typically apply to:

- the land use
- the size and type of structures that may be placed on the property
- minimum costs of structures
- engineering, architectural, and aesthetic standards, such as setbacks or specific standards of construction

Deed restrictions in a subdivision, for example, might include a minimum size for the residential structure, setback requirements for the home, and prohibitions against secondary structures such as sheds or cottages.

Deed restrictions are either covenants or conditions. A **condition** can only be created within a transfer of ownership. If a condition is later violated, a suit can force the owner to forfeit ownership to the previous owner. A **covenant** can be created by mutual agreement. If a covenant is breached, an injunction can force compliance or payment of compensatory damages.

LIENS

Lien types
Lien priority
Superior liens
Junior liens

A lien is a creditor's **claim** against personal or real property as security for a debt of the property owner. If the owner defaults, the lien gives the creditor the right to force the sale of the property to satisfy the debt.

For example, a homeowner borrows $50,000 to pay for a new roof. The lender funds the loan in exchange for the borrower's promissory note to repay the loan. At the same time, the lender places a lien on the property for $50,000 as security for the debt. If the borrower defaults, the lien allows the lender to force the sale of the house to satisfy the debt.

The example illustrates that a lien is an encumbrance that restricts free and clear ownership by securing the liened property as **collateral** for a debt. If the owner sells the property, the lienholder is entitled to that portion of the sales proceeds needed to pay off the debt. In addition, a defaulting owner may lose ownership altogether if the creditor forecloses.

In addition to restricting the owner's bundle of rights, a recorded lien effectively reduces the owner's equity in the property to the extent of the lien amount.

The creditor who places a lien on a property is called the **lienor**, and the debtor who owns the property is the **lienee**.

Liens have the following legal features:

- **a lien does not convey ownership, with one exception**

  A lienor generally has an equitable interest in the property, but not legal ownership. The exception is a **mortgage lien** on a property in a title-theory state. In these states, the mortgage transaction conveys legal title to the lender, who holds it until the mortgage obligations are satisfied. During the mortgage loan period, the borrower has equitable title to the property.

- **a lien attaches to the property**

  If the property is transferred, the *new owner acquires the lien securing the payment of the debt.* In addition, the creditor may take foreclosure action against the new owner for satisfaction of the debt.

- **a property may be subject to multiple liens**

  There may be numerous liens against a particular property. The more liens there are recorded against property, the less secure the collateral is for a creditor, since the total value of all liens may approach or exceed the total value of the property.

- **a lien terminates on payment of the debt and recording of documents**

  Payment of the debt and recording of the appropriate satisfaction documents ordinarily terminate a lien. If a default occurs, a suit for judgment or foreclosure enforces the lien. These actions force the sale of the property.

Lien types

Liens may be voluntary or involuntary, general or specific, and superior or inferior.

Voluntary and involuntary. A property owner may create a **voluntary** lien to borrow money or some other asset secured by a mortgage. An **involuntary** lien is one that a legal process places against a property regardless of the owner's desires.

If statutory law imposes an involuntary lien, the lien is a **statutory lien**. A real estate tax lien is a common example. If court action imposes an involuntary lien, the lien is an **equitable lien**. An example is a judgment lien placed on a property as security for a money judgment.

General and specific. A general lien is one *placed against any and all real and personal property* owned by a particular debtor. An example is an inheritance tax lien placed against all property owned by the heir. **A specific** lien *attaches to a single item* of real or personal property, and does not affect other property owned by the debtor. A conventional mortgage lien is an example, where the property is the only asset attached by the lien.

Superior and inferior lien. The category of superior, or **senior**, liens ranks above the category of inferior, or **junior**, liens, meaning that superior liens receive first payment from the proceeds of a foreclosure. The superior category includes liens for real estate tax, special assessments, and inheritance tax. Other liens, including income tax liens, are inferior.

Lien priority

Within the superior and inferior categories, a ranking of lien priority determines the order of the liens' claims on the security underlying the debt. The highest ranking lien is first to receive proceeds from the foreclosed and liquidated security. The lien with lowest priority is last in line. The owner receives any sale proceeds that remain after all lienors receive their due.

Lien priority is of paramount concern to the creditor, since it establishes the level of risk in recovering loaned assets in the event of default.

Establishment of priority. Two factors primarily determine lien priority:

- the lien's categorization as superior or junior
- the date of recordation of the lien

Exhibit 5.4 Priority of Real Estate Liens

Superior liens in rank order
1. Real estate tax liens
2. Special assessment liens
3. Federal estate tax liens
4. State inheritance tax liens

Junior liens: priority by date of recording
Federal income tax liens
State corporate income tax liens
State intangible tax liens
Judgment liens
Mortgage liens
Vendor's liens
Mechanic's liens (by date work was performed)
Broker's liens

All superior liens take precedence over all junior liens regardless of recording date, since they are considered to be matters of public record not requiring further constructive notice. Thus, a real estate tax lien (senior) recorded on June 15 has priority over an income tax lien (junior) recorded on June 1.

A junior lien is automatically inferior, or **subordinate**, to a superior lien. Among junior liens, date of recording determines priority. The rule is: *the earlier the recording date of the lien, the higher its priority*. For example, if a judgment lien is recorded against a property on Friday, and a mortgage lien is recorded on the following Tuesday, the judgment lien has priority and must be satisfied in a foreclosure ahead of the mortgage lien.

The mechanic's lien is an exception to the recording rule. Its priority dates from the point in time when the work commenced or ended, as state law determines, rather than from when it was recorded.

The following example illustrates how lien priority works in paying off secured debts. A homeowner is foreclosed on a second mortgage taken out in 2018 for $25,000. The first mortgage, taken in 2016, has a balance of $150,000. Unpaid real estate taxes for the current year are $1,000. There is a $3,000 mechanic's lien on the property for work performed in 2017. The home sells for $183,000.

The proceeds are distributed in the following order:

1. $1,000 real estate taxes
2. $150,000 first mortgage
3. $3,000 mechanic's lien
4. $25,000 second mortgage
5. $4,000 balance to the homeowner

Note the risky position of the second mortgage holder: the property had to sell for at least $179,000 for the lender to recover the $25,000.

Subordination. A lienor can change the priority of a junior lien by voluntarily agreeing to subordinate, or lower, the lien's position in the hierarchy. This change is often necessary when working with a mortgage lender who will not originate a mortgage loan unless it is senior to all other junior liens on the property. The lender may require the borrower to obtain agreements from other lien holders to subordinate their liens to the new mortgage.

For example, interest rates fall from 8% to 6.5% on first mortgages for principal residences. A homeowner wants to refinance her mortgage, but she also has a separate home-equity loan on the house. Since the first-mortgage lender will not accept a lien priority inferior to a home equity loan, the homeowner must persuade the home equity lender to subordinate the home equity lien to the new first-mortgage lien.

Superior liens

Real estate tax lien. The local legal taxing authority annually places a real estate tax lien, also called an **ad valorem tax lien**, against properties as security for payment of the annual property tax. The amount of a particular lien is based on the taxed property's assessed value and the local tax rate.

Special assessment lien. Local government entities place assessment liens against certain properties to ensure payment for local improvement projects such as new roads, schools, sewers, or libraries. An assessment lien applies only to properties that are expected to benefit from the municipal improvement.

Federal and state inheritance tax liens. Inheritance tax liens arise from taxes owed by a decedent's estate. The lien amount is determined through probate and attaches to both real and personal property.

Junior liens

Tax liens. All tax liens other than those for ad valorem, assessment, and estate tax are junior liens. They include:

- **federal income tax lien**

  placed on a taxpayer's real and personal property for failure to pay income taxes

- **state corporate income tax lien**

  filed against corporate property for failure to pay taxes

- **state intangible tax lien**

  filed for non-payment of taxes on intangible property

- **state corporation franchise tax lien**

  filed to ensure collection of fees to do business within a state

Judgment lien. A judgment lien attaches to real and personal property as a result of a money judgment issued by a court in favor of a creditor. The creditor may obtain a **writ of execution** to force the sale of attached property and collect the debt. After paying the debt from the sale proceeds, the debtor may obtain a **satisfaction of judgment** to clear the title records on other real property that remains unsold.

During the course of a lawsuit, the plaintiff creditor may secure a **writ of attachment** to prevent the debtor from selling or concealing property. In such a case, there must be a clear likelihood that the debt is valid and that the defendant has made attempts to sell or hide property.

Certain properties are exempt from judgment liens, such as homestead property and joint tenancy estates.

Mortgage and trust deed lien. In lien-theory states, mortgages and trust deeds secure loans made on real property. In these states, the lender records a lien as soon as possible after disbursing the funds in order to establish lien priority.

Vendor's lien. A vendor's lien, also called a **seller's lien**, secures a purchase money mortgage, a seller's loan to a buyer to finance the sale of a property.

Municipal utility lien. A municipality may place a utility lien against a resident's real property for failure to pay utility bills.

Mechanic's lien. A mechanic's lien secures the costs of labor, materials, and supplies incurred in the repair or construction of real property improvements. If a property owner fails to pay for work performed or materials supplied, a worker or supplier can file a lien to force the sale of the property and collect the debt.

Any individual who performs approved work may place a mechanic's lien on the property to the extent of the direct costs incurred. Note that unpaid subcontractors may record mechanic's liens *whether the general contractor has been paid or not*. Thus it is possible for an owner to have to double-pay a bill in order to eliminate the mechanic's lien if the general contractor neglects to pay the subcontractors. The mechanic's lienor must enforce the lien within a certain time period, or the lien expires.

In contrast to other junior liens, the priority of a mechanic's lien *dates from the time when the work was begun or completed*. For example, a carpenter finishes a job on May 15. The owner refuses to pay the carpenter in spite of the carpenter's two-month collection effort. Finally, on August 1, the carpenter places a mechanic's lien on the property. The effective date of the lien for purposes of lien priority is May 15, not August 1.

Broker's lien. Many states allow a broker in specified circumstances to file a broker's lien against a property in a transaction in case the party obligated to pay the broker a commission refuses to pay. The lien attaches to the real estate interest owned by the obligated party.

FORECLOSURE

Mortgage lien foreclosure
Judicial foreclosure
Non-judicial foreclosure
Strict foreclosure
Deed in lieu of foreclosure
Short sale

All liens can be enforced by the sale or other transfer of title of the secured property, whether by court action, operation of law, or through powers granted in the original loan agreement. The enforcement proceedings are referred to as foreclosure.

State law governs the foreclosure process. Broadly, a statutory or court-ordered sale enforces a general lien, including a judgment lien. A lawsuit or loan provision authorizing the sale or direct transfer of the attached property enforces a specific lien, such as a mortgage. Real estate tax liens are enforced through **tax foreclosure sales**, or **tax sales**.

Mortgage lien foreclosure

Three types of foreclosure process enforce mortgage liens:

- judicial foreclosure
- non-judicial foreclosure
- strict foreclosure

Exhibit 5.5 Foreclosure Processes

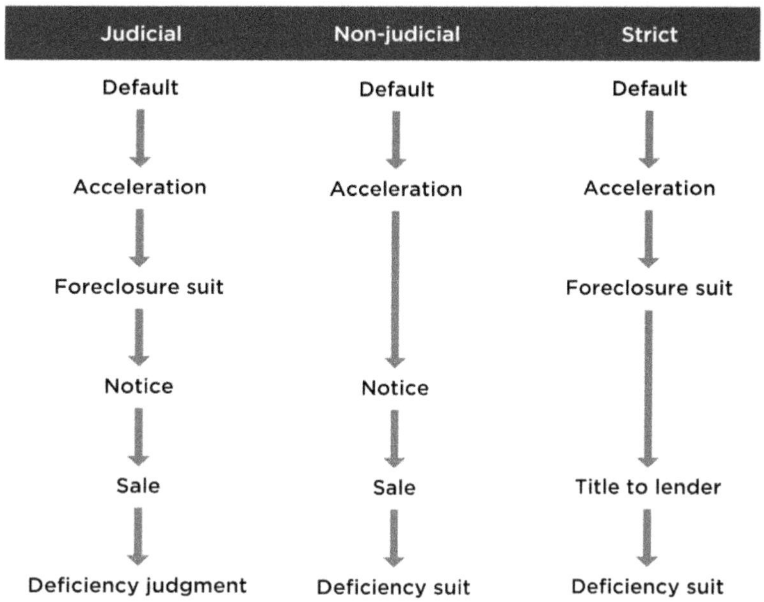

Judicial foreclosure

Judicial foreclosure occurs in states that use a two-party mortgage document (borrower and lender) that does not contain a "power of sale" provision. Lacking this provision, a lender must file a **foreclosure suit** and undertake a court proceeding to enforce the lien.

Acceleration and filing. If a borrower has failed to meet loan obligations in spite of proper notice and applicable grace periods, the lender can **accelerate** the loan, or declare that the loan balance and all other sums due on the loan are payable immediately.

If the borrower does not pay off the loan in full, the lender then files a foreclosure suit, naming the borrower as defendant. The suit asks the court to:

- terminate the defendant's interests in the property
- order the property sold publicly to the highest bidder
- order the proceeds applied to the debt

Lis Pendens. In the foreclosure suit, a **lis pendens** gives public notice that the mortgaged property may soon have a judgment issued against it. This notice enables other lienholders to join in the suit against the defendant.

Writ of execution. If the defendant fails to meet the demands of the suit during a prescribed period, the court orders the termination of interests of any and all parties in the property, and orders the property to be sold. The court's **writ of execution** authorizes an official, such as the county sheriff, to seize and sell the foreclosed property.

Public sale and sale proceeds. After public notice of the sale, the property is auctioned to the highest bidder. The new owner receives title free and clear of all previous liens, whether the lienholders have been paid or not. Proceeds of the sale are applied to payment of liens according to priority. After payment of real estate taxes, lienholders' claims and costs of the sale, any remaining funds go to the mortgagor (borrower).

Deficiency judgment. If the sale does not yield sufficient funds to cover the amounts owed, the mortgagee may ask the court for a deficiency judgment. This enables the lender to attach and foreclose a judgment lien on other real or personal property the borrower owns.

Right of redemption. The borrower's right of redemption, also called equity of redemption, is the right to *reclaim a property* that has been foreclosed by paying off amounts owed to creditors, including interest and costs. Redemption is possible within a **redemption period**. Some states allow redemption during the foreclosure proceeding at any time "until the gavel drops" at the sale. Other states have statutory periods of up to a year following the sale for the owner of a foreclosed property to redeem the estate. Also see **right to reinstate** on page 256 in Chapter 17.

Non-judicial foreclosure

When there is a "power of sale" provision in the mortgage or trust deed document, a non-judicial foreclosure can force the sale of the liened property *without a foreclosure suit*. The "power of sale" clause in effect enables the mortgagee to order a public sale without court decree.

Foreclosure process. On default, the foreclosing mortgagee records and delivers notice to the borrower and other lienholders. After the proper period, a "notice of sale" is published, the sale is conducted, and all liens are extinguished. The highest bidder then receives unencumbered title to the property.

Deficiency suit. The lender does not obtain a deficiency judgment or lien in a non-judicial foreclosure action. The lender instead must file a new deficiency suit against the borrower.

Re-instatement and redemption. During the notice of default and notice of sale periods, the borrower may pay the lender and terminate the proceedings. Exact re-instatement periods vary from state to state. There is no redemption right in non-judicial foreclosure.

Strict foreclosure

Strict foreclosure is a court proceeding that gives the lender title directly, by court order, instead of giving cash proceeds from a public sale.

On default, the lender gives the borrower official notice. After a prescribed period, the lender files suit in court, whereupon the court establishes a period within which the defaulting party must repay the amounts owed. If the defaulter does not repay the funds, the court orders transfer of full, legal title to the lender.

Deed in lieu of foreclosure

A defaulting borrower who faces foreclosure may avoid court actions and costs by voluntarily deeding the property to the mortgagee. This is accomplished with a deed in lieu of foreclosure , which transfers legal title to the lienholder. The transfer, however, does not terminate any existing liens on the property.

Short sale

A **short sale** occurs when a property owner owes more than resale value and loan pay-off for a property and agrees to let the lender sell the property in exchange for release from the lien. The lender may or may not agree to accept the deficient price as satisfaction and may require the seller to pay the deficiency by way of a deficiency judgment. There may also be tax consequences for the seller. To avoid the deficiency, the seller must make sure that the agreements include a full release of the underlying debt and a statement that it was fully satisfied.

After the property is retaken by foreclosure or short sale, it becomes "bank owned." **Forbearance** or a **loan modification** allows the borrower to avoid legal action and keep the property under a new agreement with the lender.

The parties to a short sale are the buyer and seller. The lender is a third party contingency who must approve the sale. The process is generally as follows.

Short sale procedure

1. The borrower or borrower's agents contact the lender to discuss the short sale option.
2. If willing, the lender sets the required terms of the short sale.
3. The real estate agent provides the lender a Broker's Price Opinion (BPO).
4. The agent lists the property for sale at the price that will cover the mortgage.
5. The agent places a note in the Multiple Listing Service (MLS) stating that the lender will consider a short sale.
6. A buyer submits an offer.
7. The owner agrees to the contract
8. The lender approves the short sale.
9. The transaction closes.
10. The lender may take action to recover the deficiency.

5 Encumbrances and Liens Snapshot Review

ENCUMBRANCES	• non-possessory interests limiting the legal owner's rights
EASEMENTS	• a right to use portions of another's property
Easement appurtenant	• dominant tenement's right to use or restrict adjacent servient tenement; attaches to the real estate
	• easement by necessity: granted by necessity, e.g. to landlocked owners
	• party wall: negative easement in a shared structure
Easement in gross	• a right to use property that does not attach to the real estate
	• personal: not revocable or transferrable; ends upon death of easement holder
	• commercial: granted to businesses; transferrable
Easement creation	• voluntary grant, court decree by necessity or prescription, eminent domain
	• by prescription: obtainable through continuous, open, adverse use over a period
Easement termination	• release; merger; abandonment; condemnation; change of purpose; destruction; non-use
ENCROACHMENTS	• intrusions of real estate into adjoining property; can become easements
LICENSES	• personal rights to use a property; do not attach; non-transferrable; revocable
DEED RESTRICTIONS	• conditions and covenants imposed on a property by deed or subdivision plat
LIENS	• claims attaching to real and personal property as security for debt
Lien types	• voluntary and involuntary; general and specific; superior and junior
Lien priority	• rank ordering of claims established by lien classification and date of recording; determines who gets paid first if lienee defaults
Superior liens	• rank over junior liens; not ranked by recording date; real estate tax and assessment liens and inheritance taxes
Junior liens	• rank by recording date: judgment; mortgage, vendor's, utility, mechanic's, broker's, other tax liens; mechanic's lien priority "dates back" to when work or sale transpired
FORECLOSURE	• enforcement of liens through liquidation or transfer of encumbered property
Mortgage lien foreclosure	• liquidation or transfer of collateral property by judicial, non-judicial, or strict foreclosure
Judicial foreclosure	• lawsuit and court-ordered public sale; deficiency judgments, redemption rights
Non-judicial foreclosure	• "power of sale" granted to lender; no suit; no deficiency judgment; no redemption period after sale
Strict foreclosure	• court orders legal transfer of title directly to lender without public sale
Deed in lieu of foreclosure	• defaulted borrower deeds property to lender to avoid foreclosure
Short sale	• sale at a price that does not cover a borrower's loan balance

6 Transferring & Recording Title To Real Estate

Title to Real Estate
Deeds of Conveyance
Wills
Involuntary Title Transfer
Title Records

TITLE TO REAL ESTATE

Legal and equitable title
Notice of title
Transferring title

Legal and equitable title

Owning title to real property commonly connotes owning the complete bundle of rights that attach to the property, including the right to possession. More accurately, someone who possesses all ownership interests owns **legal title** to the property. Legal title is distinct from **equitable title**, which is the interest or *right to obtain legal title* to a property in accordance with a sale or mortgage contract between the legal owner and a buyer or creditor. During the contractual period of time when ownership of legal title is contingent upon the contract, the buyer or lender owns equitable title to the property.

For example, a buyer enters into a contract for deed to purchase a house. The seller lends the bulk of the purchase price to the buyer for a term of three years. The buyer takes possession of the property, and makes payments on the loan. During this period, the seller retains legal title, and the buyer owns equitable title. If the buyer fulfills the terms of the agreement over the three year period, the buyer has an enforceable contract to obtain legal title.

Another common example is a mortgage loan transaction that gives the lender the right to execute a strict foreclosure, which transfers legal title to the lender in the event of a default. With this contractual right, the lender has equitable title to the property.

In practice, the terms "title" and "legal title" are often used interchangeably.

Notice of title

In any legal system that permits private ownership of real property, there will always be disputes as to who truly owns a particular parcel of real estate. For example, an owner might "sell" his property to three unrelated parties. The first party buys the property at the earliest date, the second party pays the highest price, and the third party receives the best deed, a warranty deed. Who owns legal title to the property?

Ownership of legal title is a function of evidence. A court will generally rule that the person who has the preponderance of evidence of ownership is the owner of the property. In the example, if the first two buyers did not receive a deed while the third party did, the third party may have the best evidence and be ruled the legal title-holder. However, what if the first buyer had moved into the house and occupied it for six months before the original owner sold the property to the second and third buyers? And what if the second buyer, after searching title records, reports that the seller never really owned the property and therefore could not legally sell it to anyone! Now who owns the property?

The illustration underscores the difficulty of proving title to real estate: there is no absolute and irrefutable proof that a party holds legal title. Our legal system has developed two forms of title evidence-- actual notice and constructive notice-- to assist in the determination.

Actual notice. The term "notice" is synonymous with "knowledge." A person who has received *actual* notice has *actual knowledge* of something. Receiving actual notice means learning of something through direct experience or communication. In proving real estate ownership, a person provides actual notice by producing direct evidence, such as by showing a valid will. Another party receives actual notice by seeing direct evidence, such as by reviewing the deed, reading title records, or physically visiting the property to see who is in possession. Thus if Mary Pierce drives to a property and sees directly that John Doe is in possession of the home, Mary then has received actual notice of John Doe's claim of ownership. Her knowledge is obtained through direct experience.

Constructive notice. Constructive notice, or **legal notice**, is knowledge of a fact that a person *could have or should have obtained*. The foremost method of imparting constructive notice is by recordation of ownership documents in public records, specifically, *title records*. Since public records are open to everyone, the law generally presumes that when evidence of ownership is recorded, the public at large *has received constructive notice* of ownership. By the same token, the law presumes that the owner of record is in fact the legal owner. Thus, if John Doe records the deed of conveyance, he has imparted, and Mary Pierce has received, constructive notice of ownership. Possession of the property can also be construed as constructive notice, since a court may rule that Mary *should have visited the property* to ascertain whether it was occupied.

A combination of actual and constructive notice generally provides the most indisputable evidence of real property ownership.

Transferring title

Transfer of title to real estate, also called **alienation**, occurs voluntarily and involuntarily. When the transfer uses a written instrument, the transfer is called a **conveyance.**

Exhibit 6.1 Transferring Title to Real Estate

Voluntary	Involuntary
public grant deed will	descent escheat foreclosure eminent domain adverse possession estoppel

Voluntary alienation. Voluntary alienation is an unforced transfer of title by sale or gift from an owner to another party. If the transferor is a government entity and the recipient is a private party, the conveyance is a **public grant**. If the transferor is a private party, the conveyance is a **private grant**.

A living owner makes a private grant by means of a **deed of conveyance**, or **deed**. A private grant that occurs when the owner dies is a **transfer by will**.

Involuntary alienation. Involuntary alienation is a transfer of title to real property without the owner's consent. Involuntary alienation occurs primarily by the processes of descent and distribution, escheat, foreclosure, eminent domain, adverse possession, and estoppel.

DEEDS OF CONVEYANCE

Delivery and acceptance
Validity
Deed clauses and covenants
Statutory deeds
Special purpose deeds
Transfer tax

A deed is a legal instrument used by an owner, the **grantor**, to transfer title to real estate voluntarily to another party, the **grantee**.

Delivery and acceptance

Execution of a valid deed in itself does not convey title. It is necessary for the deed to be *delivered to and accepted by the grantee* for title to pass. To be legally valid, delivery of the deed requires that the grantor

- be *competent* at the time of delivery
- *intend to deliver* the deed, beyond the act of making physical delivery

Validity of the grantee's acceptance requires only that the grantee have physical possession of the deed or record the deed.

Once accepted, title passes to the grantee. The deed has fulfilled its legal purpose and it cannot be used again to transfer the property. If the grantee loses the deed, there is no effect on the grantee's title to the estate. The grantor, for example, cannot reclaim the estate on the grounds that the grantee has lost the deed after it was delivered and accepted. Nor can the grantee return the property by returning the deed. To do so, the grantee would need to execute a new deed.

In states that use the Torrens system, title passes only when the *deed has been registered on the certificate of title and a transfer certificate has been issued to the new owner.*

Validity

Depending on state law, a deed must meet the following requirements for validity. The deed must:

- be delivered and accepted
- have a competent grantor and legitimate grantee

  The grantor must be living, of legal age, and mentally competent. If grantor is a corporation, the signing party must be duly authorized. The grantee must be living or have legal existence, but need not be of legal age or mentally competent.

- be in writing
- contain a legal description
- contain a granting clause

  The deed must express the grantor's present desire and intention to transfer legal title to the grantee.

- include consideration

  The deed must be accompanied by valuable (monetary) or good (love and affection) consideration, but the amount need not reflect the actual price in most cases.

- be signed by the grantor

  The deed must be signed by the grantor, but need not be signed by the grantee unless the deed contains special provisions requiring the grantee's acceptance. Grantors may give power of attorney to other parties, authorizing them to execute deeds on their behalf. The power of attorney authorization should be recorded to ensure a valid conveyance.

- be acknowledged

  The grantor must declare before a notary or other authorized person that the grantor's identity and signature are genuine, and that the deed execution was a free, voluntary act. The grantor then receives a certificate of acknowledgment signed by the notary. Some states require acknowledgment to complete a valid conveyance. Most states require it before they will record the deed. A deed without an acknowledgement, therefore, tends to endanger one's claim to a property.

Recording. Recording is *not* necessary to make a deed valid. However, it is in the grantee's best interests to do so. Recording the deed gives the public constructive notice of the grantee's ownership.

Deed clauses and covenants

Conveyance clauses and covenant, or warrant clauses set forth all the necessary provisions of the conveyance.

Conveyance clauses. Conveyance clauses describe the details of the transfer. The principal conveyance clauses are:

- **granting clause, or premises clause**

  the only required clause; contains the conveyance intentions; names the parties; describes the property; indicates nominal consideration

- **habendum clause**

  describes the type of estate being conveyed (fee simple, life, etc.)

- **reddendum clause, or reserving clause**

  recites restrictions and limitations to the estate being conveyed, e.g., deed restrictions, liens, easements, encroachments, etc.

- **tenendum clause**

  identifies property being conveyed in addition to land

Covenant, or warrant, clauses. Covenant clauses present the grantor's assurances to the grantee. A deed of conveyance usually contains one or more of the following covenants, depending on the type of deed.

- **warrant of seisin**

  assures that the grantor owns the estate to be conveyed, and has the right to do so

- **warrant of quiet enjoyment**

  assures that the grantee will not be disturbed by third party title disputes

- **warrant of further assurance**

  assures that the grantor will assist in clearing any title problems discovered later

- **warranty forever; warranty of title**

  assures that the grantee will receive good title, and that grantor will assist in defending any claims to the contrary

- **warrant of encumbrances**

  assures that there are no encumbrances on the property except those expressly named

- **warranty against grantor's acts**

  states the assurance of a trustee, acting as grantor on behalf of the owner, that nothing has been done to impair title during the fiduciary period

Statutory Deeds

A deed of conveyance can make a variety of warranties and convey a range of interests. The most common deeds are statutory deeds, in which the covenants are defined in law and do not need to be fully stated in the deed. The prominent types are the following.

Bargain and sale deed. In a bargain and sale deed, the grantor covenants that the title is valid but may or may not warrant against encumbrances or promise to defend against claims by other parties. If there *is* a warrant of defense, the deed is a full warranty bargain and sale deed.

The overall bargain and sale covenant is: *"I own, but won't defend."*

General warranty deed. The general warranty deed, or **warranty deed** for short, is the most commonly used deed. It contains the fullest possible assurances of good title and protection for the grantee. The deed is technically a bargain and sale deed in which the grantor promises to defend against any and all claims to the title.

The overall general warranty covenant is: *"I own and will defend."*

Special warranty deed. In a special warranty deed, the grantor warrants only against title defects or encumbrances not noted on the deed that may have occurred during the grantor's period of ownership or trusteeship. The deed does not protect the grantee against claims that predate the owner's period of ownership. Special warranty deeds are often used by trustees and grantors who acquired the property through a tax sale.

The overall special warranty covenant is: *"I own and will defend against my acts only."*

Quitclaim deed. A quitclaim deed transfers real and potential interests in a property, whether an interest is known to exist or not. The grantor makes no claim to any interest in the property being conveyed and offers no warrants to protect the grantee.

The quitclaim is typically used to clear title rather than convey it. Where there is a possibility that prior errors in deeds or other recorded documents might **cloud** (encumber) the title, the relevant parties execute a quitclaim deed to convey "any and all" interest to the grantee.

If a party responsible for encumbering title refuses to quitclaim the interest, the owner may file a **quiet title suit.** This requires the lienor to prove the validity of an interest. If the defendant is unable to do so, the court removes the cloud by decree.

The overall quit claim covenant is: *"I may or may not own, and I won't defend."*

Special purpose deeds

A special purpose deed is one tailored to the requirements of specific parties, properties, and purposes. The principal types are:

- **personal representative's deed**

  used by an executor to convey a decedent's estate; also called an executor's deed

- **guardian's deed**

  used by a court-appointed guardian to transfer property of minors or mentally incompetent persons

- **sheriff's deed**

  used to convey foreclosed property sold at public auction

- **deed *of* trust**

  used to convey property to a third party trustee as collateral for a loan; on satisfaction of the loan terms, the trustee uses a **reconveyance deed** to convey the property back to the borrower

- **deed *in* trust**

  used to convey property to the trustee of a land trust. not to be confused with deed *of* trust

- **master deed**

  used to convey land to a condominium developer; accompanied by the condominium declaration when recorded

- **partition deed**

  used to convey co-owned property in compliance with a court order resulting from a partition suit; a partition suit terminates an estate when one or more co-owners want to dissolve their relationship and are unable to do so without the assistance of a court.

- **patent deed**

  used to transfer government property to private parties

- **tax deed**

  used to convey property sold at a tax sale

Transfer tax

State law usually requires payment of a **documentary stamp tax** on a conveyance of real property. The tax is based on the actual price of the property conveyed, thus enabling taxing authorities to ascertain current market value for ad valorem tax purposes. Payment of the tax is evidenced on the deed.

Exemptions from transfer tax include:

- transfer within the immediate family
- consideration less than a certain amount
- transfer between government entities or non-profit organizations
- trust deed transfer and reconveyance
- tax deed

WILLS

Types of will
Validity
Probate

A will, or more properly, a **last will and testament**, is a legal instrument for the voluntary transfer of real and personal property after the owner's death. It describes how the maker of the will, called the **testator** or **devisor,** wants the property distributed. A beneficiary of a will is called an **heir** or **devisee**. The property transferred by the will is the **devise**.

A will takes effect only after the testator's death. It is an **amendatory** instrument, meaning that it can be changed at any time during the maker's lifetime.

Commonly, the testator names an **executor**, or **personal representative**, to oversee the settlement of the estate. If a minor is involved, the testator may identify a **guardian** to handle legal affairs on behalf of the minor.

Types of will

A will generally takes one of the following forms:

- **witnessed**

  in writing and witnessed by two people

- **holographic**

  in the testator's handwriting, dated and signed

- **approved**

  on pre-printed forms meeting the requirements of state law

- **nuncupative**

  made orally, and written down by a witness; generally *not valid* for the transfer of real property

Validity

State law establishes requirements for a valid will. The law generally requires that:

- the testator be of legal age and mentally competent
- the testator indicate that the will is the "last will and testament"
- the will be signed
- the completion of the will be witnessed and signed by the witnesses
- the will be completed voluntarily, without duress or coercion

Probate

A court proceeding called **probate** generally settles a decedent's estate, whether the person has died **testate** (having left a valid will) or **intestate** (having failed to do so). Real property may be exempted from probate if it is held in a land trust. Probate of real property occurs *under jurisdiction of courts in the state where the property is located, regardless of where the deceased resided.*

The probate court's objectives are to:

- validate the will, if one exists
- identify and settle all claims and
  outstanding debts against the estate
- distribute the remainder of the estate to the rightful heirs If the will does not name an executor, the court will appoint an **administrator** to fulfill this role.

Exhibit 6.2 Transfer of a Decedent's Estate by Probate

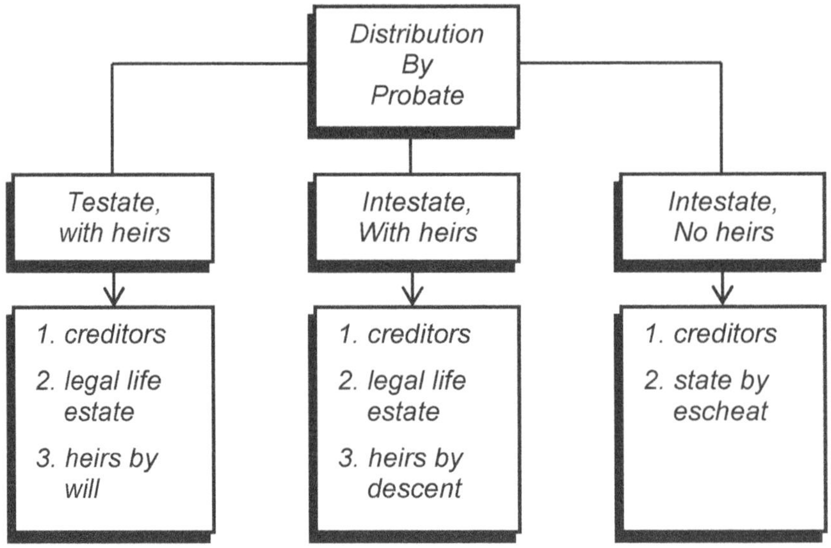

The exhibit shows three possible channels of probate deliberation, depending on whether there is a will and heirs.

Testate proceeding. If the decedent died with a valid will, the court hears the claims of lienors and creditors and determines their validity. First in line are the superior liens: those for real estate taxes, assessment taxes, federal estate taxes, and state inheritance taxes. If the estate's liquid assets are insufficient to pay all obligations, the court may order the sale of personal or real property to satisfy the obligations.

The court must also hear and satisfy legal life estate claims, including those for dower, curtesy, homestead, and elective share. These interests may prevail even if the will does not provide for them.

Once all claims have been satisfied, the balance of the estate's assets passes to the rightful heirs *free and clear of all liens and debts*.

Intestate proceeding with heirs. If the decedent died without a valid will, the estate passes to lawful heirs according to the state's laws of **descent and distribution**, or **succession**. Laws of descent stipulate *who inherits and what share they receive,* without regard to the desires of the heirs or the intentions of the deceased.

For example, John Astor dies intestate, leaving a wife and four children. The laws of descent in his state provide that the surviving spouse receives one-third of the estate, and the four children receive equal shares of the remaining two thirds.

Intestate proceeding with no heirs. If an intestate decedent has no heirs, the estate **escheats**, or reverts, to the state or county after all claims and debts have been validated and settled.

INVOLUNTARY TITLE TRANSFER

Laws of descent
Abandonment
Foreclosure
Eminent domain
Adverse possession
Estoppel

State law regulates all forms of involuntary alienation, whether such transfer occurs by the laws of descent, abandonment, foreclosure, eminent domain, adverse possession, or estoppel.

Laws of descent

Involuntary alienation occurs when a title-holder dies without a valid will. The state's statutes of descent and distribution identify heirs and the respective shares of the estate they will receive. In the absence of heirs, title transfers to the state or county by escheat.

Abandonment

Property that has been abandoned for a statutory period may also escheat to the state or county.

Foreclosure

A property owner who fails to fulfill loan obligations or pay taxes may lose an estate through foreclosure.

Eminent domain

Various government and public entities can transfer private property to the public sphere by the power of eminent domain. The transfer is involuntary, even though the owner receives compensation. For example, a city government wants to widen a highway to accommodate growth. The government uses eminent domain to condemn and purchase all properties abutting the thoroughfare in order to complete the construction project.

Adverse possession

State laws may allow a real property owner to lose legal title to an **adverse possessor**. An adverse possessor is someone who enters, occupies, and uses another's property without the knowledge or consent of the owner, or with the knowledge of an owner who fails to take any action over a statutory period of time.

To claim legal title, the adverse possessor must:

- be able to show a **claim of right** or **color of title** as reason for the possession
- have **notorious possession**, which is possession without concealment
- maintain a consistent claim of **hostile possession**, which is a claim to ownership and possession regardless of the owner's claims or consent
- occupy the property *continuously* for a statutory period of time
- in some states, *pay taxes*

A **claim of right** is based on the adverse possessor's occupying and maintaining the property as if he or she were the legal owner. **Color of title** results when a grantee has obtained defective title, or received title by defective means, but occupies the property as if he or she were the legal owner. A court may hold that a claim of right or a claim of colored title is a valid reason for the possession.

Notorious possession and **hostile possession** give constructive notice to the public, including the legal owner, that a party other than the legal owner is occupying and claiming to own the property. It is possible for such notice to prevail over notice by recordation as the dominant evidence of legal ownership, provided the possessor has occupied the property continuously for the statutory period of time.

In some states, the possessor must have paid taxes over a prescribed period to obtain title. However, if the possessor has paid rent of any kind, the claim of ownership might be refuted.

Avoiding adverse possession. An owner can avert the danger of involuntary alienation by adverse possession by *periodically inspecting the property within statutory deadlines* and evicting any trespassers found. The owner may also sue to quiet title, which would eliminate the threat of the adverse possessor's claim to legal title.

A property registered in the Torrens system cannot be lost to adverse possession.

Estoppel

Estoppel prevents a person from claiming a right or interest that is inconsistent with the person's previous statements or acts. As a basis for involuntary alienation, the doctrine of estoppel can prevent an owner from re-claiming a property that was transferred under false pretenses. For example, an owner conveys a property with a defective title. The grantor is fully aware of the defect but makes no disclosure to the grantee. The grantor later cures the defect and then claims to be the rightful owner of the property on the basis of the effort and expense of clearing the title. Estoppel disallows the grantor's claim because of the prior conveyance action. The grantee remains legal owner and benefits from the cleared title as well.

TITLE RECORDS

Chain of title
Recording system
Title evidence

State laws require the recording of all documents that affect rights and interests in real estate in the public real estate records of the county where the property is located. These public records, or **title records**, contain a history of every parcel of real estate in the county, including names of previous owners, liens, easements, and other encumbrances that have been recorded.

Deeds, mortgages, liens, easements, and sale contracts are among the documents that must be recorded. Other public records that affect real estate title are marriage, probate, and tax records.

Generally, a County Recorder's Office or other similarly named office maintains the title records.

Title records serve a number of purposes, not the least of which is to avoid ownership disputes. Other important purposes are:

- **Public notice**

  Title records protect the public by giving all concerned parties **constructive notice** of the condition of a property's legal title: who owns the property, who maintains claims and encumbrances against the property.

- **Buyer protection**

  Title records protect the buyer by revealing whether a property has **marketable title**, one free of undesirable encumbrances. The buyer is legally responsible for knowing the condition of title, since it is a matter of public record. Recording a transaction also protects a buyer by replacing the deed as evidence of ownership.

- **Lienholder protection**

  Title records protect the lienholder by putting the public on notice that the lien exists, and that it may be the basis for a foreclosure action. Recording also establishes the lien's priority.

Chain of title

Chain of title refers to the succession of property owners *of record* dating back to the original grant of title from the state to a private party. If there is a missing link in the chronology of owners, or if there was a defective conveyance, the chain is said to be broken, resulting in a **clouded title** to the property. To remove the cloud, an owner may need to initiate a **suit to quiet title**, which clears the title record of any unrecorded claims.

Abstract of Title. An abstract of title is a written, chronological summary of the property's title records and other public records affecting rights and interests in the property. It includes the property's chain of title and all current recorded liens and encumbrances, by date of filing. A title abstractor or title company analyst conducts the search of public records, called a **title search**, needed to produce an abstract. Insurers and lenders generally require the search to identify title defects and ascertain the current status of encumbrances.

A **title plant** is a duplicate set of records of a property copied from public records and maintained by a private company, such as a title company.

Recording system

There are no federal recording standards. Each state prescribes procedures and requirements for recording in public title records: forms, proper execution, acknowledgment, and witnessing.

The Torrens system. Certain states and counties use the Torrens system of recording. The Torrens system differs from other title recording systems in that *title passes only when the conveyance has been duly registered on the title certificate itself.* Encumbrances likewise have no legal effect until they are recorded. In effect, the Torrens title record is the title itself. It is not necessary to search public records to ascertain the status of title; it is all reflected on the title certificate.

To enter a property in the Torrens system, a court action must first clear title by giving notice to all potential interest holders that they must express their claims. At the end of the proceeding, the court decrees that the title is accepted into Torrens registration. The Torrens registry retains the original registration documents and provides copies to the recorder or other appropriate office. All subsequent transactions affecting title must follow the proper Torrens recording procedures and requirements.

Title evidence

Marketable title. Since the value of a property is only as good as the marketability of its title, the evidence supporting the status of title is a significant issue. To demonstrate marketable title to a buyer, a seller must show that the title is free of

- doubts about the identity of the current owner
- defects, such as an erroneous legal description
- claims that could affect value
- undisclosed or unacceptable encumbrances

In the conventional residential transaction, a buyer's best assurance of marketable title is the title company itself. The title company's due diligence in preparing for closing is to investigate the status of the property's title, complete with liens, claims and encumbrances. This process involves various forms of title search and chain-of-title investigation. In essence, if any of these activities uncover title clouds or claims prior to closing, the title company will stop the closing process until the problem is cleared up.

The culmination of the pre-closing title work is obtaining a completed title insurance policy, which in itself is one of the best available assurances of clear, marketable title.

The four principal forms of evidence in support of the status of marketable title are:

- a Torrens certificate
- a title insurance policy
- an attorney's opinion of the title abstract
- a title certificate

Torrens certificate. If available, the Torrens certificate is the best evidence, for the reasons given earlier-- it is not merely a record, but is the title itself.

Title insurance. In the absence of Torrens registration, a title insurance policy is commonly accepted as the best evidence of marketable title. A title insurance policy indemnifies the policy holder against losses arising from defects in the insured title.

The common policy types are the lender's policy and the owner's policy, which protect the respective policy holders' interests in the property. Thus, a lender who holds an $800,000 mortgage on a property will obtain protection worth $800,000 against the possibility that the lender's lien cannot be enforced. The owner's policy will insure against defective title to the extent of the property's initial or appreciated value.

An owner's policy may have *standard coverage* or *extended coverage*. Standard coverage protects against title defects such as incompetent grantors, invalid deeds, fraudulent transaction documents, and defects in the chain of title. Extended coverage protects against liabilities that may not be of public record, including fraud, unrecorded ownership claims, unintentional recording errors, and unrecorded liens. Extended coverage may also protect against adverse possessors, boundary disputes, and prescriptive easements. Neither standard nor extended coverage insures against defects expressly excluded by the policy or defects that the owner might have been aware of but did not disclose.

Before issuing a title insurance policy, a title company conducts a *title search* to uncover defects in title or unrecorded breaks in the chain of title. If the search fails to discover any uninsurable defects, the company issues a **binder**, or commitment to insure. The binder recapitulates the property description, interest to be insured, names of insured parties, and exceptions to coverage.

Attorney's opinion of abstract. An attorney's opinion of abstract states that the attorney has examined a title abstract, and gives the attorney's opinion of the condition and marketability of the title. Generally, an opinion is not a proof or guarantee of clear title. Further, it offers no protection in the event title turns out to be defective. Also known as *opinion of title*.

Title certificate. A title certificate is a summary of the condition of title as of the date of the certificate, based on a search of public records by an abstractor or title analyst. The certificate does not guarantee clear title against defects, unrecorded encumbrances or encroachments.

6 Transferring and Recording Title to Real Estate Snapshot Review

TITLE TO REAL ESTATE

Legal and equitable title	• legal title: ownership of the bundle of rights
	• equitable title: a conditional right to legal title subject to an owner's agreements with buyers and creditors
Notice of title	• how ownership is evidenced to the public
	• actual notice: knowledge acquired or imparted directly through demonstrable evidence, e.g., presenting or inspecting a deed, visiting a party in possession
	• constructive notice: knowledge one could or should have obtained, as presumed by law; imparted by recording in public records "for all to see"
Transferring title	• voluntary by grant, deed, or will
	• involuntary by descent, escheat, eminent domain, foreclosure, adverse possession, estoppel
DEEDS OF CONVEYANCE	• instruments of voluntary conveyance by grantor to grantee
Delivery and acceptance	• legal title transfers upon competent grantor's intentional delivery and grantee's acceptance; in Torrens, title transfers upon registration
Validity	• grantor, grantee, in writing, legal description, granting clause, consideration, grantor's signature, acknowledgement, delivery and acceptance
Deed clauses and covenants	• premises clause: granting
	• habendum clause: type of estate
	• reddendum clause: restrictions
	• tenendum clause: other property included
	• warrants: seizen; quiet enjoyment; further assurance; forever; encumbrances; grantor's acts
Statutory deeds	• bargain and sale: "I own but won't defend"
	• general warranty: "I own and will defend"
	• special warranty: "I own and warrant myself only"
	• quitclaim: "I may or may not own, and won't defend"
Special purpose deeds	• used for different purposes, to convey certain interests, or by certain parties
Transfer tax	• state tax on conveyances based on price
WILLS	• last will and testament: voluntary transfer to heirs after death
	• maker: devisor or testator; heir: devisee; estate: devise
Types of will	• witnessed; holographic; approved; nuncupative

Validity

- adult; competent; indicates "last will and testament"; signed; witnessed; voluntary

Probate

- if testate, estate passes to heirs; if intestate, to successors by descent; if intestate with no heirs, estate escheats to state or county
- process: validate will; validate, settle claims and pay taxes; transfer balance of estate to heirs

INVOLUNTARY TITLE TRANSFER

- descent and escheat: no will
- foreclosure: lose title by forfeiture
- eminent domain: lose title to public for the greater good
- adverse possession: by claim of right or color of title; continuous, notorious, hostile possession; may have to pay taxes
- estoppel: barred by prior acts or claims

TITLE RECORDS

- all instruments affecting title must be recorded
- give public notice; protect owners; protect lienholders' claims

Chain of title

- successive property owners from original grant to present owner
- abstract of title: chronology of recorded owners, transfers, encumbrances

Recording system

- local property recording system governed by state law
- Torrens registry: requires court action initially: legal title does not pass until recordation occurs

Title evidence

- needed to prove marketable title as well as who owns
- forms of evidence: Torrens; title insurance; attorney's opinion of abstract; title certificates

7 Leasing Essentials

The Lease Contract
Types of Lease
Default and Termination
Uniform Residential Landlord and Tenant Act

THE LEASE CONTRACT

Leasehold rights and obligations
Contract requirements
Lease clauses

A lease is both *an instrument of conveyance* and *a contract* between principal parties to uphold certain covenants and obligations. As a conveyance, a lease conveys an interest, called the leasehold estate, but does not convey legal title to the property. For this reason, a leasehold is also called a **less-than-freehold** estate.

The four principal types of leasehold estate are:

- **estate for years**: has a specific lease term
- **estate from period-to-period**: the lease term automatically renews
- **estate at will**: has no specified lease term
- **estate at sufferance**: a tenancy without consent

The legal essence of a valid lease is that *it conveys an exclusive right to use and occupy a property for a limited period of time in exchange for rent and the return of the property after the lease term is over.* Leasehold estates are distinguished from freeholds by their temporary nature. Every leasehold has a limited duration, whether the term is 99 years or not stated at all, as in an estate at will. While the lease conveys exclusive use, it may also *restrict such use* to conform to the landlord's desires. For example, an apartment lease may prohibit a tenant from using or storing hazardous materials within the premises.

Like other contracts, a lease becomes a binding agreement when the parties accept the terms of the agreement and communicate their agreement to the other party. Recording of a leasehold conveyance is not a requirement for validity, although it is usually good procedure to do so.

In a lease arrangement, the owner is the **landlord**, or **lessor**, and the renter is the **tenant**, or **lessee**.

Leasehold rights and obligations

Tenant's rights and obligations. A lease conveys a **leasehold interest** or **estate** that grants the tenant the following rights during the lease term:

- exclusive possession and occupancy
- exclusive use
- quiet enjoyment
- profits from use

A tenant has the sole right to occupy and use the premises without interference from outside parties, including the landlord. The landlord may enter the premises for specified purposes such as inspections, but the interference must be reasonable and limited. In addition, the landlord can do nothing outside of the lease's express provisions that would impair the tenant's enjoyment of income deriving from use of the premises. For example, the landlord can not place a kiosk in front of a retail tenant's entry in such a way as to prevent customers from entering the store.

The lease defines the tenant's obligations, which principally are to:

- pay the rent on time
- maintain the property's condition
- comply with the rules and regulations of the building

Landlord's rights and obligations. In conveying the leasehold estate, the landlord acquires a **leased fee estate,** which entails the rights to:

- receive rent
- re-possess the property following the lease term
- monitor the tenant's obligations to maintain the premises

The lease defines the landlord's obligations, which principally are to:

- provide the necessary building support and services
- maintain the condition of the property

Death of tenant or landlord. A valid lease creates obligations that survive the death of the landlord or tenant, with certain exceptions. A tenant's estate *remains liable for payment of rent if the tenant dies;* the landlord's estate *remains bound to provide occupancy despite the landlord's death.*

Conveyance of leased property. The landlord may sell, assign, or mortgage the leased fee interest. However, transferring and encumbering the leased property do not extinguish the obligations and covenants of a lease. Buyers and creditors, therefore, must take their respective interests subject to the terms of the lease.

Contract requirements

State contract laws determine the requirements for a valid lease. These laws generally require the following conditions.

Parties. The principal parties must be legally able to enter into the agreement; i.e., meet certain age, sanity, and other requirements.

Property description. The lease must identify the property by legal description or other locally accepted reference.

Exclusive possession. The landlord must provide an irrevocable right to exclusive possession during the lease term, provided the tenant meets all obligations.

Legal and permitted use. The intended use of the property must be legal. A use that is legal but not permitted does not invalidate the lease but constitutes grounds for default.

Consideration. The lease contract must be accompanied by consideration to the landlord for the rights conveyed. How the consideration is paid does not affect the lease's validity, so long as the parties comply with the terms of the lease.

Offer and acceptance. The parties must accept the lease, and communicate their acceptance to the other party, for the lease to take legal effect.

Signatures. The landlord must sign the lease to convey the leasehold interest. A tenant need not sign the lease, although it is prudent to do so in order to enforce the terms of the lease. Multiple tenants who sign a single lease are jointly and severally responsible for fulfilling lease obligations. Thus, if one renter abandons an apartment, the other renters remain liable for rent.

Oral versus written form. Generally, a *lease for a period exceeding one year cannot be oral but must be in writing to be enforceable* because of the Statute of Frauds. An oral lease or rental agreement is legally construed to be a tenancy at will, having no specified term. Further, an oral lease terminates on the death of either principal party.

Lease clauses

The clauses of a lease define the contractual relationship between landlord and tenant. The most important and basic clauses are the following.

Rent and security deposit. A rent clause stipulates the time, place, manner and amount of rent payment. It defines any grace period that is allowed, and states the penalties for delinquency.

The lease may also call for a security deposit to protect the landlord against losses from property damage or the tenant's default. State law regulates the handling of the security deposit: where it is deposited, and whether the tenant receives interest on the deposit. A landlord may require additional financial security from a tenant of dubious creditworthiness in the form of personal guarantees, third party guarantees, or pledges of other property as collateral.

Lease term. In the absence of an explicit term with beginning and ending date, a court will generally construe the lease to be a tenancy at will, cancelable upon proper notice.

Repairs and maintenance. Repairs and maintenance provisions define the landlord's and tenant's respective responsibilities for property repairs and maintenance. Generally, the tenant is responsible for routine maintenance of the premises while the landlord is responsible for general repairs. In residential leases, the landlord is responsible for major repairs and capital improvements. Payment of repairs and maintenance costs, however, is entirely negotiable between landlord and tenant.

Subletting and assignment. Subletting (subleasing) is the transfer by a tenant, the **sublessor**, of a *portion* of the leasehold interest to another party, the **sublessee**, through the execution of a **sublease**. The sublease spells out all of the rights and obligations of the sublessor and sublessee, including the payment of rent to the sublessor. The sublessor remains *primarily liable* for the original lease with the landlord. The subtenant is *liable* only to the sublessor.

For example, a sublessor subleases a portion of the occupied premises for a portion of the remaining term. The sublessee pays sublease rent to the sublessor, who in turn pays lease rent to the landlord.

An assignment of the lease is a transfer of the *entire leasehold interest* by a tenant, the **assignor**, to a third party, the **assignee**. There is no second lease, and the assignor retains no residual rights of occupancy or other leasehold rights unless expressly stated in the assignment agreement. The assignee becomes primarily liable for the lease and rent, and the assignor, the original tenant, remains secondarily liable. The assignee pays rent directly to the landlord.

All leases clarify the rights and restrictions of the tenant regarding subleasing and assigning the leasehold interest. Generally, the landlord cannot prohibit either act, but the tenant must obtain the landlord's written approval. The reason for this requirement is that the landlord has a financial stake in the creditworthiness of any prospective tenant.

Rules and regulations. A tenant must abide by all usage restrictions imposed by the lease's rules and regulations for the property. These rules aim to protect the property's condition as well as the rights of other tenants.

Improvements and alterations. A landlord typically wants to prevent a tenant from making alterations that later tenants may not desire. By the same token, a tenant who pays for an improvement wants to know who will own it at the end of the lease term. An improvements and alterations clause therefore identifies necessary permissions and procedures, and who owns improvements. Customarily, tenant improvements become the property of the landlord in the absence of an express agreement to the contrary.

Options. An option clause offers a tenant the opportunity to choose a course of action at some time in the future under certain terms. Typical options are the right to renew the lease, buy the property, and lease additional adjacent space. A tenant does not have to exercise an option, but the landlord must comply if the tenant does exercise it.

Damage and destruction. A damage and destruction provision defines the rights and obligations of the parties in the event the leased premises are damaged or destroyed. State laws regulate such provisions.

TYPES OF LEASE

Gross lease
Net lease
Percentage lease
Residential lease
Commercial lease
Ground lease
Proprietary lease
Leasing of rights

Gross lease

A gross lease, or **full service** lease, requires the landlord to pay the property's operating expenses, including utilities, repairs, and maintenance, while the tenant pays only rent. Rent levels under a gross lease are higher than under a net lease, since the landlord recoups expense outlays in the form of added rent.

Gross leases are common for office and industrial properties. Residential leases are usually gross leases with the exception that the tenants often pay utilities expenses.

Net lease

A net lease requires a tenant to pay for utilities, internal repairs, and a proportionate share of taxes, insurance, and operating expenses in addition to rent. In effect, the landlord "passes through" actual property expenses to the tenant rather than charging a higher rent level. Net leases vary as to exactly what expenses the tenant is responsible for. The extreme form of net lease requires tenants to cover all expenses, including major repairs and property taxes.

Net leases are common for office and industrial properties. They are sometimes also used for single family dwellings.

In practice, the terms net and gross lease can be misleading: some gross leases still require tenants to pay some expenses such as utilities and repairs. Similarly, some net leases require the landlord to pay certain expenses. Prudent tenants and landlords look at all expense obligations in relation to the level of rent to be charged.

Percentage lease

A percentage lease allows the landlord to share in the income generated from the use of the property. A tenant pays **percentage rent**, or an amount of rent equal to a percentage of the tenant's periodic gross sales. The percentage rent may be:

- a fixed percent of gross revenue without a minimum rent
- a fixed minimum rent plus an additional percent of gross sales
- a percentage rent or minimum rent, whichever is greater

Percentage leases are used only for retail properties.

Residential lease

A residential lease may be a net lease or a gross lease. Usually, it is a form of gross lease in which the landlord pays all property expenses except the tenant's utilities and water. Since residential leases tend to be short in term, tenants cannot be expected to pay for major repairs and improvements. The landlord, rather, absorbs these expenses and recoups the outlays through higher rent.

Residential leases differ from commercial and other types of lease in that:

- lease terms are shorter, typically one or two years
- lease clauses are fairly standard from one property to the next, in order to reflect compliance with local landlord-tenant relations laws
- lease clauses are generally not negotiable, particularly in larger apartment complexes where owners want uniform leases for all residents

Commercial lease

A commercial lease may be a net, gross, or percentage lease, if the tenant is a retail business. As a rule, a commercial lease is a significant and complex business proposition. It may involve hundreds of thousands of dollars for improving the property to the tenant's specifications. Since the lease terms are often long, total rent liabilities for the tenant can easily be millions of dollars.

Some important features of commercial leases are:

- long term, ranging up to 25 years
- require tenant improvements to meet particular usage needs
- virtually all lease clauses are negotiable due to the financial magnitude of the transaction
- default can have serious financial consequences; therefore, lease clauses must express all points of agreement and be very precise

Ground lease

A ground lease, or **land lease**, concerns the land portion of a real property. The owner grants the tenant a leasehold interest in the land only, in exchange for rent.

Ground leases are primarily used in three circumstances:

- an owner wishes to lease raw land to an agricultural or mining interest
- unimproved property is to be developed and either the owner wants to retain ownership of the land, or the developer or future users of the property do not want to own the land
- the owner of an improved property wishes to sell an interest in the improvements while retaining ownership of the underlying land

In the latter two instances, a ground lease offers owners, developers, and users various financing, appreciation, and tax advantages. For example, a ground lease lessor can take advantage of the increase in value of the land due to the new improvements developed on it, without incurring the risks of developing and owning the improvements. Land leases executed for the purpose of development or to segregate ownership of land from ownership of improvements are inherently long term leases, often ranging from thirty to fifty years.

Proprietary lease

A proprietary lease conveys a leasehold interest to an owner of a cooperative. The proprietary lease does not stipulate rent, as the rent is equal to the owner's share of the periodic expenses of the entire cooperative. The term of the lease is likewise unspecified, as it coincides with the ownership period of the cooperative tenant: when an interest is sold, the proprietary lease for the seller's unit is assigned to the new buyer.

Leasing of rights

The practice of leasing property rights other than the rights to exclusive occupancy and possession occurs most commonly in the leasing of water rights, air rights, and mineral rights.

For example, an owner of land that has deposits of coal might lease the mineral rights to a mining company, giving the mining company the limited right to extract the coal. The rights lease may be very specific, stating how much of a mineral or other resource may be extracted, how the rights may be exercised, for what period of time, and on what portions of the property. The lessee's rights do not include common leasehold interests such as occupancy, exclusion, quiet enjoyment, or possession of the leased premises.

Another example of a rights lease is where a railroad wants to erect a bridge over a thoroughfare owned by a municipality. The railroad must obtain an air rights agreement of some kind, whether it be an easement, a purchase, or a lease, before it can construct the bridge.

DEFAULT AND TERMINATION

Remedies for default
Default by tenant
Default by landlord
Causes for lease termination

Remedies for default

A landlord or tenant who violates any of the terms and covenants of the lease has breached the contract and is in default. In the event of a default, the damaged party may pursue court action, including suing for

- damages
- cancellation of the lease
- specific performance

A successful suit for **specific performance** compels the defaulting party to perform the contract obligation that was breached. For example, if a landlord fails to replace carpeting as promised in the lease, the tenant can sue to obtain the landlord's specific performance of installing a new carpet.

Default by tenant

Tenant default occurs most commonly from failure to pay rent or maintain the premises. If a tenant is in default, the landlord may file a **suit for possession**, also called a **suit for eviction**. If successful in this suit, the landlord can repossess the property and evict the tenant. The landlord also has the right to sue for damages.

Before filing a suit for possession, the landlord must give the tenant proper notice to pay monies due or otherwise cure the default before a deadline, or else vacate the premises. If the deadline passes without satisfaction, the landlord may file the suit and obtain a judgment for possession. The landlord may then obtain an order directing the sheriff to complete the eviction, forcibly if necessary.

Default by landlord

The most common form of landlord default is failure to provide services and maintain the property condition. When a landlord defaults on the terms of the lease, tenants may sue for damages. In an instance where the landlord's negligence or disruptive action has rendered the property unoccupiable, a tenant may vacate the premises and declare that the lease is cancelled by default. This action, called **constructive eviction**, can nullify the tenant's lease obligations if the claim succeeds in court. In order to obtain a constructive eviction judgment, the tenant *must vacate* the premises.

For example, a landlord will not repair a roof and will not allow an office tenant to make the repair and deduct the cost from the rent. A thunderstorm soaks the suite and ruins several pieces of office equipment. By refusing to act, the landlord has breached the lease covenant to maintain the premises. The tenant moves out, claiming the lease null and void. The tenant also sues the landlord for damages to the equipment and for recovery of relocation expenses.

Causes for lease termination

A lease may terminate for any of the following causes.

Breach or default. Breach of contract or default, as previously discussed, may terminate a lease.

Term expiration. In a tenancy for years, the lease automatically terminates at the end of the lease term.

Notice. Proper notice by either party may terminate a periodic leasehold, or a tenancy at will.

Voluntary agreement. Both parties can agree to terminate a lease at any time.

Property destruction. Destruction of the property is grounds for terminating lease obligations.

Condemnation. A taking by eminent domain proceedings generally terminates a lease.

Foreclosure. A foreclosure extinguishes all prior interests in a property, including a leasehold.

Death of tenant or landlord, with qualifications. A lease for tenancy at will terminates on the death of either landlord or tenant. A lease also terminates on the death of the landlord if the landlord held a life estate interest in the property, since the landlord could not have conveyed an interest that extended beyond his or her own interest.

Except in the circumstances mentioned, a lease *does not* terminate on the death of the landlord or tenant. Sale of the property also does not terminate a lease.

Abandonment. If a tenant abandons a leased property and demonstrates no intention of fulfilling the obligations of the lease, the landlord may re-take possession and pursue legal recourses for default. In such a case, the tenant remains liable for payment of rent. The landlord also has the option of terminating the lease, which releases the tenant from responsibility for rent.

However, the landlord may be able to sue for damages and at the same time re-let the property.

It is important to note that vacating leased premises does not in itself constitute abandonment, and certainly not if the tenant continues to abide by the lease obligations.

UNIFORM RESIDENTIAL LANDLORD AND TENANT ACT (URLTA)

Areas of regulation

The **Uniform Residential Landlord and Tenant Act (URLTA)** is a model law enacted as a blueprint for state laws to *regulate leasing and management practices of landlords with residential properties*. Numerous states have enacted tenant-landlord regulations in response to the law.

The act aims to:

- equalize and standardize rights of landlord and tenant
- protect tenants from unethical practices
- prevent unfair, complex leases and their enforceability

One important effect of URLTA is that it prompted legislation at the state level that empowered the courts to nullify residential leases that violated URLTA guidelines, particularly where a lease gave unfair advantage to the landlord.

Areas of regulation

URLTA legislation primarily addresses the lease contract, deposits and advances, obligations of landlord and tenant, the landlord's rights of access, and standards for eviction.

Lease agreements. URLTA sets standards for improving oral, vague, or unbalanced lease agreements. The law's positions on these issues are:

- unclear lease term: becomes a periodic tenancy
- rent amount: fair market value or court's opinion
- waiving of rights: certain rights cannot be waived

The law intends to avoid irregularities and vagueness in the lease term and rent obligations, as these can cause exaggeration in a landlord's claim for the amount of rent due from a defaulting tenant. A vague lease term can also lead to a dispute about the duration of a tenant's possession rights. A landlord, for example, could claim that a lease has expired in order to acquire a higher-paying tenant. URLTA also discourages the landlord practice of persuading tenants to waive rights they do not understand or are unaware of.

Deposit and advance. URLTA requires leases to be clear about:

- maximum deposit amount
- the tenant's right to earn interest on the deposit

- commingling deposit or advance with other monies
- deadline for returning deposits
- procedures and criteria for return of the deposit to the tenant

Although URLTA applies to how landlords can handle deposits and advances, state laws also strictly regulate how brokers and agents may handle tenant monies.

Landlord's obligations. Under URLTA, a landlord must:

- bargain in good faith with the tenant
- provide required maintenance
- make repairs
- comply with local building codes
- provide access and safety services: elevator; fire escapes, etc.
- provide a procedure for delivery of official notices

Tenant's obligations. A tenant must:

- bargain in good faith
- maintain the condition of the leased premises
- abide by (legitimate) rules and regulations of the building
- refrain from abusing or causing destruction to the property
- limit uses to those approved
- avoid unduly disturbing other tenants

Access. URLTA attempts to balance the landlord's right to access the premises with the tenant's right of quiet enjoyment. The landlord has the right to enter the premises at any time when acting to prevent damage or destruction; to make repairs or show the property, on giving proper notice; if the purpose is not arbitrary and the time is reasonable The tenant may not refuse the landlord entry for acceptable reasons such as emergencies, repairs, inspections, and showings.

Default and eviction. URLTA attempts to establish equitable procedures for dealing with lease defaults. If the landlord defaults, a tenant may sue for damages, terminate the agreement, or negotiate a rent abatement. Tenants generally are not released of liability for rent during a dispute. Rents, however, may be paid to a court impound pending judgment. If a tenant defaults, the landlord may terminate and evict, provided proper notice is made and the landlord can justify the cause for the action.

Exemptions. State laws based on URLTA generally do not apply to transient occupancies, such as hotel and motel rentals, proprietary leases in cooperatives, or to occupancy in a residence that is under a contract for deed.

7 Leasing Essentials Snapshot Review

THE LEASE CONTRACT	• instrument of leasehold conveyance; contract of covenants and obligations
	• landlord grants temporary, exclusive use in trade for rent and reversion
Leasehold rights and obligations	• tenant rights: exclusive use and possession; quiet enjoyment; profits
	• tenant obligations: pay rent; maintain premises; follow rules
	• landlord rights: receive rent; repossess; monitor property condition
	• landlord obligations: support and services; maintenance
	• leasehold rights survive death and conveyance or encumbrance
Contract requirements	• parties; legal description; exclusive possession; legal use; lease term; consideration; offer and acceptance; signatures; written if over one year in term
Lease clauses	• rent; deposit; term; repairs and maintenance; subletting and assignment; rules and regulations; improvements; alterations; options; damage; destruction
TYPES OF LEASE	• based on expense responsibility; how rent is paid; property type; rights leased
Gross lease	• landlord pays expenses; tenant pays more rent
Net lease	• tenant pays some or all expenses; rent is less
Percentage lease	• landlord receives rent minimum plus percentage of retailer's sales
Residential lease	• gross lease hybrid; short term; uniform terms reflect landlord-tenant standards
Commercial lease	• longer term; entails tenant improvements; complex, negotiable lease terms
Ground lease	• landlord owns and leases ground but does not own improvements
Proprietary lease	• for cooperative unit owners; indefinite term; assigned to new unit owner on sale
Leasing of rights	• leasehold transfer of rights for limited use; examples: air, mineral, water rights
DEFAULT AND TERMINATION	
Remedies for default	• sue for damages, lease cancellation, and/or specific performance
Default by tenant	• cancellation; damages; suit for possession; must give proper notice
Default by landlord	• suit for constructive eviction; must vacate premises to uphold
Causes for lease termination	• default; term expiration; notice; voluntary agreement; property destruction; condemnation; death, in some cases; abandonment
UNIFORM RESIDENTIAL LANDLORD AND TENANT ACT	• aims to balance landlord and tenant rights; to standardize leases and eviction procedures; to protect tenants; serve as model for state-level legislation
Areas of regulation	• contract language; waiver of rights; deposit; obligations of landlord and tenant; default and eviction

8 Land Use Planning And Control

Real Estate Planning
Public Land Use Control
Private Land Use Control
Environmental Controls

REAL ESTATE PLANNING

Goals of land use control
The master plan
Planning objectives
Plan development
Planning management

While the Constitution guarantees the right of individual ownership of real estate, it does not guarantee the uncontrolled sale, use, and development of real estate. As American history demonstrates, unregulated use of real estate has significant potential for eventual damage to property values as well as to the environment. Moreover, with the explosive urban growth in this century, it has become clear that regulation of land use is necessary to preserve the interests, safety, and welfare of the community.

Without a central authority to exert control, land use tends to be chaotic. For example, rapid growth can outpace the support capabilities of basic municipal services such as sewers, power, water, schools, roads and communications. On an aesthetic level, communities need controls to keep certain commercial and industrial land uses away from residential areas to avoid the undermining of property values by pollution, noise, and traffic congestion.

Goals of land use control

Over time, public and private control of land use has come to focus on certain core purposes. These are:

- preservation of property values
- promotion of the highest and best use of property
- balance between individual property rights and the public good, i.e., its health, safety and welfare
- control of growth to remain within infrastructure capabilities
- incorporation of community consensus into regulatory and planning activities

The optimum management of real property usage must take into account both the interests of the individual and the interests of the surrounding community. While maintaining the value of an individual estate is important, the owner of an estate must realize that unregulated use and development can jeopardize the value not only of the owner's estate but of neighboring properties. Similarly, the community must keep in mind the effect of government actions on individual property values, since local government is largely supported by taxes based on the value of property.

Exhibit 8.1 Public Land Use Control

A community achieves its land usage goals through a three-phase process, as the exhibit illustrates:

- *development of a master plan* for the jurisdiction
- *administration of the plan* by a municipal, county, or regional planning commission
- *implementation of the plan* through public control of zoning, building codes, permits, and other measures

Municipal, county, and regional authorities develop comprehensive land use plans for a particular community with the input of property owners. A planning commission manages the master plan and enforces it by exercising its power to establish zones, control building permits, and create building codes.

In addition to public land use planning and control, some private entities, such as subdivision associations, can impose additional standards of land use on owners within the private entity's legal jurisdiction. Private controls are primarily implemented by deed restrictions.

The master plan

Public land use planning incorporates long-term usage strategies and growth policies in a **land use plan**, or **master plan**. In many states, the process of land use planning begins when the state legislature enacts laws *requiring all counties and municipalities to adopt a land use plan*. The land use plan must not only reflect the needs of the local area, but also conform to state and federal environmental laws and the plans of regional and state planning agencies. The state enforces its planning mandates by giving state agencies the power to approve county and local plans.

The master plan therefore fuses state and regional land use laws with local land use objectives that correspond to the municipality's social and economic conditions. The completed plan becomes the overall guideline for creating and enforcing zones, building codes, and development requirements.

Planning objectives

The primary objectives of a master plan are generally to control and accommodate social and economic growth.

Amount of growth. A master plan *sets specific guidelines on how much growth the jurisdiction will allow*. While all communities desire a certain degree of growth, too much growth can overwhelm services and infrastructure.

To formulate a growth strategy, a plan initially forecasts growth trends, then estimates how well the municipality can keep pace with the growth forecast. The outcome is a policy position that limits building permits and development projects to desired growth parameters. A growth plan considers:

- nature, location and extent of permitted uses
- availability of sanitation facilities
- adequacy of drainage, waste collection, and potable water systems
- adequacy of utilities companies
- adequacy and patterns of thoroughfares
- housing availability
- conservation of natural resources
- adequacy of recreational facilities
- ability and willingness of the community to absorb new taxes, bond issues, and assessments

Growth patterns. In addition to the quantity of growth, a master plan also *defines what type of growth will occur, and where*. Major considerations are:

- the type of enterprises and developments to allow
- residential density and commercial intensity
- effects of industrial and commercial land uses on residential and public sectors, i.e., where to allow such uses
- effect of new developments on traffic patterns and thoroughfares
- effects on the environment and environmental quality (air, water, soil, noise, visual aspects)
- effect on natural resources that support the community
- code specifications for specific construction projects

Accommodating demand. As the master plan sets forth guidelines for how much growth will be allowed, it must also *make plans for accommodating expanding or contracting demand for services and infrastructure*. The plan must identify:

- facilities requirements for local government
- new construction requirements for streets, schools, and social services facilities such as libraries, civic centers, etc.
- new construction required to provide power, water and sewer services

Plan development

In response to land use objectives, community attitudes, and conclusions drawn from research, the planning personnel formulate their plan. In the course of planning, they analyze

- population and demographic trends
- economic trends
- existing land use
- existing support facilities
- traffic patterns

Planning management

Public land use management takes place within county and municipal **planning departments**. These departments are responsible for:

- long-term implementation of the master plan
- creating rules and restrictions that support plans and policies
- enforcing and administering land use regulation on an everyday basis

The planning commission. In most jurisdictions, a planning commission or board comprised of officials appointed by the government's legislative entity handles the planning function.

The commission oversees the operations of the department's professional planning staff and support personnel. In addition, the commission makes recommendations to elected officials concerning land use policy and policy administration.

The planning commission is responsible for:

- approving site plans and subdivision plans
- approving building permits
- ruling on zoning issues

PUBLIC LAND USE CONTROL

Zoning
Zoning administration
Subdivision regulation
Building codes
Public acquisition and ownership
Environmental restrictions

At the state level, the legislature enacts laws that control and restrict land use, particularly from the environmental perspective. At the local level, county and city governments control land use through the authority known as **police power**. The most common expressions of police power are county and municipal **zoning**. Other examples of public land use control are:

- subdivision regulations
- building codes
- eminent domain
- environmental restrictions
- development requirements

Governments also have the right to **own** real property for public use and welfare. In exercising its ownership rights, a municipality may **annex** property adjacent to its existing property or purchase other tracts of land through conventional transfers. Where necessary, it may force property owners to sell their property through the power of **eminent domain**.

Zoning

Zoning is the primary tool by which cities and counties regulate land use and implement their respective master plans. The Constitution grants the states the legal authority to regulate, and the states delegate the authority to counties and municipalities through legislation called **enabling acts**.

The zoning ordinance. The vehicle for zoning a city or county is the **zoning ordinance**, a regulation enacted by the local government. The intent of zoning ordinances is to specify land usage for every parcel within the jurisdiction. In some areas, state laws permit zoning ordinances to apply to areas immediately beyond the legal boundaries of the city or county.

Zoning ordinances implement the master plan by regulating density, land use intensity, aesthetics, and highest and best use. Ordinances typically address:

- the nature of land use-- office, commercial, residential, etc.
- size and configuration of a building site, including setbacks, sidewalk requirements, parking requirements, and access
- site development procedures
- construction and design methods and materials, including height restrictions, building-to-site area ratios, and architectural styles
- use of space within the building
- signage

Ordinance validity. Local planners do not have unlimited authority to do whatever they want. Their zoning ordinances must be clear in import, apply to all parties equally, and promote health, safety, and welfare of the community in a reasonable manner.

Building permits. Local governments enforce zoning ordinances by issuing building permits to those who want to improve, repair, or refurbish a property. To receive a permit, the project must comply with all relevant ordinances and codes. Further zoning enforcement is achieved through periodic inspections.

Types of zones. One of the primary applications of zoning power is the separation of residential properties from commercial and industrial uses. Proper design of land use in this manner preserves the aesthetics and value of neighborhoods and promotes the success of commercial enterprises through intelligently located zones.

Six common types of zone are

- residential
- commercial
- industrial
- agricultural
- public
- planned unit development (PUD)

Residential. Residential zoning restricts land use to private, non-commercial dwellings. Sub-zones in this category further stipulate the types of residences allowed, whether single-family, multi-unit complexes, condominiums, publicly subsidized housing, or other form of housing.

Residential zoning regulates:

- *density,* by limiting the number and size of dwelling units and lots in an area
- values and aesthetics, by limiting the type of residences allowed. Some areas adopt **buffer zones** to separate residential areas from commercial and industrial zones.

Commercial. Commercial zoning regulates the location of office and retail land usage. Some commercial zones allow combinations of office and retail uses on a single site. Sub-zones in this category may limit the type of retail or office activity permitted, for example, a department store versus a strip center.

Commercial zoning regulates:

- intensity of usage, by limiting the area of store or office per site area. Intensity regulation is further achieved by minimum parking requirements, setbacks, and building height restrictions.

Industrial. Industrial zoning regulates:

- intensity of usage
- type of industrial activity
- environmental consequences

A municipality may not allow some industrial zones, such as heavy industrial, at all. The industrial park is a relatively recent concept in industrial zoning.

Agricultural. Agricultural zoning restricts land use to farming, ranching, and other agricultural enterprises.

Public. Public zoning restricts land use to public services and recreation. Parks, post offices, government buildings, schools, and libraries are examples of uses allowed in a public zone.

Planned Unit Development (PUD). planned unit development zoning restricts use to development of whole tracts that are designed to use space efficiently and maximize open space. A PUD zone may be for residential, commercial, or industrial uses, or combinations thereof.

Zoning administration

Zoning Board of Adjustment. A county or local board, usually called the zoning board of adjustment or zoning appeals board, administers zoning ordinances. The board rules on interpretations of zoning ordinances as they apply to specific land use cases presented by property owners in the jurisdiction. In effect, the zoning board is a court of appeals for owners and developers who desire to use land in a manner that is not entirely consistent with existing ordinances.

The board conducts hearings of specific cases and renders official decisions regarding the land use based on evidence presented.

A zoning board generally deals with such issues and appeals as:

- nonconforming use
- variance
- special exception or conditional use permit
- zoning amendment

If the board rejects an appeal, the party may appeal the ruling further in a court of law.

Exhibit 8.2 Zoning Appeals

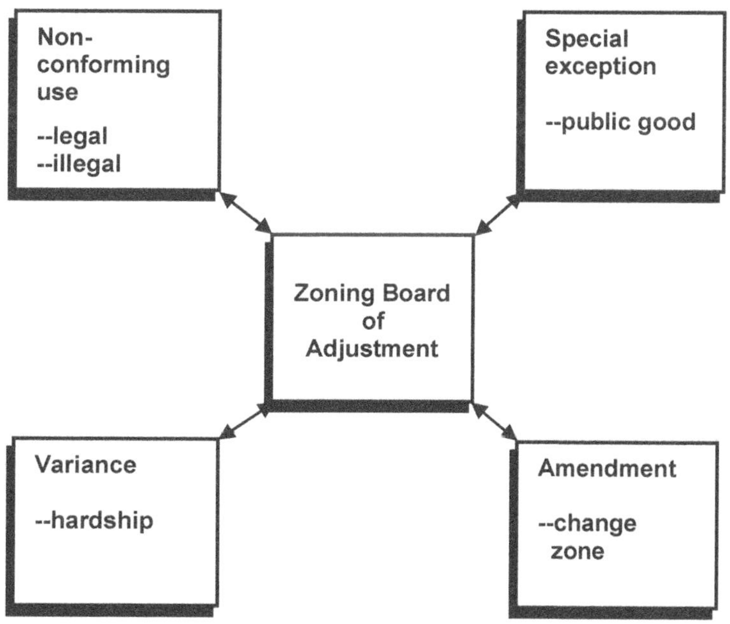

Nonconforming use. A nonconforming use is one *that clearly differs from current zoning*. Usually, nonconforming uses result when a zoning change leaves existing properties in violation of the new ordinance. This type of nonconforming use is a **legal** nonconforming use. A board usually treats this kind of situation by allowing it to continue either

- indefinitely
- until the structures are torn down
- only while the same use continues, or
- until the property is sold

For instance, a motel is situated in a residential area that no longer allows commercial activity. The zoning board rules that the motel may continue to operate until it is sold, destroyed or used for any other commercial purpose.

An **illegal nonconforming use** is one that conflicts with ordinances that were in place before the use commenced. For instance, if the motel in the previous example is sold, and the new owner continues to operate the property as a motel, the motel is now an illegal, nonconforming use.

Variance. A zoning variance allows a use that differs from the applicable ordinance for a variety of *justifiable* reasons, including that:

- compliance will cause unreasonable hardship
- the use will not change the essential character of the area
- the use does not conflict with the general intent of the ordinance

For example, an owner mistakenly violates a setback requirement by two feet. His house is already constructed, and complying with the full setback now would be extremely expensive, if not impossible. The zoning board grants a variance on the grounds that compliance would cause an unreasonable hardship.

A grant of a zoning variance may be unconditional, or it may require conditions to be fulfilled, such as removing the violation after a certain time.

Special exception. A special exception grant authorizes a use that is not consistent with the zoning ordinance in a literal sense, yet is clearly *beneficial or essential to the public welfare* and does not materially impair other uses in the zone.

A possible example is an old house in a residential zone adjacent to a retail zone. The zoning board might grant a special exception to a local group that proposes to renovate the house and convert it to a local museum, which is a retail use, since the community stands to benefit from the museum.

Amendment. A current or potential property owner may petition the zoning board for an outright change in the zoning of a particular property. For example, a property zoned for agricultural use has been idle for years. A major employer desires to develop the property for a local distribution facility, which would create numerous jobs, and petitions for an amendment. The board changes the zoning from agricultural to light industrial to permit the development. Since a change in zoning can have significant economic and social impact, an appeal for an amendment is a difficult process that often involves public hearings.

Subdivision regulation

In addition to complying with zoning ordinances, a developer of multiple properties in a subdivision must meet requirements for subdivisions.

Subdivision plat approval. The developer submits a plat of subdivision containing surveyed plat maps and comprehensive building specifications. The plat, as a minimum, shows that the plan complies with local zoning and building ordinances. The project can commence only after the relevant authority has approved the plat.

Subdivision requirements typically regulate:

- location, grading, alignment, surfacing, street width, highways
- sewers and water mains
- lot and block dimensions
- building and setback lines
- public use dedications
- utility easements
- ground percolation
- environmental impact report
- zoned density

Concurrency. Many states have adopted policies that require developers, especially of subdivisions, to take responsibility for the impact of their projects on the local infrastructure by taking corrective action. Concurrency is a policy that requires the developer to make accommodations *concurrently* with the development of the project itself, not afterwards. For example, if a project will create a traffic overload in an area, the developer may have to widen the road while constructing the project.

FHA requirements. In addition to local regulation, subdivisions must meet FHA (Federal Housing Authority) requirements to qualify for FHA financing insurance. The FHA sets standards similar to local ordinances to ensure an adequate level of construction quality, aesthetics, and infrastructure services.

Building codes

Building codes allow the county and municipality to protect the public against the hazards of unregulated construction. Building codes establish standards for virtually every aspect of a construction project, including offsite improvements such as streets, curbs, gutters, drainage systems, and onsite improvements such as the building itself.

Building codes typically address:

- architectural and engineering standards
- construction materials standards
- building support systems such as life safety, electrical, mechanical, and utility systems

Certificate of occupancy. Building inspectors inspect a new development or improvement for code compliance. If the work complies, the municipality or county issues a **certificate of occupancy** which officially clears the property for occupation and use.

Public acquisition and ownership

If efforts to regulate privately owned property are inadequate or impractical in a particular situation, or if there is a compelling public need, a county or local government may acquire property by means of direct purchase.

A government body might acquire land because of the public need for:

- thoroughfares and public rights-of-way
- recreational facilities
- schools
- essential public facilities
- urban renewal or redevelopment

In many cases, public acquisition of property is a voluntary transaction between the government entity and the private owner. However, if the private party is unwilling to sell, the government may purchase the property anyway. The power to do this is called **eminent domain**.

Eminent domain. Eminent domain allows a government entity to purchase a fee, leasehold, or easement interest in privately owned real property for the **public good** and for **public use**, regardless of the owner's desire to sell or otherwise transfer any interest. In exchange for the interest, the government must pay the owner "just compensation."

To acquire a property, the public entity initiates a condemnation suit. Transfer of title extinguishes all existing leases, liens, and other encumbrances on the property. Tenants affected by the condemnation sale may or may not receive compensation, depending on the terms of their agreement with the landlord.

Public entities that have the power of eminent domain include:

- all levels of government
- public districts (schools, etc.)
- public utilities
- public service corporations (power companies, etc.)
- public housing and redevelopment agencies
- other government agencies

To acquire a property, the public entity must first adopt a formal resolution to acquire the property, variously called a “resolution of necessity.” The resolution must be adopted at a formal hearing where the owner may voice an opinion. Once adopted, the government agency may commence a condemnation suit in court. Subsequently, the property is purchased and the title is transferred in exchange for just compensation. Transfer of title extinguishes all existing leases, liens, and other encumbrances on the property. Tenants affected by the condemnation sale may or may not receive compensation, depending on the terms of their agreement with the landlord.

In order to proceed with condemnation, the government agency must demonstrate that the project is necessary, the property is necessary for the project, and that the location offers the greatest public benefit with the least detriment.

As an eminent domain proceeding is generally an involuntary acquisition, the condemnation proceeding must accord with due process of law to ensure that it does not violate individual property rights. Further, the public entity must justify its use of eminent domain in court by demonstrating the validity of the intended public use and the resulting “public good” or “public purpose” ultimately served.

The issue of eminent domain versus individual property rights has recently come under scrutiny in light of a 2005 Supreme Court ruling that affirmed the rights of state and local governments to use the power of eminent domain for urban re-development and revitalization. The ruling allowed that private parties could undertake a project for profit without any public guarantee that the project would be satisfactorily completed. The ruling brought the issue of "public use" into question, as the use of the re-development could well be private and even a private for-profit enterprise. The winning argument was that the "public purpose" is served when redevelopment creates much needed jobs in a depressed urban area. As a result of this decision, many see the power of eminent domain and the definition of public good as being in conflict with the constitutional rights of private property ownership. New and different interpretations of the public's right to pre-empt private property ownership by eminent domain may be expected.

PRIVATE LAND USE CONTROL

Deed restriction
Declaration restriction
Deed condition
HOA regulation

Property owners in the private sector can regulate land use to some extent through deed restrictions and deed conditions.

Deed restriction

A restriction expressed in a conveyance (deed or lease) of a residential, commercial, or industrial property places limits on the use of the property. Such restrictions are also referred to as "covenants, conditions, and restrictions," or CCRs. A quitclaim deed can terminate a private deed restriction.

Typical restrictions concern:

- required minimum area of a residence
- setback
- prohibition against construction of sheds or secondary buildings
- prohibition against conducting certain commercial activities

Deed restrictions may not be discriminatory by restricting ownership or use on the basis of race, religion, marital status, or gender.

Restrictions on commercial property use may not violate fair trade and anti-trust laws.

Declaration restriction

The declaration of a subdivision, Planned Unit Development, condominium, and commercial or industrial park contains private use restrictions. These have the same legal effect as a deed restriction, as the declaration attaches to the rights in the property. A private party cannot, however, extinguish a declaration restriction by agreement or quitclaim deed.

The kinds of restrictions found in declarations are much the same as those found in deeds: construction restraints, aesthetics standards, etc.

The underlying purpose of restrictions is to preserve the value and quality of the neighborhood, commercial center, or industrial park.

Injunction. A private usage restriction can be enforced by filing for a court injunction. A court can order the violator to cease and desist, or to correct the infraction. If, however, owners in a subdivision or park allow a violation to continue for a sufficient length of time, they can lose their right to legal recourse.

Deed condition

A deed condition may restrict certain uses of a property, much like a deed restriction. However, violation of a deed condition gives the grantor the right to re- take possession of the property and file suit for legal title.

HOA regulation

Homeowners' associations (HOAs) are bodies, usually established by developers, that determine rules and regulations for the operation of a housing development. The rules are presented in a Declaration of Covenants, Conditions, and Restrictions (CC&Rs) for the development and in association by-laws. Common regulations include:

- fee obligations
- pet restrictions
- rental guidelines
- maintenance standards
- occupancy limits
- parking
- noise
- required insurance

An HOA may not impose a rule that conflicts with the law or violates homeowner rights. Infringements of rules and regulations may be enforced by the action of a civil court.

ENVIRONMENTAL CONTROLS

Areas of concern
Major legislation
Responsibilities and liabilities

In recent years, federal and state legislatures have enacted laws to conserve and protect the environment against the hazards of growth and development, particularly in terms of air, water, and soil quality.

Regional, county, and local planners must integrate environmental laws into their respective land use plans and regulations. Private property owners are responsible for complying with these laws.

Areas of concern

Air. Air quality, both indoor and outdoor, has been a matter of concern since the 1960's. With today's construction methods creating airtight, energy-efficient structures, attention to sources of indoor air pollution is more important than ever. Off-gassing from synthetic materials and lack of ventilation can lead to such consequences as Sick Building Syndrome (SBS) and Building-Related Illness (BRI) as well as other health problems. Among the significant threats are:

- *asbestos*, a powdery mineral once commonly used as a fireproof insulating material around pipes, in floor tiles and linoleum, in siding and roofing, in wallboard, joint compound, and many other applications.

  When airborne, it is a health hazard. Its use today is highly restricted, and removal can be expensive and dangerous. Inspection by a certified asbestos inspector is the best way to determine whether a building needs treatment.

- *carbon monoxide*, a colorless, odorless, poisonous gas that may result from faulty heating equipment. Home and commercial detection devices are available.

- *formaldehyde,* a chemical used in building materials and in other items such as fabrics and carpeting. As it ages, formaldehyde gives off a colorless, pungent gas.

  Its use in urea-formaldehyde foam insulation (UFFI) was banned 1982 (ban later reduced to a warning) but the material is still present in many structures. *Other substances known in general as volatile organic compounds (VOCs) and* used in construction materials such as adhesives emit toxic fumes. Professional testing can identify levels and, in some cases, sources of formaldehyde gas and other VOCs.

- *lead,* a heavy metal once widely used in paints and plumbing materials. It has been banned in paint since 1978 and in new plumbing since 1988.

  It continues to be a health threat, particularly to children, as it occurs in airborne paint particles, paint chips, and soil and groundwater polluted by various external sources of emission. Inspection should be performed by licensed lead inspectors.

- *mold,* a fungus that grows in the presence of moisture and oxygen on virtually any kind of organic surface.

  It often destroys the material it grows on and emits toxic irritants into the air. Tightly sealed structures with inadequate ventilation are most susceptible. Roof leaks, improper venting of appliances, runoff from gutters and downspouts, and flood damage are common contributors. In recent years, mold- and mildew-related lawsuits and claims have become substantial.

- *radon*, a colorless, odorless, radioactive gas that occurs naturally in the soil throughout the United States.

  It enters buildings through foundation and floor cracks, wall seams, sump pits, and windows, among other ways. At accumulations above certain levels, it is suspected of contributing to cancer. Excessive radon can be removed by special ventilation systems. Professional and home inspections are available.

Soil and water. Soil, groundwater, and drinking water supplies are vulnerable to pollution from leaking landfills; improper waste disposal; agricultural runoff; industrial dumping in waterways; highway and rail spills; industrial emissions; internal combustion emissions; and underground tanks leaking fuels and chemicals, to mention but a few sources. Some of the problems subject to controls are:

- dioxins, a family of compounds produced as a byproduct of manufacturing and incinerating materials that contain chlorine
- lead and *mercury*
- MTBE, Methyl Tertiary Butyl Ether, a gasoline additive
- PCB, Polychlorinated Biphenyl, a substance formerly widely used as an electrical insulation
- *Underground Storage Tanks* (USTs), regulated since 1984
- *Wetlands,* considered part of the natural water filtering system as well as special habitats, subject to restrictions on development and use.

Other ambient and natural conditions. Other regulated and controlled environmental conditions include:

- *Electromagnetic Fields* (EMFs) created by powerlines
- *noise* created by airports, air, rail and highway traffic
- *earthquake and flood hazards* that affect hazard insurance, lending practices, and construction requirements for buildings in designated flood and earthquake zones.

Exhibit 8.3 Environmental Concerns

	Indoors	Outdoors
Air	asbestos, BRI, carbon monoxide, formaldehyde, lead-based paint, mold, radon, SBS, VOCs	airborne lead, carbon dioxide, mercury, sulfur, dioxins
Soil		dioxins, lead, PCBs, waste, hazardous materials
Water	dioxins, lead plumbing, lead-paint, mercury, MTBE, PCBs	dioxins, lead, mercury, MTBE, PCBs, USTs, waste, hazardous materials
Ambience		EMFs, noise
Structure	UFFI	flood, earthquake

BRI: Building-Related Illness
SBS: Sick Building Syndrome
VOC: Volatile Organic Compound
MTBE: Methyl Tertiary Butyl Ether
PCB: Polychlorinated Biphenyl
UST: Underground Storage Tank
EMF: Electromagnetic Field
UFFI: Urea-Formaldehyde Foam Insulation

Major legislation

National Environmental Policy Act (1969). This act created the Environmental Protection Agency (EPA) and the Council for Environmental Quality, giving them a mandate to establish environmental standards for land use planning. The act also required environmental impact surveys on large development projects.

Clean Air Amendment (1970). This act authorized the EPA to establish air quality standards for industrial land uses as well as for automobile and airplane emissions.

Water Quality Improvement Act (1970), the Water Pollution Control Act amendment (1972), the Clean Water Act Amendment (1977). These acts addressed standards to control water pollution and industrial wastes from the standpoints of future prevention as well as remediation of existing pollution.

Resource Recovery Act (1970), the Resource Conservation and Recovery Act (1976), the Comprehensive Environmental Response, Compensation and Liability Act (Superfund) (1980), the Superfund Amendment and Reauthorization Act (1986). These acts addressed disposal of solid and toxic wastes and measures for managing waste. In addition, the Superfund act provided money for hazardous waste disposal and the authority to charge cleanup costs to responsible parties.

Lead-based paint ban (1978) and Residential Lead-based Paint Hazard Reduction Act (1992, 1996). These regulations banned lead in the manufacture of paint and established disclosure requirements and guidelines for testing and remediation.

Exhibit 8.4 Landmarks in Environmental Control Legislation

Legislation	Date	Regulated
Solid Waste Disposal Act (later part of RCRA)	1965 (1976, 1999, 2002)	landfills
Air Quality Act, Clean Air Act	1967 (1970)	air quality standards
National Environmental Policy Act (NEPA)	1969 (1970)	created EPA
Flood Control Act	amended 1969	building in flood zones; flood insurance
Resource Recovery Act	1970	solid waste disposal
Water Quality Improvement Act	1970	dumping in navigable waters; wetlands
Water Pollution Control Act amendment	1972	dumping in navigable waters; wetlands
Marine Protection Research and Sanctuaries Act	1972	offshore waste dumping
Noise control legislation	1972	airport- and transportation-related noise
Coastal Zone Management Act	1972	beaches, marine habitats
Clean Water Act	1972 (1977)	dumping in navigable waters; wetlands
Safe Drinking Water Act	1974	public water supply, lead
Resource Conservation and Recovery Act (RCRA)	1976	hazardous waste, solid waste
Toxic Substances Control Act	1976	industrial chemicals
Lead-based paint ban (US Consumer Product Safety Commission rule)	1978	lead-based paint in residences
PCB ban (EPA rule)	1979	polychlorinated biphenyls
RCRA amendment	1984	underground storage tanks
Comprehensive Environmental Response, Compensation and Liability Act	1980	hazardous waste disposal
UFFI ban	1982	formaldehyde in insulation materials
Superfund Amendment and Reauthorization Act	1986	hazardous waste cleanup costs
Asbestos ban (EPA rule)	1989	asbestos in building materials
Residential Lead-based Paint Hazard Reduction Act (EPA and HUD rule)	1992 (1996)	lead-based paint disclosure and treatment
Flood Insurance Reform Act	1994	flood insurance in flood zones
Brownfields legislation	2002	industrial site cleanup

Responsibilities & liabilities

Licensees are expected to be aware of environmental issues and to know where to look for professional help. They are not expected to have expert knowledge of environmental law nor of physical conditions in a property. Rather, they must treat potential environmental hazards in the same way that they treat other material facts about a property: disclosure.

In sum, for their own protection, licensees should be careful to:

- be aware of potential hazards
- disclose known material facts
- distribute the HUD booklet (below)
- know where to seek professional help.

Lead. The Lead-based Paint Act of 1992 requires a seller or seller's agent to disclose known lead problems in properties built before 1978. The licensee must give the buyer or lessee a copy of the EPA-HUD-US Consumer Product Safety Commission booklet, "Protect Your Family from Lead in your home."

Further, the 1996 lead-based paint regulation requires sellers or lessors of almost all residential properties built before 1978 to disclose known lead-based paint hazards and provide any relevant records available. The seller is not required to test for lead but must allow the buyer a ten-day period for lead inspection. Only a licensed lead professional is permitted to deal with testing, removal or encapsulation. It is the real estate practitioner's responsibility to ensure compliance.

CERCLA/Superfund. Under CERCLA and the Superfund Amendment of 1986, current landowners as well as previous owners of a property may be held liable for environmental violations, even if "innocent" of a violation. Sellers often carry the greatest exposure, and real estate licensees may be held liable for improper disclosure.

A real property owner can be held liable for the entire cost of remediating soil, groundwater, or indoor air contamination. A tenant can be held liable for cleanup costs as an "operator" if tenant operations are linked to contamination

Sale of a contaminated property. Selling a property with an environmental problem does not avoid liability for the seller, although seller and buyer may agree to share or transfer some liability. If there is a concern, a Phase I audit or Environmental Site Assessment (ESA) should be conducted before proceeding with the transaction. A Phase I audit identifies

- prior uses
- presence of hazardous materials

The Phase I ESA reviews environmental documents; conducts a title search for environmental liens and restrictions; and includes a visual inspection of the site and surrounding properties. There is no sampling or testing. Fannie Mae, Freddie Mac, and HUD require special Phase I ESAs on certain properties.

A Phase II audit (ESA) is conducted if a site is considered contaminated. This is a more detailed investigation using chemical analysis to uncover hazardous substances and/or petroleum hydrocarbons in samples of soil, groundwater or building materials.

A Phase III audit (ESA) involves remediation. Intensive testing, sampling, monitoring, and modeling are applied to design plans for remediation, cleanup, and follow-up monitoring. Remediation may use a variety of techniques and technologies, such as excavation and removal, dredging, chemical treatment, pumping, and solidification. Major remediation efforts usually require extensive consultation with the surrounding community. Federal funding may be available.

See Chapter 20 for further discussion. For more information, also check these sources:

asbestos	https://www.epa.gov/asbestos
carbon monoxide	https://www.epa.gov/indoor-air-quality-iaq/what-carbon-monoxide
formaldehyde	https://www.epa.gov/formaldehyde
lead	https://www.epa.gov/lead
	https://www.hud.gov/program_offices/healthy_homes/enforcement/disclosure
	https://www.epa.gov/lead/real-estate-disclosure
mold	https://www.epa.gov/mold/mold-and-your-home
radon	https://www.epa.gov/radon
	https://www.hud.gov/program_offices/healthy_homes/healthyhomes/radon
CERCLA	https://www.epa.gov/superfund

8 Land Use Planning and Control Snapshot Review

REAL ESTATE PLANNING	
Goals of land use control	• preserve property values; promote highest and best use; safeguard public health, safety and welfare; control growth; incorporate community consensus
	• process: develop plan; create administration; authorize controls
The master plan	• long term growth and usage strategies; often required by state law
	• local plans fuse municipal goals and needs with state and regional laws
Planning objectives	• control growth rates: how much growth will occur and at what rate
	• control growth patterns: type of growth desired, where it should be located
	• accommodate demand for services and infrastructure
Plan development	• research trends and conditions; blend local and state objectives into master plan
Planning management	• commission makes rules, approves permits, codes, and development plans
PUBLIC LAND USE CONTROL	• state laws; local regulations, zones, codes; public ownership; private restrictions
Zoning	• "police power" granted by state-level enabling acts; zoning ordinance: creates zones, usage restrictions, regulations, requirements
Types of zone	• residential, commercial, industrial, agricultural, public, PUD
Zoning administration	• Zoning Board of Adjustment oversees rule administration and appeals
	• nonconforming use: legal if use prior to zone creation; variance: exception based on hardship; special exception: based on public interest; amendment: change of zones; rezoning
Subdivision regulation	• plat of subdivision and relevant requirements must be met and approved; must meet FHA requirements for insured financing
Building codes	• comprehensive onsite and offsite construction and materials standards; must be met to receive certificate of occupancy
Public acquisition and ownership	• eminent domain: public power to acquire property for public use
PRIVATE LAND USE CONTROL	
Deed restriction	• single-property use restriction as stipulated in a deed; may not be discriminatory
Declaration restriction	• use restriction in multiple-property declarations; enforced by court injunction
Deed condition	• usage restriction that can trigger repossession by a previous owner if violated
HOA regulation	• homeowner's association rules require conformity to CCRs
ENVIRONMENTAL CONTROLS	
Areas of concern	• air, soil, water quality; ambient health hazards; natural hazards
Major legislation	• limits damage to environment; standards for air, land, water, materials use
Responsibilities & liabilities	• disclosure and information for practitioners; remediation for owners; lead disclosure; CERCLA/Superfund exposure; Phase I, II, III Environmental Site Assessments to detect and mitigate contamination

9 Legal Descriptions

Methods of Legal Description
Metes and Bounds
The Rectangular Survey System
Recorded Plat Method
Describing Elevation

METHODS OF LEGAL DESCRIPTION

There are many common ways of describing properties: address (100 Main Street), name (Buckingham Palace), and general description ("the south forty acres"). Such informal descriptions are not acceptable for use in public recordation or, generally speaking, in a court of law because they lack both permanence and sufficient information for a surveyor to locate the property.

Even if a legal document or public record refers to an address, the reference is always supported by an accepted legal description.

A legal description of real property is one which *accurately locates and identifies the boundaries of the subject parcel to a degree acceptable by courts of law in the state where the property is located.*

The general criterion for a legal description is that it alone provides sufficient data for a surveyor to locate the parcel. A legal description identifies the property as unique and distinct from all other properties.

Legal description provides accuracy and consistency over time. Systems of legal description, in theory, facilitate transfers of ownership and prevent boundary disputes and problems with chain of title.

A legal description is required for:

- public recording
- creating a valid deed of conveyance or lease
- completing mortgage documents
- executing and recording other legal documents

In addition, a legal description provides a basis for court rulings on encroachments and easements.

The three accepted methods of legally describing parcels of real estate are:

- metes and bounds
- rectangular survey system, or government survey method
- recorded plat method, or lot and block method

Since the metes and bounds method preceded the inception of the rectangular survey system, the older East Coast states generally employ metes and bounds descriptions. States in the Midwest and West predominantly use the rectangular survey system. Some states combine methods.

METES AND BOUNDS

A metes and bounds description identifies the boundaries of a parcel of real estate using reference points, distances, and angles. The description always identifies an *enclosed* area by starting at an origination point, called **point of beginning**, or POB, and returning to the POB at the end of the description. A metes and bounds description *must return to the POB in order to be valid.*

The term "metes" refers to distance and direction, and the term "bounds" refers to fixed reference points, or **monuments** and **landmarks**, which may be natural and artificial. Natural landmarks include trees, rocks, rivers, and lakes. Artificial landmarks are typically surveyor stakes.

Many states use metes and bounds description to describe properties within the rectangular survey system.

A metes and bounds description begins with an identification of the city, county, and state where the property is located. Next, it identifies the POB and describes the distance and direction from the POB to the first monument, and then to subsequent monuments that *define the property's enclosed perimeter*.

Exhibit 9.1 Metes and Bounds Description

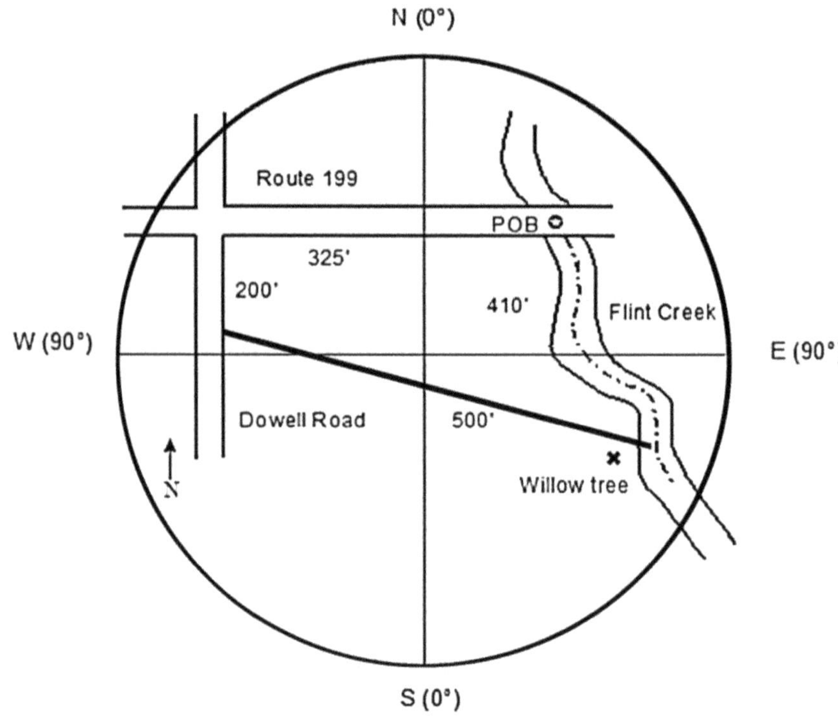

A parcel of land located in Bucks County, Pennsylvania, having the following description: commencing at the intersection of the south line of Route 199 and the middle of Flint Creek, thence southeasterly along the center thread of Flint Creek 410 feet, more or less, to the willow tree landmark, thence north 65 degrees west 500 feet, more or less to the east line of Dowell Road, thence north 2 degrees east 200 feet, more or less, along the east line of Dowell Road to the south line of Route 199, thence north 90 degrees east 325 feet, more or less, along the south line of Route 199 to the point of beginning.

THE RECTANGULAR SURVEY SYSTEM

The survey grid
Sections of township
Fractions of a section
Converting section fractions to acres

The federal government developed the **rectangular survey system**, or **government survey method**, to simplify and standardize property descriptions as a replacement for the cumbersome and often inaccurate metes and bounds method. The system was further modified to facilitate the transfer of large quantities of government-owned western lands to private parties.

To institute the system, all affected land was surveyed using latitude (east-west) and longitude (north-south) lines. The object was to create uniform grids of squares, called townships, which would have equal size and be given a numerical reference for identification.

Exhibit 9.2 Principal Meridians and Base Parallels

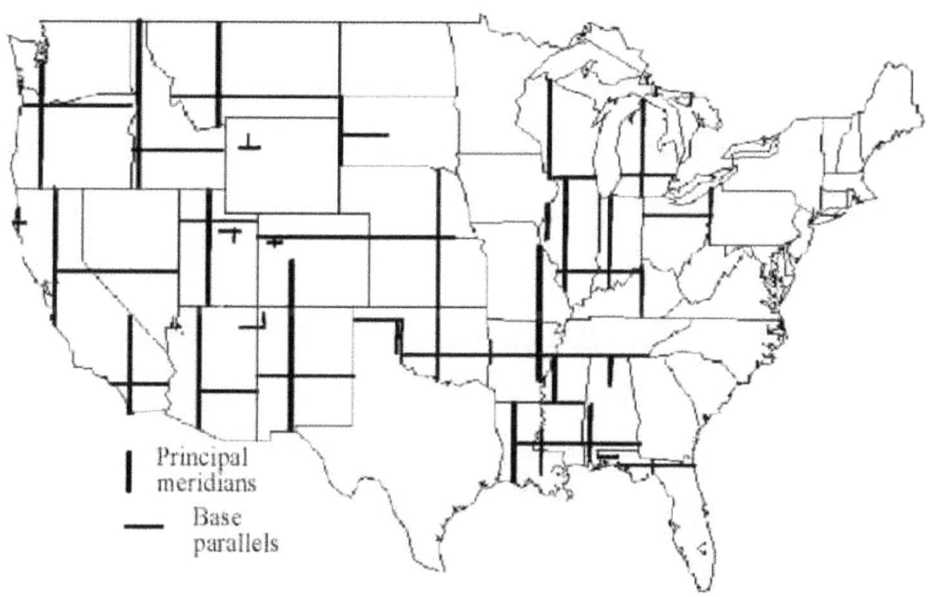

The rectangular survey system works well for describing properties that are square or rectangular in shape, since these can be described as fractions of sections. However, for an irregular shape, such as a triangle, the rectangular system is inadequate as a method of legal description. The full description has to include a metes and bounds or lot and block description.

The survey grid

The following exhibit shows a portion of the rectangular survey system.

Exhibit 9.3 A Sample Survey Grid: Florida

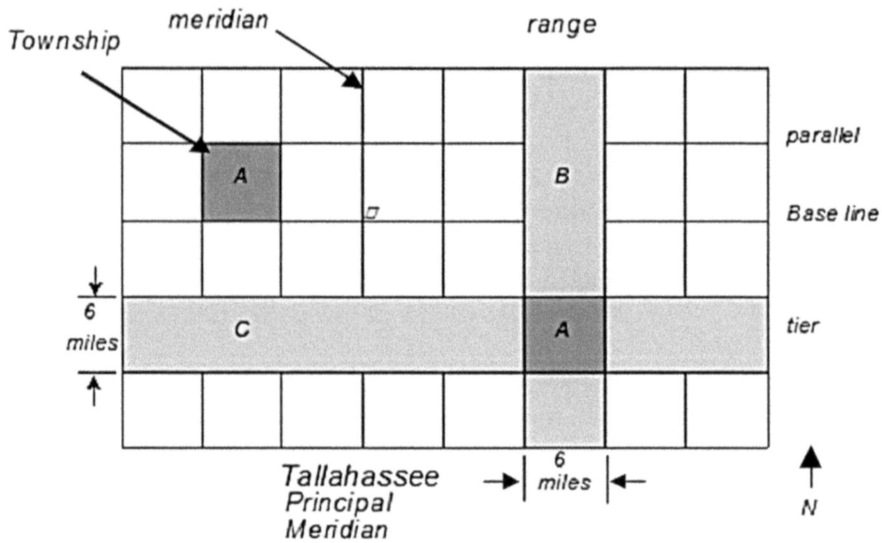

Meridian. The north-south, longitudinal lines on the survey grid are **meridians**. The **principal meridian** is the single designated meridian for identifying townships in the principal meridian's geographical "jurisdiction." There are 37 principal meridians in the national survey. In the exhibit, the principal meridian is the Tallahassee Principal Meridian.

Parallel. The east-west, latitudinal lines are called **parallels.** The **base parallel** or **base line** is the designated line for identifying townships. There is a base parallel for each principal meridian

Range. The north-south area between consecutive meridians is called a **range**. The area labeled "B" in the exhibit is a range. A range is identified by its relationship to the principal meridian. All ranges are six miles wide.

Tier. The east-west area between two parallels is called a **tier**, or a **township strip**. The area marked "C" in the exhibit is a tier. A tier is identified by its relationship to the base parallel. All tiers are six miles wide.

Township. A township is the area enclosed by the intersection of two consecutive meridians and two consecutive parallels, as the shaded square marked "A" in the exhibit illustrates. Since the parallels and meridians are six miles apart, a township is a square with six miles on each side. Its area is therefore 36 square miles.

Sections of a township

The rectangular survey system divides a township into thirty-six squares called **sections**. Each side of a section is one mile in length. Thus the area of a section is one square mile, or 640 acres. As the next exhibit illustrates, the sections in a township are numbered sequentially starting with Section 1 in the northeast corner, proceeding east to west across the top row, continuing from west to east across the next lower row, and so on, alternately, ending with Section 36 in the southeast corner.

Exhibit 9.4 Sections of a Township

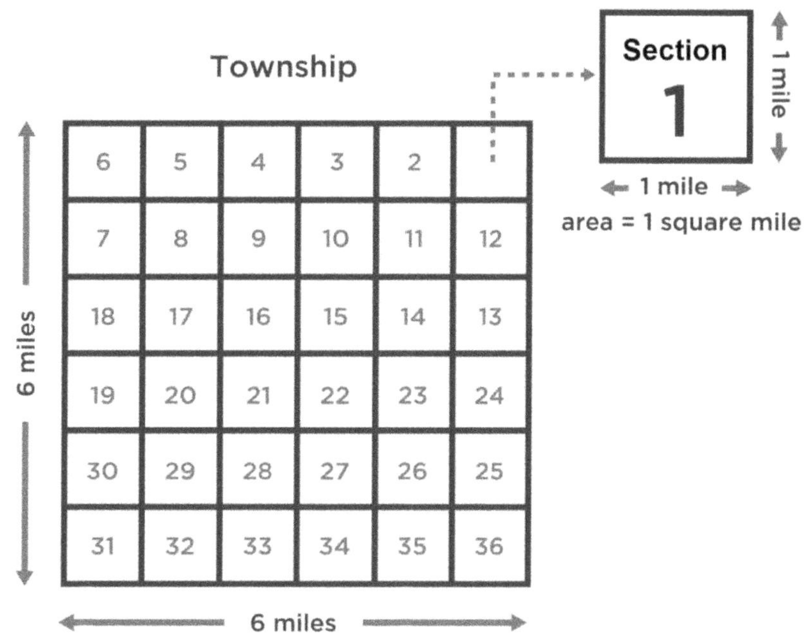

Fractions of a section

A section of a township can be divided into fractions as the next exhibit shows.

Exhibit 9.5 Fractions of Sections and Acreage

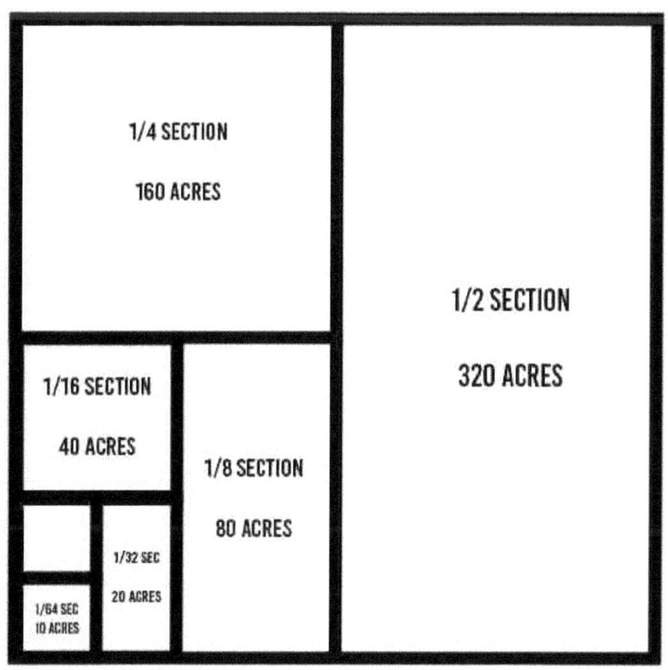

Converting section fractions to acres

The size in acres of a subsection of a township is a fraction of 640 acres, since there are 640 acres in a section.

For example, the SW 1/4 of a section is one quarter section. Thus, its acreage is one quarter of 640, or 160 acres. Going further, the E 1/2 of the SW 1/4 is one half of that one quarter, or 80 acres. The E 1/2 of the SW 1/4 of the SW ¼ is 20 acres.

A quick method of calculating the acreage of a parcel from its legal description is as follows:

(1) *Multiply the denominators* of the fractional descriptions together.

(2) Divide 640 by the resulting number.

Applying this method to the foregoing descriptions, we get:

SW 1/4 of a section: $\frac{640}{4} = 160\ acres$

E 1/2 of the SW 1/4 of a section: $\frac{640}{(2x4)} = 80\ acres$

E 1/2 of the SW 1/4 of the SW 1/4 of a section $\frac{640}{(2x4x4)} = 20\ acres$

RECORDED PLAT METHOD

Subdivision plat map
Description format

Subdivision plat map The recorded plat method, also called the **lot and block system**, is used to describe properties in residential, commercial, and industrial *subdivisions*.

Under this system, tracts of land are subdivided into lots. The entire group of lots comprises the subdivision. In a large subdivision, lots may be grouped together into **blocks** for ease of reference. The entire subdivision is surveyed to specify the size and location of each lot and block. The surveyor then incorporates the survey data into a **plat of survey**, or **subdivision plat map**, which must comply with local surveying standards and ordinances.

If local authorities accept it, the subdivision plat map is recorded in the county where the subdivision is located. The recorded lot and block numbers of a subdivision parcel, along with its section, township and meridian reference, become the property's legal description. The exhibit shows a sample subdivision plat map.

Exhibit 9.6 Subdivision Plat Map

Panther Ridge "The Forest" Subdivision

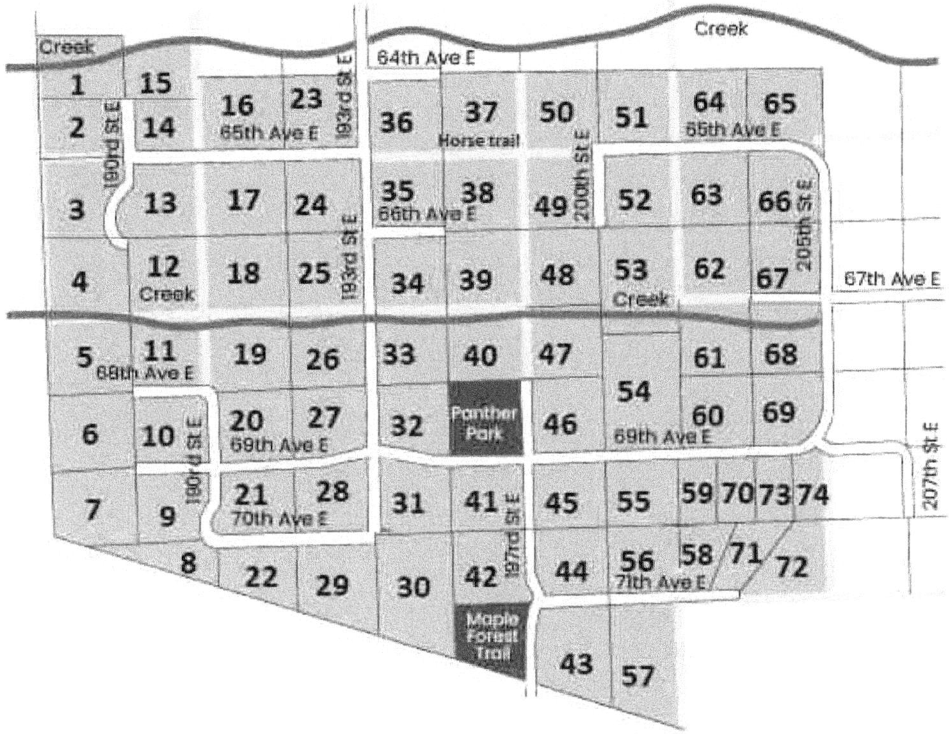

Description format The description of a recorded plat property first presents the property's lot number or letter, then the block identifier and the subdivision name. Note that this is only a portion of the full legal description, which must describe the subdivision's location within a section, a township, a county, and a state. For example, if the subdivision in the exhibit is situated in the southeast quarter of Section 35 of Township T28S, R19E, of the Tallahassee Principal Meridian and its block number is 8, the legal description of the lot marked "7" would be:

> "Lot 7, Block 8 of the Panther Ridge, the Forest Subdivision of the SE 1/4 of Section 35, Township T28S, R19E of the Tallahassee Principal Meridian in Manatee County, Florida."

DESCRIBING ELEVATION

To describe property located above or below the earth's surface, such as the air rights of a condominium, a surveyor must know the property's elevation. Standard elevation reference points, called **datums**, have been established throughout the country. The original datum was defined by the U.S. Geological Survey as mean sea level at New York harbor. A surveyor uses a datum as an official elevation point to describe the height or depth of a property. If, for example, the datum for an area is a point 100 feet above sea level, all surveys in the area will indicate elevation as a distance above or below 100 feet above sea level.

In many cases it is impractical for a surveyor to rely on a single datum for an entire surveying area. To simplify matters, surveyors have identified local elevation markers, called **benchmarks,** to provide reference elevations for nearby properties. Once a benchmark is registered, it provides a valid reference point for surveying other elevations in the immediate area.

9 Legal Descriptions Snapshot Review

METHODS OF LEGAL DESCRIPTION	• metes and bounds; rectangular survey system or government survey; recorded plat or lot and block
	• legal description is sufficiently accurate, acceptable in court of law; facilitates transfers; avoids disputes; used in legal contracts
METES AND BOUNDS	• describes property perimeter by landmarks, monuments, distances, angles
	• from point of beginning (POB), describes perimeter and returns to POB; usable within rectangular survey system
RECTANGULAR SURVEY SYSTEM	
The survey grid	• meridians: north-south lines six miles apart
	• parallels: east-west lines six miles apart
	• ranges: north-south strips of area between meridians; tiers: east-west strips of area between parallels; townships: the area representing the intersection of a range and a tier, consisting of six-mile by six-mile squares of land
Sections of a township	• 36 sections per township, each one-mile square (1 mile on each side)
Fractions of a section	• 1 section = 640 acres; fractions of sections described by size and location within progressively larger quarters of section
Converting section fractions to acres	• formula: multiply denominators of section fractions; divide product into 640
RECORDED PLAT METHOD	• or lot and block system; used in surveyed subdivisions
Subdivision plat map	• surveyed plat of subdivided tract; legal descriptor if approved and recorded
Description format	• lots within subdivision are identified by lot reference and block reference: "Lot 7 Block B of the Grand Oaks Subdivision"
DESCRIBING ELEVATION	• datum: a standard elevation reference point; benchmark: elevation marker officially surveyed and registered

10 Fundamentals of Contract Law

Contract Validity and Enforceability
Contract Creation
Classifications of Contracts
Contract Termination

Real estate contracts are the legal agreements that underlie the transfer and financing of real estate, as well as the real estate brokerage business. Sale and lease contracts and option agreements are used to transfer real estate interests from one party to another. Mortgage contracts and promissory agreements are part of financing real estate. Listing and representation contracts establish client relationships and provide for compensation.

In order to work with real estate contracts, it is imperative first to grasp basic concepts that apply to all contracts in general. These concepts provide a foundation for understanding the specifics of particular types of real estate contract.

CONTRACT VALIDITY AND ENFORCEABILITY

Legal status of contracts
Criteria for validity
Validity of a conveyance contract
Enforcement limitations
Electronic contracting

A **contract** is an agreement between two or more parties who, in a "meeting of the minds," have pledged to perform or refrain from performing some act. A *valid* contract is one that is *legally enforceable* by virtue of meeting certain requirements of contract law. If a contract does not meet the requirements, it is not valid and the parties to it cannot resort to a court of law to enforce its provisions.

Note that a contract is not a legal form or a prescribed set of words in a document, but rather the intangible agreement that was made in "the meeting of the minds" of the parties to the contract.

Legal status of contracts

In terms of validity and enforceability, a court may construe the legal status of a contract in one of four ways:

- valid
- valid but unenforceable
- void
- voidable

Valid. A valid contract is one which meets the legal requirements for validity. These requirements are explained in the next section.

A valid contract that is in writing is enforceable within a statutory time period. A valid contract that is made orally is also generally enforceable within a statutory period, with the exceptions noted below.

Valid but unenforceable. State laws declare that some contracts are enforceable only if they are in writing. These laws apply in particular to the transfer of interests in real estate. Thus, while an oral contract may meet the tests for validity, if it falls under the laws requiring a written contract, the parties will not have legal recourse to enforce performance. An oral long-term lease and an oral real estate sales contract are examples of contracts that may be valid but not enforceable.

Note that such contracts, if valid, remain so even though not enforceable. This means that if the parties fully execute and perform the contract, the outcome may not be altered.

Void. A void contract is an agreement that does not meet the tests for validity, and therefore is no contract at all. If a contract is void, neither party can enforce it.

For example, a contract that does not include consideration is void. Likewise, a contract to extort money from a business is void. Void contracts and instruments are also described as "null and void."

Voidable. A voidable contract is one which initially appears to be valid, but is subject to rescission by a party to the contract who is deemed to have acted under some kind of disability. Only the party who claims the disability may rescind the legal effect of the contract.

For example, a party who was the victim of duress, coercion, or fraud in creation of a contract, and can prove it, may disaffirm the contract. However, the disaffirmation must occur within a legal time frame for the act of rescission to be valid. Similarly, if the party who has cause to disaffirm the contract elects instead to perform it, the contract is no longer voidable but valid.

A voidable contract differs from a void contract in that the latter does not require an act of disaffirmation to render it unenforceable.

Criteria for validity

A contract is valid only if it meets all of the following criteria.

Exhibit 10.1 Contract Validity Requirements

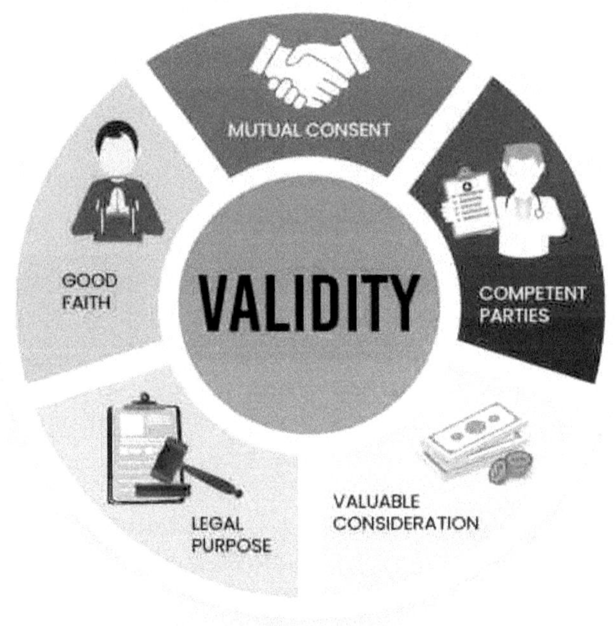

Competent parties. The parties to a contract must have the capacity to contract, and there must be at least two such parties. Thus, the owner of a tenancy for life cannot deed his interest to himself in the form of a fee simple, as this would involve only one party. Capacity to contract is determined by three factors:

- legal age
- mental competency
- legitimate authority

Depending on state law, a contract involving a minor as a party may be either void or voidable. If the law allows a minor to contract, the contract will generally be voidable and the minor can disaffirm the contract.

To be mentally competent, a party must have sufficient understanding of the import and consequences of a contract. Competency in this context is separate and distinct from sanity. Incompetent parties, or parties of "unsound mind," may not enter into enforceable contracts. The incompetency of a party may be ruled by a court of law or by other means. In some areas, convicted felons may be deemed incompetent, depending on the nature of the crime.

During the period of one's incompetency, a court may appoint a guardian who may act on the incompetent party's behalf with court approval.

If the contracting party is representing another person or business entity, the representative must have the *legal authority* to contract. If representing another person, the party must have a bona fide power of attorney. If the contracting party is representing a corporation, the person must have the appropriate power and approval to act, such as would be conferred in a duly executed resolution of the Board of Directors. If the contracting entity is a general partnership, any partner may validly contract for the partnership. In a limited partnership, only general partners may be parties to a contract.

Mutual consent. Mutual consent, also known as *offer and acceptance* and *meeting of the minds,* requires that a contract involve a clear and definite offer and an intentional, unqualified acceptance of the offer. In effect, the parties must agree to the terms without equivocation. A court may nullify a contract where the acceptance of terms by either party was partial, accidental, or vague.

Valuable consideration. A contract must contain a two-way exchange of valuable consideration as compensation for performance by the other party. The exchange of considerations must be two-way. The contract is not valid or enforceable if just one party provides consideration.

Valuable consideration can be something of tangible value, such as money or something a party promises to do or not do. For example, a home builder may promise to build a house for a party as consideration for receiving money from the home buyer. Or, a landowner may agree not to sell a property as consideration for a developer's option money. Also, valuable consideration can be something intangible that a party must give up, such as a homeowner's occupancy of the house in exchange for rent. In effect, consideration is the price one party must pay to obtain performance from the other party.

Valuable consideration may be contrasted with good consideration, or "love and affection," which does not qualify as consideration in a valid contract. Good consideration is something of questionable value, such as a child's love for her mother. Good consideration disqualifies a contract because, while one's love or affection is certainly valuable to the other party, it is not something that is specifically offered in exchange for something else. Good consideration can, however, serve as a nominal consideration in transferring a real property interest as a gift.

In some cases, what is promised as valuable consideration must also be deemed to be *sufficient* consideration. Grossly insufficient consideration, such as $50,000 for a $2 million property, may invalidate a contract on the grounds that the agreement is a gift rather than a contract. In other cases where there is an extreme imbalance in the considerations exchanged, a contract may be invalidated as a violation of good faith bargaining.

Exhibit 10.2 Consideration

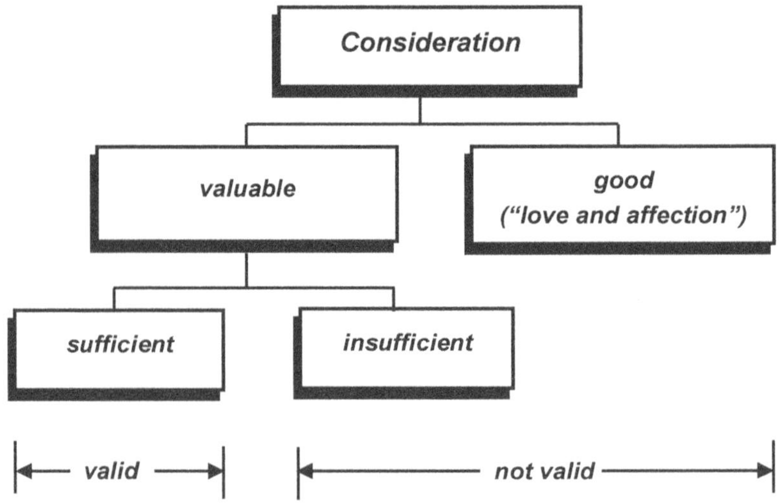

Legal purpose. The content, promise, or intent of a contract must be lawful. A contract that proposes an illegal act is void.

Voluntary, good faith act. The parties must create the contract in good faith as a free and voluntary act. A contract is thus voidable if one party acted under duress, coercion, fraud, or misrepresentation.

For example, if a property seller induces a buyer to purchase a house based on assurances that the roof is new, the buyer may rescind the agreement if the roof turns out to be twenty years old and leaky.

Validity of a conveyance contract

In addition to satisfying the foregoing requirements, a contract that conveys an interest in real estate must:

- be in writing
- contain a legal description of the property
- be signed by one or more of the parties

A lease contract that has a term of one year or less is an exception. Such leases do not have to be in writing to be enforceable.

Enforcement limitations

Certain contracts that fail to meet the validity requirements are voidable if a damaged party takes appropriate action. The enforcement of voidable contracts, however, is limited by **statutes of limitation.** Certain other contracts which are valid may not be enforceable due to the **statute of frauds**.

Statute of limitations. The statute of limitations restricts the time period for which an injured party in a contract has the right to rescind or disaffirm the contract. A party to a voidable contract must act within the statutory period.

Statute of frauds. The statute of frauds requires that certain contracts *must be in writing* to be enforceable. Real estate contracts that convey an interest in real property fall in this category, with the exception that a lease of one year's duration or less may be oral. All other contracts to buy, sell, exchange, or lease interests in real property must be in writing to be enforceable. In addition, *listing agreements* in most states must be in writing.

The statute of frauds concerns the enforceability of a contract, not its validity. Once the parties to a valid oral contract have executed and performed it, even if the contract was unenforceable, a party cannot use the Statute of Frauds to rescind the contract.

For example, a broker and a seller have an oral agreement. Following the terms of the agreement, the broker finds a buyer, and the seller pays the commission. They have now executed the contract, and the seller cannot later force the broker to return the commission based on the statute of frauds.

Electronic contracting

Contracting electronically through email and fax greatly facilitates the completion of transactions. Clients, lenders, title agents, inspectors, brokers, and other participants in a transaction can quickly share documentation and information. Electronic contracting is made possible by the Uniform Electronic Transactions Act (UETA) and the Electronic Signatures in Global and National Commerce Act (E-Sign), which are federal laws. UETA, which has been accepted in most states, provides that electronic records and signatures are legal and must be accepted. E-Sign makes contracts, records, and signatures legally enforceable, regardless of medium, even where UETA is not accepted.

CONTRACT CREATION

Offer and acceptance
Counteroffer
Revocation of an offer
Termination of an offer
Assignment of a contract
Contract preparation

Offer and acceptance

The mutual consent required for a valid contract is reached through the process of offer and acceptance: The **offeror** proposes contract terms in an **offer** to the **offeree**. If the offeree accepts all terms without amendment, the offer becomes a contract. The exact point at which the offer becomes a contract is when the offeree gives the offeror notice of the acceptance.

Exhibit 10.3 Offer, Counter Offer and Acceptance

Offer. An offer expresses the offeror's intention to enter into a contract with an offeree to perform the terms of the agreement in exchange for the offeree's performance. In a real estate sale or lease contract, the offer must clearly contain all intended terms of the contract in writing and be communicated to the offeree.

If an offer contains an expiration date and the phrase "time is of the essence," the offer expires at exactly the time specified. In the absence of a stated time period, the offeree has a "reasonable" time to accept an offer.

Acceptance. An offer gives the offeree the power of accepting. For an acceptance to be valid, the offeree must manifestly and unequivocally accept all terms of the offer without change, and so indicate by signing the offer, preferably with a date of signing. The acceptance must then be communicated to the offeror. If the communication of acceptance is by mail, the offer is considered to be communicated as soon as it is placed in the mail.

Counteroffer

By changing any of the terms of an offer, the offeree creates a counteroffer, and the original offer is void. At this point, the offeree becomes the offeror, and the new offeree gains the right of acceptance. If accepted, the counteroffer becomes a valid contract provided all other requirements are met.

For example, a seller changes the expiration date of a buyer's offer by one day, signs the offer and returns it to the buyer. The single amendment extinguishes the buyer's offer, and the buyer is no longer bound by any agreement. The seller's amended offer is a counteroffer which now gives the buyer the right of acceptance. If the buyer accepts the counteroffer, the counteroffer becomes a binding contract.

Revocation of an offer

An offer may be revoked, or withdrawn, at any time before the offeree has communicated acceptance. The revocation extinguishes the offer and the offeree's right to accept it.

For example, a buyer has offered to purchase a house for the listed price. Three hours later, a family death radically changes the buyer's plans. She immediately calls the seller and revokes the offer, stating she is no longer interested in the house. Since the seller had not communicated acceptance of the offer to the buyer, the offer is legally cancelled.

If the offeree has paid consideration to the offeror to leave an offer open, and the offeror accepts, an option has been created which cancels the offeror's right to revoke the offer over the period of the option.

Termination of an offer

Any of the following actions or circumstances can terminate an offer:

- acceptance: the offeree accepts the offer, converting it to a contract
- rejection: the offeree rejects the offer
- revocation: the offeror withdraws the offer before acceptance
- lapse of time: the offer expires
- counteroffer: the offeree changes the offer
- death or insanity of either party

Assignment of a contract

A real estate contract that is not a personal contract for services can be assigned to another party unless the terms of the agreement specifically prohibit assignment.

Listing agreements, for example, are not assignable, since they are personal service agreements between agent and principal. Sales contracts, however, are assignable, because they involve the purchase of real property rather than a personal service.

Contract preparation

State laws define the extent to which real estate brokers and agents may legally prepare real estate contracts. Such laws, referred to as "broker-lawyer accords," also define what types of contracts brokers and agents may prepare. In some states, brokers and agents may not draft contracts, but they may use standard promulgated forms and complete the blanks in the form.

As a rule, a broker or agent who completes real estate contracts is engaging in the unauthorized practice of law unless the broker is a party to the agreement, such as a in a listing agreement or sales contract. Brokers and agents may not complete leases, mortgages, contracts for deed, or promissory notes to which they are not a party.

Agents must be fully aware of what they are legally allowed to do and not do in preparing and interpreting contracts for clients. In addition to practicing law without a license, agents expose themselves to lawsuits from clients who relied on a contract as being legally acceptable.

CLASSIFICATIONS OF CONTRACTS

Oral vs. written
Express vs. implied
Unilateral vs. bilateral
Executed vs. executory

Oral vs. written

A contract may be in writing or it may be an oral, or **parol**, contract. Certain oral contracts are valid and enforceable, others are not enforceable, even if valid. For example, most states require listing agreements, sales contracts, and leases exceeding one year to be in writing to be enforceable.

Express vs. implied

An **express contract** is one in which all the terms and covenants of the agreement have been manifestly stated and agreed to by all parties, whether verbally or in writing.

An **implied contract** is an unstated or unintentional agreement that may be deemed to exist when the *actions of any of the parties* suggest the existence of an agreement.

A common example of an implied contract is an implied agency agreement. In implied agency, an agent who does not have a contract with a buyer performs acts on the buyer's behalf, such as negotiating a price that is less than the listing price. In so doing, the agent has possibly created an implied contract with the buyer, albeit unintended. If the buyer compensates the agent for the negotiating efforts, the existence of an implied agency agreement becomes even less disputable.

Bilateral vs. unilateral

A **bilateral contract** is one in which both parties promise to perform their respective parts of an agreement in exchange for performance by the other party.

An example of a bilateral contract is an exclusive listing: the broker promises to exercise due diligence in the efforts to sell a property, and the seller promises to compensate the broker when and if the property sells.

In a **unilateral contract**, only one party promises to do something, provided the other party does something. The latter party is not obligated to perform any act, but the promising party must fulfill the promise if the other party chooses to perform.

An option is an example of a unilateral contract: in an option-to-buy, the party offering the option (optionor) promises to sell a property if the optionee decides to exercise the option. While the potential buyer does not have to buy, the owner must sell if the option is exercised.

Executed vs. executory

An **executed contract** is one that has been fully performed and fulfilled: neither party bears any further obligation. A completed and expired lease contract is an executed contract: the landlord may re-possess the premises and the tenant has no further obligation to pay rent.

An **executory contract** is one in which performance is yet to be completed. A sales contract prior to closing is executory: while the parties have agreed to buy and sell, the buyer has yet to pay the seller and the seller has yet to deed the property to the buyer.

CONTRACT TERMINATION

Forms of contract termination
Breach of contract

Forms of contract termination

Termination of a contract, also called **cancellation** and **discharge**, may occur for any of the following causes.

Performance. A contract terminates when fully performed by the parties. It may also terminate for:

- partial performance, if the parties agree
- sufficient performance, if a court determines a party has sufficiently performed the contract, even though not to the full extent of every provision

Infeasibility. An otherwise valid contract can be canceled if it is not possible to perform. Certain personal services contracts, for example, depend on the unique capabilities of one person which cannot be substituted by someone else. If such a person dies or is sufficiently disabled, the contract is cancelable.

Mutual agreement. Parties to a contract can agree to terminate, or renounce, the contract. If the parties wish to create a new contract to replace the cancelled contract, they must comply with the validity requirements for the new contract. Such substitution is called **novation**.

Cooling-period rescission. Rescission is the act of nullifying a contract. In many states, parties to certain contracts are allowed a statutory amount of time after entering into a contract, or "cooling period", to rescind the contract without cause. No reason need be stated for the cancellation, and the cancelling party incurs no liability for performance.

For example, consider the unsuspecting buyer of a lot in a new resort development. Such buyers are often the targets of hard-sell tactics which lead to a completed sales contract and a deposit. The statutory cooling period gives the buyer an opportunity to reconsider the investment in the absence of the persistent salesperson.

Revocation. Revocation is cancellation of the contract by one party without the consent of the other. For example, a seller may revoke a listing to take the property off the market. While all parties have the *power* to revoke, they may not have a defensible *right*. In the absence of justifiable grounds, a revocation may not relieve the revoking party of contract obligations.

For example, a seller who revokes a listing without grounds may be required to pay a commission if the broker found a buyer, or reimburse the broker's marketing expenses if no buyer was found.

Abandonment. Abandonment occurs when parties fail to perform contract obligations. This situation may allow the parties to cancel the contract.

Lapse of time. If a contract contains an expiration provision and date, the contract automatically expires on the deadline.

Invalidity of contract. If a contract is void, it terminates without the need for disaffirmation. A voidable contract can be cancelled by operation of law or by rescission.

Breach of contract

A breach of contract is a failure to perform according to the terms of the agreement. Also called **default**, a breach of contract gives the damaged party the right to take legal action.

The damaged party may elect the following legal remedies:

- rescission
- forfeiture
- suit for damages
- suit for specific performance

Rescission. A damaged party may rescind the contract. This cancels the contract and returns the parties to their pre-contract condition, including the refunding of any monies already transferred.

Forfeiture. A forfeiture requires the breaching party to give up something, according to the terms of the contract. For example, a buyer who defaults on a sales contract may have to forfeit the earnest money deposit.

Suit for damages. A damaged party may sue for money damages in civil court. The suit must be initiated within the time period allowed by the statute of limitations. When a contract states the total amount due to a damaged party in the event of a breach, the compensation is known as **liquidated damages**. If the contract does not specify the amount, the damaged party may sue in court for **unliquidated damages**.

Suit for specific performance. A suit for specific performance is an attempt to force the defaulting party to comply with the terms of the contract. Specific performance suits occur when it is difficult to identify damages because of the unique circumstances of the real property in question. The most common instance is a defaulted sale or lease contract where the buyer or seller wants the court to compel the defaulting party to go through with the transaction, even when the defaulter would prefer to pay a damage award.

10 Fundamentals of Contract Law Snapshot Review

CONTRACT VALIDITY AND ENFORCEABILITY	• contract: mutual promises based on "meeting of the minds" to do or refrain from doing something; potentially enforceable if created validly
Legal status of contracts	• valid: meets criteria
	• void: does not meet criteria
	• voidable: invalid if disaffirmed
	• valid yet unenforceable: certain oral contracts
Criteria for validity	• competent parties; mutual consent; valuable consideration; legal purpose; voluntary, good faith act
Validity of a conveyance contract	• must be in writing; contain a legal description; be signed by one or more parties
Enforcement limitations	• statute of frauds: must be written to be enforceable
	• statute of limitations: must act within time frame
Electronic contracting	• federal law: electronic records and signatures are legal and must be accepted; enforceable regardless of medium
CONTRACT CREATION	
Offer and acceptance	• valid offer and valid acceptance creates contract
	• offer becomes contract on communication of acceptance by offeree to offeror
Counteroffer	• any offer in response to an offer or any altered original offer; nullifies original offer
Revocation of an offer	• offeror may revoke offer prior to communication of acceptance by offeree
Termination of an offer	• acceptance; rejection; revocation; expiration; counteroffer; death or insanity
Assignment of a contract	• assignable unless expressly prohibited or a personal service
Contract preparation	• restricted unless licensed as attorney or a party to the contract
CLASSIFICATIONS OF CONTRACTS	• oral or written; express or implied; unilateral or bilateral; executed or executory
CONTRACT TERMINATION	
Forms of contract termination	• performance; infeasibility; mutual agreement; cooling-period rescission; revocation; abandonment; lapse of time; invalidity of contract; breach of contract
Breach of contract	• default without cause
	• legal remedies: rescission; forfeiture; suit for damages; specific performance

11 National Agency

The Agency Relationship
Fiduciary Duties
Forms of Real Estate Agency
Agency Disclosure Rules

THE AGENCY RELATIONSHIP

Basic roles
Types of agency
Creating an agency relationship
Terminating an agency relationship

The most primary of relationships in real estate brokerage is that between broker and client, the relationship known in law as the **agency relationship**. In every state, a body of law, generally called the **law of agency,** defines and regulates the legal roles of this relationship. The parties to the relationship are the **principal** (a client), the **agent** (a broker), and the **customer** (a third party).

The laws of agency are distinct from laws of contracts, although the two groups of laws interact with each other. For example, the listing agreement -- a contract -establishes an agency relationship. Thus the relationship is subject to contract law. However, agency law dictates how the relationship will achieve its purposes, regardless of what the listing contract states.

The essence of the agency relationship is *trust, confidence, and mutual good faith*. The principal trusts the agent to exercise the utmost skill and care in fulfilling the authorized activity, and to promote the principal's best interests. The agent undertakes to strive in good faith to achieve the desired objective, and to fulfill the fiduciary duties.

It is important to understand that the agency relationship does *not* require compensation or any form of consideration. Nor does compensation define an agency relationship: a party other than the principal may compensate the agent.

Basic roles

In an agency relationship, a principal hires an agent as a *fiduciary* to perform a desired service on the principal's behalf. As a fiduciary, the agent has a legal obligation to fulfill specific *fiduciary duties* throughout the term of the relationship.

The **principal,** or **client**, is the party who hires the agent. The agent works *for* the client. The principal may be a seller, a buyer, a landlord, or a tenant.

The **agent** is the fiduciary of the principal, hired to perform the authorized work and bound to fulfill fiduciary duties. In real estate brokerage the agent *must* be a licensed broker.

The **customer** or **prospect** is a third party in the transaction whom the agent does not represent. The agent works *with* a customer in fulfilling the client's objectives. A seller, buyer, landlord, or tenant may be a customer. A third party who is a potential customer is a **prospect**.

Types of agency

According to the level of authority delegated to the agent, there are three types of agency: *universal, general, and special*.

Universal agency. In a universal agency relationship, the principal empowers the agent to perform any and all actions that may be legally delegated to an agency representative. The instrument of authorization is the power of attorney.

General agency. In a general agency, the principal delegates to the agent ongoing tasks and duties within a particular business or enterprise. Such delegation may include the authority to enter into contracts.

Special, or **limited, agency.** Under a special agency agreement, the principal delegates authority to conduct a specific activity, after which the agency relationship terminates. In most cases, the special agent *may not* bind the principal to a contract.

In most instances, real estate brokerage is based on a special agency. The principal hires a licensed broker to procure a ready, willing, and able buyer or seller. When the objective is achieved, the relationship terminates, although certain fiduciary duties survive the relationship.

Creating an agency relationship

An agency relationship may arise from an express oral or written agreement between the principal and the agent, or from the actions of the parties by implication.

Written or oral listing agreement. The most common way of creating an agency relationship is by listing agreement, which may be oral or written. The agreement sets forth the various authorizations and duties, as well as requirements for compensation. A listing agreement establishes an agency for a specified transaction and has a stated expiration.

Implied agency. An agency relationship can arise by implication, intentionally or unintentionally. Implication means that the parties act *as if* there were an agreement. For example, if an agent promises a buyer to do everything possible to find a property at the lowest possible price, and the buyer accepts the proposition, there may be an implied agency relationship even though there is no specific agreement. Even if the agent does not wish to establish an agency relationship, the agent's actions may be construed to imply a relationship. Whether intended or accidental, the creation of implied agency obligates the agent to fiduciary duties and professional standards of care. If these are not fulfilled, the agent may be held liable

Terminating an agency relationship

Full performance of all obligations by the parties terminates an agency relationship. In addition, the parties may terminate the relationship at any time by *mutual agreement*. Thirdly, the agency relationship automatically terminates on the *expiration* date, whether the obligations were performed or not.

Involuntary termination. An agency relationship may terminate contrary to the wishes of the parties by reason of:

- death or incapacity of either party
- abandonment by the agent
- condemnation or destruction of the property
- renunciation
- breach
- bankruptcy
- revocation of the agent's license

Involuntary termination of the relationship may create legal and financial liability for a party who defaults or cancels. For example, a client may renounce an agreement but then be held liable for the agent's expenses or commission.

FIDUCIARY DUTIES

Agent's duties to the client
Agent's duties to the customer
Principal's duties
Breach of duty

The agency relationship imposes fiduciary duties on the client and agent, but particularly on the agent. An agent must also observe certain standards of conduct in dealing with customers and other outside parties.

Agent's duties to the client

Skill, care, and diligence. The agent is hired to do a job, and is therefore expected to do it with diligence and reasonable competence. Competence is generally defined as a level of real estate marketing skills and knowledge comparable to those of other practitioners in the area.

The notion of care extends to observing the limited scope of authority granted to the agent. A conventional listing agreement does not authorize an agent to obligate the client to contracts, and it does not allow the agent to conceal offers to buy, sell, or lease coming from a customer or another agent. Further, since a client relies on a broker's representations, a broker must exercise care not to offer advice outside of his or her field of expertise. Violations of this standard may expose the agent to liability for the unlicensed practice of a profession such as law, engineering, or accounting.

Exhibit 11.1 Fiduciary Duties

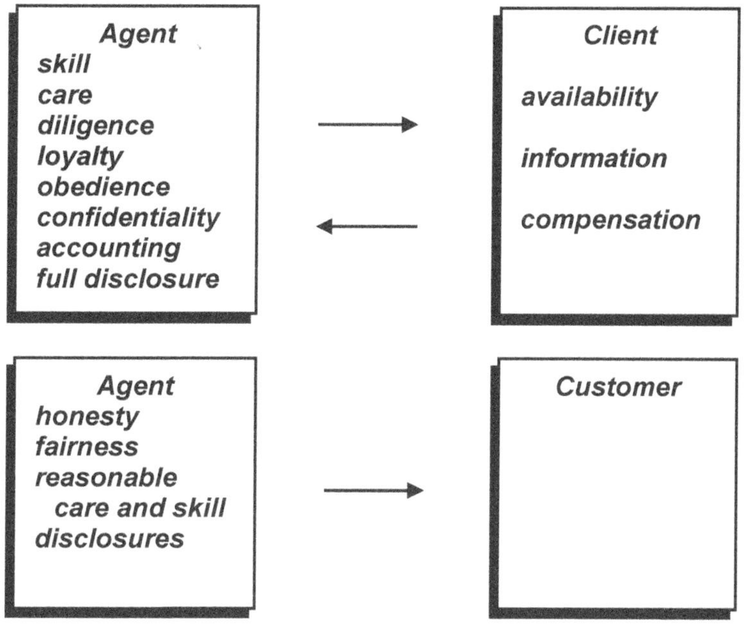

Loyalty. The duty of loyalty requires the agent to place the interests of the client above those of all others, particularly the agent's own. This standard is particularly relevant whenever an agent discusses transaction terms with a prospect.

Obedience. An agent must comply with the client's directions and instructions, *provided they are legal*. An agent who cannot obey a legal directive, for whatever reason, must withdraw from the relationship. If the directive is illegal, the agent must also immediately withdraw.

Confidentiality. An agent must hold in confidence any personal or business information received from the client during the term of employment. An agent may not disclose any information that would harm the client's interests or bargaining position, or anything else the client wishes to keep secret.

The confidentiality standard is one of the duties that extends *beyond the termination of the listing*: at *no time* in the future may the agent disclose confidential information.

An agent must exercise care in fulfilling this duty: if confidentiality conflicts with the agent's legal requirements to disclose material facts, the agent must inform the client of this obligation and make the required disclosures. If such a conflict cannot be resolved, the agent must withdraw from the relationship.

Accounting. An agent must safeguard and account for all monies, documents, and other property received from a client or customer. State license laws regulate the broker's accounting obligations and escrow practices.

Full disclosure. An agent has the duty to inform the client of all material facts, reports, and rumors that might affect the client's interests in the property transaction.

In recent years, the disclosure standard has been raised to require an agent to disclose items that a practicing agent *should know,* whether the agent actually had the knowledge or not, and regardless of whether the disclosure furthers or impedes the progress of the transaction.

The most obvious example of a "should have known" disclosure is a property defect, such as an inoperative central air conditioner, that the agent failed to notice. If the air conditioner becomes a problem, the agent may be held liable for failing to disclose a material fact if a court rules that the typical agent in that area would detect and recognize a faulty air conditioner.

There is no obligation to obtain or disclose information related to a customer's race, creed, color, religion, sex or national origin: anti-discrimination laws hold such information to be immaterial to the transaction.

Some states have recently enacted laws requiring a seller to make a written disclosure about property condition to a prospective buyer. This seller disclosure may or may not relieve the agent of some liabilities for disclosure.

Exhibit 11.2 Disclosure of Material Facts

Critical material facts for disclosure include:

- the agent's opinion of the property's condition
- information about the buyer's motivations and financial qualifications
- discussions between agent and buyer regarding the possibility of the agent's representing the buyer in another transaction.
- adverse material facts, including property condition, title defects, environmental hazards, and property defects

Agent's duties to the customer

The traditional notion of *caveat emptor*-- let the buyer beware-- no longer applies unequivocally to real estate transactions. Agents *do* have certain obligations to customers, even though they do not represent them. In general, they owe a third party:

- honesty and fair dealing
- reasonable care and skill
- proper disclosure

An agent has a duty to deal fairly and honestly with a customer. Thus, an agent may not deceive, defraud, or otherwise take advantage of a customer.

"Reasonable care and skill" means that an agent will be held to the standards of knowledge, expertise, and ethics that are commonly maintained by other agents in the area.

Proper disclosure primarily concerns disclosure of agency, property condition, and environmental hazards.

An agent who fails to live up to prevailing standards may be held liable for negligence, fraud, or violation of state real estate license laws and regulations. Agents should be particularly careful about misrepresenting and offering inappropriate expert advice when working with customers.

Intentional misrepresentation. An agent may intentionally or unintentionally defraud a buyer by misrepresenting or concealing facts. While it is acceptable to promote the features of a property to a buyer or the virtues of a buyer to a seller, it is a fine line that divides promotion from misrepresentation. Silent misrepresentation, which is intentionally failing to reveal a material fact, is just as fraudulent as a false statement.

Negligent misrepresentation. An agent can be held liable for failure to disclose facts the agent was not aware of if it can be demonstrated that the agent *should have known* such facts. For example, if it is a common standard that agents inspect property, then an agent can be held liable for failing to disclose a leaky roof that was not inspected.

Misrepresentation of expertise. An agent should not act or speak outside the agent's area of expertise. A customer may rely on anything an agent says, and the agent will be held accountable. For example, an agent represents that a property will appreciate. The buyer interprets this as expert investment advice and buys the property. If the property does not appreciate, the buyer may hold the agent liable.

Principal's duties

The obligations of a principal in an agency relationship concern the following:

Availability. In a special agency, the power and decision-making authority of the agent are limited. Therefore, the principal must be available for consultation, direction, and decision-making. Otherwise the agent cannot complete the job.

Information. The principal must provide the agent with a sufficient amount of information to complete the desired activity. This may include property data, financial data, and the client's timing requirements.

Compensation. If an agreement includes a provision for compensating the agent and the agent performs in accordance with the agreement, the client is obligated to compensate the agent. As indicated earlier, however, the agency relationship does not necessarily include compensation.

Breach of duty

An agent is liable for a breach of duty to client or customer. Since clients and customers rely on the expertise and actions of agents performing within the scope of their authority, regulatory agencies and courts aggressively enforce agency laws, standards, and regulations.

A breach of duty may result in:

- rescission of the listing agreement (causing a loss of a potential commission)
- forfeiture of any compensation that may have already been earned
- disciplinary action by state license law authorities, including license suspension or revocation
- suit for damages in court

FORMS OF REAL ESTATE AGENCY

Single agency
Subagency
Dual agency
Designated agency
No agency
No subagency

The primary forms of agency relationship between brokers and principals are: *single agency, dual agency, and subagency*. In a fourth kind of relationship, referred to as *transaction brokerage*, no agency relationship exists in the transaction. Finally, some states are beginning to disallow subagency altogether. Students are advised to ascertain which agency relationships are allowed and practiced in their particular state.

Exhibit 11.3 Forms of Agency and No Agency in Real Estate Brokerage

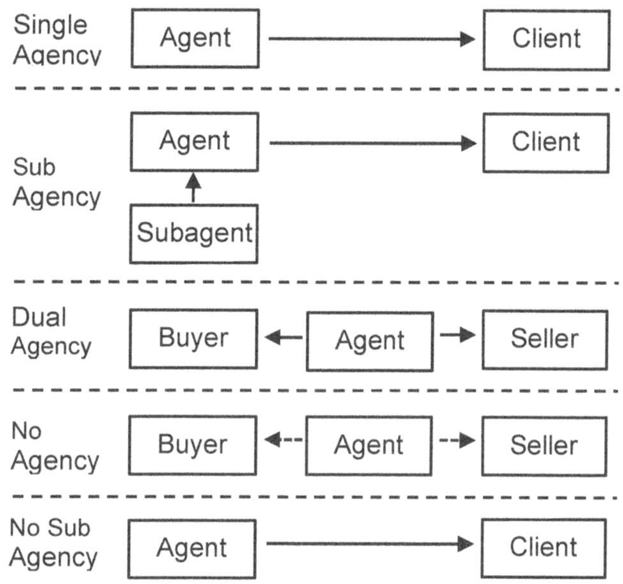

Single agency

The agent represents one party in a transaction. The client may be either seller or buyer.

Seller agency. In the traditional situation, a seller or landlord is the agent's client. A buyer or tenant is the customer.

Buyer agency. Recently, it has become common for an agent to represent a buyer or tenant. In this relationship, the property buyer or tenant is the client and the property owner is the customer.

Real estate vernacular calls an agent of the seller or owner the **listing broker**. An agent who works for the listing broker and who obtained the listing is the **listing agent**. A broker who represents a buyer is the **buyer's broker.** One who does this as a specialization is a **buyer broker**. A broker or salesperson who represents tenants is a **tenant representative**.

Subagency

In a subagency, a broker or licensed salesperson works as the agent of a broker who is the agent of a client. Subagents might include a cooperating licensed broker, that broker's licensed salespeople, and the listing broker's licensed salespeople, all of whom agree to work for the listing broker on behalf of the client. In effect, a subagent is an agent of the broker who is agent of the client. The subagent owes the same duties to the agent as the agent owes to the client. By extension, a subagent owes all the fiduciary duties to the client.

Outside "co-brokers" and agents. It is common practice for brokers and salespersons to "cooperate" with a listing broker in finding buyers or tenants. A listing broker, in return, agrees to share the commission with a cooperating broker.

It is cooperating brokers who form multiple listing services to facilitate the process of bringing together buyers and sellers.

The broker's salespersons. All of the listing broker's salespeople who have agreed to work for the broker to find a customer are subagents of the listing broker and owe the fiduciary duties to the broker and, by extension, to the broker's client.

Dual agency

Dual agency means representing both principal parties to a transaction. The agent represents both buyer and seller or tenant and owner. For instance, if a salesperson completes a buyer agency agreement with a party on behalf of a broker, and the party then becomes interested in a property listed by the broker, the broker becomes a dual agent.

Dual agency has become increasingly prevalent with the advent of buyer and tenant representation. Dual agency may arise from voluntary, specific agreement between the principal parties or from the parties' actions, much like implied single agency.

Conflict of interest. Dual agency contains an inherent conflict of interest. Since many of an agent's fiduciary duties can only be rendered to one party, dual agency is, by definition, difficult, if not impossible.

Written, informed consent. In states that permit dual agency, the agent must meet strict disclosure requirements, and principals must agree *in writing* to proceed with the dual agency relationship.

Disclosed (voluntary) dual agency. The parties to a transaction may create a dual agency by giving written consent in disclosure forms, confirmation forms, and sale contract forms. For example, an agent represents a buyer who becomes interested in a property that the agent has listed with the seller. The agent then discloses the relationship with the principals to both principals, and the principals agree in writing to move ahead. A disclosed dual agency is thus voluntarily created.

Implied and undisclosed dual agency. If a broker or agent acts in any way that leads a customer to believe that the agent is representing the customer, a dual agency has potentially been created. For example, a buyer makes confidential disclosures to the agent who works for the seller and exhorts the agent to keep them confidential. The buyer wants the house but knows he is going to lose his job in a month and probably will not qualify for financing. If the agent agrees to keep the information confidential, the agent has not only created an agency relationship with the buyer, but is now in a dual agency situation. Moreover, if the agent fails to disclose the buyer's confidence to the seller, the agent has violated fiduciary duty to the seller.

Duties of a disclosed dual agent. A dual agent's first duty is to disclose the agency relationship to both principal parties or to withdraw from one side of the duality. After disclosing, the agent must obtain the written consent of both parties.

If both parties accept the dual agency, the agent owes all the fiduciary duties to both parties except full disclosure, undivided loyalty, and exclusive representation of one principal's interests.

Designated agency

A designated agent is a salesperson or an associate broker selected by the broker and client as the client's legal agent pursuant to a designated agency agreement. Under a designated agency agreement, the client has no agency relationship with any licensee other than those specified in the designated agency agreement. Absent such an agreement, the client has an agency relationship with the broker and all affiliated licensees in the brokerage firm. The designated agency agreement allows a broker to select a salesperson and associate brokers to act as the client's agent.

A designated agency agreement must contain the name of all associate brokers who are authorized to act as supervisory brokers. A listing agreement or a buyer's agency agreement may be amended to establish a designated agency relationship, to change a designated agent, or to change supervisory brokers at any time pursuant to a written addendum.

The designated agent's knowledge of a client's confidential information is not imputed to any affiliated licensee not having an agency relationship with that client. A designated agent cannot disclose a client's confidential information to any licensee, whether or not an affiliated licensee, except that a designated agent may disclose to any supervisory broker confidential information of a client for purposes of seeking advice or assistance for the benefit of the client. A licensee who represents a client in an agency capacity does not breach any duty or obligation owed to that client by failing to disclose to that client information obtained through a present or prior agency relationship.

Two designated agents may each represent a different party in the same transaction and will not be considered dual agents. For example, one designated agent can represent the buyer and another designated agent can represent the seller in the same transaction, and neither is a dual agent. The broker and all supervisory brokers are considered disclosed consensual dual agents for that real estate transaction. Before an offer is made or presented, designated agents representing different parties in the same transaction must notify their clients that their broker represents both buyer and seller.

Exhibit 11.4 Dual vs. Designated Agency

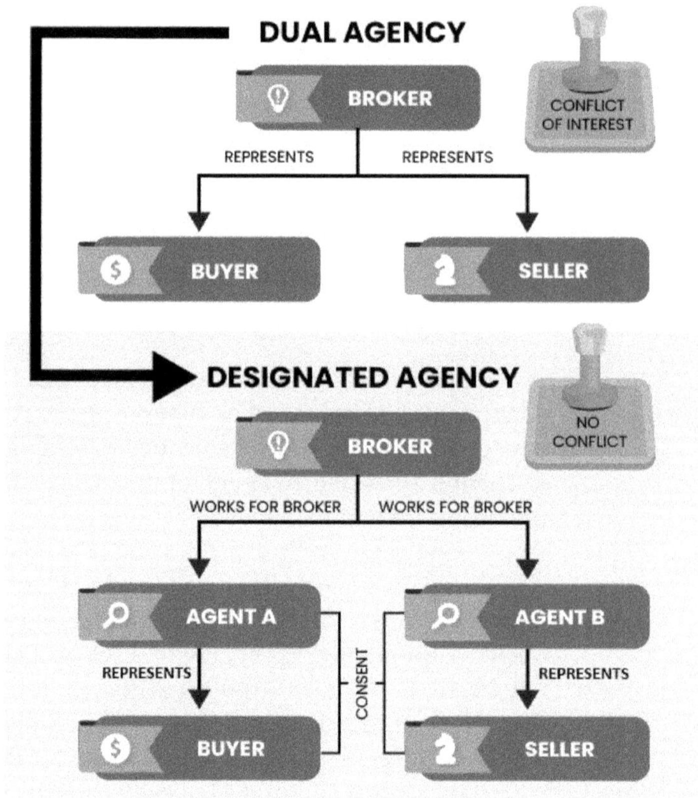

No agency

In recent years, the brokerage industry has striven to clear up the question of who works for whom, and who owes fiduciary duties to whom. A recent solution allows a broker to represent *no one* in a transaction. That is, the broker acts as a **transaction broker**, or **facilitator**, and is not an agent of either the buyer or seller. In this relationship, the facilitator does not advocate the interests of either party.

Duties of the transaction broker, or facilitator. In the role of transaction broker, the broker's duties and standards of conduct are to

- account for all money and property received or handled
- exercise reasonable skill and care
- provide honesty and fair dealing
- present all offers in a timely fashion
- assist the parties in closing the transaction
- keep the parties fully informed
- advise the parties to obtain expert advice or counsel
- disclose to both parties in residential sale transactions all material facts affecting the property's value
- protect the confidences of both parties in matters that would materially disadvantage one party over the other.

Duties not imposed on the transaction broker. Since there are no fiduciary duties binding the transaction broker, the broker is held to standards for dealing with customers as opposed to clients. These include honesty, fair dealing, and reasonable care. The transaction broker is under no obligation to inspect the property for the benefit of a party or verify the accuracy of statements made by a party.

As state regulatory authorities formalize the facilitator role, it is expected that brokers will have to obtain written consent from the principal parties, just as in the case of dual agency.

No subagency

As another response to the problem of 'who works for whom,' some states have recently moved in the direction of disallowing subagency. In this scenario, subagency is replaced by buyer agency and seller agency *only*. In other words, an agent either represents the buyer directly, or the seller directly. An agent who shows a buyer a property either represents the buyer, or is in fact the listing agent. Note that this arrangement need not change traditional compensation structures: an agent may represent a buyer and still receive a portion of the commission paid by the seller.

AGENCY DISCLOSURE RULES

Objectives of disclosure
Seller agent disclosures
Buyer agent disclosures
Dual agent disclosures
Facilitator disclosures

Traditionally, brokers and agents have disclosed to customers whose interests it is that they are serving. This traditional ethic is now, in many states, required by law. Agents must know what agency disclosures they have to make, to whom, and when in the business relationship they must make them.

Objectives of disclosure

Disclosure removes confusion about who an agent is working for. It may prevent complaints arising from customers and clients who feel they have been deceived.

Specifically, the requirement to disclose aims to:

- notify clients and customers about whom the agent represents
- inform clients and customers of the fiduciary duties and standards of care the agent owes them
- inform prospective clients and customers that they have a choice in how they are represented
- obtain acknowledgement and acceptance of the disclosure from the principal parties

Recent legislation requires an agent to disclose to all parties the fact that the agent represents one party and does not represent the other. In other words, an agent must inform client and customer that the agent represents the client and does not represent the customer (unless it is a dual agency). An agent must disclose agency relationships whenever there is a transfer of a real estate interest, whether the interest is a fee, partial fee, exchange, leasehold, sublease, assignment, air right or subsurface right.

Seller agent disclosures

Client disclosure. Depending on state regulations, an agent who intends to represent a seller or owner must disclose the import of the proposed agency relationship in writing before the listing agreement is executed. The agent must inform the seller or landlord in writing that the agent will be representing the client's interests as a fiduciary, and will not be representing the interests of any potential buyer. Any subsequent sale or lease contract with a customer should confirm this disclosure.

Customer disclosure. A listing agent must disclose in writing to a buyer or tenant that the agent represents the owner in the transaction. This disclosure must occur before or at the first "substantive contact" with the customer prospect. The disclosure must also be confirmed in any subsequent sale or lease contract.

Substantive contact. Subject to variations in state regulation, "substantive contact" between listing agent and customer occurs whenever the agent is:

- showing the prospect a property
- eliciting confidential information from a prospect regarding needs, motivation, or financial qualification
- executing a contractual offer to sell or lease

Exclusions. Interaction between a seller's agent and a customer is not always substantive. Possible instances that might be excluded from the requirement of disclosure are:

- attendance at, or supervision of, an open house, providing the agent does not engage in any of the contacts described above
- preliminary "small talk" concerning price ranges, locations, and architectural styles
- responding to questions of fact regarding advertised properties

Oral disclosure. If an agent becomes involved in a substantive contact over the phone or in a such way that it is not feasible to make written disclosure, the agent must make the disclosure orally and follow up with a written disclosure at the first face-to-face meeting.

Buyer agent disclosures

Client disclosure. An agent who plans to represent a buyer or tenant must disclose the import of the proposed agency relationship in writing before the representation agreement is executed.

Customer disclosure. A buyer agent must disclose the agency relationship to the seller or seller's agent on first contact. Substantive contact is assumed.

Dual agent disclosures

Informed written consent. An agent who desires to operate in a dual agency capacity must obtain the informed written consent of all parties. Subsequent contracts should confirm the disclosure. "Informed written consent" means both parties have read, understood, and signed an acceptable disclosure form.

Prohibited disclosures. State regulations prohibit a dual agent from making certain disclosures. For instance, a dual agent, unless expressly instructed by the relevant party, usually cannot disclose:

- to the buyer that the seller will accept less than the listed price
- to the seller that the buyer will pay more than the price submitted in a written offer to the seller
- the motivation of any party concerning the transaction
- that a seller or buyer will agree to financing terms other than those offered

Facilitator disclosures

Rules for disclosing a transaction broker's status of non-agency are similar to those of dual agency. The agent must provide written notice to all parties or their agents on first becoming a transaction broker or on the first substantive contact, whichever comes first.

11 National Agency Snapshot Review

THE AGENCY RELATIONSHIP

Basic roles
- principal, or client, hires agent (broker) to find a ready, willing, and able customer (buyer, seller, tenant); client-agent fiduciary foundations: trust, confidence, good faith

Types of agency
- universal: represent in business and personal matters; can contract for principal
- general: represent in business matters; agent can contract for principal
- special: represent in single business transaction; normally agent cannot contract for principal; the brokerage relationship is usually special agency

Creating an agency relationship
- created by express written or oral agreement or as an implied agreement by actions of either party

Terminating an agency relationship
- causes: fulfillment; expiration; mutual agreement; incapacity; abandonment; or destruction of property; renunciation; breach; bankruptcy; revocation of license

FIDUCIARY DUTIES

Agent's duties to the client
- skill, care, diligence; loyalty; obedience; confidentiality; disclosure; accounting

Agent's duties to the customer
- honesty and fair dealing; exercise of reasonable care and skill; proper disclosures; danger areas: misrepresentation; advising beyond expertise

Principal's duties
- availability; provide information; compensation

Breach of duty
- liabilities: loss of listing, compensation, license; suit for damages

FORMS OF REAL ESTATE AGENCY

Single agency
- seller agency; buyer agency; tenant representation

Subagency
- outside brokers and agents who help listing agent; listing broker's own agents

Dual agency
- representing both sides; potential conflict of interest; must disclose, obtain written consent; types: voluntary by consent; involuntary by actions of parties (implied agency); duties: all but full disclosure and loyalty

Designated agency
- an agent is designated to represent a client exclusively; no other licensees in the firm have any agency relationship with the client unless named in the agreement

No agency
- "facilitator" or "transaction broker"; representing neither party in the transaction; duties to both parties: accounting; skill, care and diligence; honesty and fair dealing; disclosures affecting property value

AGENCY DISCLOSURE

Objectives of disclosure
- declare; explain; offer choice; obtain documented consent

Seller agent disclosures
- to client: in writing on or before listing is executed; to customer: prior to substantive contact, in writing; oral permitted but must have written follow-up

Buyer agent disclosures
- in writing; upon first contact with listing agent or seller

Dual agent disclosures
- "informed, written consent"; may not disclose: price or financing positions or motivations unless authorized

Facilitator disclosures
- on becoming transaction broker or on substantive contact whichever is first

12 Listing Agreements: an Overview

Review of Legal Foundations
Types of Listing Agreement
Fulfillment and Termination
Agreement Clauses

REVIEW OF LEGAL FOUNDATIONS

Agency law
Contract law

A listing agreement, the document that puts an agent or broker in business, is a legally enforceable real estate agency agreement between a real estate broker and a client, authorizing the broker to perform a stated service for compensation. The unique characteristic of a listing agreement is that it is governed both by agency law and by contract law.

Agency law

The cornerstones of agency law in the context of a listing agreement are:

- definition of the roles of parties involved
- fiduciary duties of the agent
- agent's scope of authority

Parties. The principal parties to the contract are the **listing broker** and the **client**. The client may be buyer, seller, landlord or tenant in the proposed transaction. Legally, the broker is the client's **agent**. The principal party on the other side of the transaction is a **customer** or a potential customer, called a **prospect**. A broker or salesperson who assists the listing broker in finding a customer is an **agent** of the listing broker and a **subagent** of the client. A broker who represents the party on the other side of the transaction is an agent of that party, and not an agent of the listing broker, unless a dual agency arrangement is specifically allowed.

Fiduciary duties. A listing agreement establishes an agency relationship between agent and client that commits the agent to the full complement of fiduciary duties to the client in fulfilling the agreement.

Scope of authority. Customarily, a listing is a *special agency,* or *limited agency,* agreement. Special agency *limits* the scope of the broker's authority to specific activities, generally those which generate customers and catalyze the transaction. A special agency agreement usually *does not* authorize a broker to obligate the client to a contract as a principal party, unless the agreement expressly grants such authorization or the client has granted power of attorney to the broker. For example, a listing broker may not tell a buyer that the seller will accept an offer regardless of its terms. Telling the offeror that the offer *is* accepted would be an even more serious breach of the agreement.

Under agency law, a client is liable for actions the broker performs that are within the scope of authority granted by the listing agreement. A client is *not liable* for acts of the broker which go beyond the stated or implied scope of authority.

Thus, in the previous example, the seller would not be liable for the broker's statements that the offer would be accepted or was accepted, since the broker did not have the authority to make such statements. A broker who exceeds the scope of authority in the listing agreement risks forfeiting compensation and perhaps even greater liabilities.

Contract law

Bilateral or unilateral agreement. Listings may be bilateral or unilateral, depending on the type of listing and the wording of the agreement. An open listing is a unilateral agreement in that the seller promises to pay a commission to any agent who produces a buyer but no agent promises or is obligated to take any action. On the other hand, most exclusive listings are bilateral agreements because of wording that promises the due diligence of the agent to procure a buyer in return for the seller's promise to pay a commission if a buyer is produced.

Validity. A listing agreement must meet the requirements for a valid contract to be enforceable.

Termination. A listing, like any contract, may terminate for any of the following causes: performance, infeasibility, mutual agreement, rescission, revocation, abandonment, lapse of time, invalidity, and breach.

Legal form. A valid listing may be oral or written. However, many states consider only a written listing to be enforceable, particularly an exclusive right-to-sell listing. In practice, a broker should get every listing in writing and make sure it clearly states what the broker is authorized to do and how the broker will be paid. An oral listing, even if enforceable, limits a broker's ability to remedy problems:

- a contested oral listing must be supported by considerable evidence to be enforced
- a broker may not be able to sue a principal for damages incurred under an oral lease
- if the client dies, the broker may not be able to obtain compensation for a successfully performed oral listing

An express listing, verbal or written, manifestly authorizes the broker to pursue certain actions for the client. Clients and agents may also create an *implied agency listing* based on substantive actions rather than on an express agreement. For example, if a seller allows a broker to undertake certain activities toward effecting a transaction without a specific authorization, but with full knowledge and consent, an implied agency may have been created. Consequently, if the principal proceeds with a customer procured in this manner, he or she may be liable to the broker for compensation. Conversely, the agent may be held responsible for fulfilling fiduciary duties imposed by the implied agency.

Assignment. Since a listing agreement is a personal service contract, it is *not assignable*. In particular, a broker cannot assign a listing to another broker.

TYPES OF LISTING AGREEMENT

Exclusive right-to-sell (or lease)
Exclusive agency
Open listing
Net listing
Buyer and tenant agency agreement
Transaction broker agreement
Multiple listing
Limited services agreement

A broker may represent any principal party of a transaction: seller, landlord, buyer, tenant. An **owner listing** authorizes a broker to represent an owner or landlord. There are three main types of owner listing agreement: *exclusive right-to-sell (or lease)*; *exclusive agency*; and *open listing*. Another type of listing, rarely used today and illegal in many states, is a *net listing*. The first three forms differ in their statement of conditions under which the broker will be paid. The net listing is a variation on how much the broker will be paid.

A **buyer agency** or **tenant representation agreement** authorizes a broker to represent a buyer or tenant. The most commonly used form is an *exclusive right-to-represent* agreement, the equivalent of an exclusive right-to-sell. However, exclusive agency and open types of agreement may be also used to secure a relationship on this side of a transaction.

Though not a distinct type of listing agreement, *multiple listing* is a significant feature of brokerage practice. Multiple listing is an authorization to enter a listing in a multiple listing service.

Exclusive right-to-sell (or lease)

The exclusive right-to-sell, also called **exclusive authorization-to-sell** and, simply, the **exclusive**, is the most widely used owner agreement. Under the terms of this listing, a seller contracts exclusively with a single broker to procure a buyer or effect a sale transaction. If a buyer is procured during the listing period, the broker is entitled to a commission, *regardless of who is procuring cause*. Thus, if anyone-the owner, another broker-- sells the property, the owner must pay the listing broker the contracted commission.

The exclusive right-to-lease is a similar contract for a leasing transaction. Under the terms of this listing, the owner or landlord must pay the listing broker a commission if anyone procures a tenant for the named premises.

The exclusive listing gives the listing broker the greatest assurance of receiving compensation for marketing efforts.

In some states, an exclusive right-to-sell listing is enforceable only if it is in writing and has an expiration date. Some states do not require the agreement to be in writing, but if it is in writing, it must have an expiration date.

Exclusive agency

An exclusive agency listing authorizes a single broker to sell the property and earn a commission, but *leaves the owner the right to sell the property without the broker's assistance*, in which case no commission is owed. Thus, if any party other than the owner is procuring cause in a completed sale of the property, including another broker, the contracted broker has earned the commission. This arrangement may also be used in a leasing transaction: if any party other than the owner procures the tenant, the owner must compensate the listing broker.

An exclusive agency listing generally must have an expiration date. Most states allow either an oral or written agreement.

Open listing

An open listing, or, simply, **open**, is a *non-exclusive* authorization to sell or lease a property. The owner may offer such agreements to any number of brokers in the marketplace. With an open listing, the broker who is the first to perform under the terms of the listing is the sole party entitled to a commission. Performance usually consists of being the procuring cause in the finding of a ready, willing, and able customer. If the transaction occurs without a procuring broker, no commissions are payable.

Open listings are rare in residential brokerage. Brokers generally shy away from them because they offer no assurance of compensation for marketing efforts. In addition, open listings cause commission disputes. To avoid such disputes, a broker has to register prospects with the owner to provide evidence of procuring cause in case a transaction results.

An open listing may be oral or written.

Net listing

A net listing is one in which an owner sets a minimum acceptable amount to be received from the transaction and allows the broker to have any amount received in excess as a commission, assuming the broker has earned a commission according to the other terms of the agreement. The owner's "net" may or may not account for closing costs.

For example, a seller requires $750,000 for a property. A broker sells the property for $830,000 and receives the difference, $80,000, as commission.

Net listings are generally regarded as unprofessional today, and many states have outlawed them. The argument against the net listing is that it creates a conflict of interest for the broker. It is in the broker's interest to encourage the owner to put the lowest possible acceptable price in the listing, regardless of market value. Thus the agent violates fiduciary duty by failing to place the client's interests above those of the agent.

Exhibit 12.1 Types of Listing

Exclusive Right	*$ ➡ Broker*	***IF customer is procured***
Exclusive Agency	*$ ➡ Broker*	***IF customer is procured and client does not procure***
Open	*$ ➡ Broker*	***IF broker procures customer***
Net	*$ ➡ Broker*	***IF customer is due commission, receives proceeds over seller's minimum***
"Multiple Listing"	*$ ➡ Broker*	***Authority to enter listing in multiple listing service***

Buyer and tenant agency agreements

Buyer and tenant agency agreements create a fiduciary relationship with the buyer or tenant just as seller listings create a fiduciary relationship with the seller. Generally, buyer and tenant representation agreements are subject to the same laws and regulations as those applying to owner listings. Thus:

- a representation agreement may be an exclusive, exclusive agency, or open listing. As with owner listings, the most widely used agreement is the exclusive. In this arrangement, the buyer agrees to only work with the buyer representative in procuring a property.
- an exclusive listing generally must have an expiration date along with other requirements of a valid listing.
- state laws require an exclusive authorization to be in writing

Duties of the Agent. At the formation of the relationship, the buyer agent has the duty to explain how buyer or tenant agency relationships work. This is culminated by a signed agreement where the principal understands and accepts these circumstances. During the listing term, the buyer or tenant agent's principal duties are to diligently locate a property that meets the principal's requirements. In addition, the agent must comply with his or her state agency-disclosure laws which may differ from those of traditional listing agents. This involves timely disclosures to prospective sellers and their agents, usually upon initial contact.

Transaction broker agreement

In terms of agency, a transaction broker is in a non-agency relationship with the seller or buyer. The agent is not bound by fiduciary duties to either party. Nevertheless, transaction brokers enter into binding agreements with buyers and sellers to complete transactions. Such agreements may be exclusive or non-exclusive. Like conventional listings, the transaction brokerage agreement binds the principal to a compensation agreement in the event the broker procures a property or a buyer. Typical agreements affirm the nature of the relationship, contain expiration dates, and describe the terms of the agreement, such as the type of property desired or the price a seller deems acceptable.

Like other listing agreements, transaction broker agreements vary among the states where this form of relationship is practiced.

Multiple listing

A multiple listing is not a listing contract in and of itself, but rather a provision in an exclusive listing authorizing the broker to place the listing into a multiple listing service.

A multiple listing service, or an MLS, is an organization of member brokers who agree to cooperate by sharing listing information and facilitating the showing and sale of listed properties. Under current rules, the REALTOR®-sponsored MLS does not publish or require offers of cooperative compensation. Compensation arrangements between brokers and buyers or sellers are negotiated outside the purview of, and separate from, the MLS.

The MLS authorizations enable and require the broker to disseminate the listing information in a timely fashion so that participating members in the organization can participate in the sale of the property as subagents.

Limited services agreement

Rather than provide the full services due a client under a standard listing agreement, a licensee may enter into an agreement to provide limited services selected by the client. The agreement must:

- be in writing
- disclose that the licensee is acting as a limited service representative
- list the specific services the licensee will provide
- state the duties of a standard agent that the limited service representative will not provide.

Some states require a limited service listing agreement to comply with minimum service requirements.

FULFILLMENT AND TERMINATION

Agent's performance
Compensation
Causes for termination
Revoking a listing

A listing agreement may terminate in many ways. The only desirable and favorable way is by fulfillment of the contract. Fulfillment results when both parties have performed the actions they have promised to perform.

Agent's performance

An agent performs a listing agreement by achieving the result specified in the agreement. When and if the result is achieved, the agent's performance is complete.

Find a customer or effect a transaction. A listing generally specifies the result to be either finding a customer or effecting a completed transaction.

Finding a customer means locating a party who is *ready, willing, and able* to transact under the client's terms. Effecting a completed transaction means finding a customer who is not only ready, willing, and able, but one who makes an acceptable offer.

A ready, willing, and able customer is one who is:

- amenable to the terms of the transaction (ready and willing)
- financially capable of paying the price and legally capable of completing the transaction (able)

Specific responsibilities. A listing agreement authorizes a broker to undertake actions relevant to achieving the performance objective. Authorized activities usually include the following:

- show or seek property
- locate buyer, seller, tenant, or landlord
- communicate the client's transaction terms
- promote features and advantages of the terms to customers
- assist in negotiating a meeting of the minds between parties

Due diligence. Due diligence in the listing context refers to verifying the accuracy of the statements in the listing regarding the property, the owner, and the owner's representations. Especially important facts for a broker or agent to verify are:

- the property condition
- ownership status
- the client's authority to act

Failure to perform a reasonable degree of due diligence may increase an agent's exposure to liability in the event that the property is not as represented or that the client cannot perform as promised.

Delegation of responsibilities. In the normal course of business, a listing broker *delegates* marketing responsibilities to salespeople. A salesperson may not, however, seek compensation directly from a client. Only the broker can obtain and disburse the compensation.

Compensation

The main item of performance for the client is payment of compensation, if the agreement calls for it. A broker's compensation is earned and payable when the broker has performed according to the agreement. The amount and structure of the compensation, potential disputes over who has earned compensation, and the client's liability for multiple commissions are other matters that agency agreements should address.

Negotiated compensation. The amount of a broker's commission is whatever amount the client and broker have agreed to. Compensation may be in the form of a percentage of the sale or lease price, or a flat fee. In practice, commissions vary for different geographical areas, types of property and transaction, and services performed.

Procuring cause. Disputes often arise as to whether an agent is owed a commission. Many such disputes involve open listings where numerous agents are working to find customers for the principal, and none has a clear claim on a commission. In other cases, a client may claim to have found the customer alone and therefore to have no responsibility for paying a commission. There are also situations where cooperating brokers and subagents working under an exclusive listing dispute about which one(s) deserve a share of the broker's commission.

The concept that decides such disputes is that the party who was the "procuring cause" in finding the customer is entitled to the commission or commission share. The two principal determinants of procuring cause are:

- being first to find the customer
- being the one who induces the customer to complete the transaction

For example, Broker A and Broker B each have an open listing with a property owner. Broker A shows Joe the property on Monday. Broker B shows Joe the same property on Friday, and then Joe buys the property. Broker A will probably be deemed to be the procuring cause by virtue of having first introduced Joe to the property.

Compensation for buyer brokers. Buyer agency agreements specify how a buyer's agent will be compensated and under what conditions compensation is earned. Under current industry rules, compensation for buyer brokers must be negotiated directly between the buyer and the buyer broker in a written buyer-broker agreement before the agent provides brokerage services such as showing properties.

The buyer-broker agreement may provide for various forms of compensation, including:

- a client-paid retainer fee,
- an hourly or flat fee, or
- a commission that becomes payable upon the successful completion of a transaction.

Sellers may still choose to offer concessions or contribute funds toward the buyer's closing costs, which the buyer may use, in turn, to pay their broker, the buyer broker's compensation is no longer determined or communicated through the MLS, and listing brokers are not permitted to offer cooperative compensation within the MLS.

In all cases, the buyer-broker agreement must clearly state:

1. How much compensation the buyer broker is entitled to,
2. Who is responsible for paying it, and
3. How the broker may receive payment, including whether the buyer will request seller concessions to offset the cost.

The buyer-broker agreement also defines when compensation is earned. Typically, a commission is earned once the buyer enters into a binding sales contract with a seller. Depending on the agreement's terms, the buyer broker may be entitled to compensation even if the buyer defaults, although payment customarily occurs at closing.

Causes for termination

A listing may terminate on grounds of:

- *performance*: all parties perform; the intended outcome
- *infeasibility*: it is not possible to perform under the terms of the agreement
- *mutual agreement*: both parties agree to cancel the listing
- *revocation*: either party cancels the listing, with or without the right
- *abandonment*: the broker does not attempt to perform
- *breach*: the terms of the listing are violated
- *lapse of time*: the listing expires
- *invalidity of contract*: the listing does not meet the criteria for validity
- *incapacitation or death of either party*
- *involuntary title transfer*: condemnation, bankruptcy, foreclosure
- *destruction of the property*

Listing expiration regulations. In most states, open listings do not require a stated expiration date. Rather, they expire after a "reasonable" period of time as locally defined.

The other types of listing generally must specify a termination date and may not have an automatic renewal mechanism. Courts in many states construe any listing that has no expiration as an open listing. However, some states make these requirements only of written listings, and may not require exclusives to be in writing.

Revoking a listing

Power vs. right. Both principals to the listing agreement have the power to revoke the contract at any time. They do not, however, always have the right. That is, client or broker may cancel a listing but remain liable for damages to the other party.

Revocation by the client. If the client revokes the listing after the broker has already earned a commission, the client must pay the commission, no matter what type of listing it was.

If the broker has not fully performed prior to the revocation, the following guidelines apply:

- exclusive right-to-sell: if the property sells during the term of the revoked listing, the client is liable for the commission. If the property does not sell, the client is liable for the broker's actual costs.
- exclusive agency: if the property sells during the term of the revoked listing, the client is liable at least for the broker's costs

- and possibly for the commission. If the property does not sell during the term, the client is liable for the broker's costs.
- open: if revoked prior to performance, the client is generally not liable for any payment

Revocation by the broker. If the broker cancels the listing or otherwise defaults, the client may sue the broker for money damages.

LISTING AGREEMENT CLAUSES

Exclusive right-to-sell clauses
Exclusive buyer agency clauses
Transaction brokerage clauses

A written listing, particularly an exclusive, is a formal contract which contains the entirety of all agreements between the parties. If an agreement is left out, it is assumed not to exist. An agreement that is included is assumed to exist and is generally enforceable. If a written agreement contains mistakes, it is probably not valid or enforceable. For these reasons, it is extremely important for a listing agreement to be accurate, error-free, and complete.

Students are cautioned to note that listing agreements vary in language and form from state to state. For that reason it is important to ascertain the legal requirements and required clauses for certain types of listings, particularly exclusive listings, in your state. In addition, some states require that if agents use pre-printed forms, such forms must contain certain provisions.

Exclusive right-to-sell clauses

Requirements for exclusive listing agreements vary from state to state. Generally, a written listing agreement requires as a minimum:

- names of all owners
- address or legal description of the listed property
- listing price
- expiration date
- commission terms
- authority granted

The following clause descriptions are found in a typical exclusive right-to-sell listing agreement.

Parties and authorization. The agreement should name all legal owners of the property, or duly authorized representatives of the owners, as the client party. It must also name the broker.

An authorization clause sets forth the nature of what the broker is allowed to do, i.e., the type of listing. Note that the phrase "right-to-sell" is a misnomer. A broker cannot legally sell the property without proper power of attorney. The usual right is to effect a sale or find a buyer.

Real Property. The real property description may include an address, but in some states it must include the *legal description*.

It is critical to identify both the real property and any personal property that are for sale and included in the listing price.

Fixtures. Typical agreements list what fixtures are included in the sale specifically, and "all other things attached or affixed to the property" generally. The seller must then enter which items are excluded from the sale.

Personal Property. The listing agreement should include all personal property that is to be included in the transaction and listing price.

Listing price. A clause usually sets forth the gross price for the property and possibly the financing terms the owner will accept, particularly if seller financing or assumption of the seller's loan is involved.

The listing price is the seller's asking price for the property. This may or may not be the price the seller ultimately accepts. The full listing price does not have to be obtained for the broker to earn a commission. The listing price clause may also state the seller's agreement to pay customary closing costs.

Listing term. In most states, exclusive listings must have a specific beginning and ending date of the listing agreement. In many states, failure to name a termination date in a written listing is grounds for revocation of the real estate license. Any provision for renewal of the listing term should be very specific. Automatic renewals are illegal in many states.

To protect the broker, some listings contain a provision to extend the listing period in the event an expiration occurs during the period in which a sale contract is pending.

Agent's duties. This clause specifies the broker's responsibilities and authorization to carry out certain activities. These typically include marketing activities, multiple listing service activities, property access and showings, authority to allow other parties access, permission to inspect existing mortgage financing documents, and authority to accept deposits. Commonly, the clause specifically bars the broker from executing any contract on behalf of the owner.

Agent's compensation. A clause will identify the broker's fee and the necessary conditions for the fee to be earned. For instance, it may state that a commission is earned if a buyer is procured, a contract is executed, or the seller voluntarily transfers the property for any price during the listing period.

A fee clause usually provides for remedies in the event of default by the buyer or seller. In effect, if the seller breaches the listing without grounds after a buyer has been procured, the commission is payable. If the owner cannot sell the property for reasons beyond the owner's control, the owner is not liable for a commission. If the buyer breaches a sale contract, the owner and broker may split the buyer's earnest money deposit as liquidated damages, depending on state law.

Protection period. Many listings include a protection clause stating that, for a certain period after expiration, the owner is liable for the commission if the property sells to a party that the broker procured, unless the seller has since listed the property with another broker.

Multiple listing. This provision obtains the seller's consent to placing the listing in a multiple listing service and authorization to disseminate information about the listing to members.

Cooperation with other agents. This clause requires the seller to agree or refuse to cooperate with subagents or buyer agents in selling the property and under what terms (cooperation without compensation through MLS). Recent agreements stipulate that subagents and buyer agents must disclose their relationships to the buyer upon initial contact and subsequently in writing. There may also be a warning to the seller not to disclose confidential information to a buyer broker insofar as this agent is required to disclose all relevant information to the buyer.

Non-discrimination. Most exclusive listings contain an affirmation that the agent will conduct all affairs in compliance with state and federal fair housing and nondiscrimination laws.

Dual agency. In the absence of disclosure and consent, dual agency represents a conflict of interest for the broker. A good agreement specifically asks the owner to consent to or refuse to allow the broker's representation of both parties.

If the clause states that the owner refuses to accept dual agency, the broker agrees not to show the property to any buyers the broker represents.

If the seller accepts dual agency, the broker may represent both parties under the restrictions set forth in the listing. The restrictions are generally to protect the confidentialities of either party, particularly those relating to price and terms. Additionally, the broker covenants to deal honestly and impartially with the parties.

Other disclosures by agent. In addition to agency, other disclosures might be included to cover any direct or indirect interest the broker has in the transaction and special compensation the broker might be receiving from other parties connected with the transaction.

Seller's representations and promises. In this clause, the owner represents that he or she in fact owns the property in the manner stated in the listing, and is legally capable of delivering fee simple, marketable title.

The clause may further require the owner to warrant that he or she

- is not represented by another party and will not list the property elsewhere during the listing period
- will not lease the property during the listing period without approval
- agrees to provide necessary information

- will refer all prospects directly to the broker without prior direct negotiation
- has reviewed a sample "Offer to Purchase and Sell" contract
- will make the property presentable and available for showing at reasonable times upon notice by agent.

Seller's property condition disclosure. Most current listing forms require the seller to disclose the condition of the property to prospective buyers. New laws in most states allow buyers to cancel a sale contract if they have not received the seller's property condition disclosure before closing or occupancy or other deadline. In addition, the listing may include among the seller's duties the requirement to complete and provide the agent with a Lead Paint Hazard addendum. A copy of the required notice to buyers may be attached to the listing agreement as part of the agreement.

Seller's title and deed. A provision usually requires the owner to promise to deliver good and marketable title, title insurance, and to convey the property using a general warranty deed to a buyer. Without this covenant, the broker has no assurance that a transaction will occur, and in turn that he or she will be paid for procuring a buyer.

Flood hazard insurance. This clause requires the seller to disclose whether he or she is required to or presently maintains flood insurance on the property.

Limitation of liability. There is often a clause requiring the owner to indemnify the broker against liability resulting from casualty, loss, and owner misrepresentation during the listing period.

In practice, liability and indemnification clauses do not necessarily absolve a broker from liability.

Escrow authorization. The seller authorizes escrow officers to disburse earned commission funds to the broker upon the broker's instructions to do so.

IRS requirements; alien seller withholding. A clause may state that the seller will comply with IRS requirements for providing tax-related information. This ensures that a seller who is an alien understands that a buyer will be required to withhold a percentage of the sale price for the IRS.

Other listing provisions. An exclusive listing might also provide for:

- *mediation*: in the event of a dispute, the owner agrees to arbitrate differences before filing a lawsuit
- *attorney fees*: the losing party in a lawsuit must pay court costs and attorney fees
- *acknowledgment*: the owner acknowledges reading and understanding the agreement
- *entire agreement*: the listing cannot be changed without written agreement; the listing sets forth all agreements made
- *binding effect*: listing is binding and enforceable

- *saving clause*: if a portion of the agreement is invalid or unenforceable, the balance of the agreement remains valid as permitted by law

Notices to owner. Some listing agreements include notices to the seller concerning:

- *fee negotiability*: the broker's fee is the result of negotiations with the seller
- *fair housing laws*: the broker and seller must comply with discrimination laws
- *keyboxes; security*: the seller should take prudent measures to protect personal property and remove dangerous items that could cause injury
- *legal advice disclaimer*: the broker cannot give legal advice

Signatures. All owners and the broker must sign the listing and indicate the date of signing.

Exclusive buyer agency clauses

The exclusive buyer agency agreement is very similar to the exclusive right-to-sell agreement, the only significant differences being the agent's objectives and the fact that the principal is the buyer instead of the seller. The notable exception is how the agent is paid, as previously discussed.

The clauses which are virtually identical to the exclusive right-to-sell are:

- the identity of the principal and the agent's authorized activity
- the description of the property desired in terms of location, price, size, etc.
- the term of the agreement and its automatic termination
- the buyer's agreement to work exclusively through the agent
- the agent's duties to locate a suitable property according to the buyer's specifications
- the non-discrimination clause
- signatures of the parties

The following clauses distinguish the buyer agency agreement from the exclusive right-to sell agreement.

Buyer's representation of exclusivity. Here the buyer affirms that he or she is not represented by another agent. In addition the buyer acknowledges an understanding of the agency relationship.

Agent compensation clause. This clause sets forth how the agent is to be paid, whether by retainer or commission, and the negotiated amount of the commission. Second, clause provisions establish the circumstances under which the agent has earned the commission. This includes finding a property during the agreement term or the buyer contracting to buy a property shown by the agent within a stipulated period of time following expiration. In addition, the clause provides that the agent will be paid in the event the buyer defaults on a sale contract.

Other buyers acknowledged. In this provision, the buyer acknowledges that the agent is working with other buyers who may be in competition for any property the buyer is shown by the agent.

Transaction brokerage clauses

Transaction brokerage agreements vary greatly among the states where this brokerage relationship is practiced. The agreement may be exclusive or non-exclusive. Despite the lack of standardization and uniformity, these agreements contain the following principal provisions.

Parties and property identification. The agreement identifies the principals and if a seller, the description of the property to be sold, or if a buyer a description of the property desired.

Agent's authorized activity. This clause gives the agent the exclusive right and authority to sell or locate property for the principal.

Non-agency declaration. The agreement clearly sets forth that it is a non-agency personal services contract with a legally binding effect. This provision expressly states that the broker is not an agent of the buyer or seller and is not acting in a fiduciary capacity. In addition, the principal agrees that the agent is not working for the benefit of either party nor advocating the interests of either party. Usually this clause requires the principal's acknowledgment that he or she has read a state-level approved document describing and explaining the forms of agency or non-agency relationships practiced in that state.

Transaction broker duties. Like other listings, this clause defines what activities the agent will undertake to earn compensation. Key words are 'assist,' or 'offer information' or 'facilitate' as opposed to 'represent.' Activities include web searches, showings, advertising, etc.

Other buyers acknowledged. If a buyer agreement, the buyer will acknowledge that the agent is working with other buyers who may be in competition for any property the buyer is shown by the agent.

Compensation. This clause stipulates what the agent will be paid, by whom, and upon what circumstances, much like the buyer agency agreement. In addition, the clause provides that, if the buyer purchases a property that was previously shown by the agent within a certain amount of time following the listing's expiration date, then the agent is owed the commission.

Buyer or seller duties. Here the agreement states what the buyer or seller commits to do during the listing term, most notably to compensate the agent for fulfilling the agreement. In addition, the seller typically agrees to show the property, and provide property condition disclosures. The buyer agrees to work exclusively with the agent (if an exclusive agreement) and provide information regarding the desired property and certain financial information.

Agreement term. Like other listings, the transaction agreement contains a beginning and ending date for the listing term. The term is extendable to closing if the principal buys or sells a property for which the settlement date is beyond the original expiration date.

Non-discrimination. The agreement affirms that the agent will conduct all affairs in compliance with state and federal fair housing and non-discrimination laws.

Signatures of parties. The signatures of the principal and agent affirm the agreement as well as acknowledge that the principal has received a copy of the agreement.

12 Listing Agreements: An Overview Snapshot Review

REVIEW OF LEGAL FOUNDATIONS

- listing: broker's enforceable contract of employment with client establishing special agency relationship to procure a customer

Agency law

- parties: listing broker and client; broker's subagents; customers and prospects
- fiduciary duties: loyalty; obedience; disclosure; care; diligence; accounting
- scope of authority: listings are special or limited agency, not general agency agreements; broker may not contract for client unless specifically authorized; clients liable only for broker's acts within scope of authority

Contract law

- listings are unilateral contracts; listing must be valid to be enforceable; legal form: oral listings are valid and enforceable except, in many states, exclusive right-to-sell listings which must be written to be enforceable
- listings are not assignable since they are personal service contracts

TYPES OF LISTING AGREEMENT

- owner listing: authorization to sell or lease; buyer or tenant listing: authorization to represent buyer or tenant

Exclusive right-to-sell (or lease)

- most prevalent; given to one broker; must usually be written; must expire; broker gets commission if property transfers during period

Exclusive agency

- exclusive excepting owner; oral or written; must expire; broker gets commission unless owner sells

Open listing

- non-exclusive; oral or written; no stated expiration; procuring cause gets commission; no commission if client procures customer

Net listing

- all sale proceeds above a seller's minimum price go to the broker; discouraged, if not illegal

Buyer and tenant agency agreements

- open or exclusive listings with buyers or tenants to represent their interests compensation in form stipulated by agreement; payable if buyer defaults; agent has fiduciary and disclosure duties

Transaction broker agreements

- non-agency; no fiduciary duties; agent does not work in the interests of or for the benefit of either party

Multiple listing

- listing placed in MLS; owners consent to rules and provisions of MLS

Limited services agreement

- agreement that commits licensee to provide a limited, specified list of services to a client instead of the full set due under a standard agreement

FULFILLMENT AND TERMINATION

Agent's performance

- based on results: find ready willing and able customer or effect a sale; may perform only authorized tasks to achieve result; must verify owner and property data; may delegate duties to salespeople and other brokers

Compensation

- negotiated; where disputed, procuring cause is owed commission

Causes for termination

- performance; infeasibility; mutual agreement; revocation; abandonment; breach; expiration; invalidity; incapacitation or death; involuntary transfer; destruction of property

Revoking a listing

- clients always have power to revoke during period, but may incur liability for commission or damages

LISTING AGREEMENT CLAUSES

Exclusive right-to-sell clauses

- minimal requirements: broker's and owners' names; address and/or legal description; listing price; expiration date; agent's duties; compensation terms; authority granted; agency and non-agency disclosures: seller's representations and condition disclosures

Exclusive buyer agency clauses

- minimal requirements virtually identical to exclusive right-to-sell; distinguishing features: buyer's representation of exclusivity; agent compensation; buyer's acknowledgment of other buyers

Transaction broker clauses

- may be exclusive or non-exclusive; typical principle provisions: identification of parties and property; agent's authorized activity; declaration of non-agency; broker's duties; buyer's acknowledgment of other buyers; compensation; buyer or seller duties; expiration date

13 General Brokerage Practices

Function and Organization
The Broker-Salesperson Relationship
Operating a Real Estate Brokerage
Business Brokerage

FUNCTION AND ORGANIZATION

The core activity of brokerage
Who may legally broker real estate?
Types of brokerage organization
Trade organizations

The core activity of brokerage

Effecting a transaction. The core activity of real estate brokerage is the business of procuring a buyer, seller, tenant, or property on behalf of a client for the purpose of completing a transaction. If successful, the broker receives a commission according to the provisions of a listing agreement. A broker's compensation for effecting a transaction is usually a negotiated percentage of the purchase price.

Broker cooperation. Real estate transactions commonly involve cooperation between brokers from different brokerage companies, particularly when an outside broker represents a prospective buyer. Most listing agreements authorize the listing broker to cooperate with other brokers for the purpose of marketing the property and facilitating showings and offers. In such cases, the cooperating broker acts on behalf of the buyer rather than as a subagent of the seller. Cooperation may involve sharing property information, providing access for showings, and coordinating the negotiation process.

While the listing broker may cooperate with a broker representing a buyer or tenant, compensation arrangements are no longer predetermined or offered through the multiple listing service. Instead, a buyer's broker is compensated according to the buyer–broker agreement and any concessions negotiated within the purchase contract. The listing broker's role is to cooperate in the transaction, not to offer or split commissions with other brokers.

Multiple listing service (MLS). Another common form of broker cooperation is participation in a multiple listing service, or MLS. An MLS is an organization of brokers who agree to cooperate by sharing listing information and making property data widely available to other member brokers. Members also agree to enter their exclusive listings into the MLS distribution system so that all participants are promptly informed when new properties come on the market.

The listing agreement used for MLS participation outlines the procedures and policies governing submission of the property to the service, and ensuring that all principal parties understand how listing information will be shared. A broker involved in an MLS-listed transaction continues to owe all duties and responsibilities required by agency law to their respective client. The listing agreement identifies these duties and the broker's fiduciary obligations in the transaction.

Critical brokerage skills. To generate business, as well as achieve the transactional objectives of clients, a broker must be proficient in four skill areas:

- obtaining a client listing
- marketing a listing
- facilitating the closing of a transaction
- managing market information

A client hires a broker by executing a listing agreement. Once hired, the broker or agent implements a marketing plan to procure the other principal party for the transaction. The broker then plays an important role in pre-closing activities to ensure successful closing of the transaction.

To serve clients and locate customers, a broker must become expert in local real estate market conditions. A fundamental part of maintaining market expertise is organizing and managing an information system.

Types of transactions and properties brokered. Brokers and salespeople are licensed to broker all types of real property for clients in any form of transaction. In practice, it is common for brokers and agents to specialize in a type of property, a type of transaction, or a geographical area.

Brokerage vs. trading. The distinction between brokerage and trading for one's own account is important for determining whether one must be licensed to perform the real estate activity in question. To be considered brokerage, an agent's activity must generally be conducted on behalf of a person or business entity other than the agent. Buying, selling, and leasing real estate for one's own account or for one's company are generally not considered brokerage.

Brokerage vs. advisory services. Technically, brokerage is distinct from the practice of rendering real estate advisory services. A licensed broker acting as a consultant for a fee usually is not working to effect a particular transaction. Since the objective is not purely transaction-oriented, the activity is not really brokerage. Examples of advisory services include:

- providing an estimate of value
- performing market analysis
- managing property

Even though fee consulting is not brokerage in the strict sense, real estate consultants who offer advisory services to the public must have a real estate license in most states.

Exhibit 13.1 Common Brokerage Specialties

Transaction type	
sales rentals assignments	exchanges subleases options
Property type	
Residential single family condominiums cooperatives mobile homes apartments	**Commercial** retail office industrial
Land undeveloped developed agricultural	**Special purpose** government religious recreational
Businesses	**Real estate securities**

Who may legally broker real estate?

Real estate license laws. All fifty states (and Canada) impose legal licensing requirements on any person or business entity desiring to broker real estate. To obtain a broker's license, an applicant must complete required education, meet experience requirements as a salesperson, and pass a state examination. There may be additional requirements concerning age, criminal record, and professional background. Practicing real estate brokerage without a valid license is illegal. Anyone who plans to obtain a real estate license should become familiar with the real estate license law of the relevant state.

Range of business entities. Some business entities may legally broker real estate, and others may not. The principal types of business organization and the legal restrictions on their ability to broker real estate are described below. Note that all the business entities may own, buy, and sell *their own* real estate in varying degrees without violating license laws.

Sole proprietorship. A sole proprietorship is a business owned by a single individual. When the proprietor dies, the business terminates. Sole proprietorships must follow state licensing and registration laws to conduct business, such as fictitious name laws. Other distinguishing characteristics of sole proprietorships are:

- liability: sole proprietors are personally liable for their own debts and actions and those of employees while performing business duties; proprietors may be sued personally

- taxation: business profits are taxed once as the proprietor's personal income

A sole proprietorship *may broker* real estate if properly licensed.

Corporation for profit. A corporation is a legal entity owned by stockholders. A corporation for profit consists of one or more persons authorized to conduct business for profit. A board of directors elected by stockholders oversees the business. Officers (president, vice president, secretary, treasurer) and managers conduct day-to-day affairs. Other distinguishing characteristics are:

- "perpetual" existence: the corporation survives the death of any of the stockholders, directors, or officers
- formation: to incorporate, principal parties must complete and file articles of incorporation in accordance with state law; a corporation is domestic if it is headquartered in the state where the articles of incorporation were filed. Otherwise, the corporation is a foreign corporation
- liability: shareholders of the corporation are only liable to the extent of the value of one's shares; officers and directors may be held personally liable for the corporation's actions under the Sarbanes-Oxley Act of 2002
- taxation: owners are double-taxed on business profits; corporate profits are taxed and after-tax dividends distributed to shareholders are taxed again as personal income

A corporation *may broker* real estate if it is legally authorized to do business in a state and licensed to broker there. State license laws may require one or more officers to hold active or inactive broker's licenses. Generally, shareholders may not broker real estate for the corporation.

Non-profit corporation. A non-profit corporation is a corporate entity which is not legally entitled to generate profit. A board of directors and officers manage operations. Non-profit organizations are not subject to taxation.

A non-profit organization *may not* broker real estate.

General partnership. A general partnership is a for-profit business consisting of two or more co-owners who have agreed to share business profits. Unlike a corporation, the general partnership is not a distinct, legal entity, although a corporation may be a partner in a general partnership. Additional distinguishing features are:

- formation: the partnership is formed by a written or oral partnership agreement with or without a financial investment by either partner
- dissolution: the partnership may be terminated through mutual agreement, withdrawal or death of a partner, or by legal action
- liability: all partners bear full liability for debts and obligations jointly and severally
- taxation: partners are taxed once on their respective partnership profits; partnerships do not have double-taxation

A general partnership *may* broker real estate if properly licensed. State law may require one or all partners to hold active or inactive broker's licenses.

Limited partnership. A limited partnership consists of general partners and limited partners. General partners are wholly responsible for business operations, while limited partners are investors who participate only in business profits. The general partners typically receive compensation for their management responsibilities. Other defining features are:

- limited partners: a limited partner must make an investment, which subsequently comprises the extent of the partner's liability. Limited partners are taxed once, on profits distributed by the partnership.

- general partners: bear sole liability for debts and obligations

A limited partnership *may* broker real estate. However, limited partners may not broker real estate for the partnership. State laws may require the general partners to have active or inactive broker's licenses. Limited partners need not be licensed for the partnership to broker real estate.

Joint venture. A joint venture is a partnership formed to complete a specific business endeavor, such as a real estate development. Individuals, general and limited partnerships, and corporations may participate. In forming the entity, the partners identify how they will conduct business and share profits. Principal parties in the joint venture share liability, but may not obligate the other co-venturers to agreements outside of the joint venture project.

A joint venture *may* broker real estate, provided the co-venturers are duly licensed.

Business trust and real estate investment trust. A business trust is a group of investors who invest in a pooled trust fund managed by their elected trustee. The trustee purchases investment assets and distributes profits and gains to the trustors. A business trust that invests primarily in real estate and meets certain other requirements is a real estate investment trust (REIT) and receives special tax treatment.

A business trust may *not* broker real estate, but it may buy and sell its own real estate assets.

Cooperative association. A cooperative association is a non-profit, tax-exempt alliance of individuals or companies formed to promote common goods or services.

A cooperative association *may not* broker real estate.

Exhibit 13.2 Who may broker real estate

May broker	May not broker
individual sole proprietor for-profit corporation general partnership limited partnership joint venture	non-profit corporation business trust co-operative association

Types of brokerage organization

In addition to being organized as a sole proprietorship, partnership, corporation or joint venture, a brokerage may be:

- independent or affiliated
- specialized in a type of property
- specialized in a type of transaction
- specialized in a type of client

These variations in brokerage organization are usually a response to competitive conditions in the local real estate market.

Independent brokerage. A brokerage that is not affiliated with a franchise is an independent agency. Many independent agencies participate in networks on a local, regional, or national basis. Such networks expose the independent broker to a larger market without compromising individual identity.

Franchise. A franchised brokerage is an independently-owned company that enters into a licensing arrangement with a franchisor to participate in various benefits offered in exchange for compensation. Franchisors generally offer local franchisees:

- the use of a recognized trade name
- national and regional advertising
- training programs
- standardized operating procedures
- a national referral system

In exchange, a franchisee pays the franchisor start-up fees and a portion of gross income.

Commercial and residential brokerages. Many brokerages deal primarily with limited types of property: residential, commercial, industrial, undeveloped land, etc. In practice, most residential companies conduct a small amount of commercial brokerage, while commercial brokerages tend to deal strictly with retail, office, industrial, or land properties. A large company may handle all types of properties but will probably have a separate organizational division for each property type.

Transaction-specialized brokerages. Brokerages often organize around a particular type of transaction. Thus, there are companies that specialize in apartment rentals, office rentals, exchanges, business brokerage, and, most commonly, residential sales.

Buyer- and seller-oriented brokerages. Companies sometimes specialize even further by choosing to represent only one side in a transaction. Thus a brokerage may represent only commercial tenants, or only residential buyers, or some other limited type of client.

Trade organizations

Numerous trade organizations serve the real estate brokerage industry and all of its areas of specialization. The largest is the National Association of Realtors® (NAR). NAR is comprised of a national headquarters, a state association in each state, and within each state, local Realtor® boards.

One should note that the term Realtor® is a protected trade name of NAR. *Only members of the organization may use the term to refer to themselves*. More specifically, there are two identities within NAR: Realtor, and Realtor-Associate. By definition, a Realtor® is a member broker and a Realtor-Associate® is a member sales agent. (In some states, Realtor applies to both broker and sales agent.) Membership in the local board automatically includes membership in the local MLS, the state association, and NAR.

THE BROKER-SALESPERSON RELATIONSHIP

Legal relationships
Salesperson's employment status
Obligations and responsibilities
Agent compensation

Legal relationships

Only a broker with an active broker's license can hire and employ a licensed salesperson. A licensed salesperson may work only for the employing broker and may not work for or receive direct compensation from any other broker.

Agent's scope of authority. State real estate license laws provide for two distinct licenses to conduct real estate brokerage: the broker license and the salesperson or sales agent license.

A licensed real estate broker is duly authorized to represent clients directly in brokering real estate. A sales agent, on the other hand, is only authorized to represent a broker and carry out such duties as the broker may legitimately delegate. In other words, a sales agent does not directly represent the client in a transaction but is rather the agent of the broker and subagent of the client. A sales agent is therefore a fiduciary of the employing broker.

As agent of a broker, a salesperson may offer properties for sale or lease, procure buyers, negotiate transaction terms, and otherwise conduct the business of brokerage. The agent, however, must act entirely on the broker's behalf.

A salesperson *may not*:

- bind a client to any contract
- receive compensation directly from a client
- accept a listing or deposit that is not in the name of the broker

Salesperson's employment status

A sales agent may be an independent contractor (IC) or an employee. In either case, the broker is responsible and liable for the sales agent's actions. Brokers are subject to guidelines of the U.S. Equal Employment Opportunity Commission (EEOC), a federal agency that enforces laws against workplace discrimination.

Independent contractor / broker relationship. Generally, a broker has limited control over the actions of a contractor. Specifically:

- a broker can require performance results, but is limited in demanding *how* a contractor performs the work. For example, a broker may not prescribe selling methods, meeting attendance, or office hours.
- an IC is responsible for income and social security taxes; the broker does not withhold taxes
- a broker cannot provide an IC with employee benefits such as health insurance or pension plans

Employee / broker relationship. A broker has greater control over the actions of an employee. Specifically:

- a broker can impose a sales methodology. In addition, a broker can enforce all office policies, including hours, meeting attendance, and telephone coverage.
- a broker must withhold income taxes and pay unemployment compensation tax on behalf of an employee
- an employee may receive the benefits enjoyed by the broker's non-selling employees

A written agreement between broker and employee or independent contractor should clearly state each party's duties and responsibilities to the other. In addition, the agreement should clarify the agent's compensation program as well as who is to pay for incidental business expenses.

Real estate assistant or personal assistant. Brokers and salespersons may hire licensed or unlicensed employees to assist them with a variety of tasks. Unlicensed assistants may perform clerical or ministerial acts, but nothing requiring a license. Licensed assistants may perform tasks requiring a license. Unlicensed assistants usually may be compensated directly by the sales associate they work for, but licensed assistants must be compensated by the employing broker and are subject to that broker's supervision.

Obligations and responsibilities

Sales agent's duties and responsibilities. In accepting employment from a broker, a salesperson generally makes a commitment to:

- work diligently to sell the broker's listings
- work diligently to procure new listings
- promote the business reputation of the broker
- abide by the broker's established policies
- fulfill the fiduciary duties owed clients as their subagent
- maintain insurance policies as required by the broker
- have transportation for conducting business, as required by the broker
- conform to ethical standards imposed by broker and trade organization
- uphold all covenants and provisions of the employment agreement

Broker's obligations to the sales agent. In employing a salesperson, a broker generally makes a commitment to:

- make the brokerage's listings available
- make the brokerage's market and property data available
- provide whatever training was promised at the time of hiring
- provide whatever office support was promised at the time of hiring
- uphold the commission structure and expense reimbursement policy
- conform to ethical standards imposed by the broker's trade organization
- uphold all covenants and provisions of the employment agreement

Agent compensation

An agent employee of a broker may receive wages, salary, additional commissions, expense reimbursements, and benefit plans. An independent contractor's compensation is a normally a combination of commissions and free office support. Most sales agents work as independent contractors who earn a commission.

Commission splits. A sales agent earns compensation for procuring listings and for representing buyers or tenants when a completed transaction results. Brokerages typically view these activities as two "sides" of a commission: the listing side and the buyer-representation side. An agent who procures a listing receives a share of the broker's listing-side commission according to the agent's compensation agreement. A buyer agent who completes a purchase receives a share of the broker's buyer-side commission, as established in the buyer-broker agreement and the brokerage's commission schedule. If an agent represents both the seller and the buyer in the same transaction (where permitted), the agent may receive a share of both sides of the commission earned by the brokerage.

Commission schedules. An agent's commission schedule is a comprehensive summary of commission splits under various circumstances, including:

- representation of sellers and representation of buyers
- salesperson's level of sales performance
- broker's level of expense reimbursement to agent
- the particular policies or organization of the agency
- prevailing commission splits in the market

In view of these circumstances, an agent's commission schedule can vary widely. For example, an agent who is the highest sales producer in the market may be able to secure a 70% or 80% commission split with the broker, regardless of whether the agent is representing the seller or the buyer. If the broker is paying an inordinate amount of selling expenses, an agent's commission split may only be 40%. Some brokerages have a policy of not paying any expenses except the rent. In such cases, agents may receive an 80% or 90% commission split. In almost all cases, broker and agent negotiate the schedule of commissions in the environment of competitive market conditions.

Calculating commissions. The following exhibit illustrates how commissions might be split in a hypothetical transaction.

Exhibit 13.3 Calculating Commissions

Sale price: $500,000
Total commission paid by seller to listing broker: 6% ($30,000)
Buyer-broker compensation (if applicable): as negotiated in buyer-broker agreement
Agent splits (example): 50%

Situation A: buyer is represented by a separate brokerage

	Commission $	Commission %
Listing broker	7,500	1.5%
Listing agent	7,500	1.5%
Buyer broker	7,500	1.5%
Buyer agent	7,500	1.5%

Situation B: buyer has no broker; listing agent finds buyer

Listing broker	15,000	3.0%
Listing agent	15,000	3.0%

Situation C: buyer represented by another agent in the same brokerage

Listing broker	15,000	3.0%
Listing agent	7,500	1.5%
Buyer agent	7,500	1.5%

OPERATING A REAL ESTATE BROKERAGE

Obtaining listings
Marketing listings
Pre-closing activities
Handling trust funds
Managing information
Policy manual
Advertisement regulations
Anti-trust laws

Obtaining listings

Listings are the traditional source of a broker's income. By obtaining a listing, a broker secures the opportunity to earn the commission paid by the seller when the property is sold. In contrast, working with buyers does not guarantee compensation unless the buyer has entered into a written buyer representation agreement. Without such an agreement, a buyer may move from one agent to another with no obligation to any particular broker. Agents can spend considerable time with a buyer and earn nothing. Hence the special value of a listing: it remains the most predictable source of revenue for a brokerage.

Listing procedures. The marketing and self-promotional efforts of agents generate listings. New agents usually focus on becoming well known in a small geographical area and hope to encounter clients there who are willing to list with them. More experienced and better-known agents are able to rely to a greater extent on referrals in obtaining listings.

New or experienced, an agent needs certain skills at each step in the process of obtaining a listing.

Exhibit 13.4 Listing Steps

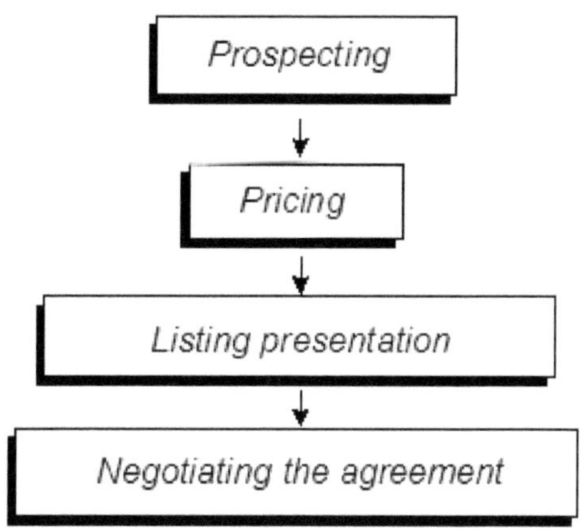

Prospecting. Prospecting is any activity designed to generate listing prospects: parties who intend to sell or lease property and who have not yet committed to a broker. Prospecting activities include mailing newsletters and flyers, selling directly and person-to-person, advertising, and selling indirectly via community involvement.

The goal of prospecting is to reach a potential seller or landlord, make that person aware of the agent's and brokerage's services, and obtain permission to discuss the benefits of listing, often in the form of a formal selling presentation.

Pricing. It is almost always necessary for an agent seeking a listing to suggest a listing price or price range for the property. It is important to make a careful estimate, because underpricing a property is not in the best interests of the seller, and overpricing it often prevents a transaction altogether.

The "Appraisal" chapter describes methods of estimating value. In brief, an agent usually relies on an analysis of comparable properties which have recently sold in the same neighborhood. By making adjustments for the differences between the subject property and the comparables, the agent arrives at a general price range.

Agents must be careful to caution sellers that they are not appraisers, and that the suggested price range is not an expert opinion of market value. If a more precise estimate of market value is desired, the seller should hire a licensed appraiser.

Listing presentation and negotiation of agreement. A listing presentation is an agent's opportunity to meet with a seller and present the merits of the agent's marketing plan, personal expertise, and company strengths. At the same time, an agent can explain the many phases and details of a real estate transaction and point out how the provisions of the listing agreement and the agent-principal relationship work to ensure a smooth transaction.

Ultimately, the agent's aim in a presentation meeting is to have the principal execute a listing agreement. The agent must then submit the listing to the broker for approval and signing. This result will set in motion the process of marketing the property. In practice, it may take an agent many meetings with a prospect before the prospect signs an agreement.

Marketing listings

The process of marketing a listed property occurs in three broad steps, leading to the desired end of a completed sale contract. At each of these steps, there are critical skills an agent must master.

Exhibit 13.5 Marketing Steps

Marketing plan. After the broker formalizes the listing agreement, the sales agent initiates a marketing plan for the property. An ideal marketing plan is a cohesive combination of promotional and selling activities directed at potential customers. The best combination is one that aims to have maximum impact on the marketplace in relation to the time and money expended.

Selling the prospect. When marketing activities produce prospects, the agent's marketing role becomes more interpersonal. An agent must now:

- qualify prospects' plans, preferences, and financial capabilities
- show properties that meet the customer's needs
- elicit the buyer's reactions to properties
- report material results to the seller or listing agent

At the earliest appropriate time, an agent must make certain disclosures to a prospective customer. Depending on state laws, an agent may have to disclose the relevant agency relationship, the property's physical condition, and the possible presence of hazardous materials.

Obtaining offers. If a buyer is interested in purchasing a property, an agent obtains the buyer's offer of transaction terms, including price, down payment, desired closing date, and financing requirements.

An agent must be extremely careful at this point to abide by fiduciary obligations to the client, whoever that party may be. Discussions of price are particularly delicate: whether the client is buyer or seller, the agent's duty is to uphold the client's best interests. Thus it is not acceptable to suggest to a customer what price the client will or will not accept. With pricing and other issues, it is always a good practice to understand what role the client wants the agent to assume in the offering phase of the transaction; in other words, exactly how far the agent may go in developing terms on the client's behalf.

When a buyer or tenant makes an offer, the agent *must* present it to the seller or landlord at the earliest possible moment. If the terms of the offer are unacceptable, the agent may assist the seller in developing a counteroffer, which the agent would subsequently submit to the customer or customer's agent. The offering and counteroffering process continues until a meeting of the minds results in a sale contract.

Pre-closing activities

Between the execution of the sale contract and the closing of the transaction, the property is "under contract" or "contract pending." During this period, buyer and seller have certain things to do to achieve a successful closing. The buyer often needs to arrange financing and dispose of other property; the seller may need to clear up title encumbrances and make certain property repairs. The sale contract should specify all such required tasks.

The time period between contracting and closing is referred to as the **contingency period**, or **pre-closing period**.

Agent's responsibilities. As dictated by custom and the circumstances of a transaction, an agent has a range of duties and responsibilities during the pre-closing period.

An agent's foremost duty following acceptance of an offer is to submit the contract and the earnest money to the employing broker without delay. Most states impose deadlines for this requirement, usually within twenty-four hours from the agent's receipt of the deposit.

Other possible responsibilities are:

- assisting the buyer in obtaining financing
- assisting the seller in clearing title
- assisting the seller in completing property repairs
- recommending inspectors, appraisers, attorneys, and title companies
- assisting in communications between principals
- assisting in the exchange of transaction documents

Broker's responsibilities. The listing broker has the primary responsibility for handling deposit monies and for overseeing the agent's pre-closing activities. State license laws require that earnest money deposits be placed in an account which is separate from the broker's operating accounts. They also require the broker to keep accurate records and follow accepted accounting procedures. These precautions protect the buyer and seller and safeguard the deposited funds. A broker must be careful to avoid two common violations of escrow regulations: commingling and conversion, described below.

Handling trust funds

General account requirements. Brokers who receive and hold earnest money deposits or money belonging to others, particularly clients and customers, must maintain a trust account. Typically, trust accounts must

- designate the real estate broker as trustee
- provide for withdrawal of funds without prior notice

State or national depository institution. According to state law, brokers must maintain their escrow accounts in a state- or federally-chartered savings and loan association or credit union. A broker may maintain more than one trust account to meet business requirements.

Non-trust funds. Brokers may maintain nominal amounts of operating funds in their trust accounts sufficient to cover bank service charges and minimum balance requirements. Such non-trust funds must be identified as such in the trust account.

Commingling. Commingling is the act of mixing the broker's personal or business funds with escrow funds. To avoid committing a violation, a broker must not deposit any money belonging to others in the broker's business or personal account. Also, a broker must not deposit operating funds into any trust account. The definition of commingling includes the failure to deposit earnest money into escrow in a timely manner. In most states, commingling funds constitutes grounds for license suspension or revocation and is a serious violation of the law.

Conversion. Conversion is the act of misappropriating escrow funds for the broker's business or personal use. More serious than mere commingling, conversion is effectively an act of theft: using monies which do not belong to the broker. Conversion carries serious consequences, including license revocation.

Deposit deadlines. A real estate broker must deposit trust funds received within a required deadline after receiving notice that an offer to purchase is accepted by all parties. The deadline varies from state-to-state, so licensees must be familiar with local regulations to remain in compliance with escrow laws.

Holding funds. Brokers must retain the trust monies in the trust account until the transaction involved is consummated or terminated, at which time the broker must account for the full amount received and disbursed.

If a purchase agreement signed by a seller and purchaser provides for someone other than a real estate broker to hold a deposit, a licensee in possession of that deposit must deliver the deposit to that person within the required number of banking days after the licensee receives notice that an offer to purchase is accepted by all parties.

Return of earnest money deposit. Generally, escrow funds are disbursed to the respective parties at closing, or according to escrow instructions. However, if any trust fund disbursement is disputed, the broker must follow very specific procedures for handling the dispute. Depending on the jurisdiction, these can range from arbitration to court-ordered resolutions. In any case, the broker must rely on state regulations and legal solutions instituted by the courts.

Salesperson receiving trust funds. A real estate salesperson must deliver to the real estate broker, on receipt, a deposit or other money paid in connection with a transaction in which the real estate salesperson is engaged on behalf of the real estate broker.

Communications and technology

Multiple listing services and websites. The posting and sharing of property listings and data among broker websites, firm websites, and multiple listing services (MLS) is one of the most effective marketing tools available to today's licensees. Broker cooperation assures sellers of maximum exposure for their properties, just as it assures buyers of seeing the widest possible range of listed properties.

To ensure fair use of MLS facilities, the National Association of REALTORS® has developed an Internet Data Exchange (IDX) policy that enables MLS members to display and use MLS data while respecting the rights of property owners and brokers to market their properties however they want.

Basically, persons who want to make use of MLS data have to share their own data as well. They can opt out of the sharing policy so that competitors cannot post their properties on competing websites, but then they cannot post competitors' properties on their own sites.

There are a number of websites that provide consumers with the capability to search through listings all over the country and even the world. Of course, it is always wise to recognize that information posted on the internet is not necessarily reliable and that the source of the information should be considered carefully.

Email and texting. Frequent and virtually instantaneous contact between real estate practitioners and consumers is possible via email and texting. As both these forms of communication fall under the category of advertising, practitioners need to carefully observe their state's advertising regulations. In brief, be truthful, direct, and concise. Provide the information required by law, and do not violate prohibitions against unsolicited emails and messages.

Social media. Social media websites allow rapid exchange of information, documents, photos, messages and data with a select group of contacts. They also represent another form of advertising and so are subject to real estate commission advertising regulations in most states.

Smartphones. Smartphones facilitate the use, not only of email, texting, and social media, but also of immediate internet access, document review, photo and document sharing, data storage, and video conferencing. They offer, in fact, an almost complete mobile office.

Managing information

The ability to satisfy the needs of clients and customers is largely dependent on a broker's ability to obtain, organize, and manage information. Information is a cornerstone of the broker's perceived value in the marketplace and a major reason why buyers and sellers seek a broker out. Systematic collection and updating of relevant information is therefore a business priority.

Property data. Most brokerages maintain two categories of property data: available properties, and all properties in the market area. In residential brokerage, available property basically consists of the listings in the MLS and for-sale-by-owner properties. Records for all properties in an area are accessible in tax records. Commercial brokerages usually keep track of available and occupied commercial properties in a proprietary database.

Buyer data. Buyer information is usually compiled and maintained, often informally, by each agent in a brokerage. An agency's base of prospects who are looking for property at any given time is valuable for marketing new listings.

Tenant data. In residential and commercial leasing companies, information is compiled and maintained on all tenants in an area, by property type used. Such files contain a tenant's lease expiration, property size, and rent.

Client data. It is important to keep track of both current and former clients. Former clients are likely prospects to become clients again or customers. They are also a source of referrals. Current clients, of course, should be the broker's primary concern.

Market data. Today's clients and customers expect a broker to know the market intimately. It is often the broker or agent with the best market knowledge who dominates business in the market. Knowing a market includes keeping up to date on:

- pricing and appreciation trends
- financing rates and terms
- demographic patterns and trends
- construction trends
- general economic trends

Policy manual

A well-managed brokerage relies on a written policy manual to keep the business running smoothly and professionally. A policy manual sets forth company rules, regulations, and policies.

Advertisement regulations

Advertising is an important tool in marketing properties and procuring buyers. It is, however, subject to regulation and restrictions. In general, state laws and regulations require that:

- advertising must not be misleading
- the broker is responsible for the content of advertising done by agents
- all advertising must reveal the identity of the broker; licensed brokers and agents may not use blind ads that conceal their identities
- brokers selling their own property through the brokerage must disclose the brokerage identity
- salespersons must include the broker's business identity in any advertising; they may not advertise in their own name solely (unless selling their own property through channels other than the agency)

Telephone Consumer Protection Act. The TCPA (Telephone Consumer Protection Act) addresses the regulation of unsolicited telemarketing phone calls. Rules include the following:

- telephone solicitors must identify themselves, on whose behalf they are calling, and how they can be contacted
- telemarketers must comply with any do-not-call request made during the solicitation call
- consumers can place their home and wireless phone numbers on a national Do-Not-Call list which prohibits future solicitations from telemarketers.

CAN-SPAM Act. The CAN-SPAM Act (Controlling the Assault of Non-Solicited Pornography and Marketing Act of 2003) supplements the Telephone Consumer Protection Act (TCPA). It

- bans sending unwanted email 'commercial messages' to wireless devices
- requires express prior authorization

- requires giving an 'opt out' choice to terminate the sender's messages

Anti-trust laws

Brokerage companies, like other businesses, are subject to anti-trust laws designed to prevent monopolies and unfair trade practices.

Sherman Antitrust Act. Enacted in 1890, the Sherman Antitrust Act prohibits restraint of interstate and foreign trade by conspiracy, monopolistic practice, and certain forms of business combinations, or mergers. The Sherman Act empowers the federal government to proceed against antitrust violators.

Clayton Antitrust Act. The Clayton Antitrust Act of 1914 reinforces and broadens the provisions of the Sherman Act. Among its prohibitions are certain exclusive contracts, predatory price cutting to eliminate competitors, and inter-related boards of directors and stock holdings between same-industry corporations. The Clayton Act also legalizes certain labor strikes, picketing, and boycotts.

Anti-competitive behavior. The effect of antitrust legislation is to prohibit trade practice and trade restraints that unfairly disadvantage open competition. Business practices and behaviors which violate antitrust laws include collusion, price fixing, market allocation, bid rigging, restricting market entry, exclusive dealing, group boycotts, and predatory pricing.

Collusion. Collusion is the illegal practice of two or more businesses joining forces or making joint decisions which have the effect of putting another business at a competitive disadvantage. Businesses may not collude to fix prices, allocate markets, create monopolies, or otherwise interfere with free market operations.

Price fixing. Price fixing is the practice of two or more brokers agreeing to charge certain commission rates or fees for their services, regardless of market conditions or competitors. In essence, such pricing avoids and disturbs the dynamics of a free, open market.

For instance, the two largest brokerages in a market jointly decide to cut commission rates by 50% in order to draw clients away from competitors. The cut-rate pricing could destroy smaller agencies that lack the staying power of the large companies.

Market allocation. Market allocation is the practice of colluding to restrict competitive activity in portions of a market in exchange for a reciprocal restriction from a competitor: "we won't compete against you here if you won't compete against us there."

For example, Broker A agrees to trade only in single family re-sales, provided that Broker B agrees to focus exclusively on apartment rentals and condominium sales. The net effect is an illegally restricted market where collusion and monopoly supplant market forces.

Group boycott. Group boycotting is the illegal activity of a number of competitors in a given market "ganging up" on a competitor in that market to limit the boycotted party's access to customers and patrons of the competitor's business. For instance, a group of brokers might collectively refuse to show a boycotted broker's listings to potential buyers. Over time, the boycotted company is essentially "starved" out of the market.

Tie-in agreements. In a tie-in agreement, the sale of one product or performance of a service is tied to the sale of another, less desirable product or service. For instance, "I will sell you this car, but you have to hire my brother-in-law to drive it." Or, more likely, "I will list and sell your old home if you hire me to find you a new home to purchase." Tie-ins restrict competition and limit the freedom of the consumer.

Violations of fair trade and anti-trust laws may be treated as felonies, and penalties can be substantial. Loss of one's license is also at stake. Brokers are well-advised to understand and recognize these laws.

BUSINESS BROKERAGE

Business brokerage vs. real property brokerage
Transaction knowledge
Accounting
Determining a price
Business brokerage regulation

Business brokerage is *effecting a sale or exchange of an existing business*. In most cases, the sale of a business entails the simultaneous transfer of an estate in land, whether a leasehold or a fee. Thus to sell businesses, a broker must generally hold a real estate license.

In some states, business brokerage is classified into *opportunity brokerage* and *enterprise brokerage* in accordance with the size of the business being sold. **Opportunity brokerage** concerns a small business, usually a proprietorship or partnership, where the transaction consists of a sale of assets and an assignment of a lease. **Enterprise brokerage** concerns a larger company, usually a corporation, where the transaction involves the sale of stock and multiple real estate parcels leased or owned by the seller.

The process of business brokerage is similar to real estate brokerage: a broker secures a listing, procures a purchaser, and facilitates the closing. Once a ready, willing, and able buyer is found, the broker earns a commission.

Business brokerage vs real property brokerage

The critical difference between selling a business and selling real estate is that selling a business includes the transfer of *business income, personal property assets*, and, possibly, *liabilities*, in addition to real property. To be competent in this brokerage specialty, a business broker must have specialized skills concerning transactions, accounting, and pricing. A business broker must also rely on a professional team to complete the transaction. Members of this team would include the client's legal counsel, accountant, and, preferably, a professional appraiser.

Transaction knowledge

Types of sale. There are generally two types of business sale transaction for a business broker to be aware of: the *asset sale* and the *stock sale*. In an **asset sale**, the purchaser takes possession of some or all of the assets of the business, as well as the real estate, in exchange for the sale price. The purchase usually does not include acquiring the existing business entity or its liabilities. An asset sale is preferred by buyers who want to buy only portions of a business, or to avoid liabilities inherent in a stock purchase.

In a **stock sale**, a purchaser acquires complete ownership of a business, including the legal corporate entity, all assets, all financial liabilities, and any current or future legal liabilities arising from incidents that have occurred prior to the sale. A purchaser may prefer a stock sale to avoid creating a new business entity or to benefit from a possible tax advantage. In addition, a stock sale keeps a business identity intact, which can be very valuable.

Transaction documents. The most common transaction documents in business brokerage are a *sale contract,* an *assignment* or *real estate sale contract,* a *no-compete agreement,* and a *consulting agreement*.

A **sale contract** sets forth all terms and conditions of the agreement, including exactly what is being sold. An **assignment** or **real estate sale agreement** is an agreement for transferring any and all real property involved in the transaction. A **no-compete agreement** is a seller's covenant, for compensation, not to compete with the buyer under prescribed conditions and time periods. A **consulting agreement** is an employment agreement that hires the seller to assist the buyer in taking over business operations.

For the most part, transaction documents in business brokerage are not fully standardized. For that reason, a business broker must exercise caution in dealing with document language so as to avoid the unauthorized practice of law.

Accounting

A broker or agent who wants to undertake business brokerage needs basic proficiency in accounting. In particular, one must know how to read and interpret:

- income, expenses, and profit on an income statement
- assets, liabilities, and net worth on a balance sheet

Income, expenses, and profit. A business's profit is the revenue remaining from gross income after all expenses have been paid. A business broker must evaluate an owner's income and expenses in order to determine what the business may be worth to a buyer. This often involves interpreting which income and expense items will change after the business is sold. For example, a seller owns a grocery store and uses family members to perform clerical work without pay. If a buyer is a bachelor without children, much of the clerical work will have to be hired out. The additional payroll suddenly changes the store's profitability significantly. Neglecting to consider how income and expenses might change is likely to lead to serious problems in working with buyers.

Business assets. The assets of a business include **tangible** assets and **intangible** assets. Tangible assets include:

- cash and marketable securities
- inventory
- trade fixtures and equipment
- real property
- accounts receivable

Intangible assets include:

- the company name
- trademarks
- copyrights
- licenses
- contracts for future sales of goods or services
- goodwill

In valuing a business, both tangible and intangible assets must be taken into account, even though intangible assets may be very difficult to appraise.

Business liabilities. Business liabilities acquired in a corporate stock sale include short-term debt, such as accounts payable, and long-term liabilities, such as mortgages and leases.

Goodwill. Goodwill is a business brokerage term with two meanings. In one sense, goodwill is an intangible asset consisting of any factor that an owner values in the business, apart from any other specific asset. For example, goodwill might include reputation, a long history of success in a market, name recognition, a dominant market share, and an excellent business location. In the second sense, which is more familiar to accountants, goodwill is the difference in value between an owner's price and the value of all other business assets. For example, if an owner wants $400,000 for a business, and the totality of tangible and intangible assets is valued at $320,000, the goodwill is an $80,000 asset.

Determining a price

The most difficult task for a business broker is often finding the proper price range for a business. An owner of a smaller business has probably built the business from scratch and tends to overvalue it. Moreover, such an owner may have incomplete and disorganized accounting records, making the valuation of assets quite difficult. Finally, a business's true income may be different for one owner than it would be for another because of variations in management style and ability.

In any case, the value of the business is a function of the following:

- past, present, and future net profits, and capitalized value of these
- amount of risk and certainty associated with realizing future profits
- value of all assets as reflected in the books of account
- impact of goodwill on the value of the business
- prices paid for similar businesses
- all other risks associated with the business

Business brokerage regulation

Licensing. A business broker generally must have an active real estate license. In addition, the broker may need to have a valid securities license since a transaction may entail the sale of securities.

Uniform Commercial Code (UCC). The Uniform Commercial Code regulates the sale of personal property on a state-by-state basis, and forms the basis for standardized sale documents. Standard documents include promissory notes, security agreements, and bills of sale.

Bulk Sales Act. The Bulk Sales Act protects creditors against loss of collateral in an indebted business through the undisclosed sale of the business's inventory. If a business sells over half of its inventory to a buyer, the act declares that the sale is a bulk sale, and, as such, is potentially an asset sale. Since a creditor could lose security in such a sale, the seller must disclose the names of creditors to the buyer in a Bulk Sales Affidavit. The buyer must notify the creditors of the sale, who may then take appropriate action to secure their loans.

13 General Brokerage Practices Snapshot Review

FUNCTION AND ORGANIZATION

The core activity of brokerage

- procuring buyer, seller, tenant, or leased property for a client, often with the help of other brokers and a multiple listing service
- skills: listing, marketing, facilitating, managing information
- Multiple Listing Service: network of brokers who share listings

Who may legally broker real estate?

- yes: sole proprietorship, for-profit corp., general or limited partnership, joint venture. no: non-profit corp., business trust, cooperative association

Types of brokerage organization

- independents; franchises; agencies by property type, by transaction type, and by client type; limited and full service agencies

THE BROKER-SALESPERSON RELATIONSHIP

Legal relationships

- salesperson is agent, fiduciary of broker; acts in broker's name; subagent of client
- **may not:** have two employers; be paid by other parties; bind clients contractually

Salesperson's employment status

- may be employee or contractor; relationship defined by agreement; assistant may be licensed or unlicensed; if licensed, supervised and paid by employing broker

Obligations and responsibilities

- agent to broker: obtain & sell listings; follow policies and employment provisions; promote ethics and broker's reputation
- broker to agent: provide data, office support, compensation, training; uphold ethics, policies, and employment agreement

Agent compensation

- commissions are negotiated in listing and buyer broker agreements

OPERATING A REAL ESTATE BROKERAGE

Obtaining listings

- generate prospects; develop price range; complete listing presentation; negotiate execute and agreement

Marketing listings

- develop marketing plan; sell and qualify prospective buyers; complete necessary disclosures; obtain offers

Pre-closing activities

- facilitate fulfillment of contract contingencies and provisions
- no commingling or conversion of escrow funds

Handling trust funds

- trust funds to be held in trust account in state- or federally-chartered institution; no commingling or conversion; timely deposit and withdrawal; full accounting

Communications and technology

- marketing techniques using technology: broker cooperation via MLS and competitors' websites; email and texting; social media websites; smartphone communication capabilities; all must be used carefully and in conformity with advertising rules and other laws

Managing information	• property data; buyer and tenant files; market data files
Policy manual	• written procedures **and** policies on all aspects of the business to ensure smooth, consistent operations
Advertisement regulations	• no misleading ads; must contain broker's ID; broker responsible for content; no blind ads
Anti-trust laws	• Sherman Act and Clayton Act pioneered antitrust laws to prohibit unfair trade practices, trade restraints, and monopolies
	• illegal to collude, disadvantage competitors; fix prices; allocate markets; force tie-ins
BUSINESS BROKERAGE	• sale of existing business and its real estate; opportunity and enterprise brokerage
Business brokerage vs. real estate brokerage	• special skills: transaction knowledge; accounting; determining the price
Transaction knowledge	• types of sale: asset sale and stock sale
	• documents: sale contract; real estate sale contract or assignment; no-compete agreement; consulting agreement
Accounting	• income, expenses, and profit
	• balance sheet: assets, liabilities, net worth
	• assets: tangible and intangible
	• goodwill: intangible asset--difference between price & other assets
Determining a price	• reconciliation of income, cost, and market data approaches; influenced by risk and stability of future income
Business brokerage regulation	• may need securities license; must comply with Bulk Sales law

14 Overview of Conveyance Contracts

Contract for Sale
Sale Contract Provisions
Option-To-Buy Contract
Contract for Deed

CONTRACT FOR SALE

Legal characteristics
Contract creation
Earnest money escrow
Contract contingencies
Default

A real estate sale contract is a binding and enforceable agreement wherein a buyer, the **vendee**, agrees to buy an identified parcel of real estate, and a seller, the **vendor**, agrees to sell it under certain terms and conditions. It is the document that is at the center of the transaction.

The conventional transfer of real estate ownership takes place in three stages. First, there is the negotiating period where buyers and sellers exchange offers in an effort to agree to all transfer terms that will appear in the sale contract. Second, when both parties have accepted all terms, the offer becomes a binding sale contract and the transaction enters the pre-closing stage, during which each party makes arrangements to complete the sale according to the sale contract's terms. Third is the closing of the transaction, when the seller deeds title to the buyer, the buyer pays the purchase price, and all necessary documents are completed. At this stage, the sale contract has served its purpose and terminates.

Other names for the sale contract are *agreement of sale, contract for purchase, contract of purchase and sale*, and *earnest money contract*.

Legal characteristics

Executory contract. A sale contract is *executory:* the signatories have yet to perform their respective obligations and promises. Upon closing, the sale contract is fully performed and no longer exists as a binding agreement.

Signatures. All owners of the property should sign the sale contract. If the sellers are married, both spouses should sign to ensure that both spouses release homestead, dower, and curtesy rights to the buyer at closing. Failure to do so does not invalidate the contract but can lead to encumbered title and legal disputes.

Enforceability criteria. To be enforceable, a sale contract must:

- be validly created (mutual consent, consideration, legal purpose, competent parties, voluntary act)
- be in writing
- identify the principal parties
- clearly identify the property, preferably by legal description
- contain a purchase price
- be signed by the principal parties

Written vs. oral form. A contract for the sale of real estate is enforceable only if it is in writing. A buyer or seller cannot sue to force the other to comply with an oral contract for sale, even if the contract is valid.

Assignment. Either party to a sale transaction can assign the sale contract to another party, subject to the provisions and conditions contained in the agreement.

Who may complete. A broker or agent may assist buyer and seller in completing an offer to purchase, provided the broker represents the client faithfully and does not charge a separate fee for the assistance. It is advisable, and legally required in most states, for a broker to use a standard contract form promulgated by state agencies or real estate boards, as such forms contain generally accepted language. This relieves the broker of the dangers of creating new contract language, which can be construed as a practice of law for which the broker is not licensed.

Contract creation

Offer and acceptance. A contract of sale is created by full and unequivocal acceptance of an offer. Offer and acceptance may come from either buyer or seller. The offeree must accept the offer without making any changes whatsoever. A change terminates the offer and creates a new offer, or counteroffer. An offeror may revoke an offer for any reason prior to communication of acceptance by the offeree.

Equitable title. A sale contract gives the buyer an interest in the property that is called equitable title, or *ownership in equity*. If the seller defaults and the buyer can show good faith performance, the buyer can sue for specific performance, that is, to compel the seller to transfer legal title upon payment of the contract price.

Earnest money escrow

The buyer's earnest money deposit fulfills the consideration requirements for a valid sale contract. In addition, it provides potential compensation for damages to the seller if the buyer fails to perform. The amount of the deposit varies according to local custom. It should be noted that the earnest money deposit is not the only form of consideration that satisfies the requirement.

The sale contract provides the *escrow instructions* for handling and disbursing escrow funds. The earnest money is placed in a third party trust account or escrow. A licensed escrow agent employed by a title company, financial institution, or brokerage company usually manages the escrow. An individual broker may also serve as the escrow agent.

The escrow holder acts as an impartial fiduciary for buyer and seller. If the buyer performs under the sale contract, the deposit is applied to the purchase price.

Strict rules govern the handling of earnest money deposits, particularly if a broker is the escrow agent. For example, state laws direct the broker when to deposit the funds, how to account for them, and how to keep them separate from the broker's own funds.

Contract contingencies

A sale contract often contains contingencies. A contingency is a condition that must be met before the contract is enforceable.

The most common contingency concerns financing. A buyer makes an offer contingent upon securing financing for the property under certain terms on or before a certain date. If unable to secure the specified loan commitment by the deadline, the buyer may cancel the contract and recover the deposit. An appropriate and timely loan commitment eliminates the contingency, and the buyer must proceed with the purchase.

It is possible for both buyers and sellers to abuse contingencies in order to leave themselves a convenient way to cancel without defaulting. To avoid problems, the statement of a contingency should:

- be explicit and clear
- have an expiration date
- expressly require diligence in the effort to fulfill the requirement

A contingency that is too broad, vague, or excessive in duration may invalidate the entire contract on the grounds of insufficiency of mutual agreement.

Default

A sale contract is bilateral, since both parties promise to perform. As a result, either party may default by failing to perform. Note that a party's failure to meet a contingency does not constitute default, but rather entitles the parties to cancel the contract.

Buyer default. If a buyer fails to perform under the terms of a sale contract, the breach entitles the seller to legal recourse for damages. In most cases, the contract itself stipulates the seller's remedies. The usual remedy is forfeiture of the buyer's deposit as **liquidated damages**, provided the deposit is not grossly in excess of the seller's actual damages. It is also customary to provide for the seller and broker to share the liquidated damages. The broker may not, however, receive liquidated damages in excess of what the commission would have been on the full listing price.

If the contract does not provide for liquidated damages, the seller may sue for damages, cancellation, or specific performance.

Seller default. If a seller defaults, the buyer may sue for specific performance, damages, or cancellation.

SALE CONTRACT PROVISIONS

Primary provisions
Secondary provisions

Sale contracts can vary significantly in length and thoroughness. They also vary according to the type of sale transaction they describe. Some of the varieties are:

- Residential Contract of Sale
- Commercial Contract of Sale
- Foreclosure Contract of Sale
- Contract of Sale for New Construction
- Contract of Sale for Land
- Exchange Agreement

As the most common sale transaction is a residential sale, a Residential Contract of Sale is the type with which a licensee should first become familiar.

Primary provisions

A typical residential sale contract contains provisions of the following kind.

Parties, consideration, and property. One or more clauses will identify the parties, the property, and the basic consideration, which is the sale of the property in return for a purchase price.

There must be at least two parties to a sale contract: one cannot convey property to oneself. All parties must be identified, be of legal age, and have the capacity to contract.

The property clause also identifies fixtures and personal property included in the sale. Unless expressly excluded, items commonly construed as fixtures are *included* in the sale. Similarly, items commonly considered personal property are *not included* unless expressly included.

Legal description. A legal description must be sufficient for a competent surveyor to identify the property.

Price and terms. A clause states the final price and details how the purchase will occur. Of particular interest to the seller is the buyer's down payment, since the greater the buyer's equity, the more likely the buyer will be able to secure financing. In addition, a large deposit represents a buyer's commitment to complete the sale.

If seller financing is involved, the sale contract sets forth the terms of the arrangement: the amount and type of loan, the rate and term, and how the loan will be paid off.

It is important for all parties to verify that the buyer's earnest money deposit, down payment, loan proceeds, and other promised funds together equal the purchase price stated in the contract.

Loan approval. A financing contingency clause states under what conditions the buyer can cancel the contract without default and receive a refund of the earnest money. If the buyer cannot secure the stated financing by the deadline, the parties may agree to extend the contingency by signing next to the changed dates.

Earnest money deposit. A clause specifies how the buyer will pay the earnest money. It may allow the buyer to pay it in installments. Such an option enables a buyer to hold on to the property briefly while obtaining the additional deposit funds. For example, a buyer who wants to buy a house makes an initial deposit of $200, to be followed in twenty-four hours with an additional $2,000. The sale contract includes the seller's acknowledgment of receipt of the deposit.

Escrow. An escrow clause provides for the custody and disbursement of the earnest money deposit, and releases the escrow agent from certain liabilities in the performance of escrow duties.

Closing and possession dates. The contract states when title will transfer, as well as when the buyer will take physical possession. Customarily, possession occurs on the date when the deed is recorded, unless the buyer has agreed to other arrangements.

The closing clause generally describes what must take place at closing to avoid default. A seller must provide clear and marketable title. A buyer must produce purchase funds. Failure to complete any pre-closing requirements stated in the sale contract is default and grounds for the aggrieved party to seek recourse.

Conveyed interest; type of deed. One or more provisions will state what type of deed the seller will use to convey the property, and what conditions the deed will be subject to. Among common "subject to" conditions are easements, association memberships, encumbrances, mortgages, liens, and special assessments. Typically, the seller conveys a fee simple interest by means of a general warranty deed.

Title evidence. The seller covenants to produce the best possible evidence of property ownership. This is commonly in the form of title insurance.

Closing costs. The contract identifies which closing costs each party will pay. Customarily, the seller pays title and property-related costs, and the buyer pays financing-related costs. Annual costs such as taxes and insurance are prorated between the parties. Note that who pays any particular closing cost is an item for negotiation.

Damage and destruction. A clause stipulates the obligations of the parties in case the property is damaged or destroyed. The parties may negotiate alternatives, including seller's obligation to repair, buyer's obligation to buy if repairs are made, and the option for either party to cancel.

Default. A default clause identifies remedies for default. Generally, a buyer may sue for damages, specific performance, or cancellation. A seller may do likewise or claim the earnest money as liquidated damages.

Broker's representation and commission. The broker discloses the applicable agency relationships in the transaction and names the party who must pay the brokerage commission.

Seller's representations. The seller warrants that there will be no liens on the property that cannot be settled and extinguished at closing. In addition, the seller warrants that all representations are true, and if found otherwise, the buyer may cancel the contract and reclaim the deposit.

Secondary provisions

A sale contract may contain numerous additional clauses, depending on the complexity of the transaction. The following are some of the common provisions.

Inspections. The parties agree to inspections and remedial action based on findings.

Owner's association disclosure. The seller discloses existence of an association and the obligations it imposes.

Survey. The parties agree to a survey to satisfy financing requirements.

Environmental hazards. The seller notifies the buyer that there may be hazards that could affect the use and value of the property.

Compliance with laws. The seller warrants that there are no undisclosed building code or zoning violations.

Due-on-sale clause. The parties state their understanding that loans that survive the closing may be called due by the lender. Both parties agree to hold the other party harmless for the consequences of an acceleration.

Seller financing disclosure. The parties agree to comply with applicable state and local disclosure laws concerning seller financing.

Rental property; tenants rights. The buyer acknowledges the rights of tenants following closing.

FHA or VA financing condition. A contingency allows the buyer to cancel the contract if the price exceeds FHA or VA estimates of the property's value.

Flood plain; flood insurance. Seller discloses that the property is in a flood plain and that it must carry flood insurance if the buyer uses certain lenders for financing.

Condominium assessments. Seller discloses assessments the owner must pay.

Foreign seller withholding. The seller acknowledges that the buyer must withhold 15% of the purchase price at closing if the seller is a foreign person or entity and forward the withheld amount to the Internal Revenue Service. Certain limitations and exemptions apply.

Tax deferred exchange. For income properties only, buyer and seller disclose their intentions to participate in an exchange and agree to cooperate in completing necessary procedures.

Merger of agreements. Buyer and seller state that there are no other agreements between the parties that are not expressed in the contract.

Notices. The parties agree on how they will give notice to each other and what they will consider to be delivery of notice.

Time is of the essence. The parties agree that they can amend dates and deadlines only if they both give written approval.

Fax transmission. The parties agree to accept facsimile transmission of the offer, provided receipt is acknowledged and original copies of the contract are subsequently delivered.

Survival. The parties continue to be liable for the truthfulness of representations and warranties after the closing.

Dispute resolution. The parties agree to resolve disputes through arbitration as opposed to court proceedings.

C.L.U.E. Report. CLUE (Comprehensive Loss Underwriting Exchange) is a claims history database used by insurance companies in underwriting or rating insurance policies. A CLUE Home Seller's Disclosure Report shows a five-year insurance loss history for a specific property. Among other things, it describes the types of any losses and the amounts paid. Many home buyers now require sellers to provide a CLUE Report (which only the property owner or an insurer can order) as a contingency appended to the purchase offer. A report showing no insurance loss within the previous five years is an indication that the availability and pricing of homeowner's insurance will not present an obstacle to the purchase transaction.

Addenda. Addenda to the sale contract become binding components of the overall agreement. The most common addendum is the seller's property condition disclosure. Examples of other addenda are:

agency disclosure	asbestos / hazardous materials
liquidated damages	radon disclosure
flood plain disclosure	tenant's lease

OPTION-TO-BUY CONTRACT

Contract requirements
Common provisions
Legal aspects

An option-to-buy is an enforceable contract in which a potential seller, the **optionor**, grants a potential buyer, the **optionee**, the right to purchase a property before a stated time for a stated price and terms. In exchange for the right of option, the optionee pays the optionor valuable consideration.

For example, a buyer wants to purchase a property for $150,000, but needs to sell a boat to raise the down payment. The boat will take two or three months to sell. To accommodate the buyer, the seller offers the buyer an option to purchase the property at any time before midnight on the day that is ninety days from the date of signing the option. The buyer pays the seller $1,000 for the option. If buyer exercises the option, the seller will apply the $1,000 toward the earnest money deposit and subsequent down payment. If the optionee lets the option expire, the seller keeps the $1,000. Both parties agree to the arrangement by completing a sale contract as an addendum to the option, then executing the option agreement itself.

An option-to-buy places the optionee *under no obligation* to purchase the property. However, the seller must perform under the terms of the contract if the buyer exercises the option. An option is thus a *unilateral* agreement. Exercise of the option creates a bilateral sale contract where both parties are bound to perform. An unused option terminates at the expiration date.

An optionee can use an option to prevent the sale of a property to another party while seeking to raise funds for the purchase. A renter with a **lease option-to-buy** can accumulate down payment funds while paying rent to the landlord. For example, an owner may lease a condominium to a tenant with an option to buy. If the tenant takes the option, the landlord agrees to apply $100 of the monthly rent paid prior to the option date toward the purchase price. The tenant pays the landlord the nominal sum of $200 for the option.

Options can also facilitate commercial property acquisition. The option period gives a buyer time to investigate zoning, space planning, building permits, environmental impacts, and other feasibility issues prior to the purchase without losing the property to another party in the meantime.

Contract requirements

To be valid and enforceable, an option-to-buy must:

- include actual, non-refundable consideration

  The option must require the optionee to pay a specific consideration *that is separate from the purchase price*. The consideration cannot be refunded if the option is not exercised. If the option is exercised, the consideration may be applied to the purchase price. If the option is a lease option, portions of the rent may qualify as separate consideration.

- include price and terms of the sale

  The price and terms of the potential transaction must be clearly expressed and cannot change over the option period. It is customary practice for the parties to complete and attach a sale contract to the option as satisfaction of this requirement.

- have an expiration date

  The option must automatically expire at the end of a specific period.

- be in writing

  Since a potential transfer of real estate is involved, most state statutes of fraud require an option to be in writing.

- include a legal description

- meet general contract validity requirements

  The basics include competent parties, the optionor's promise to perform, and the optionor's signature. Note that it is not necessary for the optionee to sign the option.

Common provisions Beyond the required elements, it is common for an option to include provisions covering:

- how to deliver notice of election

  A clause clarifies how to make the option election, exactly when the election must be completed, and any additional terms required such as an earnest money deposit.

- forfeiture terms

  A clause provides that the optionor is entitled to the consideration if the option term expires.

- property and title condition warranties

  The optionor warrants that the property will be maintained in a certain condition, and that title will be marketable and insurable.

- how option consideration will be credited

  A clause states how the optionor will apply the option consideration toward the purchase price.

Legal aspects

Equitable interest. The optionee enjoys an equitable interest in the property because the option creates the right to obtain legal title. However, the option does not in itself convey an interest in real property, only a right to do something governed by contract law.

Recording. An option should be recorded, because the equitable interest it creates can affect the marketability of title.

Assignment. An option-to-buy is assignable unless the contract expressly prohibits assignment.

CONTRACT FOR DEED

Interests and rights
Legal form
Default and recourse
Usage guidelines

A contract for deed is also called a *land contract*, an *installment sale*, a *conditional sales contract,* and an *agreement for deed*. It is a bilateral agreement between a seller, the **vendor,** and a buyer, the **vendee**, in which the vendor defers receipt of some or all of the purchase price of a property over a specified period of time. During the period, the *vendor retains legal title* and the vendee acquires equitable title. The vendee takes possession of the property, makes stipulated payments of principal and interest to the vendor, and otherwise fulfills obligations as the contract requires. At the end of the period, the buyer pays the vendor the full purchase price and the vendor deeds legal title to the vendee.

Like an option, a contract for deed offers a means for a marginally qualified buyer to acquire property. In essence, the seller acts as lender, allowing the buyer to take possession and pay off the purchase price over time. A buyer may thus avoid conventional down payment and income requirements imposed by institutional lenders. During the contract period, the buyer can work to raise the necessary cash to complete the purchase or to qualify for a conventional mortgage.

A contract for deed serves two primary purposes for a seller. First, it facilitates a sale that might otherwise be impossible. Second, it may give the seller certain tax benefits. Since the seller is not liable for capital gains tax until the purchase price is received, the installment sale lowers the seller's tax liability in the year of the sale.

Interests and rights

Vendor's rights and obligations. During the contract period, the seller may:

- mortgage the property
- sell or assign whatever interests he or she owns in the property to another party
- incur judgment liens against the property

The vendor, however, is bound to the obligations imposed by the contract for deed. In particular, the vendor may not breach the obligation to convey legal title to the vendee upon receipt of the total purchase price. In addition, the vendor remains liable for underlying mortgage loans.

Vendee's rights and obligations. During the contract period, the buyer may occupy, use, enjoy, and profit from the property, subject to the provisions of the written agreement. The vendee must make periodic payments of principal and interest and maintain the property. In addition, a vendee may have to pay property taxes and hazard insurance.

Legal form

Like other conveyance contracts, a contract for deed instrument identifies:

- the principal parties
- the property's legal description
- consideration: specifically what the parties promise to do
- the terms of the sale
- obligations for property maintenance
- default and remedies
- signatures and acknowledgment

The contract specifies the vendee's payments, payment deadlines, when the balance of the purchase price is due, and how the property may be used.

Default and recourse

Seller default. If the seller defaults, such as by failing to deliver the deed, the buyer may sue for specific performance, or for cancellation of the agreement and damages.

Buyer default. States differ in the remedies they prescribe for the seller in case of buyer default. Some states consider the default a breach of contract that may be remedied by cancellation, retention of monies received, and eviction. Others provide foreclosure proceedings as a remedy.

Usage guidelines

Many areas have no standardized contract for deed or any form sanctioned by associations and agencies. Therefore, this kind of conveyance presents certain pitfalls for buyer and seller.

In some states, a breach of the contract for deed is remedied under *local contract law* rather than foreclosure law. The buyer may not have the protections of a redemption period or other buyer-protection laws which accompany formal foreclosure proceedings. The vendor might sue the vendee for breach of contract for the slightest infraction of the contract terms.

A second danger for the vendee is that the vendor has the power and the right to encumber the property in ways that may not be desirable for the buyer. For example, the seller could place a home equity loan on the property, then fail to make periodic payments. The bank could then foreclose on the vendor, thus jeopardizing the vendee's eventual purchase.

For the seller, the principal danger is that the buyer acquires possession in exchange for a minimal down payment. A buyer might damage or even vacate the property, leaving the seller to make repairs and retake possession. Further, since the contract is recorded, the seller must also bear the time and expense of clearing the title.

To minimize risk, principal parties in a contract for deed should observe the following guidelines:

- use an attorney to draft the agreement
- adopt the standard forms, if available
- become familiar with how the contract will be enforced
- utilize professional escrow and title services
- record the transaction properly
- be prepared for the possible effect on existing financing

14 Overview Of Conveyance Contracts Snapshot Review

CONTRACT FOR SALE	
Legal characteristics	• binding, bilateral contract for purchase and sale; enforceable; executory, or to be fulfilled; expires upon closing; must be in writing; contain valuable consideration; identify property; be signed by all; be a valid contract
Contract creation	• by unqualified acceptance of an offer; gives buyer equitable title, power to force specific performance
Earnest money escrow	• secures contract validity and buyer's equitable interest; varies in amount; deposit controlled by disinterested party who must act according to escrow instructions
Contract contingencies	• conditions that must be met for the contract to be enforceable
Default	• buyer may sue for cancellation and damages or for specific performance; seller may claim deposit as liquidated damages, or may sue for cancellation, other damages, or for specific performance
SALE CONTRACT PROVISIONS	
Primary provisions	• parties, consideration, legal description, price and terms, loan approval, earnest money, escrow, closing and possession dates, conveyed interest, type of deed, title evidence, property condition warranty, closing costs, damage and destruction, default, broker's representation, commission, seller's representations
Secondary provisions	• inspections, owner's association disclosure, survey, environmental hazards, compliance with laws, due-on-sale, seller financing disclosure, rental property tenant's rights, FHA or VA financing condition, flood plain and flood insurance, condominium assessments, foreign seller withholding, tax-deferred exchange, merger of agreements, notices, time of the essence, fax transmission, survival, dispute resolution, addenda
THE OPTION-TO-BUY CONTRACT	• optionor gives option to optionee; unilateral contract: seller must perform; buyer need not; if option exercised, option becomes bilateral sale contract
Contract requirements	• must include: non-refundable consideration for the option right; price and terms of the sale; option period expiration date; legal description; must be in writing and meet contract validity requirements
Common clause provisions	• special provisions: how to exercise option; terms of option money forfeiture; how option money will be applied to purchase price
Legal aspects	• creates equitable interest; is assignable; should be recorded
CONTRACT FOR DEED	• purchase price is paid over time in installments; seller retains title; buyer takes possession; at end of period, buyer pays balance of price, gets legal title
Interests and rights	• seller may encumber or assign interest; remains liable for underlying mortgage • buyer may use, possess, profit; must make periodic payments, maintain the property, and purchase at end of term
Default and recourse	• if seller defaults, buyer may sue for cancellation and damages or specific performance; seller's default remedies vary by area; may sue for specific performance or damages, or may need to foreclose

15 Real Estate Market Economics

The Market System
Real Estate Market Dynamics

Real estate is an economic product that is subject to economic laws and influences, much like all of the other goods and services in our economic system.

Real estate professionals do not have to be economists; in fact, they are better off leaving complex economic theories to those professing expertise in that often confusing field. However, brokers and agents do need a basic understanding of how our economy works, and particularly, how real estate as an economic product fits into the real estate marketplace.

Understanding the fundamentals of real estate economics enables one to:

- recognize the effect of current economic conditions in the real estate market on transactions, prices, and values
- apply economic principles to estimates of future conditions in the real estate market
- apply economic principles to specific geographical areas and property types in order to assess economic conditions for a particular property and site

These are abilities that will benefit the clients of any real estate professional.

THE MARKET SYSTEM

Supply and demand
Price and value
Productivity and costs
Market interaction
Market equilibrium

Supply and demand

The goal of an economic system is to produce and distribute a *supply* of goods and services to satisfy the *demand* of its constituents. Economic activity therefore centers on the production, distribution and sale of goods and services to meet consumer demand.

Supply is *the quantity of a product or service available for sale, lease, or trade at any given time.*

Demand is *the quantity of a product or service that is desired for purchase, lease, or trade at any given time*.

The interplay of supply and demand is what makes an economy work: consumers demand goods and services; suppliers and sellers produce and distribute the goods and services for a negotiated price.

Exhibit 15.1 Supply, Demand, Price

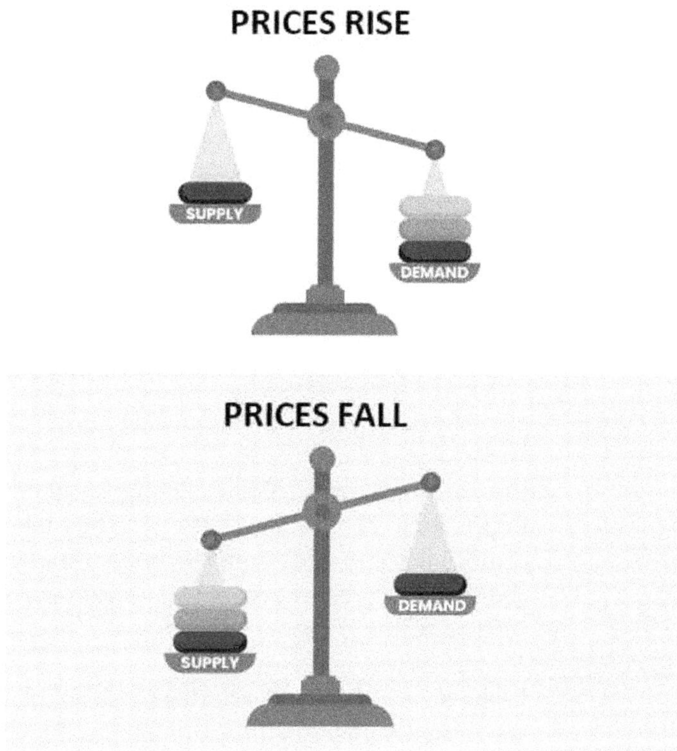

Price and value

The price mechanism. In addition to supply and demand, the other critical component of an economic system is the price mechanism, or simply, price. A **price** is the amount of money or other asset that a buyer has agreed to pay and a seller has agreed to accept to complete the exchange of a good or service. It is a quantification of the value of an item traded.

Price in this context means the final trading price; it is not the preliminary asking price of the seller nor the initial bidding price of the purchaser. Asking and bidding prices are pricing positions in a negotiation between the parties prior to the exchange. The true price of an item or service is the final number the parties agree to.

Value and value determinants. Price is not something of value in itself. It is only a number that *quantifies value*. The economic issue underlying the interplay of supply and demand is, how do trading parties arrive at the value of a good or service as indicated by the price?

Consider consumer demand for air conditioners. Why do air conditioners have value? How do they command the price they do?

The value of something is based on the answers to four questions:

- How much do I desire it?
- How useful is it?
- How scarce is it?
- Am I able to pay for it?

Desire. One determinant of value is how dear the item is to the purchaser. Returning to the air conditioner example, the question becomes "how much do I desire to be cool, dry, and comfortable?" To a person who lives in the tropics, it is safe to say that air conditioning is *more valuable* than a heating system. It is also safe to say the opposite is true for residents of northern Alaska.

Utility. The second determinant of value is the product's *ability to do the job*. Can the air conditioner satisfy my need to stay cool? How cool does it make my house? Does it even work properly? Of course, I won't pay as much if it is old or ineffectual.

Scarcity. The third critical element of value is a product's *availability in relation to demand.* The air conditioner is quite valuable if there are only five units in the entire city and everyone is hot. On the other hand, the value of an air conditioner goes down if there are ten thousand units for sale in a 500-person market.

Purchasing power. A fourth component of value is the *consumer's ability to pay* for the item. If one cannot afford to buy the air conditioner, the value of the air conditioner is diminished, since it is financially out of reach. If all air conditioners are too expensive, consumers are forced to consider alternatives such as ceiling fans.

In the marketplace, the relative presence or absence of the four elements of value is constantly changing due to innumerable factors. Since price is a reflection of the total of all value factors at any time, changes in the underlying factors of value trigger changes in price.

Productivity and costs

To produce a good or service, a supplier incurs **costs**, or those expenses necessary to generate and deliver the item to the market. The essential production costs are the costs of capital, materials, and supplies; labor; management; and overhead.

Costs play an important role in the dynamics of supply, demand, and value. Since a producer has limited resources, it is imperative to maximize the efficiency of the production process and minimize its costs. Moreover, since consumers will pay the lowest possible price for comparable goods and services, the producer must be price-competitive to stay in business. A competitor who can produce an item of similar quality for less will eventually force higher-priced items out of the market.

Cost and price. Consider a producer who is efficient and produces the product or service in demand at the lowest possible cost. Adding to the cost a required profit margin, the producer establishes a minimum price for the item. In this scenario, cost essentially equals price. To the efficient producer, costs and sufficient profit are paramount, since a lower price puts the producer out of business. At that point, the elements of value-- desire, utility, scarcity, and purchasing power-- do not matter: if the consumer wants the item at all, he or she must cover the producer's costs and profit.

In summary, supply, demand, and price interact continuously in a market. Underlying and influencing these forces are the dynamics of value and the costs of producing goods and services.

Market interaction

What is a market? A market is a place where supply and demand encounter one another: suppliers sell or trade their goods and services to demanders, who are consumers and buyers. It is a *transaction arena* where the price mechanism is constantly defining and quantifying the value produced by the relative elements of supply and demand.

Supply, demand and price interrelationships. In a market economy, the primary interactions between supply, demand and price are:

- if supply increases relative to demand, price decreases
- if supply decreases relative to demand, price increases
- if demand increases relative to supply, price increases
- if demand decreases relative to supply, price decreases

These relationships reflect simple common sense: if a valued product becomes increasingly scarce, its value and price go up as consumers compete for the limited supply. If there is an overabundance of a product, the price falls, as demand is largely met. On the other side, if demand for a product or service increases in relation to supply, prices will go up as consumers compete for the popular item. If demand diminishes, the price drops with it.

The inverse of these principles also applies. By tracking a price trend, one can draw conclusions about supply and demand trends:

- if price decreases, demand is declining in relation to supply
- if price increases, demand is increasing in relation to supply

To assess price movements, the supply and demand of a product or service must always be considered together. It is always possible for demand and supply to rise and fall together at the same rate, with no detectable price change resulting.

For example, if demand for bicycles jumps a million units, and manufacturers easily produce the necessary new supply, there may be no increase in price. The price may even go down as manufacturers obtain better prices on the larger quantities of raw materials they now use.

Market equilibrium

Another significant principle of supply/demand/price interaction is **market equilibrium**:

- a market tends toward a state of equilibrium in which supply equals demand, and price, cost, and value are identical

According to this principle, market demand moves to meet supply, and supply moves to meet demand. If there is an extreme shortage of an item for which there is normally a strong demand, suppliers will rush to increase production to close the gap. If inventories of an item are very high, suppliers will stop production until the oversupply has been depleted.

Similarly, if the price of an item far exceeds its cost, new suppliers will enter the market with lower prices. If the price of an item is far less than its perceived value, either consumers will bid up the price or the perceived value will decline.

For example, a new convenience store opens on the edge of a rapidly growing town. The owners know demand will increase, so they anticipate the demand with their increment of supply. Initially, the store creates excess supply, so business is slow. However, as people move in, demand increases, and the store begins to make substantial profits. After some time, other retailers hear that the store is profitable: demand now significantly exceeds supply, and the operator's costs are out of line with values and prices. A second retailer opens a store to equalize the imbalance. The new competitor, an addition of supply, now forces prices, costs, and profits into closer proximity.

The equilibrium time lag. In theory, markets strive for equilibrium, but in reality there is always a time lag between a recognized imbalance and the completion of the market adjustment. Since the underlying determinants of supply and demand (scarcity, desire, utility, purchasing power and costs) are constantly changing, a market is usually in some condition of imbalance.

REAL ESTATE MARKET DYNAMICS

Economic characteristics of real estate
Real estate supply and demand
Market influences on supply and demand

As an economic commodity, real estate is bought, sold, traded, and leased as a product within a real estate market.

Economic characteristics of real estate

Real estate, like other products and services, is:

- subject to the laws of supply and demand
- governed in the market by the price mechanism
- influenced by the producer's costs to bring the product to market
- influenced by the determinants of value: utility, scarcity, desire, and purchasing power

Distinguishing features. In comparison with other economic products and services, real estate has certain unique traits. These include:

- **inherent product value**

  Land is a scarce resource as well as a required factor of production. Like gold and silver, it has both inherent value and utility value.

- **unique appeal of product**

  Since no two parcels of real estate can be alike (each has a different location), every parcel of real property has its own appeal. Likewise, no two parcels of real estate can have exactly the same value, except by coincidence.

- **demand must come to the supply**

  Since real property cannot be moved, real property investors and users must come to the supply. This creates risk, because if demand drops, the supply cannot be transported to a higher demand market.

- **illiquid**

  Real estate is a relatively illiquid economic product, meaning it cannot always be readily sold for cash. Since it is a large, long-term investment that has no exact duplicate, buyers must go through a complex process to evaluate and purchase the right parcel of real estate.

- **slow to respond to changes**

  Real estate is relatively slow to respond to market imbalances. Because new construction is a large-scale, time-consuming process, the market is slow to respond to increases in demand. The market is similarly slow to respond to sharp declines in demand, since the product cannot be moved and sold elsewhere. Instead, owners must wait out slow periods and simply hope for the best.

- **decentralized, local market**

  A real property cannot be shipped to a large, central real estate marketplace. Real estate markets are thus local in nature and highly susceptible to swings in the local economy.

Real estate supply and demand

Supply. In real estate, supply is the *amount of property available* for sale or lease at any given time. Note that supply is generally not the number of properties available, except in the case of residential real estate. The units of supply used to quantify the amount of property available differ for different categories of property. These supply units, by property type, are:

- residential: dwelling units
- commercial and industrial: square feet
- agricultural: acreage

Factors influencing supply. In addition to the influences of demand and the underlying determinants of value, real estate supply responds to

- development costs, particularly labor
- availability of financing
- investment returns
- a community's master plan
- government police powers and regulation

Demand. Real estate demand is the amount of property buyers and tenants wish to acquire by purchase, lease or trade at any given time. Units of demand, by property classification, are:

- residential: households
- commercial and industrial: square feet
- agricultural: acreage

The unit of residential demand is the household, which is an individual or family who would occupy a dwelling unit. Residential demand can be further broken down into demand to lease versus buy, and demand for single family homes versus apartments.

Residential demand can be very difficult to quantify. One measure is the number of buyers employing agents to locate property. Another measure is the net population change in an area, plus families that attempted to move in but could not.

The unit of commercial (retail and office) and industrial real estate demand is the square foot, further broken down into demand for leased space versus purchased space. In most instances, the area demanded refers to the improved area rather than the total lot area.

Demand for office and industrial real estate is calculated by identifying employment growth or shrinkage in a market, then multiplying the employment change times the average area of floor space a typical employee uses. For example, consider an office property market where employment in the community increases by 500 employees. If each employee uses an average of 120 square feet, the increased demand for space is 60,000 square feet.

Factors affecting demand. The demand for particular types of real estate relates to the specific concerns of users. These concerns revolve around the components of value: desire, utility, scarcity, and purchasing power.

Residential users are concerned with:

- quality of life
- neighborhood quality
- convenience and access to services and other facilities
- dwelling amenities in relation to household size, lifestyle, and costs

Retail users are concerned with:

- sufficient trade area population and income
- the level of trade area competition
- sales volume per square foot of rented area
- consumer spending patterns
- growth patterns in the trade area

Office users are concerned with:

- costs of occupancy to the business
- efficiency of the building and the suite in accommodating the business's functions
- accessibility by employees and suppliers
- matching building quality to the image and function of the business

Industrial users are concerned with:

- functionality
- the availability and proximity of the labor pool
- compliance with environmental regulations
- permissible zoning
- health and safety of the workers
- access to suppliers and distribution channels

Base employment and total employment. The engine that drives demand for real estate of all types in a market is employment-- *base* employment and *total* employment.

Exhibit 15.2 Basis of Real Estate Demand

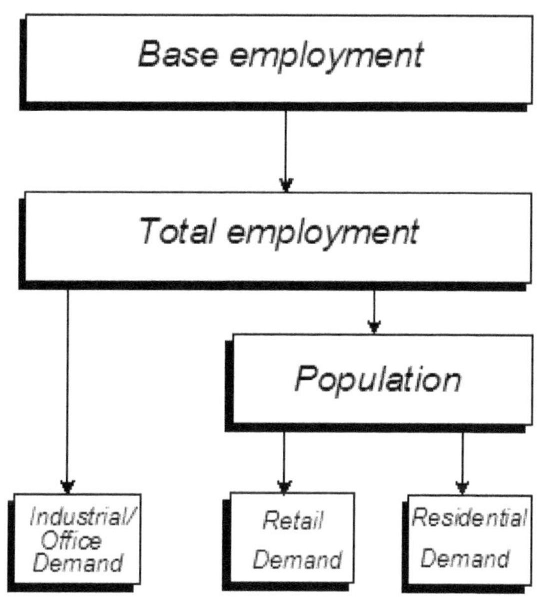

Base employment is the number of persons employed in the businesses that represent the economic foundation of the area. For example, the auto industry has traditionally been the primary base employer of the Detroit metropolitan area.

Base industries lead to the rise of supporting and secondary industries in the market. If the auto industry is the base, auto parts manufacturers and assembly industries will develop to support the auto manufacturing plants. In addition, service businesses emerge to support the many needs of the local population engaged in primary and secondary employment.

Thus, base employment feeds total employment. Total employment in a market includes base, secondary, and support industries. Total employment creates a demand for a labor force. From total employment derives demand for industrial and office space on the one hand; on the other hand, as employment grows, so grows the population, leading to the demand for housing and for retail support. In addition to creating demand for real estate, employment creates the purchasing power necessary for households to acquire dwellings and retail products.

Without employment, a real estate market evaporates, as there is no demand for commercial or industrial facilities, nor is there demand for retail services or housing. The best example of this phenomenon is a gold rush boom town: as soon as the gold runs out, there is no more mining. Without mining employment, everyone moves away and the town becomes a ghost town.

Supply and demand interaction. Real estate supply and demand, like supply and demand for other economic products, interact in the marketplace to produce *price movements.*

Exhibit 15.3 Real Estate Supply-Demand Cycle

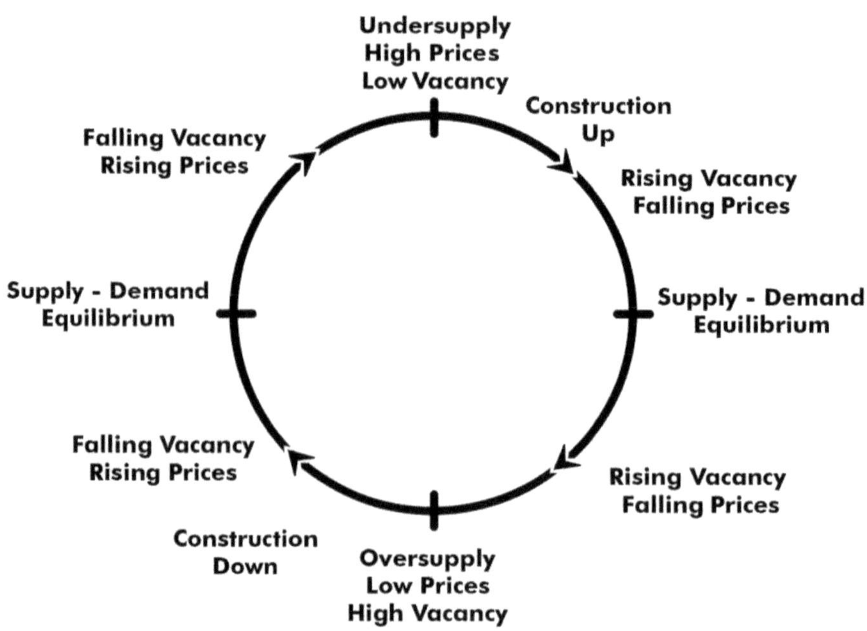

As the exhibit illustrates, prices, construction, and vacancy move up and down in the cycle. Construction represents the addition of new supply. **Vacancy** is the amount of total real estate inventory of a certain type that is unoccupied at a given time. **Absorption** is the amount of available property that becomes occupied over a period of time.

Taking the point of undersupply, or high demand, as a starting point in the cycle, vacancy is low and prices are high. This situation stimulates suppliers to construct additional housing or commercial space. New construction, by adding supply, causes vacancy to rise and prices to fall until supply-demand equilibrium results. As more new space is added, supply begins to outstrip demand, vacancy continues to rise, and prices continue to fall. At the bottom of the cycle, prices and vacancy are at unacceptable levels, and construction ceases. The market "dies" until excess supply can be absorbed. The absorption process continues through the equilibrium point until price and vacancy conditions are sufficiently attractive to encourage renewed construction. Then the cycle repeats.

Market influences On supply and demand

Numerous factors in a market influence the real estate cycle to speed up or slow down. These influences can be local or national, and from the public or private economic sector.

Local market influences. Since the real estate market is local by definition, local factors weigh heavily in local real estate market conditions. Among these are:

- cost of financing
- availability of developable land
- construction costs
- capacity of the municipality's infrastructure to handle growth
- governmental regulation and police powers
- changes in the economic base
- in- and out-migrations of major employers

National trends. Regional and national economic forces influence the local real estate market in the form of:

- changes in money supply
- inflation
- national economic cycles

In recent years international economic trends have increasingly influenced local real estate markets, particularly in border states, large metropolitan areas, and in markets where the economic base is tied to foreign trade. In these instances, currency fluctuations have significant impact on the local economy.

Governmental influences. Governments at every level exert significant influence over local real estate markets. The primary forms of government influence are:

- local zoning power
- local control and permitting of new development
- local taxing power

- federal influence on interest rates
- environmental legislation and regulations

A good example of government influence over the local real estate market is a city government's power to declare a moratorium on new construction, regardless of demand. Such officially declared stoppages may occur because of water or power shortages, insufficiency of thoroughfares, or incompatibility with the master plan.

15 Real Estate Market Economics Snapshot Review

THE MARKET SYSTEM

Supply and demand

- supply: goods or services available for sale, lease, or trade
- demand: goods or services desired for purchase, lease, or trade

Price and value

- price mechanism: quantified value of an exchange
- value components: desire; utility; scarcity; purchasing power

Productivity and costs

- cost plus profit equals minimum price; production cost possible component of value

Market interaction

- market: transaction arena where suppliers and demanders define value through the price mechanism
- if supply increases relative to demand, price decreases; if demand increases relative to supply, price increases

Market equilibrium

- supply and demand tend toward balance where they are equal
- market equilibrium: price, cost, value theoretically the same; market imbalances are caused by changes in supply or demand

REAL ESTATE MARKET DYNAMICS

Economic characteristics of real estate

- governed by supply, demand, price, costs, value components, government influence
- inherent value; unique appeal; immovable supply; illiquid; slow response to cycles; decentralized market

Real estate supply and demand

- supply: property available for sale or lease; measured in dwelling units, square feet, acres; influenced by costs, finance, returns, government regulation
- demand: property buyers and tenants wish to acquire; measured in households, square feet, acres; influences: residential-- quality, amenities, price convenience; retail-trade area, sales, competition, site access, visibility; growth patterns; office-efficiency, costs, functionality; industrial-- functionality, labor, regulatory compliance, access to labor, supplies, distribution channels
- base employment, total employment, population determine overall demand
- if employment and population increase, demand and prices increase; if they decrease, the opposite occurs
- supply-demand indicators are price, vacancy, and absorption; vacancy is existing, unoccupied supply; absorption is the "filling up" of vacancy
- real estate supply-demand cycle: undersupply > accelerated construction adds supply > equilibrium > construction adds more supply > oversupply > construction stops > equilibrium > demand absorbs supply

Market influences on supply and demand

- local economic factors; national economic trends in money supply, inflation; government regulation at all levels

16 Appraising and Estimating Market Value

Real Estate Value
Appraising Market Value
The Sales Comparison Approach
The Cost Approach
The Income Capitalization Approach
Regulation of Appraisal Practice

REAL ESTATE VALUE

Foundations of real estate value
Types of value

The valuation of real property is one of the most fundamental activities in the real estate business. Its role is particularly critical in the transfer of real property, since the value of a parcel establishes the general price range for the principal parties to negotiate.

Real estate value in general is *the present monetary worth of benefits arising from the ownership of real estate*. The primary benefits that contribute to real estate value are:

- income
- appreciation
- use
- tax benefits

Ownership of real estate produces income when there are leases on the land, the improvements, or on air, surface, or subsurface rights. Such income is part of real estate value because an investor will pay money to buy the income stream generated by ownership of the property.

Appreciation is an increase in the market value of a parcel of land over time, usually resulting from a general rise in sale prices of real estate throughout a market area. Such an increase, whether actual or projected, is another investment benefit that contributes to real estate value.

The way a property is used -- whether residential, commercial, agricultural, recreational, etc. -- in large part determines the property's value. Each kind of use has its own benefits.

Depending on current tax law, tax benefits from ownership of a property may take the form of preferred treatment of capital gain, tax losses, depreciation, and deferrals of tax liability. These tax benefits contribute to the income and potential sale price of a property.

Foundations of real estate value

A number of economic forces interact in the marketplace to contribute to real estate value. Among the most recognized of these principles are those listed below.

Exhibit 16.1 Economic Principles Underlying Real Estate Value

supply and demand	change
utility transferability	highest and best use
anticipation substitution	conformity
contribution	progression and regression
	assemblage
	subdivision

Supply and demand. The availability of certain properties interacts with the strength of the demand for those properties to establish prices. When demand for properties exceeds supply, a condition of scarcity exists, and real estate values rise. When supply exceeds demand, a condition of surplus exists, and real estate values decline. When supply and demand are generally equivalent, the market is considered to be in balance, and real estate values stabilize.

Utility. The fact that a property has a use in a certain marketplace contributes to the demand for it. Use is not the same as function. For instance, a swampy area may have an ecological function as a wetland, but it may have no economic utility if it cannot be put to some use that people in the marketplace are willing to pay for.

Transferability. How readily or easily title or rights to real estate can be transferred affects the property's value. Property that is encumbered has a value impairment since buyers do not want unmarketable title. Similarly, property that cannot be transferred due to disputes among owners may cause the value to decline, because the investment is wholly illiquid until the disputes are resolved.

Anticipation. The benefits a buyer *expects to derive from a property over a holding period* influence what the buyer is willing to pay for it. For example, if an investor anticipates an annual rental income from a leased property to be one million dollars, this expected sum has a direct bearing on what the investor will pay for the property.

Substitution. According to the principle of substitution, a buyer will *pay no more for a property than the buyer would have to pay for an equally desirable and available substitute property*. For example, if three houses for sale are essentially similar in size, quality and location, a potential buyer is unlikely to choose the one that is priced significantly higher than the other two.

Contribution. The principal of contribution focuses on the degree to which a particular improvement affects market value of the overall property. In essence, the contribution of the improvement is *equal to the change in market value that the addition of the improvement causes*. For example, adding a bathroom to a house may contribute an additional $15,000 to the appraised value. Thus the contribution of the bathroom is $15,000. Note that an improvement's contribution to value has little to do with the improvement's cost. The foregoing bathroom may have cost $5,000 or $20,000. Contribution is what the market recognizes as the change in value, not what an item cost. If continuous improvements are added to a property, it is possible that, at some point, the cost of adding improvements to a property no longer contributes a corresponding increase in the value of the property. When this occurs, the property suffers from *diminishing marginal return,* where the costs to improve exceed contribution.

Change. Market conditions are in a state of flux over time, just as the condition of a property itself changes. These fluctuations and changes will affect the benefits that can arise from the property, and should be reflected in an estimate of the property's value. For example, the construction of a neighborhood shopping center in the vicinity of a certain house may increase the desirability of the house's location, and hence, its value.

Highest and best use. This principle holds that there is, theoretically, a single use for a property that produces the greatest income and return. A property achieves its maximum value when it is put to this use. If the actual use is not the highest and best use, the value of the property is correspondingly less than optimal. Technically, highest and best use must be legally permissible, physically possible, financially feasible, and maximally productive.

For example, a property with an old house on it may not be in its highest and best use if it is surrounded by retail properties. If zoning permits the property to be converted to a retail use, its highest and best use may well be retail rather than residential.

Conformity. This principle holds that a property's maximal value is attained when its form and use are in tune with surrounding properties and uses. For example, a two-bedroom, one-bathroom house surrounded by four-bedroom, three-bathroom homes may derive maximal value from a room addition.

Progression and regression. The value of a property influences, and is influenced by, the values of neighboring properties. If a property is surrounded by properties with higher values, its value will tend to rise (progression); if it is surrounded by properties with lower values, its value will tend to fall (regression).

Assemblage. Assemblage, or the conjoining of adjacent properties, sometimes creates a combined value that is greater than the values of the unassembled properties. The excess value created by assemblage is called **plottage value.**

Subdivision. The division of a single property into smaller properties can also result in a higher total value. For instance, a one-acre suburban site appraised at $50,000 may be subdivided into four quarter-acre lots worth $30,000 each. This principle contributes significantly to the financial feasibility of subdivision development.

Types of value

The purpose of an appraisal influences an estimate of the value of a parcel of real estate. This is because there are different types of value related to different appraisal purposes. Some of the possibilities are listed below.

Exhibit 16.2 Types of Real Estate Value

market	reversionary
reproduction	appraised
replacement	rental
salvage	leasehold
plottage	insured
assessed	book
condemned	mortgage

Market value. Market value is an estimate of the price at which a property will sell at a particular time. This type of value is the one generally sought in appraisals and used in brokers' estimates of value.

Reproduction value. Reproduction value is the value based on the cost of constructing a precise duplicate of the subject property's improvements, assuming current construction costs.

Replacement value. Replacement value is the value based on the cost of constructing a functional equivalent of the subject property's improvements, assuming current construction costs.

Salvage value. Salvage value refers to the nominal value of a property that has reached the end of its economic life. Salvage value is also an estimate of the price at which a structure will sell if it is dismantled and moved.

Plottage value. Plottage value is an estimate of the value that the process of assemblage adds to the combined values of the assembled properties.

Assessed value. Assessed value is the value of a property as estimated by a taxing authority as the basis for ad valorem taxation.

Condemned value. Condemned value is the value set by a county or municipal authority for a property which may be taken by eminent domain.

Depreciated value. Depreciated value is a value established by subtracting accumulated depreciation from the purchase price of a property.

Reversionary value. Reversionary value is the estimated selling price of a property at some time in the future. This value is used most commonly in a proforma investment analysis where, at the end of a holding period, the property is sold and the investor's capital reverts to the investor.

Appraised value. Appraised value is an appraiser's opinion of a property's value.

Rental value. Rental value is an estimate of the rental rate a property can command for a specific period of time.

Leasehold value. Leasehold value is an estimate of the market value of a lessee's interest in a property.

Insured value. Insured value is the face amount a casualty or hazard insurance policy will pay in case a property is rendered unusable.

Book value. Book value is the value of the property as carried on the accounts of the owner. The value is generally equal to the acquisition price plus capital improvements minus accumulated depreciation.

Mortgage value. Mortgage value is the value of the property as collateral for a loan.

APPRAISING MARKET VALUE

Market value
The appraisal and its uses
Measuring living area
Steps in the appraisal process

Market value

Market value is an opinion of the price that a willing seller and willing buyer would probably agree on for a property at a given time if:

- the transaction is a cash transaction
- the property is exposed on the open market for a reasonable period
- buyer and seller have full information about market conditions and about potential uses
- there is no abnormal pressure on either party to complete the transaction
- buyer and seller are not related (it is an "arm's length" transaction)
- title is marketable and conveyable by the seller
- the price is a "normal consideration," that is, it does not include hidden influences such as special financing deals, concessions, terms, services, fees, credits, costs, or other types of consideration.

Another way of describing market value is that it is the highest price that a buyer would pay and the lowest price that the seller would accept for the property.

The market price, as opposed to market value, is what a property actually sells for. Market price should theoretically be the same as market value if all the conditions essential for market value were present. Market price, however, may not reflect the analysis of comparables and of investment value that an estimate of market value includes.

The appraisal and its uses

While most appraisals seek to estimate market value, any of the types of value described earlier may be the objective of an appraisal. An appraisal is distinguished from other estimates of value in that it is an opinion of value supported by data and performed by a professional, disinterested third party. Appraisers acting in a professional capacity are also regulated by state laws and bound to standards set by the appraisal industry.

Broker's opinion of value. A broker's opinion of value may resemble an appraisal, but it differs from an appraisal in that it is not necessarily performed by a disinterested third party or licensed professional and it generally uses only a limited form of one of the three appraisal approaches. In addition, the opinion is not subject to regulation, nor does it follow any particular professional standards.

Uses. The appraisal itself is used in real estate decision-making to estimate one or more types of value, depending on the kind of decision to be made. Appraisals may be ordered and used by mortgage lenders, government agencies, investors, utilities companies, and real estate buyers and sellers.

An appraisal helps in setting selling prices and rental rates, determining the level of insurance coverage, establishing investment values, and establishing the value of the real estate as collateral for a loan.

Appraisals may be developed and reported in a narrative format or on a prescribed form with attachments. The most commonly used form for residential appraisals is the "Uniform Residential Appraisal Report" (URAR) promoted by the Federal National Mortgage Association (FNMA) and Federal Home Loan Mortgage Corporation (FHLMC) (known as Fannie Mae and Freddie Mac, respectively).

Measuring living area

The concept of living area is fundamental to estimating residential property value, since a subject's living area is a major component of its desirability and market value. But what is living area, and how is it measured? Standards differ from state to state.

ANSI and Fannie Mae standards. ANSI (American National Standards Institute) and Fannie Mae are the two most prominent organizations which originate and propound modern measuring standards in national real estate practice. Current living area measurement standards can be found in ANSI and Fannie Mae literature. The following guidelines are general and not intended to be rigid or comprehensive. Practitioners must always be aware of and follow local measurement standards..

The principal ANSI and Fannie Mae standards for measuring gross living area (GLA) include the following. These standards mainly apply to single-family residential properties.

1. **Gross living area** is based on the dimensions of all rooms "above grade" as measured from the exterior walls of the premises, including stairwells but excluding "open areas." Space should be measured to the inch or to 1/10th of a foot and living areas calculated and totaled.
2. **Above grade** is defined as above the surface of the ground. Living area below-grade (one foot or more) must be counted as basement area – thus not as 100% living area.
3. **Minimum ceiling height** for living area is 7 feet. In two-story properties (or more) with sloped ceilings, at least 50% of the ceiling area must have a height of 7 feet or more.
4. **Finished space:** To be counted in GLA footage, a space must be finished, i.e., have a floor covering and a ceiling. Entry areas may be counted, but seasonal porches are excluded.

5. **Under heat and attached:** Countable living area must be heated. In addition, it must be attached to the main house itself. For example, an unattached outbuilding cannot be counted in the total.
6. **Attics and basements**: Partially finished or only partially heated areas may not be counted as 100% GLA footage. Since these standards can vary widely from state to state, practitioners should ascertain the local standards that apply.
7. **Garage areas** are not fully countable if they are unattached, or attached but not heated. However, they may meet a local standard if fully heated, finished and improved for other household uses.
8. **Stairs and closets**: Both these improvement areas are generally fully countable in GLA.

Ultimately, the most accurate measurement of living areas relies heavily on adherence to local standards and practices, and to practices dictated by mortgage underwriters.

Steps in the appraisal process

A systematic procedure enables an appraiser to collect, organize and analyze the necessary data to produce an appraisal report.

Exhibit 16.3 Steps in the Appraisal Process

1. Identify the purpose
2. Assimilate relevant data
3. Assess the highest and best use
4. Estimate the value of the land
5. Apply the three approaches to estimating value
6. Reconcile the values from the approaches
7. Compile the report

Purpose. The first step in the process is to define the appraisal problem and the purpose of the appraisal. This involves

- identifying the subject property by legal description
- specifying the interest to be appraised
- specifying the purpose of the appraisal, for example, to identify market value for a purchase, identify rental levels, or establish a value as collateral for a loan
- specifying the date for which the appraisal is valid
- identifying the type of value to be estimated

Data. The second step is to collect, organize and analyze relevant data about the subject property. Information relevant to the property includes notes and drawings from physical inspection of the subject, public tax and title records, and reproduction costs. Relevant information about the market includes environmental, demographic, and economic reports concerning the neighborhood, community, and region.

Highest and best use. The third step is to analyze market conditions to identify the most profitable use for the subject property. This use may or may not be the existing use.

Land value. The fourth step is to estimate the land value of the subject. An appraiser does this by comparing the subject site, but not its buildings, with similar sites in the area, and making adjustments for significant differences.

Three approaches. The fifth step is to apply the three basic approaches to value to the subject: *the sales comparison approach, the cost approach, and the income capitalization approach*. Using multiple methods serves to guard against errors and to set a range of values for the final estimate.

Reconciliation. The sixth step is to reconcile the value estimates produced by the three approaches to value into a final value estimate. To do this, an appraiser must

- weigh the appropriateness of a particular approach to the type of property being appraised
- take into account the quality and quantity of data obtained in each method

Report. The final step is to present the estimate of value in the format requested by the client.

THE SALES COMPARISON APPROACH

Steps in the approach
Identifying comparables
Adjusting comparables
Weighting comparables
Broker's comparative market analysis

The sales comparison approach, also known as the *market data approach*, is used for almost all properties. It also serves as the basis for a broker's opinion of value. It is based on the principle of substitution-- that a buyer will pay no more for the subject property than would be sufficient to purchase a comparable property-- and contribution-- that specific characteristics add value to a property.

The sales comparison approach is widely used because it takes into account the subject property's specific amenities in relation to competing properties. In addition, because of the currency of its data, the approach incorporates present market realities.

The sales comparison approach is limited in that every property is unique. As a result, it is difficult to find good comparables, especially for special-purpose properties. In addition, the market must be active; otherwise, sale prices lack currency and reliability.

Steps in the approach

The sales comparison approach consists of comparing sale prices of recently sold properties that are comparable with the subject and making dollar adjustments to the price of each comparable to account for competitive differences with the subject. After identifying the adjusted value of each comparable, the appraiser weights the reliability of each comparable and the factors underlying how the adjustments were made. The weighting yields a final value range based on the most reliable factors in the analysis.

Exhibit 16.4 Steps in the Sales Comparison Approach

1. Identify comparable sales.
2. Compare comparables to the subject and make adjustments to comparables.
3. Weight values indicated by adjusted comparables for the final value estimate of the subject.

Identifying comparables

To qualify as a comparable, a property must:

- resemble the subject in size, shape, design, utility and location
- have sold recently, generally within six months of the appraisal
- have sold in an arm's-length transaction

An appraiser considers three to six comparables, and usually includes at least three in the appraisal report.

Appraisers have specific guidelines within the foregoing criteria for selecting comparables, many of which are set by secondary market organizations such as FNMA. For example, to qualify as a comparable for a mortgage loan appraisal, a property might have to be located within one mile of the subject. Or perhaps the size of the comparable must be within a certain percentage of improved area in relation to the subject.

The time-of-sale criterion is important because transactions that occurred too far in the past will not reflect appreciation or recent changes in market conditions.

An arm's length sale involves objective, disinterested parties who are presumed to have negotiated a market price for the property. If the sale of a house occurred between a father and a daughter, for example, one might assume that the transaction did not reflect market value.

Principal sources of data for generating the sales comparison are tax records, title records, and the local multiple listing service.

Adjusting comparables

The appraiser adjusts the sale prices of the comparables to account for competitive differences with the subject property. Note that the sale prices of the comparables are known, while the value and price of the subject are not. Therefore, adjustments can be made *only to the comparables' prices, not to the subject's*. Adjustments are made to the comparables in the form of a value deduction or a value addition.

Adding or deducting value. If the comparable is *better* than the subject in some characteristic, an amount is *deducted* from the sale price of the comparable. This neutralizes the comparable's competitive advantage in an adjustment category.

For example, a comparable has a swimming pool and the subject does not. To equalize the difference, the appraiser deducts an amount, say $6,000, from the sale price of the comparable. Note that the adjustment reflects the contribution of the swimming pool to market value. The adjustment amount is not the cost of the pool or its depreciated value.

If the comparable is *inferior* to the subject in some characteristic, an amount is *added* to the price of the comparable. This adjustment equalizes the subject's competitive advantage in this area.

Adjustment criteria. The principal factors for comparison and adjustment are *time of sale, location, physical characteristics, and transaction characteristics.*

- **time of sale**

  An adjustment may be made if market conditions, market prices, or financing availability have changed significantly since the date of the comparable's sale. Most often, this adjustment is to account for appreciation.

- **location**

  An adjustment may be made if there are differences between the comparable's location and the subject's, including neighborhood desirability and appearance, zoning restrictions, and general price levels.

- **physical characteristics**

  Adjustments may be made for marketable differences between the comparable's and subject's lot size, square feet of livable area (or other appropriate measure for the property type), number of rooms, layout, age, condition, construction type and quality, landscaping, and special amenities.

- **transaction characteristics**

  An adjustment may be made for such differences as mortgage loan terms, mortgage assumability, and owner financing.

Weighting comparables

Adding and subtracting the appropriate adjustments to the sale price of each comparable results in an adjusted price for the comparables that indicates the value of the subject. The last step in the approach is to perform a weighted analysis of the indicated values of each comparable. The appraiser, in other words, must identify which comparable values are more indicative of the subject and which are less indicative.

An appraiser primarily relies on experience and judgment to weight comparables. There is no formula for selecting a value from within the range of all comparables analyzed. However, there are three quantitative guidelines: the total number of adjustments; the amount of a single adjustment; and the net value change of all adjustments.

As a rule, *the fewer the total number of adjustments, the smaller the adjustment amounts, and the less the total adjustment amount, the more reliable the comparable.*

Number of adjustments. In terms of total adjustments, the comparable with the fewest adjustments tends to be most similar to the subject, hence the best indicator of value. If a comparable requires excessive adjustments, it is increasingly less reliable as an indicator of value. The underlying rationale is that there is a margin of error involved in making any adjustment. Whenever a number of adjustments must be made, the margin of error compounds. By the time six or seven adjustments are made, the margin becomes significant, and the reliability of the final value estimate is greatly reduced.

Single adjustment amounts. The dollar amount of an adjustment represents the variance between the subject and the comparable for a given item. If a large adjustment is called for, the comparable becomes less of an indicator of value. The smaller the adjustment, the better the comparable is as an indicator of value. If an appraisal is performed for mortgage qualification, the appraiser may be restricted from making adjustments in excess of a certain amount, for example, anything in excess of 10-15% of the sale price of the comparable. If such an adjustment would be necessary, the property is no longer considered comparable.

Total net adjustment amount. The third reliability factor in weighting comparables is the total net value change of all adjustments added together. If a comparable's total adjustments alter the indicated value only slightly, the comparable is a good indicator of value. If total adjustments create a large dollar amount between the sale price and the adjusted value, the comparable is a poorer indicator of value. Fannie Mae, for instance, will not accept the use of a comparable where total net adjustments are in excess of 15% of the sale price.

For example, an appraiser is considering a property that sold for $500,000 as a comparable. After all adjustments are made, the indicated value of the comparable is $605,000, a 21% difference in the comparable's sale price. This property, if allowed at all, would be a weak indicator of value.

Broker's comparative market analysis

A broker or salesperson who is attempting to establish a listing price or range of prices for a property uses a scaled-down version of the appraiser's sales comparison approach called a comparative market analysis, or CMA (also called a competitive market analysis). While the CMA serves a useful purpose in setting general price ranges, brokers and agents need to exercise caution in presenting a CMA as an appraisal, which it is not. Two important distinctions between the two are objectivity and comprehensiveness.

First, the broker is not unbiased: he or she is motivated by the desire to obtain a listing, which can lead one to distort the estimated price. Secondly, the broker's CMA is not comprehensive: the broker does not usually consider the full range of data about market conditions and comparable sales that the appraiser must consider and document. Therefore, the broker's opinion will be less reliable than the appraiser's.

The following exhibit illustrates the sales comparison approach. An appraiser is estimating market value for a certain house. Four comparables are adjusted to find an indicated value for the subject. The grid which follows the property and market data shows the appraiser's adjustments for the differences between the four comparables and the subject.

For practice with the sales comparison approach, see the exercise on page 412 in the math chapter.

Exhibit 16.5 Sales Comparison Approach Illustration

Data

Subject property:	8 rooms-- 3 bedrooms, two baths, kitchen, living room, family room; 2,000 square feet of gross living area; 2-car attached garage; landscaping is good. Construction is frame with aluminum siding.
Comparable A:	Sold for 1,000,000 within previous month; conventional financing at current rates; located in subject's neighborhood with similar locational advantages; house approximately same age as subject; lot size smaller than subject; view similar to subject; design less appealing than subject's; construction similar to subject; condition similar to subject; 7 rooms-- two bedrooms, one bath; 1,900 square feet of gross living area; 2-car attached garage; landscaping similar to subject.
Comparable B:	Sold for 1,200,000 within previous month; conventional financing at current rates; located in subject's neighborhood with similar locational advantages; house six years newer than subject; lot size smaller than subject; view is better than the subject's; design is more appealing than subject's; construction (brick and frame) better than subject's; better condition than subject; 10 rooms-four bedrooms, three baths; 2,300 square feet of gross living area; 2-car attached garage; landscaping similar to subject.
Comparable C:	Sold for 1,150,000 within previous month; conventional financing at current rates; located in subject's neighborhood with similar locational advantages; house five years older than subject; lot size larger than subject; view similar to subject; design and appeal similar to subject's; construction similar to subject; condition similar to subject; 8 rooms-- three bedrooms, two baths; 2,000 square feet of gross living area; 2-car attached garage; landscaping similar to subject.
Comparable D:	Sold for 1,090,000 within previous month; conventional financing at current rates; located in a neighborhood close to subject's, but more desirable than subject's; house approximately same age as subject; lot size same as subject; view similar to subject; design less appealing than subject's; construction (frame) poorer than subject's; poorer condition than subject; 7 rooms-- two bedrooms, one and one half baths; 1,900 square feet of gross living area; 2-car attached garage; landscaping similar to subject.

Exhibit 16.5, cont. Sales Comparison Approach Illustration

Adjustments

	Subject	A	B	C	D
Sale price		1,000,000	1,200,000	1,150,000	1,090,000
Financing terms		standard	standard	standard	standard
Sale date	NOW	equal	equal	equal	equal
Location		equal	equal	equal	-20,000
Age		equal	-12,000	+10,000	equal
Lot size		+10,000	+10,000	-10,000	equal
Site/view		equal	-10,000	equal	equal
Design/appeal		+10,000	-12,000	equal	+5,000
Construction quality	good	equal	-30,000	equal	+10,000
Condition	good	equal	-50,000	equal	+20,000
No. of rooms	8				
No. of bedrooms	3	+5,000	-5,000	equal	+5,000
No. of baths	2	+10,000	-15,000	equal	+5,000
Gross living area	2,000	+10,000	-20,000	equal	+10,000
Other space					
Garage	2 car/attd.	equal	equal	equal	equal
Other improvements					
Landscaping	good	equal	equal	equal	equal
Net adjustments		+45,000	-144,000	0	+35,000
Indicated value	1,120,000	1,045,000	1,056,000	1,150,000	1,125,000

For comparable A, the appraiser has made additions to the lot value, design, number of bedrooms and baths, and for gross living area. This accounts for the comparable's *deficiencies* in these areas relative to the subject. A total of five adjustments amount to $45,000, or 4.5% of the purchase price.

For comparable B, the appraiser has deducted values for age, site, design, construction quality, condition, bedrooms, baths, and living area. This accounts for the comparable's superior qualities relative to the subject. The only addition is the lot size, since the subject's is larger. A total of nine adjustments amount to $144,000, or 12% of the sale price.

For comparable C, the appraiser has added value for the age and deducted value for the lot size. The two adjustments offset one another for a net adjustment of zero.

For comparable D, one deduction has been made for the comparable's superior location. This is offset by six additions reflecting the various areas where the comparable is inferior to the subject. A total of seven adjustments amount to $35,000, or 3.2% of the sale price.

In view of all adjusted comparables, the appraiser developed a final indication of value of $1,120,000 for the subject. Underlying this conclusion is the fact that Comparable C, since it only has two minor adjustments which offset each other, it is by far the best indicator of value. Comparable D might be the second best indicator, since the net adjustments are very close to the sale price. Comparable A might be the third best indicator, since it has the second fewest number of total adjustments. Comparable B is the least reliable indicator, since there are numerous adjustments, three of which are of a significant amount. In addition, Comparable B is questionable altogether as a comparable, since total adjustments alter the sale price by 12%.

THE COST APPROACH

Types of cost appraised
Depreciation
Steps in the approach

The cost approach is most often used for recently built properties where the actual costs of development and construction are known. It is also used for special-purpose buildings which cannot be valued by the other methods because of lack of comparable sales or income data.

The strengths of the cost approach are that it:

- provides an upper limit for the subject's value based on the undepreciated cost of reproducing the improvements
- is very accurate for a property with new improvements which are the highest and best use of the property.

The limitations of the cost approach are that:

- the cost to create improvements is not necessarily the same as market value
- depreciation is difficult to measure, especially for older buildings

Types of cost appraised

The cost approach generally aims to estimate either the *reproduction cost* or the *replacement cost* of the subject property.

Reproduction cost is the cost of constructing, at current prices, a *precise duplicate* of the subject improvements. **Replacement cost** is the cost of constructing, at current prices and using current materials and methods, a *functional equivalent* of the subject improvements.

Replacement cost is used primarily for appraising older structures, since it is impractical to consider reproducing outmoded features and materials. However, reproduction cost is preferable whenever possible because it facilitates the calculation of depreciation on a structure.

Depreciation

A cornerstone of the cost approach is the concept of depreciation. Depreciation is the *loss of value in an improvement over time*. Since land is assumed to retain its value indefinitely, depreciation only applies to the improved portion of real property. The loss of an improvement's value can come from any cause, such as deterioration, obsolescence, or changes in the neighborhood. The sum of depreciation from all causes is accrued depreciation.

An appraiser considers depreciation as having three causes: physical deterioration, functional obsolescence, and economic obsolescence.

Physical deterioration. Physical deterioration is wear and tear from use, decay, and structural deterioration. Such deterioration may be either *curable or incurable*.

Curable deterioration occurs when the costs of repair of the item are less than or equal to the resulting increase in the property's value. For example, if a paint job costs $6,000, and the resulting value increase is $8,000, the deterioration is considered curable. Incurable deterioration is the opposite: the repair will cost more than can be recovered by its contribution to the value of the building. For example, if the foregoing paint job cost $10,000, the deterioration would be considered incurable.

Functional obsolescence. Functional obsolescence occurs when a property has outmoded physical or design features which are no longer desirable to current users. If the obsolescence is curable, the cost of replacing or redesigning the outmoded feature would be offset by the contribution to overall value, for example, a lack of central air conditioning. If the functional obsolescence is incurable, the cost of the cure would exceed the contribution to overall value, for example, a floor layout with a bad traffic pattern that would cost three times as much as the ending contribution to value.

Economic obsolescence. Economic (or **external**) obsolescence is the loss of value due to adverse changes in the surroundings of the subject property that make the subject less desirable. Since such changes are usually beyond the control of the property owner, economic obsolescence is considered *an incurable value loss*. Examples of economic obsolescence include a deteriorating neighborhood, a rezoning of adjacent properties, or the bankruptcy of a large employer.

Steps in the approach

The cost approach consists of estimating the value of the land "as if vacant;" estimating the cost of improvements; estimating and deducting accrued depreciation; and adding the estimated land value to the estimated depreciated cost of the improvements.

Exhibit 16.6 Steps in the Cost Approach

1. Estimate land value.
2. Estimate reproduction or replacement cost of improvements.
3. Estimate accrued depreciation.
4. Subtract accrued depreciation from reproduction or replacement cost.
5. Add land value to depreciated reproduction or replacement cost.

Estimate land value. To estimate land value, the appraiser uses the sales comparison method: find properties which are comparable to the subject property in terms of land and adjust the sale prices of the comparables to account for competitive differences with the subject property. Common adjustments concern location, physical characteristics, and time of sale. The indicated values of the comparable properties are used to estimate the land value of the subject. The implicit assumption is that the subject land is vacant (unimproved) and available for the highest and best use.

Estimate reproduction or replacement cost of improvements. There are several methods for estimating the reproduction or replacement cost of improvements. These are as follows.

- **unit comparison method (square-foot method)**

  The appraiser examines one or more new structures that are similar to the subject's improvements, determines a cost per unit for the benchmark structures, and multiplies this cost per unit times the number of units in the subject. The unit of measurement is most commonly denominated in square feet.

- **unit-in-place method**

  The appraiser uses materials cost manuals and estimates of labor costs, overhead, and builder's profit to estimate the cost of constructing separate components of the subject. The overall cost estimate is the sum of the estimated costs of individual components.

- **quantity survey method**

  The appraiser considers in detail all materials, labor, supplies, overhead and profit to get an accurate estimate of the actual cost to build the improvement. More thorough than the unit-in-place method, this method is used less by appraisers than it is by engineers and architects.

- **cost indexing method**

  The original cost of constructing the improvement is updated by applying a percentage increase factor to account for increases in nominal costs over time.

Estimate accrued depreciation. Accrued depreciation is often estimated by the **straight-line** method, also called the **economic age-life method**. This method assumes that depreciation occurs at a steady rate over the economic life of the structure. Therefore, a property suffers the same incremental loss of value each year.

The **economic life** is the period during which the structure is expected to remain useful in its original use. The cost of the structure is divided by the number of years of economic life to determine an annual amount for depreciation. The straight-line method is primarily relevant to depreciation from physical deterioration.

Subtract accrued depreciation from reproduction or replacement cost. The sum of accrued depreciation from all sources is subtracted from the estimated cost of reproducing or replacing the structure. This produces an estimate of the current value of the improvements.

Add land value to depreciated reproduction or replacement cost. To complete the cost approach, the estimated value of the land "as if vacant" is added to the estimated value of the depreciated reproduction or replacement cost of the improvements. This yields the final value estimate for the property by the cost approach.

Exhibit 16.7 Cost Approach Illustration

I. LAND VALUE	
Land value, by direct sales comparison	80,000
II. IMPROVEMENTS COST	
Main building (by one or more of the four methods)	260,000
Plus: other structures	16,000
Total cost new	276,000
III. ACCRUED DEPRECIATION	
Physical depreciation	
Curable	10,000
Incurable	14,000
Functional obsolescence	6,000
External obsolescence	
Total depreciation	30,000
IV. IMPROVEMENTS COST MINUS DEPRECIATION	
Total cost new	276,000
Less: total depreciation	30,000
Depreciated value of improvements	246,000
V. OVERALL ESTIMATED VALUE	
Total land value	80,000
Depreciated value of improvements	246,000
Indicated value by cost approach	326,000

THE INCOME CAPITALIZATION APPROACH

Steps in the approach
Gross rent and gross income multiplier approach

The income capitalization approach, or income approach, is used for income properties and sometimes for other properties in a rental market where the appraiser can find rental data. The approach is based on the principle of anticipation: the expected future income stream of a property underlies what an investor will pay for the property. It is also based on the principle of substitution: that an investor will pay no more for a subject property with a certain income stream than the investor would have to pay for another property with a similar income stream.

The strength of the income approach is that it is used by investors themselves to determine how much they should pay for a property. Thus, in the right circumstances, it provides a good basis for estimating market value.

The income capitalization approach is limited in two ways. First, it is difficult to determine an appropriate capitalization rate. This is often a matter of judgment and experience on the part of the appraiser. Secondly, the income approach relies on market information about income and expenses, and it can be difficult to find such information.

Steps in the approach

The income capitalization method consists of estimating annual net operating income from the subject property, then applying a capitalization rate to the income. This produces a principal amount that the investor would pay for the property.

Exhibit 16.8 Steps in the Income Capitalization Approach

1. Estimate potential gross income.
2. Estimate effective gross income.
3. Estimate net operating income.
4. Select a capitalization rate.
5. Apply the capitalization rate.

Estimate potential gross income. Potential gross income is the scheduled rent of the subject plus income from miscellaneous sources such as vending machines and telephones. Scheduled rent is the total rent a property will produce if fully leased at the established rental rates.

Scheduled rent
\+ Other income
____

Potential gross income

An appraiser may estimate potential gross rental income using current market rental rates (market rent), the rent specified by leases in effect on the property (contract rent), or a combination of both. Market rent is determined by market studies in a process similar to the sales comparison method. Contract rent is used primarily if the existing leases are not due to expire in the short term and the tenants are unlikely to fail or leave the lease.

Estimate effective gross income. Effective gross income is potential gross income minus an allowance for vacancy and credit losses.

Potential gross income
\- Vacancy & credit losses
____

Effective gross income

Vacancy loss refers to an amount of potential income lost because of unrented space. Credit loss refers to an amount lost because of tenants' failure to pay rent for any reason. Both are estimated on the basis of the subject property's history, comparable properties in the market, and assuming typical management quality. The allowance for vacancy and credit loss is usually estimated as a percentage of potential gross income.

Estimate net operating income. Net operating income is effective gross income minus total operating expenses.

Effective gross income
\- Total operating expenses

Net operating income

Operating expenses include fixed expenses and variable expenses. Fixed expenses are those that are incurred whether the property is occupied or vacant, for example, real estate taxes and hazard insurance. Variable expenses are those that relate to actual operation of the building, for example, utilities, janitorial service, management, and repairs.

Operating expenses typically include an annual reserve fund for replacement of equipment and other items that wear out periodically, such as carpets and heating systems. Operating expenses do not include debt service, expenditures for capital improvements, or expenses not related to operation of the property.

Select a capitalization rate. The capitalization rate is an estimate of the *rate of return* an investor will demand on the investment of capital in a property such as the subject. The judgment and market knowledge of the appraiser play an essential role in the selection of an appropriate rate for the subject property. In most cases, the appraiser will research capitalization rates used on similar properties in the market.

Apply the capitalization rate. An appraiser now obtains an indication of value from the income capitalization method by dividing the estimated net operating income for the subject by the selected capitalization rate

$$\frac{NOI}{capitalization\ rate} = value$$

Using traditional symbols for income (I), rate (R) and value (V), the formula for value is

$$\frac{I}{R} = V$$

Exhibit 16.9 Income Capitalization Method Illustration

I. ESTIMATE POTENTIAL GROSS INCOME

Potential gross rental income	192,000
Plus: other income	2,000
Potential gross income	194,000

II. ESTIMATE EFFECTIVE GROSS INCOME

Less: vacancy and collection losses	9,600
Effective gross income	184,400

III. ESTIMATE NET OPERATING INCOME

Operating expenses	
Real estate taxes	32,000
Insurance	4,400
Utilities	12,000
Repairs	4,000
Maintenance	16,000
Management	12,000
Reserves	1,600
Legal and accounting	2,000
Total expenses	84,000

Effective gross income	184,400
Less: total expenses	84,000
Net operating income	100,400

IV. SELECT CAPITALIZATION RATE

Capitalization rate: 7%

V. APPLY CAPITALIZATION RATE

$$\frac{I}{R} = V = \frac{100,400}{.07} = 1,434,300 \text{ (rounded)}$$

Indicated value by income approach: 1,434,300

Gross rent and gross income multiplier approach

The gross rent multiplier (GRM) and gross income multiplier (GIM) approaches are simplified income-based methods used primarily for properties that produce or might produce income but are not primarily income properties. Examples are single-family homes and duplexes.

The methods consist of applying a multiplier to the estimated gross income or gross rent of the subject. The multiplier is derived from market data on sale prices and gross income or gross rent.

The advantage of the income multiplier is that it offers a relatively quick indication of value using an informal methodology. However, the approach leaves many variables out of consideration such as vacancies, credit losses, and operating expenses. In addition, the appraiser must have market rental data to establish multipliers.

Steps in the gross rent multiplier approach. There are two steps in the gross rent multiplier approach.

First, select a gross rent multiplier by examining the sale prices and monthly rents of comparable properties which have sold recently. The appraiser's judgment and market knowledge are critical in determining an appropriate gross rent multiplier for the subject. The gross rent multiplier for a property is:

$$\frac{Price}{Monthly\ rent} = GRM$$

Second, estimate the value of the subject by multiplying the selected GRM by the subject's monthly income.

GRM x Subject monthly rent = estimated value

Exhibit 16.10 Gross Rent Multiplier Illustration

Property	Sale price	Monthly rent	GRM
Comparable A	250,000	1660	151
Comparable B	248,000	1500	165
Comparable C	324,000	2,200	147
Comparable D	304,000	1,800	169
Subject	320,000	2,000	160

In the illustration, the indicated GRM for the subject is 160, based on the appraiser's research and judgment. Applying the GRM to a rental rate of $2,000, the indicated value for the subject is $320,000.

Steps in the gross income multiplier approach. The GIM approach is identical to the GRM approach, except that a different denominator is used in the formula. Step one is to select a gross income multiplier by examining the sale prices and gross annual incomes of comparable properties which have sold recently. The gross income multiplier for a property is:

$$\frac{Price}{Gross\ annual\ income} = GIM$$

Step two is to estimate the value of the subject by multiplying the selected GIM by the subject's gross annual income:

GIM x Subject gross annual income = estimated value

Exhibit 16.11 Gross Income Multiplier Illustration

Property	Sale price	Gross income	GIM
Comparable A	250,000	19,920	12.55
Comparable B	248,000	18,000	13.78
Comparable C	324,000	26,400	12.27
Comparable D	304,000	21,600	14.07
Subject	324,000	24,000	13.50

In the illustration, the indicated GIM for the subject is 13.5 , based on the appraiser's research and judgment. Applying the GIM to the property's gross annual income gives an indicated value for the subject of $324,000.

REGULATION OF APPRAISAL PRACTICE

Licensure
Professional standards
Professional associations and designations

Licensure

In 1989, Congress passed the Financial Institutions Reform, Recovery and Enforcement Act (FIRREA) in response to the savings and loan crisis. This act included provisions to regulate appraisal.

Title XI of FIRREA requires that competent individuals whose professional conduct is properly supervised perform all appraisals used in federally-related transactions. Such federally-related appraisals must be performed only by state-certified appraisers. A state-certified appraiser is one who has passed the necessary examinations and competency standards as established by each state in conformance with the federal standards stated in FIRREA and USPAP (Uniform Standards of Professional Appraisal Practice). The criteria for certification as a minimum must follow those established by the Appraiser Qualifications Board of the Appraisal Foundation.

Professional standards

The Uniform Standards of Professional Appraisal Practice (USPAP) is a set of standards, guidelines and provisions for the appraisal industry. It resulted from the cooperation of nine national appraisal organizations in 1985.

The "competence" provision requires appraisers to assess whether they have the necessary knowledge and competence to perform a specific assignment. If they do not, they must disclose this fact.

The "departure" provision permits appraisers to perform an appraisal that does not meet all the USPAP guidelines provided they have informed the client of the limitations of the incomplete appraisal and if the partial appraisal will not be misleading.

The "standards" concern:

- recognized appraisal methods
- definition of due diligence
- how appraisal results are reported
- disclosures and assumptions
- appraisal review
- real estate analysis
- mass appraisals
- personal property appraisals
- business appraisals
- compliance with USPAP
- compliance with the Code of Professional Ethics and Standards of Professional Practice

Professional associations and designations

Prior to the establishment of state certification programs, the only indication of professional competence for an appraiser was membership in and designation by one of the national appraisal associations. These associations continue to provide education and recognition of professional accomplishment for appraisers.

The appraisal organizations who jointly formed the Appraisal Foundation in 1987 are:

- American Institute of Real Estate Appraisers
- American Society of Appraisers
- American Society of Farm Managers and Rural Appraisers
- International Association of Assessing Officers
- International Right of Way Association
- National Association of Independent Fee Appraisers
- National Society of Real Estate Appraisers
- Society of Real Estate Appraisers

The American Institute of Real Estate Appraisers and the Society of Real Estate Appraisers have since joined to become the Appraisal Institute.

16 Appraising and Estimating Market Value Snapshot Review

REAL ESTATE VALUE	•	present monetary worth of benefits arising from ownership, including: income, appreciation, use, tax benefits
Foundations of real estate value	•	anticipation, substitution, contribution, change, highest and best use, conformity, supply, demand, progression, regression, assemblage, subdivision, utility, transferability
Types of value	•	market, reproduction, replacement, salvage, plottage, assessed, condemned, depreciated, reversionary, appraised, rental, leasehold, insured, book, mortgage
APPRAISING MARKET VALUE		
Market value	•	price willing buyer and seller would agree on given: cash transaction, exposure, information, no pressure, arm's length, marketable title, no hidden influences
The appraisal and its uses	•	a professional's opinion of value, supported by data, regulated, following professional standards; used in real estate decision-making
Measuring living area	•	standards vary by locality; national guidelines from ANSI and Fannie Mae
Steps in the appraisal process	•	define purpose, collect and analyze data, identify highest and best use, estimate land value, apply basic appraisal approaches, reconcile, compile report
SALES COMPARISON APPROACH	•	most commonly used; relies on principles of substitution and contribution
Steps in the approach	•	compare sale prices, adjust comparables to account for differences with subject
Identifying comparables	•	must be physically similar, in subject's vicinity, recently sold in arm's length sale
Adjusting comparables	•	deduct from comp if better than subject; add to comp if worse than subject
Weighting adjustments	•	best indicator has fewest and smallest adjustments, least net adjustment from the sale price
Broker's comparative market analysis	•	abridged sales comparison approach by brokers and agents to find a price range
COST APPROACH	•	most often used for recently built properties and special-purpose buildings
Types of cost appraised	•	reproduction: precise duplicate; replacement: functional equivalent
Depreciation	•	loss of value from deterioration, or functional or economic obsolescence
Steps in the approach	•	land value plus depreciated reproduction or replacement cost of improvements
INCOME APPROACH	•	used for income properties and in a rental market with available rental data
Steps in the approach	•	value = NOI divided by the capitalization rate
GRM and GIM approach	•	GRM: price divided by monthly rent; value: GRM times monthly rent; GIM: price divided by gross annual income; value: GIM times annual income
REGULATION OF APPRAISAL		
Licensure	•	state-licensed or -certified per FIRREA/USPAP for federally-related appraisals
Professional standards	•	USPAP establishes appraisal standards, guidelines and provisions
Professional associations and designations	•	founders of Appraisal Foundation offer education and professional designations

17 Real Estate Finance

Anatomy of Mortgage Lending
Initiating a Mortgage Loan
Qualifying for a Mortgage Loan
Closing a Loan
Laws Affecting Mortgage Lending
The Mortgage Market
Types of Real Estate Loans

ANATOMY OF MORTGAGE LENDING

Mechanics of a loan transaction
Financial components of a loan
Promissory note
Mortgage document and trust deed

Mechanics of a loan transaction

It is common to use borrowed money to purchase real estate. When a borrower gives a note promising to repay the borrowed money and executes a mortgage on the real estate for which the money is being borrowed as security, the financing method is called mortgage financing. The term "mortgage financing" also applies to real estate loans secured by a deed of trust. The process of securing a loan by pledging a property without giving up ownership of the property is called **hypothecation**.

States differ in their interpretation of who owns mortgaged property. Those that regard the mortgage as a lien held by the mortgagee (lender) against the property owned by the mortgagor (borrower) are called **lien-theory** states. Those that regard the mortgage document as a conveyance of ownership from the mortgagor to the mortgagee are called **title-theory** states. Some states interpret ownership of mortgaged property from a point of view that combines aspects of both title and lien theory.

A valid mortgage or trust deed financing arrangement requires

- a *note* as evidence of the debt
- the *mortgage or trust deed* as evidence of the collateral pledge

Note. In addition to executing a mortgage or trust deed, the borrower signs a promissory note for the amount borrowed. The amount of the loan is typically the difference between the purchase price and the down payment. A promissory note creates a personal liability for the borrower to repay the loan.

Mortgage. A mortgage is a legal document stating the pledge of the borrower (the **mortgagor**) to the lender (the **mortgagee**). The mortgage document pledges the borrower's ownership interest in the real estate in question as collateral against performance of the debt obligation.

The flow of funds and obligations in a mortgage transaction is as follows:

Exhibit 17.1 Flow of a Mortgage Transaction

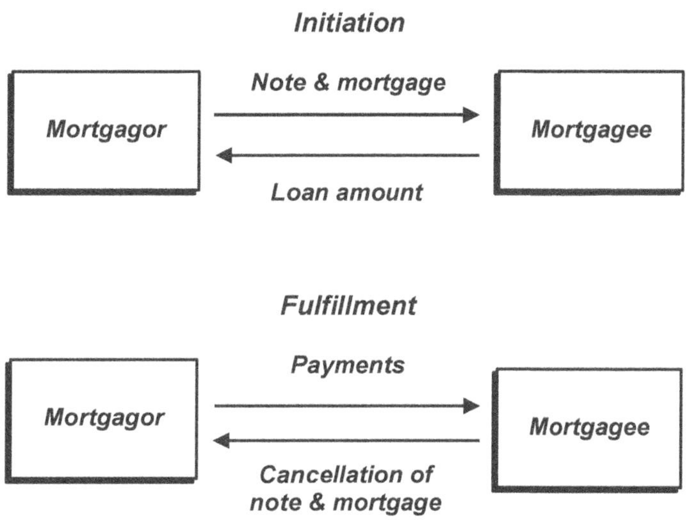

The deed of trust. A deed of trust conveys title to the property in question from the borrower (**trustor**) to a **trustee** as security for the loan. The trustee is a third party fiduciary to the trust. While the loan is in place, the trustee holds the title on behalf of the lender, who is the **beneficiary** of the trust. On repayment of the loan, the borrower receives the title from the trustee in the form of a deed of reconveyance.

The flow of funds and obligations in a trust deed transaction is as follows:

Exhibit 17.2 Flow of a Trust Deed Transaction

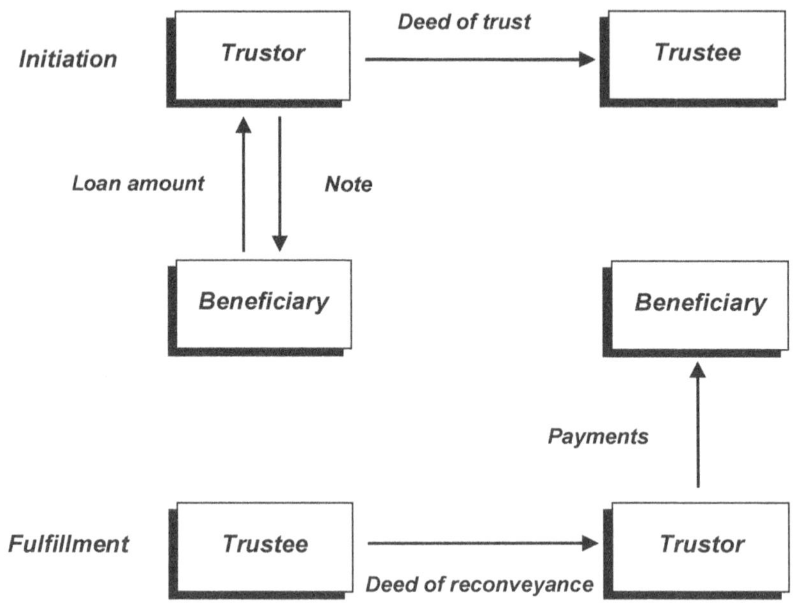

Financial components of a loan

The financial components of a mortgage loan include:

- principal
- interest and interest rate
- points
- term
- payments

Principal. The capital amount borrowed, on which interest payments are calculated, is the original loan **principal**. In an amortizing loan, part of the principal is repaid periodically along with interest, so that the principal balance decreases over the life of the loan. At any point during the life of a mortgage loan, the remaining unpaid principal is called the **loan balance**, or **remaining balance**.

Interest and interest rate. Interest is a charge for the use of the lender's money. Interest may be paid in *advance* at the beginning of the payment period, or in *arrears* at the end of the payment period, according to the terms of the note. Mortgage interest is most commonly paid in arrears. The **interest rate** is a percentage applied to the principal to determine the amount of interest due. The rate may be *fixed* for the term of the loan, or it may be *variable*, according to the terms of the note. A loan with a fixed interest rate is called a fixed-rate loan; a loan with a variable interest rate is commonly called an adjustable rate loan.

Because the interest rate on a mortgage loan does not reflect the full cost of the loan to the borrower, federal law requires a lender on a residential property to compute and disclose an **Annual Percentage Rate (APR)** that includes other finance charges in addition to the basic interest rate in the calculation.

Many states have laws against **usury**, which is the charging of excessive interest rates on loans. Such states have a maximum rate that is either a flat rate or a variable rate tied to an index such as the prime lending rate.

Points. From the point of view of a lender or investor, the amount loaned in a mortgage loan is the lender's capital investment, and the interest paid by the borrower is the return earned by the invested capital. It is often the case that a lender needs to earn a greater return than the interest rate alone provides. For example, a lender may require additional yield on a low-interest VA loan which has an interest rate maximum. In such a case, the lender charges up-front **discount points** to make up the difference between the interest rate on the loan and the required return. This effectively raises the yield of the loan to the lender.

A discount point is *one percent of the loan amount*. Thus, one point on a $100,000 loan equals $1,000. The lender charges this as *pre-paid interest* at closing by funding only the face amount of the loan minus the discount points. The borrower, however, must repay the full loan amount, along with interest calculated on the full amount.

The value of one discount point to a lender is usually estimated to be equivalent to raising the interest rate on the loan by 1/8%. Thus, a lender has to charge eight points to raise the yield by 1%. If a lender needs to earn 7% on a loan offered at 6.5%, the number of points necessary would be figured as follows:

7.0% - 6.5% = .5%
.5% x 8 (points per 1%) = 4 points

On a loan of $100,000, the 4 points would cost the borrower:

100,000 x .04 = $4,000.

The borrower would effectively receive from the lender $96,000, and owe principal and interest based on $100,000. For tax reasons, it is usually advisable for the borrower to receive the full loan amount from the lender and pay the points in a check which is separate from that used for other closing costs. As pre-paid interest, points paid in this way may be deductible on the borrower's income tax return for the year of the purchase. The borrower should seek the advice of a tax consultant concerning this matter.

Term. The loan term is the period of time over which the loan must be repaid. A "30-year loan" is a loan whose balance must be fully paid off at the end of thirty years. A "five-year balloon loan" is a loan whose balance must be paid off at the end of five years, although its payments may be calculated on a term of another length, such as fifteen or thirty years. Such a loan is also sometimes described as a 30-year loan with a five-year "call."

Payments. The loan term, loan amount, and interest rate combine to determine the periodic payment amount. When these three quantities are known, it is possible to identify the periodic payment from a mortgage table or with a financial calculator. Mortgage payments are usually made on a monthly basis. On an amortizing loan, a portion of the payment goes to repay the loan balance in advance, and a portion goes to payment of interest in arrears.

For example, Mary and Jerry King borrow $400,000 to finance the purchase of a home. The loan has a term of thirty years at an interest rate of 5% and is amortizing. The monthly payment for this loan will be $2,147. For the first payment at the end of the month, the Kings owe interest on $400,000 for the monthly period. At 5%, this amounts to $1,666.67. Since their payment is $2,147 and the interest charge is $1,666.67, the difference, which is $480.33, is applied to an advance payment of principal. The following month, the Kings will pay interest on the new, smaller loan balance of $399,519.67 ($400,000.00 – 480.33).

If a borrower pays more than the scheduled payment amount, the excess is credited to repayment of the principal, which is reduced by the amount of the excess payment. The required minimum payment amount remains constant for the life of the loan, but the loan term can be reduced by this means, thereby also reducing the total amount of interest paid over the life of the loan.

Promissory note

A borrower who executes a promissory note is the **maker** or **payer** of the note. The lender is the **payee**. To be properly executed, all parties who have an interest in the property should sign the note. The note sets forth:

- the loan amount
- the term of the loan
- the method and timing of repayment
- the interest rate to be paid
- the borrower's promise to pay

The note may also state that it is payable to the bearer, if used with a deed of trust, or to the mortgagee, if used with a mortgage. Other items in the mortgage document or deed of trust may be repeated in the promissory note, especially:

- the right to prepay the loan balance
- charges for late payment
- conditions for default
- notifications and cures for default
- other charges

A promissory note is a **negotiable instrument**, which means the payee may *assign* it to a third party. The assignee would then have the right to receive the borrower's periodic payments.

Mortgage document and trust deed

A borrower who executes a mortgage is a **mortgagor**. The lender named in the mortgage is the **mortgagee**. In a trust deed, the borrower is the **trustor** and the lender is **beneficiary**. The mortgage or trust document identifies the property being given as security, giving both its legal description and mailing address. The document contains much of the same information as the note, including:

- the debt amount
- the term of the loan
- method and timing of payments

The document does not usually provide details about the payment amount, interest rate, or charges.

Among the major clauses of a typical mortgage are the following.

Payment of Principal and Interest: Prepayment and Late Charges. The borrower must make timely payments according to the terms of the note.

Funds for Taxes and Insurance. Unless waived by the lender or prohibited by law, the borrower must make monthly payments to cover taxes and hazard insurance. If applicable, the borrower must also pay flood insurance and mortgage insurance installments.

Periodic payments of taxes and insurance are held in a reserve fund called the **escrow account**. The Real Estate Settlement Procedures Act (RESPA) limits the amount of funds that the lender can require and hold for this purpose.

The borrower's monthly payment to the lender for principal and interest is called the **P&I** payment (principal and interest). The amount which also includes the escrow payment is called **PITI** (principal, interest, taxes, insurance).

Application of Payments. The amount of each payment is applied to various items in order of priority. Unless local law provides otherwise, this order is: 1) prepayment charges; 2) escrow; 3) interest; 4) principal; 5) late charges.

Charges and Liens. The borrower is liable for paying any charges, liens, or other expenses that may have priority over the mortgage or trust instrument.

Hazard or Property Insurance. The borrower must keep the property insured as the lender requires to protect the lender's collateral. **Homeowners' insurance** policies typically provide coverage for losses due to fire, lightning, wind, hail, explosions, glass breakage, smoke, riots, vandalism, theft, and other perils. Insurance proceeds, in case of a claim, are applied first to restoring the property, or, if that is not feasible, to payment of the debt.

Occupancy, Preservation, Maintenance and Protection of the Property. The borrower must take and maintain occupancy of the property as the borrower's principal residence according to the lender's requirements. The borrower must not use or neglect the property in such a way as to impair the lender's lien on the property. This could include using the property for illegal purposes, creating hazardous waste on the property, or destroying the improvements.

Protection of Lender's Rights in the Property. The lender may take actions it believes are necessary to protect its rights in the property if the borrower's actions threaten them. The costs of these actions would be charged to the borrower, and become part of the monthly payment.

Mortgage Insurance. The lender may require the borrower to obtain **private mortgage insurance**, or **PMI**. Mortgage insurance protects the lender against loss of a portion of the loan (typically 20-25%) in case of borrower default. Private mortgage insurance generally applies to loans that are not backed by the Federal Housing Administration (FHA) or Veterans Administration (VA) and that have a down payment of less than 20% of the property value.

Inspection. With proper notice, the lender may inspect the property if there is reasonable cause to fear damage to its lien.

Condemnation. If the property is condemned or taken by eminent domain, the lender declares a claim on any resulting proceeds.

Borrower Not Released; Forbearance by Lender Not a Waiver. The lender reserves the right to take future action against the borrower for default, even if the lender decides not to take immediate action. If the lender agrees to change the terms of the loan, it does not release the borrower from the original liability.

Transfer of the Property or a Beneficial Interest in Borrower. If the borrower sells or transfers its interest in the property without the lender's approval, the lender may demand immediate and full repayment of the loan balance. This is an **alienation** clause, also known as a **due-on-sale** clause and a **call** clause. It allows the lender to prevent the assumption of the mortgage by a buyer if the borrower sells the property. The requirement to repay the loan before the scheduled date is called **acceleration**.

Borrower's Right to Reinstate. If the lender holds the borrower in default under the terms of the mortgage and proceeds to enforce its rights under the document, such as by foreclosing, the borrower has the right to reinstate his or her interest by performing certain actions. This usually means paying overdue mortgage payments and any other expenses the lender may have incurred in protecting its rights. The clause, also known as a **redemption** clause, gives the borrower a period of time to satisfy obligations and prevent the lender from forcing a sale of the property. See **foreclosure** in Chapter Five.

Release. The lender agrees to release the mortgage or trust document to the borrower when the borrower has paid off the loan and all other sums secured by the document. The release clause, also known as a **defeasance** clause, may specify that the mortgagee will execute a **satisfaction of mortgage** (also known as **release of mortgage** and **mortgage discharge**) to the mortgagor. In the case of a deed of trust, the lender as beneficiary requests the trustee to execute a **release deed** or **deed of reconveyance** to the borrower as trustor. The release deed or satisfaction should be recorded as necessary in county records to show that the mortgagee/trustee has extinguished all liens against the property.

INITIATING A MORTGAGE LOAN

The loan application
Mortgage loan underwriting

The process of initiating a mortgage loan begins when a borrower completes a loan application and submits it to a lender for evaluation by the lender's underwriters.

The loan application

Forms. Most lenders use some version of the "Uniform Residential Loan Application" promulgated by Fannie Mae. This form requests the borrower to provide information about the property and the borrower. In addition, the application must include supporting documentation, as indicated in the following exhibit.

Exhibit 17.3 Property and Borrower Information

Property information	age & year built original cost	year acquired current loan balance
Borrower information	age employment history assets	education monthly income & expenses debts
Supporting documentation	appraisal report purchase contract	credit report income and employment verification

The standard form includes the loan amount requested, based on an estimate of the purchase, refinance, or other underlying transaction.

Completion. The application must be complete for the lender to consider it. The form must be signed and dated by the applicant(s) and delivered to the lending institution. The **initiation** of the application process occurs when the lender receives the completed application package from the applicant. Federal law requires the lender to accept all applications and to give applicants notice concerning the disposition of the application. If the lender denies the loan application because of fraudulent information on the application form, the borrower has no claim to a refund of the application fee.

Mortgage loan underwriting

Loan underwriting is the process of assessing the lender's risk in giving a loan. Mortgage underwriting includes:

- evaluating the borrower's ability to repay the loan
- appraising the value of the property offered as security
- determining the terms of the loan

Risk. A lender undertakes a number of risks in lending money. The principal risks are that the borrower will default on repayment of the loan, and that the borrower will damage the value of the property as security. In addition, the lender runs the risk that, in the event of a foreclosure, the sales proceeds from the property will be insufficient to cover the lender's loss.

Qualification. A lender assesses risks by examining, or *qualifying*, both borrower and property. In qualifying a borrower, an underwriter weighs the ability of the borrower to repay the loan. This requires an analysis of whether the borrower's income, cash resources, creditworthiness, net worth, and employment stability meet the lender's standards.

Loan-to-value ratio, or LTV. In qualifying a property, an underwriter assesses the ability of the property value to cover potential losses. In this evaluation, a lender requires that the appraised value of the property be more than adequate to cover the contemplated loan and costs. To protect further against loss, a lender will usually lend only a portion of the property's value. The relationship of the loan amount to the property value, expressed as a percentage, is called the **loan-to-value ratio, or LTV**. If the lender's loan to value ratio is 80%, the lender will lend only $80,000 on a home appraised at $100,000. The difference between what the lender will lend and what the borrower must pay for the property is the amount the borrower must provide in cash as a down payment.

Even if borrower and property qualify, a lender may, under certain circumstances, seek further protection against risk by requiring the borrower to obtain private mortgage insurance. This is frequently the case with loans requiring a relatively small down payment, leading to a high loan-to-value ratio.

Private mortgage insurance. As mentioned earlier, if a loan's LTV ratio is too high, a lender may require that the borrower purchase private mortgage insurance, commonly called PMI. This insurance secures whatever portion of the loan amount takes the LTV ratio above the typical ratio limit – which is usually 80% of the property's value. This protects the lender from the borrower's default – which can become more likely if the borrower has very little equity in the property.

To illustrate, take a $500,000 property with an 90-10% LTV loan on it. At 90%, this loan would be 90% times $500,000, or $450,000. Next, consider that the lender requires 20% equity, or an 80-20% LTV. Such an LTV would cap the loan limit at $400,000. In this case, to get this lender to lend $450,000, the borrower would have to purchase PMI to insure the "top" portion of the loan, or $50,000. With this PMI safety net, the lender can lend the funds, and the borrower closes with a 90-10 LTV loan.

In practice, a borrower who has to obtain PMI must retain the insurance policy and continue the premium payments until the LTV ratio on the loan has dropped to within acceptable levels, such as the 80-20 level. This happens by the property's value appreciating as well as the loan balance being paid off over time. Finally, if the borrower can assimilate enough funds to pay down the loan balance, the lender will be obligated to drop the PMI requirement, since, as we have seen, a prepayment of principal changes the loan-to-value ratio.

QUALIFYING FOR A MORTGAGE LOAN

Equal Credit Opportunity Act
Income qualification
Loan constant
Cash qualification
Net worth
Credit evaluation
Loan commitment

To qualify for a mortgage loan, a borrower must meet the lender's qualifications in terms of *income, debt, cash, and net worth*. In addition, a borrower must demonstrate sufficient *creditworthiness* to be an acceptable risk.

Equal Credit Opportunity Act

The Equal Credit Opportunity Act (ECOA) requires a lender to evaluate a loan applicant on the basis of that applicant's own income and credit rating, unless the applicant requests the inclusion of another's income and credit rating in the application. In addition, ECOA has prohibited a number of practices in mortgage loan underwriting. Accordingly, a lender may not:

- discount or disregard income from part-time work, a spouse, child support, alimony, or separate maintenance. Further, the loan officer may not ask whether any of the applicant's income is derived from these sources.
- assume that income for a certain type of person will be reduced because of an employment interruption due to child-bearing or child-raising. The loan officer may not ask about the applicant's plans or behavior concerning child-bearing or birth control.
- refuse a loan solely on the basis that the security is located in a certain geographical area.
- ask applicants any question about their age, sex, religion, race or national origin, except as the law may require.
- require a spouse to sign any document unless the spouse's income is to be included in the qualifying income, or unless the spouse agrees to become contractually obligated, or the state requires the signature for some purpose such as clearing clouded title.

If a lender denies a request for a loan, or offers a loan under different terms than those requested by an applicant, the lender must give the applicant written notice providing specific reasons for the action.

Qualifying the borrower. The lender must rely on eight types of information to determine that the borrower has the ability to repay the loan:

1. current income or assets (excluding the value of the mortgaged property)
2. current employment status
3. credit history
4. monthly payment for the mortgage
5. monthly payments being made on other loans on the same property
6. monthly payments for other mortgage-related expenses
7. other debts
8. monthly debt payments compared to monthly income (debt-to-income ratio)

The lender cannot use a temporarily low rate (introductory or "teaser" rate) to determine qualification. For an adjustable rate mortgage (ARM), the highest rate the borrower might have to pay is generally to be used.

The "ability to repay" requirements are relaxed in certain circumstances where the borrower is attempting to refinance from a riskier loan (such as an interest-only loan) to a less risky one (such as a fixed-rate mortgage loan.

Qualified Mortgage. A Qualified Mortgage is one that meets the "ability-to-repay" requirements, has certain required features and is not allowed to have others. There are exceptions to these rules for certain kinds of small lenders. Issuing a Qualified Mortgage gives the lender certain legal protections in case the borrower fails to repay the loan.

Generally not allowed:

- an "interest-only" period--when interest, but not principal, is being repaid
- negative amortization–when principal increases over time
- balloon payment–larger than normal payment at the end of the loan term
- loan term longer than 30 years
- excessive upfront fees and points

Generally required:

- monthly debt no more than 43 % of monthly pre-tax income
- limits on points

Qualified Mortgages include loans that can be bought by Fannie Mae or Freddie Mac or insured by certain government agencies, such as the Department of Agriculture, even if the debt ratio is higher than 43 percent. Also, loans that are insured or guaranteed by the Department of Housing and Urban Development, including through the Federal Housing Administration, are qualified mortgages under rules issued by that agency.

Valuations. Before issuing a first mortgage loan, a lender must

- notify the borrower within three days of the loan application that a copy of any appraisal will be promptly provided
- provide the borrower with a free copy of any valuation used, including appraisal reports, automated valuation model reports, and broker's price opinions, promptly when completed and no later than three days before closing
- provide these copies even if the loan does not close

The lender may ask for the deadline to be waived so that the copies may be delivered at closing, and may charge a reasonable fee for obtaining the valuation.

Discovery and disclosure requirements. Creditors are required to provide applicants with free copies of all appraisals and other written valuations developed in connection with an application for a loan to be secured by a first lien on a dwelling and must notify applicants in writing that copies of appraisals will be provided to them promptly.

High cost loans. When the annual percentage rate (APR) or points and fees on a home loan, home equity loan, or home equity line of credit (HELOC) exceed certain limits, special consumer protections apply. The lender must provide information in advance that explains the costs, terms, and associated fees, and get a housing counselor to certify that the borrower has received counseling about the high-cost mortgage.

With high-cost mortgages, lenders are not allowed to add many kinds of fees and charges to the loan amount, namely:

- prepayment penalties for early loan payoff
- balloon payments
- late fees larger than 4 percent of the regular payment
- fees for payoff statements (statements of loan balance)
- loan modification fees

Income qualification

Lenders want to be assured that the borrower has adequate means to make all necessary periodic payments on the loan in addition to other housing expenses and debts such as credit card payments and car payments. Most lenders use two ratios to estimate an applicant's ability to fulfill a loan obligation: an *income ratio,* or *housing ratio*, and a *debt ratio*, or *housing plus debt ratio*. They also consider the stability of an applicant's income. Please note that the income and debt ratios in the discussion below do not necessarily reflect the latest ratios used by FHA, VA, or other lenders. Check for updates on the websites of those agencies.

Income ratio. The income ratio, or housing expense ratio, establishes borrowing capacity by limiting the percent of gross income a borrower may spend on housing costs. Housing costs include principal, interest, taxes, and homeowner's insurance, and may include monthly assessments, mortgage insurance, and utilities. The income ratio formula is:

Income Ratio

$$\frac{monthly\ housing\ expense}{monthly\ GROSS\ income} = income\ ratio$$

To identify the maximum monthly housing expense an income ratio allows, modify the formula as follows:

monthly gross income x income ratio = monthly housing expense

Most conventional lenders require that this ratio be *no greater than 25-28%*. In other words, a borrower's total housing expenses cannot exceed 28% of gross income. For an FHA-backed loan, the ratio is 31%. VA-guaranteed loans do not use this qualifying ratio.

For example, if a couple has combined monthly gross income of $12,000, and a lender's maximum income ratio is 28%, the couple's monthly housing expense cannot exceed $3,360:

$$\$12{,}000 \times 28\% = \$3{,}360$$

Debt ratio. The debt ratio considers all of the monthly obligations of the income ratio *plus any additional monthly payments the applicant must make for other debts*. The lender will look specifically at minimum monthly payments due on revolving credit debts and other consumer loans. The debt ratio formula is:

Debt Ratio

$$\frac{\textit{monthly housing expense} + \textit{monthly debt obligations}}{\textit{monthly GROSS income}} = \textit{debt ratio}$$

To identify the housing expenses plus debt a debt ratio allows, modify the formula as follows:

monthly gross income x debt ratio = monthly housing expense + monthly debt obligations

Most conventional lenders require that this debt ratio be *no greater than 36%*. For an FHA-backed loan, the debt ratio may not exceed 43%. The VA uses 41% and a variable "residual income" calculation. The FHA and VA include in the debt figure any obligation costing more than $100 per month and any debt with a remaining term exceeding six months.

Using the 36% debt ratio, the couple whose monthly income is $12,000 will be allowed to have monthly housing and debt obligations of $4,320:

$12,000 gross income x 36% = $4,320 expenses and debt

VA-guaranteed loans also require a borrower to meet certain qualifications based on net income after paying federal, state, and social security taxes, housing maintenance and utilities expenses. Such **residual income requirements** vary by family size, loan amount, and geographical region.

Income stability. A lender looks beyond income and debt ratios to assess an applicant's income stability. Important factors are:

- how long the applicant has been employed at the present job
- how frequently and for what reasons the applicant has changed jobs in the past
- how likely secondary income such as bonuses and overtime is to continue on a regular basis
- how educational level, training and skills, age, and type of occupation may affect the continuation of the present income level in the future.

Loan constant

A loan constant is a pre-calculated, unchanging number that relates the principal and interest payment amount of a loan to the amount of the loan at a given interest rate and term.

With the loan constant in hand, one can easily derive

- the amount of a loan from its principal and interest payment
- the amount of the principal and interest payment from the loan amount .

By way of these calculations, homebuyers can easily determine how much they can pay per month on a loan or how much loan they can get given their payment affordability. By extension, they can answer two essential homebuyer questions: (a) Can I afford to buy that house? And (b) How much house can I afford to buy?

Loan constants are presented as the monthly payment amount in dollars needed to amortize a loan of a $1,000 for a certain term at a certain interest rate. The constant must be multiplied by the number of thousands in the loan amount to derive a monthly payment for a larger loan amount. Loan constants can be found in readily available loan constant tables, such as the following.

Monthly Payment Needed to Amortize a $1,000 loan (Loan Constant)

	Loan Term in Years				
Interest Rate	**10**	**15**	**20**	**25**	**30**
3.0	**9.65**	**6.9**	**5.54**	**4.74**	**4.21**
3.5	**9.88**	**7.14**	**5.79**	**5**	**4.49**
4.0	**10.13**	**7.4**	**6.06**	**5.28**	**4.78**
4.5	**10.37**	**7.65**	**6.33**	**5.56**	**5.07**
5.0	**10.61**	**7.91**	**6.6**	**5.85**	**5.37**
5.5	**10.86**	**8.18**	**6.88**	**6.15**	**5.68**
6.0	**11.1**	**8.44**	**7.16**	**6.44**	**6**
6.5	**11.35**	**8.71**	**7.46**	**6.75**	**6.32**
7.0	**11.61**	**8.99**	**7.75**	**7.07**	**6.65**

Solving for the monthly principal and interest payment (PI). The periodic principal and interest payment (PI) on an amortized loan is the total of the payments for interest and principal over that period. In the following examples, the derived number PI does not include any escrow amounts for taxes or interest.

To derive a monthly payment for a given loan amount, interest rate, and term, select the loan constant for that loan from the "Monthly Payment Needed to Amortize a Loan of $1,000" charts. Then multiply *the number of thousand dollar increments in the loan amount (in other words, the loan amount divided by 1,000) by the loan constant.*

(Loan amount L ÷ 1,000) x Constant C = Payment PI

or

(L ÷ 1,000) x C = PI

1. A borrower's interest rate is 5.5% and she needs a 30-year loan in the amount of $350,000. What will her monthly PI payment be?

Answer

(a) the monthly loan constant C for a 30-year loan at 5.5% is **5.68.**
(b) the monthly PI payment for a **$350,000** loan = ($350,000 L ÷ 1,000) x 5.68 C = (350 x 5.68) = **$1,988.00** PI

2. A borrower's interest rate is 6.0% and she prefers to get a 20-year loan. To buy the house, she must borrow $280,000. What will her payment be?

Answer

(a) the monthly loan constant C for a 20-year loan at 6.0% is **7.16.**
(b) the monthly PI payment for **a $280,000** loan L = (280,000 L ÷ 1,000) x 7.16 C = (280 x 7.16) = **$2,004.80** PI

Solving for the loan amount. The loan amount in the present context is the beginning principal balance of the loan.

To derive a loan amount when you know the monthly PI payment, the interest rate and the term, identify the loan's constant, divide the PI amount by that constant, *then multiply the result by 1,000.*

(Payment PI ÷ Constant C) x 1,000 = Loan amount L

or

(PI ÷ C) x 1,000 = L

1. A borrower's interest rate is 5.5% and he wants a 30-year loan. His banker said he could afford to pay $1,988 PI per month. How much can he borrow at this budget (to the nearest thousand)?

Answer

(a) the monthly loan constant C for a 30-year loan at 5.5% is **5.68.**
(b) the loan amount L = payment PI **$1,988** ÷ loan constant C **5.68** x 1000 = **$350,000** L.

2. A borrower's interest rate is 6.0% and she prefers to get a 20-year loan. Her banker said she could afford a monthly PI payment of $2,000. How much can she borrow with this payment budget?

Answer

(a) the monthly loan constant C for a 20-year loan at 6.0% is **7.16.**
(b) the loan amount L = payment PI **$2,000** ÷ loan constant C **7.16** x 1,000 = $279,329, or **$280,000** rounded.

Cash qualification

Since a lender lends only part of the purchase price of a property according to the lender's loan-to-value ratio, a lender will verify that a borrower has the cash resources to make the required down payment. If some of a borrower's cash for the down payment comes as a gift from a relative or friend, a lender may require a **gift letter** from the donor stating the amount of the gift and lack of any requirement to repay the gift. On the other hand, if someone is lending an applicant a portion of the down payment with a provision for repayment, a lender will consider this another debt obligation and adjust the debt ratio accordingly. This can lower the amount a lender is willing to lend.

Net worth

An applicant's **net worth** shows a lender the depth of the applicant's cash reserves, the value and liquidity of assets, and the extent to which assets exceed liabilities. These facts are important to a lender as an indication of the applicant's ability to sustain debt payment in the event of loss of employment.

Credit evaluation

Credit report and credit score. A lender must obtain a written credit report on any applicant who submits a completed loan application. The credit report will contain the applicant's history regarding:

- outstanding debts
- payment behavior (timeliness, collection problems)
- legal information of public record (lawsuits, judgments, bankruptcies, divorces, foreclosures, garnishments, repossessions, defaults)

Problems with payment behavior and legal actions are likely to cause a lender to deny the application, unless the applicant can provide an acceptable explanation of mitigating and temporary circumstances that caused the problem.

If a lender denies a loan on the basis of a credit report, the lender must disclose in writing that the applicant is entitled to a statement of reason from any creditor responsible for the negative report.

Since 1995, the Federal Home Loan Mortgage Corporation and the Federal National Mortgage Association have been encouraging lenders to use *credit scoring* to evaluate loan applicants. **Credit scoring** is a computer-based method of assigning a numerical value to an applicant's credit. The credit score is a statistical prediction of a borrower's likelihood of defaulting on a loan.

Loan commitment

When a lender's underwriters have qualified an applicant and the lender has decided to offer the loan, the lender gives the applicant a written notice of the agreement to lend under specific terms. This written promise is the **loan commitment**. The commitment may take a number of common forms, including *a firm commitment, a lock-in commitment, a conditional commitment, and a take-out commitment*.

A **firm commitment** is a straight forward offer to make a specific loan at a specific interest rate for a specific term. This kind of commitment is the one most commonly offered to home buyers.

A **"lock-in" commitment** is an offer to lend a specific amount for a specific term at a specific interest rate, *but the interest rate is subject to an expiration* *date*, for instance, sixty days. This guarantees that the lender will not raise the interest rate during the application and closing periods. The borrower may have to pay points or some other charge for the lock-in.

A **conditional commitment** offers to make a loan if certain provisions are met. This kind of commitment generally applies to construction loans. A typical condition for funding the loan is completion of a development phase.

A **take-out commitment** offers to make a loan that will "take out" another lender's loan, i.e., pay it off and replace it. The take-out loan is most often used to retire a construction loan. The take-out lender agrees to pay off the short-term construction loan by issuing a long-term permanent loan.

CLOSING A LOAN

Closing of a mortgage loan normally occurs with the closing of the real estate transaction. At the real estate closing, the lender typically has deposited the funded amount with an escrow agent, along with instructions for disbursing the funds. The borrower deposits necessary funds with the escrow agent, executes final documents, and receives signed copies of all relevant documents.

Title to the mortgaged property is transferred and recorded according to legal procedures in effect at the time of closing. The borrower receives a package containing copies of all documents relevant to the transaction.

LAWS AFFECTING MORTGAGE LENDING

Truth-in-Lending and Regulation Z
Equal Credit Opportunity Act
Real Estate Settlement Procedures Act
National Flood Insurance Act

Truth-in-Lending and Regulation Z

The Consumer Credit Protection Act, enacted in 1969 and since amended by the Truth-in-Lending Simplification and Reform Act, is implemented by the Federal Reserve's **Regulation Z**. Regulation Z applies to all loans secured by a residence. It does not apply to commercial loans or to agricultural loans over $25,000. Its provisions cover *the disclosure of costs, the right to rescind the credit transaction, advertising credit offers, and penalties for non-compliance with the act.*

The Dodd-Frank Wall Street Reform and Consumer Protection Act of 2010 (Dodd-Frank Act) established the Consumer Financial Protection Bureau (CFPB.) to protect consumers by carrying out federal consumer financial laws. The CFPB consolidates most Federal consumer financial protection authority in one place, including enforcement of RESPA, ECOA, and Truth in Lending.

Disclosure of costs. Under Regulation Z, a lender must disclose all finance charges as well as the true Annualized Percentage Rate (APR) in advance of closing. A lender does not have to show the total interest payable over the loan term or include in finance charges such settlement costs as fees for appraisal, title, credit report, survey, or legal work. Disclosure must be distinctly presented in writing.

Rescission. A borrower has a limited right to cancel the credit transaction, usually within three days of completion of the transaction. The right of rescission does not apply to "residential mortgage transactions," that is, to mortgage loans used to finance the purchase or construction of the borrower's primary residence. However, state law may require a rescission period and notice on these transactions as well.

Advertising. Any type of advertising to offer credit is subject to requirements of full disclosure if it includes:

- a down payment percentage or amount
- an installment payment amount
- a specific amount for a finance charge
- a specific number of payments
- a specific repayment period
- a statement that there is no charge for credit

If any of these items appears in the advertising, the lender must disclose the down payment amount or percentage, repayment terms, the APR, and whether the rate can be increased after consummation of the loan.

Noncompliance. Willful violation of Regulation Z is punishable by imprisonment of up to a year and/or a fine of up to $5,000. Other violations may be punished by requiring payment of court costs, attorneys' fees, damages, and a fine of up to $1,000.

Equal Credit Opportunity Act

ECOA prohibits discrimination in extending credit based on race, color, religion, national origin, sex, marital status, age, or dependency upon public assistance. A creditor may not make any statements to discourage an applicant on the basis of such discrimination or ask any questions of an applicant concerning these discriminatory items. A real estate licensee who assists a seller in qualifying a potential buyer may fall within the reach of this prohibition. A lender must also inform a rejected applicant in writing of reasons for denial within 30 days. A creditor who fails to comply is liable for punitive and actual damages.

Real Estate Settlement Procedures Act

RESPA is a federal law which aims to *standardize settlement practices and ensure that buyers understand settlement costs*. RESPA applies to purchases of residential real estate (one- to four-family homes) to be financed by "federally related" first mortgage loans. Federally related loans include:

- VA- and FHA-backed loans
- other government-backed or -assisted loans
- loans that are intended to be sold to FNMA, FHLMC, GNMA, or other government-controlled secondary market institutions
- loans made by lenders who originate more than one million dollars per year in residential loans.

In addition to imposing settlement procedures, RESPA provisions prohibit lenders from paying kickbacks and unearned fees to parties who may have helped the lender obtain the borrower's business. This would include, for example, a fee paid to a real estate agent for referring a borrower to the lender.

To assist in informing and educating borrowers, RESPA requires that lenders provide a loan applicant with a **loan information booklet** and a **loan estimate**. The booklet, produced by the Consumer Financial Protection Bureau, explains RESPA provisions, general settlement costs, and the required **Closing Disclosure** form. The lender must provide the estimate of closing costs within three days following the borrower's application. RESPA is discussed further in the chapter on "Closings."

Disclosures. The Consumer Financial Protection Bureau (CFPB) requires lenders to use two specific forms to disclose settlement costs to the buyer. A lender must provide a Loan Estimate (H-24) within three days of receiving the loan application and allow the buyer to see the Closing Disclosure (H-25) three days before loan consummation. A lender must also provide a buyer with a copy of the information booklet, "Your Home Loan Toolkit," concerning mortgage loan, closing costs and closing procedures. The disclosures specify:

- settlement charges
- title charges
- recording and transfer fees
- reserve deposits required
- tax and insurance escrow deposits required
- any other fees or charges
- total closing costs

The disclosure forms vary, depending on loan type. The costs in the Closing Disclosure must match those in the Loan Estimate within certain standards. A sample of the H-25 Closing Disclosure is provided in Chapter 21.

National Flood Insurance Act

Federal law requires that borrowers seeking to finance real estate through federally related loans obtain flood insurance if the property is located in a designated flood-hazard area. The Department of Housing and Urban Development administers a program to subsidize flood insurance for borrowers in communities that have entered the program and complied with its construction standards. The Army Corps of Engineers has prepared flood-zone maps for the entire country.

THE MORTGAGE MARKET

Supply and demand for money
The primary mortgage market
The secondary mortgage market
Role of FNMA, GNMA, FHLMC AND FAMC

Mortgage loans provide borrowers with funds to purchase real estate. Money for mortgages primarily comes from cash savings of individuals, government, and businesses. This money may become available through the process of **intermediation**, in which funds on deposit with financial institutions are loaned out to borrowers, or **disintermediation**, in which the owners of the savings invest their money directly by making loans or other investments. Government actions and investor activities affect the supply of money for mortgage loans and encourage or discourage the market for mortgage loans as an investment.

Supply and demand for money

Money is a limited commodity subject to the effects of supply and demand. The federal government's monetary policy *controls the supply of money* in order to achieve the country's economic goals. An excessive supply of money usually causes interest rates to fall and consumer prices to rise. Conversely, an excessive demand for money, such as for mortgage loans, causes interest rates to rise and prices to fall. Regulation of the money supply addresses these fluctuations with the aim to control and limit wide swings in the supply and demand cycle. These efforts, in turn, help to buffer the economy from severe inflationary or recessionary trends.

Regulating the money supply. The Federal Reserve System regulates the money supply by means of three methods:

- *selling or re-purchasing government securities*, primarily Treasury bills
- changing the *reserve requirement* for member banks. The reserve is a percentage of depositors' funds that banks and other regulated financial institutions may not lend out.
- changing the interest rate, or *discount rate,* the system charges member institutions for borrowing funds from the Federal Reserve System central banks

When the Federal Reserve sells Treasury bills, the money paid for the securities is removed from the economy's money supply. Conversely, when it repurchases Treasury bills, the cash paid out to investors puts money back into the economy.

The second control, regulating reserve requirements, effectively restricts how much money banks can put into the economy through the disbursement of loans. When the Federal Reserve *raises* reserve requirements, banks have less money to lend, decreasing the money supply. When the Fed *lowers* reserve requirements, banks have more money to lend, increasing the money supply.

The third control, and perhaps the most effective, is regulation of the discount rate which member banks must pay to borrow money. If the discount rate goes up, it becomes more cost-prohibitive to borrow. Therefore the money supply tightens. If the discount rate is lowered, banks have an incentive to borrow more money to lend to customers.

The primary mortgage market

The **primary mortgage market** consists of lenders who originate mortgage loans directly to borrowers. Primary mortgage market lenders include:

- savings and loans
- commercial banks
- mutual savings banks

- life insurance companies
- mortgage bankers
- credit unions

Mortgage brokers are also part of the primary mortgage market, even though they do not lend to customers directly. Rather, they are instrumental in procuring borrowers for primary mortgage lenders.

The primary lender assumes the initial risk of the long-term investment in the mortgage loan. Primary lenders sometimes also **service** the loan until it is paid off. Servicing loans entails collecting the borrower's periodic payments, maintaining and disbursing funds in escrow accounts for taxes and insurance, supervising the borrower's performance, and releasing the mortgage on repayment. In many cases, primary lenders employ mortgage servicing companies, which service loans for a fee.

Portfolio lenders. A primary mortgage market lender may or may not sell its loans into the secondary market. Many lenders originate loans for the purpose of retaining the investments in their own loan *portfolio.* These loans are referred to as *portfolio loans*, and lenders originating loans for their own portfolio are called *portfolio lenders*. Portfolio lenders are less restricted by the standards and forms imposed on other lenders by secondary market organizations. In retaining their portfolio loans, portfolio lenders may vary underwriting criteria and hold independent standards for down payment requirements and the condition of the collateral.

The secondary mortgage market

Lenders, investors and government agencies that buy loans already originated by someone else, or originate loans indirectly through someone else, constitute the **secondary mortgage market**.

Secondary mortgage market organizations include:

- Federal National Mortgage Association (FNMA, or Fannie Mae)
- Federal Home Loan Mortgage Corporation (FHLMC, or Freddie Mac)
- Government National Mortgage Association (GNMA, or Ginnie Mae)
- investment firms that assemble loans into packages and sell securities based on the pooled mortgages
- life insurance companies
- pension funds
- primary market institutions who also invest as secondary lenders

Secondary mortgage market organizations buy pools of mortgages from primary lenders and sell securities backed by these pooled mortgages to investors. By selling securities, the secondary market brings investor money into the mortgage market. By purchasing loans from primary lenders, the secondary market returns funds to the primary lenders, thereby enabling the primary lender to originate more mortgage loans.

Exhibit 17.4 Money Flow in the Mortgage Market

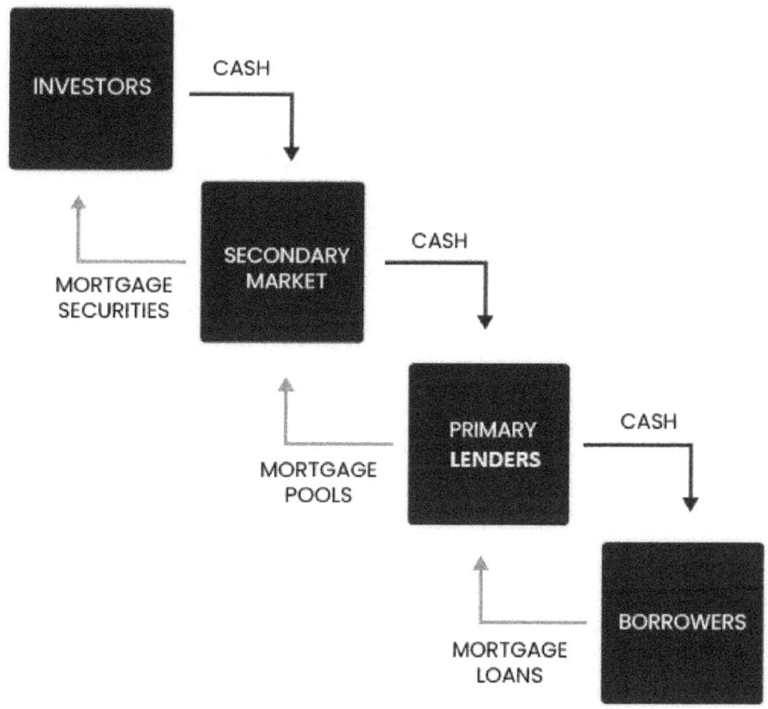

Primary lenders make a profit on the sale of loans to the secondary market. The secondary market acquires a profitable long-term investment without having to underwrite, originate, and service the loans. Secondary market organizations customarily hire primary lenders or loan servicing companies to service mortgage pools.

Secondary market loan requirements. The secondary market only buys loans that meet established requirements for quality of collateral, borrower and documentation. Since many primary lenders intend to sell their loans to the secondary market, the qualification standards of the secondary market limit and effectively regulate the kind of loans the primary lender will originate.

Role of FNMA GNMA, FHLMC AND FAMC

As major players in the secondary market, the Federal National Mortgage Association (FNMA, "Fannie Mae"), Government National Mortgage Association (GNMA, "Ginnie Mae), Federal Home Loan Mortgage Corporation (FHLMC, "Freddie Mac") and Federal Agricultural Mortgage Corporation (FAMC, “Farmer Mac”) tend to set the standards for the primary market.

Federal National Mortgage Association, or Fannie Mae. Fannie Mae is a government-sponsored enterprise, originally organized as a privately-owned corporation. As a secondary market player, it:

- buys conventional, FHA-backed and VA-backed loans
- gives banks mortgage-backed securities in exchange for blocks of mortgages

- offers lenders firm loan purchase commitments, provided they conform to Fannie Mae's lending standards
- sells bonds and mortgage-backed securities
- guarantees payment of interest and principal on mortgage-backed securities

Government National Mortgage Association, or Ginnie Mae. Ginnie Mae is a division of the Department of Housing and Urban Development. Its purpose is to administer special assistance programs and to help Fannie Mae in its secondary market activities. Specifically, GNMA

- guarantees payment on FNMA high-risk, low-yield mortgages and absorbs the difference in yield between the mortgages and market rates
- guarantees privately generated securities backed by pools of VA-and FHA-guaranteed loans

Federal Home Loan Mortgage Corporation, or Freddie Mac. Freddie Mac is a government-sponsored enterprise, originally chartered as an corporation in 1970. As a secondary market player, FHLMC buys mortgages and pools them, selling bonds backed by the mortgages in the open market. Freddie Mac guarantees performance on FHLMC mortgages.

A federal conservator, the Federal Housing Finance Authority (FHFA), now operates Fannie Mae and Freddie Mac as conservator with the U.S. Treasury a majority owner of both organizations.

The Federal Agricultural Mortgage Corporation, or Farmer Mac. Farmer Mac (FAMC) is a federal agency whose central function is to increase the availability and affordability of credit for American agriculture and American rural communities. In effect, Farmer Mac is the secondary loan market for American agricultural businesses. More specifically, Farmer Mac provides rural lenders and cooperatives with liquidity and lower-cost capital for funding agricultural assets, businesses and other related capital requirements within the farming community.

Farmer Mac's central activities within the agricultural credit market include purchasing ag loans; enhancing USDA loan guarantees; providing credit guarantees for loans and credit; and providing flexible, wholesale credit for ag lenders, agribusinesses, and applicable investment firms.

TYPES OF REAL ESTATE LOANS

Conventional loans
FHA-insured loans
VA-guaranteed loans
Common loan structures
Seller financing
Special-purpose loans

Conventional loans

A **conventional mortgage** loan is a permanent long-term loan that is not FHA-insured or VA-guaranteed. Market rates usually determine the interest rate on the loan. Because of the lack of insurance or guarantee by a government agency, the risk to a lender is greater for a conventional loan than for a non-conventional loan. This risk is usually reflected in higher interest rates and stricter requirements for the down payment and the borrower's income qualification. At the same time, conventional loans allow greater flexibility in fees, rates, and terms than do insured and guaranteed loans.

The primary sources of conventional loans are banks and savings and loan associations. Other conventional lenders include credit unions, life insurance companies, pension funds, mortgage bankers, and private individuals. Various types of lenders specialize in mortgage lending for specific purposes and type of borrower, such as commercial, construction, or single-family residential loans.

FHA-insured loans

The Federal Housing Administration (FHA) is an agency of the Department of Housing and Urban Development (HUD). It does not lend money, but *insures* permanent long-term loans made by others. The lender must be approved by the FHA, and the borrower must meet certain FHA qualifications. In addition, the property used to secure the loan must meet FHA standards. The FHA insures that the lender will not suffer significant loss in the case of borrower default. To provide this security, FHA provides insurance and charges the borrower an insurance premium. FHA loans typically have a higher loan-to-value ratio than conventional loans, enabling a borrower to make a smaller down payment.
The basic FHA-insured loan program is the **Title II, Section 203(b)** program for loans on one- to four-family residential properties. Among the features of this program are the following.

FHA mortgage insurance. The FHA determines how much mortgage insurance must be provided and charges the borrower an appropriate mortgage insurance premium (MIP). The initial premium is payable at closing or is added to the borrower's loan balance and financed. Further annual premiums are charged monthly. The amount of the premium varies according to the loan term and the applicable loan-to-value ratio.

Borrower default. The FHA reimburses the lender for losses due to default by the borrower, including costs of foreclosure.

Appraisal. The property must be appraised by an FHA-approved appraiser. The property must also meet the FHA's standards for type and quality of construction, neighborhood quality, and other features.

Maximum loan amount. The FHA has set maximum loan amounts for over 80 regions. Borrowers within a region are limited to the loan ceiling amount in effect for the region. In addition, the maximum loan amount is restricted by the loan-to-value ratios in effect. The maximum FHA-backed loan a borrower can obtain will be the lesser of the regional ceiling amount or the amount dictated by the loan-to-value standard. Calculations are based on the lesser of sale price or appraised value.

Down payment requirement. The minimum down payment for an FHA-backed loan is based on the lower of the appraised value or the sales price. The present requirement for single-family residential loans is 3.5%.

Maximum loan term. Thirty years is the maximum length of the repayment period.

Prepayment privilege. The borrower has the right to pay off the loan at any time without penalty, provided the lender is given prior notice. The lender may charge up to 30 days' interest if the borrower provides less than 30 days' notice.

Assumability. FHA-backed loans on owner-occupied properties are assumable if the buyer is qualified. Lenders and borrowers should check with FHA for current requirements.

Interest rate. The lender and borrower negotiate the interest rate on an FHA-backed loan without any involvement by FHA.

Points, fees and costs. The lender may charge discount points, a loan origination fee, and other such charges. These may be paid by buyer or seller. However, if the seller pays more than a specified percentage of the costs normally paid by a buyer, the FHA may regard these as sales concessions and lower the sales price on which the loan insurance amount is based.

In addition to Section 203(b) loan programs, FHA offers insurance coverage for other loan products. These include:

- home improvement loans
- subsidized loans for low- and middle-income families
- loans for condominiums
- loans for multi-family projects
- graduated-payment loans
- adjustable-rate loans

VA-guaranteed loans

The Department of Veterans Affairs (formerly Veterans Administration) offers *loan guarantees to qualified veterans*. The VA, like the FHA, does not lend money except in certain areas where other financing is not generally available. Instead, the VA partially guarantees permanent long-term loans originated by VA-approved lenders on properties that meet VA standards. The VA's guarantee enables lenders to issue loans with higher loan-to-value ratios than would otherwise be possible. The interest rate on a VA-guaranteed loan is usually lower than one on a conventional loan. The borrower does not pay any premium for the loan guarantee, but does pay a VA funding fee at closing.

Borrower default. The VA reimburses the lender for losses up to the guaranteed amount if foreclosure sale proceeds fail to cover the loan balance.

Appraisal. The property must be appraised by a VA-approved appraiser. The VA issues a *Certificate of Reasonable Value* which creates a maximum value on which the VA-guaranteed portion of the loan will be based. The property must meet certain VA specifications.

Down payment requirement. The VA usually requires no down payment, although the lender may require one.

Maximum loan amount. The VA does not cap the loan amount, but it does limit the liability it can assume, which usually influences the amount an institution will lend. The amount a qualified veteran with full entitlement can borrow without making a downpayment determines the practical loan limits. This amount varies by county. The basic entitlement available to each eligible veteran is $36,000. Lenders will generally lend a maximum of 4 times that amount without a down payment if the veteran is fully qualified and the property appraises for the asking price.

A veteran must apply for a *Certificate of Eligibility* to find out how much the VA will guarantee in a particular situation.

Maximum loan term. The maximum loan term for one- to four-family residences is 30 years. For loans secured by farms, the maximum loan term is 40 years.

Prepayment privilege. The loan may be paid off early without penalty.

Assumability. VA loans are assumable with lender approval. Usually, the person assuming the loan must have VA eligibility, and the assumption may have to be approved by the VA.

Interest rate. Lender and borrower negotiate the interest rate for all VA-insured loans.

Points, fees and costs. The lender may charge discount points, origination fees, and other reasonable costs. These may be paid by seller (with some limits) or buyer, but may not be financed. The VA funding fee, however, may be included in the loan amount. The funding fee is a percentage of the loan amount which varies based on the type of loan, military category, whether the loan is a first-time loan, and whether there is a down payment.

Other VA programs. In addition to insuring loans to veterans, the VA may insure loans for lenders who set up a special account with the VA. The VA may also actually lend money directly when an eligible veteran cannot find other mortgage money locally.

Common loan structures

Variations in the structure of interest rate, term, payments, and principal payback produce a number of commonly recognized loan types. Among these are the following.

Amortizing loan. Amortization provides for gradual repayment of principal and payment of interest over the term of the loan. The borrower's periodic payments to the lender include a portion for interest and a portion for principal. In a fully amortizing mortgage, the principal balance is zero at the end of the term. In a partially amortizing loan, the payments are not sufficient to retire the debt. At the end of the loan term, there is still a principal balance to be paid off.

Negatively amortized loan. Negative amortization causes the loan balance to increase over the term. This occurs if the borrower's periodic payment is insufficient to cover the interest owed for the period. The lender adds the amount of unpaid interest to the borrower's loan balance. Temporary negative amortization occurs on graduated payment loans, and may occur on an adjustable rate mortgage.

Adjustable and fixed rate loans. Loans may have fixed or variable rates of interest over the loan term. Adjustable rate mortgages (ARMs) allow the lender to change the interest rate at specified intervals and by a specified amount. Federal regulations place limits, called rate caps, on incremental interest rate increases and on the total amount by which the rate may be increased over the loan term.

Senior and junior loans. When there are multiple loans on a single property, there is an order of priority in the liens which the mortgages create. The first, or senior, loan generally has priority over any subsequent loans. Second loans are riskier than first loans because the senior lender will be satisfied first in case of default. Therefore, interest rates on second mortgages are generally higher than on first mortgages.

Fixed and graduated payment loans. Loans may have variable payment amounts over the term of the loan, or a single fixed payment amount. With a graduated payment mortgage, the payments at the beginning of the loan term are not sufficient to amortize the loan fully, and unpaid interest is added to the principal balance. Payments are later adjusted to a level that will fully amortize the loan's increased balance over the remaining loan term.

Interest-only loan. In an interest-only loan, periodic payments over the loan term apply only to interest owed, not to principal. At the end of the term, the full balance must be paid off in a lump-sum, "balloon" payment. Since these loans have no periodic principal payback, their monthly payments are smaller than amortizing loans for the same amount at the same rate of interest.

Buydown loan. A buydown loan entails a prepayment of interest on a loan. The prepayment effectively lowers the interest rate and the periodic payments for the borrower. Buydowns typically occur in a circumstance where a builder wants to market a new development to a buyer who cannot quite qualify for the necessary loan at market rates. By "buying down" a borrower's mortgage, a builder enables the borrower to obtain the loan. The builder may then pass the costs of the buydown through to the buyer in the form of a higher purchase price.

Seller financing

The seller may provide some or all of the financing for the buyer's purchase. Some of the most common methods of seller financing are purchase money mortgages, including the wraparound, and the contract for deed.

Purchase money mortgage. With a purchase money mortgage, the borrower gives a mortgage and note to the seller to finance some or all of the purchase price of the property. The seller in this case is said to "take back" a note, or to "carry paper," on the property. Purchase money mortgages may be either senior or junior liens.

Wraparound. In a wraparound loan arrangement, the seller receives a junior mortgage from the buyer, and uses the buyer's payments to make the payments on the original first mortgage. A wraparound enables the buyer to obtain financing with a minimum cash investment. It also potentially enables the seller to profit from any difference between a lower interest rate on the senior loan and a higher rate on the wraparound loan. A wraparound is possible only if the senior mortgagee allows it.

Contract for deed. Under a contract for deed arrangement, the seller retains title and the buyer receives possession and equitable title while making payments under the terms of the contract. The seller conveys title when the contract has been fully performed.

Special-purpose loans

Home equity loan. The ostensible purpose of this type of loan is to obtain funds for home improvement. Structurally, the home equity loan is a junior mortgage secured by the homeowner's equity, **equity** in general being the portion of the property's value actually owned by the homeowner, expressed as the difference between the property's market value and all loan balances outstanding on the property.

For some lenders, the maximum home equity loan amount is based on the difference between the property's appraised value and the maximum loan-to-value ratio the lender allows on the property, inclusive of all existing mortgage loans. Thus if a home is appraised at $500,000 and the lender's maximum LTV is 80%, the lender will lend a total of $400,000. If the owner's existing mortgage balance is $325,000, the owner would qualify for a $75,000 home equity loan.

Package loan. A package loan finances the purchase of real estate and personal property. For example, a package loan might finance a furnished condominium, complete with all fixtures and decor.

Construction loan. A construction loan finances construction of improvements. This type of loan is paid out by the lender in installments linked to stages of the construction process. The loan is usually interest-only, and the borrower makes periodic payments based on the amount disbursed so far. As short-term, high-risk financing, the interest rates are usually higher than those for long-term financing. The borrower is expected to find permanent ("take out") financing elsewhere to pay off the temporary loan when construction is complete.

Bridge loan. A bridge, or gap, loan is used to cover a gap in financing between short-term construction financing and long-term permanent financing. For instance, a developer may have difficulty finding a long-term lender to take out the construction lender. However, as the construction loan is expensive and must be paid off as soon as possible, the developer may find an interim lender who will pay off the construction loan but not agree to a long-term loan.

Participation loan. In a participation loan, the lender participates in the income and/or equity of the property, in return for giving the borrower more favorable loan terms than would otherwise be justified. For instance, the borrower makes smaller periodic payments than the interest rate and loan amount require, and the lender makes up the difference by receiving some of the property's income. This type of loan usually involves an income property.

Permanent (take-out) loan. A permanent loan is a long-term loan that "takes out" a construction or short-term lender. The long-term lender pays off the balance on the construction loan when the project is completed, leaving the borrower with a long-term loan under more favorable terms than the construction loan offered.

Reverse annuity. In a reverse annuity mortgage, a homeowner pledges the equity in the home as security for a loan which is paid out in regular monthly amounts over the term of the loan. The homeowner, in effect, is able to convert the equity to cash without losing ownership and possession.

Blanket. A blanket mortgage is secured by more than one property, such as multiple parcels of real estate in a development.

For more information:

FHA loans:	https://entp.hud.gov/idapp/html/hicostlook.cfm
VA loans:	https://www.va.gov/housing-assistance/
HUD:	https://www.hud.gov/resources
FNMA:	http://www.fanniemae.com/portal/index.html
FHLMC:	www.freddiemac.com
GNMA:	https://www.ginniemae.gov/pages/default.aspx
FAMC	https://www.farmermac.com/
ECOA:	https://www.consumer.ftc.gov/articles/0347-your-equal-credit-opportunity-rights
CFPB:	https://www.consumerfinance.gov/policy-compliance/guidance/tila-respa-disclosure-rule/

17 Real Estate Finance Snapshot Review

ANATOMY OF MORTGAGE LENDING

Mechanics of a loan transaction

- mortgage financing: using borrowed money secured by a mortgage to finance the purchase of real estate
- instruments: note and mortgage or trust deed
- mortgage mechanics: borrower gives lender note and mortgage; lender gives borrower funds and records a lien
- trust deed mechanics: trust deed conveys title from the borrower/trustor to a third-party trustee who holds title on behalf of the lender/beneficiary until the debt is repaid

Financial components of a loan

- original principal: capital amount borrowed on which interest payments are calculated
- loan balance: remaining unpaid principal at any point in the life of the loan
- interest: charge for the use of money; rate fixed or variable
- Annual Percentage Rate (APR) includes interest and all other finance charges; lender must disclose on residential properties
- point: one percent of the loan amount, charged by lender at origination to obtain required return
- term: period of time for repayment of interest and principal
- payment: the periodic payment of interest and/or principal

Promissory note

- legal instrument executed by borrower stating debt amount, loan term, method and timing of repayment, interest rate, promise to pay; may repeat other provisions from mortgage document or deed of trust; negotiable instrument assignable to a third party

Mortgage document and trust deed

- the legal documents which pledge the property as collateral for the loan
- may include clauses covering payment of principal and interest, prepayment, late charges, escrow for taxes and insurance, liens, insurance requirements, occupancy and maintenance, lender's rights, private mortgage insurance, inspection, and other conditions of performance

INITIATING A MORTGAGE LOAN

The loan application

- borrower provides personal and property data; supporting documentation: appraisal report, credit report, purchase contract, income and/or employment verification
- lenders must accept all completed applications and notify applicants about disposition of application

Mortgage loan underwriting

- process of evaluating borrower's ability to repay and value of the property
- loan-to-value ratio: relationship of loan amount to property value, expressed as a percentage

QUALIFYING FOR A MORTGAGE LOAN

Equal Credit Opportunity Act
- lender must evaluate applicant according to applicant's own income and credit information

Income qualification
- income ratio and debt ratio qualify borrower's income; income ratio applied to gross income determines housing expense maximum; debt ratio takes revolving debt into account

Loan constant
- monthly or annual payment amount needed to amortize a $1,000 loan given interest rate and term; used to derive loan amount or payment amount with known interest rate and loan term

Cash qualification
- lender verifies applicant's sources of cash for down payment; extra cash enhances income qualification evaluation

Net worth
- extent to which applicant's assets exceed liabilities as a further source of reserves

Credit evaluation
- lender obtains credit reports to evaluate applicant's payment behavior

Loan commitment
- written pledge by lender to grant loan under specific terms; firm, lock-in, conditional, take-out

CLOSING A LOAN
- usually simultaneous with closing of real estate transaction; transfer of funds, signing of documents, escrow deposits

LAWS AFFECTING MORTGAGE LENDING

Truth-in-Lending and Regulation Z
- Reg Z implements Truth-in-Lending Simplification and Reform Act and Consumer Credit Protection Act
- provisions: lender must disclose finance charges and APR prior to closing; borrower has limited right of rescission; lender must follow disclosure requirements in advertising

Equal Credit Opportunity Act
- ECOA prohibits discrimination in lending

Real Estate Settlements and Procedures Act
- RESPA standardizes settlement practices
- provisions: lender must provide CFPB booklet explaining loans, settlement costs and procedures; lender must provide CFPB Loan Estimate of settlement costs within three days of application; lender must provide CFPB Closing Disclosure three days before loan consummation

National Flood Insurance Act
- borrowers of "federally-related loans" must obtain flood insurance if property is in designated flood-hazard area

THE MORTGAGE MARKET

Supply and demand for money
- relationship between money supply and demand affects interest rates, consumer prices, availability of mortgage money
- Federal Reserve controls: T-bills; reserve requirement, discount rate

The primary mortgage market
- originates mortgage loans directly to borrowers; savings and loans, commercial banks, mutual savings banks, life insurance companies, mortgage bankers, credit unions

The secondary mortgage market	• buys existing loans to provide liquidity to primary lenders; Fannie Mae, Ginnie Mae, Freddie Mac, investment firms, life insurance companies, pension funds
Role of FNMA, GNMA, FHLMC, and FAMC	• FNMA buys conventional, FHA- and VA-backed loans and pooled mortgages; guarantees payment on mortgage-backed securities; GNMA guarantees payment on certain types of loans; FHLMC buys and pools mortgages; sells mortgage-backed securities; FAMC funds agricultural assets, businesses and related capital requirements for the farming community
TYPES OF REAL ESTATE LOANS	
Conventional loans	• permanent, long-term loans not insured by FHA or guaranteed by VA
FHA-insured loans	• insured loans granted by FHA-approved lenders to borrowers who meet FHA qualifications
VA-guaranteed loans	• guaranteed loans granted by VA-approved lenders to qualified veterans
Common loan structures	• amortizing, negative amortizing, interest only, fixed rate, adjustable rate, senior, junior, fixed or graduated payment, balloon, buydown
Seller financing	• purchase money mortgages: loans by the seller to the property buyer for all or part of the purchase price; contract for deed: installment sale where seller finances buyer and retains title until contract terms are met
Special-purpose loans	• home equity, package, construction, bridge, equity participation, take-out, reverse annuity, and blanket

18 Real Estate Investment

Investment Fundamentals
Real Estate as an Investment
Real Estate Investment Entities
Taxation of Real Estate Investments
Investment Analysis of a Residence
Investment Analysis of an Income Property

INVESTMENT FUNDAMENTALS

Investment characteristics
Rewards
Risks
Types of investments

Investment characteristics

The idea of investment is simple: take something of value and put it to work in some way to increase its value over time. With any investment, one wants the original investment to grow, without losing it. This idea is called **conservation of capital**. Unfortunately, no investment is truly secure. External conditions change, and the investment itself can change. Even if you do nothing with it, its value does not remain constant.

Risk versus return. The general rule in investments is that the safer the investment, the more slowly it gains in value. The more you want it to gain, and the more quickly, the more you must risk losing it. How much do you want to earn, and how much are you willing to risk to earn it? Reward in investing corresponds directly to the degree of risk.

Management. Another aspect of investment is the amount of attention you must pay to it to make it work. You can deposit cash in a passbook account and forget about it. You can use your cash to buy a business and then run the business yourself to make your asset grow and earn. How much do you want to be involved in managing your investment?

Liquidity. The issue of exchangeability is an important one in investment. How easy is it to recover your invested resource, without loss, and exchange it for another one that you want? If there is a **market** for the type of resource you have- other people want to buy and sell it for themselves-- your investment is **liquid**. The most liquid form of financial investment is generally cash, since cash is itself a medium of exchange and people always want it. A more illiquid investment is one which takes a long time to exchange for something you prefer to own. How long are you willing to wait to recover your invested resource and its earnings?

Rewards

The basic aim of financial investment is to increase one's wealth, to add value to what you have. This can occur in several ways.

Income. An investment can generate income in some way on a periodic basis. You may consume this cash, spending it for goods and services that, when used up, have no further value. Or, you may use the cash to put into another investment.

Appreciation. Your invested asset itself may gain value over time because of an increase in market demand for it. When you sell or exchange it for something else you prefer to have, you get more than you originally put into the investment.

Leverage. You may pledge the value of your resource to borrow funds in order to make an investment that is larger than your own resource permits you to do directly. The small resource is used as a lever to make a larger investment, and thus increases your opportunity to benefit from income, appreciation, and the other rewards of investment.

Tax benefits. Some investments receive treatment under tax laws that enables the investor to reduce or defer the amount of tax owed. Tax dollars you don't have to pay are dollars you have available for some other use, such as consuming or further investing.

Risks

Investment risks come from a variety of general sources, including the market, business operations, the value of money, and changes in the interest rate.

Market risk. Changes in the demand for your invested resource may cause your investment to lose value and to become illiquid.

Business risk. Changes in the operation of a business with which your investment is connected may reduce or eliminate the income- and appreciation-earning capacity of your investment.

Purchasing power risk. Changes in the value of money as an exchange medium, such as through inflation, may decrease the practical value of your invested resource.

Financial risk. Changes in financial markets, particularly in interest rates, may reduce the value of your investment by making it less desirable to others and by making it more expensive for you to maintain.

An investment may fail to produce any or all of the desired investment rewards listed earlier. The expected income may not be realized. The invested asset may fail to appreciate as expected. It may even decline in value. Perhaps even worse, you may be called on to **add** to the investment just to keep it in place. Your leverage may turn against you, becoming **negative leverage**. This is the situation when your cost of borrowing funds to make the investment becomes greater than the income the investment returns to you. Finally, your expectation of a tax advantage may be disappointed. Tax laws are constantly changing.

Types of investments

Four of the most important types of investment are investments in money, equity, debt, and real estate.

Money investments. A money investment is one in which the basic form of the investment remains money. Examples are: deposit accounts, certificates of deposit, money funds, and annuities. The basic reward from a money investment comes in the form of interest. Money investments are relatively safe, with correspondingly conservative rates of return.

Debt investments. A debt investment is one in which an investor buys a debt instrument. Examples are bonds, notes, mortgages, and bond mutual funds. The basic reward comes in the form of interest. Debt investments are usually riskier than money investments and less risky than stocks or real estate.

Equity investments. An equity investment is one in which an investor buys an ownership interest in a business concern. Examples are stocks and stock mutual funds. The basic rewards come in the form of dividends and appreciation of share value. Equity investments are generally riskier than money and debt investments.

Real estate investments. A real estate investment is one in which an investor *buys real estate for its investment benefits rather than primarily for its utility*. It may have the features of both an equity and debt investment, depending on the type of real estate involved and numerous other factors, such as the type of interest one owns. A real estate investor may invest in an income-producing property or a non-income producing property.

- **Non-income property**

  a residential property used as the investor's primary residence. The basic reward, beyond the enjoyment of use, comes in the form of appreciation. There may also be tax benefits, depending on how the purchase is financed.

- **Income property**

  a property owned specifically for the investment rewards it offers. Examples are multi-family residential properties, retail stores, industrial properties, and office buildings. Rewards come in any or all of the forms mentioned earlier: income, appreciation, leverage and tax advantages.

REAL ESTATE AS AN INVESTMENT

Risk and reward
Illiquidity
Management requirements

Real estate investments participate in the general risks and rewards of all investments. However, real estate investments are often complex. They are also distinguished by their lack of liquidity and by the amount of management they require. In addition, each investor has specific aims and circumstances that affect the viability of any particular real estate investment for that individual. Licensees who lack expertise in the area of real estate investment analysis should refer potential investors to a competent advisor. Nevertheless, a licensee should be familiar with the basics of real estate as an investment.

Risk and reward

Capital put into real estate is always subject to the full range of risk factors: market changes, income shortfalls, negative leverage, tax law changes, and poor overall return.

Market demand for a specific type of property can decline. For example, a business district's retailers may vacate stores in an area in order to obtain better space in a new shopping center. Market downturns leave the income property investor with an unmarketable property or one which can only be re-leased at a loss of some portion of the original investment. Thus the expected reward from income or appreciation may never be obtained.

Another risk of the investment property is the cost of development or operation. If start-up costs or ongoing operating costs exceed rental income, the owner must dip into additional capital resources to maintain the investment until its income increases. If income does not rise, or if costs do not decline, the investor can simply run out of money.

Leverage is a constant risk in real estate investment. If the property fails to generate sufficient revenue, the costs of borrowed money can bankrupt the owner, just as development and operating costs can. Investors often overlook the fact that leverage only works when the yield on the investment exceeds the costs of borrowed funds.

Tax law is an ongoing risk in long-term real estate investment. If the investor's tax circumstances change, or if the tax laws do, the investor may end up paying more capital gains and income taxes than planned, undermining the return on the investment. An investor needs to consider carefully the value of such potential tax benefits as deductions for mortgage interest, tax losses, deferred gains, exemptions, and tax credits for certain types of real estate investment.

Another consideration is *opportunity cost*. Opportunity cost is the return that an investor could earn on capital invested with minimal risk. If the real estate investment, with all its attendant risk, cannot yield a greater return than an investment elsewhere involving less risk, then the opportunity cost is too high for the real estate investment. Despite all the risks, real estate remains a popular investment, because, historically, the rewards have outweighed the risks. Real estate has proven to be relatively resistant to adverse inflationary trends that have hurt money, debt, and stock investments. In addition, real estate has proven to be a viable investment in view of the economy's continued expansion over the last fifty years.

Illiquidity

Compared with other classes of investment, real estate is relatively illiquid. Even in the case of liquidating a single-family residence, one can expect a marketing period of at least several months in most markets. In addition, it takes time for the buyer to obtain financing and to complete all the other phases of closing the transaction. Commercial and investment properties can take much longer, depending on market conditions, leases, construction, permitting, and a host of other factors. The investor who is in a hurry to dispose of such an investment can expect to receive a lower sales price than may be ideal. Compare this with the ease of drawing money out of a bank account or selling a stock.

Management requirements

Real estate tends to require a high degree of investor involvement in management of the investment. Even raw land requires some degree of maintenance to preserve its value: drainage, fencing, payment of taxes, and periodic inspection, to name a few tasks. Improved properties often require extensive management, including repairs, maintenance, onsite leasing, tenant relations, security, and fiscal management.

REAL ESTATE INVESTMENT ENTITIES

Direct
Syndicate and partnership
Real Estate Investment Trust
Real Estate Mortgage Investment Conduit

Direct

Individuals, corporations or other investor entities may invest as **active investors** in a property by buying it directly and taking responsibility for managing and operating the property.

Syndicate and partnership

A real estate **syndicate** is a group of investors who combine resources to buy, develop, and/or operate a property.

A **general partnership** is a syndicate in which all members participate equally in managing the investment and in the profits or losses it generates. The group designates a trustee to hold title in the name of the syndicate.

A **limited partnership** is a syndicate in which a **general partner** organizes, operates and is generally responsible for the partnership's interests in the property. **Limited partners** invest money in the partnership but do not participate in operating the property. These limited partners are **passive investors**.

Real Estate Investment Trust (REIT)

In a Real Estate Investment Trust, investors buy certificates in the trust, and the trust in turn invests in mortgages or real estate. Investors receive income according to the number of shares they own. A trust must receive at least 75% of its income from real estate to qualify as a REIT, and if certain other conditions are met, the trust does not have to pay any corporate income tax.

Real Estate Mortgage Investment Conduit (REMIC)

A REMIC is a kind of partnership entity formed to hold a fixed pool of mortgages that are secured by real property. The entity issues two kinds of interest. Holders of residual interests are treated, for tax purposes, as partners. Holders of regular interests are regarded as owning debt instruments. Income (or loss) received by regular or residual interest holders is treated as **portfolio** income or loss, and is not included in determining losses from **passive** activities.

TAXATION OF REAL ESTATE INVESTMENTS

Taxable income
Cost recovery
Gain on sale
Interest
Passive activities

Real estate investments are taxed on the income they produce and on the increase in value, or gain, when the investment is sold. These forms of taxation are distinct from the ad valorem taxation of real estate.

Taxable Income

Taxable income from investment real estate is *the gross income received minus any expenses, deductions or exclusions that current tax law allows*. Taxable income from real estate is added to the investor's other income and taxed at the investor's marginal tax rate. The "Investment Analysis of an Income Property" section below gives details.

Cost recovery

Cost recovery, or **depreciation**, allows the owner of income property to deduct a portion of the property's value from gross income each year over the life of the asset. The "life of the asset" and the deductible portion are defined by law. In theory, the owner recovers the full cost of the investment if it is held to the end of the asset's economic life as defined by the Internal Revenue Service. At the time of selling the asset, the accumulated cost recovery is subtracted from the investment's original value as part of determining the taxable capital gain.

Cost recovery is allowed only for income properties and that portion of a non-income property which is used to produce income. It applies only to improvements. Land cannot be depreciated. The part of a property which can be depreciated is called the **depreciable basis**.

Depreciation schedules. Residential rental properties are depreciated over a period of 27.5 years. The basic annual deduction for such property is 3.636%, with adjustments for the month of the taxable year in which the property was placed in service. Non-residential income properties placed in service after 1994 are depreciated over a period of 39 years (basic annual percentage is 2.564%). The proper method of depreciation should be determined in consultation with a qualified tax advisor.

Gain on sale

When real estate, whether non-income or income, is sold, a *taxable event* occurs. If the sale proceeds *exceed* the original cost of the investment, subject to some adjustments, there is a **capital gain** that is subject to tax. If the sales proceeds are less than the original cost with adjustments, there is a **capital loss**.

1031 (Starker) exchange. An investor can sometimes defer the reporting of gain or loss, and, hence, taxation of gain, by participating in an exchange of like-kind assets. The legislation that deals with like-kind exchanges is contained in Section 1031 of the IRS code. These tax-deferred exchanges are sometimes called **Section 1031 exchanges** and **Starker exchanges**, named for an investor who won a case against the IRS.

To qualify under Section 1031, there must have been a legitimate exchange of the assets involved. The property being transferred must have been held for productive use in a trade or business or held as an investment and must be exchanged for property that will also be used in a trade or business or be held as an investment. Tax on gain is deferred until the investment or business property is sold and not exchanged.

Interest

Mortgage interest incurred by loans to buy, build, or materially improve a primary or secondary residence is deductible from gross income, subject to limitations based on the loan amount and when it was incurred . The interest on a home equity loan may be deducted only if the loan is used to "buy, build or substantially improve" the home that secures the loan. Principal payments on a loan are *not* deductible. Licensees should consult the latest IRS publications for current rules on mortgage interest deduction.

For income properties that are held as investments, interest on debts incurred to finance the investment is deductible as **investment interest** up to the amount of net income received from the property.

Passive activities

Passive activities are business activities in which the taxpayer does not materially participate. Included are interests in **limited partnerships** and **rental** activities. Losses from such activities may be used to offset income from other passive activities. Passive losses, with certain limitations, may be carried forward to future years or accumulated and deducted from capital gain at the time of sale.

INVESTMENT ANALYSIS OF A RESIDENCE

Appreciation
Deductibles
Tax liability
Gains tax exclusion

Investment analysis examines the economic performance of an investment. The analysis includes costs, income, taxation, appreciation, and return.

A property acquired and used as a primary residence is an example of a non-income property. If a portion of a residence is used for business (i.e., a home office), this portion only may be treated as an income property for tax purposes. Since, by definition, a non-income property does not generate income, its value as an investment must come from one or more of the other sources: appreciation, leverage, or tax benefits.

Appreciation

Appreciation is the increase in value of an asset over time. A simple way to estimate appreciation on a primary residence is to subtract the price originally paid from the estimated current market value:

Current value - original price = total appreciation

For example, if a house was bought for $300,000 and its estimated market value now is $400,000, it has appreciated by $100,000.

Original price:	$300,000
Current market value:	$400,000
Total appreciation:	$100,000

Total appreciation can be stated as a percentage increase over the original price by dividing the estimated total appreciation by the original price.

The house in the last example has appreciated by 33%:

$$\frac{(Total\ appreciation)}{Original\ price} = \%\ appreciated$$

$$\frac{100{,}000}{300{,}000} = 33\%$$

To estimate the percentage of *annual appreciation*, divide the percent appreciated by the number of years the house has been owned:

$$\frac{\%\ total\ appreciation}{years\ owned} = \%\ appreciation\ per\ year$$

If the house in the previous example has been owned for three years, the annual appreciation has been 11%.

$$\frac{33\%}{3\ years} = 11\%\ appreciation\ per\ year$$

Deductibles

The primary tax benefit available to the owner of a non-income property is the *annual deduction for mortgage interest*. The portion of annual mortgage payments that goes to repay principal must be subtracted to determine the amount paid for interest. Principal repayment is not deductible. Furthermore, depreciation is not allowed for non-income properties. Consult IRS publications for current conditions and limitations for mortgage interest deductibility.

Tax liability

The seller of a principal residence may owe tax on capital gain that results from the sale. The IRS defines gain on the sale of a home as **amount realized** from the sale minus the **adjusted basis** of the home sold.

Amount realized. The amount realized, also known as **net proceeds from sale**, is expressed by the formula:

$$\begin{array}{rl} & \text{sale price} \\ - & \text{costs of sale} \\ \hline & \text{amount realized} \end{array}$$

The sale price is the total amount the seller receives for the home. This includes money, notes, mortgages or other debts the buyer assumes as part of the sale.

Costs of sale include brokerage commissions, relevant advertising, legal fees, seller-paid points and other closing costs. Certain *fixing-up expenses*, as discussed further below, can be deducted from the amount realized to derive an **adjusted sale price** for the purpose of postponing taxation on gain.

For example, Larry and Mary sold their home for $350,000. Their selling costs, including the commission they paid Broker Betty and amounts paid to inspectors, a surveyor, and the title company, amounted to ten percent of the selling price, or $35,000. The amount they realized from the sale was therefore $315,000.

Adjusted basis. Basis is a measurement of how much is invested in the property for tax purposes. Assuming that the property was acquired through purchase, the **beginning basis** is the cost of acquiring the property. Cost includes cash and debt obligations, and such other settlement costs as legal and recording fees, abstract fees, surveys, charges for installing utilities, transfer taxes, title insurance, and any other amounts the buyer pays for the seller.

The beginning basis is increased or decreased by certain types of expenditures made while the property is owned. Basis is increased by the cost of **capital improvements** made to the property. Assessments for local improvements such as roads and sidewalks also increase the basis. Examples of capital improvements are: putting on an addition, paving a driveway, replacing a roof, adding central air conditioning, and rewiring the home.

Basis is decreased by any amounts the owner received for such things as easements.

The basic formula for **adjusted basis** is:

	Beginning basis
+	capital improvements
-	exclusions, credits or other amounts received
	adjusted basis

For example, Mary and Larry originally paid $200,000 for their home. They spent an additional $10,000 on a new central heating and cooling unit. Their adjusted basis at the time of selling it is therefore $210,000.

Gain on sale. The gain on sale of a primary residence is represented by the basic formula:

	amount realized (net sales proceeds)
-	adjusted basis
	gain on sale

Gain on sale, if it does not qualify for an exclusion under current tax law, is taxable.

Exhibit 18.1 Gain on Sale

	Selling price of old home	$350,000
-	Selling costs	35,000
=	Amount realized	315,000
	Beginning basis of old home	200,000
+	Capital improvements	10,000
=	Adjusted basis of old home	210,000
	Amount realized	315,000
-	Adjusted basis	210,000
=	Gain on sale	105,000

In the case of Mary and Larry, their capital gain was $315,000 - $210,000, or $105,000. They will owe tax on this amount in the year of the sale unless they qualify for the exclusion described below.

Gains tax exclusion

Tax law provides an exclusion of $250,000 for an individual taxpayer and $500,000 for married taxpayers filing jointly. The exclusion of gain from sale of a residence can be claimed *every two years*, provided the taxpayer

1. owned the property for at least two years during the five years preceding the date of sale;

2. used the property as principal residence for a total of two years during that five-year period;

3. has waited two years since the last use of the exclusion for any sale.

Losses are not deductible, and there is no carry-over of any unused portion of the exclusion. Postponed gains from a previous home sale under the earlier rollover rules reduce the basis of the current home if that home was a qualifying replacement home under the old rule.

INVESTMENT ANALYSIS OF AN INCOME PROPERTY

Pre-tax cash flow
Tax liability
After-tax cash flow
Investment performance

Income properties are those which are held primarily for the generation of income. In addition to commercial and investment properties such as office buildings, this category includes residential rental properties. An important difference between income and non-income properties is that deductions for depreciation are allowed on income properties. Income properties, like non-income properties, generate a gain (or loss) on sale, and they also create an annual income stream. The annual income streams are determined on both a pre-tax and after-tax basis in order to determine the productivity of the investment.

Pre-tax cash flow

Cash flow is the difference between the amount of actual cash flowing into the investment as revenue and out of the investment for expenses, debt service, and all other items. Cash flow concerns cash items only, and therefore excludes depreciation, which is not a cash expense **Pre-tax cash flow**, or cash flow before taxation, is calculated as follows:

	potential rental income
-	vacancy and collection loss
=	effective rental income
+	other income
=	gross operating income (GOI)
-	operating expenses
-	reserves
=	net operating income (NOI)
-	debt service
=	pre-tax cash flow

Potential rental income is the annual amount that would be realized if the property is fully leased or rented at the scheduled rate. **Vacancy and collection loss** is rental income lost because of vacancies or tenants' failure to pay rent. **Effective rental income** is the potential income adjusted for these losses. To that is added any **other income** the property generates, such as from laundry or parking charges, to obtain **gross operating income**. **Operating expenses** paid by the landlord include such items as utilities and maintenance. These are deducted from gross operating income. Some owners also set aside a cash **reserve** each year to build up a fund for capital replacements in the future, for example, to replace a roof or a furnace. Cash reserves are not deductible for tax purposes until spent as deductible repairs or maintenance. The remainder is **net operating income (NOI)**. When the annual amount paid for **debt service**, including principal and interest, is subtracted, the remainder is the **pre-tax cash flow**.

For instance, a small office building of 3,500 square feet rents at $20 per square foot. If fully rented, the annual rental income would be $70,000. Historically, the property averages $4,200 in vacancy and collection losses. Equipment rental will provide an additional $2,000 per year in income. The owner will have to pay operating expenses amounting to ten dollars per square foot, or $35,000 per year. The owner sets aside one dollar per square foot, or $3,500 per year, for reserves. The owner financed the purchase of the building with a loan that requires annual debt service in the amount of $20,000. The pre-tax cash flow for the building is illustrated in the following exhibit.

Exhibit 18.2 Pre-tax Cash Flow

	potential rental income	$70,000
-	vacancy and collection loss	4,200
=	effective rental income	65,800
+	other income	2,000
=	gross operating income (GOI)	67,800
-	operating expenses	35,000
-	reserves	3,500
=	net operating income (NOI)	29,300
-	debt service	20,000
=	pre-tax cash flow	9,300

Tax liability

The owner's tax liability on taxable income from the property is based on *taxable income* rather than cash flow. Taxable income and tax liability are calculated as follows:

	net operating income (NOI)
+	reserves
-	interest expense
-	cost recovery expense
=	taxable income
x	tax rate
=	tax liability

Taxable income is net operating income minus all allowable deductions. Cost recovery expense is allowed as a deduction, while allowances for reserves and payments on loan principal payback are not allowed. Thus, since reserves were deducted from gross operating income to determine NOI, this amount must be added back in. As only the interest portion of debt service is deductible, the principal amount must be removed from the debt service payments and the *interest expense* deducted from NOI. Taxable income, multiplied by the owner's marginal tax bracket, gives the **tax liability**.

Note on tax rate: when a rental property is owned as an individual or by way of a pass-through entity (partnership, LLC treated as a partnership for tax purposes, or S corporation), its net income is taxed at the individual's personal marginal income tax rate. The next exhibit shows the tax liability for the previous example using an individual rate of 24%.

Exhibit 18.3 Tax Liability

	net operating income (NOI)	29,300
+	reserves	3,500
-	interest expense	10,000
-	cost recovery expense	22,000
=	taxable income	800
x	tax rate (24%)	
=	tax liability	192

After-tax cash flow

After-tax cash flow is the amount of income from the property that actually goes into the owner's pocket *after income tax is paid*. It is figured as:

	pre-tax cash flow
-	tax liability
=	after-tax cash flow

The after-tax cash flow for the sample property is illustrated in the following exhibit.

Exhibit 18.4 After-tax Cash Flow

	pre-tax cash flow	9,300
-	tax liability	192
=	after-tax cash flow	9,108

Investment performance

Investors measure the investment performance of an income property in many different ways, depending on their needs. A few of the common measures are:

$$\frac{\textbf{Net operating income}}{\textbf{price}} = \textbf{return on investment (ROI)}$$

$$\frac{\textbf{cash flow}}{\textbf{cash invested}} = \textbf{cash-on-cash return (C on C)}$$

$$\frac{\textbf{cash flow}}{\textbf{equity}} = \textbf{return on equity (ROE)}$$

Other measures of return use the process of **discounted cash flow analysis**. These methods, chief of which is probably **internal rate of return (IRR)**, require an estimate of projected after-tax proceeds from sale of the property. A licensee who does not have the expertise necessary for these more complicated measures should refer clients to a qualified investment expert.

18 Real Estate Investment Snapshot Review

INVESTMENT FUNDAMENTALS

Investment characteristics
- the greater the risk, the higher the expected return
- some investments require more investor involvement than others
- some investments are more liquid (convertible to cash) than others

Rewards
- investors seek to increase wealth through income, appreciation, leverage and tax benefits

Risks
- risks: changes in supply and demand for the investment (market risk), changes in businesses with which the investment is connected (business risk), changes in the value of money (purchasing power risk), and changes in interest rates (financial risk)

Types of investments
- among the investor's choices are investments in money (e.g., certificates of deposit), equity (e.g., stocks), debt (e.g., bonds and mortgages), and real estate (income and non-income properties)

REAL ESTATE AS AN INVESTMENT

Risk and reward
- the real estate investor must weigh the potential risks and returns inherent in market variability, expected vs. real income, use of borrowing leverage, changes in tax treatment of capital gains and income, and the cost of capital

Illiquidity
- real estate is generally less liquid than other investment types: it takes time to market a property

Management requirements
- real estate tends to require more investor involvement than other investments do: maintenance, management, operation

REAL ESTATE INVESTMENT ENTITIES

Direct
- buying a property and taking responsibility for management and operation

Syndicate and partnership
- a group of investors pool resources to buy, develop and/or operate a property

Real Estate Investment Trust
- REIT: investors buy certificates in a trust that invests in mortgages or real estate and receive income according to shares owned

Real Estate Mortgage Investment Conduit
- REMIC: investors hold residual or regular interests in an entity that holds a pool of mortgages secured by real property

TAXATION OF REAL ESTATE INVESTMENTS

Taxable income
- gross income received minus allowable expenses, deductions and exclusions

Cost recovery
- deduction of a portion of a property's value from gross income each year over the

Gain on sale
- an excess of proceeds from sale of a property over the original cost of the property, subject to adjustments

Interest
- mortgage interest is deductible from annual gross income from a property, subject to limitations

Passive activities
- business activities in which the taxpayer does not materially participate, including interests in limited partnerships and rental activities; losses from such activities can be used to offset income from other passive activities

INVESTMENT ANALYSIS OF A RESIDENTIAL PROPERTY

Appreciation
- increase in the value of an asset over time; may be stated as a difference between the original price and current market value, or as a percentage increase over the original price; not a true measure of investment return

Deductibles
- for non-income properties, primary tax benefit is annual deduction for mortgage

Tax liability
- the seller of a principle residence owes tax on any capital gain that results from the sale unless excluded; capital gain is defined as the amount realized minus the adjusted basis

Gains tax exclusion
- up to $250,000 for a single seller and $500,000 for a married couple can be excluded from gains tax every two years

INVESTMENT ANALYSIS OF AN INCOME PROPERTY

Pre-tax cash flow
- annual pre-tax cash flow is net operating income minus debt service

Tax liability
- tax liability on income from a property is based on taxable income: net operating income minus interest expense and cost recovery

After-tax cash flow
- annual after-tax cash flow is pre-tax cash flow minus tax liability

Investment performance
- a few common measures of investment performance are:
  - return on investment (net operating income divided by price)
  - cash-on-cash return (cash flow divided by cash invested)
  - return on equity (cash flow divided by equity)
  - discounted cash flow analysis
  - internal rate of return

19 Real Estate Taxation

Taxing Entities
Ad Valorem Taxation
Special Assessments
Tax Lien Enforcement

TAXING ENTITIES

State government
County and local government
Tax districts

Real estate taxation refers to the taxation of real estate as property. Real estate property taxes are imposed by "taxing entities" or "taxing districts" at county and local levels of government.

There are *no federal taxes on real property*. The Constitution of the United States specifically prohibits such taxes. The federal government does, however, tax income derived from real property and gains realized on the sale of real property. The federal government can impose a tax lien against property for failure to pay any tax due the Internal Revenue Service.

State government

States may legally levy taxes on real property, but most delegate this power to counties, cities, townships and local taxing districts. Some states place limits on how local governments may levy such taxes. States may impose a tax lien against property for failure to pay any real property taxes which the state has levied or delegated to local taxing bodies.

County and local government

Counties, cities and municipalities, townships and special tax districts levy taxes on real property to raise funds for providing local services. It is common for the county to collect all real property taxes and distribute it among the other taxing bodies.

Tax districts

County and local governments establish **tax districts** to collect funds for providing specific services. The boundaries of such districts typically do not coincide with municipal boundaries. The major tax district in most areas is the school district. Other important tax districts are those for fire protection, community colleges, and parks.

A property tax bill might include tax levies from such districts as the following

- bridge and highway
- nursing home
- storm water management
- township
- fire district
- school district
- retirement fund
- health services
- historical museum
- sanitorium
- forest preserve/land management
- public library district
- park district
- community college district

In addition to generally established tax districts, a local government authority may establish a **special tax district** to pay for the cost of a specific improvement or service that benefits that area. For instance, a special tax district might be created to fund extension of municipal water service to a newly incorporated area. Unlike a permanent tax district such as the school district, a special tax district is temporary, ceasing to exist once the costs of the specific project have been paid for.

AD VALOREM TAXATION

Tax base totalling
Homestead exemption
Other exemptions
Tax rate derivation
Tax billing and collection

General property taxes are levied on an ad valorem basis, meaning that they are based on the **assessed value** of the property. Assessed value is determined according to state law, usually by a county or township assessor or appraiser. The actual tax, though based on assessed value, may be derived as a legislated percentage of the assessed value. Land and improvements may be assessed separately. Ad valorem taxes are paid annually.

Tax base totalling

The **tax base** of an area is the total of the appraised or assessed values of all real property within the area's boundaries, excluding partially or totally exempt properties:

tax base = assessed values - exemptions

Taxing entities generate the annual revenues they require by levying taxes on the tax base. The **tax rate**, or **millage rate**, determines how much of a tax levy the tax base will receive. The tax rate for each taxing entity is calculated by dividing the amount of revenue required by the tax base. This rate is then applied to the taxable value of each individual real property to determine its tax levy.

Value assessment. County or township officers, called assessors or appraisers, value the real property within their jurisdiction for purposes of levying taxes. This valuation process results in an **assessed value**. Assessment practices differ from state to state. In many states, assessed value does not reflect the market value that an appraisal for other purposes might aim to estimate. For instance, in some areas, assessors use a sales comparison approach to assess the value of land and a cost approach to value improvements.

The role of the assessor in the taxing process is limited to making the valuation and notifying the owner of the assessed value; other tax officials determine the tax rate and the tax levy.

Equalization. Some taxing bodies recognize that local assessments can lead to unfairly high or low values for properties in certain areas. Therefore the jurisdiction may establish **equalization factors** to level out the unevenness of valuations. For instance, if assessed values of properties in one county are consistently ten percent below the average for other counties, an **equalization board** may multiply each assessed value in that county by a factor of 110% to raise them to the average level for the state.

Appeals. Property owners may object to the assessed value of their property, but not to the tax rate. An owner usually has a certain period to protest after receiving notice of the assessed value. According to local law, a property owner must present evidence that the assessor made an error to a review board or appeal board. Typical evidence would include market data on comparable properties that sold recently, or evidence that neighboring properties had less appreciation or even declined in assessed value in comparison with the protestor's property. An owner who is dissatisfied with the actions of the appeals or review board can take the protest to court.

Homestead exemption

A homestead is a parcel of real property that is owned and occupied as a family home. Some states exempt a portion of the value of the homestead from judgments to protect families against eviction by creditors. States and counties may *exempt a portion of the assessed value of the principal residence from property taxation*.

A property owner generally qualifies for a homestead exemption by meeting two criteria:

- is head of a family
- resides on the property for a required length of time

Some states also allow a single person to claim the homestead exemption.

Depending on state law, home owners may have to apply every year for the exemption, or they may receive it automatically without filing.

Other exemptions

Properties. Most states exempt certain types of property from property taxes. Certain classes of property owner may also be exempted or have a reduced liability. Exempted are:

- **government-owned properties**

  real properties owned by federal, state, and local governments are **immune** from real property taxation

- **properties owned by non-profit organizations**

  real properties owned by churches and non-profit organizations are **exempt** from real property taxation

Owner classes. Miscellaneous exemptions may be granted to classes of property owner, such as: senior citizens, widows, and disabled individuals.

States and municipalities may also offer property tax reductions or exemptions to certain industries to encourage economic growth.

Tax rate derivation

Tax district budgeting. The derivation of a tax rate, or millage rate, begins with the taxing body determining its funding requirements to provide services for the year. This requirement is formalized in the annual budget. Then the county or district looks at its sources of revenue, such as sales taxes, business taxes, income taxes, state and federal grants, fees, and so forth. The part of the budgeted expenditures that cannot be funded from other income sources *must come from real property taxes.* This budgetary shortfall becomes the ad valorem **tax levy**. The tax levy is derived every year, since budget requirements and revenue tallies are performed on an annual cycle.

Tax rate. Each individual taxing body has its own tax rate. The tax rate is determined by dividing the taxing body's budgeted amount to be collected from real estate taxes by the tax base:

$$\frac{\text{tax requirement}}{\text{tax base}} = \text{tax rate (millage rate)}$$

If, for example, a taxing body needs $500,000 from property taxes, and the tax base for the district is $15,000,000, the tax rate for this body is:

$$\frac{500{,}000}{15{,}000{,}000} = .03$$

This tax rate of .03 or 3% may be expressed in a number of ways, depending on local practice: as **mills**, as dollars per $100 of assessed value, or as dollars per $1,000 of assessed value. A mill is one one-thousandth of a dollar ($.001). A tax rate of one mill means that the owner pays one dollar for every thousand dollars of assessed value. Thus the rate of .03 above could be expressed as:

30 mills
$3 per $100
$30 per $1,000
3 percent

Tax rate limitations. Some states, counties or other taxing districts place limitations or **caps** on the absolute millage rate or the annual increase in millage for property taxes. In such situations, taxing bodies are *forced to limit their budget requirements*, unless there has been a sufficient increase in tax base to produce the required funds without raising the millage rate.

Tax billing and collection

Individual owner billings. Each property owner's tax bill is determined by multiplying the tax rate for each taxing district times the **taxable value** of the property. Taxable value is *the assessed value after all exemptions and adjustments have been taken into account*.

For example, a certain property is owned and occupied as a primary residence and qualifies for a homestead exemption. The assessed value of the property is $240,000, and the exemption is $75,000. The property is taxed by the school district at a rate of 5 mills, and by the county at a rate of 2 mills. The property tax bill for these items would be calculated as follows.

Exhibit 19.1 Tax Bill Calculation

I. Taxable Value

	assessed value	$ 240,000
-	homestead exemption	$ 75,000
	taxable value	$ 165,000

II. Tax Calculations

	taxable value	$ 165,000
x	5 mills—school dist.	.005
	school tax	$ 825
	taxable value	$ 165,000
x	2 mills—county	.002
	county tax	$ 330

III. Totaling

	school tax	$ 825
+	county tax	$ 330
	total tax bill	$ 1,155

Payment deadlines are usually set by law and differ from region to region. Different taxing bodies may have different fiscal years, and as a result may issue tax bills at different times of the year. It is more common for a county to issue a bill that consolidates the bills of all the lesser taxing bodies. The consolidated bill may be payable annually, semi-annually, quarterly, or on some other schedule as prescribed by law. In many cases where the owner has a mortgage and a required escrow account, the escrow officer will pay the tax bill. The owner will only receive notice of the assessed value and the tax statement.

SPECIAL ASSESSMENTS

A special assessment is a tax levied against specific properties that will benefit from a public improvement. Common examples are assessments for sidewalks, water service and sewers. Special assessments are based on the cost of the improvement and apportioned on a pro rata basis among benefiting properties according to the value that each parcel will receive from the improvement.

For example, a dredging project is approved to deepen the canals for a canal-front subdivision. The project cost is $200,000. Although there are 100 properties in the subdivision, only the 50 that are directly on the canal stand to benefit. Therefore, assuming each canal-front lot receives equal benefit, the 50 properties are each assessed $4,000 as a special assessment tax. Note that once the work is completed and paid, the assessment is discontinued.

If a taxing entity initiates an assessment, the assessment creates an **involuntary tax lien**. If property owners initiate the assessment by requesting the local government to provide the improvement, the assessment creates a **voluntary tax lien.**

Special assessments are usually paid in installments over a number of years. However, taxpayers generally have the option of paying the tax in one lump sum or otherwise accelerating payment.

TAX LIEN ENFORCEMENT

Sale of tax certificates
Tax deed
Tax sale

If taxes remain unpaid for a period of time specified by state law, the tax collecting agency may enforce the tax lien in several ways, depending on what the law prescribes.

Sale of tax certificates

Some states sell **tax certificates**. The buyer of a tax certificate agrees to pay the taxes due. After a period of time specified by law, the holder of the tax certificate on a property may then apply for a **tax deed**.

Tax deed

A tax deed is a legal instrument for conveying title when a property is sold for non-payment of taxes. The application for a tax deed causes the taxing agency to institute a **tax sale** or **tax foreclosure**.

Tax sale

A tax sale is frequently some type of auction. If the tax has not already been paid through the tax certificate process, the buyer of the property must pay the taxes due. There is usually a legally-prescribed **redemption period** during which the defaulted taxpayer has the right to buy back the property and reclaim title. If the taxpayer can redeem the property by paying the delinquent taxes and any other charges before the tax sale occurs, this right is known as an **equitable right of redemption**. If the taxpayer can redeem the property after the tax sale, this right is known as a **statutory right of redemption**. In this case, the taxpayer must pay the amount paid by the winning bidder at the tax sale, plus any charges, additional taxes, or interest that may have accumulated. If the defaulted taxpayer does not redeem the property within the allotted time, the state issues the tax deed to convey title.

Exhibit 19.2 Tax Lien Enforcement

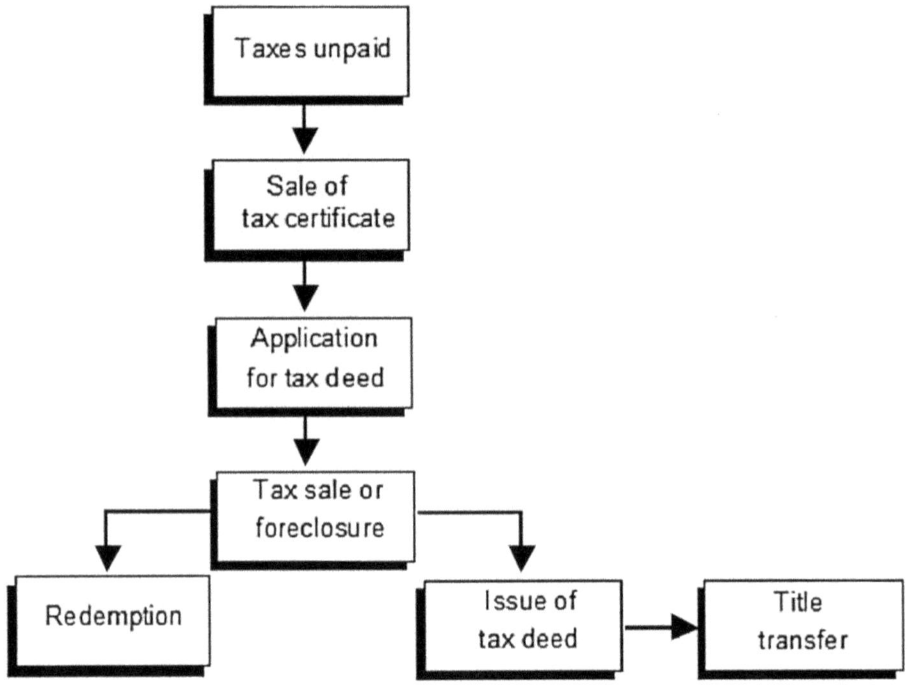

19 Real Estate Taxation Snapshot Review

TAXING ENTITIES	• no federal ad valorem taxes, only federal tax on income and gain; federal government can impose a tax lien against real property
State government	• states may levy property taxes but many delegate this power to county and local government; states can impose a tax lien against real property
County and local government	• counties, cities, municipalities, townships and special tax districts levy taxes on real property
Tax districts	• established to collect funds for providing specific services, e.g., schools, fire protection, parks, community colleges, libraries, road maintenance
AD VALOREM TAXATION	• property tax levied annually on the taxable value of a property in order to help fund government and public services
Tax base totalling	• tax base equals the total of assessed values of all real property within the area, excluding exemptions
Homestead exemption	• a tax exemption of a portion of the assessed value of a property owned and occupied as a family home
Other exemptions	• immune from tax: government-owned properties; exempt from taxes: properties owned by non-profit-organizations
Tax rate derivation	• (1) taxing entity determines what budget requirements must be met by ad valorem tax; (2) divide tax requirement by the tax base
	• tax rate stated as mills ($.001), or dollars per $100 of assessed value, or dollars per $1,000 of assessed value, or as a percentage of assessed value
Tax billing and collection	• individual tax bill: tax rate times taxable value
	• taxable value: assessed value minus exemptions and adjustments
SPECIAL ASSESSMENTS	• tax levied against specific properties that will benefit from a public improvement; amount is based on a pro rata share of the cost of the improvement and the value each parcel will receive from the improvement
TAX LIEN ENFORCEMENT	
Sale of tax certificates	• the buyer of a tax certificate agrees to pay the taxes due and after a period of time may apply for a tax deed on the property
Tax deed	• conveys title in the tax sale
Tax sale	• the buyer must pay the taxes due, if still unpaid; the defaulted taxpayer may be able to redeem the property and reclaim title; if not redeemed, the state issues the tax deed to convey title to the buyer

20 Professional Practices

Fair Housing Laws
Property Disclosures
Other Professional Practices

FAIR HOUSING LAWS

Civil Rights Act of 1866
Civil Rights Act of 1968
Forms of illegal discrimination
Title VIII exemptions
Jones v. Mayer
Equal Opportunity in Housing poster
Fair Housing Amendments Act of 1988
Discrimination by the client
Violations and enforcement
Fair financing laws
Americans with Disabilities Act

Federal and state governments have enacted laws prohibiting discrimination in the national housing market. The aim of these **fair housing laws,** or **equal opportunity housing laws,** is to give all people in the country an equal opportunity to live wherever they wish, provided they can afford to do so, without impediments of discrimination in the purchase, sale, rental, or financing of property.

State Fair Housing Laws. While states have enacted fair housing laws that generally reflect the provisions of national law, each state may have slight modifications of national law. For that reason, it is incumbent upon real estate students to learn their state laws and, in particular, note where these laws differ from national fair housing laws.

Fair Housing and Local Zoning. The Fair Housing Act prohibits a broad range of practices that discriminate against individuals on the basis of race, color, religion, sex, national origin, familial status, and disability. The Act does not pre-empt local zoning laws. However, the Act applies to municipalities and other local government entities and prohibits them from making zoning or land use decisions or implementing land use policies that exclude or otherwise discriminate against protected persons, including individuals with disabilities.

Civil Rights Act of 1866

The original fair housing statute, the Civil Rights Act of 1866, prohibits discrimination in housing *based on race.* The prohibition relates to selling, renting, inheriting, and conveying real estate.

Executive Order 11063. While the Civil Rights Act of 1866 prohibited discrimination, it was only marginally enforced. In 1962, the President issued Executive Order 11063 to *prevent discrimination in residential properties financed by FHA and VA loans*. The order facilitated enforcement of fair housing where federal funding was involved.

Civil Rights Act of 1968

Title VIII (Fair Housing Act). Title VIII of the Civil Rights Act of 1968, known today as the Fair Housing Act, prohibits discrimination in housing *based on race, color, religion, or national origin*. The Office of Fair Housing and Equal Opportunity (FHEO) administers and enforces Title VIII under the supervision of the Department of Housing and Urban Development (HUD).

Forms of illegal discrimination

The Fair Housing Act specifically prohibits such activities in residential brokerage and financing as the following.

Discriminatory misrepresentation. An agent may not conceal available properties, represent that they are not for sale or rent, or change the sale terms for the purpose of discriminating. For example, an agent may not inform a minority buyer that the seller has recently decided not to carry back second mortgage financing when in fact the owner has made no such decision.

Discriminatory advertising. An agent may not advertise residential properties in such a way as to restrict their availability to any prospective buyer or tenant.

Providing unequal services. An agent may not alter the nature or quality of brokerage services to any party based on race, color, sex, national origin, or religion. For example, if it is customary for an agent to show a customer the latest MLS publication, the agent may not refuse to show it to any party. Similarly, if it is customary to show qualified buyers prospective properties immediately, an agent may not alter that practice for purposes of discrimination.

Steering. Steering is the practice of directly or indirectly channeling customers toward or away from homes and neighborhoods. Broadly interpreted, steering occurs if an agent describes an area in a subjective way for the purpose of encouraging or discouraging a buyer about the suitability of the area.

For example, an agent tells Buyer A that a neighborhood is extremely attractive, and that desirable families are moving in every week. The next day, the agent tells Buyer B that the same neighborhood is deteriorating, and that values are starting to fall. The agent has blatantly steered Buyer B *away* from the area and Buyer A *into* it.

Blockbusting. Blockbusting is the practice of inducing owners in an area to sell or rent to avoid an impending change in the ethnic or social makeup of the neighborhood that will cause values to go down.

For example, Agent Smith tells neighborhood owners that several minority families are moving in, and that they will be bringing their relatives next year. Smith informs homeowners that, in anticipation of a value decline, several families have already made plans to move.

Restricting MLS participation. It is discriminatory to restrict participation in any multiple listing service based on one's race, religion, national origin, color, or sex.

Redlining. Redlining is the residential financing practice of refusing to make loans on properties in a certain neighborhood regardless of a mortgagor's qualifications. In effect, the lender draws a red line around an area on the map and denies all financing to applicants within the encircled area.

Title VIII exemptions

The Fair Housing Act allows for exemptions under a few specific circumstances. These are:

- a privately owned single-family home where no broker is used and no discriminatory advertising is used, with certain additional conditions
- rental of an apartment in a 1-4 unit building where the owner is also an occupant, provided the advertising is not discriminatory
- facilities owned by private clubs and leased non-commercially to members
- facilities owned by religious organizations and leased non-commercially to members, provided membership requirements are not discriminatory

Jones v. Mayer

In 1968, the Supreme Court ruled in *Jones v. Mayer* that all discrimination in selling or renting residential property based on race is prohibited under the provisions of the Civil Rights Act of 1866. Thus, while the Federal Fair Housing Act exempts certain kinds of discrimination, anyone who feels victimized by discrimination *based on race* may seek legal recourse under the 1866 law.

Equal Opportunity in Housing poster

In 1972, HUD instituted a requirement that brokers display a standard HUD poster. The poster affirms the broker's compliance with fair housing laws in selling, renting, advertising, and financing residential properties. Failure to display the poster may be construed as discrimination.

Fair Housing Amendments Act of 1988

Amendments to federal fair housing laws prohibit discrimination based on sex and discrimination against handicapped persons and families with children.

Exemptions. Federal fair housing laws do not prohibit age and family status discrimination under the following circumstances:

- in government-designated retirement housing
- in a retirement community if all residents are 62 years of age or older
- in a retirement community if 80 % of the dwellings have one person who is 55 years of age or older, provided there are amenities for elderly residents

- in residential dwellings of four units or less, and single family houses if sold or rented by owners who have no more than three houses

Discrimination by the client

Fair housing laws apply to home sellers as well as to agents, with the exception of the exemptions previously cited. If an agent goes along with a client's discriminatory act, the agent is equally liable for violation of fair housing laws. It is thus imperative to avoid complicity with client discrimination. Further, an agent should withdraw from any relationship where client discrimination occurs.

Examples of potential client discrimination are:

- refusing a full-price offer from a party
- removing the property from the market to sidestep a potential purchase by a party
- accepting an offer from one party that is lower than one from another party

Violations and enforcement

Persons who feel they have been discriminated against under federal fair housing laws may file a complaint with the Office of Fair Housing and Equal Opportunity (FHEO) within HUD, or they may file suit in a federal or state court.

Filing an FHEO complaint. Complaints alleging fair housing violations must be filed with the Office of Fair Housing and Equal Opportunity within one year of the violation. HUD then initiates an investigation in conjunction with federal or local enforcement authorities.

If HUD decides that the complaint merits further action, it will attempt to resolve the matter out of court. If efforts to resolve the problem fail, the aggrieved party may file suit in state or federal court.

Filing suit. In addition to or instead of filing a complaint with HUD, a party may file suit in state or federal court within two years of the alleged violation.

Penalties. If discrimination is confirmed in court, the respondent may be enjoined to cease practicing his or her business. For example, a discriminating home builder may be restrained from selling available properties to buyers. Also, the plaintiff may be compensated for damages including humiliation, suffering, and pain. In addition, the injured party may seek equitable relief, including forcing the guilty party to complete a denied action such as selling or renting the property. Finally, the courts may impose civil penalties for first-time or repeat offenders.

Fair financing laws

Parallel anti-discrimination and consumer protection laws have been enacted in the mortgage financing field to promote equal opportunity in housing.

Equal Credit Opportunity Act (ECOA). Enacted in 1974, the Equal Credit Opportunity Act requires lenders to be fair and impartial in determining who qualifies for a loan. A lender may not discriminate on the basis of race, color, religion, national origin, sex, marital status, or age. The act also requires lenders to inform prospective borrowers who are being denied credit of the reasons for the denial.

Home Mortgage Disclosure Act. This statute requires lenders involved with federally guaranteed or insured loans to exercise impartiality and non-discrimination in the geographical distribution of their loan portfolio. In other words, the act is designed to prohibit redlining. It is enforced in part by requiring lenders to report to authorities where they have placed their loans.

Exhibit 20.1 Equal Opportunity in Housing Poster

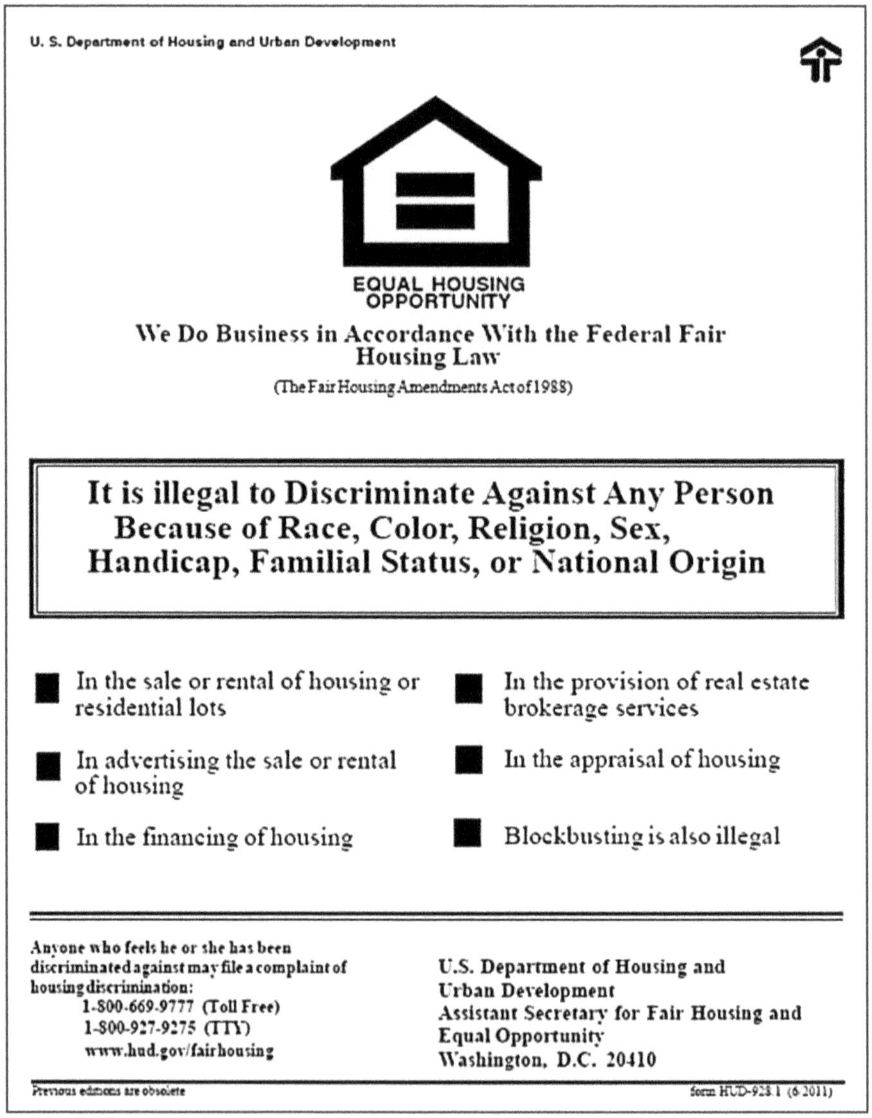
U. S. Department of Housing and Urban Development

EQUAL HOUSING OPPORTUNITY

We Do Business in Accordance With the Federal Fair Housing Law

(The Fair Housing Amendments Act of 1988)

It is illegal to Discriminate Against Any Person Because of Race, Color, Religion, Sex, Handicap, Familial Status, or National Origin

- In the sale or rental of housing or residential lots
- In advertising the sale or rental of housing
- In the financing of housing
- In the provision of real estate brokerage services
- In the appraisal of housing
- Blockbusting is also illegal

Anyone who feels he or she has been discriminated against may file a complaint of housing discrimination:
1-800-669-9777 (Toll Free)
1-800-927-9275 (TTY)
www.hud.gov/fairhousing

U.S. Department of Housing and Urban Development
Assistant Secretary for Fair Housing and Equal Opportunity
Washington, D.C. 20410

Previous editions are obsolete

form HUD-928.1 (6/2011)

Americans with Disabilities Act (ADA)

Purpose. The ADA, which became law in 1990, is a civil rights law that prohibits discrimination against individuals with disabilities in all areas of public life, including employment, education, transportation, and facilities that are open to the general public. The purpose of the law is to make sure that people with disabilities have the same rights and opportunities as everyone else.

The Americans with Disabilities Act Amendments Act (ADAAA) became effective on January 1, 2009. Among other things, the ADAAA clarified that a disability is "a physical or mental impairment that substantially limits one or more major life activities." This definition applies to all titles of the ADA and covers private employers with 15 or more employees, state and local governments, employment agencies, labor unions, agents of the employer, joint management labor committees, and private entities considered places of public accommodation. Examples of the latter include hotels, restaurants, retail stores, doctor's offices, golf courses, private schools, day care centers, health clubs, sports stadiums, and movie theaters.

Components. The law consists of five parts.

- Title I (Employment) concerns equal employment opportunity. It is enforced by the U.S. Equal Employment Opportunity Commission.

- Title II (State and Local government) concerns nondiscrimination in state and local government services. It is enforced by the U.S. Department of Justice.

- Title III (Public Accommodations) concerns nondiscrimination in public accommodations and commercial facilities. It is enforced by the U.S. Department of Justice.

- Title IV (Telecommunications) concerns accommodations in telecommunications and public service messaging. It is enforced by the Federal Communications Commission.

- Title V (Miscellaneous) concerns a variety of general situations including how the ADA affects other laws, insurance providers, and lawyers.

Real estate practitioners are most likely to encounter Titles I and III and should acquire familiarity with these. In advising clients, licensees are well-advised to seek qualified legal counsel.

Requirements. As noted in Chapter 23 under "Management Functions," the act requires landlords in certain circumstances to modify housing and facilities so that disabled persons can access them without hindrance.

The ADA also requires that disabled employees and members of the public be provided access that is equivalent to that provided to those who are not disabled.

- Employers with at least fifteen employees must follow nondiscriminatory employment and hiring practices.

- Reasonable accommodations must be made to enable disabled employees to perform essential functions of their jobs.

- Modifications to the physical components of a building may be necessary to provide the required access to tenants and their customers, such as widening doorways, changing door hardware, changing how doors open, installing ramps, lowering wall-mounted telephones and keypads, supplying Braille signage, and providing auditory signals.

- Existing barriers must be removed when the removal is "readily achievable," that is, when cost is not prohibitive. New construction and remodeling must meet a higher standard.
- If a building or facility does not meet requirements, the landlord must determine whether restructuring or retrofitting or some other kind of accommodation is most practical.

Penalties. Violations of ADA requirements can result in citations, business license restrictions, fines, and injunctions requiring remediation of the offending conditions. Business owners may also be held liable for personal injury damages to an injured plaintiff.

PROPERTY DISCLOSURES

Residential property condition
Environmental issues
Warranties
Inspections
Homeowners' associations

Residential property condition

Seller's disclosure form. Many states require sellers to make a written disclosure about property condition to a prospective buyer. This seller disclosure may or may not relieve the agent of some liabilities for disclosure. The residential property condition disclosure is the seller's written summary of the property's condition at the time of contracting for sale. The disclosure is entered on state-approved forms.

Owner's role. State legislation requires owners of previously occupied single family homes and buildings containing 1-4 dwelling units to provide the disclosure to prospective buyers if they are selling, exchanging, or optioning their property. Some exceptions and exemptions apply. When required, the disclosure must be transmitted to the prospective buyer no later than when the buyer makes an offer.

A typical form requires the seller to affirm whether or not problems exist in any of the listed features and systems of the property. In denying that a problem exists, the seller claims to have no knowledge of a defect. If a defect does in fact exist, the seller can be held liable for intentional misrepresentation. A third possible response to a property condition question is that of "no representation." Here, the seller makes no claim of knowledge as to whether a problem exists. With this answer, the seller is no longer held liable for a disclosure of any kind relating to a particular feature, whether a defect is known or otherwise.

Once the seller has signed the form and delivered it to the buyer, the buyer must acknowledge receipt and knowledge of the property condition disclosures, along with other provisions set forth on the form.

Licensee's role. The residential property re-seller must comply with the property condition disclosure requirement whether an agent is employed in the transaction or not. If an agent is involved in the transaction, the agent must disclose any and all material facts he or she knows or should reasonably know about the property, regardless of what the seller may have disclosed on the form.

Right of rescission. Sellers who fail to complete and deliver the property condition disclosure statement to buyers in a timely fashion effectively give the buyer a subsequent right under certain conditions to rescind the sale contract and re-claim their deposits. The buyer must follow certain procedures and meet certain deadlines in order to legitimately effect the cancellation. The buyer's right to cancel persists until closing or occupancy, whichever comes first.

Property condition and material facts. As explained in the chapter on agency, an agent has the duty to inform the client of all material facts, reports, and rumors that might affect the client's interests in the property transaction. A material fact is one that might affect the value or desirability of the property to a buyer if the buyer knew it. Material facts include

- the agent's opinion of the property's condition
- adverse facts about property condition, title defects, environmental hazards, and property defects

In recent years, the disclosure standard has been raised to require an agent to disclose items that a practicing agent *should know,* whether the agent actually had the knowledge or not, and regardless of whether the disclosure furthers or impedes the progress of the transaction.

Facts not considered to be material, and therefore not usually subject to required disclosure, include such items as property stigmatization (e.g., that a crime or death occurred on the property) and the presence of registered sex offenders in the neighborhood (in accordance with Megan's Law, federal legislation that requires convicted offenders to register with the state of residence; in some states, agents must provide registry information to buyers).

The agent may be held liable for failing to disclose a material fact if a court rules that the typical agent in that area would detect and recognize the adverse condition. There is no obligation to obtain or disclose information that is immaterial to the transaction, such as property stigmas.

An agent who sees a "red flag" issue such as a potential structural or mechanical problem should advise the seller to seek expert advice. Red flags can seriously impact the value of the property and/or the cost of remediation. In addition to property condition per se, they may include such things as

- environmental concerns
- property anomalies, such as over-sized or peculiarly shaped lot
- neighborhood issues

- poor construction
- signs of flooding
- poor floorplan
- adjacent property features

The following exhibit is part of a typical property condition disclosure form showing the level of detail that is expected in a seller's disclosure.

Exhibit 20.2 Property Condition Disclosure Form

Buyers and seller should be aware that any agreement executed between the parties will supercede this form as to any abligations on the part of the seller to repair items identified below and/or the obligation of the buyer to accept such items "as is".

INSTRUCTIONS TO THE SELLER

Complete this form yourself and answer each question to the best of your knowledge. If an answer is an estimate, clearly label it as such. The Seller hereby authorizes any agent(s) representing any party in this transaction to provide a copy of this statement to any person or entity in connection with any actual or anticipated sale of the subject property.

PROPERTY ADDRESS ______________________________ CITY ____________________

SELLER'S NAMES(S) ______________________________ PROPERTY AGE ____________

DATE SELLER ACQUIRED THE PROPERTY________________ DO YOU OCCUPY THE PROPERTY? ________

IF NOT OWNER–OCCUPIED. HOW LONG HAS IT BEEN SINCE THE SELLER OCCUPIED THE PROPERTY? ____________

(Check the one that applies) THIS PROPERTY IS A ☐ SITE BUILT HOME ☐ NONSITE BUILT HOME

☐ Range
☐ Oven
☐ Microwave
☐ Dishwasher
☐ Garbage Disposal
☐ Trash Compactor
☐ Water Softener Alarm
☐ 220 Volt Wiring
☐ Washer/Dryer Hookups
☐ Central Heating
☐ Heat Pump
☐ Central Air Conditioning
☐ Wall/Window Air Conditioning
☐ Window Screens
☐ Rain Gutters
☐ Fireplace(s) (Number_______)
☐ Gas Starter for Fireplace
☐ Smoke Detector/Fire
☐ Burglar Alarm
☐ Patio/Decking/Gazebo
☐ Irrigation System
☐ Sump Pump
☐ Garage Door Opener(s)
☐ (Number of openers _________)
☐ Intercom
☐ TV Antenna/Satellite Dish
☐ Pool
☐ Spa/Whirlpool Tub
☐ Hot Tub
☐ Sauna
☐ Current Termite Contract
☐ Access to Public Streets
☐ Other________________
☐ Other________________

Garage:	☐ Attached	☐ Not Attached	☐ Carport	
Water Heater:	☐ Gas	☐ Solar	☐ Electric	
Water Supply:	☐ City	☐ Well	☐ Private Utility	Other__________
Waste Disposal:	☐ City Sewer	☐ Septic Tank	☐ Other ________	
Gas Supply:	☐ Utility	☐ Bottled	☐ Other ________	

Roof(s): Type ______________________________ Age(approx) ____________________

Other Items: ____

To the best of your knowledge, are any of the above NOT in operating condition? ☐ YES ☐ NO
If YES, then describe (Attach additional sheets if necessary);

ARE YOU (SELLER) AWARE OF ANY DEFECTS/AMLFUNCTIONS IN ANY OF THE FOLLOWING?

	YES	NO	UNKNOWN		YES	NO	UNKNOWN
Interior Walls	☐	☐	☐	Central Heating	☐	☐	☐
Ceilings	☐	☐	☐	Central Air Conditioning	☐	☐	☐
Floors	☐	☐	☐	Electrical System	☐	☐	☐
Windows	☐	☐	☐	Exterior Walls	☐	☐	☐
Doors	☐	☐	☐	Roof	☐	☐	☐
Insulation	☐	☐	☐	Basement	☐	☐	☐
Plumbing	☐	☐	☐	Foundation	☐	☐	☐
Sewer/Septic	☐	☐	☐	Slab	☐	☐	☐
Heat Pump	☐	☐	☐	Driveway	☐	☐	☐
				Sidewalks	☐	☐	☐

If any of the above is/are marked YES, Please explain:

____
____
____

This Form Compliments of Kirkland, Rothman-Branning & Associates, PLLC
901-758-558

ww. kr-ba.com
jtk10-02

Exhibit 20.2 Property Condition Disclosure Form, page 2

C. ARE YOU (SELLER) AWARE OF ANY OF THE FOLLOWING?

	YES	NO	UNKNOWN
1. Substances, materials, or products which may be an environmental hazard such as, but not limited to: asbestos, radon gas, lead-based paint, fuel or chemical storage tanks, and/or contaminated water on the subject property	❑	❑	❑
2. Features shared in common with adjoining landowners, such as, but not limited to, walls, fences, and driveways, whose use or responsibility for maintenance may have an effect on the subject property	❑	❑	❑
3. Any authorized changes in roads, drainage, or utilities affecting the property, or contiguous to the property	❑	❑	❑
4. Any changes since the most recent survey of this property was done	❑	❑	❑
Most recent survey of the property: ____________ [check here ❑ if unknown]			
5. Any encroachments, easements, or similar items that may affect your ownership interest in the property	❑	❑	❑
6. Room additions, structural modifications, or other alterations or repairs made without necessary permits	❑	❑	❑
7. Room additions, structural modifications, or other alterations or repairs not in compliance with building codes	❑	❑	❑
8. Is heating and air conditioning supplied to all finished rooms?	❑	❑	❑
If the same type of system is not used for all finished rooms, please explain. ____________			
9. Landfill (compacted or otherwise) on the property or any portion thereof	❑	❑	❑
10. Any settling from any cause, or slippage, sliding, or other soil problems	❑	❑	❑
11. Flooding, drainage, or grading problems	❑	❑	❑
12. Any requirement that flood insurance be maintained on the property	❑	❑	❑
13. Property or structural damage from fire, water, wind, storm, earthquake/tremor, landslide or wood destroying organisms	❑	❑	❑
14. Any zoning violations, nonconforming uses, and/or violations of "setback" requirements	❑	❑	❑
15. Neighborhood noise problems or other nuisances	❑	❑	❑
16. Subdivisions and/or deed restrictions or obligations	❑	❑	❑
17. A Homeowners Association (HOA) which has any authority over the subject property	❑	❑	❑
Name of HOA: ____________			
HOA Address: ____________			
Monthly Dues: ____________ Special Assessments: ____________			
18. Any "common area" (facilities such as, but not limited to, pools, tennis courts, walkways, or other areas co-owned in undivided interest with others)	❑	❑	❑
19. Any notices of abatement or citations against the property	❑	❑	❑
20. Any lawsuit(s) or proposed lawsuit(s) by or against the seller which affect or will affect the property	❑	❑	❑
21. Is any system, equipment or part of the property being leased	❑	❑	❑
If yes, please explain, and include a written statement regarding payment information.			
22. Any exterior wall covering of the structure covered with exterior insulation and finishing systems (EIFS), also known as "synthetic stucco"	❑	❑	❑
If yes, has there been a recent inspection to determine whether the structure has excessive moisture accumulation and/or moisture related damage? (The Tennessee Real Estate Commission urges any buyer or seller who encounters this product to have a qualified professional inspect the structure in question for the preceding concern and provide a written report of their finding.)	❑	❑	❑

If yes, please explain. If necessary, please attach an additional sheet.

____

____

D. CERTIFICATION: I/we certify that the information herein, concerning the real property located at ____________, is true and correct to the best of my/our knowledge as of the date signed. Should any of these conditions change prior to conveyance of title to this property, these changes will be disclosed in addendum(a) to this document.

______________________ ______________________
Transferor (Seller) Date

______________________ ______________________
Transferor (Seller) Date

Parties may wish to obtain professional advice and/or inspections of the property and to negotiate appropriate provisions in the purchase agreement regarding advice, inspections, or defects.

TRANSFEREE/BUYER'S ACKNOWLEDGMENT: I/we understand that this disclosure statement is not intended as a substitute for any inspection, and that I/we have a responsibility to pay diligent attention to and inquire about those material defects which are evident by careful observation.

I/we acknowledge receipt of a copy of this disclosure.

______________________ ______________________
Transferee (Buyer) Date

______________________ ______________________
Transferee (Buyer) Date

This Form Compliments of Kirkland, Rothman-Branning & Associates, PLLC 901-758-5588	www.kr-ba.com jtk10-02

Environmental issues

Health hazards occur within structures, on real estate parcels, and in the area surrounding real estate. They may occur naturally or as a result of human activity. Environmental laws regulate some, but not all, health hazards that affect real estate. Real estate agents, owners, and sellers have various responsibilities for detecting, disclosing, and remediating regulated hazards. Some important issues are reviewed below. There is further information in the "Environmental Controls" section of Chapter 8.

Lead-based paint. This hazard cannot be absorbed through the skin, but it becomes dangerous when it is ingested or inhaled. It can be found in most homes built before 1978 and can be present in the air, drinking water, food, contaminated soil, deteriorating paint, and dust from the paint. Children are particularly susceptible because young children are known to eat chips of the paint, allowing the lead to enter their bloodstreams. Homebuyers and renters are required to be given the EPA-HUD-US Consumer Product Safety Commission's booklet, "Protect Your Family from Lead in Your Home" and must be informed if lead-based paint is present in the home. Buyers may have a risk assessment performed prior to purchasing the home.

Mold. This is a fungus that grows under moist conditions and causes allergic reaction for some people. The presence of mold in the home must be disclosed as a latent defect. Flooding and water damage must also be disclosed as both of those can lead to mold growth. Inspections do not always find mold because it often grows inside walls and ductwork. Most molds require removal by a professional.

Asbestos. While harmless in its original condition, it can cause lung cancer if its dust filters into the air. If it is found in a home during remodeling, it must be removed by professionals to prevent contamination. It can be found in roofing and siding, older insulation, textured paint, artificial ashes sold for gas fireplaces, some vinyl floor tiles, coatings for older hot water and steam pipes.

Air quality. The quality of air in a home can be adversely impacted by the presence of carbon monoxide, radon, deteriorating asbestos and lead-based paint, methamphetamine production, formaldehyde, and other toxic chemicals. Homes can and should be tested for many of these contaminants prior to purchase.

Water quality. Ground water is easily contaminated from septic tanks, agricultural runoff, highway de-icing, landfills, pesticides, animal waste, etc. Many people rely on ground water for drinking so must be aware that contaminated water can cause problems from mild stomach problems to cancer and death. The Environmental Protection Agency (EPA) sets standards for protecting ground water from contamination. It also offers advice and resources to facilitate the rehabilitation of contaminated ground water sources. One such means of protection is to advise private well users to have the water tested at least once a year.

Carbon monoxide. This is an odorless, colorless, toxic gas that can kill a person before its presence is known. It can be caused by unvented kerosene and gas space heaters; leaking chimneys; back-drafting from furnaces, gas water heaters, wood stoves, and fireplaces; gas stoves, gasoline powered equipment, vehicle exhaust in garages, tobacco smoke. Carbon monoxide can be detected in a structure by a unit similar to a smoke alarm which should be included in every home, especially those with gas equipment and fireplaces or furnaces.

Faulty septic systems. Inspections of septic systems are important because these systems take wastewater from the property, remove most of the contaminants, and then put the water into the soil. If the system is faulty, it can be releasing contaminated water into the soil, thereby contaminating the soil. Potential buyers and septic system users should have the county health department conduct an inspection of the system.

Illegal drug manufacturing. Manufacturing illegal drugs such as methamphetamine produces highly toxic fumes that last a long time. Continued exposure to the fumes can cause fatal burns to the lungs, can damage the liver and spleen, and can lead to learning disabilities. Any property suspected as having been a place for drug manufacturing should be investigated prior to being sold or leased, and the possible health hazards must be disclosed to the potential buyer or renter.

Radon. This is the easiest hazard to detect and mitigate. It is an odorless, colorless, tasteless, and radioactive gas that is created in the ground where uranium and radium exist. Prolonged exposure to radon can cause lung cancer. It can enter the home through any cracks, gaps, or cavities, including crawl spaces and openings around pipes. It can be easily detected by a radon test, so home inspections should include this test.

Urea formaldehyde. This type of hazard is found in foam thermal insulation in homes built before 1980. The formaldehyde gas emissions from the insulation decrease over time, so most homes with the insulation no longer pose a threat. The most common sources of formaldehyde in a home are pressed wood products such as particleboard, hardwood plywood paneling, and medium density fiberboard. Plastic furniture, new carpeting, and other vinyl materials also emit formaldehyde gases during the first few months after installation. Formaldehyde can cause eye problems, nausea, breathing problems, and allergic reactions.

Leaking underground storage tanks. USTs have at least 10 percent of their volume underground and are used to store fuel oil, gasoline, and other toxic fluids. Tanks made of steel can corrode over time and leak their contents into the surrounding soil, contaminating groundwater. They also provide a potential for fire and explosion. Tank removal is expensive, so removal is not common. Therefore, potential buyers must be informed of the presence of a UST on the property and of the health and financial risks of purchasing a property that contains a UST.

Clean Air and Clean Water Acts. The Clean Air Act of 1963, since amended a number of times, was designed to control air pollution on a national level. Among other things, the act authorizes the setting of standards for controlling the emission of pollutants and monitoring air quality. It identifies hazardous air pollutants such as formaldehyde and regulates their use. Importantly, the act allows private citizens to sue other citizens to enforce the law.

The Clean Water Act, officially known as the Federal Water Pollution Control Act Amendments of 1972, together with revisions contained in the Clean Water

Act of 1977 and the Water Quality Act of 1987, is the primary federal law governing water pollution. It applies to all waters connected with navigable waters, but the interpretation of exactly which waters are covered remains open to dispute. The Clean Water Act does not directly deal with groundwater contamination, which is addressed in the Safe Drinking Water Act, Resource Conservation and Recovery Act, and the Superfund act.

Safe Drinking Water Act. Congress passed the Safe Drinking Water Act (SDWA) in 1974 (amended 1986 and 1996) to regulate and protect the public supply of drinking water. The act authorizes the setting of standards, protection of water sources, training of operators, funding of improvements, and dissemination of information. Under the act, water suppliers must report health risks to the EPA within 24 hours of discovery. Hydraulic fracturing (fracking) oil and gas production poses one of the greatest current threats to groundwater.

Property sellers generally must disclose the source of drinking water for the property and the presence, type and location of any septic system on the property. A water supply other than a municipal one and any septic system other than a standard one should be tested.

Brownfields Law. Brownfields are abandoned commercial or industrial sites that are likely to contain toxic material. The Small Business Liability Relief and Brownfields Revitalization Act (known as the Brownfields Law), passed in 2002 provides clean-up funds, liability protections, and tax incentives to reclaim contaminated properties. Under this law, owners who neither caused nor contributed to the contamination are released from liability for the clean up.

Environmental Protection Agency. The EPA was established on December 2, 1970 to bring together federal research, monitoring, standard-setting and enforcement activities into one agency dedicated to environmental protection. The EPA, working with state, local, and tribal governments, enforces the Clean Air and Clean Water Acts along with other environmental laws.

Disclosure obligations and liabilities. As discussed in an earlier chapter, licensees are expected to be aware of environmental issues and to know where to look for professional help. They are not expected to have expert knowledge of environmental law nor of physical conditions in a property. Rather, they must treat potential environmental hazards in the same way that they treat other material facts about a property: disclosure. It is advisable to have an attorney draft the appropriate disclosures to lessen the broker's liability should problems occur in the future.

The Lead-based Paint Act of 1992 requires a seller or seller's agent to disclose known lead problems in properties built before 1978. The licensee must give the buyer or lessee a copy of the EPA-HUD-US Consumer Product Safety Commission booklet, "Protect Your Family from Lead in your home."

Further, the 1996 lead-based paint regulation requires sellers or lessors of almost all residential properties built before 1978 to disclose known lead-based paint hazards and provide any relevant records available. The seller is not required to test for lead but must allow the buyer a ten-day period for lead inspection. Only a licensed lead professional is permitted to deal with testing, removal or encapsulation. It is the real estate practitioner's responsibility to ensure compliance.

Under CERCLA and the Superfund Amendment of 1986, current landowners as well as previous owners of a property may be held liable for environmental violations, even if "innocent" of a violation. Sellers often carry the greatest exposure, and real estate licensees may be held liable for improper disclosure.

In sum, for their own protection, licensees should be careful to:

- be aware of potential hazards
- disclose known material facts
- distribute the HUD booklet
- know where to seek professional help.

Warranties

Purpose and scope. Home warranties, or home service contracts, cover service, repair, or replacement of a home's major systems and appliances. Warranties are usually purchased for one year at a time with the annual cost determined by the following:

- the location of the property – prices vary from state to state due to cost of living and property regulations in the specific area
- the type of property – single family homes have different price points than mobile homes or multifamily properties
- the size of the property – smaller homes have cheaper coverage options than large homes. often, the home's square footage determines the cost of the warranty
- the amount of coverage – standard coverage plans may exclude certain parts of the property, resulting in a lower price for the plan. The excluded items can be covered with a more extensive plan at a higher cost

Home warranties are often included in the purchase price of a home or are purchased by the buyer at the time of the home purchase.

Limitations. Purchasers of home warranties need to fully understand their coverage limitations in order to have realistic expectations of the warranty. Similarly, it is important for a homeowner to understand what may not be covered in the warranty. These items may include

- conditions that existed prior to the effective coverage of the warranty
- failures caused by something other than normal wear and tear
- improperly installed or modified items
- damages caused by failure of another system or appliance, such as kitchen cabinets being damaged from a plumbing leak in the pipes under the sink, called consequential damages
- outdoor items such as sprinklers or swimming pool
- repairs to faucets
- refrigerators, washers and dryers, or garage door openers are often not covered

Basically, unless an item is specifically listed in the warranty contract, it will not be covered.

With a home warranty, the homeowner must go through the warranty company to have the service performed. The company usually has established relationships with specific service providers and may use only those providers for service under the warranty. The homeowner is typically charged a service fee on top of the annual fee for each repair job.

Inspections

Process. Property inspections may identify builder oversights or the need for major repairs. They may also identify the need for regular maintenance to keep the property in good condition. In addition to looking for structural issues, plumbing and electrical problems, and roof and foundation issues, inspections can uncover termites or other pests that are damaging the structure. Inspections can also uncover environmental issues that have a detrimental impact on the property.

Termite inspections. Termites are destructive pests that exist in all states except Alaska. They cause an estimated $50 billion in damage to buildings each year. They often cause extensive damage to the property before the owner even realizes there is a problem. Termites eat wood from the inside out, so they are not easily discovered except by professional inspectors. Having homes inspected annually for termites can prevent substantial damage and cost.

The most common type of termite is the subterranean termite. They are often confused with winged ants, but they are much more destructive. Termite inspectors look for the following indications that termites are present in the structure:

- swarms of termites inside the home
- termite excrement
- termite bodies found in spider webs near the structure
- the presence of termite mud tubes by which termites traverse open spaces between sources of wood; the tubes protect the termites from dehydration and predators; their diameter is similar to that of a drinking straws
- areas on the property that serve to harbor termites, such as wood fencing, mulch, piles of firewood, dead tree limbs, etc.
- a hollow sound when a wood beam is tapped
- long, deep grooves in wood

Because termites cause such extensive damage and can live inside the structure of a home for years, a termite inspection should be part of any home buying transaction as well as a periodic event.

Exhibit 20.3 For Your Protection…

CAUTION

U.S. Department of Housing and Urban Development
Federal Housing Administration (FHA)

OMB Approval No: 2502-0538 (exp. 04/30/2018)

For Your Protection: Get a Home Inspection

Why a Buyer Needs a Home Inspection

A home inspection gives the buyer more detailed information about the overall condition of the home prior to purchase. In a home inspection, a qualified inspector takes an in-depth, unbiased look at your potential new home to:

Evaluate the physical condition: structure, construction, and mechanical systems; Identify items that need to be repaired or replaced; and
Estimate the remaining useful life of the major systems, equipment, structure, and finishes.

You Must Ask for a Home Inspection

A home inspection will only occur if you arrange for one. FHA does not perform a home inspection.

Decide early. You may be able to make your contract contingent on the results of the inspection.

Appraisals are Different from Home Inspections

An appraisal is different from a home inspection and does not replace a home inspection. Appraisals estimate the value of the property for lenders. An appraisal is required to ensure the property is marketable. Home inspections evaluate the condition of the home for buyers.

FHA Does Not Guarantee the Value or Condition of your Potential New Home

If you find problems with your new home after closing, FHA cannot give or lend you money for repairs, and FHA cannot buy the home back from you. Ask a qualified home inspector to inspect your potential new home and give you the information you need to make a wise decision.

Radon Gas Testing and other safety/health issues

The United States Environmental Protection Agency and the Surgeon General of the United States have recommended that all houses should be tested for radon. For more information on radon testing, call the toll-free National Radon Information Line at 1-800-SOS-Radon or 1-800-767-7236.

Ask your home inspector about additional health and safety tests that may be relevant for your home.

Be an Informed Buyer

It is your responsibility to be an informed buyer. You have the right to carefully examine your potential new home with a qualified home inspector. To find a qualified home inspector ask for references from friends, realtors, local licensing authorities and organizations that qualify and test home inspectors.

HUD-92564-CN (6/14)

Environmental inspections. Home inspections should include looking for common environmental issues that can affect the property and the residents of the property. Environmental hazards can have a significant impact on the sale of a property. An environmental site assessment (ESA) may be conducted to identify environmental impairments and protect parties against becoming involved in contamination issues. Such assessments are performed in three phases. A Phase 1 ESA identifies potential problems on or near the subject property. A Phase 2 ESA involves active testing of soil, water, and other components of the subject property.

Environmental impact statements. When a project is federally funded, the responsible parties must provide an environmental impact statement (EIS) detailing how the project will affect the environment. Privately funded projects are also often required to prepare an EIS before any permits are issued. An EIS is expected to address air and water quality issues, noise, health and safety, wildlife, vegetation, water and sewer requirements, traffic, population density, and other issues as appropriate.

Agent disclosure duties. Most states require disclosure of known material facts regarding residential properties of one to four units. If a licensee knows the result of an inspection, this is a material fact to be disclosed. Disclosure of environmental issues on commercial and industrial properties is often not mandated. Where disclosure is not required, real estate licensees should suggest the use of a professional environmental audit.

Homeowners' associations

States have various requirements for a seller's property condition disclosure statement to be completed by the seller and furnished to the buyer. Any such disclosure is likely to include whether the property is subject to a common interest property plan (e.g. condominium), whether the plan imposes any restrictions, whether membership in a Homeowners' Association (HOA) is obligatory, and the identity of the HOA, if any.

State law will typically require the association or management company to provide association documents to the buyer to satisfy the seller disclosure requirements. These documents may be attached to or delivered in conjunction with the sale contract. The contract itself usually specifies the timing of the disclosures. There may be a place on the contract for the buyer to acknowledge receipt and knowledge of the HOA disclosures. In some states, the seller's agent gathers and provides the documents to a buyer or buyer's agent before the writing of an offer.

A typical HOA disclosure package includes

- declarations
- articles of incorporation
- bylaws
- articles of organization
- operating agreements
- rules and regulations
- party wall agreements
- minutes of annual owners' meeting

- minutes of directors' or managers' meetings
- financial documents: balance sheet, income and expenditures, budget, reserve study, unpaid assessments, audit report, list of fees and charges
- list of insurance policies
- list of assessments by unit type

The seller is responsible for making the disclosures, but the buyer must exercise due diligence in the reading and understanding of them. The agent's responsibility is to make sure the disclosures are made.

OTHER PROFESSIONAL PRACTICES

Codes of ethics
Job performance
Duties to clients
Duties to customers
Disclosure
Wholesaling
Love letters
Professional relationships

Codes of ethics

The real estate industry has developed a code of professional standards and ethics as a guideline in serving the real estate needs of consumers. This professional code has emerged from three primary sources:

- federal and state legislation
- state real estate licensing regulation
- industry self-regulation through trade associations and institutes

Federal legislation focuses primarily on anti-discrimination laws and fair trade practices. State laws and licensing regulations focus on agency and disclosure requirements and regulating certain brokerage practices within the state jurisdiction. Real estate trade groups focus on professional standards of conduct in every facet of the business.

By observing professional ethics and standards, licensees will serve clients and customers better, foster a professional image in the community, and avoid regulatory sanctions and lawsuits.

Today's professional ethics are not only important for one's career; they are also legal imperatives.

Trade associations representing the real estate industry have instituted their own codes of ethics and professional practices covering every facet of brokerage activity. For the latest Code of Ethics of the National Association of REALTORS®, see https://www.nar.realtor/about-nar/governing-documents/code-of-ethics/2025-code-of-ethics-standards-of-practice .

The standards of most codes for real estate licensees concern the following general areas of practice.

Job performance

A professional real estate agent must understand the skills and knowledge the profession requires and make a commitment to maintain and improve expertise in these areas. Of particular importance are:

- market knowledge
- real estate laws
- evolving standards of practice

Other aspects of professional performance that are usually supported include:

- promoting exclusive listings
- promoting the professionalism of the real estate industry
- promoting arbitration of disagreements rather than litigation
- obtaining transactional agreements between parties in writing
- submitting offers and counteroffers in a timely and objective manner
- keeping the funds of others separate from broker and personal funds
- providing equal professional services to all persons
- providing services only within the agent's area of competence or with the assistance of a specialist
- observing the highest standards of truthfulness in advertising
- cooperating with real estate boards and commissions in their enforcement of standards

A real estate professional must recognize the limits of the agent's role and avoid practicing other professions beyond the agent's qualifications, such as law, investment counseling, securities brokerage, and tax advising.

Duties to clients

Most codes of ethics uphold the commitment to fulfill fiduciary duties. Specific applications include:

- honestly representing market value and property condition
- respecting rights and duties of other client-agent relationships
- submitting all offers
- avoiding commingling and conversion
- keeping transaction documents current
- maintaining confidentiality
- managing client property competently

Duties to customers

Some of the guidelines for working with customers are:

- honestly representing market value and property condition
- avoiding calling a service "free" that in fact is contingent on receiving a commission
- advertising truthfully

Disclosure

In compliance with applicable laws and to promote respect for the real estate profession, licensees should be careful to disclose

- that the agent is going to receive compensation from more than one party in a transaction
- property defects if they are reasonably apparent; however there is no duty to disclose a defect which it would require technical expertise to discover
- any interest the agent has in a listed property if the agent is representing a party concerning the property
- any profits made on a client's money
- the agent's identity in advertisements
- the agent's representation of both parties in a transaction
- the existence of accepted offers
- identity of broker and firm in advertising as required by state law

Wholesaling

Real estate wholesaling is a method of profiting from a real estate transaction without actually buying any real estate. The wholesaler finds a willing seller, puts the property under contract, and finds a third-party buyer willing to buy at a higher price than what the wholesaler has agreed to pay the original seller. At closing, the wholesaler assigns the contract to the ultimate buyer; the ultimate buyer settles with the original seller and pays the wholesaler the difference in the two contracts as a fee.

Some states require the wholesaler in such transactions to hold a real estate license.

Love letters

Buyers sometimes try to enhance the attractiveness of a purchase offer by attaching a personal note to the offer. This appeal to the seller, called a "love letter," typically mentions such things as why the buyer particularly likes the home, how the buyer imagines family life in the home, and how well the buyer will care for the home.

The practice is discouraged in some states and by some real estate associations as creating the possibility of liability for fair housing violations. Since the letter may divulge information about such characteristics of the buyer as race, religion, or familial status, it could be construed as providing an unlawful basis for the seller's decision to accept or reject an offer.

Some sellers explicitly refuse to accept these love letters. Best practice is to avoid the use of love letters and find other ways to make the offer attractive.

Professional relationships

Professional conduct excludes disparagement of competitors. Real estate professionals also

- forgo pursuit of unfair advantage
- arbitrate rather than litigate disputes
- respect the agency relationships of others
- conform to accepted standards of co-brokerage practices

For more Fair Housing information:

HUD's central fair housing site:
www.hud.gov/program_offices/fair_housing_equal_opp

Fair housing laws:
www.hud.gov/program_offices/fair_housing_equal_opp/fair_housing_and_related_law
www.hud.gov/program_offices/fair_housing_equal_opp/fair_housing_act_overview

Complaint procedures, with state links:
www.hud.gov/program_offices/fair_housing_equal_opp/online-complaint

Advertising guidelines vis a vis fair housing:
www.hud.gov/program_offices/fair_housing_equal_opp/advertising_and_marketing

20 Professional Practices Snapshot Review

FAIR HOUSING LAWS	•	enacted to create equal opportunity and access to housing and housing finance
	•	state laws generally reflect federal fair housing laws; federal laws do not pre-empt local zoning laws but prohibit them from discriminating
Civil Rights Act of 1866	•	no discrimination in selling or leasing housing *based on race*
	•	Executive Order 11063: no race discrimination involving FHA- or VA-backed loans
Civil Rights Act of 1968	•	Title VIII (Fair Housing Act): no housing discrimination *based on race, color, religion, national origin*
	•	certain exceptions permitted
Forms of illegal discrimination	•	discriminatory misrepresentation, advertising, and financing; unequal services; steering; blockbusting; restricting access to market; redlining
Title VIII exemptions	•	privately-owned single-family with no broker and no discriminatory advertising; 1-4 unit apartment building where owner is resident and no discriminatory advertising; private club facilities leased to members; religious organization-owned facilities for members and no discrimination
Jones v. Mayer	•	no race discrimination, without exception
Equal Opportunity in Housing Poster	•	must be displayed by brokers
Fair Housing Amendments Act of 1988	•	no discrimination *based on sex or against the handicapped or families with children*
Discrimination by the client	•	agent liable for complying with client's discriminatory acts
Violations and enforcement	•	file HUD complaint, sue in court, or both; may obtain injunction, damages; violators subject to prosecution
Fair financing laws	•	Equal Credit Opportunity Act: no discrimination in housing finance based on race, color, religion, sex, marital status, age; Home Mortgage Disclosure Act: no redlining
Americans with Disabilities Act	•	no discrimination against those with disabilities; applies to employment, education, transportation, public facilities; equivalent access
	•	Titles I (employment) and III (public accommodation) most common for real estate agents
PROPERTY DISCLOSURES		
Residential property condition	•	written seller disclosure may be required; may or may not relieve agent of some liabilities
	•	seller discloses known problems; agent discloses known material facts known or should have known; failure to disclose grants right of rescission to buyer
	•	agent should advise seller of red flag issues detected; may include environmental concerns, property size and shape, neighborhood, construction quality, flooding, floorplan, adjacent property

Environmental issues	•	duties of detecting, disclosing, remediating for owner and agent vary; typically include: lead-based paint, mold, asbestos, air quality, water quality, carbon monoxide, septic system, drug manufacturing, radon, formaldehyde, underground tanks
	•	agents need to be familiar with requirements of EPA, CERCLA/Superfund Act, Clean Air and Water Acts, Lead-based Paint Act, among others
	•	licensees must be aware of issues, know where to find professional help, disclose
Warranties	•	agents should inform clients of limitations of home warranties; not a substitute for inspection
Inspections	•	inspections can reveal structural, electrical, plumbing, roof, foundation, pest, environmental issues; agent must disclose inspection results if known
Homeowners' Associations	•	agent must make sure existence, requirements, mandates, costs of homeowners' association are disclosed
OTHER PROFESSIONAL PRACTICES	•	codes of ethics provide self-regulating standards of conduct covering all facets of the profession; serve clients, customers, and the public; avoid sanctions and liability; cover practices such as job performance, duties to clients and customers, disclosures, non-discrimination, professional relationships
Job performance	•	maintain knowledge of market, laws, practices; recognize limits of agent's role
Duties to clients	•	fiduciary duties; truthful representation of facts; respect client relationships; submit offers; avoid illegal practices; document transaction
Duties to customers	•	truthful representation of facts; truthful advertising
Disclosure	•	compensating parties; property defects; agent's interest in property; use of client funds; agent's identity in advertising
Wholesaling	•	acting as an intermediary in a transaction by contracting to purchase, assigning the contract to another buying, and taking the difference as a fee; licensing may or may not be required
Love letters	•	personal notes from buyers to sellers to enhance attractiveness of an offer
Non-discrimination	•	compliance with fair housing laws
Professional relationships	•	no disparagement of competitors; no unfair advantage; respect for others; arbitration of disputes
Residential property condition disclosure	•	where required, re-seller of residential property must complete and deliver to buyer on or before offering; failure gives buyer right to rescind prior to closing or occupancy; agents must disclose material facts; buyers must acknowledge receipt

21 Closings

The Closing Event
Real Estate Settlement Procedures Act
Financial Settlement of the Transaction
Computing Prorations
Taxes Due at Closing
Closing Cost Calculations: Case Study
TILA/RESPA Integrated Disclosure Rule
Reporting Requirements

THE CLOSING EVENT

The setting
The closing process
Transfer of title
Transfer of purchase funds
Escrow procedures
Lender closing requirements
Broker's role

The setting

The closing event is the culmination of the real estate transaction. During this event, the buyer pays the purchase price and receives title to the purchased real estate. At the same time, the buyer completes financing arrangements, and buyer and seller pay all required taxes, fees, and charges.

Customary Practices. Procedures and customary practices for conducting real estate closings vary from state to state. For example, it is common in some states for sellers to pay title insurance, while in other states the buyer and seller might share this expense. Students should refer to supplemental state materials to ascertain prevailing practices in their state.

Time. The sale contract sets the date of the closing, usually within sixty days of signing. The time period between signing and closing is expected to be sufficient for the removal of any contingencies, such as the buyer's obtaining of financing, the performance of inspections, and the correction of identified physical defects. Failure of either buyer or seller to perform pre-closing actions specified in the contract can delay or terminate the transaction. If the contract includes a statement that "time is of the essence," all parties agree to meet the time limitations exactly as stated. If both parties consent, however, they can re-schedule the closing date.

Location. Closings occur at various locations, such as the office of the title company, the lender, the escrow agent, one of the attorneys, the broker, or the county recorder. The sale contract specifies the location.

Parties at closing. The primary parties at the closing are normally buyer, seller, and a closing agent or escrow officer. Other parties who might be present include the title officer, attorneys, brokers or agents, and the lender's representative. It is not actually necessary for any of these parties to attend the meeting. The closing agent can complete the transaction, provided all documents have been duly executed in advance.

The closing process

The closing process consists of buyer and seller verifying that each has fulfilled the terms of the sale contract. If they have, then the mortgage loan, if any, is closed, all expenses are apportioned and paid, the consideration is exchanged for the title, final documents are signed, and arrangements are made to record the transaction according to local laws.

Exhibit 21.1 The Closing Process

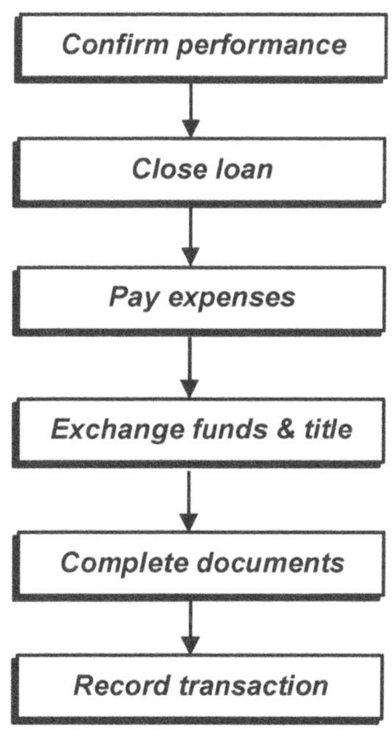

Transfer of title

The seller must produce evidence of marketable title, such as a commitment for title insurance by a title insurer. Before making a title commitment, a title company performs a title search to discover any liens, encumbrances, restrictions, conditions, or easements attaching to the title.

If there are any encumbrances or liens that damage the title, the seller is expected to remove these prior to the date specified in the contract. The most common title cloud is an unpaid lien.

The seller may also be asked to execute an affidavit of title stating that, since the date of the original title search, the seller has incurred no new liens, judgments, unpaid bills for repairs or improvements, no unrecorded deeds or contracts, no bankruptcies or divorces that would affect title, or any other defects the seller is aware of.

The purchaser, purchaser's lender, or title company may require a survey to verify the location and size of the property. The survey also identifies any easements, encroachments, or flood plain hazard.

The buyer should inspect the property to make certain that the property is in the condition in which the seller states that it is, and that any repairs or other required actions have been performed. A final inspection, called a **buyer's walk-through**, should be conducted as close to the closing date as possible.

If the seller's mortgage lien(s) are to be satisfied at closing, the lender will provide a **payoff statement**, also called an **offset statement**, specifying the amount of unpaid principal and any interest due as of the closing date, plus fees that will be due the lender and any credits or penalties that may apply. The holder of a note secured by a trust deed will provide a similar statement, called a **beneficiary statement**, to show any unpaid balance. Even if the buyer is assuming the seller's mortgage loan, the buyer will want to know the exact amount of the unpaid balance as of the closing date.

Finally, the seller produces and/or deposits with the escrow agent the deed that conveys the property to the buyer.

Transfer of purchase funds

The buyer usually produces and/or deposits with the escrow agent the following:

- earnest money
- loan funds and documents
- any other cash needed to complete the purchase

Escrow procedures

If the closing occurs "in escrow" rather than face-to-face, the principal parties deposit funds and documents with the appointed escrow agent, and the escrow agent disburses funds and releases documents to the appropriate parties when all the conditions of the escrow have been met. If for any reason the transaction cannot be completed, for instance if the buyer refuses the title as it is offered, or the buyer fails to produce the necessary cash, the escrow instructions usually provide a mechanism for reconveying title to the seller and funds to the buyer. In such a case, both parties return to their original status as if no sale had occurred.

Lender closing requirements

A lender is concerned about the quality of the collateral a borrower is providing in return for the mortgage loan. The collateral would be endangered by defects in the title, by liens that would take precedence over the mortgage lien, such as a tax lien, and by physical damage to the property which is not repaired. Consequently, the lender typically requires a survey; a property inspection; hazard insurance; a title insurance policy; a reserve account for taxes and insurance; and possibly, private mortgage insurance. In some cases the lender may also require a *certificate of occupancy* verifying that any new construction performed complies with local building codes.

Broker's role

A broker usually continues to provide service between the signing of the sale contract and the closing by helping to make arrangements for pre-closing activities such as inspections, surveys, appraisals and repairs and generally taking steps to ensure that the closing can proceed as scheduled.

A broker may conduct proceedings at the closing meeting, or may have no further role in the transaction after the sale contract is signed, depending on local practices and the transaction in question. In many states, the broker is charged with the responsibility for accuracy and timely delivery of the closing documents to the principal parties. A broker may also have the responsibility for reporting the transaction to the Internal Revenue Service.

Finally, if the seller of the property is a non-resident alien, U.S. law may require the broker to withhold and transmit to the Internal Revenue Service a portion of the sale proceeds to cover the alien seller's income tax liability. There are also special reporting requirements when the transaction involves a non-resident alien.

REAL ESTATE SETTLEMENT PROCEDURES ACT (RESPA)

TRID
Information booklet
Loan Estimate
Mortgage servicing disclosure
Closing Disclosure
Disclosures after settlement
Limits on escrow accounts
Referral fees and kickbacks

The **Real Estate Settlement Procedures Act** (RESPA) is a consumer protection statute enacted in 1974. Its purpose is to clarify settlement costs and to eliminate kickbacks and fees that increase settlement costs. RESPA specifies certain closing procedures when a purchase:

- involves a residential property, including one- to four-family residences, cooperatives and condominiums;
- involves a first or second mortgage lien; and
- is being financed by a "federally-related" mortgage loan, which includes loans made by a federally-insured lender; loans insured or guaranteed by the VA or FHA, loans administered by HUD, and loans intended to be sold to FNMA, FHLMC, or GNMA.

RESPA regulations do not apply to transactions being otherwise financed except in the case of an assumption in which the terms of the assumed loan are modified or the lender's charges for the assumption are greater than $50.

RESPA is directed at lenders and settlement companies, but licensees should be familiar with requirements and changes implemented as of January, 2014. The Dodd-Frank Act of 2010 granted rule-making authority under RESPA to the Consumer Financial Protection Bureau (CFPB) and generally granted the CFPB authority to supervise and enforce compliance with RESPA and its implementing regulations. In 2013, the CFPB made substantive and technical changes to the existing regulations. Substantive changes included modifying the servicing transfer notice requirements and implementing new procedures and notice requirements related to borrowers' error resolution requests and information requests. The amendments also included new provisions related to escrow payments, force-placed insurance, general servicing policies, procedures, and requirements, early intervention, continuity of contact, loss mitigation and the relation of RESPA's servicing provisions to State law. These RESPA amendments went into effect on January 10, 2014.

TRID Effective October 3, 2015, a TILA/RESPA Integrated Disclosure Rule (TRID) integrates the disclosure requirements of RESPA and Truth-in-Lending, replacing the old Good Faith Estimate form and HUD-1 Uniform Settlement Statement a new Loan Estimate form and Closing Disclosure form, respectively.

Information booklet A lender subject to RESPA must give loan applicants the CFPB booklet, "Your Home Loan Toolkit," within three days of receiving a loan application. This booklet describes loans, closing costs, and the Closing Disclosure form.

Loan Estimate A lender must give the applicant, at the time of application or within three business days of application, a Loan Estimate (H-24) of likely settlement costs. This estimate is usually based on comparable transactions completed in the area. The terms stated in the Closing Disclosure must agree with those of the Loan Estimate within certain limits.

Mortgage servicing disclosure The lender must disclose to the buyer whether the lender intends to service the loan or convey it to another lender for servicing. This disclosure must also be accompanied by information as to how the buyer can resolve complaints.

Closing Disclosure Under CFPB rules, a lender must use the Closing Disclosure (H-25) to disclose settlement costs to the buyer. This form covers all costs that the buyer will have to pay at closing, whether to the lender or to other parties. Use of this form enforces RESPA's prohibitions against a lender's requiring a buyer to deposit an excessive amount in the tax and insurance escrow account or to use a particular title company for title insurance. The consumer must receive the completed form not later than three business days before closing and has the right to inspect a revised form one business day before closing. A description and example of this form are provided later in this chapter.

Disclosures after settlement Loan servicers must provide borrowers with an annual escrow statement which summarizes all inflows and outflows in the prior 12-month period. The statement must also disclose shortfalls or overages in the account, and how the discrepancies will be resolved.

Limits on escrow accounts Section 10 of RESPA limits the amounts lenders can require borrowers to place in escrow for purposes of paying taxes, hazard insurance, and other property-related expenses. The limitation applies to the initial deposits as well as deposits made over the course of the loan's term.

Referral fees and kickbacks RESPA prohibits the payment of fees as part of a real estate settlement when no services are actually rendered. This prohibition includes referral fees for such services as title searches, title insurance, mortgage loans, appraisals, credit reports, inspections, surveys, and legal services.

Business relationships and affiliations among real estate firms, mortgage brokers, title insurance firms and other such companies that are involved in a transaction are permitted, provided the relationships are disclosed in writing to the consumer, the consumer is free to go elsewhere for the relevant service, and the companies do not exchange fees for referrals.

FINANCIAL SETTLEMENT OF THE TRANSACTION

Settlement process
Selling terms and closing costs
Debits and credits
Non-prorated items
Prorated items

Settlement process

The process of settlement consists of five basic steps:

1. Identify selling terms and closing costs.
2. Determine non-prorated debits and credits.
3. Determine prorated debits and credits.
4. Complete the closing statement.
5. Disburse funds.

Selling terms and closing costs

Selling terms are the price of the property, the buyer's deposit and downpayment, and the terms and amounts of the buyer's financing arrangements. Closing costs are final expenses that buyer or seller must pay at closing to complete the transaction. The sale contract identifies all selling terms and who pays which costs. The apportionment of expenses is subject to negotiation, and in the absence of a specific agreement, is determined by custom. Closing costs include such items as brokerage fees, mortgage-related fees, title-related expenses, and real estate taxes.

Debits and credits

The closing statement accounts for the debits and credits of the buyer and seller to settle and complete the transaction. A debit is an amount that one party must pay at closing or has already paid prior to closing. A credit is an amount that a party must receive at closing or that has already been received prior to closing.

Exhibit 21.2 Debit and Credit

The excess of the buyer's debits over the buyer's credits is the amount the buyer must bring to the closing. The excess of the seller's credits over the seller's debits is the amount the seller will receive at closing.

An individual expense item that one party owes to a party unrelated to the transaction, such as an attorney or the state, is treated as *a debit to that party only*. An income or expense item that affects both parties is apportioned, or **prorated**, to each party to reflect the proper amount that each owes or should receive. A prorated item is treated as *a debit to one party and a credit to the other party for the same amount*.

Buyer's debits and credits. To determine how much money the buyer owes at closing, the buyer's debits are totaled and compared with the total of the buyer's credits. The excess of debits over credits is the amount the buyer must bring to the closing, usually in the form of a cashier's check or certified check. The items typically debited and credited to the buyer are illustrated in the following exhibit.

Exhibit 21.3 Buyer's Credits and Debits

Buyer's Credits

earnest money
loan amount (borrowed or assumed)
seller's share of prorated items the buyer will pay

Buyer's Debits

purchase price
expenses (per agreement or custom)
buyer's share of prorated items prepaid by seller

Seller's credits and debits. To determine how much the seller will receive at closing, the same procedure is followed for the seller's debits and credits. The excess of credits over debits is what the seller will receive. The items typically debited and credited to the seller are illustrated in the following exhibit.

Exhibit 21.4 Seller's Debits and Credits

Seller's Debits

expenses (per agreement or custom)
seller's share of prorated items the buyer will pay
loan balance or other lien to be paid off

Seller's Credits

purchase price
buyer's share of prorated items prepaid by seller

Non-prorated items

Non-prorated items are costs *incurred by one party only.* Items not prorated include those listed in the next exhibit.

Exhibit 21.5 Non-Prorated Items

Buyer usually pays	Seller usually pays
Mortgage recording fees Documentary stamp tax Intangible tax on mortgage Mortgage-related fees: appraisal, credit, survey, loan Impound reserves: insurance, taxes Attorney fees	Stamp tax on deed Title insurance Brokerage fee Inspection fees Title-related expenses Attorney fees

Prorated items

Many of the items to be settled at the closing are partly the responsibility of the buyer and partly of the seller. Some are expense items that the seller has *paid in advance*, where the buyer owes the seller part of the expense. Some are income items that the seller received in advance, and the seller owes the buyer a part of the income. Others are items the buyer will have to pay *in arrears*, and the seller owes the buyer part of the expense. The method of dividing financial responsibility for such items is **proration**. With a prorated item, there is always a debit to one party and a corresponding credit for the same amount to the other party.

Items paid in advance. At the time of closing, the seller has paid some items in advance that cover a period of time that goes beyond the closing date. In effect, the seller has prepaid some of the buyer's expenses, and the buyer must reimburse the seller. Heating oil and natural gas are typical items. By the same token, the seller of a rental property may have received rent or rental deposits in advance, and must reimburse the buyer for the part that belongs to the buyer. For an expense the seller paid in advance, *the buyer receives a debit and the seller receives a credit.*

For income the seller received in advance, *the buyer receives a credit and the seller receives a debit.*

Items paid in arrears. At the time of closing, the seller has incurred certain expenses that have not been billed or paid at the time of closing and that the buyer will have to pay later. A typical item is real estate taxes.

For an item the buyer will pay in arrears, *the buyer receives a credit and the seller receives a debit.*

Exhibit 21.6 Items Paid in Arrears and Advance

	arrears	advance
real estate taxes	x	
mortgage interest	x	
rents received by seller		x
utilities	x	

Charging shares. If the seller has paid the buyer's share of an item, *charge the buyer for the buyer's share of the period.* If the buyer will pay the seller's share of an item, *charge the seller for the seller's share of the period.* If the seller has received the buyer's share of an income item, *charge the seller for the buyer's share of the period.*

Exhibit 21.7 Who Gets Charged

Seller paid for the year: charge buyer for buyer's share

Annual expense – closing August 7												
Jan	Feb	Mar	Apr	May	Jun	Jul	Aug		Sep	Oct	Nov	Dec
							7	8				
Seller's share								Buyer's share				

Buyer will pay for the month: charge seller for seller's share

Monthly expense – closing August 7							
August							
1	2	3	4	5	6	7	8-31
Seller's share							Buyer's share

COMPUTING PRORATIONS

12-month/30-day method
365-day method

The primary methods of calculating prorations are the 360/30-day method, which computes prorations on the basis of a 360-day year and 30-day month, and the 365-day method, which computes prorations on the basis of a 365-day year. The 360/30-day method is commonly used for prorating mortgage interest. Either method may be used for real estate taxes, depending on local practice.

It is customary in most states that the seller owns the property up to and including the day of closing unless stated otherwise in the contract. Thus the closing day is apportioned to the seller in computing prorations. The method of prorating, if not specified in the contract, will follow local custom.

12-month / 30 day method

The 12-month/30-day method determines an average daily rate of payment for an item to be prorated *based on a 30-day month and a 360-day year*. The method consists of the following steps for annual and monthly items.

Annual items

1. Identify the total amount to be prorated.
2. Divide this amount by 12 to obtain an average monthly rate.
3. Divide the monthly rate by 30 to obtain an average daily rate.
4. Multiply the monthly amount times the seller's number of months of ownership in the year of the sale up to the month of closing. For the month of closing, multiply the seller's number of days of ownership times the daily amount and add the result to the previous result. The final result is the seller's pro rata share of this item.
5. The buyer's pro rata share of an item is the total amount less the seller's pro rata share.

Monthly items

1. Identify the total amount to be prorated.
2. Divide this amount by 30 to obtain the average daily amount.
3. Multiply the daily amount times the seller's number of days of ownership. The result is the seller's pro rata share of this item.
4. The buyer's pro rata share of an item is the total amount less the seller's pro rata share.

Exhibit 21.8 Prorating Annual Item: Real Estate Tax 12-month/30-day Method

A sale transaction on a single-family house closes on March 2. County taxes for the previous year, to be paid in arrears, amount to $1,730. The seller owns the house through the day of closing. What are the seller's and buyer's prorated shares of this item?

Total amount due:		=	$ 1,730.00
Monthly amount:	1,730 ÷ 12	=	$ 144.17
Daily amount:	144.17 ÷ 30	=	$ 4.81
Seller's share:	144.17 x 2 mo.	=	$ 288.34
	4.81 x 2 days	=	$ 9.62
	288.34 + 9.62	=	$ 297.96
Buyer's share	1,730 - 297.96	=	$ 1,432.04

Closing statement entries. The seller will be charged for the seller's share of the proration; an amount of $297.96 will be entered as a debit to the seller and a credit to the buyer because the buyer will have to pay the seller's share when the tax bill is received.

Exhibit 21.9 Prorating Monthly Item: Rent Received 12-month/30-day Method

The house in the previous example has been rented during the listing and selling period at a rate of $1800 per month. Rent for the month of March was paid to the seller on March 1. What is the buyer's prorated share of this rent? The day of closing, March 2, belongs to the seller.

Total received:		=	$ 1,800.00
Daily amount:	1800 ÷ 30	=	$ 60.00
Seller's share:	60.00 x 2 days	=	$ 120.00
Buyer's share	1800.00 – 120.00	=	$ 1,680.00

Closing statement entries. The seller will be charged for the buyer's share of the proration; an amount of $1,680.00 will be debited to the seller's account and credited to the buyer's account because the seller has received rent that belongs to the new owner after closing.

365-day method

The 365-day method uses the actual number of days in the calendar. The steps in the calculation are the same for annual and monthly prorations. The steps are:

1. Identify the total annual or monthly amount to be prorated.
2. For an annual proration, divide the total amount by 365 to obtain a daily amount (366 in a Leap Year). For a monthly proration, divide the total amount by the actual number of days in the month to obtain the daily amount.
3. Multiply the daily amount times the seller's number of days of ownership. The result is the seller's pro rata share of the item.
4. The buyer's pro rata share of an item is the total amount less the seller's pro rata share.

Exhibit 21.10 Prorating an Annual Tax Bill, 365-day Method

The seller in the previous example has a $1,730 tax bill, paid annually in arrears on December 31. Closing is on March 2, and the seller owns the day of closing. What is the seller's prorated share of this item?

Total amount due:		=	$ 1.730.00
Daily amount:	1730 ÷ 365	=	$ 4.75
Seller's share:	61 days x 4.75	=	$ 289.14
Buyer's share:	1730 - 289.14	=	$ 1,440.86

Closing statement entries. The seller will be charged for the seller's share of the proration; an amount of $289.14 will be debited to the seller's account and credited to the buyer's account because the buyer will have paid the seller's share of the tax bill in arrears.

TAXES DUE AT CLOSING

State taxes on the deed
State taxes on the mortgage

Certain transfer taxes that are due in connection with the closing appear and are accounted for on the closing statement. These include state taxes relating to the deed and to the buyer's mortgage. In addition to state-imposed taxes, counties and municipalities may also impose a tax on the real estate transfer.

State taxes on the deed

Most states impose a **transfer tax** when real estate is conveyed. The tax is usually paid when the deed is recorded, often in the form of **documentary stamps** purchased from the recorder where the deed is recorded. The stamps must be attached to deeds and conveyances before they are recorded.

Tax rates are specific to each state. Methods of stating the transfer tax due include quoting the tax as a percentage of the taxable consideration and as a dollar rate per $100.00 of total selling price. If the number of 100's is not a whole number, it must be rounded up to the next 100. For instance, if a property sells for $350,120 and the tax rate is $.55 per $100.00 "or any fraction thereof," the tax stamps will cost:

350,120 ÷ 100.00	=	3,501.20
3,501.20 *rounded up*	=	3,502
3,502 x $.55	=	$1,926.10

State taxes on the mortgage

Some states also impose a tax on instruments that contain promises to pay money, such as mortgages, notes, and contracts. Such taxes may be paid by the purchase of documentary stamps from the agency which will record the instrument. In addition, some states impose a further tax on the mortgage as an item of intangible personal property.

Taxes on the mortgage are typically paid by the buyer/borrower.

CLOSING COST ITEMIZATION: CASE ILLUSTRATION

Selling terms and closing costs
Prorations and charges

The Closing Disclosure summarizes the financial settlement of a transaction. At closing, the closing agent also generally provides a statement to the buyer and/or seller detailing receipts and disbursements from relevant escrow accounts to which the buyer and seller have contributed funds as part of the transaction. The following illustration shows how some of these cost components are calculated and allocated in a sample transaction.

Selling terms and closing costs

Lawrence and Sandy Binder have accepted an offer on their house located at 928 Elm Street, Littleburg. The buyers, Bill and Dillis Waite, offered $450,000, with earnest money of $70,000 and the remaining $380,000 of the purchase price to come from a new conventional loan from Scepter Mortgage Company. The loan is for 30 years at 5.5% interest, with a monthly principal plus interest payment of $2,158. The lender is charging 1.5 points and a 1% origination fee. Closing is set to occur at Alta Title Company at 4 p.m. on May 10 of the current (non-leap) year.

The Binders have an agreement to pay a broker's commission of 6% to Littleburg Realty. Their unpaid mortgage loan balance as of May 1 will be $184,000. Their monthly interest payments are $613.00. The annual interest rate is 4%. The previous year's county taxes, amounting to $2,572, have been paid by the seller in arrears. The current year's taxes, not yet billed or paid, are assumed to be the same as the previous year's. The parties agree to prorate using the 365-day method, and that the day of closing belongs to the seller. The relevant facts and costs, and who pays them according to the terms of the sale contract, are summarized below.

Selling terms	
Sale price:	$450,000
Deposit/downpayment	$70,000
Loan amount	$380,000
Seller-paid Costs	
Commissions:	6% of sale price (.06)
Real estate taxes:	$2,572, to be prorated
Title insurance:	$900 owner's coverage
Seller's attorney:	$1,500
Record Release Deed:	$25
Survey:	$550
Transfer stamps	
state:	$162
county:	$162
Seller's loan payoff:	$184,000 + 10 days' prorated May interest @ $613/month
Buyer- paid Costs	
Sale price:	$450,000 ($70,000 earnest money already deposited by buyer)
Appraisal fee:	$400 already paid by buyer
Credit report:	$50 already paid by buyer
Closing fee:	$350
Recording fees:	$55
Title insurance:	$250 for lender's coverage
Buyer's attorney:	$1200
Pest inspection:	$100
Buyer's loan:	$380,000; 30-year fixed @ 5.5% (.055) points: 1.5% of loan amount (.015) origination fee: 1.0% of loan amount (.01)
Hazard insurance:	$2,400/year
Real estate taxes:	$2,572.00, to be prorated
Tax and insurance escrow:	8 months' taxes, 4 months' insurance
Prepaid interest:	from day after closing to end of month

Prorations and charges

According to the summarized sale contract, the only cost to be prorated and shared between seller and buyer is the real estate tax. Other costs to be computed are the broker's commission, the seller's unpaid mortgage interest, the buyer's loan fees and points, the buyer's tax and insurance escrows, and the buyer's prepaid mortgage interest.

Commission. The commission paid by the seller is:

$450,000 x 6% = $27,000.00

At closing this amount will be charged, or debited, to the seller.

Real estate taxes. Using the 365-day method, the daily amount is \$2,572 ÷ 365, or \$7.05 (rounded). The total number of days is the number of days in January, February, March and April, plus 10 days in May, or (31+28+31+30+10), or 130 days. At closing, the seller's share of \$916.50 is charged to the seller and the buyer is credited with the same amount.

Total amount due:		=	\$	2,572.00
Daily amount:	2,572 ÷ 365	=	\$	7.05
Seller's share	7.051 x 130	=	\$	916.50
Buyer's share:	2,572 – 916.50	=	\$	1,655.50

Seller's unpaid mortgage interest. Since mortgage interest is paid in arrears, the seller owes the lender for interest not yet charged for the ten days of the month of closing. This amount is therefore debited to the seller.

Daily amount:	613 ÷ 31 days	=	\$	19.77
Seller's charge:	19.77 x 10 days	=	\$	197.70

Buyer's loan origination and points. The buyer's debits for loan fees and points are:

Fee:	380,000 x 1%	=	\$	3,800
Points:	380,000 x 1.5%	=	\$	5,700

Buyer's escrow. The lender requires the buyer to establish an escrow account to cover eight months of real estate taxes and four months of hazard insurance. The debits charged to the buyer are therefore:

Taxes:				
Annual amount:		=	\$	2,572.00
Monthly amount:	2,572 ÷ 12	=	\$	214.33
Amount due:	214.33 x 8 mo.	=	\$	1,714.64
Insurance:				
Annual amount:		=	\$	2400.00
Monthly amount:	2400 ÷ 12	=	\$	200.00
Amount due:	200 x 4 mo.	=	\$	800.00

Prepaid interest. The lender requires the buyer (borrower) to pay, in advance, the interest on the loan amount disbursed at closing to cover the 21 days of the closing month that would be due in arrears later. Note that the lender is not charging the borrower for interest for the day of closing. The buyer's first mortgage payment, which will cover the month of June, will not be due until July 1. Charged to buyer:

Monthly amount:	380K x 5.5% ÷ 12	=	\$	1741.67
Daily amount:	1,741.67 ÷ 31	=	\$	56.18
Total prepaid interest	56.18 x 21 days	=	\$	1179.78

TILA/RESPA INTEGRATED DISCLOSURE RULE

Forms and procedures
Good faith
Types of charges
Applicable transactions
The H-25 Closing Disclosure form

Forms and procedures

As mentioned earlier, the TILA/RESPA Integrated Disclosures (TRID) rule is in effect as of October 3, 2015. These changes introduce new mandatory forms and procedures to replace the old ones, as follows.

- Lenders must give the consumer a copy of the **booklet**, "Your Home Loan Toolkit" **at the time** of loan application.

- Lenders must deliver or mail the **Loan Estimate** (Form H-24) to the consumer **no later than the third business day** after receiving a loan application. (A "business day" in this context is any day on which the lender's offices are open for business. An "application" exists when the consumer has given the lender or mortgage broker six pieces of information: name; income; Social Security number; property address; estimated value of property; loan amount sought).

- Lenders must provide the **Closing Disclosure** (Form H-25) to the consumer **at least three business days** before consummation of the loan. (A "business day" in this context is any calendar day except a Sunday or the day on which a legal public holiday is observed. "Consummation" refers to the day on which the borrower becomes indebted to the creditor; this may or may not correspond to the day of closing the transaction.)

Exhibit 21. 11 TILA/RESPA Disclosures

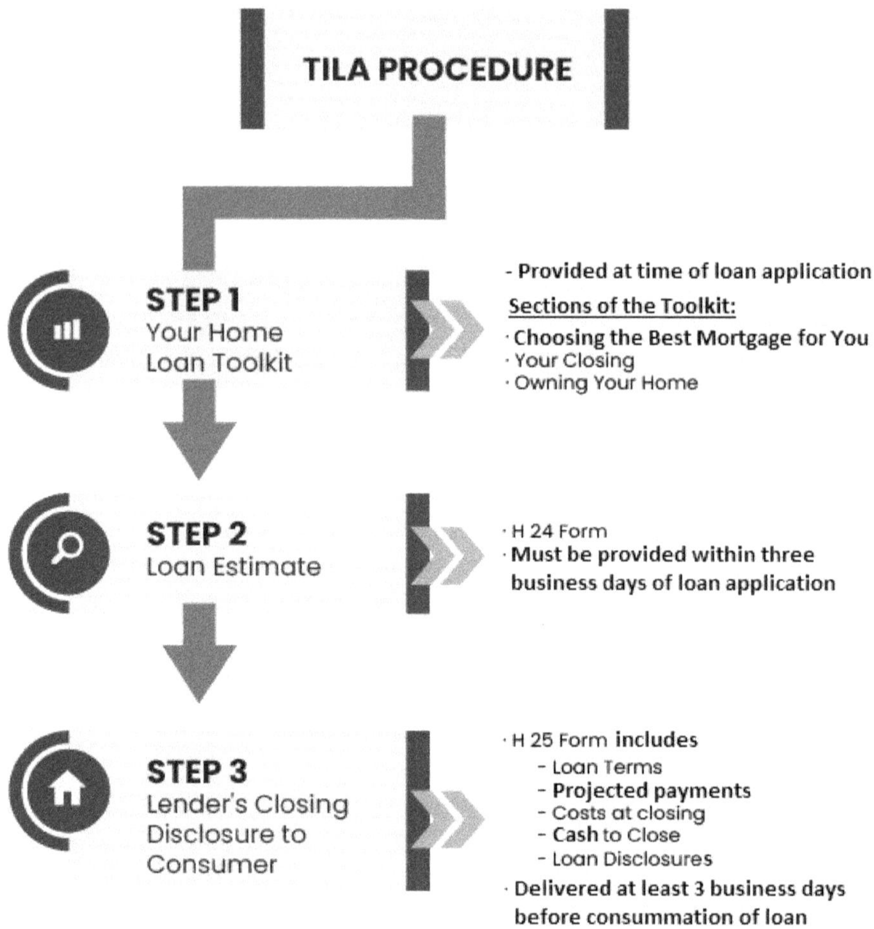

Good faith

Creditors are responsible for ensuring that the figures stated in the Loan Estimate are made in good faith and consistent with the best information reasonably available to the creditor at the time they are disclosed.

Good faith is measured by calculating the difference between the estimated charges originally provided in the Loan Estimate and the actual charges paid by or imposed on the consumer in the Closing Disclosure.

Generally, if the charge paid by or imposed on the consumer exceeds the amount originally disclosed on the Loan Estimate it is not in good faith, regardless of whether the creditor later discovers a technical error, miscalculation, or underestimation of a charge, although there are exceptions.

Types of charges

For certain costs or terms, creditors are permitted to charge consumers more than the amount disclosed on the Loan Estimate without any tolerance limitation.

These charges are:

- prepaid interest; property insurance premiums; amounts placed into an escrow, impound, reserve or similar account
- charges for services required by the creditor if the creditor permits the consumer to shop and the consumer selects a third-party service provider not on the creditor's written list of service providers
- charges paid to third-party service providers for services not required by the creditor (may be paid to affiliates of the creditor)

However, creditors may only charge consumers more than the amount disclosed when the original estimated charge, or lack of an estimated charge for a particular service, was based on the best information reasonably available to the creditor at the time the disclosure was provided.

Charges for third-party services and recording fees paid by or imposed on the consumer are grouped together and subject to a 10% cumulative tolerance ("10% tolerance" charges). This means the creditor may charge the consumer more than the amount disclosed on the Loan Estimate for any of these charges so long as the total sum of the charges added together does not exceed the sum of all such charges disclosed on the Loan Estimate by more than 10%.

For all other charges ("zero tolerance" charges), creditors are not permitted to charge consumers more than the amount disclosed on the Loan Estimate under any circumstances other than changed circumstances that permit a revised Loan Estimate.

If the amounts paid by the consumer at closing exceed the amounts disclosed on the Loan Estimate beyond the applicable tolerance threshold, the creditor must refund the excess to the consumer no later than 60 calendar days after consummation.

Applicable transactions

The Integrated Disclosures rule applies to most closed-end consumer mortgages. It does not apply to:

- home equity lines of credit (HELOCs)
- reverse mortgages
- mortgages secured by a mobile home or by a dwelling that is not attached to real property (i.e., land)
- loans made by persons who are not considered "creditors" by virtue of the fact they make five or fewer mortgages in a year.

However, certain types of loans that used to be subject to TILA but not RESPA are now subject to the TILA-RESPA rule's integrated disclosure requirements, including:

- construction-only loans
- loans secured by vacant land or by 25 or more acres
- credit extended to certain trusts for tax or estate planning

Guides and detailed information about the current TILA-RESPA rule can be found on the Consumer Financial Protection Bureau (CFPB) website at

https://www.consumerfinance.gov/policy-compliance/guidance/tila-respa-disclosure-rule/

The H-25 Closing Disclosure form

The H-25 Closing Disclosure form consists of five pages. Pages 1, 4, and 5 vary, depending on the loan type. To illustrate the form, we use a sample disclosure for a ***30-year fixed rate*** loan that is presented on the CFPB website.

Page 1 has four sections: general information, Loan Terms, Projected Payments, and Costs at Closing.

General information. This section has three columns:

- Closing information –issue date, closing date, disbursement date, settlement agent, file number, property address, and sale price
- Transaction information – names and addresses for borrower, seller and lender
- Loan information – loan term, loan purpose, product type, loan type and loan ID number

Loan Terms. This section states the loan amount, interest rate, and monthly principal and interest payment, and indicates whether any of those amounts can increase after closing. It also gives specifics of any prepayment penalty or balloon payment.

Projected Payment. This section displays the borrower's payment for principal and interest and mortgage insurance, an estimated escrow payment, and the total estimated monthly mortgage payment for years 1-7 and 8-30 of the loan term. It also provides an estimate of monthly tax, insurance, and assessment payments and indicates whether the payments will be held in escrow.

Costs at Closing. The last section of page 1 shows the borrowers' total closing costs (brought forward from page 2) and the total amount of cash the buyer needs to close (brought forward from page 3).

Page 2 details the closing costs. There are two sections divided into four columns:

- Description of the costs—loan costs and other costs
- Costs paid by the borrower – "at closing" or "before closing"
- Costs paid by the seller – "at closing" or "before closing"
- Costs paid by others (in the example, someone other than buyer or seller pays for the appraisal)

Loan Costs. The first section deals with the loan costs:

A. Origination charges, such as points, application fee, and underwriting fee

B. Charges for services the borrower did not shop for - items the lender requires, such as appraisals and credit reports

C. Services the borrower did shop for - items the borrower orders on his own, such as pest inspections, survey fees, and title insurance

D. The total of A, B, and C above

Other Costs. The second section deals with additional transaction-related costs:

E. Taxes and other government fees, such as recording fees and transfer taxes

F. Prepaid items, such as homeowner's insurance, mortgage insurance, prepaid interest, and property taxes to be paid before the first scheduled loan payment

G. Initial escrow payment at closing – an amount the borrower will pay the lender each month to be held in escrow until due, typically for insurance premiums and tax instalments

H. Other costs not covered elsewhere on the disclosure, such as items as association fees, home warranty fees, home inspection fees, real estate commission, and prorated items

I. The total of the costs of E, F, G, and H above

J. The total borrower-paid closing costs from D + I above. This total is carried to the bottom of page 1 as "Costs at Closing – Closing Costs."

Page 3 has two sections, one for calculating cash to close, the other for summarizing the transactions of borrower and seller.

Calculating Cash to Close. The first section compares the final costs of the loan with the lender's original Loan Estimate. This calculation considers costs paid before closing, down payment, deposits, seller credits, adjustments, and other credits. The last line of the calculation is "Cash to close," the amount the borrower needs to produce at closing.

When an amount has changed, the creditor must indicate where the consumer can find the amounts that have changed on the Loan Estimate. For example, if the Seller Credit amount changed, the creditor can indicate that the consumer should "See Seller Credits in Section L." When the increase in Total Closing Costs exceeds the legal limits, the creditor must disclose this fact and the dollar amount of the excess in the "Did this change?" column. A statement directing the consumer to the Lender Credit on page 2 must also be included if the creditor owes a credit to the consumer at closing for the excess amount.

Summaries of Transactions. The second section of page 3 is divided into two columns (or subsections), one to summarize the borrower's transaction and the other for the seller's transaction. The borrower's column includes:

K. amounts due from the borrower at closing, including the sale price and adjustments for items paid by the seller in advance.

L. amounts already paid by or on behalf of the borrower at closing, such as deposit, loan amount, loan assumptions, seller credits, other credits, and adjustments for items unpaid by the seller, such as taxes and assessments.

The calculation at the bottom of the left column subtracts the totals already paid by the borrower (line L) from the total due from the borrower (line K) to derive the Cash to Close due from the borrower at closing. This figure is the same as that at the bottom of page 1 under "Costs at Closing – Cash to Close."

The seller's column of the Summaries section includes:

M. amounts due to the seller at closing, including the sale price of the property and adjustments for items paid by the seller in advance.

N. amounts due from the seller at closing, such as closing costs the seller will pay, payoff of first or second mortgages, seller credit, and adjustments for items unpaid by the seller, such as taxes and assessments.

The calculation at the bottom of the right column subtracts the total due from the seller (line N) from the total due to the seller (line M) to derive the Cash to Seller, which is the amount the seller will receive at closing.

Page 4 provides additional Loan Disclosures:

- Assumption –whether the lender will allow a loan assumption on a future transfer
- Demand feature –whether the lender can require early repayment
- Late payment – the fee the lender will charge for a late payment
- Negative amortization –whether the loan is negatively amortized, which increases loan amount and diminishes the borrower's equity over the term
- Partial payments –whether the lender accepts partial payments and applies them to the loan
- Security interest –identifies the property securing the loan
- Escrow account – itemizes what is included in the escrow account and states the monthly escrow payment

Page 5 provides additional calculations, disclosures, and contact information:

- Loan Calculations –the total amount of all payments on the loan, the dollar amount of the finance charges over the life of the loan, the amount financed, the annual percentage rate (APR), and the total interest percentage (TIP)
- Other Disclosures –other important information for the borrower, including the right to a copy of the appraisal report and an indication of whether the borrower is protected against liability for the unpaid balance in the event of a foreclosure
- Contact Information –names, addresses, license numbers, contact names, email addresses, and phone numbers for persons involved in the transaction.
- Confirm Receipt –the borrowers' signatures confirming receipt of the Closing Disclosure document. **Signing the document does not indicate acceptance of the loan.**

Exhibit 21.12 Sample H-25 Closing Disclosure, Page 1

Closing Disclosure

This form is a statement of final loan terms and closing costs. Compare this document with your Loan Estimate.

Closing Information		Transaction Information		Loan Information	
Date Issued	4/15/2013	**Borrower**	Michael Jones and Mary Stone 123 Anywhere Street Anytown, ST 12345	**Loan Term**	30 years
Closing Date	4/15/2013			**Purpose**	Purchase
Disbursement Date	4/15/2013			**Product**	Fixed Rate
Settlement Agent	Epsilon Title Co.	**Seller**	Steve Cole and Amy Doe 321 Somewhere Drive Anytown, ST 12345		
File #	12-3456			**Loan Type**	☒ Conventional ☐ FHA ☐ VA ☐ ______
Property	456 Somewhere Ave Anytown, ST 12345	**Lender**	Ficus Bank	**Loan ID #**	123456789
Sale Price	$180,000			**MIC #**	000654321

Loan Terms		**Can this amount increase after closing?**
Loan Amount	$162,000	NO
Interest Rate	3.875%	NO
Monthly Principal & Interest *See Projected Payments below for your Estimated Total Monthly Payment*	$761.78	NO
		Does the loan have these features?
Prepayment Penalty		YES • **As high as $3,240** if you pay off the loan during the first 2 years
Balloon Payment		NO

Projected Payments		
Payment Calculation	**Years 1-7**	**Years 8-30**
Principal & Interest	$761.78	$761.78
Mortgage Insurance	+ 82.35	+ —
Estimated Escrow *Amount can increase over time*	+ 206.13	+ 206.13
Estimated Total Monthly Payment	$1,050.26	$967.91

Estimated Taxes, Insurance & Assessments *Amount can increase over time* *See page 4 for details*	$356.13 a month	**This estimate includes** ☒ Property Taxes ☒ Homeowner's Insurance ☒ Other: Homeowner's Association Dues *See Escrow Account on page 4 for details. You must pay for other property costs separately.*	**In escrow?** YES YES NO

Costs at Closing		
Closing Costs	$9,712.10	Includes $4,694.05 in Loan Costs + $5,018.05 in Other Costs – $0 in Lender Credits. *See page 2 for details.*
Cash to Close	$14,147.26	Includes Closing Costs. *See Calculating Cash to Close on page 3 for details.*

CLOSING DISCLOSURE PAGE 1 OF 5 • LOAN ID # 123456789

Exhibit 21.13 Sample H-25 Closing Disclosure, Page 2

Closing Cost Details

Loan Costs	Borrower-Paid At Closing	Borrower-Paid Before Closing	Seller-Paid At Closing	Seller-Paid Before Closing	Paid by Others
A. Origination Charges	**$1,802.00**				
01 0.25 % of Loan Amount (Points)	$405.00				
02 Application Fee	$300.00				
03 Underwriting Fee	$1,097.00				
04					
05					
06					
07					
08					
B. Services Borrower Did Not Shop For	**$236.55**				
01 Appraisal Fee to John Smith Appraisers Inc.					$405.00
02 Credit Report Fee to Information Inc.		$29.80			
03 Flood Determination Fee to Info Co.	$20.00				
04 Flood Monitoring Fee to Info Co.	$31.75				
05 Tax Monitoring Fee to Info Co.	$75.00				
06 Tax Status Research Fee to Info Co.	$80.00				
07					
08					
09					
10					
C. Services Borrower Did Shop For	**$2,655.50**				
01 Pest Inspection Fee to Pests Co.	$120.50				
02 Survey Fee to Surveys Co.	$85.00				
03 Title – Insurance Binder to Epsilon Title Co.	$650.00				
04 Title – Lender's Title Insurance to Epsilon Title Co.	$500.00				
05 Title – Settlement Agent Fee to Epsilon Title Co.	$500.00				
06 Title – Title Search to Epsilon Title Co.	$800.00				
07					
08					
D. TOTAL LOAN COSTS (Borrower-Paid)	**$4,694.05**				
Loan Costs Subtotals (A + B + C)	$4,664.25	$29.80			
Other Costs					
E. Taxes and Other Government Fees	**$85.00**				
01 Recording Fees Deed: $40.00 Mortgage: $45.00	$85.00				
02 Transfer Tax to Any State			$950.00		
F. Prepaids	**$2,120.80**				
01 Homeowner's Insurance Premium (12 mo.) to Insurance Co.	$1,209.96				
02 Mortgage Insurance Premium (mo.)					
03 Prepaid Interest ($17.44 per day from 4/15/13 to 5/1/13)	$279.04				
04 Property Taxes (6 mo.) to Any County USA	$631.80				
05					
G. Initial Escrow Payment at Closing	**$412.25**				
01 Homeowner's Insurance $100.83 per month for 2 mo.	$201.66				
02 Mortgage Insurance per month for mo.					
03 Property Taxes $105.30 per month for 2 mo.	$210.60				
04					
05					
06					
07					
08 Aggregate Adjustment	– 0.01				
H. Other	**$2,400.00**				
01 HOA Capital Contribution to HOA Acre Inc.	$500.00				
02 HOA Processing Fee to HOA Acre Inc.	$150.00				
03 Home Inspection Fee to Engineers Inc.	$750.00			$750.00	
04 Home Warranty Fee to XYZ Warranty Inc.			$450.00		
05 Real Estate Commission to Alpha Real Estate Broker			$5,700.00		
06 Real Estate Commission to Omega Real Estate Broker			$5,700.00		
07 Title – Owner's Title Insurance (optional) to Epsilon Title Co.	$1,000.00				
08					
I. TOTAL OTHER COSTS (Borrower-Paid)	**$5,018.05**				
Other Costs Subtotals (E + F + G + H)	$5,018.05				
J. TOTAL CLOSING COSTS (Borrower-Paid)	**$9,712.10**				
Closing Costs Subtotals (D + I)	$9,682.30	$29.80	$12,800.00	$750.00	$405.00
Lender Credits					

CLOSING DISCLOSURE PAGE 2 OF 5 • LOAN ID # 123456789

Exhibit 21.14 Sample H-25 Closing Disclosure, Page 3

Calculating Cash to Close Use this table to see what has changed from your Loan Estimate.

	Loan Estimate	Final	Did this change?
Total Closing Costs (J)	$8,054.00	$9,712.10	YES • See Total Loan Costs (D) and Total Other Costs (I)
Closing Costs Paid Before Closing	$0	– $29.80	YES • You paid these Closing Costs **before closing**
Closing Costs Financed (Paid from your Loan Amount)	$0	$0	NO
Down Payment/Funds from Borrower	$18,000.00	$18,000.00	NO
Deposit	– $10,000.00	– $10,000.00	NO
Funds for Borrower	$0	$0	NO
Seller Credits	$0	– $2,500.00	YES • See Seller Credits in **Section L**
Adjustments and Other Credits	$0	– $1,035.04	YES • See details in **Sections K and L**
Cash to Close	$16,054.00	$14,147.26	

Summaries of Transactions Use this table to see a summary of your transaction.

BORROWER'S TRANSACTION

K. Due from Borrower at Closing				**$189,762.30**
01 Sale Price of Property				$180,000.00
02 Sale Price of Any Personal Property Included in Sale				
03 Closing Costs Paid at Closing (J)				$9,682.30
04				
Adjustments				
05				
06				
07				
Adjustments for Items Paid by Seller in Advance				
08 City/Town Taxes		to		
09 County Taxes		to		
10 Assessments		to		
11 HOA Dues	4/15/13	to	4/30/13	$80.00
12				
13				
14				
15				
L. Paid Already by or on Behalf of Borrower at Closing				**$175,615.04**
01 Deposit				$10,000.00
02 Loan Amount				$162,000.00
03 Existing Loan(s) Assumed or Taken Subject to				
04				
05 Seller Credit				$2,500.00
Other Credits				
06 Rebate from Epsilon Title Co.				$750.00
07				
Adjustments				
08				
09				
10				
11				
Adjustments for Items Unpaid by Seller				
12 City/Town Taxes	1/1/13	to	4/14/13	$365.04
13 County Taxes		to		
14 Assessments		to		
15				
16				
17				
CALCULATION				
Total Due from Borrower at Closing (K)				$189,762.30
Total Paid Already by or on Behalf of Borrower at Closing (L)				– $175,615.04
Cash to Close ☒ From ☐ To Borrower				**$14,147.26**

SELLER'S TRANSACTION

M. Due to Seller at Closing				**$180,080.00**
01 Sale Price of Property				$180,000.00
02 Sale Price of Any Personal Property Included in Sale				
03				
04				
05				
06				
07				
08				
Adjustments for Items Paid by Seller in Advance				
09 City/Town Taxes		to		
10 County Taxes		to		
11 Assessments		to		
12 HOA Dues	4/15/13	to	4/30/13	$80.00
13				
14				
15				
16				
N. Due from Seller at Closing				**$115,665.04**
01 Excess Deposit				
02 Closing Costs Paid at Closing (J)				$12,800.00
03 Existing Loan(s) Assumed or Taken Subject to				
04 Payoff of First Mortgage Loan				$100,000.00
05 Payoff of Second Mortgage Loan				
06				
07				
08 Seller Credit				$2,500.00
09				
10				
11				
12				
13				
Adjustments for Items Unpaid by Seller				
14 City/Town Taxes	1/1/13	to	4/14/13	$365.04
15 County Taxes		to		
16 Assessments		to		
17				
18				
19				
CALCULATION				
Total Due to Seller at Closing (M)				$180,080.00
Total Due from Seller at Closing (N)				– $115,665.04
Cash ☐ From ☒ To Seller				**$64,414.96**

CLOSING DISCLOSURE PAGE 3 OF 5 • LOAN ID # 123456789

Exhibit 21.15 Sample H-25 Closing Disclosure, Page 4

Additional Information About This Loan

Loan Disclosures

Assumption
If you sell or transfer this property to another person, your lender
☐ will allow, under certain conditions, this person to assume this loan on the original terms.
☒ will not allow assumption of this loan on the original terms.

Demand Feature
Your loan
☐ has a demand feature, which permits your lender to require early repayment of the loan. You should review your note for details.
☒ does not have a demand feature.

Late Payment
If your payment is more than *15* days late, your lender will charge a late fee of *5% of the monthly principal and interest payment.*

Negative Amortization (Increase in Loan Amount)
Under your loan terms, you
☐ are scheduled to make monthly payments that do not pay all of the interest due that month. As a result, your loan amount will increase (negatively amortize), and your loan amount will likely become larger than your original loan amount. Increases in your loan amount lower the equity you have in this property.
☐ may have monthly payments that do not pay all of the interest due that month. If you do, your loan amount will increase (negatively amortize), and, as a result, your loan amount may become larger than your original loan amount. Increases in your loan amount lower the equity you have in this property.
☒ do not have a negative amortization feature.

Partial Payments
Your lender
☒ may accept payments that are less than the full amount due (partial payments) and apply them to your loan.
☐ may hold them in a separate account until you pay the rest of the payment, and then apply the full payment to your loan.
☐ does not accept any partial payments.
If this loan is sold, your new lender may have a different policy.

Security Interest
You are granting a security interest in
456 Somewhere Ave., Anytown, ST 12345

You may lose this property if you do not make your payments or satisfy other obligations for this loan.

Escrow Account
For now, your loan
☒ will have an escrow account (also called an "impound" or "trust" account) to pay the property costs listed below. Without an escrow account, you would pay them directly, possibly in one or two large payments a year. Your lender may be liable for penalties and interest for failing to make a payment.

Escrow		
Escrowed Property Costs over Year 1	$2,473.56	Estimated total amount over year 1 for your escrowed property costs: *Homeowner's Insurance* *Property Taxes*
Non-Escrowed Property Costs over Year 1	$1,800.00	Estimated total amount over year 1 for your non-escrowed property costs: *Homeowner's Association Dues* You may have other property costs.
Initial Escrow Payment	$412.25	A cushion for the escrow account you pay at closing. See Section G on page 2.
Monthly Escrow Payment	$206.13	The amount included in your total monthly payment.

☐ will not have an escrow account because ☐ you declined it ☐ your lender does not offer one. You must directly pay your property costs, such as taxes and homeowner's insurance. Contact your lender to ask if your loan can have an escrow account.

No Escrow		
Estimated Property Costs over Year 1		Estimated total amount over year 1. You must pay these costs directly, possibly in one or two large payments a year.
Escrow Waiver Fee		

In the future,
Your property costs may change and, as a result, your escrow payment may change. You may be able to cancel your escrow account, but if you do, you must pay your property costs directly. If you fail to pay your property taxes, your state or local government may (1) impose fines and penalties or (2) place a tax lien on this property. If you fail to pay any of your property costs, your lender may (1) add the amounts to your loan balance, (2) add an escrow account to your loan, or (3) require you to pay for property insurance that the lender buys on your behalf, which likely would cost more and provide fewer benefits than what you could buy on your own.

CLOSING DISCLOSURE PAGE 4 OF 5 • LOAN ID # 123456789

Exhibit 21.16 Sample H-25 Closing Disclosure, Page 5

Loan Calculations

Total of Payments. Total you will have paid after you make all payments of principal, interest, mortgage insurance, and loan costs, as scheduled.	$285,803.36
Finance Charge. The dollar amount the loan will cost you.	$118,830.27
Amount Financed. The loan amount available after paying your upfront finance charge.	$162,000.00
Annual Percentage Rate (APR). Your costs over the loan term expressed as a rate. This is not your interest rate.	4.174%
Total Interest Percentage (TIP). The total amount of interest that you will pay over the loan term as a percentage of your loan amount.	69.46%

Questions? If you have questions about the loan terms or costs on this form, use the contact information below. To get more information or make a complaint, contact the Consumer Financial Protection Bureau at **www.consumerfinance.gov/mortgage-closing**

Other Disclosures

Appraisal
If the property was appraised for your loan, your lender is required to give you a copy at no additional cost at least 3 days before closing. If you have not yet received it, please contact your lender at the information listed below.

Contract Details
See your note and security instrument for information about
- what happens if you fail to make your payments,
- what is a default on the loan,
- situations in which your lender can require early repayment of the loan, and
- the rules for making payments before they are due.

Liability after Foreclosure
If your lender forecloses on this property and the foreclosure does not cover the amount of unpaid balance on this loan,

☒ state law may protect you from liability for the unpaid balance. If you refinance or take on any additional debt on this property, you may lose this protection and have to pay any debt remaining even after foreclosure. You may want to consult a lawyer for more information.

☐ state law does not protect you from liability for the unpaid balance.

Refinance
Refinancing this loan will depend on your future financial situation, the property value, and market conditions. You may not be able to refinance this loan.

Tax Deductions
If you borrow more than this property is worth, the interest on the loan amount above this property's fair market value is not deductible from your federal income taxes. You should consult a tax advisor for more information.

Contact Information

	Lender	Mortgage Broker	Real Estate Broker (B)	Real Estate Broker (S)	Settlement Agent
Name	Ficus Bank		Omega Real Estate Broker Inc.	Alpha Real Estate Broker Co.	Epsilon Title Co.
Address	4321 Random Blvd. Somecity, ST 12340		789 Local Lane Sometown, ST 12345	987 Suburb Ct. Someplace, ST 12340	123 Commerce Pl. Somecity, ST 12344
NMLS ID					
ST License ID			Z765416	Z61456	Z61616
Contact	Joe Smith		Samuel Green	Joseph Cain	Sarah Arnold
Contact NMLS ID	12345				
Contact ST License ID			P16415	P51461	PT1234
Email	joesmith@ ficusbank.com		sam@omegare.biz	joe@alphare.biz	sarah@ epsilontitle.com
Phone	123-456-7890		123-555-1717	321-555-7171	987-555-4321

Confirm Receipt

By signing, you are only confirming that you have received this form. You do not have to accept this loan because you have signed or received this form.

Applicant Signature Date Co-Applicant Signature Date

CLOSING DISCLOSURE PAGE 5 OF 5 • LOAN ID # 123456789

REPORTING REQUIREMENTS

Who must report
What must be filed

Who must report

The Tax Reform Act of 1986 requires that persons designated by the act as "real estate brokers" must report a closed real estate transaction to the Internal Revenue Service and provide the information contained in the report to each party to the transaction. The act defines "real estate broker" as any of the following:

- the seller's broker
- the buyer's broker
- the settlement agent, escrow agent, attorney, title company or other party responsible for closing the transaction
- the mortgage lender
- anyone so designated by the Internal Revenue Service

What must be filed

The person reporting files a Form 1099-S information return with the Internal Revenue Service. This form includes the names and addresses of the parties to the transaction and information about the sale proceeds.

The reporting person also provides each party to the transaction with a written statement showing the name and address of the reporting party as well as the information reported in the 1099.

If the transaction involves a non-resident alien, the reporting person may also have tax reporting and withholding responsibilities under the Foreign Investment and Real Property Tax Act of 1980 (FIRPTA), the Deficit Reduction Act of 1984 (DEFRA), and/or the Branch Profits Tax and Technical and Miscellaneous Revenue Act of 1988 (TAMRA).

21 Closings Snapshot Review

THE CLOSING EVENT

The setting	• sale contract sets date, location, and who participates
The closing process	• verify contract fulfillment; exchange consideration and title; pay expenses; sign final documents; arrange for recording the transaction
Transfer of title	• seller gives evidence of marketability-- title abstract or title insurance commitment; may also need affidavit stating no new encumbrances incurred; seller must remove encumbrances or liens prior to the specified date; if seller is paying off mortgage lien, lender provides a payoff statement
Transfer of purchase funds	• buyer produces funds and documents needed to complete the transaction
Escrow procedures	• if closing "in escrow," escrow agent holds and disburses funds and releases documents when escrow conditions have been met
Lender closing requirements	• common: survey, inspections, hazard insurance, title insurance, certificate of occupancy, reserves for taxes and insurance, private mortgage insurance
Broker's role	• broker's role ranges from nil to conducting the proceedings to reporting the transaction
REAL ESTATE SETTLEMENT PROCEDURES ACT	• for residential property, first or second mortgage, federally-related mortgage, assumption modifying loan terms, lender charging over $50 for assumption
Information booklet	• lender must provide borrower with CFPB booklet, "Your Home Loan Toolkit"
Loan Estimate	• lender must provide CFPB's H-24 Loan Estimate of settlement costs
Mortgage servicing disclosure	• lender must disclose who will be servicing loan
Closing Disclosure	• lender must use CFPB's H-25 Closing disclosure
Disclosures after settlement	• loan servicers must provide annual escrow statements to borrowers
Limits on escrow accounts	• places ceiling on amounts lenders may compel borrowers to place in escrow
Referral fees and kickbacks	• RESPA prohibits payment of referral fees and kickbacks; business relationships between firms involved in the transaction must be disclosed

FINANCIAL SETTLEMENT OF THE TRANSACTION

Settlement process	• identify closing costs; determine who pays what; do prorations; assign debits and credits; complete closing statement; disburse funds
Selling terms and closing costs	• price, deposits, downpayment, financing, final expenses to be paid at closing; apportionment of expenses determined by sale contract or custom
Debits and credits	• excess of buyer's debits over credits is amount buyer must produce at closing; excess of seller's credits over debits is amount seller must receive
Non-prorated items	• incurred by one party only; not shared

Prorated items
- incurred by buyer or seller in advance or arrears; shared by buyer and seller; typical: real estate taxes, insurance premiums, mortgage interest, rents

COMPUTING PRORATIONS
- sale contract or local custom establishes methods of proration to be used for particular items

12-month/30-day method
- determines average daily amount based on 12-month year and 30-day month

365-day method
- determines an amount using the actual number of calendar days

TAXES DUE AT CLOSING

State taxes on deed
- state, counties and municipalities may impose taxes on transfer

State taxes on mortgage
- state may impose taxes on mortgages, notes and contracts

TILA/RESPA INTEGRATED DISCLOSURES RULE

Forms and procedures
- effective October 3, 2015
- mandatory: Your Home Loan Toolkit booklet at loan application; Loan Estimate form 3 business days after loan application; Closing disclosure 3 business days before consummation

Good faith
- Loan Estimate costs based an best information available
- Closing Disclosure costs equal estimate costs within certain tolerances

Types of charges
- no limitation on increase over estimate
- 10% tolerance charges
- 0 tolerance charges

Applicable transactions
- most closed-end consumer mortgages, including: construction loans, loans secured by vacant land, loans to trusts
- not covered: home equity loans, reverse mortgages, loans on mobile homes, loans by small lenders (no more than 5 loans per year)

The H-25 form
- 5 pages, variable by loan type

REPORTING REQUIREMENTS

Who must report
- "real estate broker" defined by the Tax Reform Act of 1986; buyer's or seller's broker, settlement agent, mortgage lender, other IRS-designated party

What must be filed
- Form 1099-S Information Return
- statements to each party
- tax reporting and withholding if FIRPTA applies (non-resident alien)

22 Risk Management

Risk Management Strategies
Risk Management Procedures
Primary Areas of Risk

Risk is the chance of losing something. Its two dimensions are the probability of occurrence and the extent of exposure to monetary or non-monetary consequences. Since most risks are related to judgments and decisions, the real estate licensee, who makes numerous complex decisions every day, faces a high degree of ***risk potential***.

Risk management is a structured approach to dealing with the uncertainties and consequences of risk. In real estate practice, the aim is to reduce risk to an acceptable level through anticipation and planning.

RISK MANAGEMENT STRATEGIES

Avoidance
Reduction
Transference
Retention

Four well-established strategies for managing risk are:

- Avoidance (elimination)
- Reduction (mitigation, sharing)
- Transference (outsourcing, insuring)
- Retention (acceptance and budgeting)

Not all of these strategies are always possible or available, but a real estate firm or licensee who fails to make a conscious effort to employ one or more of them increases the likelihood of loss from the many potential risks that are always present in the real estate business.

Avoidance

Avoidance includes refraining from an activity that carries risk. One can avoid the risks of being in an automobile accident by not riding in automobiles. Avoiding risks also means missing the opportunity to benefit from the avoided activity. By avoiding automobile travel, one is confined to modes of transportation, such as buses and walking, that do not offer the same high degree of personal freedom and efficiency. Complete avoidance of risk in real estate practice is almost impossible. A broker, for instance, may believe that hiring only experienced affiliates eliminates the risk that affiliates will commit license law violations. However, even experienced practitioners may not know the law, and, sometimes, people break the law deliberately. The risk may be reduced, but it remains.

Reduction

Reduction involves taking steps to reduce the probability or the severity of a potential loss. However, this strategy may result in reducing risk in one area only to increase it in another. A familiar example is a sprinkler system that dispenses water to reduce the risk of fire but at the same time increases the risk of water damage.

In real estate practice, one risk reduction tactic is to share responsibility for making a decision. The agent provides the consumer with expertise, and perhaps some advice, but lets the consumer decide how much to offer. In this way, the agent gets some relief from the risks inherent in the buyer's decision to purchase.

Transference

Transference means passing the risk to another party, by contract or other means. An insurance policy is the common example, but sometimes the wording of a sales or personal services contract can transfer risk without resorting to insurance.

In the real estate business, transference is typically and most successfully accomplished by means of an errors and omissions (E&O) insurance policy, either on the individuals in a firm or on the firm itself. State law may require such insurance.

Retention

Retention of risk means entering into an activity in spite of known risks and taking full responsibility for the consequences. This is, in effect, self-insurance, the only strategy left when risk cannot be reduced or transferred and one has decided not to avoid it because of the desirability of the potential benefits.

Exhibit 22.1 Risk Management Strategies and Procedures

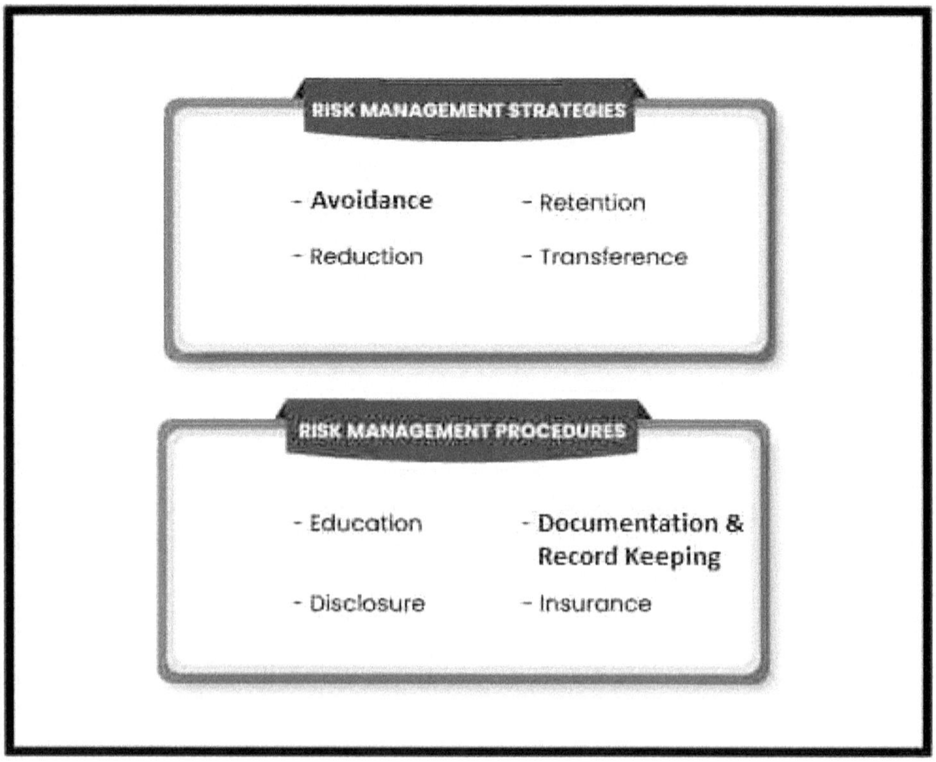

RISK MANAGEMENT PROCEDURES

Education
Disclosure
Documentation and record keeping
Insurance

Experience shows that the most practical strategies for risk management in real estate practice are reduction and transference, with procedures focusing on:

- Education
- Disclosure
- Documentation
- Insurance

Education

Education is the first line of defense against risk. When agents are familiar with the forms provided by the office, how and when to complete them and where to send them, the likelihood of errors is reduced. Likewise, agents need to be able to identify and understand common contract elements, complete contract forms developed by attorneys, and evaluate offers received from co-op agents on their listings without committing a license violation or breach of law.

In most states, brokers have a legal obligation to provide training to affiliated licensees. Licensees also have the obligation to seek out appropriate education and training outside the brokerage to ensure that they know how to comply with the law. In addition, licensees must satisfy legal requirements for continuing education, while those who care about personal excellence will seek further education and training to enhance their professional skills.

Disclosure

By ensuring that all parties have the information they are entitled to, proper disclosure reduces the risk that clients and customers will accuse a licensee of misleading or inducing them to make a decision with incomplete information. Further, laws in every state require disclosures of one kind or another.

Disclosure may be made in writing or verbally and may or may not require written acknowledgment from the receiving party.

Required disclosures usually include:

- agency relationships
- property condition
- duties and obligations
- personal interest in the transaction
- personal interest in referrals

Documentation and Record keeping

Documentation provides evidence of compliance with laws and regulations. It proves what clients and customers and licensees said and did in a transaction. Some documentation is required by law.

The components of a thoroughly documented paper trail include:

- Policy and procedure manuals
- Standard forms
- Communication records
- Transaction records
- Contracts
- Accounting
- Other important documents

Policy manual. A written and uniformly enforced company policy lets everyone in the firm know what to expect before problems arise. The policy manual should cover the company's rules in such areas as floor duty privileges, assignment of relocation properties to agents, referrals between agents within the company, and requirements for continuing education, sales meeting participation, and property tours.

Procedures manual. A company procedures manual should spell out how to handle every aspect of the company's business that agents and brokers need to know—from handling consumers' funds and documents, conducting consumer transactions, dealing with MLS-related matters, and placing signage, to all procedures prescribed by state or federal law, especially license, banking and fair housing laws. Adherence to a procedures manual reduces the risk that an individual will inadvertently commit an unlawful act. Whenever changes are made to the policy or procedures manual, each agent should sign the revised manual as evidence that the agent has examined it.

Standard forms. Standard forms save time and protect against the unauthorized practice of law. Since they are most often prepared by lawyers familiar with the market area, they can address contingencies that are common in the area in a manner that reflects the real estate laws of the state. On the other hand, a licensee often needs to adapt a standardized form for a client by assisting with filling in blanks, modifying terms, and attaching addenda. The licensee must always remain aware of the limitations the state has placed on such activities.

Here are a few of the standard forms a brokerage should provide for its agents and affiliates:

- buyer and seller representation agreements
- agreement to show property
- purchase and sale agreement
- agency disclosure form
- property condition disclosure, disclaimer, and exemption form
- lease agreement
- personal interest disclosure form
- referral for service disclosure form
- lead-based paint disclosure form
- special disclosure forms (mold, radon, subsurface sewage system, impact fees/adequate facilities taxes, etc.)
- referral agreement
- independent contractor agreement
- closing checklist

Communication records. Some communications with transaction parties are good and necessary for business. Others are required by law, such as certain disclosures. A transaction checklist is a good tool for managing risk associated with the failure to make required communications to all principals and for keeping track of required communications from co-op agents.

Retaining evidence that information has been communicated is a necessary procedure. Electronic communications should be archived on suitable electronic media. Copies of mailed or faxed communications should be maintained in the transaction folder.

It is always difficult to document telephone or face-to-face conversations, especially with the constant use of cell phones from a variety of locations. It is a good practice to make brief notes at the time and then write them up later for mailing or faxing to the other party. Be sure, however, that you can produce these notes on demand, lest you be accused later of withholding documentation that has been promised.

Maintaining a good record of communications is useful for resolving disagreements where parties dispute what has been said because it allows the agent to produce a dated document that resolves the issue definitively.

Transaction records. State laws require licensees to document transactions. Firms are required to keep written records of all real estate transactions for a number of years (usually three to five) after closing or termination. Required records typically include:

- listing agreements
- offers
- contracts
- closing statements
- agency agreements
- disclosure documents
- correspondence and other communication records
- notes and any other relevant information

Accounting. In addition to other accounting records, there is the requirement to maintain written accounting of escrow funds. For each transaction, property, and principal, escrow records will include:

- depositor
- date of deposit
- date of withdrawal
- payee
- other information deemed pertinent by the real estate commission

Other documents. Additional documents may be required by law or regulation, or should be kept simply as protection in case of disputes and lawsuits. These would include copies of advertising materials, materials used in training agents, records of compliance with continuing education requirements, safety manuals, and anything else that shows how the firm conducts its business and safeguards its staff as well as the rights of consumers.

Insurance

Many forms of insurance are available for property owners and managers. Some of these types are also used to manage certain risks of brokers and licensees.

General Liability. General liability insurance provides coverage for risks incurred by a property owner when the public or a licensee enters the owned property (**public liability**). The insurer pays the covered claim and legal fees, costs, and expenses, including medical expenses, resulting from owner negligence or other causes. This type of insurance does not cover **professional liability,** for which an Errors & Omissions policy is necessary.

Errors and Omissions. Professional liability is of two general types:

1. Unprofessional conduct – a claim that one has failed to carry out fiduciary duties and provide an acceptable standard of care
2. Breach of contract – a claim that one has failed to perform services under the terms of a contract in a timely manner

The primary method for transferring the professional liability risks of brokers, managers, and licensees is Errors & Omissions (E&O) insurance. A standard E&O policy provides coverage for "damages resulting from any negligent act, error or omission arising out of Professional Services." A standard policy does NOT cover:

- violations of law
- fraudulent, dishonest, criminal or malicious acts
- mishandling of escrow moneys, earnest money deposits, or security deposits
- antitrust violations
- sexual harassment
- Fair Housing violations
- agent-owned properties
- environmental violations
- failure to detect or disclose environmental conditions, including mold
- acts committed prior to licensure or after termination of active status
- activities as an appraiser if licensing other than a real estate license is required

E&O insurance, in short, covers "mistakes" but not crimes.

Fire and hazard. The risks of property damage caused by fire, wind, hail, smoke, civil disturbance, and other such causes are covered by fire and hazard insurance.

Flood. The risks of property damage caused by floods, heavy rains, snow, drainage failures, and failed public infrastructures such as dams and levies are covered by a specialized flood policy. Regular hazard policies do not include flood coverage.

Other insurance. Other common types of insurance coverage for income and commercial properties include:

- **casualty**—coverage for specific risks, such as theft, vandalism, burglary, illness and accident, machinery damage
- **workers' compensation**—hospital and medical coverage for employees injured in the course of employment, mandated by state laws
- **contents and personal property**—coverage for building contents and personal property when they are not actually on the building premises
- **consequential loss, use, and occupancy**—coverage for the business losses resulting from a disaster, such as loss of rent and other revenue, when the property cannot be used for business
- **surety bond**—coverage against losses resulting from criminal or negligent acts of an employee

---

PRIMARY AREAS OF RISK

Agency
Property disclosures
Listing and selling process
Contracting process
Fair Housing
Antitrust
Rules and regulations
Misrepresentation
Recommending providers
Financing and closing
Trust fund handling
Safety And security

Risks for licensees are present every day in business transactions. Many of these risks carry legal implications as well as possible financial and professional consequences.

Exhibit 22.2 Real Estate Management Risks

Agency	Finance	Compliance
Disclosures	Trust Funds	Referrals
Contracting	Listing / Selling	Closing
Misrepresentation	Fair Housing / Antitrust	

Agency

The risks of agency will occur in one of two areas:

- the requirement to inform and disclose
- the requirement to carry out an agency duty.

Most states require agency relationships to be in writing and to be disclosed to all parties to a transaction. State law may spell out agency duties, or the duties may be a part of general agency law. In states that do not use agency, there is still the obligation to explain and disclose the nature of the relationship.

Disclosure requirements. A licensee may be acting in a transaction as facilitator, agent, subagent, designated agent, single agent, dual agent, non-agent or in some capacity. Regardless of status, the licensee must follow state disclosure requirements. These are, typically, to:

- disclose status ***verbally*** to other licensees on initial contact
- disclose status ***verbally*** to buyer and seller before providing real estate services
- confirm the disclosure ***in writing*** before signing a listing agreement or presenting a purchase offer (to an unrepresented seller) or before preparing a purchase offer (to an unrepresented buyer)
- get a ***signed receipt*** indicating the written disclosure has been made

Carrying out the duties of agency also require disclosures of :

- personal interest the agent has in a transaction (such as owner or buyer)
- personal benefit the agent will derive from a service referral
- required property and market information
- information about customers a client is entitled to have

Duties. A licensee who acts for a principal in a real estate transaction is required by law to assume certain responsibilities toward the parties to the transaction. Whether a state applies the fiduciary duties of agency law or specifies its own duties toward clients and consumers, the basic duties remain:

To all parties

- honesty
- fairness
- reasonable care and skill
- disclosures

To clients

- skill
- care
- diligence
- loyalty
- obedience
- confidentiality
- accounting
- full disclosure

The duty to exercise **skill, care and diligence** means that licensees may not be casual or negligent in their actions. Licensee negligence is actionable when principals are harmed by the licensee's failure.

The duty of **loyalty** requires the agent to *put the client's interests above those of everyone else*, including his or her own.

The duty of **obedience** requires the agent to act on the principal's wishes regarding the transaction as long as they do not result in any illegal action. The duty of obedience never overrides the legal obligation of agents to deal fairly and honestly with all parties.

The duty of **confidentiality** requires the agent to hold in confidence any information that would harm the client's interests or bargaining position or anything else the client wishes to keep secret, unless the law requires disclosure. The duty of confidentiality survives the termination of the listing contract.

The duty of **accounting** applies to all funds involved in a real estate transaction. Accounts must be maintained as required by law, and escrow funds are to be handled strictly in accordance with the law.

The duty of **disclosure** applies to both parties to a transaction, although usually with some differences. Proper disclosure to customers primarily concerns agency, property condition, and environmental hazards. To the client, it generally concerns all known facts regarding the property and the transaction, including information about the other transaction party. State laws prescribe what may, must, and must not be disclosed. Licensees must be vigilant to avoid oversights and conflicts of interest that can lead to a disclosure to the wrong party or disclosure of information that is confidential.

Conflicts of interest. Conflicts of interest arise when an agent forgets to put the best interests of a client ahead of those of everyone else. This can happen in situations involving undisclosed dual agencies, broker-owned listings, licensees buying for their own account, vendor referrals, and property management subcontracting of services, among many others. Even ordinary, everyday transactions carry a built-in risk of conflict of interest. Consider the fact that a licensee usually receives no compensation for a failed transaction. Therefore, it is in the licensee's interest to see the transaction completed, even if it may not be in the client's best interest. A negative result from a home inspection or other test has the potential to cause a buyer to back out of a contract. A licensee who has forgotten whose best interest should be primary might be tempted to recommend inspectors who will overlook problems in exchange for receiving referrals. Licensees must always disclose any self-interest they have in a transaction, and always remember their duties to clients and consumers.

Confidentiality. Licensees have a responsibility to maintain the confidentiality of certain kinds of information they obtain concerning clients and customers. The duty to maintain confidentiality generally survives the termination of a listing agreement into perpetuity. If it seems that revealing confidential information might benefit the client, the licensee should obtain the client's written permission to proceed.

Confidential information generally includes information about a client's motivations in a transaction, financial and personal details, and information specifically designated as confidential by the client. Public information, such as that contained in public records, information that becomes known without the licensee's participation, or that the client reveals to another, is not considered confidential.

State laws often require businesses to provide security for the personal information they obtain about consumers. Security procedures should protect personal information from unauthorized access, destruction, use, modification, or disclosure. Confidential information, when it is not to be retained, must be disposed of in a secure manner.

Penalties. Possible penalties for breach of agency relationships include:

- rescission of transaction
- loss of compensation
- fees and costs
- punitive damages
- ethics discipline
- license discipline

Property disclosures

Property condition. Most states require the seller of a residential property to deliver to the buyer a written disclosure or disclaimer about the property's condition, including any material defects the owner knows about. The disclosure is usually required before any purchase contract is accepted.. A second disclosure may be required at closing. The licensee should always obtain the parties' signatures acknowledging receipt of these disclosures.

Depending on the state, the licensee may have no further duty to disclose property condition after properly informing parties of their rights and obligations. However, the licensee may still be subject to legal action for

- deliberately distorting the facts (intentional misrepresentation)
- cheating any party (fraud)
- concealing or failing to disclose adverse facts which the licensee knew about or should have known about (intentional or unintentional misrepresentation)

Lead-based paint and other disclosures. Federal law requires sellers of houses built before 1978 to make a lead-based paint disclosure before accepting an offer to purchase. The licensee must tell the seller about this requirement, give the seller the proper disclosure form, and make sure that the buyer receives it.

The licensee must also make sure the seller discloses any other circumstances the situation and the law require, which may include:

- wood infestation inspection report
- soil test report
- subsurface sewage disposal system permit disclosure
- impact fees or adequate facilities taxes disclosure

- mold and radon reports or treatments

Listing and selling process

Nature and accuracy of the listing agreement. In most states, a listing agreement is enforceable only if it is in writing. Most states forbid net listings, because they violate the requirement that a valid listing agreement must specify a selling price and the agent's compensation. The licensee, in accordance with the duty of due diligence, must verify the accuracy of the statements in the listing regarding the property, the owner, and the owner's representations. Especially important facts for a broker or agent to verify are:

- the property condition
- ownership status
- the client's authority to act

An agent who does not to act with a reasonable degree of due diligence in these matters may be exposed to liability if it turns out that the property is not as represented or the client cannot perform the contract as promised.

Comparative Market Analysis (CMA). In preparing a Comparative Market Analysis, licensees should guard against using the terms "appraisal" and "value," which are reserved for the use of certified appraisers. Misuse of these terms could lead to a charge of misrepresenting oneself as an appraiser. In discussing listed properties with clients or customers, real estate licensees should be careful to use guarded terms such as "recommended listing price," "recommended purchase price,' and "recommended listing price range."

Agents should make every effort to help the sellers find a reasonable listing price based on the current market. If the CMA leads the seller to list at a price that is too high, the seller may blame the agent when the transaction fails because of an appraisal that comes in below the selling price. To minimize this risk, it is best to be conservative in the CMA and retain documentation that the seller went above the recommended price in spite of the agent's advice.

Estimate of Closing Costs. In preparing an estimate of closing costs for a seller or buyer, there is the risk of forgetting something, leading to an unpleasant surprise when the consumer suddenly faces unexpected costs or conditions. Licensees should use their broker's form, if there is one, and make it clear to the consumer that it is only an estimate of likely costs, not a statement of actual costs. In some states, brokers and agents do not prepare closing cost estimates, leaving that task to the lender.

Advertising. State and federal laws regulate advertising, including the federal Fair Housing laws as they pertain to discriminatory advertising and providing of services. Advertising includes electronic communication, social media/networking, and internet marketing. Usage must be consistent with company image and legal requirements. The license laws of most states list illegal advertising actions subject to discipline such as:

- making any substantial and intentional misrepresentation
- making any promise that might cause a person to enter into a contract or agreement when the promise is one the licensee cannot or will not abide by
- making continued and blatant misrepresentations or false promises through affiliate brokers, other persons, or any advertising medium
- making misleading or untruthful statements in any advertising, including using the term "Realtor" when not authorized to do so and using any other trade name, insignia or membership in a real estate organization when the licensee is not a member.

Committing such acts may result in license suspension or revocation.

Authorizations and Permissions. Licensees should stay within the bounds of the authority granted by the agency agreement or must not do anything requiring permission without first getting that permission in writing. For instance, permission should be obtained before doing any of the following unless the listing agreement specifically grants the authority:

- post a sign on the property
- remove other signs
- show the property
- hand out the property condition disclosure
- distribute marketing materials
- advertise in various media
- use a multiple listing service
- cooperate with other licensees
- divide the commission or negotiate a commission split
- share final sales data with the MLS
- place a lock box on the property
- appoint subagents
- appoint a designated agent
- change agency status

Scope of expertise. Real estate licensees are not, by nature, financial consultants, accountants, appraisers, soil scientists, well diggers, lawyers, decorators, contractors, builders, plumbers, carpenters, inspectors, prognosticators, and a number of other kinds of expert. However, in today's competitive environment, consumers often demand much more from a licensee than the traditional basic services. An agent who fails to live up to prevailing standards may be held liable for negligence, fraud, or violation of state real estate license laws and regulations. At the same time, agents must be particularly careful about the temptation to misrepresent themselves as experts and offer inappropriate expert advice. Disclaimer and referral are always the best risk control procedures to forestall an accusation of misrepresentation from a consumer who claims to have been harmed by reliance on the licensee's non-existent expertise. The exact nature of the services to be provided should be stated as clearly as possible in the listing agreement.

Contracting process According to the Statute of Frauds, all contacts for real estate must be in writing to be enforceable. Contracts that contain incorrect information or are inadequately prepared can pose a serious liability for a licensee. To avoid such a situation, it is imperative for the contract to reflect the terms that the parties have agreed upon in the most accurate and honest manner. The agent must also be careful to comply with the letter of the real estate law. Violations can jeopardize the enforceability of a listing or sales contract, in addition to resulting in criminal prosecution.

Common risks and errors in the contracting process include:

- using an illegal form

  A licensee may be punished for using any real estate listing agreement form, sales contract form, or offer to purchase form that lacks a ***definite termination date***.

- failing to state inclusions and exclusions

  The parties should identify as included in or excluded from the transfer any ambiguous items. Unwritten agreements between the parties are a source of later dispute and trouble.

- failing to track the progress of contingency satisfaction

  The time period for completing contingencies such as inspections is specific and limited. Failure to meet or waive a condition may terminate the contract. A "time is of the essence" clause in the standard agreement makes the time period for contingencies critical.

- mistakes in entering data in a form

  All data should be checked and verified: dates, times, amounts, warranties, descriptions, names, representations, promises, procedures, authority, etc. One way to reduce risk in the contracting process is to use a checklist that covers all the contract items.

Unauthorized practice of law. The unintentional practice of law without a license is a great risk in the contracting process, as well as in the representation process. It is illegal for real estate professionals who are not attorneys to draw up contracts for transactions they are not involved in or to charge a separate fee for preparing a contract.

Such licensees may fill in blanks or make deletions on a preprinted contract form prepared by a lawyer. While a licensee may make deletions, additions to a form should be drafted by an attorney. The principals themselves can make changes as long as each change is signed or initialed by all signers. Preprinted riders can often be attached as addenda to a contract without an attorney.

It is also illegal for real estate licensees who are not lawyers to give legal advice or interpret contract language. Licensees, however, may express opinions. For instance, if a licensee believes that a party has grasped the meaning of a contract, it is permissible to say something like, "Though I am not an attorney, in my opinion your understanding of this contract is correct." It would be questionable to make a definitive statement like, "That's correct."

Fair Housing

The risk of violating fair housing laws can be minimized through ongoing education that addresses both the content and the intent of the laws. It is especially necessary for paperwork and documentation to be accurate and concise in a situation where a fair housing issue could arise.

Advertising. The Fair Housing Act forbids real estate advertising that mentions race, color, religion, national origin, sex, handicap, or familial status in any way that suggests preference or discrimination. State laws may add other protected categories, such as creed and age.

Risk can be reduced by the use of street names or other non-biased geographical references when stating where the property is located, and by describing the property rather than the type of persons who might live in or around it. Even if a home appears "ideal for a young family," it is best not to advertise it as such. Such advertising would exclude other groups such as singles, the elderly, and older families.

In advertising the sale or rental of housing covered by the Fair Housing Act, HUD recommends using the Fair Housing Logo or phrase "Equal Housing Opportunity."

Answering questions. When faced with questions that might lead to a ***steering*** charge or other violation of fair housing laws, it is best for the licensee to limit the response to features of the home and to the process of selling, buying, and listing properties, and refer the questioner to someone else to answer questions about such matters as the demographic make-up of the neighborhood. It is illegal for the licensee to voice an opinion based on race, religion, color, creed, national origin, sex, handicap, elderliness, or familial status. The agent should explain this fact to the buyer and be wary of any situation where the agent's behavior might be construed as discriminatory.

Listing agreements. Before entering into a listing agreement, a licensee should explain that it is necessary to comply with fair housing laws and obtain the potential client's acknowledgment and agreement. The agent should make it clear that the agent will

- reject the use of terms indicating race, religion, creed, color, national origin, sex, handicap, age or familial status to describe prospective buyers.
- terminate the listing if the seller uses race, religion, creed, color, national origin, sex, handicap, age, or familial status in the consideration of an offer.
- inform the broker if the seller makes any attempt to discriminate illegally.

Offers. A seller cannot refuse to sell a property to an individual based on the individual's belonging to a protected class, and if this is attempted, the real estate professional must not be involved. If the seller asks about the color, religion, creed, national origin, ethnicity, age, or familial status of a buyer, the agent must explain that it is illegal to give out such information. The best risk reduction procedure is to treat all buyers and sellers equally, showing no preference for one over another.

Antitrust

Antitrust laws forbid brokers to band together to set a price on their services in listing and selling property. Even being overheard discussing commission rates or being present at such a conversation can lead to charges of ***price fixing***.

The law recognizes that some cooperative arrangements between firms – such as joint development projects – may help consumers by allowing these firms to compete more effectively against each other. Even so the government does not prosecute all agreements between companies, but only those that will raise prices for the public or deny the public new and better products.

Sherman Antitrust Act. The ***Sherman Antitrust Act*** makes illegal all contracts, agreements, and conspiracies among competitors that would unfairly restrict interstate trade by fixing prices, rigging bids, or other means. An unlawful monopoly is created when one company becomes the only supplier of a product or service by getting rid of competition via secret agreements with other companies.
Clayton Act. The ***Clayton Act*** prohibits mergers or acquisitions that are likely to lessen competition and increase prices to consumers. The Act also prohibits certain other business practices that under certain circumstances may harm competition. Private parties injured by an antitrust violation may sue in federal court for three times their actual damages, plus court costs and attorneys' fees.

Federal Trade Commission Act. The ***Federal Trade Commission Act*** forbids unfair competition in interstate commerce but establishes no criminal penalties.

Enforcement. Federal antitrust laws are enforced in three main ways:

- the Antitrust Division of the Department of Justice (DOJ) brings criminal and civil enforcement actions
- the FTC brings civil enforcement actions
- private parties bring lawsuits claiming damages

To collect evidence, Department of Justice lawyers often work with the Federal Bureau of Investigation (FBI) on court-authorized searches of a business, monitoring phone calls and employing informants equipped with secret listening devices.

State attorneys general may sue under the Clayton Act on behalf of injured consumers in their states, and groups of consumers often bring lawsuits on their own.

Anyone associated with an organization found guilty of an antitrust violation and determined to have had knowledge of that violation may also suffer legal consequences.

Penalties. Penalties for Violation of Antitrust Laws include:

- fines for individuals and corporations, as well as possible imprisonment.
- Under the Clayton Antitrust Act, parties can sue antitrust violators and recover three times the damages they incurred plus court costs and attorneys' fees.

Rules and regulations

State real estate laws and commissioners' rules and regulations attempt to cover every possible risky situation. Non-compliance poses a direct threat to the legal and financial status of licensee and license in the following general ways:

- license expiration
- license revocation or suspension
- licensee discipline
- suit for damages

License expiration. Licenses expire because licensees neglect to:

- maintain E & O insurance when required
- meet education requirements
- observe correct renewal procedures

License revocation or suspension. Licenses are typically revoked or suspended when a licensee is found guilty of:

- obtaining a license under false pretenses
- committing a "prohibited act"
- neglecting to present every written offer as required
- neglecting to deliver signed copies of accepted offers to transaction parties as required
- failing to make sure that all required terms and conditions are present in a contract to purchase
- handling earnest money and other escrow funds improperly

Licensee discipline. A state real estate commission may assess a civil penalty for violations of a statute, rule, or order. Licensees are disciplined for:

- acting without a license when a license is required
- demanding a referral fee without reasonable cause
- entering into a net listing
- trying to induce another licensee's client to end or change an existing agency contract
- paying a commission to an unlicensed individual or company
- receiving an illegal referral fee, rebate or kickback
- practicing with an expired license

Licensee lawsuits. A licensee may be sued by the Department of Justice, Federal Trade Commission, a state real estate commission, a human rights commission, another licensee or firm, or an individual consumer. Licensees are mainly sued for:

- fair housing violations
- antitrust violations
- license law and other state law violations
- breach of contract
- agency duty violations
- illegal practice of law
- failures to disclose
- customer or client dissatisfaction
- fraud
- theft

Misrepresentation

Misrepresentation may be unintentional or intentional.

Unintentional misrepresentation. This type of misrepresentation occurs when a licensee *unknowingly* conveys inaccurate information to a consumer concerning a property, financing or agency service. False or inaccurate information that the licensee, as a professional, should have known to be false or inaccurate may be included in the definition. Those found guilty generally have to pay fines and may be disciplined by state real estate regulators and professional organizations.

Risky areas for unintentional misrepresentation include:

- making and reporting measurements
- describing property
- offering opinions about future growth and development of a neighborhood or neighboring property
- making declarative statements about the presence or absence of hazardous materials

The risks of unintentional misrepresentation are reduced if an agent

- learns to measure and calculate areas accurately
- relies on measurements reported by others only with extreme caution and specific disclaimers
- refrains from exaggeration
- avoids stating opinions a consumer might take for expertise

Intentional misrepresentation. Also known as fraud, this kind of misrepresentation occurs when a licensee *knowingly* conveys false information about a property, financing or service. Fraud is a criminal act that may result in fines and incarceration, in addition to discipline from state regulators and professional organizations.

Recommending providers

There are several risks attending the recommendation of vendors and service providers to a consumer. First, the consumer may not be satisfied with the performance of the recommended party and blame the licensee. Second, in cases where a recommended provider performs illegal acts, there may be legal consequences for the licensee. Third, if a licensee has a business relationship with a recommended vendor or provider and neglects to disclose the fact, there are license violation consequences.

The major risk management technique is to shift the responsibility for choosing a vendor to the consumer. This can be done by refusing to recommend vendors at all; by presenting a broad range of choices and allowing the consumer to select; or by presenting a short list of thoroughly vetted vendors and allowing the consumer to make the decision, always with the disclaimer that ***to the best of the licensee's knowledge***, the vendors on the list are competent and honest, but that the consumer is responsible for investigating and making his or her own judgment before hiring or buying.

Financing and closing

In the financing and closing phases of a transaction, a consumer may feel that a licensee has been incompetent or misleading. Licensees have an obligation to inform and educate their clients throughout the transaction process. Surprises and accusations of incompetence or misrepresentation are among possible results of failing to keep the party informed.

Discrimination. Of course, it is important to comply with relevant laws. Licensees must be mindful of the requirements of ECOA and refrain from participating in any manner of discriminatory lending. It is illegal to:

- threaten, coerce, intimidate or interfere with a person who is exercising a fair housing right or assisting another other to exercise that right.

- indicate a limitation or preference based on race, color, national origin, religion, sex, familial status, or handicap in any advertisement or communication. Single-family and owner-occupied housing that is otherwise exempt from the Fair Housing Act is subject to this prohibition against discriminatory advertising.

Progress reporting. All inspections and tests must comply with local and state laws and with the purchase contract. Progress reports should be accurate, timely, in writing, and free of speculation. If a consumer has a question about the meaning of something in an inspection report, the licensee should refer the consumer to the person who wrote the report rather than trying to explain it. This method transfers some of the risk inherent in interpreting the report.

Qualifying buyers. Many transactions fail because a buyer has been improperly qualified before the offer is presented. Using a lender to qualify the buyer saves time and protects the agent against leading a seller to believe a purchaser is fully qualified when this may not be the case. Also, lenders and loan agents are better able to look into the buyer's qualifications than a real estate licensee is. If it becomes necessary to show a property to a potential buyer who has not been qualified by a lender, the licensee can gain some protection by performing an informal qualification and documenting the fact that it was based on the information provided by the buyer. The buyer's signature on this documentation indicates the buyer's acceptance of at least partial responsibility for the qualification.

Lending fees disclosure. The licensee should explain loan fees, charges,

amounts, timing, and responsibilities. Agents can assist in the loan decision by explaining how to compare loans with differing charges and interest rates. The fact that a high origination fee and points may make a loan with a low interest rate unattractive to a borrower is important information for the agent to provide, and providing it may protect the agent against a later complaint that the buyer suffered a loss because of the agent's failure to inform.

Appraisal problems. Delays and appraised value are the typical problem areas. Failure to inform parties about delays can compromise the transaction. An under-appraisal will require the buyer to make a larger down payment or the seller to lower the price. If the property appraises for more than the purchase price, the seller may blame the agent for suggesting the lower price. In such a case, the seller's agent's defense is that the seller agreed to the listing price and that the price was a factor in attracting the buyer to the property.

RESPA Violations. The **Real Estate Settlement Procedures Act (RESPA)** stipulates that the parties to certain purchase transactions must be given accurate information reflecting their closing costs. It also prohibits certain business practices that are not considered to be in the consumer's best interest.

The licensee's risks regarding RESPA primarily relate to

- failing to ensure that the consumer is informed about his or her rights under the law
- giving or receiving an illegal kickback.

RESPA currently requires lenders to:

- give a copy of a Consumer Financial Protection Bureau loan information booklet to the applicant. The booklet explains RESPA provisions, general settlement costs, and the required **Closing Disclosure** form. The lender must provide the estimate of closing costs within three business days following the borrower's application.
- give the applicant a Loan Estimate (Form H-24) of expected closing costs within three business days of receiving the application. Actual closing costs may not vary from the estimate beyond certain limits.
- give the buyer the Closing Disclosure (Form H-25) specifying costs to be paid by buyer and seller at closing three business days before consummation.
- give the ***buyer*** the opportunity to review the final settlement statement *one business day prior to closing*.

RESPA specifically ***prohibits*** any fee or kickback paid to a party for a service when the party has not actually rendered the service. For example, it is prohibited for an insurance company to pay a real estate agent or a lender for referring a client.

Fees for referring clients to the following services are strictly forbidden:

- title services (search, insurance)
- appraisals
- inspections
- surveys
- loan issue
- credit report
- attorney services

The sharing of commissions and the payment of referral fees among cooperating brokers and multiple-listing services are not RESPA violations.

Trust fund handling

State laws prescribe how licensees must handle any escrow or earnest money deposits they receive. Those laws usually state that a broker must hold money received in connection with the purchase or lease of real property in a trust fund account. The type of account and financial depository are specified. The broker must record receipt of the money and place that money in the trust account within a specified time period. Usually, the law allows the broker to hold an earnest money check uncashed until the offer is accepted, provided the buyer gives written permission and the seller is informed.

Typical trust fund handling requirements include:

- the broker named as trustee of the account
- a federally-insured bank or recognized depository located in the state
- an account that is not interest-bearing if the financial institution ever requires prior written notice for withdrawals
- maintenance of records in a particular accounting format
- separate records kept for each beneficiary, property, or transaction
- records of funds received and paid out regularly reconciled with bank statements
- withdrawals only by the broker-trustee or other specifically authorized person

Commingling and conversion. Mixing of personal or company funds with client funds is grounds for the revocation or suspension of a real estate license. Depositing client funds in a personal or business account, or using them for any purpose other than the client's business, is also grounds for suspension or revocation of a license. It is important for the broker to remove commissions, fees or other income earned by the broker from a trust account within the period specified by law to avoid committing an act of commingling.

22 Risk Management Snapshot Review

RISK MANAGEMENT STRATEGIES	• two dimensions of risk: size, probability; risk management: structured approach to uncertainty
Avoidance	• refrain from risky activity
Reduction	• reduce probability; share responsibility
Transference	• pass risk by contract; insurance
Retention	• accept risk; self-insurance
RISK MANAGEMENT PROCEDURES	
Education	• train in laws, forms and procedures, job performance
Disclosure	• provide information to reduce misunderstanding & lawsuits; agency, property condition, duties, personal interest
Documentation and record keeping	• maintain evidence of compliance; manuals, forms, records, contracts, accounting, other documents
Insurance	• general liability, E & O, fire and hazard, flood, casualty, workers, personal property, consequential loss, surety bond
PRIMARY AREAS OF RISK	
Agency	• main failures: to inform and disclose, to fulfill duties
	• disclosures: verbal, written, signed receipt; agency relationship and duties; personal interest in transaction; required information
	• duties: to all– honesty, fairness, care, skill, required disclosures; additional to clients– diligence, loyalty, obedience, confidentiality, accounting, full disclosure
	• conflicts of interest arise from failing to put client's interest first
	• confidentiality duty lasts forever; laws define what is confidential, how to treat and dispose of information
	• penalties include loss of transaction, compensation, fees and costs, damages, license
Property disclosures	• property condition, lead-based paint, other conditions; disclosure may discharge liability; failure to disclose may be construed as misrepresentation
Listing and selling process	• areas of risk include listing agreement accuracy, Comparative Market Analysis results, closing cost estimates, advertising, authorizations and permissions, exceeding expertise
Contracting process	• contracts for real estate must be in writing; inaccuracy endangers contract; other risks: illegal form, omitted elements, lapsed contingencies, wrong data
	• unauthorized practice of law: non-lawyers may fill in blanks and delete words on standard contract forms; no legal advice to public allowed
Fair Housing	• advertising may not state preference, limitation or discrimination based on race, color, religion, national origin, sex, handicap, familial status
	• agent must not be involved with discriminatory actions of a client or customer

Antitrust

- government prosecutes cooperative arrangements that raise prices or reduce consumer choices: Sherman Antitrust Act outlaws restraint of trade; Clayton Act outlaws practices that harm competition; Federal Trade Commission Act outlaws unfair methods of competition
- violations punishable by government criminal and civil actions as well as by private lawsuits; fines, damages, and imprisonment possible

Rules and regulations

- violators of state rules and regulations risk license expiration, revocation, suspension, and other discipline
- prime causes of discipline include commission of prohibited acts, practicing with an expired license, disclosure failures, earnest money mishandling

Misrepresentation

- unintentional: inaccurate information conveyed unknowingly; subject to fines and license discipline; occurs most often in measurements, property descriptions
- intentional: fraud, knowingly conveying false information; criminal act subject to fines, license discipline, and incarceration

Recommending providers

- risks include consumer dissatisfaction, possible vicarious liability for illegal acts committed by a recommended provider, undisclosed business relationship (RESPA violation as well as license violation)
- best practice: do not recommend any vendors, or provide a list of trusted vendors with no recommendation and a disclaimer

Financing and closing

- risk areas include fair housing and ECOA violations; failed transactions because of agent failure to monitor contingency period; failure to ensure proper disclosure of closing costs; RESPA violations

Trust fund handling

- risk areas include mishandling of earnest money deposits; commingling and conversion of trust funds; errors in use of trust accounts

23 Property Management

Management Functions
The Management Agreement
Leasing Considerations
The Management Business

MANAGEMENT FUNCTIONS

Reporting
Budgeting
Renting
Property maintenance
Construction
Risk management

Property management is a specialty within the real estate profession. Many states require persons who manage real estate on behalf of other persons or entities to be licensed as real estate brokers. Other states license such persons specifically as property managers. Real estate firms that handle the sale of commercial and investment properties are in a natural position to manage those properties for their owners. Some property managers work for firms that manage multiple properties under blanket management contracts. Others are independent agents. Some are employees of the owner. They generally fall into one of the following categories:

- **individual property manager**-- usually a real estate broker who manages properties for one or more owners; may belong to a small property management firm devoted to full-time property management, be self-employed, or be one of several managers in a large real estate firm.

- **individual building manager**-- usually manages a single large property; may be employed by a property manager or directly by an owner; may or may not have a real estate license.

- **resident manager** (residential properties only)-- lives on the property and may be employed by a real estate broker, a managing agent or an owner to manage a property on a part-time or full-time basis; may be required by state law for properties of certain types and sizes.

A manager has a fiduciary relationship with the principal and, in general, is charged with producing the greatest possible net return on the owner's investment while safeguarding the value of the investment for the owner/investor. At the same time, the manager has some responsibilities to tenants, who want the best value and the best space for their money. Professional managers are therefore much more than rent collectors. They need technical expertise in marketing, accounting, finance, and construction. Property managers often specialize in one type of property - apartment, office, retail, industrial, farm, single-family-and acquire specialized knowledge of that property type. Whatever the property type and management arrangement, the manager's work involves leasing, managing, marketing, and maintaining the property. The services a manager provides thus can be seen to fall into three areas: financial, physical, and administrative. Specific functions, duties, and responsibilities are determined by the management agreement, although most agreements will include at least the following functions.

Reporting

Financial reporting to the principal is a fundamental responsibility of the property manager. Reports may be required monthly, quarterly, and annually. Required reports typically include an annual operating budget (see below); monthly cash flow reports indicating income, expenses, net operating income, and net cash flow; profit and loss statements based on the cash flow reports and showing net profit; and budget comparison statements showing how actual results match the original budget.

Budgeting

An operating budget based on expected expenses and revenues is a necessity for management. The budget will determine rental rates, amounts available for capital expenditures, required reserve funds, salaries and wages of employees, amounts to be paid for property taxes and insurance premiums and mortgage or debt service. It will indicate the expected return, based on the previous year's performance. A typical budget will contain a projection, also based on past performance and on current market information, of income from all sources, such as rents and other services, and of expenses for all purposes, such as operating expenses, maintenance services, utilities, taxes, and capital expenditures. Operating statements itemizing income and expenses are then presented to the owner on a regular basis so that the owner can evaluate the manager's performance against the budget.

Income. The total of scheduled rents plus revenues from such sources as vending services, storage charges, late fees, utilities, and contracts is the ***potential gross income***. Subtracting losses caused by uncollected rents, vacancies and evictions gives ***effective gross income***. Operating expenses are subtracted from this total to show ***net operating income***. When debt service and reserves (which are not counted as operating expenses) are subtracted, the result is ***cash flow***.

Expenses. Expenses may be fixed or variable. Fixed expenses are those that remain constant and may include operating expenses, regular maintenance costs, and administration. Variable expenses are those that may change from month to month or occur sporadically, such as specific repairs or capital expenditures.

Capital expenditures. Expected expenditures for major items such as renovation or expansion should be included as a budgeting item. Large-scale projects are typically budgeted over a period of years.

Cash reserve. A cash reserve is a fund set aside from operating revenues for variable expenses, such as supplies, redecorating, and repairs. The amount of the reserve is based on experience with variable expenses in previous years.

Renting

The property manager, whose full responsibilities include maintaining and managing the property in accordance with the owner's financial goals, include seeing that the property is properly rented and tenanted. The manager may use the services of a leasing agent, whose concern is solely to rent the space. In such a situation, some of the manager's tasks may be performed by the leasing agent. Renting the property includes the following tasks, regardless of which party is actually performing them.

Controlling vacancies. There are many possible reasons for vacancies in a building:

- rent too high or too low
- ineffective marketing
- management quality
- poor tenant-retention program
- image and appearance problems
- high market vacancy rate

Successful managers look for these factors and take steps to limit or counteract their effects.

Marketing. Finding and attracting the right kind of tenants for a property is the aim of a marketing program. A marketing plan based on the property's features and the relationship between supply and demand in the market area, and consonant with the money available, will determine the best mix of advertising and promotional activities. Marketing methods include:

- billboard advertising
- brochures and fliers
- meetings and presentations
- networking
- newspaper ads
- radio and television advertising
- signs
- tenant referrals
- websites and online services

The efficiency of marketing activities can be judged in terms of how many prospects per completed lease they generate. The lower the cost per prospect per lease, the more effective and efficient the program.

Setting rents. Rental income must be sufficient to cover fixed expenses, operating expenses, and desired return on investment. But rental rates must also be realistic, taking into account what is happening in the market. The manager must consider prevailing rents in comparable properties as well as vacancy rates in the market and in the property. The manager makes a detailed survey of competitive space and makes adjustments for differences between the subject property and competing properties before setting the rental rates for the property. Residential apartment rates are stated in monthly amounts per unit, while commercial rates are usually stated as an annual or monthly amount per square foot. If vacancy rates in the managed property are too high, the manager may have to lower rates or identify problems in the property or its management that are contributing to vacancy level. On the other hand, if the property's vacancy rate is significantly lower than market rates, the manager may conclude that higher rental rates are called for.

Selecting tenants. To ensure that the property produces the desired level of income from rent, it is essential to find the most suitable tenants. For commercial space, the manager must determine that:

- the space meets the tenant's needs for size, configuration, location, and quality.
- the tenant will be able to pay for the space.
- the tenant's business is compatible with that of other tenants.
- there is room for expansion if the tenant's need for space is likely to grow.

For residential space, in addition to ascertaining the tenant's creditworthiness, the manager must be careful to comply with all federal and local fair housing laws. A manager should collect the same type of information on all prospective tenants. However, even though the law prohibits discrimination on the basis of race, sex, age and other protected classes, a manager may discriminate in certain other ways. For example, a manager has the right to refuse to rent to a person who has a history paying rent late, damaging property, fighting with other tenants, or spotty employment.

Collecting rents. The lease agreement should clearly specify the terms of rental payment. The manager must establish a system of notices and records as well as a method of collecting rents on schedule. Compliance with all state laws and regulations concerning collecting and accounting for rents is a necessity to avoid unwanted legal complications. As for monies received, the manager must follow trust fund handling procedures established by law and laid out in the rental and management agreements. If authorized by the management agreement, the manager may also collect security deposits and handle them as required by law.

Maintaining tenant relations. Happy tenants remain in a rented space longer than unhappy tenants. High tenant turnover adds to increased advertising and redecorating expenses. For these reasons, it is incumbent on the manager to

- communicate regularly with tenants
- respond promptly and satisfactorily to maintenance and service requests
- enforce rules and lease terms consistently and fairly
- comply with all relevant laws, such as fair housing and ADA (Americans with Disabilities Act) regulations

Legal issues (Fair Housing, ADA, and ECOA). Fair housing laws govern landlords and tenants just as they do sellers and buyers. They ensure that persons receive fair treatment regardless of race, color, religion, national origin, sex, handicap, or familial status. Families with children must receive equal treatment with those who do not have children. Landlords cannot charge higher rents or security deposits because of the presence of children. Managers must make sure that their marketing and leasing practices are in accordance with fair housing laws.

The Americans with Disabilities Act similarly requires landlords in certain circumstances to make housing and facilities available to disabled persons without hindrance. Familiarity with this law and with the latest state, federal, and local fair housing laws is essential.

The Equal Credit Opportunity Act, which prohibits discrimination in lending, applies to how property managers evaluate potential tenants. The manager must be consistent in evaluating the creditworthiness of applicants. The same application forms and the same credit requirements should be used with all applicants.

Property maintenance

Physical maintenance of the property is one of the property manager's primary functions. The costs of services provided must always be balanced with financial objectives and the need to satisfy tenant needs. The manager will also be concerned with staffing and scheduling requirements, in accordance with maintenance objectives.

Maintenance objectives. The foremost maintenance objective is generally to preserve the value of the physical asset for the owner over the long term. Although not every property is best served by vast expenditures on top-level maintenance, it is almost always important to maintain the viability of the property as a rental. Three general types of maintenance are required to keep a property in serviceable condition: routine, preventive, and corrective.

Routine maintenance. Routine maintenance activities are those necessary for the day-to-day functioning of the property. Regular performance of these activities helps to keep tenants satisfied as well as forestall serious problems requiring repair or correction. Routine activities are such things as:

- regular inspections
- scheduled upkeep of mechanical systems-heating, air-conditioning, rest rooms, lighting, landscaping
- regular cleaning of common areas
- minor repairs
- supervision of purchasing

Preventive maintenance. Preventive maintenance goes beyond the routine in attempting to deal with situations that can become serious problems if ignored. Seasonal or scheduled replacement of appliances and equipment, regular painting of exterior and interior areas, and planned replacement of a roof are a few examples.

Corrective maintenance. When routine and preventive maintenance fail, repairs and replacements become mandatory to keep the property operational. A boiler may develop a leak, an air-conditioning unit may break down, an elevator may cease to function properly.

Maintenance contracting. Depending on building type and size, tenant needs, and budgetary constraints, a manager may decide to hire an outside firm to handle maintenance services rather than hiring on-site employees. Efficiency, competence, responsiveness, and effective cost will be major deciding factors.

Construction

Commercial and industrial property managers are regularly called upon to make alterations to existing space to accommodate a tenant's needs. They may also have to undertake or oversee construction that alters or expands common areas or the entire building itself. Again, such work may be contracted out or done by in-house employees.

Tenant improvements. Alterations made specifically for certain tenants are called build-outs or tenant improvements. The work may involve merely painting and re-carpeting a rental space, or erecting new walls and installing special electrical or other systems. In new buildings, spaces are often left incomplete so that they can be finished to an individual tenant's specifications. In such cases, it is important to clarify which improvements will be considered tenant property (trade fixtures) and which will belong to the building.

Renovations. When buildings lose functionality (become functionally obsolescent), they generally also lose tenants, drop in class, and suffer declining rental rates. Maintenance becomes more expensive because of the difficulties of servicing out-of-date building components. Renovation may solve some of these problems, but the manager will have to help the owner determine whether the costs of renovation can be recovered by increased revenues resulting from the renovation.

Environmental concerns. A variety of environmental concerns confronts a property manager, ranging from air quality to waste disposal, tenant concerns, and federal, state and local environmental regulations. The managed property may contain asbestos, radon, mold, lead, and other problematic substances. Tenants may produce hazardous waste. The manager must be aware of the issues and see that proper procedures are in place to deal with them, including providing means for proper disposal of hazardous materials, arranging for environmental audits and undertaking possible remediation. For instance, an audit may show that a building is causing tenants to become sick because of off-gassing from construction materials combined with a lack of ventilation. Remediation may consist of nothing more than replacing carpets and improving ventilation, and the manager, if empowered to do so, should take the necessary steps.

Legal concerns (ADA). The Americans with Disabilities Act requires managers to ensure that disabled employees and members of the public have the same level of access to facilities as is provided for those who are not disabled. Employers with at least fifteen employees must follow nondiscriminatory employment and hiring practices. Reasonable accommodations must be made to enable disabled employees to perform essential functions of their jobs. Modifications to the physical components of the building may be necessary to provide the required access to tenants and their customers, such as widening doorways, changing door hardware, changing how doors open, installing ramps, lowering wall-mounted telephones and keypads, supplying Braille signage, and providing auditory signals. Existing barriers must be removed when the removal is "readily achievable," that is, when cost is not prohibitive. New construction and remodeling must meet a higher standard, Managers must be aware of the laws and determine whether their buildings meet requirements. If not, the manager must determine whether restructuring or retrofitting or some other kind of accommodation is most practical.

Risk management

Many things can go wrong in a rented property, from natural disaster to personal injury to terrorism to malfeasance by employees. Huge monetary losses for the owner, in the form of civil and criminal penalties, legal costs, fines, damages, and costs of remediation can be the result. A manager must consider the possibility of such events and have a plan for dealing with them.

Risk management strategies. Depending on the nature of the risk, the size of the potential losses, the likelihood of its happening, and the costs of doing something about it, a manager and owner will generally choose one or more of the following risk management strategies:

- avoidance-removing the source of the risk, such as by closing off a dangerous area of the building
- reduction-taking action to forestall the event before it happens, such as by installing fire alarms, sprinklers, and security systems
- transference-shifting the risk to someone else by buying an insurance policy
- retention-taking the chance that the event is not likely enough to occur to justify the expense of one of the other strategies; self-insurance

Security and safety. A court may hold a manager and owner responsible for the physical safety of employees, tenants, and customers in leased premises. In addition to standard life safety and security systems such as sprinklers, fire doors, smoke alarms, fire escapes, and door locks, a manager may have to provide electronic and human monitoring systems (security cameras, security guards) and be prepared to take action against tenants who allow, conduct or contribute to dangerous criminal activities such as assault and drug use.

Insurance. Many types of insurance are available to allow for the shifting of liability away from the owner. An insurance audit by a competent insurance agent will indicate what kind of and how much coverage is advisable. Common types of insurance coverage for income and commercial properties include:

- casualty-coverage for specific risks, such as theft, vandalism, burglary, illness and accident, machinery damage

- liability-coverage for risks incurred by the owner when the public enters the building; medical expenses resulting from owner negligence or other causes

- workers' compensation-hospital and medical coverage for employees injured in the course of employment, mandated by state laws

- fire and hazard-coverage for damage to the property by fire, wind, hail, smoke, civil disturbance, and other causes

- flood-coverage for damages caused by heavy rains, snow, drainage failures, and failed public infrastructures such as dams and levies; flood insurance is not included in regular hazard policies

- contents and personal property-coverage for building contents and personal property when they are not actually on the building premises

- consequential loss, use, and occupancy-coverage for the business losses resulting from a disaster, such as loss of rent and other revenue, when the property cannot be used for business

- surety bond-coverage against losses resulting from criminal or negligent acts of an employee

The owner may opt for a multi-peril policy which combines standard types of commercial policies and may allow special coverage for floods, earthquakes, and terrorism.

The amount of coverage provided by certain types of policies may be based on whether the property is insured at depreciated value or current replacement value. Depreciated value is its original value minus the loss in value over time. Current replacement value, which is more expensive, is the amount it would cost to rebuild or replace the property at current rates.

Commercial policies include coinsurance clauses requiring the insured to bear a portion of the loss. Fire and hazard policies usually require the coverage to be in an amount equal to at least 80 percent of the replacement value.

Owner's policies do not cover what is owned by the tenant. Tenants should obtain their own renter's or tenant's insurance to cover personal belongings. Residential and commercial or business variants are available. The question of who owns tenant improvements is not only important when it is time for the tenant to leave the premises. It is also likely to determine whether the tenant's or the landlord's insurance company will be paying if the improvements are damaged or destroyed.

Handling of trust funds. Managers are responsible for proper handling of monies belonging to other parties that come into the manager's hands in the course of doing business. For property managers, such funds include rents collected from tenants, security deposits, and capital contributions from the property owner. State laws, usually incorporated into real estate commission rules and the state's real estate law, specify how a property manager is to manage trust funds. In general, the agent is to maintain a separate bank account for these funds, with special accounting, in a qualified depository institution. The rules for how long an agent may hold trust funds before depositing them, and how the funds are to be disbursed, are spelled out. The fundamental requirements are that the owners of all funds must be identified, and there must be no commingling or conversion of client funds and agent funds. Mishandling carries heavy penalties.

THE MANAGEMENT AGREEMENT

Components
Rights, Duties, and Liabilities

Components

The management agreement establishes an agency agreement between manager and owner as well as specifying such essentials as the manager's scope of authority, responsibilities, objectives, compensation, and the term of the agreement. Property managers are usually considered to be general agents empowered to perform some or all of the ongoing tasks and duties of operating the property, including the authority to enter into contracts. The agency relationship creates the fiduciary duties of obedience, care, loyalty, accounting, and disclosure. The contractual relationship ensures that the manager will strive to realize the highest return for the owner consistent with the owner's objectives and instructions. The agreement should be in writing and include at least the basics of any real estate contract, as follows.

- **names of the parties**--owner, landlord, manager, tenant or other party to be bound by the contract

- **property description**--street address, unit number and location, square footage, and other information that specifies the leased premises

- **term**--time period (**months**, years) covered by the contract; termination conditions and provisions

- **owner's purpose--maximize** net income, maximize asset value, maximize return, minimize expenditure, maintain property quality, etc.; long-term goals for the property

- **owner's responsibilities--management** fees, plus any management expenses such as payroll, advertising and insurance that the manager will not be expected to pay

- **manager's authority**--the **scope** of powers being conveyed to the manager: hiring and staffing, setting rents, contracting with vendors, ordering repairs, limits on expenditures without seeking owner permission

- **manager's responsibilities--specification** of duties, such as marketing, leasing, maintenance, budgeting, reporting, collecting and handling rents; the manager should be included as an additional insured on the liability policy for the property

- **budget**--amounts, or percentages of revenues, allotted for operations, taxes, insurance, capital expenditures, etc.

- **allocation of costs**--who is to pay certain expenses, that is, which will be treated as expenses of the manager vs. which will be paid directly by the owner

- **reporting**--how often and what kind of reports are to be made

- **compensation**--the management fee or other means of compensation to the manager; there may be a flat fee based on square footage, a rental commission based on a percentage of annual rent, a combination of these, or some other arrangement; in compliance with anti-trust laws, management fees are not standardized but must be negotiated by agent and principal

- **equal opportunity statement**--the HUD statement or equivalent concerning availability to all persons and classes protected by law, incorporated into the agreement in the case of a residential property

Rights, duties, liabilities

Both the manager and the landlord have rights, duties and liabilities under the terms of the management contract. How these are apportioned should be clearly stated in the agreement.

Landlord. The landlord has the right to receive rent according to the agreement, and to receive the premises in the specified condition at the end of the agreement term. The landlord and his or her agents may have the right to enter and inspect the premises, examine the books, hire and fire staff, and choose vendors. The landlord may retain or grant the power to enter into contracts, to set rents, and to select tenants. The landlord will have the right to terminate the management contract according to the terms of the contract. The landlord will have the duty to pay the agreed management fee, and to make other such payments as detailed in the agreement. State law will determine to what extent a principal is liable for the acts of the manager and the manager's employees. As owner, the landlord is liable for failures to comply with certain local, state, and federal laws, particularly the Environmental Protection Act and fair housing laws.

Manager. Depending on the degree of authority granted by the agreement, the manager may have the right to hire and fire, enter into contracts, and perform routine management tasks without interference from the owner. The manager has the duties described earlier: to maintain financial records and make reports; to budget; to find, retain, and collect from tenants; to maintain and secure the property; to meet the owner's objectives. The manager's liabilities include the consequences of mishandling trust funds, violating fiduciary responsibilities, and violating fair housing laws, credit laws, and employment laws.

Exhibit 23.1 Abbreviated Sample Management Agreement

MANAGEMENT AGREEMENT

Agreement made_______*[date],* between________, a corporation organized under the laws of the State of ________, having its principal office at_______*[address],*_______*[city],*_________*[state],* here referred to as owner, and_________________, a corporation organized under the laws of the State of________, having its principal office at *address],*_____________________________*[city],*_________*[state],* here referred to as agent.

RECITALS

1. Owner holds title to the following-described real property:_____*[insert legal or other appropriate description],* here referred to as the property.
2. Agent is experienced in the business of operating and managing real estate similar to the above-described property.
3. Owner desires to engage the services of agent to manage and operate the property, and agent desires to provide such services on the following terms and conditions.

In consideration of the mutual covenants contained herein, the parties agree:

EMPLOYMENT OF AGENT. Agent shall act as the exclusive agent of owner to manage, operate, and maintain the property.

BEST EFFORTS OF AGENT. On assuming the management and operation of the property, agent shall thoroughly inspect the property and submit a written report to owner concerning the present efficiency under which the property is being managed and operated, and recommended changes, if necessary.

LEASING OF PROPERTY. Agent shall make reasonable efforts to lease available space of the property, and shall be responsible for all negotiations with prospective tenants. Agent shall also have the right to execute and enter into, on behalf of owner, month-to-month tenancies of units of the property.

ADVERTISING AND PROMOTION. Agent shall advertise vacancies by all reasonable and proper means; provided, agent shall not incur expenses for advertising in excess of____Dollars ($_____) during any calendar quarter without the prior written consent of owner.

MAINTENANCE, REPAIRS, AND OPERATIONS. Agent shall use its best efforts to insure that the property is maintained in an attractive condition and in a good state of repair. Expenditures for repairs, alterations, decorations or furnishings in excess of_____Dollars ($_____) shall not be made without prior written consent of owner.

EMPLOYEES. Agent shall employ, discharge, and supervise all on-site employees or contractors required for the efficient operation and maintenance of the property. All on-site personnel, except independent contractors and employees of independent contractors, shall be the employees of agent.

INSURANCE. Agent shall obtain the following insurance at the expense of owner, and such insurance shall be maintained in force during the full term of this agreement:

1. Comprehensive public liability property insurance of _______Dollars ($___) single limit for bodily injury, death, and property damage;

2. Comprehensive automobile insurance of _____ Dollars ($_______) single limit for bodily injury, death,
and property damage;

3. Fire and extended coverage hazard insurance in an amount equal to the full replacement cost of the structure and other improvements situated on the property; and

4. A fidelity bond in the amount of_____________ Dollars ($______) on each employee who handles cash, and workers' compensation and employer liability insurance to cover the agents and employees of both employer and agent.

Exhibit 23.1 Abbreviated Sample Management Agreement, continued

COLLECTION OF INCOME. Agent shall use its best efforts to collect promptly all rents and other income issuing from the property when such amounts become due. It is understood that agent does not guarantee the collection of rents.

BANK ACCOUNTS. Agent shall deposit (either directly or in a depositary bank for transmittal) all revenues from the property into the general property management trust fund of agent, here referred to as the trust account. From the revenues deposited in the trust account, agent shall pay all items with respect to the property for which payment is provided in this agreement, including the compensation of agent and deposits to the reserve accounts as provided for. Agent shall remit any balance of monthly revenues to owner concurrently with the delivery of the monthly report.

RESERVE ACCOUNT. Agent shall establish a reserve account for the following items: taxes, assessments, debt service, insurance premiums, repairs (other than normal maintenance), replacement of personal property, and refundable deposits.

RECORDS AND REPORTS. Agent shall furnish owner, no later than the end of the next succeeding month, a detailed statement of all revenues and expenditures for each preceding month. Within days after the end of each calendar year, agent shall prepare and deliver to owner a detailed statement of revenues received and expenditures incurred and paid during the calendar year that result from operations of the property.

COMPENSATION OF AGENT. Agent shall receive a management fee equal to___percent (__%) of the gross receipts collected from the operation of the property. Any management fee due agent hereunder shall be paid to agent within _______days after the end of each month.

TERMINATION AND RENEWAL. This agreement shall be for a term commencing on_________*[date]*, and ending on _________*[date]*.

MODIFICATION. This agreement may not be modified unless such modification is in writing and signed by both parties to this agreement.

IN WITNESS WHEREOF, the parties have executed this agreement at_*[designate place of execution]* the day and year first above written.

____

____

LEASING CONSIDERATIONS

Lease types
Owned and leased inclusions
Reversionary rights of owners
Landlord rights and responsibilities
Tenant rights and responsibilities
Evictions
Tenant improvements
Termination of a lease
Security deposit procedures
Universal Residential Landlord-Tenant Act

Lease types

Recall from the chapter on leases that a leasehold estate may grant tenancy for years, from period-to-period, at will, and at sufferance.

For years. An estate for years may be for any definite period—years, months, weeks, days. When the estate expires, the lessee must return the premises to the lessor and vacate the premises. Most commercial leases grant this type of estate.

Periodic. An estate from period-to-period does not have any definite period. Such an estate begins as a lease for a definite period but continues after the expiration of the lease, as long as the lessee continues to pay rent at the regular interval, the lessor accepts it, and no one gives notice to terminate the lease. This type of leasehold is common with residential properties.

At will. A tenancy at will is similar to the periodic tenancy, except that it does not begin with a definite period. It continues, with the consent of the lessor, as long as the tenant pays rent at regular intervals. It is terminated by the death of either party. The tenancy at will is rarely, if ever, used in a written lease.

At sufferance. A tenancy or estate at sufferance comes into existence when a tenant stays beyond the expiration of another type of lease without the lessor's permission. This type of tenancy is never intentionally used in a written lease.

Leases, depending on how rent is determined, are also defined as gross, net, percentage leases, and graduated leases.

Gross. In a gross lease, the tenant pays an established, fixed rent, and the landlord pays all property operating expenses, such as taxes, insurance, utilities, and other services. This is the arrangement commonly used in residential leases.

Net. Net leases have the tenant paying rent plus some or all of the operating expenses attributable to the rented space. This arrangement is commonly used in office and industrial leases.

Percentage. A percentage lease may be gross or net, but the rent is not fixed, but depends on the income generated by the tenant in the leased property. A common arrangement is to set a fixed base rent plus a percentage of the tenant's gross income or sales at the site. The percentage calculation may take effect only when the income reaches a certain level. This arrangement is commonly used in retail leases.

Graduated. Either a gross or a net lease may also be a graduated lease, in which the rental rate increases at specified times over the lease term.

Owned and leased inclusions

The lease should set forth items that are excluded or included in the leased property. For instance, a residential lease may include built-in appliances such as dishwashers but exclude freestanding ones, such as refrigerators. Furniture may be included or excluded. At issue for the landlord is the cost of maintenance. If a refrigerator is not included, it does not have to be maintained by the property manager.

Ownership also relates to insurance policies: one can only insure what one owns, so if a property item is destroyed by fire, the owner's policy will not provide any coverage for an item that is not included in the lease as belonging to the property. This may be of critical importance in a commercial lease where certain improvements might be owned by either the landlord or the tenant, according to the lease.

The lease should also have clear rules about making alterations. If the tenant is not satisfied with an item that is part of the property, the lease may provide for the tenant to make changes only with permission or with the obligation to return the premises to their original condition on termination, or that any alterations made to fixtures become the property of the landlord. Trade fixtures, by definition, belong to the tenant and can be removed when the tenant leaves.

Inclusions may also be of a financial nature-what is included in the rent. Principal and interest on a mortgage loan, homeowner's association dues, common area maintenance charges, liability and hazard insurance, and various operating expenses are items that might be included in the lease as the owner's or the tenant's responsibilities.

Reversionary rights of owners

Like the grantor of a life estate, the grantor of a leasehold estate retains a future interest in the estate. The lease grants a number of rights to the property, including, primarily, the rights to enter, possess, and use the property for the term of the lease. The lessee does not enjoy the full bundle of rights to the property. For instance, the lessee may not encumber or sell the property. When the lease expires (a condition subsequent), all rights revert to the original owner. A common example is the leasing of an apartment for a one-year period. When the lease expires, the lessee has no further rights in the property and full ownership reverts to the lessor. Another condition subsequent that may cause reversion of rights is tenant default.

Landlord rights and responsibilities

State law, often incorporating or modeling the Universal Residential Landlord Tenant Act (see below) prescribes rights and responsibilities for residential landlords and tenants.

Rights. Commonly, the landlord retains a right of entry into the premises in order to perform needed repairs and maintenance on a property. The lease and/or the law may specify that a landlord may enter the tenant's property only under one or more of the following conditions:

- An emergency requires the landlord to enter.
- The tenant gives consent to enter.
- The landlord enters during normal business hours and only after giving notice to either make repairs or to show the property to prospective tenants, purchasers or contractors.
- The tenant has abandoned or surrendered the property.
- The landlord has a court order allowing the entry.

Likewise, the landlord has the right to expect prompt payment of rent and adherence to building rules. At the end of the lease term, the landlord has the right to retake possession of the premises. In case of tenant breach or default, the landlord has the right to pursue the remedies provided by law, such as eviction, to take possession.

Responsibilities. The landlord (by way of the property manager), is expected to deliver a property that is habitable. This means that the landlord at the very least must:

- keep the heating, cooling, electrical, and plumbing systems in good working condition
- keep floors, stairways and railings safe and in good repair
- provide pest control as needed
- repair roof leaks and broken windows promptly.

Tenant rights and responsibilities

Rights. Beyond the right to quiet enjoyment (privacy) of a property received and maintained in a habitable condition, the tenant has other rights, depending on state law. For instance, a tenant may be able to take any of the following actions if a landlord fails to correct a problem that is the landlord's responsibility:

- move out without liability for back rent or the unexpired portion of the lease
- refer the problem to mediation, arbitration or small claims court
- after giving the owner written notification of an emergency situation, call a professional repair person and deduct the cost from the next month's rent.

Responsibilities. Depending on state law, a tenant generally must:

- Pay rent on time
- Follow the rules and regulations set out by the landlord
- Give a 30-day notice when terminating a month-to-month lease
- Return all door and mailbox keys when leaving the property
- Leave the unit in as clean a condition as it was at the start of the lease
- Keep the unit clean and sanitary
- Dispose of all rubbish, garbage and other waste in a sanitary manner
- Use and operate all electrical, gas and plumbing fixtures properly

- Refrain from destroying or damaging the property
- Prevent others from destroying or damaging the property
- Use the property and the rooms only for their intended purposes

Evictions

An ***actual eviction*** follows a procedure prescribed in state law and stated in the lease contract. The landlord must serve notice on the tenant a specified number of days before beginning the eviction suit. A court issues a judgment for possession, which requires the tenant to vacate. A court officer, such as a sheriff, may forcibly remove the tenant and possessions if the tenant refuses to vacate. The landlord can then enter and take possession.

A ***constructive eviction*** occurs when a tenant vacates the leased premises and declares the lease void, claiming that the landlord's actions have made the premises unfit for the purpose described in the lease. The tenant must prove that it was the landlord's actions that were responsible and may be able to recover damages.

Tenant improvements

As discussed earlier, leased spaces are often modified to a tenant's specifications. Such alternations may be made by the landlord on the tenant's behalf or by the tenant. Buildings usually have "standard" improvements, which any tenant improvements must equal or improve on. Many leases have a clause that requires the tenant to return the premises to the condition in which they were received at the end of the lease term. Who pays for improvements and who owns them are major matters for negotiation.

Termination of a lease

Like contracts in general, leases may terminate in a number of ways. Principal among these are the following. See the chapters on leases and contract law for more information.

Expiration. A lease with a term (estate for years) automatically expires at the end of the term.

Performance. Any contract terminates when all parties have performed their obligations.

Agreement. The parties may agree to terminate the lease before the end of the term.

Abandonment. The landlord may retake possession and pursue the tenant for default if the tenant abandons the premises and fails to fulfill lease obligations. The tenant's obligation to pay rent continues.

Default or Breach. A default occurs when either the tenant or landlord violates any of the terms or covenants of the lease. The damaged party may sue for damages, specific performance (of the breached obligation), or cancellation of the lease. When the default arises from the tenant's failure to pay rent or maintain the premises, the landlord may sue for possession and for eviction. Before filing suit, the landlord must give proper notice and allow the tenant to remedy the breach. The most common form of landlord default is failure to maintain the property and provide services. The tenant may vacate the premises and declare the lease cancelled if the landlord's default has made the premises unoccupiable. This action is called constructive eviction.

Notice. A periodic leasehold or tenancy at will may be terminated by proper notice given by either party.

Destruction. Property destruction is grounds for termination of the lease.

Condemnation. Eminent domain proceedings terminate leases.

Foreclosure. Foreclosure actions terminate lease obligations.

Death. A tenancy at will terminates on the death of either party. The landlord's death terminates any lease if the landlord held the leased property under a life estate, since the landlord cannot convey an interest that extends beyond the landlord's life.

Security deposit Procedures

As previously mentioned in the context of handling trust funds, state laws, real estate commission rules, and the state's real estate law, usually specify how a property manager is to manage security deposits. Such funds are normally held in a special trust account and may not be used for any purpose other than the intended one. Whether the deposit can earn interest, and to whom that interest belongs, are likewise prescribed by law. The law also prescribes when the deposit must be returned to the tenant, and under what circumstances any of it may be withheld. The contract language should clearly state the rules, among other things, governing what happens to the deposit when the lease terminates.

Uniform Residential Landlord-Tenant Act

The Uniform Residential Landlord-Tenant Act is model legislation that has been adopted to a greater or lessor extent in many states. In addition to addressing fair and equitable remedies for breaches by both landlord and tenant, the act aims to clarify imprecise language in residential leases that can lead to confusion or exploitation in such areas as:

- lease term
- rental amount
- security deposit
- landlord access
- procedures for default and eviction
- general obligations of landlord and tenant.

See the chapter on "Real Estate Leases" for more detail.

THE MANAGEMENT BUSINESS

Sources of business
Securing business
Professional development

Sources of business

Property management is increasingly a specialization within real estate. There is a growing need for skilled managers because of the increasing number and complexity of properties.

Specialist opportunities. Property managers with specialized training are in demand in a wide variety of property types, including shopping centers, commercial buildings, residential properties, and industrial parks. Within these property specialties are opportunities to specialize even further in such areas as:

- leasing
- asset management
- corporate property management
- resort management
- association management
- housing program management
- mobile home park management
- office building management

Owners and investors in these various property types are among the consumers of management services who represent potential clients for a professional property manager. Such owners and investors may be individuals, corporations, developers, landlords, banks, trusts, homeowners' associations, condominium associations, or investment syndicates

Securing business

Reputation, demonstrated competence, professional training, and smart advertising are keys to finding management business. Before entering into a management agreement, the manager should make sure that the owner's management objectives are clear and that they are realistic.

Management plan. Developing a management plan is a necessary step in beginning a management project, and it may also be part of obtaining a management contract. The manager must consider the owner's objectives, including financial goals; the competitive market for the property, both local and regional, depending on the property type; and the features of the particular property. The plan will take into account market indicators such as vacancy rates, occupancy rates, absorption rates, and new supply coming onto the market. It will also include a budgetary component that considers sources of revenue and anticipated expenses. Finally, the plan will indicate what the manager intends to do with the property, given these considerations, to manage the property in a way that will meet the owner's objectives.

Professional development

A number of organizations provide valuable information and training in subjects related to property management. The certifications and designations provided by these organizations are often viewed as valuable signs of competence and can be a significant factor in getting hired as a manager. Important associations include:

- IREM-The Institute of Real Estate Management, offering the CPM (Certified Property Manager) designation
- BOMA and BOMI-The Building Owners and Managers Association International and the affiliated Building Managers and Owners Institute International, offering the RPA (Real Property Administrator), SMA (Systems Maintenance Administrator), and FMA (Facilities Management Administrator) designations
- NAA-The National Apartment Association, offering designations in apartment building management, maintenance, leasing, portfolio supervision and other related areas
- NARPM-The National Association of Residential Property Managers, offering the RPM (Residential Property Manager), MPM (Master Property Manager) and other related designations
- ICSC-The International Council of Shopping Centers, offering designations in retail property leadership, management, marketing, leasing, and development
- NACM-The National Association of Condominium Managers, offering the RCM (Registered Condominium Manager) designation

23 Property Management Snapshot Review

MANAGEMENT FUNCTIONS

- main manager types: individual broker or firm managing for multiple owners; building manager, employed by owner or other manager to manage a single property; resident manager, employed by owner, broker, or management firm to live and manage on site.
- manager is a fiduciary of the principal; duty to act in principle's best interests; may specialize in a property type
- needed skills: marketing, accounting, finance, construction; financial, physical, administrative services; specific functions determined by management agreement

Reporting

- monthly, quarterly, or annually; annual operating budget, cash flow reports, profit and loss statements, budget comparison statements

Budgeting

- operating budget based on expected expenses and revenues; determines rental rates, capital expenditures, reserves, salaries and wages; projects income based on past performance and current market
- potential gross income: total of scheduled rents plus revenues from other sources; effective gross income: total gross minus losses from vacancies, evictions, uncollected rents; net operating income: effective gross minus operating expenses; cash flow: net operating income minus debt service and reserves
- expenses are variable and fixed; capital expenditures are outlays for major renovations and construction; cash reserves set aside for variable expenses

Renting

- manager must keep property properly rented and tenanted; vacancies managed by rent setting, marketing, tenant relations, good service
- selecting compatible tenants and collecting scheduled rents are top priorities
- legal issues concern compliance with fair housing laws, Americans with Disabilities Act, and ECOA

Property maintenance

- main consideration: balance between costs of services, owner financial objectives, and tenant needs
- may be routine, preventive, or corrective; staffed in-house or contracted out

Construction

- tenant alterations, renovations, and expansion; also environmental remediation
- legal concerns: Americans with Disabilities Act; applies to employers with fifteen or more employees; manager to determine feasibility of restructuring, retrofitting, new construction, or other alternatives to comply

Risk management

- risk ranges from natural disaster to personal injury, terrorism, and employee malfeasance; handled by avoiding or removing the source, installing protective systems, buying insurance, self-insuring (risk retention)
- life safety systems include sprinklers, fire doors, smoke alarms, fire escapes, monitoring systems
- insurance includes casualty, liability, workers' comp, fire and hazard, flood, contents, consequential loss, surety bonds, multi-peril; tenants need their own insurance
- handling of trust funds is a major risk area; mishandling carries heavy penalties

MANAGEMENT AGREEMENT

Components	• names of parties; property description; lease term; owner's purpose; responsibilities; authority; budget; allocation of costs; reporting; compensation; Equal Opportunity statement
Rights, duties and liabilities	• landlord: receive rent; receive premises in specified condition; enter and inspect; examine books; enter into contracts, hire vendors, set rents; pay management; comply with laws
	• manager: hire and fire; enter into contracts; perform management tasks; maintain records, make reports, budget, collect rent, find tenants, maintain the property, meet owner goals; handle trust funds; comply with laws

LEASING CONSIDERATIONS

Lease types	• for years, periodic, at will, at sufferance, gross, net, percentage, graduated
Owned and leased inclusions	• items included or excluded in the lease; owner's insurance covers only what is included; alterations to inclusions only with owner's permission
	• "inclusion" also refers to financial items included as lessee's responsibility, such as operating expenses
Reversionary rights of owners	• all rights of ownership revert to owner at end of lease term
Landlord rights and responsibilities	• rights: enter premises, receive payment, retake on termination, pursue remedies; responsibilities: provide habitable conditions; maintain heating, cooling, electrical, plumbing; keep clean and in repair
Tenant rights and responsibilities	• rights: quiet enjoyment, habitable conditions, right to take action for default; responsibilities: pay rent, obey rules, give proper notice, return property in prescribed condition, use only for intended purpose
Evictions	• actual: prescribed legal procedure; notice, suit, judgment, taking of premises; constructive: tenant vacates for landlord failure to maintain premises
Tenant improvements	• ownership of and payment for improvements according to agreement
Termination of a lease	• causes: expiration, performance, agreement, abandonment, breach, notice, destruction of premises, condemnation, foreclosure, death of either party (tenancy at will), death of landlord (life estate)
Security deposit procedures	• determined by state law, commission rules, agreement
Universal Residential Landlord-Tenant Act	• model law regulating lease language and lease terms; adopted by many states

MANAGEMENT BUSINESS

Sources of business	• leasing, asset management, corporate properties, resorts, association management, housing programs, mobile home parks, office buildings; owners, investors, corporations, developers, landlords, condo and homeowners' associations, banks, trusts, syndicates
Securing business	• develop reputation and competence; obtain training; use effective advertising; make management plan in accordance with owner objectives
Professional development	• training , designations, certifications to increase and demonstrate competence

24 Real Estate Mathematics

Basic Formulas and Functions
Real Estate Applications

Answer Key is on page 429

BASIC FORMULAS AND FUNCTIONS

Adding and multiplying fractions
Converting decimals and percentages
Converting fractions and percentages
Multiplying percentages
Calculating area

Adding and multiplying fractions

Adding

1. Formulas:

   Same denominator: $\frac{a}{c} + \frac{b}{c} = \frac{a + b}{c}$

   Different denominator: $\frac{a}{c} + \frac{b}{d} = \frac{ad + bc}{cd}$

2. Examples: $\frac{2}{5} + \frac{6}{5} = \frac{8}{5}$

   $\frac{3}{4} + \frac{4}{7} = \frac{(3 \text{ x } 7) + (4 \text{ x } 4)}{(4 \text{ x } 7)} = \frac{37}{28}$

Problem 1: $\frac{3}{19} + \frac{2}{7} = ?$

Multiplying

1. Formula: $\frac{a}{c} \times \frac{b}{d} = \frac{ab}{cd}$

2. Example: $\frac{4}{9} \times \frac{2}{3} = \frac{8}{27}$

Problem 2: $\frac{4}{14} \times \frac{3}{8} = ?$

Converting decimals and percentages

Converting a decimal to a percent

1. Formula: (decimal number) x 100 = percent number

2. Examples:
.473 x 100 = 47.3%
3.456 x 100 = 345.6%
.0042 x 100 = .42%

Problem 3: Convert the following decimals to percentages:

2.65 = %
0.294 = %
0.005 = %

Converting a percent to a decimal

1. Formula: $\frac{percentnumber}{100} = decimalnumber$

2. Examples: $\frac{47.3\%}{100} = .473$

$\frac{345.6\%}{100} = 3.456$

Problem 4: Convert the following percentages to decimals:

72.1% =
90.2% =
5.79% =

Converting fractions and percentages

Converting a fraction to a percent

1. Formulas:

(1) $\frac{a}{b}$ = a divided by b = decimal number

(2) decimal number x 100 = percent number

2. Examples: $\frac{4}{5}$ = 4 divided by 5 = 0.8 = 80%

$\frac{9}{3}$ = 9 divided by 3 = 3.0 = 300%

Problem 5: Convert the following fractions to percentages:

$\frac{8}{9} =$ %

$\frac{3}{6} =$ %

$\frac{14}{42} =$ %

Converting a percent to a fraction and reducing it

1. Formula: $X\% = \frac{X}{100}$

$\frac{X \div a}{100 \div a}$ = *reduced fraction*

where "a" is the largest number that divides *evenly* into numerator and denominator. If unknown, try 2, 3, 5, or 7.

2. Example $45\% = \frac{45}{100} = \frac{45 \div 5}{100 \div 5} \doteq \frac{9}{20}$

Problem 6: Convert and reduce the following percentages:

40% =

16% =

Multiplying Percentages

1. Formulas:

   (1) convert percent to decimal by dividing by 100

   (2) whole amount x decimal = partial amount

2. Example: 33% of 400

   (1) 33% divided by 100 = .33

   (2) 400 x .33 = 132

> Problem 7: What is 75% of 280?

Calculating area

To find the area of an irregular shape, try dividing it into triangles, rectangles, squares or trapezoids and calculate the areas of those parts; the area of the whole shape is then the sum of the areas of all of its subparts.

Base and height

1. Formulas for area of three- and four-sided shapes use a product of base and height. In the formulas, *a* represents area, *b* represents base, *h* represents height, *SF* represents square feet.

2. The base of a triangle, square, or rectangle may be any side; a trapezoid has two bases, its two parallel sides.

3. The height of a triangle is the length of a perpendicular line from the base to the triangle's opposite point. Height in a square, rectangle or trapezoid is the length of a line which is perpendicular to the base line(s).

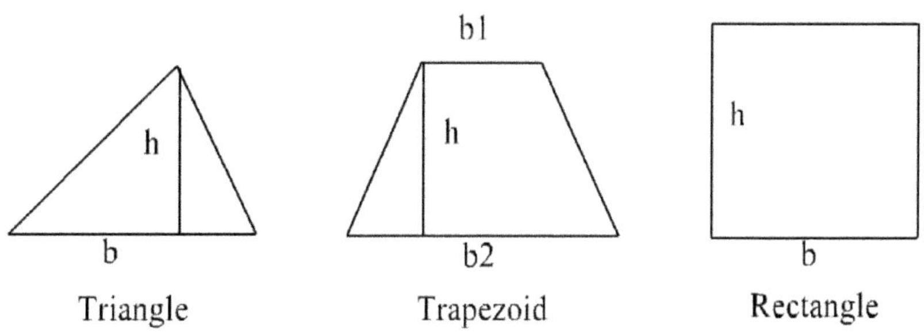

Area of a square or rectangle

1. Formula: area (a) = base (b) x height (h) $a = bxh$
2. Example: A square measures 3 feet on each side.

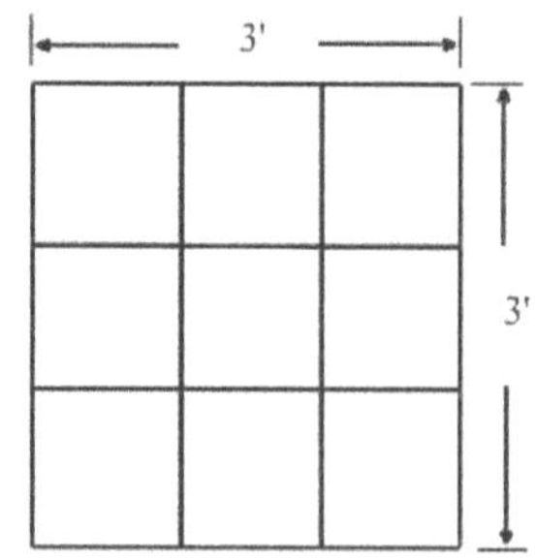

Its area is: 3 x 3 = 9 SF

Area of a triangle

1. Formula: $a = \frac{bxh}{2}$
2. Example: A triangle has a 20' base and a 4' height.

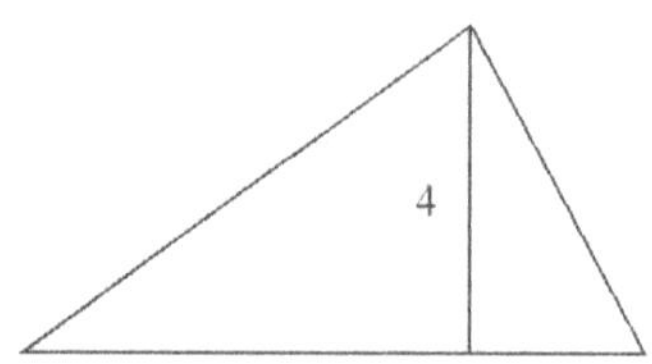

Its area is: $a = \frac{20 \times 4}{2} = 40\ SF$

Area of a trapezoid

$$A = \frac{h\,(b_1 + b_2)}{2}$$

1. Formula:
2. Example: A trapezoid's two bases are 10' and 15', and its height is 7'.

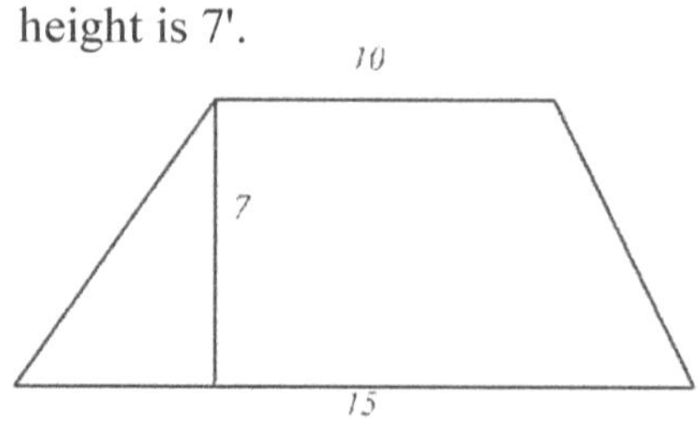

Its area is: $a = \frac{7\,(10 + 15)}{2} = 87.5\ SF$

Problem 8: Calculate the areas of the following shapes:

a rectangle with height of 4' and base of 36'

a =

a square with a side of 16'

a =

a trapezoid with height of 5' and bases of 6' and 8'

a =

REAL ESTATE APPLICATIONS

Legal descriptions (Chapter 9)
Listing agreements (Chapter 12)
Brokerage business (Chapter 13)
Sales contracts (Chapter 14)
Appraisal (Chapter 16)
Finance (Chapter 17)
Investments (Chapter 18)
Taxation (Chapter 19)
Closings (Chapter 21)

Legal descriptions (Chapter 9)

Linear measures

(cm = centimeter; m = meter; km = kilometer)

1 inch	=	1/12 foot	=	1/36 yard		
1 foot	=	12 inches	=	1/3 yard		
1 yard	=	36 inches	=	3 feet		
1 rod	=	16.5 feet	=	1/320 mile		
1 mile	=	5280 feet	=	1760 yards	=	320 rods

1 centimeter	=	1/100th m		
1 meter	=	100 cm	=	1/1000th km
1 kilometer	=	1,000 m		

Area measures

1 square inch	=	1/144th square foot
1 square foot	=	1/9th square yard
1 square yard	=	9 square feet

1 acre	=	1/640 sq. mi	=	43,560 SF	=	208.71 ft x 208.71 ft
1 square mile	=	640 acres	=	1 section	=	1/36 township
1 section	=	mile x 1 mile	=	640 acres	=	1/36 township
1 township	=	6 mi x 6 mi	=	36 sq. mi.	=	36 sections

Metric conversions

(cm = centimeter; m = meter; km = kilometer)

1 inch	=	2.54 cm						
1 foot	=	30.48 cm	=	.3048 m				
1 yard	=	91.44 cm	=	.9144 m				
1 mile	=	1609.3 m	=	1.60 km				
1 centimeter	=	.3937 inch						
1 meter	=	39.37 inches	=	3.28 feet	=	1.094 yards		
1 kilometer	=	3,281.5 feet	=	.621 mile				

Fractions of sections, acres, and linear dimensions

Fraction	# Acres	Feet X Feet
1 section	640 acres	5280 X 5280
1/2 section	320 acres	5280 X 2640
1/4 section	160 acres	2640 X 2640
1/8 section	80 acres	2640 X 1320
1/16 section	40 acres	1320 X 1320
1/32 section	20 acres	660 X 1320
1/64 section	10 acres	660 X 660

Calculating area from the legal description

1. Formula:

   (1) First multiply all the denominators of the fractions in the legal description together

   (2) Then divide 640 by the resulting product.

2. Examples:

   N 1/2 of the SW 1/4 of Section 6:

$$\frac{640}{(2 \times 4)} = \frac{640}{8} = 80 \ acres$$

   W 1/2 of the NW 1/4 of the NE 1/4 of Section 8

$$\frac{640}{(2 \times 4 \times 4)} = \frac{640}{32} = 20 \ acres$$

Problem 9: Calculate the acreage of the following:

SW 1/4 of the N 1/2 of the E 1/2 of Section 14

SE 1/4 of the NW 1/4 of the SE 1/4 of Section 20

Listing agreements (Chapter 12)

Co-brokerage commission

1. Formulas: sale price × commission rate = total listing-side commission

   buyer-broker compensation = amount agreed to in the buyer-broker agreement or negotiated in the transaction

2. Example: A house sells for $600,000. The seller agrees to pay a 6% commission to the listing broker, and the buyer and buyer broker have agreed to a 50% share of that amount as the buyer-broker's compensation,

   .

   $600,000 x 6% = $36,000 total commission x 50% = $18,000 buyer-broker's commission

Agent's commission

1. Formula: broker's commission x agent's split rate = agent's commission

2. Example: Assume an $18,000 broker's commission and a 60% - 40% agent-broker split rate.

   $18,000 x .6 = $10,800 agent's commission ($7,200 to broker)

Problem 10: A property is co-brokered by listing broker Schroeder and selling broker Hobson for $425,000. The seller agrees to pay a 6% commission to the listing broker, and the buyer and buyer broker have agreed to a 50% share of that amount as the buyer-broker's compensation, Schroeder's agent, Joachim, is on a 65% split schedule. Hobson's selling agent, Wallace, splits 50-50 with her broker. What are the participants' commissions?

Broker Schroeder:	$
Broker Hobson:	$
Schroeder's agent, Joachim:	$
Hobson's agent, Wallace:	$

Brokerage business (Chapter 13)

Goodwill calculation

1. Formula: Goodwill = Price - Value of assets

2. Example: A seller wants $1 million for a business. Assets in the business, including inventory, furniture, equipment, leasehold improvements, and working capital, have a total value of $750,000. The goodwill is:

   $1,000,000 - 750,000 = $250,000 goodwill

Problem 11: A prospective purchaser complained to a seller that the selling price had far too much goodwill: $200,000. After all, the assets only totaled $352,000. What was the price?

Sales contracts (Chapter 14)

"Percentage of listing price" calculation

1. Formula: Percentage of listing price = offer divided by listing price

2. Example: A property listed for $400,000 receives an offer for $360,000. The percentage of listing price is:

   $360,000 divided by 400,000 = 90%

Problem 12: A seller receives an offer of $674,000 on a property listed at $749,000. How much is the offer as a percent of the listing price?

Earnest money deposit calculation

1. Formula: Deposit = Listing price x required percentage

2. Example: A seller requires a 2% deposit on a property listed for $320,000. The required deposit is:

   $320,000 x 2% = $6,400

Problem 13: A seller requires a 1.5% deposit on all offers. A buyer wants to offer $312,000 for the property. What must the deposit be?

Rent escalations

1. Formula: New rent = current rent x (100% + escalation rate)

2. Example: An apartment's rent is scheduled to increase by 6%. If the current rent is $1800, the new rent is:

   $1800 x (100% + 6%) = $1,800 x 106% = $1,908

Problem 14: A tenant's rent is currently $650 per month. This rent is scheduled to increase 5% per year. What will the tenant's rent be at the beginning of the **third** year from now?

FIRPTA withholding

1. Formula: FIRPTA withholding = gross proceeds from sale x 15%

2. Example: Gross proceeds on a FIRPTA-regulated property sale are $340,000. The required withholding amount is:

   $340,000 x 15% = $51,000

Appraisal (Chapter 16)

Adjusting comparables

1. Rules:
   a. NEVER adjust the subject!
   b. If the comparable is better than the subject, subtract value from the comparable
   c. If the comparable is **worse** than the subject, **add** value to the comparable

2. Examples:
   a. A comparable has a pool and the subject does not. The appraiser estimates the value contribution to be $25,000. Adjust the comparable by entering -25,000 in the CMA.
   b. A comparable has 3 bedrooms and the subject has 4. The appraiser estimates the value contribution of a bedroom to be $15,000. Adjust the comparable by entering +15,000 in the CMA.

Problem **15:** Identify the proper adjustments for the following:

(a) The subject has a two-car garage, while the comparable does not. Value of garage is $33,000.

Adjustment:

(b) A comparable has a fireplace, and the subject does not. Value of fireplace is $8,000.

Adjustment:

(c) The subject has 1,500 square feet. The comparable has 1,600 square feet. The value of extra square feet is $200/SF.

Adjustment:

Comparative Market Analysis (CMA)

1. Steps:
   a. Identify comparable sales
   b. Compare comparables to the subject and make adjustments to comparables.
   c. Weight values indicated by adjusted comparables for the final value estimate of the subject.

Problem 16: Adjust and weigh comparables to indicate a subject value

a) Using the data and assumptions provided below, complete the worksheet by filling in value adjustments for each blank entry.

b) Total the values of each comparable's adjustments to derive a net value change for the comparable.

c) Reconcile the comparables by weighting their values against each other and estimating a value for the subject.

d) Explain your reasoning.

Comparables data

Subject:	3 bedrooms, two baths, kitchen, living room, family room; 2,500 square feet of gross living area; 3-car attached garage; condition is good.
Comparable A:	Sold for $850,000; located in subject's neighborhood with similar locational advantages; house approximately same age as subject; lot size similar to subject; condition similar to subject; two bedrooms, one bath; 2,200 square feet of gross living area.
Comparable B:	Sold for $950,000; located in subject's neighborhood with similar locational advantages; house ten years newer than subject; lot size considerably larger than the subject's; better condition than subject; four bedrooms, three baths; gross living area is similar.
Comparable C:	Sold for $1,000,000; located in subject's neighborhood with similar locational advantages; house eight years older than subject; lot size similar to subject; condition similar to subject; three bedrooms, three baths; 2,500 square feet of gross living area.
Comparable D:	Sold for 1,090,000; located in a more desirable neighborhood than subject; house approximately same age and size and condition as subject, with two bedrooms, and two baths; 1,900 square feet of gross living area.

Adjustment Assumptions

Location:	$20,000 value difference for Comparable D
Financing & terms:	no value differences
Lot size:	$10,000 value difference for Comparable B
# Bedrooms and bathrooms:	$10,000 per room
Effective age and condition:	poor -- $20,000; good – no change; excellent -- $20,000
Gross living area:	$10,000 per 100 feet

CMA Adjustment Worksheet

	Subject	A	B	C	D
Sale price	???	850,000	950,000	1,000,000	1,090,000
Location		$________	$________	$________	$________
Age		$________	$________	$________	$________
Lot size		$________	$________	$________	$________
Condition		$________	$________	$________	$________
Bedrooms	3	$________	$________	$________	$________
Baths	2	$________	$________	$________	$________
Gross living area	2,500 SF	$________	$________	$________	$________
Net adjustments		$________	$________	$________	$________
Indicated value	???	$________	$________	$________	$________

Rationale for comp adjustments:

____

____

____

____

____

Comments on weighting of adjustments and estimated value of the subject:

____

____

____

____

____

Problem 16 Answers

Completed CMA Adjustment Worksheet

	Subject	A	B	C	D
Sale price		850,000	950,000	1,000,000	1,090,000
Location		equal	equal	equal	-20,000
Age		equal	-20,000	+20,000	equal
Lot size		equal	-10,000	equal	equal
Condition	good	equal	-20,000	equal	equal
Bedrooms	3	+10,000	-10,000	equal	+10,000
Baths	2	+10,000	-10,000	-10,000	equal
Gross living area	2,500	+30,000	equal	equal	+60,000
Net adjustments		+50,000	-70,000	+10,000	+50,000
Indicated value	**1,000,000**	900,000	880,000	1,010,000	1,140,000

Discussion of Weighting, Reconciliation and Value Estimate

The completed table indicates four estimated values for the subject, ranging from $880,000 to 1,140,000.

For comparable A, the estimator has made three adjustments -- for the number of bedrooms and baths, and for gross living area -- totaling $50,000, or 5.9% of the purchase price.

For comparable B, the estimator has deducted values for age, lot, condition, bedrooms, and baths. The total of five adjustments amounts to $70,000, or 7.4% of the sale price.

For comparable C, the estimator has adjusted only for the age. The adjustment of $10,000, 1% of sale price, raises the indicated value of the subject to $1,010,000.

For comparable D, a deduction has been made for the comparable's superior location. This is offset by additions for the number of bedrooms and gross living area reflecting where the comparable is inferior to the subject. The three adjustments amount to a total of +$50,000, or 4.6% of the sale price.

Weighting the indicated values of the comparables, the estimator has developed an indicated value of $1,000,000 for the subject. Underlying this conclusion is the fact that Comparable C is by far the best indicator of value, and therefore receives the heaviest weighting as a value indicator. This property has the fewest adjustments (1) and smallest total adjustment amount (2%). Comparable D might be the second-best indicator, since it has the second-lowest number of adjustments (3), and the net adjustment is also second-best as a percent of the sale price (4.6%). Comparable A might be the third best indicator, since it has the second smallest number of total adjustments (3) but the second highest net adjustment percent (5.9%). Comparable B has the greatest number of adjustments (5) and the highest percent of sale price (7.4%) and is therefore the least reliable indicator.

Income capitalization

Gross rent multiplier (GRM)

1. Formula: gross rent x multiplier = value
2. Example: $2,000 x 135 GRM = $270,000

Gross income multiplier (GIM)

1. Formula: gross annual income x GIM = value
2. Example: $45,000 x 9 GIM = $405,000

Net income capitalization

1. Formula: annual net operating income (NOI) ÷ capitalization rate = value
2. Example: $50,000 ÷ .10 = $500,000

Problem 17: An apartment building grosses $450,000 annually, nets 350,000, and has a capitalization rate of 9%. Prevailing GIMs are 8.

(a) What is the property value using the GIM?

(b) What is the property value using net income capitalization?

Finance (Chapter 17)

Interest only loans

1. Formulas: interest payment (I) = principal (P) x interest rate (R)

   annual interest payment ÷ 12 = monthly interest payment

   monthly interest payment x 12 = annual interest payment

$$I = P \times R$$

$$R = \frac{I}{P}$$

$$P = \frac{I}{R}$$

2. Examples: A $300,000 interest-only loan @ 10% has annual payments of $30,000 and monthly payments of $2,500.

   Annual interest = $300,000 x 10% = $30,000
   Monthly interest = $30,000 ÷ 12 = $2,500

   The loan amount of an interest-only loan that has an annual interest rate of 8% and a monthly interest payment of $700 is $105,000.

   Annual interest = $700 x 12 = $8,400
   Loan amount = $8,400 ÷ .08 = $105,000

Problem 18:

(a) A $250,000 loan carries a 7% rate. What is the monthly interest payment?

(b) A $300,000 loan has monthly payments of $2,000. What is its annual interest rate?

(c) A 12% loan has annual payments of $15,000. What is the loan amount?

Loan-to-value (LTV) ratio

1. Formulas: loan amount = market value x LTV

   LTV = loan amount ÷ market value

2. Example: A 75% LTV will allow a lender to make a loan of $375,000 on a $500,000 property.

   loan amount = $500,000 x 75% = $375,000

   LTV = $375,000 ÷ $500,000 = 75%

Problem 19:

(a) A lender requires $90,000 down on a $400,000 property. Calculate the lender's required LTV.

(b) A property is valued at $600,000. The lender will allow a maximum LTV of 75%. How much can the buyer borrow on the property?

Income underwriting ratio calculation

1. Formulas: Conventional:

   monthly PITI = (25-28%) x monthly gross income

   FHA:

   monthly PITI = 31% x monthly gross income

2. Examples: A borrower has monthly gross income of $2,000. Conventional lenders are using a ratio of 28%. The borrower can afford the following monthly PITI payments:

   Conventional:

   PITI = 28% x $2,000 = $560

   FHA:

   PITI = 31% x $2,000 = $620

Problem 20: A borrower earns $4,000/month and pays $600/month in debt repayments. A conventional lender requires a 26% income ratio, and an FHA lender requires 31%. What monthly PITI can this person afford based on the income ratio?

Conventional: $

FHA: $

Debt underwriting ratio calculation

1. Formulas: Conventional:

   Expense = (36% x gross income) – monthly debt

   FHA:

   Expense = (43% x gross income) - monthly debt

2. Example: An individual has a monthly gross income of $6,000, and has monthly debt payments of $900. The borrower can afford the following monthly housing expense:

   Conventional:

   Expense = (36% x $6,000) - 900 = $1,260

   FHA:

   Expense = (43% x $6,000) – 900 = $1,680

Problem 21: A borrower earns $4,000/month and makes monthly debt payments of $600. What monthly payment for housing can this person afford based on the debt ratio?

Conventional: $

FHA: $

Points

1. Formula: 1 point = 1% (.01) of loan amount

2. Example: A lender charges 3 points (3%) on a $350,000 loan. The points charges are:

   3 points = 3%
   .03 x $350,000 = $10,500

Problem 22: A lender is charging 2.75 points on a $240,000 loan. How much must the borrower pay for points?

Investments (Chapter 18)

Appreciation

1. Formulas: total appreciation = current value – original price

   total appreciation rate = total appreciation / original price

   one-year appreciation rate = one-year appreciation / prior-year value

2. Example: A house bought for $500,000 appreciates $50,000 each Year for 3 years.

   total appreciation = $650,000 - 500,000 = $150,000

   total appreciation rate = $150,000 ÷ $500,000 = 30%

   first- year rate = $50,000 ÷ $500,000 = 10%

Problem 23: A property is purchased for $360,000. A year later it is Sold for $410,000. What is the amount of appreciation, and what is the appreciation rate?

Equity

1. Formula: equity = current value – current loan amount

2. Example: A buyer bought a property for $600,000 with a loan of $450,000. The house has appreciated $60,000 and the buyer has reduced the original loan by $30,000. The buyer's current equity is:

   Equity = ($600,000 + 60,000) - ($450,000 - 30,000) = $240,000

Problem 24: A property is purchased for $450,000 with a $75,000 downpayment. Five years later the property is worth $540,000, and the loan balance has dropped $12,500. What is the owner's new equity?

Pre-tax cash flow

1. Formula and example:

	potential rental income	$50,000
-	vacancy and collection loss	3,000
=	effective rental income	47,000
+	other income	2,000
=	gross operating income (GOI)	49,000
-	operating expenses	20,000
-	reserves	3,000
=	net operating income (NOI)	26,000
-	debt service	15,000
=	pre-tax cash flow	11,000

Problem 25: An apartment building has a potential income of $300,000 and vacancy of $12,000. Its bills total $128,000, and $12,000 has been reserved for repairs. Payments on the loan total $88,000. What is the property's pre-tax cash flow?

Tax liability

1. Formula and example:

	net operating income (NOI)	26,000
+	reserves	3,000
-	interest expense	15,000
-	cost recovery expense	5,000
=	taxable income	9,000
x	tax rate (28%)	
=	tax liability	2,520

Problem 26: The property from the previous problem has annual cost recovery of $28,000. Out of the annual debt service, $8,000 is non-interest principal payback. The property owner's tax rate is 28%. What is the property's annual tax?

Annual depreciation (cost recovery) expense

1. Calculation:
   a. identify improvements-to-land ratio

   b. identify value of improvements: ratio x property price

   c. divide value of improvements by total depreciation term

2. Example: A property was bought for $400,000. 75% of the value is allocated to the improvement. The property falls in the 39-year depreciation category.

   (1) improvements-to-land ratio = 3:1, or 75%

   (2) improvement value = $400,000 x 75% = $300,000

   (3) annual depreciation = $300,000 ÷ 39 = $7,692

Problem 27: A property is purchased for $400,000. Improvements account for 80% of the value. Given a 39-year depreciation term, what is the annual depreciation expense?

Capital gain

1. Formula and example: (residential property)

	Selling price of property	$300,000
-	Selling costs	24,000
=	Amount realized (ending basis)	$276,000
	Beginning basis (price) of property	$250,000
+	Capital improvements	10,000
-	Total depreciation expense	0
=	Adjusted basis of property	260,000
	Amount realized (ending basis)	$276,000
-	Adjusted basis of property	260,000
=	Capital gain	$ 16,000

Problem 28: A principal residence is bought for $360,000. A new tile roof is added, costing $15,000. Five years later the home sells for $440,000, and the closing costs $35,000. What is the homeowner's capital gain?

Return, rate of return, and investment amount

1. Formulas:

$$\frac{\textit{netoperatingincome}}{\textit{price}} = \textit{returnoninvestment} \ (\textit{ROI})$$

$$\frac{\textit{cash flow}}{\textit{cash invested}} = \textit{cash-on-cash return} \ (\textit{C on C})$$

$$\frac{\textit{cash flow}}{\textit{equity}} = \textit{return on equity} \ (\textit{ROE})$$

2. Example: A property is bought for $200,000 with a $50,000 down payment and a $150,000 interest-only loan. The property has a net income of $20,000 and a cash flow of $8,000. In addition, the property has appreciated $30,000.

ROI	=	$20,000 ÷ $200,000 = 10%
C on C	=	*$8,000 ÷ $50,000 = 16%*
ROE	=	$8,000 ÷ $80,000 = 10%

Problem 29: A multi-unit rental property was bought four years ago for $1,200,000 with a $200,000 down payment. The property now rents for $8,500 per month. Expenses and debt service are $1,000/month and $6,500/month respectively. An appraiser estimates the property's current value at $1,450,000. The investor pays off her principal balance at a rate of $5,000 per year. Compute the following investment returns for the investor:

ROI =
C on C =
ROE =

Taxation (Chapter 19)

Tax rate calculation

1. Formula: $\text{tax rate (millage rate)} = \frac{\text{tax requirement}}{\text{tax base}}$

2. Example: A municipality has a revenue requirement of $10,000,000 after accounting for its revenues from sale of utilities. This requirement has to be covered by property tax. The real estate tax base, after homestead exemptions, is $300,000,000. The tax rate will be:

$$\frac{10{,}000{,}000}{300{,}000{,}000} = .0333 \quad 33.33 \text{ mills}$$

Problem 30: Barrington has an annual budget of $25,000,000 to be paid by property taxes. Assessed valuations are $300,000,000, and exemptions total $25,000,000. What must the tax rate be to finance the budget?

Homestead exemption calculation

1. Formula and example

	assessed value	$360,000
-	homestead exemption	50,000
	taxable value	$310,000

Taxing the property

1. Formulas: taxable value of property x tax rate (mill rate) for each taxing authority in jurisdiction

   total tax = sum of all taxes by taxing authority

2. Example: The taxable value of a property after exemptions is 400,000 and tax rates are as shown. The property's tax bill will be:

School tax:	$400,000 x 10 mills	=	$4,000
City tax:	$400,000 x 4 mills	=	1600
County tax:	$400,000 x 3 mills	=	1200
Total tax:			$6,800

Problem 31: A homeowner's assessed valuation is $225,000. The homestead exemption is $25,000. Tax rates for the property are 8 mills for schools; 3 mills for the city; 2.5 mills for the county; and.5 mills for the local community college. What is the homeowner's tax bill?

Special assessments calculation

1. Formula: a. Identify total costs to be assessed

   b. Calculate prorated share for each property impacted

   c. Multiply cost x prorated share

2. Example: A canal will be dredged at a cost of $200,000. The improvement affects 30 properties with a total canal frontage of 4,000 feet. One property has 200' of frontage. Its assessment bill will be:

   (1) 200' ÷ 4,000' = 5% share

   (2) $200,000 x 5% = $10,000 assessment

Problem 32: A street beautification project is to cost $25,000. The project affects 20 properties having a total of 2,000 front feet. One owner's lot has 75 front feet. What will this owner's special assessment be?

Closings (Chapter 21)

Prorations

1. Formulas and rules:

Accounting for common items paid (or received) in advance vs arrears

	arrears	advance	debit	credit
real estate taxes	x		seller	buyer
rents received by seller		x	seller	buyer
utilities	x		seller	buyer

Whose share is charged to whom?

- if buyer pays taxes in arrears: charge seller, credit buyer for seller's portion
- if seller received rents in advance: charge seller, credit buyer for buyer's portion
- if seller pays utilities in advance: credit seller, charge buyer for seller's portion

Calculating the proration: 360-day method and 365-day method

1. **Calculate the daily proration amount**

   a. 360-day method: divide the annual amount by 360 or monthly amount by 30

   b. 365-day method: divide the annual proration amount by 365, or monthly amount by # days in that month

2. **Calculate # of seller's days**

   a. 360-day method: use 30 days for each month; actual number of seller days within the month, counting (or not counting) the day of closing

   b. 365-day method: use actual number of days for each month and partial month

3. **Calculate the seller's share**

   Multiply the daily amount times the number of seller's days – both methods

4. **Calculate buyer's share (both methods)**

   Subtract seller's share (from #3) from total share

2. Example: A rental property closes on January 25 and the closing day is the seller's. The 365-day method will be used for the prorations. Monthly rent already received by seller is $2,400. Annual real estate taxes to be paid in arrears by buyer are $4,000. Round to the nearest cent.

1. **Rent proration**: (monthly; 365-day method)

Daily amount:	$2,400 monthly rent ÷ 31 days in January = $77.42
# Seller's days:	25
Seller's share:	$77.42 x 25 = $1,935.50
Buyer's share:	$2,400 – 1,935.50 = $464.50

Credit buyer and debit seller for buyer's share of $464.50

2. **Tax proration**: (annual; 365-day method)

Daily amount:	$4,000 ÷ 365 = $10.96
# Seller's days:	25
Seller's share:	$10.96 x 25 = $274
Buyer's share:	$4,000 – 274 = $3,726

Credit buyer and debit seller for seller's share of $274

Problem 33: A rental property closes on March 15th. Proratable income and expenses are: rental income of $1,800/month, received in advance by seller, March 1; annual taxes of $4,800/year, to be paid in arrears by buyer, January 1 of the year after sale. The day of closing is the seller's. February has 28 days. Prorate the items using the 365-day method, and assign debits and credits.

rent:	seller's share	$
	buyer's share	$
	debit seller/credit buyer	$
	debit buyer/credit seller	$
taxes:	seller's share	$
	buyer's share	$
	debit seller/credit buyer	$
	debit buyer/credit seller	$

REAL ESTATE MATHEMATICS: ANSWER KEY

Problem 1: $\frac{3}{19}+\frac{2}{7}=\frac{21+38}{133}=\frac{59}{133}$

Problem 2: $\frac{4}{14}x\frac{3}{8}=\frac{12}{112}$

Problem 3: 2.65 = 265%
0.294 = 29.4%
0.005 = .5%

Problem 4: 72.1% = .721
90.2% = .902
5.79% = .0579

Problem 5: 8/9 = 88.8%
3/6 = 50%
14/42 = 33.3%

Problem 6: 40% = 40/100 = 2/5
16% = 16/100 = 4/25

Problem 7: 210

Problem 8: 144 SF
256 SF
35 SF

Problem 9: 40 acres
10 acres

Problem 10: Schroeder: $5,206.25
Hobson: $7,437.50
Joachim $9,668.75
Wallace: $7,437.50

Problem 11: $552,000

Problem 12: 90%

Problem 13: $4,680

Problem 14: $716.63

Problem 15: (a) +33,000 to comparable
- 8,000 to comparable
- 20,000 to comparable

Problem 16: $1,000,000

Problem 17: (a) $3,600,000
(b) $3,888,888

Problem 18: (a) $1,458
8%
$125,000

Problem 19: (a) 77.5%
(b) $450,000

Problem 20: Conventional: $1,040/month
FHA & VA: $1,240/month

Problem 21: Conventional: $840
FHA: $1,120

Problem 22: $6,600

Problem 23: $50,000; 13.89%

Problem 24: $177,500

Problem 25: $60,000

Problem 26: $14,560

Problem 27: $8,205

Problem 28: $30,000

Problem 29: (a) ROI = 7.5%
(b) C on C = 6.0%
(c) ROE = 2.55%

Problem 30: 90.9 mills, or 9.09%

Problem 31: $2,800

Problem 32: $937.50

Problem 33:

rent:	seller's share	$870.96
	buyer's share	$929.04
debit seller/credit buyer		$929.04
taxes:	seller's share	$973.16
	buyer's share	3,826.84
debit seller/credit buyer		$973.16

25 The Oklahoma Regulatory Environment

Authority of the Real Estate Commission
Licensed Activities: Acts of the Associates
Prohibited Activities and Causes for Discipline
The Complaint and Disciplinary Process
The Oklahoma Real Estate Education and Recovery Fund
OREC Notification Requirements

Every real estate transaction in Oklahoma takes place inside a framework of state law, and that framework exists for one reason: to protect the public during what is often the largest financial decision of a person's life. This chapter introduces the agency that writes and enforces those rules, the Oklahoma Real Estate Commission (OREC), together with the two bodies of law that govern daily practice: the Oklahoma Real Estate License Code, found in Title 59 of the Oklahoma Statutes, and the Commission's administrative rules, found in Title 605 of the Oklahoma Administrative Code. Knowing who holds authority, what a licensee may and may not do, how the Commission disciplines those who violate the rules, and how injured consumers are made whole forms the foundation for everything that follows.

AUTHORITY OF THE REAL ESTATE COMMISSION

The Commission and its members
Powers and duties
Two bodies of law: Code and rules

The Commission and its members

The Oklahoma Real Estate Commission, commonly abbreviated OREC, is the sole governmental body in the state with authority to regulate the real estate profession and issue real estate licenses (59 O.S. Section 858-201). No city, county, or other state agency may license real estate brokers or associates; that power belongs to OREC alone. The Commission consists of seven members appointed by the Governor with the advice and consent of the Senate, and it operates under the Oklahoma Sunset Law, which requires the Legislature to periodically re-create the agency or allow it to expire. Each member must be a United States citizen and must have lived in Oklahoma for at least three years before appointment.

Composition of the seven-member Commission. Five of the seven members must be licensed real estate brokers with at least five years of active, full-time brokerage experience before appointment. One member must be a layperson who is not in the real estate business, and one must be an active representative of an Oklahoma real estate school approved by the Commission. No more than two members may be appointed from the same congressional district.

Powers and duties

Section 858-208 of the License Code lists what the Commission may do. OREC

- issues, denies, and renews licenses;
- approves prelicense and continuing education courses, instructors, and schools;
- investigates the business dealings of licensees;
- issues cease and desist orders to anyone violating the Code; and
- disciplines licensees, instructors, and schools (59 O.S. Section 858-208).

Its disciplinary tools range from a written reprimand, to requiring additional education, to suspending or revoking a license, to imposing administrative fines. The Commission may also modify or reinstate a sanction for good cause, initiate the prosecution of those who violate the Code, and contract with debt collectors to recover unpaid fines.

Consider a practical example. If a consumer complains that a licensee advertised a home with a fabricated square footage, OREC has authority to investigate the complaint, hold a hearing, and, if it finds a violation, fine the licensee, order additional education, or suspend the license. The consumer does not have to file a private lawsuit to trigger that oversight; the Commission acts in the public interest on its own.

Two bodies of law: Code and rules

The Oklahoma Real Estate License Code are the **statutes** enacted by the Legislature and located at Title 59, Sections 858-101 and following. The Commission's **administrative rules** implement and add detail to the Code and are located at Title 605 of the Oklahoma Administrative Code. When the Code authorizes discipline for untrustworthy, improper, fraudulent, or dishonest dealing, for instance, it is the rules, specifically OREC Rule 605:10-17-4, that spell out exactly which acts fall within that phrase. A licensee is bound by both, and a violation of either can support discipline.

LICENSED ACTIVITIES: ACTS OF THE ASSOCIATES

What counts as a licensed activity
An associate works under one broker
Compensation flows through the broker

What counts as a licensed activity

A real estate license is required of anyone who, for a fee or other valuable consideration, performs or offers to perform certain acts for another person. These licensed activities include

- listing,

- selling,
- purchasing,
- exchanging,
- renting, or leasing real estate;
- negotiating any such transaction; and
- soliciting clients or prospects in connection with those services.

Performing any of these acts for compensation without a license is unlicensed activity, which the Commission may penalize directly, as a later section of this chapter explains.

An associate works under one broker

Oklahoma issues several types of license, but the working distinction for a new licensee is between a broker and an associate. The term **associate** covers the provisional sales associate, the sales associate, and the broker associate. An associate may perform licensed activities only for, and under the supervision of, the broker with whom his or her license is associated. An associate may not operate independently. Rule 605:10-17-4 makes it a prohibited dealing for an associate to perform licensed activities outside the supervision of the broker, and it is an equally serious violation for a broker to fail to supervise associates properly.

Why supervision is regulated. Tying every associate to a supervising broker gives the public an experienced, accountable professional standing behind each transaction. The broker is responsible for the associate's conduct, maintaining the trust account that holds client money, and ensuring that everyone performing licensed activities under the firm is properly licensed. The associate, in turn, gains a layer of guidance and oversight during the early years of practice.

Compensation flows through the broker

An associate may accept a commission or other valuable consideration only from the broker with whom he or she is associated. Accepting payment directly from a buyer, a seller, or another broker is a cause for discipline under the License Code (59 O.S. Section 858-312).

Picture an associate named Dana who helps a buyer close on a home. The grateful buyer offers to hand Dana a cash bonus on the spot. Dana must decline. Any compensation she earns has to be paid to her sponsoring broker, who then pays Dana under their written agreement.

The seller likewise pays the listing broker, not the individual associate. Routing all compensation through the broker keeps accountability and recordkeeping centered on the one person the Commission holds responsible for the transaction.

PROHIBITED ACTIVITIES AND CAUSES FOR DISCIPLINE

Causes for suspension or revocation
Prohibited dealings under the rules
Conduct toward the Commission

Causes for suspension or revocation

Section 858-312 of the License Code is the heart of Oklahoma's disciplinary law. It authorizes the Commission, on its own motion or upon a written complaint, to investigate any licensee, and it lists the acts that constitute cause for sanctions (59 O.S. Section 858-312). A licensee need not have completed a wrongful act; attempting it is enough. Among the causes for suspension or revocation are the following:

- making a materially false or fraudulent statement in a license application;
- making substantial misrepresentations or false promises intended to influence or induce others;
- accepting compensation as an associate from anyone other than the associate's broker;
- commingling money belonging to others with the licensee's own funds;
- placing a document on the public records to cloud a title and coerce payment of a commission;
- being unworthy or incompetent to act in a way that endangers the interest of the public.

Prohibited dealings under the rules

The Code condemns untrustworthy, improper, fraudulent, or dishonest dealing, and Rule 605:10-17-4 defines that phrase with a detailed list (OREC Rule 605:10-17-4). The list is not exhaustive, but it gives licensees concrete guidance regarding conduct the Commission will not tolerate. Prohibited dealings include the following:

- making a brokerage service contract, such as a listing, with no definite termination date;
- buying listed property for oneself without full written disclosure to, and approval of, the owner;
- failing to submit all bona fide offers to the seller before an offer is accepted in writing;
- failing to reduce an offer to writing when a prospective buyer asks that it be submitted;
- discouraging a party from obtaining a property inspection;

- failing to disclose, in writing, a known immediate family relationship to a party in the transaction.

A short scenario shows why these rules exist. Imagine a listing agent who receives two written offers on a seller's home within the same hour. The agent happens to prefer the buyer represented by a personal friend, so the agent presents only that offer to the seller. Withholding the second bona fide offer denies the seller the chance to choose the better deal and is a prohibited dealing, regardless of how the transaction eventually turns out.

Disclosing a family relationship. Now suppose an agent represents her brother as he makes an offer on a listed home. She must disclose that relationship in writing to the other party before proceeding. Failing to disclose a known immediate family relationship is an independent violation, even if the price and terms she negotiates are entirely fair. The rule protects the other side's ability to weigh the agent's loyalties for itself.

Conduct toward the Commission

Several causes for discipline concern how a licensee deals with OREC itself. Knowingly providing false or misleading information to the Commission during an investigation, interfering with an investigation by intimidating a witness or withholding evidence, and failing to respond in writing to a complaint are all violations in their own right. A licensee who ignores or obstructs the Commission compounds the original problem and invites a harsher sanction.

THE COMPLAINT AND DISCIPLINARY PROCESS

How a complaint begins
The hearing
Penalties and administrative fines

How a complaint begins

Anyone may file a complaint against a licensee, and the Commission may also open an investigation on its own motion (59 O.S. Section 858-312; OREC Rule 605:10-17-2). Complaints are submitted in writing, and Commission staff investigate by gathering documents and statements. A licensee who receives written notice of a complaint or investigation must provide an adequate written response within fifteen days. Failing to respond within that window is itself a separate cause for discipline, therefore, silence is never a safe strategy.

The hearing

If the investigation supports formal action, the matter proceeds to a hearing conducted under the Oklahoma Administrative Procedures Act and Rule 605:10-17-3. Hearings are public, a court reporter records the proceeding, and the case may be heard by the full Commission, by a panel, or by a hearing examiner. The State presents its case first, subject to cross-examination, and the respondent licensee then presents a defense. When a hearing examiner or panel hears the case, that officer prepares a proposed order for the full Commission to consider, and the Commission issues a final written order that binds the parties unless it is appealed.

Emergency or summary suspension. There is one exception to the ordinary notice-and-hearing sequence. If the Commission finds that the public health, safety, or welfare imperatively requires emergency action, it may summarily suspend a license pending revocation proceedings (OREC Rule 605:10-17-3). This power is reserved for serious, immediate threats to the public and is used sparingly.

Penalties and administrative fines

The Commission's sanctions are calibrated to the violation. For a licensee, an administrative fine must be at least one hundred dollars and may not exceed two thousand dollars for each violation, with an overall cap of five thousand dollars for all violations arising from a single incident or transaction (59 O.S. Section 858-402). Administrative fines must be paid within thirty days of notice.

What happens if a fine goes unpaid. A license may be suspended until a fine is paid. If a licensee does not pay within thirty days, the fine doubles and a second thirty-day period begins. If the doubled fine remains unpaid at the end of that period, the license is automatically revoked (59 O.S. Section 858-402). The escalating structure gives a licensee every chance to comply while making nonpayment costly.

Penalties for unlicensed activity. A person who practices real estate without a license faces a different penalty track. Section 858-401 allows a fine of up to five thousand dollars or the amount of the commissions earned, whichever is greater, for each violation, and the Commission may ask a court to enjoin the unlicensed activity (59 O.S. Section 858-401). Money collected through these penalties is deposited in the Oklahoma Real Estate Education and Recovery Fund, the subject of the next section.

THE OKLAHOMA REAL ESTATE EDUCATION AND RECOVERY FUND

Purpose of the Fund
Eligibility to recover
Payment limits and repayment

Purpose of the Fund

Discipline punishes a licensee, but by itself it does not make an injured consumer whole. The Oklahoma Real Estate Education and Recovery Fund fills that gap. Created in the State Treasury and supported largely by fees paid by licensees and by administrative fines, the Fund reimburses members of the public who win a court judgment against a licensee for damages caused by a violation of the License Code but cannot collect because the licensee will not or cannot pay (59 O.S. Section 858-601).

Eligibility to recover

A consumer cannot simply ask the Fund for money. Recovery is available only after the claimant has gone to court and met a set of conditions (59 O.S. Section 858-603). The principal requirements are these:

- the claimant must have filed an action in district court based on a violation of the License Code;
- the cause of action must have accrued no more than two years before the action was filed;
- the claimant must notify the Commission in writing when the action begins and provide a file-stamped copy of the petition, so OREC can act to protect the Fund;
- the claimant must obtain a judgment and be unable to satisfy it out of the licensee's own assets.

Who cannot recover. The Fund protects the public, not industry insiders. A licensee who acted on his or her own behalf in the transaction, the spouse or personal representative of the licensee, and a claimant who is jointly responsible for the loss are all ineligible to recover.

Payment limits and repayment

When a claim is approved, the Fund pays the unsatisfied portion of the claimant's judgment for actual or compensatory damages, or twenty-five thousand dollars, whichever is less (59 O.S. Section 858-604). Reasonable attorney fees may be reimbursed up to twenty-five percent of the approved amount, but court costs and other expenses are not recoverable. When the Fund pays a claimant, it is subrogated to that person's right to collect from the licensee, meaning the Fund steps into the claimant's shoes to pursue the debt.

The license stays revoked until the Fund is repaid. A payment from the Fund is never a gift to the licensee whose conduct caused it. The license of that licensee is revoked and remains revoked until the licensee repays the Fund in full, together with interest. Reinstatement is impossible until the debt to the Fund is satisfied.

An example ties the limits together. Suppose a court awards a defrauded buyer thirty thousand dollars against an agent, and the agent then files for bankruptcy and cannot pay. The buyer may recover twenty-five thousand dollars from the Fund, the statutory maximum, leaving five thousand dollars uncovered. The agent's license is revoked and cannot be reinstated until the agent reimburses the Fund the twenty-five thousand dollars plus interest. The Fund made the public mostly whole, and the cost ultimately falls back on the wrongdoer.

The education side of the Fund. The Fund's full name includes the word education for a reason. When the balance exceeds two hundred fifty thousand dollars, the Commission may spend the excess on real estate education and research for the benefit of the public and of licensees (59 O.S. Section 858-605). The same pool of money both compensates victims and funds the programs that help prevent future harm.

OREC NOTIFICATION REQUIREMENTS

Reporting criminal convictions
Responding to the Commission
Keeping license information current

Reporting criminal convictions

A licensee who is convicted of, or who pleads guilty or nolo contendere to, any felony must notify the Commission in writing within thirty days after the plea is entered and again within thirty days after the judgment and sentencing (59 O.S. Section 858-312). Failing to report is a separate cause for discipline, independent of the underlying crime. A licensee can therefore face sanctions for the silence itself, apart from any consequence of the conviction.

Responding to the Commission

As noted earlier, a licensee must respond in writing to a complaint or investigation within fifteen days of receiving written notice, and must produce real estate records in his or her possession when the Commission demands them in writing. Prompt, honest communication with OREC is not a courtesy; it is a regulated duty, and ignoring it is grounds for discipline on its own.

Keeping license information current

The Commission can only regulate licensees it is able to locate and identify. For that reason, a licensee must keep OREC informed of changes that affect the license record, including the following:

- a change of personal or firm mailing address;
- a change of the broker with whom an associate is associated, that is, a transfer;
- a change of the legal or trade name used in the business;
- the commencement of a Recovery Fund related lawsuit, as described in the previous section.

Why current information matters. Notices of complaints, hearings, and orders are sent to the address OREC has on file. A licensee who has moved without updating the Commission may never see a notice and may miss a deadline, and a missed deadline can turn a small problem into a suspended or revoked license. Keeping information current is a low-effort habit that protects a career.

25 The Oklahoma Regulatory Environment Snapshot Review

AUTHORITY OF THE REAL ESTATE COMMISSION

The Commission and its members
- OREC is the sole state authority to license and regulate real estate; seven members appointed by Governor with Senate consent; operates under Sunset Law (59 O.S. 858-201);
- five members brokers with 5+ years active experience, one layperson, one approved-school representative; no more than two from one congressional district;

Powers and duties
- issues, denies, renews licenses; approves courses, instructors, schools; investigates; issues cease and desist orders; disciplines by reprimand, added education, suspension, revocation, fines (59 O.S. 858-208);

Code and rules
- License Code is statute at Title 59, 858-101 et seq.; OREC rules at Title 605 OAC add detail; licensee bound by both;

LICENSED ACTIVITIES: ACTS OF THE ASSOCIATES

Licensed activity
- license required to list, sell, buy, exchange, rent, lease, negotiate, or solicit for a fee; doing so unlicensed is a penalized violation;

Associate and broker
- associate (provisional sales associate, sales associate, broker associate) acts only for and under one supervising broker; may not operate independently;

Compensation
- associate may accept compensation only from his or her own broker; payment direct from buyer, seller, or other broker is a cause for discipline (59 O.S. 858-312);

PROHIBITED ACTIVITIES AND CAUSES FOR DISCIPLINE

Causes (858-312)
- false statement on application; substantial misrepresentation or false promise; accepting pay from other than own broker; commingling; clouding title to coerce a commission; incompetency endangering public;

Prohibited dealings (605:10-17-4)
- listing with no termination date; self-purchase without written disclosure and owner approval; failing to submit all bona fide offers; not reducing an offer to writing on request; discouraging inspection; not disclosing family relationship;

Toward the Commission
- false statements during an investigation, witness intimidation, and failure to respond to a complaint are each separate violations;

THE COMPLAINT AND DISCIPLINARY PROCESS

Complaint
- anyone may file in writing; Commission may also act on its own motion; licensee must respond in writing within 15 days (59 O.S. 858-312; 605:10-17-2);

Hearing
- conducted under the APA and 605:10-17-3; public; court reporter; State presents first, then respondent; final written order by the Commission; summary suspension allowed when public welfare requires;

Fines (858-402)
- $100 to $2,000 per violation, $5,000 cap per single transaction; pay within 30 days; unpaid fine doubles, then license auto-revoked;

Unlicensed activity (858-401)
- fine up to $5,000 or commissions earned, whichever greater; injunction available; fines go to the Recovery Fund;

THE OKLAHOMA REAL ESTATE EDUCATION AND RECOVERY FUND

Purpose
- reimburses the public for unsatisfied court judgments against a licensee for Code violations; created in the State Treasury (59 O.S. 858-601);

Eligibility (858-603)
- must file in district court on a Code violation; cause of action within 2 years; notify Commission with file-stamped petition; judgment unsatisfied;
- ineligible: licensee acting on own behalf, spouse or representative of licensee, or party jointly responsible;

Payment (858-604)
- lesser of unsatisfied judgment (actual or compensatory) or $25,000; attorney fees up to 25%, no court costs; Fund subrogated; license stays revoked until repaid with interest; excess over $250,000 funds education;

OREC NOTIFICATION REQUIREMENTS

Felony
- report any felony plea or conviction in writing within 30 days of the plea and within 30 days of judgment and sentencing (59 O.S. 858-312);

Respond
- answer a complaint or investigation in writing within 15 days; produce records on written demand;

Keep current
- notify OREC of address change, broker transfer, name or trade-name change, and a Recovery Fund lawsuit; notices go to the address on file;

26 Oklahoma Licensing

Who Must Hold a License
Salesperson License Requirements
Broker and Broker Associate Requirements
Business Entity Licensing
Licensing Nonresidents
License Renewals and Continuing Education
License Transfer to a New Broker
License Types and Statuses

Chapter 25 introduced the Oklahoma Real Estate Commission and the rules that govern how licensees behave. This chapter turns to the licenses themselves: who must hold one, how each one is earned, how a license is kept current, and what happens to a license over the course of a career.

Oklahoma builds its licenses as a ladder. A newcomer enters as a provisional sales associate, advances to a renewable sales associate, and may later climb to broker associate and broker. Business entities such as corporations and partnerships hold their own broker licenses, and people licensed in other states can practice in Oklahoma as nonresidents. The License Code (Title 59 of the Oklahoma Statutes) sets the core qualifications, and the Commission's rules (Title 605 of the Oklahoma Administrative Code) supply the operating detail. Because licensing questions make up a meaningful share of the Oklahoma portion of the examination, the numbers in this chapter, the clock hours, the years of experience, and the renewal periods, are worth committing to memory.

WHO MUST HOLD A LICENSE

Licensed activity defined
The brokers and the associates
Exceptions to the license requirement

Licensed activity defined

Section 858-301 of the License Code makes it unlawful to act as a real estate broker or associate without a license. The trigger is performing, for another person and for a fee or other valuable consideration, any of the acts the Code treats as real estate brokerage: listing, selling, buying, exchanging, renting, or leasing real estate; negotiating or offering to negotiate any such transaction; and soliciting prospects in connection with those services (59 O.S. Section 858-301). A single paid act is enough to require a license. The fee does not have to be money; any valuable consideration counts.

Why the line is drawn at compensation. The license requirement protects the public from untrained people handling large, complicated transactions for hire. When a person performs these services for pay, the consumer is relying on professional skill and is owed the protections the License Code provides. Performing the same acts for one's own account, or as a favor with no expectation of compensation, does not put the public in that position, which is why the Code ties the requirement to acting for another for consideration.

The brokers and the associates

Oklahoma divides licensees into two broad groups. A **broker** is the responsible professional who may operate a real estate business, hold the trust account, and supervise others. An **associate is** a term that covers the provisional sales associate, the sales associate, and the broker associate. The associate performs licensed activities only under the sponsorship of a broker. Every associate is tied to one supervising broker at a time, and the broker answers to the Commission for the associate's conduct. The chapters that follow build out each of these license types in turn.

Exceptions to the license requirement

The Code lists people who may perform what look like licensed acts without a license because they are not acting for another for a fee. Property owners selling, renting, or leasing their own real estate do not need a license, nor do their regular salaried employees acting within the scope of ownership and management.

A person holding a recorded power of attorney who consummates a contract for an owner is exempt, as are persons acting under court order, such as executors, administrators, trustees, and receivers. These exceptions keep ordinary owners and court officers from being swept into the licensing system.

Consider a homeowner who lists and sells her own house, negotiates directly with buyers, and signs the contract herself. She performs several acts that would require a license if she did them for someone else, but because she is selling her own property she needs no license. If that same homeowner began selling neighbors' homes for a commission, she would cross the line and would need to be licensed.

A modern wrinkle: marketing an equitable interest. The Code closes a gap that has grown with so-called wholesaling. A person who signs a contract to buy a property and then publicly markets that purchase contract, the equitable interest, for sale to another buyer is treated as acting as a real estate licensee and must hold an active license to do so (59 O.S. Section 858-301). The exemption for selling one's own property does not stretch to publicly advertising a contract position the person never intends to close. New licensees should understand this distinction because consumers are increasingly approached by unlicensed wholesalers, and the licensee who works with them needs to know where the legal line falls.

It helps to remember why these rules exist at all. As Chapter 25 explained, the Commission is the sole authority that licenses real estate professionals in Oklahoma, and it does so under the state's police power to protect the public. Licensing is the gate: it ensures that anyone paid to guide a consumer through a real estate transaction has met minimum standards of education, competence, and honesty before taking on that responsibility. Every requirement in this chapter traces back to that purpose.

SALESPERSON LICENSE REQUIREMENTS

Basic qualifications
Education and examination
Application and background check
The provisional license is the entry point

Basic qualifications

The entry-level license in Oklahoma is the provisional sales associate license. To be eligible, an applicant must be at least eighteen years of age and must be a United States citizen or a lawful permanent resident whose status the Commission can verify (59 O.S. Section 858-302). An applicant must also be of good moral character, a standard the Commission evaluates through a criminal background check described below. There is no Oklahoma residency requirement to become a resident licensee; residency for license purposes is determined by where the sponsoring brokerage is located, a point that matters for nonresidents in a later section.

Education and examination

Before applying, the candidate must complete ninety clock hours of approved basic real estate instruction, known as the Basic Course of Real Estate, Part I of II (59 O.S. Section 858-302). That course completion is valid for three years; a candidate who waits longer than three years to use it must take the ninety hours again. After the Commission approves the application, the candidate sits for the licensing examination, which has a national portion and an Oklahoma portion that are scored separately. Both must be passed before a license issues.

Application and background check

Application for licensure is made on the Commission's forms and is accompanied by the required fees (59 O.S. Section 858-302). Every applicant must complete a fingerprint-based national criminal history background check, and the Commission reviews an applicant's criminal history under its rules before issuing a license (OREC Rule 605:10-7-11). A criminal record does not automatically disqualify an applicant; the Commission weighs the nature of the offense and the time that has passed. Once the application is approved, the background check is cleared, the examination is passed, and the Education and Recovery Fund fee is paid, the Commission issues the provisional sales associate license.

A typical path looks like this. Maria finishes the ninety-hour course in the spring, schedules her fingerprinting through the state vendor, and submits her application online. The Commission approves it, she passes both portions of the exam, pays her fees, and receives a provisional sales associate license. She may now perform licensed activities, provided she is sponsored by a broker who agrees to supervise her.

How the examination works. The licensing examination is delivered in two separately scored parts, a national portion and an Oklahoma portion. A candidate who passes one portion but fails the other retakes only the failed portion, and a passing score on a portion is good for a limited period while the candidate completes the rest of the process. An approved application is valid for one year, so a candidate has a defined window in which to pass both portions and place the license with a broker. Planning around these windows keeps a candidate from having to repeat completed steps.

How criminal history is weighed. A criminal record is reviewed, not used as an automatic bar. The Commission considers the nature and seriousness of an offense and how much time has passed, and Oklahoma law sets out how convictions affect eligibility and the periods that may apply (59 O.S. Section 858-301.1). An applicant with a past offense should disclose it fully and provide the supporting court documents, because a candid, well-documented application is handled far more smoothly than one in which a record surfaces unexplained during the background check.

The provisional license is the entry point, not the destination. The provisional sales associate license is non-renewable. It is a one-term license that exists to launch a new licensee, who must complete a post-license course before the license expires in order to move up to a renewable sales associate license. That post-license requirement, and the consequence of missing it, is covered in the final section of this chapter under license statuses.

BROKER AND BROKER ASSOCIATE REQUIREMENTS

The broker license
The broker associate license
Distinguishing the broker from the associate broker

The broker license

A broker license is the senior individual license. An applicant who holds a sales associate license, or who is not currently licensed, must meet four requirements (59 O.S. Section 858-303). First, the applicant must have two years of licensure within the previous five years, or its equivalent. Second, the applicant must complete ninety clock hours of approved advanced real estate instruction, the Advanced Course in Real Estate, together with the Broker in Charge course; the advanced education is valid for three years. Third, the applicant must document ten completed real estate transactions within the past five years on the Commission's forms. Fourth, the applicant must pass the broker examination.

What a broker may do. Passing the broker license requirements qualifies a person to operate a brokerage as a managing broker, proprietor broker, or branch office broker. A broker may hold and manage the trust account, supervise associates, and run a real estate office. With that authority comes responsibility: the Commission holds the broker accountable for the licensed activities of every associate the broker sponsors.

What counts as experience and a transaction. The two-year experience requirement is measured as two years of licensure within the previous five years, which gives a licensee flexibility if a career included a gap. The ten transactions must be documented on the Commission's forms, and a transaction means a completed sale, exchange, purchase, or lease of real estate (59 O.S. Section 858-303). The point is to confirm that a broker candidate has not only studied advanced material but has actually closed deals and understands how a transaction moves from contract to closing.

The Broker in Charge course. The Broker in Charge course is a fifteen-hour course focused on the supervisory and operational duties unique to running a brokerage, such as trust account handling, advertising oversight, and associate supervision. It is required of a person who will be responsible for an office, which is why it is part of the broker requirements but not the broker associate requirements.

The broker associate license

The broker associate license, governed by Section 858-303A, is for a licensee who has earned broker-level qualifications but chooses to keep practicing under another broker's supervision rather than operate a brokerage. An applicant must hold a renewable sales associate or broker associate license and have two years of licensure within the previous five years as a sales associate or provisional sales associate, must complete the ninety clock hours of advanced real estate instruction, and must pass the broker examination (59 O.S. Section 858-303A). The broker associate does not complete the Broker in Charge course and does not document ten transactions, because the broker associate is not taking on the role of running an office.

Distinguishing the broker and broker associate

Supervisory responsibility. The difference between a broker and a broker associate is about role, not raw qualification. Both pass the same broker examination and both complete the same ninety-hour advanced course. The broker has additionally completed the Broker in Charge course and documented ten transactions, and is licensed to operate a brokerage and supervise others. The broker associate has met the education and examination bar but works inside another broker's firm, much as a sales associate does, without holding the supervising-broker responsibilities.

Picture James, a sales associate with three years of experience and fifteen closed transactions. He takes the ninety-hour advanced course and passes the broker examination. If he also completes the Broker in Charge course and submits documentation of ten transactions, he can become a broker and open his own office. If he would rather keep selling under his current managing broker while holding a higher credential, he can become a broker associate instead, skipping the Broker in Charge course and the transaction documentation. A broker associate who later decides to run a brokerage can upgrade to broker by completing the Broker in Charge course and documenting the ten transactions (59 O.S. Section 858-303).

BUSINESS ENTITY LICENSING

Corporations and associations
Partnerships and sole proprietors
Teams must be registered

Corporations and associations

A real estate business does not have to be a single individual. The Commission may license a corporation or association as a broker, but only if the managing officer or managing member holds an individual broker license, and only if every member, officer, or employee who acts as a broker or sales associate also holds the appropriate individual license (59 O.S. Section 858-305). In other words, the entity itself is licensed as the broker, and a qualified individual broker stands behind it as the managing broker responsible to the Commission. The entity must also remain in good standing, which the Commission's rules tie to keeping a qualifying managing broker in place (OREC Rule 605:10-7-8).

Partnerships and sole proprietors

The rule for partnerships is stricter. The Commission may license a partnership as a broker only if each partner holds an individual broker license (59 O.S. Section 858-305). A sole proprietor, by contrast, is simply an individual broker who owns the real estate business directly rather than through an entity. Whatever the form, the licensing principle is constant: a licensed individual broker must be responsible for the firm, and everyone performing licensed activities under it must be properly licensed.

Suppose four experienced agents want to form a brokerage as a limited liability company. The entity can be licensed as a broker, but the managing member must hold an individual broker license, and every member or employee who lists or sells property must hold at least a sales associate license. If they instead chose to organize as a partnership, the Code would require all of the partners, not just the managing one, to be licensed brokers.

Teams must be registered

Many brokerages contain teams, meaning two or more licensees who work under the same broker, work together on transactions, and present themselves to the public as a unit under a team name. The Code requires every team affiliated under a brokerage to be registered with the Commission before the team performs any licensed activities, and the broker must notify the Commission when a team name is no longer used (59 O.S. Section 858-305). Registration lets the Commission see how licensees are grouped and advertised within a firm. The broker submits team name registrations and pays the associated registration fee.

Keeping the entity in good standing. An entity license depends on a qualified managing broker remaining in place. If the managing broker who qualifies a corporation or association leaves, the entity must promptly designate another qualified broker or it risks losing its good standing, because the entity has no authority to act without an individual broker standing behind it (OREC Rule 605:10-7-8). The same logic applies to a partnership that loses one of its broker partners.

Branch offices

A firm that operates from more than one location handles its additional offices as branch offices. A branch office is an extension of the main office and is supervised by a branch office broker, a person who has qualified for a broker license and is designated to direct that location on the firm's behalf. A branch office may not be owned independently of the firm's broker, and the branch office broker is treated as an associate of the managing or proprietor broker for supervision purposes. The structure lets a firm expand geographically while keeping each location under a qualified broker.

LICENSING NONRESIDENTS

The nonresident license
Consent to service of process
Cooperative brokerage as an alternative

The nonresident license

A person who wants to perform licensed activities in Oklahoma but maintains a place of business outside the state may obtain an Oklahoma nonresident license (59 O.S. Section 858-306). The applicant must comply with all applicable provisions of the Code, including passing the Oklahoma state portion of the licensing examination, and must file a certification of licensure from each jurisdiction in which the applicant holds or has held a license; that certification is valid for sixty days (OREC Rule 605:10-7-9). The nonresident pays the same examination and license fees as a resident applicant. A nonresident license stays in force only as long as the licensee remains in good standing in the home jurisdiction.

Residency is set by the brokerage, not the home address. Oklahoma classifies a licensee as resident or nonresident based on where the sponsoring brokerage is located, not where the person lives. A licensee affiliated with an Oklahoma-based brokerage is treated as a resident; a licensee affiliated with an out-of-state brokerage is treated as a nonresident. This distinction drives the continuing education a licensee must complete, as the upcoming license renewal section explains.

Consent to service of process

Before a nonresident license issues, the nonresident must give written consent that lawsuits arising from Oklahoma transactions may be brought in Oklahoma, and must appoint the Secretary-Treasurer of the Commission as the agent to receive service of summons (59 O.S. Section 858-306). Service on that agent is treated as personal service on the nonresident. This arrangement ensures that an Oklahoma consumer harmed by a nonresident licensee can pursue the licensee in an Oklahoma court without having to chase the licensee across state lines.

Cooperative brokerage as an alternative

A broker licensed in another state who does not hold an Oklahoma nonresident license is not entirely shut out. That out-of-state broker may enter a cooperative brokerage agreement with an Oklahoma-licensed broker (59 O.S. Section 858-306). Under such an arrangement each broker conducts real estate activities only in the state where that broker is licensed, and they share the cooperation by agreement. The choice between obtaining a nonresident license and cooperating with an Oklahoma broker depends on how often and how independently the out-of-state broker intends to work in Oklahoma.

For example, a Texas broker who occasionally refers clients moving to Oklahoma City might simply cooperate with an Oklahoma broker and split the resulting fee. A Texas broker who plans to list and sell Oklahoma property regularly would instead obtain an Oklahoma nonresident license, pass the state portion of the exam, and appoint the Commission's Secretary-Treasurer as a service agent.

Credit for experience in another state. An applicant who has been actively licensed in another jurisdiction can often qualify on the strength of that experience. The Commission's rules allow a nonresident applicant who has been actively licensed as a sales associate or broker for at least two of the previous three years to apply on that basis, and they provide a parallel path for a person who moves to Oklahoma and seeks a resident license after holding a license elsewhere (OREC Rule 605:10-7-9; 605:10-7-10). In every case the applicant still passes the Oklahoma state portion of the examination, because the state-specific law is what an out-of-state licensee has not yet been tested on.

LICENSE RENEWALS AND CONTINUING EDUCATION

The three-year renewal cycle
Continuing education hours and subjects
Exemptions and nonresident requirements

The three-year renewal cycle

Oklahoma real estate licenses are issued for three-year terms and must be renewed before they expire. **Continuing education** is the condition of renewal: as a condition of renewing or reactivating a license, each licensee must show the Commission evidence of completing the required continuing education within the thirty-six months immediately preceding the new term (59 O.S. Section 858-307.2). The number of hours and the required subjects are set by Commission rule, and the Commission will not issue an active renewal or reactivate a license until the requirement is met. Renewal access opens in the License Portal sixty days before the expiration date.

Continuing education hours and subjects

A resident sales associate or resident broker associate must complete thirty hours of continuing education each three-year term. Of those, thirteen hours are required subjects and seventeen hours may be electives in any approved category.

- six hours in Contracts and Forms;
- three hours in Professional Conduct;
- one hour in the Oklahoma Broker Relationships Act;

- one hour in Code and Rules;
- one hour in Fair Housing;
- one hour in a designated Hot Topic.

A resident broker also completes thirty hours, but the mix is different. A broker must complete the fifteen-hour Broker in Charge course and six hours in Contracts and Forms, with the remaining nine hours available in any approved category. The heavier supervisory content reflects the broker's responsibility for an office and a trust account.

Exemptions and nonresident requirements

Not every licensee carries the full thirty hours. A licensee on inactive status has no continuing education requirement while inactive, although any hours missed must be completed before returning to active status. Nonresident licensees carry a reduced load of eight hours: one hour in the Oklahoma Broker Relationships Act, one hour in Code and Rules, and six hours in Contracts and Forms, on the premise that the nonresident completes general continuing education in the home state. The provisional sales associate is a special case, with a post-license course rather than ordinary continuing education, covered in the next sections.

Counting hours is straightforward once the required subjects are covered. A resident sales associate might take a six-hour contracts class, a three-hour professional conduct class, and the four one-hour required classes, reaching thirteen required hours, then fill the remaining seventeen with electives on financing, fair housing practice, or technology. Completing all thirty before the expiration date keeps the license active without interruption.

Why these subjects are required. The mandated subjects track the areas where licensees are most likely to cause harm or fall out of step with changing law. Contracts and forms carry the largest required block because most consumer complaints arise from how a contract was written or explained. Professional conduct, the Broker Relationships Act, and code and rules keep licensees current on their duties and on disciplinary standards, while fair housing and the rotating hot topic address areas of active legal and market change. The required core is the Commission's way of steering continuing education toward the knowledge that protects consumers.

Reactivation and the consequence of falling short. Continuing education is required not only to renew an active license but also to reactivate one that has gone inactive; the Commission will not move a license to active status until the outstanding hours are complete. An active licensee who does not finish the required hours by the renewal date does not simply get an extension. The license moves to lapsed status, with the reinstatement consequences described in the final section, which is why experienced licensees treat the renewal date as a hard deadline and often complete their hours well in advance.

LICENSE TRANSFER TO A NEW BROKER

Filing the change of association
Continuity of practice
When a broker refuses to release

Filing the change of association

An associate's license is always tied to a sponsoring broker, so changing brokers is a regulated event. When an associate moves from one firm to another, or relocates between offices within a firm, the change must be filed with the Commission within ten days, and the new broker must provide consent to sponsor the associate (OREC Rule 605:10-11-2). The associate pays a transfer fee for the change of association. Each of these steps is now handled through the online License Portal.

Continuity of practice

An active associate who transfers in a timely manner and in compliance with the ten-day rule may continue to perform licensed activities without a gap, because the license follows the associate to the new broker once the new broker's consent is recorded. This continuity matters because an associate may not perform licensed activities except under a sponsoring broker; a lapse in sponsorship is a lapse in the ability to work.

When a broker refuses to release

Occasionally a broker will not promptly release a departing associate. The rules provide a safety valve. If a broker refuses for any reason to release an associate, the associate notifies the broker and the Commission in writing of the disassociation. The Commission then sends one additional notice to the broker and releases the associate within two business days (OREC Rule 605:10-11-2). The departing associate is therefore not held hostage by a former broker, although questions about compensation already earned are handled separately.

Suppose an associate named Priya decides to join a new brokerage. Her new broker submits consent to sponsor her, and the change is filed within ten days; Priya keeps working without interruption. If her old broker dragged his feet and refused to release her, Priya could notify both the broker and the Commission in writing, and the Commission would release her within two business days after a final notice to the old broker.

Compensation already earned. Releasing an associate and paying an associate are two different questions. The release rules keep a departing associate from being trapped, but they do not erase compensation the associate earned while at the former firm. Money owed on transactions the associate worked before leaving is handled under the agreement between the broker and the associate, separate from the mechanics of transferring the license. When an associate leaves, the former broker is also expected to make every attempt to notify the associate of the disassociation, so that no one is surprised about where the license stands.

LICENSE TYPES AND STATUSES

Active and inactive status
Lapsed licenses and reinstatement
Changing status
Post-license education for provisional sales associates

Active and inactive status

Every license sits in a status that determines what the licensee may do. An active license is a license in good standing. This status permits the licensee to perform real estate transactions under a broker. An inactive license is also in good standing, but the licensee may not perform licensed activities while inactive (59 O.S. Section 858-309). An inactive licensee must still renew every three years, although continuing education is not required to renew an inactive license. The advantage of going inactive rather than letting a license expire is that an inactive licensee can return to active status at any time simply by completing any outstanding continuing education and paying the fee, without reapplying, retesting, or repeating a background check.

Lapsed licenses and reinstatement

A license that is not renewed, or an active license whose continuing education is not completed by the renewal date, **moves to lapsed status** after expiration. A lapsed licensee is no longer in good standing and may not practice. How a lapsed license is restored depends on how long it has been lapsed:

- **lapsed less than one year**: the licensee may renew through the License Portal with additional late fees;
- **lapsed more than one year but less than three years**: the licensee must submit a reinstatement application, pay additional fees, and satisfy examination and background check requirements;
- **lapsed three years or more**: the licensee must submit a new application for licensure and start over.

Why inactive status is the safer parking spot. Because a long lapse can force a licensee to retest or even reapply from scratch, a licensee who needs to step away from the business is almost always better off moving the license to inactive status than letting it lapse. The inactive license preserves the credential and the path back to active practice.

Changing status

A licensee changes status, whether activating, inactivating, transferring, or updating personal information, through the Commission (OREC Rule 605:10-7-3). Placing a license on inactive status is done by submitting a status change request, and activation is requested the same way once any required continuing education is complete. Address, name, and contact changes are made in the licensee's portal profile, and keeping that information current is important because the Commission sends official notices to the address on file.

A status change can also be triggered from outside. Not every status change is the licensee's own choice. Oklahoma law links a real estate license to compliance with the Oklahoma Tax Commission, so a notice of tax noncompliance can affect a licensee's active status until the matter is resolved and the Commission receives confirmation that compliance has been restored.

Active licensees can retrieve their wall certificate and pocket card at any time through the portal, while an inactive licensee, who cannot practice, is not issued those credentials. These housekeeping details are easy to overlook but they signal, at a glance, whether a license is currently good to use.

Post-license education for provisional sales associates

The provisional sales associate license deserves special attention because it is non-renewable and time-limited. To convert it into a renewable sales associate license, the provisional licensee must complete a forty-five clock hour **post-license course**, the Provisional Post-license Course of Real Estate, Part II of II, before the provisional license expires (OREC Rule 605:10-3-7). The course covers practical and legal subjects, including at least three hours of laws and regulations affecting real estate practice. The Commission will not issue a renewable sales associate license until the provisional licensee submits evidence of completing the forty-five hours along with the required forms and fees.

The stakes are high because there is no grace period built into the provisional license. A provisional sales associate who completes the forty-five-hour post-license course and files the paperwork before the expiration date becomes a renewable sales associate and continues without interruption. A provisional sales associate who lets the license expire without completing the course cannot simply renew, because the provisional license is non-renewable; that licensee faces reapplying. The single most important deadline in a new Oklahoma licensee's first term is the date by which the post-license course must be finished.

.

26 Oklahoma Licensing Snapshot Review

WHO MUST HOLD A LICENSE

Licensed activity
- license required to list, sell, buy, exchange, rent, lease, negotiate, or solicit for another for a fee or valuable consideration (59 O.S. 858-301);

Two groups
- broker may operate a business, hold trust account, supervise; associate (provisional SA, SA, broker associate) works only under a sponsoring broker;

Exceptions
- owners selling or leasing own property and their employees; attorney-in-fact; executors, trustees, receivers acting under court order;

SALESPERSON LICENSE REQUIREMENTS

Qualifications
- at least 18; U.S. citizen or lawful permanent resident; good moral character via background check (59 O.S. 858-302);

Education and exam
- 90 clock hours Basic Course Part I, valid 3 years; pass national and Oklahoma exam portions;

Application
- Commission forms and fees; fingerprint background check and criminal-history review (605:10-7-11); Recovery Fund fee; then provisional license issues;
- provisional sales associate license is non-renewable; must complete 45-hour post-license course to become a renewable sales associate;

BROKER AND BROKER ASSOCIATE REQUIREMENTS

Broker (858-303)
- 2 years licensure within last 5; 90-hour advanced course plus Broker in Charge; document 10 transactions in 5 years; pass broker exam; may operate a brokerage;

Broker associate (858-303A)
- renewable SA or broker associate license plus 2 years licensure; 90-hour advanced course; pass broker exam; no BIC, no 10 transactions; works under another broker;

Difference
- same exam and advanced course; broker adds BIC and 10 transactions and runs an office; broker associate practices under a broker;

BUSINESS ENTITY LICENSING

Corp / association
- entity licensed as broker if managing officer or member is a licensed broker and every acting member, officer, or employee is licensed (59 O.S. 858-305; 605:10-7-8);

Partnership
- licensed as broker only if every partner holds a broker license; sole proprietor is an individual broker who owns the business;

Teams
- every team must be registered with the Commission before performing licensed activities; broker notifies when a team name is dropped;

LICENSING NONRESIDENTS

Nonresident license
- place of business out of state; comply with Code and pass Oklahoma state exam portion; file certification of licensure (valid 60 days); same fees; valid only while in good standing elsewhere (59 O.S. 858-306; 605:10-7-9);

Residency
- set by brokerage location: Oklahoma brokerage equals resident, out-of-state brokerage equals nonresident;

Service / cooperation
- must appoint Commission Secretary-Treasurer as service agent; out-of-state broker without OK license may use a cooperative brokerage agreement;

LICENSE RENEWALS AND CONTINUING EDUCATION

Cycle
- licenses renew every 3 years; CE is the condition of renewal, completed within the 36 months before the term (59 O.S. 858-307.2); portal opens 60 days out;

Resident SA / broker assoc.
- 30 hours: 13 required (6 contracts, 3 professional conduct, 1 BRA, 1 code and rules, 1 fair housing, 1 hot topic) plus 17 electives;

Resident broker
- 30 hours: 15-hour Broker in Charge plus 6 contracts plus 9 elective;

Exemptions
- inactive licensees need no CE while inactive; nonresidents need 8 hours (1 BRA, 1 code and rules, 6 contracts);

LICENSE TRANSFER TO A NEW BROKER

Transfer
- change of association filed within 10 days; new broker consents to sponsor; transfer fee paid; done in the License Portal (605:10-11-2);

Continuity
- active associate transferring on time keeps working without a gap; no licensed activity without a sponsoring broker;

Refusal to release
- if a broker will not release, associate notifies broker and Commission in writing; Commission releases within 2 business days after a final notice;

LICENSE TYPES AND STATUSES

Active/ inactive
- active equals good standing and may practice; inactive equals good standing but may not practice, still renews every 3 years, no CE to renew, reactivate by completing CE and fee (858-309);

Lapsed
- under 1 year: renew with late fees; 1 to 3 years: reinstatement application, fees, exam, background; 3 years or more: new application;

Changing status
- activate, inactivate, transfer, and update info through the Commission portal (605:10-7-3); notices go to the address on file;

Post-license (605:10-3-7)
- provisional SA must finish the 45-hour post-license course before expiration to earn a renewable SA license; provisional license is non-renewable;

27 The Oklahoma Broker Relationships Act

Definitions
Brokerage Service Agreements
Services Provided to the Parties
Duties Owed to All Parties
Duties Owed to the Party Served
Disclosure of Duties and Services
Disclosure of the Licensee's Status and Interest
Broker-Salesperson Relationship and Compensation

Most states still describe a real estate professional as an agent who owes a client the fiduciary duties of the common law. Oklahoma took a different road. Through the Oklahoma Broker Relationships Act, codified at Sections 858-351 through 858-363 of the License Code and implemented by the Commission's rules at Title 605, Oklahoma replaced common-law agency with a statutory set of broker relationships. Under this framework a broker is not an agent, a subagent, or a dual agent. Instead, a broker provides brokerage services to one or both parties and owes a fixed list of statutory duties, some to everyone in the transaction and some only to the party the broker is working for. This chapter walks through the definitions, the agreements that create these relationships, the duties owed, the disclosures required, and the rules on compensation. Because the Act differs so sharply from the national model, and because roughly a fifth of the Oklahoma examination is drawn from it, the precise wording in this chapter matters.

DEFINITIONS

Broker and brokerage services
Parties and the transaction
Why the definitions matter

Broker and brokerage services

The Act gives several familiar words specific meanings (59 O.S. Section 858-351). A broker, for purposes of the Act, means a real estate broker and also the broker associate, sales associate, or provisional sales associate whom the broker authorizes to provide brokerage services. In other words, when the Act says broker, it includes the individual licensee working with the public, not just the person who owns the firm. Brokerage services means simply the services a broker provides to a party in a transaction. The firm is the brokerage under which the licensees operate.

Parties and the transaction

A party is a person who is a seller, buyer, landlord, or tenant, or a person involved in an option or exchange of real estate (59 O.S. Section 858-351). Note that a party is not called a client or a principal, because the Act deliberately avoids agency language. A transaction is the activity or process of buying, selling, leasing, renting, optioning, or exchanging real estate, and it expressly includes soliciting, advertising, showing property, presenting offers and counteroffers, entering into agreements, and closing them. The breadth of that definition means the duties in the Act attach across the entire arc of a deal, not just at the closing table.

Why the definitions matter. These definitions carry real weight on the examination and in practice. Because broker includes every licensee, the statutory duties bind a brand-new sales associate exactly as they bind the managing broker. Because the Act speaks of a party rather than a client, a licensee should not assume that working with a buyer creates the kind of loyalty the common law attached to an agent. The relationship is defined by the brokerage service agreement and the statute, not by who happens to be in the car looking at houses.

A contrast with common-law agency. It helps to see what Oklahoma left behind in defining relationships by statute as opposed to common law. In a traditional agency state, a real estate agent who represents a buyer owes that buyer common-law fiduciary duties such as loyalty, obedience, and full disclosure of everything the agent knows, and the agent's knowledge is often imputed to the client. That structure forces hard questions about dual agency and subagency whenever one firm or one cooperating broker touches both sides. Oklahoma sidesteps the whole problem by declaring that a broker is simply not an agent. The duties a broker owes are the duties the statute lists, no more and no less, and they are the same kind of duties whether the broker is helping the buyer, the seller, or both.

BROKERAGE SERVICE AGREEMENTS

What a brokerage service agreement is
How long it lasts
Services to a tenant under property management

What a brokerage service agreement is

A brokerage service agreement is the contract that sets a broker relationship in motion. The Commission's rules define it as an oral or written agreement to provide brokerage services, entered into between a real estate broker and a person who is a party to a real estate transaction (OREC Rule 605:10-15-2). The category is broad: it includes **listing agreements with sellers**, **buyer broker agreements** with buyers, and **property management agreements** with landlords. Every brokerage agreement must incorporate the statutory duties of

Section 858-353 as material terms, so the duties travel with the agreement automatically (59 O.S. Section 858-355.1).

How long service agreements last

A brokerage service agreement remains in full force and effect until it expires or is otherwise terminated by an agreement of the parties (OREC Rule 605:10-15-2). This is why a listing or buyer agreement should always state a definite termination date. As Chapter 25 noted, making a brokerage service contract with no termination date is a prohibited dealing, so the duration of the agreement is not a mere formality but a compliance requirement.

Services to a tenant under property management

The rules address a recurring source of confusion. When a broker manages property for a landlord under a property management agreement, the services the broker provides to a tenant do not create a broker relationship with the tenant unless the parties agree to that in writing (OREC Rule 605:10-15-2). Even so, the broker still owes the tenant the baseline duties of honesty and reasonable skill and care.

The landlord is the party the broker works for, but the tenant is not left without protection. Consider a property manager who leases apartments for an owner. The manager works for the owner under a property management agreement, so the owner is the party served. A tenant who signs a lease is not automatically the manager's client, but the manager must still treat that tenant honestly and competently. If the manager wanted to represent the tenant as well, that arrangement would have to be put in writing.

Oral agreements and the writing the law expects. The rule recognizes that a brokerage service agreement may be oral, which means the statutory duties can attach even before anyone signs a form. As a matter of sound practice, however, brokerage relationships are reduced to writing. The subchapter that houses these rules is titled Disclosures, Brokerage Services, and Statute of Frauds, a reminder that agreements affecting real estate and the right to a commission are far easier to enforce when they are in writing. A written agreement also lets the parties fix the definite termination date the Code requires and document the compensation terms discussed later in this chapter.

The three common agreements illustrate the range. **A listing agreement** is a brokerage service agreement between the firm and a seller; **a buyer broker agreement** is one between the firm and a buyer; and a **property management agreement** is one between the firm and a landlord. Each is a contract to provide brokerage services to a party, each carries the statutory duties as material terms, and each should carry a clear start and end date. The label on the form matters less than the substance: an agreement to provide brokerage services to a party is a brokerage service agreement, whatever it is called.

SERVICES PROVIDED TO THE PARTIES

Serving one party or both
Notice when a firm serves both
Providing fewer services

Serving one party or both

A broker may provide brokerage services to one party or to both parties in a transaction (59 O.S. Section 858-355.1). This is the Oklahoma alternative to the common-law idea of dual agency. Because the broker is never an agent, there is no conflict of fiduciary loyalties to manage; instead, the same statutory duties apply to each party the broker serves. A broker who provides services to either party must describe and disclose those duties in writing before the party signs a contract to sell, purchase, lease, option, or exchange real estate.

Notice when a firm serves both

When a single firm ends up working with both sides of one transaction, the firm must give written notice to both the buyer and the seller that it is providing brokerage services to both parties, and it must do so before the parties sign the contract (59 O.S. Section 858-355.1). The mandatory duties then remain in place for each party. This commonly happens when a firm has a property listed and a buyer who is already working with that same firm wants to make an offer on it.

Picture a brokerage that has listed the Garcia family's home. A buyer who is working with an associate at that same brokerage wants to make an offer on the Garcia listing. The moment the firm is serving both sides, it must notify both the buyer and the seller in writing that it is providing brokerage services to both parties, before either side signs. The associates involved continue to owe each party the full set of statutory duties; neither side is treated as less protected because the firm is on both sides.

Providing fewer services

A broker does not have to perform every step of a transaction, but a broker who intends to provide fewer brokerage services than those needed to complete the transaction must disclose that in writing to the party being served. The disclosure has to describe the steps the broker will not handle and state that the broker assisting the other party is not required to fill those gaps. This keeps a party from assuming a level of help the broker never agreed to provide, and it is reflected in the Commission's standard disclosure form.

The firm and the individual associate. Because the Act defines broker to include both the firm's broker and the associates, a firm can serve both sides of a transaction with two different associates, one working with the buyer and another working with the seller, while still owing each party the full statutory duties. There is no agency conflict to cure, so Oklahoma does not need the elaborate designated-agency machinery that agency states rely on. What the firm must do is give the required written both-parties notice and make sure each associate honors the duties to the party that associate is serving.

A fewer-services example is common in flat-fee and limited-service arrangements. Suppose a seller hires a brokerage only to place the listing in the multiple listing service and otherwise handle the sale himself. The brokerage must disclose in writing the steps it will not perform, such as negotiating offers or coordinating the closing, and must make clear that the buyer's broker is not obligated to take over those tasks for the seller. The seller then proceeds knowing exactly where the brokerage's help stops.

DUTIES OWED TO ALL PARTIES

The mandatory duties to everyone
What confidential information means
Disclosure of property condition

The mandatory duties to everyone

Section 858-353 is the core of the Act. Its first set of duties is owed to all parties in a transaction, is mandatory, and may not be waived or abrogated by a broker (59 O.S. Section 858-353). A broker must do the following for everyone in the deal:

- **treat all parties with honesty** and exercise reasonable skill and care;
- unless specifically waived in writing by a party, receive all written offers and counteroffers, reduce offers and counteroffers to writing on request, and **present all written offers** and counteroffers in a timely manner;
- **account in a timely way for all money** and property the broker receives;
- **keep confidential information confidential**;
- **disclose information about the property** as required by the Residential Property Condition Disclosure Act;
- **comply with the License Code** and all applicable statutes and rules.

What confidential information means

The Act does something unusual: it defines confidential information narrowly and exhaustively. Only four kinds of information are confidential in an Oklahoma transaction (59 O.S. Section 858-353):

- that a party or prospective party **is willing to pay more** or accept less than the amount being offered;
- that a party is willing to agree to financing terms different from those offered;
- **the party's motivating factors for buying**, selling, leasing, optioning, or exchanging the property;
- **any information a party specifically designates as confidential** in writing, unless that information is public.

The limits of confidentiality. Because the list is exhaustive, information that does not fall within it is not confidential under the Act, and **a known material defect in the property is never confidential.** A broker may not stay silent about a leaking roof or a cracked foundation simply because the seller would prefer it kept quiet; the property-disclosure duty overrides any such wish. The broker also may share confidential information when the party consents in writing, when the law requires disclosure, or when the information has become public from a source other than the broker.

A simple example sharpens the point. If a seller privately tells the listing associate that she will accept ten thousand dollars below her asking price, that is confidential and the associate may not reveal it to a buyer. But if the same seller mentions that the home has a chronic drainage problem in the backyard, that is a property condition the associate must disclose, not a secret the associate may keep. The Act protects negotiating posture, not material facts about the property.

How the all-parties duties fit the rest of the Code. The duty to disclose property condition runs through the Residential Property Condition Disclosure Act, which sets out the Disclosure Statement and Disclaimer Statement a seller uses and the licensee's role in delivering them. The duty to account for money and property connects to the trust account rules, which govern how a broker holds earnest money and other funds. And the duty to receive, reduce to writing on request, and timely present all written offers and counteroffers is the statutory basis for the prohibited-dealing rule, discussed in Chapter 25, against failing to submit all bona fide offers. The Act is not an island; it is the relationship backbone that those other rules hang on.

Notice also who is protected. The honesty and reasonable-skill-and-care duty is owed to all parties, which means even a buyer the listing associate is not working for is entitled to honest treatment and competent handling. A listing associate who lies to a prospective buyer about the property violates the Act even though the buyer is not the associate's client, because that particular duty does not depend on a brokerage agreement. The duties owed to everyone form a floor beneath the entire transaction.

DUTIES OWED TO THE PARTY SERVED

The extra duties to the represented party
Compensation disclosure
Duties that survive the relationship

The extra duties to the represented party

Beyond the duties owed to everyone, the Act imposes a second set of mandatory duties owed only to the party for whom the broker is providing brokerage services (59 O.S. Section 858-353). These too may not be waived. The broker must inform that party in writing, when an offer is made, that the party will be expected to pay certain closing costs and brokerage service costs, along with the approximate amount of those costs, and the broker must keep that party informed regarding the transaction. When a broker works with both parties, this set of duties is owed to each of them.

Compensation disclosure

Recent amendments have added compensation transparency to the duties owed to the represented party. A broker must disclose, in writing, the compensation and fees assessed on the transaction to the represented party before the effective date of the contract for sale or lease, and must disclose the time frame for which the compensation agreement is valid. That time frame may not exceed one year, and if no time frame is stated, the agreement defaults to sixty days. These requirements, reflected in the Commission's current disclosure forms, align Oklahoma practice with the national shift toward written, up-front agreement on how a buyer's broker is paid.

In practice this means a buyer's associate cannot wait until closing to spring a fee on the buyer. Before the purchase contract takes effect, the associate puts the compensation in writing, states how long the compensation agreement lasts, and makes sure the buyer understands what the buyer may owe. If the associate forgets to state a duration, the law treats the agreement as lasting sixty days rather than leaving it open-ended.

Why compensation moved to the front of the deal. Newly formed compensation-disclosure duties reflect a **national change in how buyer representation is paid**. For decades a buyer's broker was often compensated through an offer of cooperation made by the listing side, and buyers rarely saw a separate written agreement about it.

Following industry-wide settlements that took effect in 2024, written buyer agreements with clear, up-front compensation terms became the norm, and **Oklahoma folded matching duties into the Act.** The result is that the represented party now learns, in writing and before committing, what the broker will be paid and for how long the compensation arrangement holds.

Duties that survive the relationship

Some duties do not end when the agreement does. After a brokerage relationship terminates, expires, or is completed, the broker still owes two duties (59 O.S. Section 858-358). The broker must **account for all money** and property relating to the transaction, and the broker **must keep confidential** all confidential information received during the relationship. A broker cannot reveal a former party's negotiating limits or motivations after the deal closes any more than during it. Confidentiality, in particular, outlives the relationship that created it.

DISCLOSURE OF DUTIES AND SERVICES

When and how the disclosure is made
Confirmation in the contract
The Commission's disclosure form

When and how the disclosure is made

The Act does not leave the duties unspoken. A broker who provides brokerage services to one or both parties must describe and disclose those duties and responsibilities in writing before the party or parties sign a contract to sell, purchase, lease, option, or exchange real estate (59 O.S. Section 858-355.1). The disclosure is made up front, while a party can still absorb it, rather than buried in the closing paperwork. The point is that every party should understand, before committing, exactly what the broker is required to do and not do.

Confirmation in the contract

Disclosure alone is not enough; it must be confirmed. The written disclosures required by the Act must be confirmed in writing by each party in a separate provision that is incorporated in or attached to the contract to purchase, option, or exchange real estate (59 O.S. Section 858-356). This confirmation creates a clear record that the party received the disclosure and understood the broker's role, which protects the party and the broker alike if a dispute arises later.

The Commission's disclosure form

To standardize all of this, the Commission publishes a **Disclosure of Brokerage Duties, Responsibilities and Services form**, with versions directed to buyers and to sellers. The form lists the mandatory duties in plain language, explains what happens when a firm serves both parties, addresses a broker who will provide fewer services, and provides the signature block by which each party confirms receipt. Using the current Commission form is the simplest way for a licensee to meet the disclosure and confirmation requirements correctly.

In a typical sale, the buyer's associate hands the buyer the brokerage duties disclosure at the first substantive meeting, walks through the mandatory duties, and has the buyer acknowledge receipt. When the purchase contract is later prepared, the confirmation provision is incorporated into or attached to the contract and signed. The same sequence happens on the seller's side with the seller version of the form.

Two disclosure versions, one purpose. The buyer and seller versions of the form differ in wording but share a purpose: **to put each party on notice, before signing, of exactly what the broker must do**. Both versions list the mandatory duties owed to all parties and to the party served, explain the both-parties notice, and contain the confirmation signature block. A licensee who consistently delivers the correct version, reviews it with the party, and secures the confirmation in the contract has satisfied the heart of the Act's disclosure scheme. Skipping or mishandling that step is one of the more common and avoidable ways a licensee draws a complaint.

The form can be viewed here - https://oklahoma.gov/content/dam/ok/en/orec/documents/contracts-and-forms-page/2026-contract-forms/2026%20Disclosure%20of%20Brokerage%20Service%20-%20Buyer.pdf.

DISCLOSURE OF THE LICENSEE'S STATUS AND INTEREST

Disclosing licensed status
Buying or selling with an interest
Beneficial interests and referral fees

Disclosing licensed status

A licensee must be transparent about being a licensee. Commission rules require a licensee to disclose licensed status in advertising, so that a member of the public dealing with the licensee knows a real estate professional is involved (OREC Rule 605:10-9-4). This matters most when a licensee is dealing for the licensee's own account, because the other side is entitled to know that the person across the table has professional training and is bound by the License Code.

Buying or selling with an interest

When a licensee buys or sells property in which the licensee has an interest, the licensee must make full written disclosure of that interest to all parties in the transaction. As Chapter 25 noted, purchasing property for oneself, or for an entity in which the licensee has an interest, without full written disclosure to all parties is a prohibited dealing, and buying listed property without disclosing the interest to and obtaining the approval of the owner is a separate violation (OREC Rule 605:10-15-1; 605:10-17-4). When a licensee acts as a licensee in the deal, the transaction should also be completed under the supervision of the licensee's broker.

Beneficial interests and referral fees

Financial relationships. The disclosure duty includes financial relationships as well. A licensee may not, without disclosing the fact in writing to all parties on both sides of the transaction, accept a fee, commission, rebate, kickback, or other compensation for recommending or referring a product or service, or own a beneficial interest in an entity that provides such a product or service to buyers, sellers, or tenants (OREC Rule 605:10-15-1). An associate ordinarily reports the interest to the broker, who carries the primary responsibility to make the written disclosure, and the obligation is a continuing one.

Two quick examples show the reach of these rules. First, if an associate wants to buy a home that her own brokerage has listed, she must disclose in writing to the seller that she is a licensee with an interest and obtain the owner's approval. Second, if an associate refers buyers to a title or mortgage company in which the associate holds an ownership stake, the associate must disclose that beneficial interest in writing to the parties before making the referral. In both cases the cure is the same: put the interest in writing, in front of everyone affected, before proceeding.

Family relationships. The disclosure net also includes close personal ties. As Chapter 25 noted, failing to disclose in writing a known immediate family relationship to a party in a transaction for which the broker is providing services is a prohibited dealing (OREC Rule 605:10-17-4). An associate who represents a buyer making an offer on a relative's home, or who is selling to a relative, must disclose that relationship in writing so the other side can weigh it. The principle behind status, interest, and family disclosures is identical: anything that could color the licensee's judgment belongs on the table, in writing, before the parties commit.

Acting as a licensee versus acting as an owner. Whether these rules apply turns on the capacity in which the licensee is acting. If a licensee is using professional skills in the deal, the licensee is acting as a licensee and the disclosure and supervision rules apply in full. If, by contrast, the licensee simply hires a separate, independent broker to sell the licensee's own property and pays that broker a commission, the licensee is acting as an ordinary owner. The distinction matters because it determines which set of obligations governs the transaction, and a licensee who is unsure should err toward disclosing and working under the broker's supervision.

BROKER-SALESPERSON RELATIONSHIP AND COMPENSATION

Associates work through the broker
Compensation does not determine the relationship
No agency, no vicarious liability

Associates work through the broker

Although the Act treats each licensee as a broker for duty purposes, the licensing structure still funnels everything through the firm's broker. An associate provides brokerage services under the sponsorship of a broker and is compensated by that broker, not directly by the parties. The broker, in turn, may agree on how brokerage services are priced. Nothing in the Act requires a broker to charge, or prohibits a broker from charging, a separate fee for each duty or service provided during a transaction (59 O.S. Section 858-359).

Compensation does not determine the relationship

One of the most tested points in the Act is that money does not define the relationship. The payment or promise of payment of compensation by a party to a broker does not determine what relationship, if any, has been established between the broker and that party (59 O.S. Section 858-359). **What creates the relationship is the brokerage service agreement**, not who pays. Likewise, when a broker receives a fee based on the selling price or lease cost of a transaction, that does not by itself constitute a breach of any duty.

This principle has grown more important as buyer-broker compensation has moved into the open. Suppose a seller pays the listing broker, who in turn shares part of the fee with the broker working with the buyer. That payment does not make the buyer's broker the seller's representative, and it does not make the seller a client of the buyer's broker. Each broker's relationship is set by that broker's own agreement with a party, and the flow of money between brokers does not rewrite it.

No agency, no vicarious liability

The Brokerage Relationship Act ties the overall framework together by abrogating common-law agency. The statutory duties replace and abrogate the fiduciary or other duties a broker would owe a party under common-law agency, and remedies at law and equity supplement the Act (59 O.S. Section 858-360). A broker is not an agent, subagent, or dual agent, and no offer of subagency may be made to other brokers, although brokers may cooperate with one another. Because the broker is not an agent, a party to a transaction is not vicariously liable for the acts or omissions of a licensee providing brokerage services under the Act (59 O.S. Section 858-362).

Cooperation without subagency. Cooperation and subagency are not the same thing, and the difference is central to the Oklahoma model. Two brokers may cooperate on a transaction, dividing the work and sharing compensation, without either becoming the subagent of the other or of the other's party. In an agency state, a cooperating broker historically could be a subagent of the seller, which exposed the seller to liability for that broker's conduct. **Oklahoma forbids offers of subagency** precisely to prevent that linkage, so cooperation here is an arrangement between brokers that does not pull either party into responsibility for the other broker's behavior.

A note on the word agent. Even though Oklahoma brokers are not agents in the legal sense, the Act permits a broker and the broker's associates to use the word agent in a trade name and as a common term of the trade (59 O.S. Section 858-361). Thus a licensee may still call herself a real estate agent in everyday speech and marketing. The label is allowed; what the Act removes is the common-law agency relationship and the fiduciary duties and vicarious liability that came with it.

The practical effect for a consumer is reassuring. If a buyer's licensee makes a mistake or commits a wrongful act, the seller is not on the hook for it, and neither is the buyer for the acts of the seller's licensee, because no agency relationship makes one party answerable for another's licensee. Responsibility stays with the licensee and the supervising broker, which is exactly where the License Code places accountability.

Taken together, the pieces of the Act form a coherent system. Definitions set the vocabulary, brokerage service agreements create the relationships, and the statutory duties, some owed to everyone and some owed to the party served, supply the substance. Disclosure and written confirmation make the relationship transparent, the status and interest rules keep the licensee's loyalties on the record, and the compensation and abrogation provisions settle who pays, what that payment means, and who bears responsibility when something goes wrong. A licensee who understands the Act as a system rather than a list of isolated rules will find the Oklahoma model both simpler and more protective than the common-law agency it replaced.

27 The Oklahoma Broker Relationships Act Snapshot Review

DEFINITIONS

Broker
- includes the real estate broker and the authorized broker associate, sales associate, or provisional sales associate providing brokerage services (59 O.S. 858-351);

Party/ transaction
- party is a seller, buyer, landlord, tenant, or person in an option or exchange, not a client; transaction spans soliciting through closing;

BROKERAGE SERVICE AGREEMENTS

Definition
- oral or written agreement to provide brokerage services; includes listings, buyer broker, and property management agreements; incorporates 858-353 duties as material terms (605:10-15-2; 858-355.1);

Duration
- in force until it expires or is terminated by agreement; a contract with no termination date is a prohibited dealing;

Tenant
- managing for a landlord does not create a relationship with the tenant unless agreed in writing; broker still owes the tenant honesty and reasonable skill and care;

SERVICES PROVIDED TO THE PARTIES

One or both
- broker may serve one party or both; Oklahoma substitute for dual agency; same statutory duties apply to each party served (858-355.1);

Both-party notice
- firm serving both sides must give written notice to both before signing; common when a firm's buyer offers on the firm's listing;

Fewer services
- broker providing fewer services must disclose in writing the steps not provided and that the other broker need not fill them;

DUTIES OWED TO ALL PARTIES

Mandatory (858-353A)
- honesty and reasonable skill and care; receive, reduce on request, and timely present written offers and counteroffers; account for money and property; keep confidential information confidential; disclose property condition; comply with the Code;

Confidential (only four)
- willing to pay more or accept less; willing to accept different financing; motivating factors; info designated confidential in writing unless public;
- a known material defect is never confidential; may disclose with written consent, when required by law, or when already public from another source;

DUTIES OWED TO THE PARTY SERVED

Extra duties (858-353B)
- inform in writing of costs when an offer is made; keep the party informed; owed to each party when serving both;

Compensation
- disclose compensation and fees in writing before the contract effective date; state the agreement time frame, max 1 year, default 60 days;

Survive (858-358)
- after termination the broker still accounts for money and property and keeps confidential information confidential;

DISCLOSURE OF DUTIES AND SERVICES

When
- describe and disclose duties in writing before the party signs a contract (858-355.1); made up front, not at closing;

Confirm (858-356)
- each party confirms the disclosure in writing in a separate provision incorporated in or attached to the contract;

Form
- Commission publishes buyer and seller versions of the brokerage duties disclosure form; using the current form meets the requirement;

DISCLOSURE OF THE LICENSEE'S STATUS AND INTEREST

Status
- licensee must disclose licensed status in advertising (605:10-9-4);

Interest
- buying or selling with an interest requires full written disclosure to all parties and, for listed property, the owner's approval (605:10-15-1; 605:10-17-4);

Beneficial interest
- written disclosure required to accept a referral fee or own a beneficial interest in a product or service entity; associate reports to broker; duty is continuing;

BROKER-SALESPERSON RELATIONSHIP AND COMPENSATION

Through the broker
- associate works under and is paid by the broker; broker may or may not charge separate fees per service (858-359);

Relationship
- payment does not determine the relationship; the brokerage service agreement does; a price-based fee is not a breach (858-359);

No agency (858-360-362)
- statutory duties abrogate common-law agency; broker is not agent, subagent, or dual agent; parties not vicariously liable; may use agent in a trade name (858-361);

28 Regulation of Brokerage Practices

Advertising Regulation
Unlicensed Assistants and Licensed Activity
Broker Supervision
Place of Business Requirements
Trade Names
Teams
Cessation of Brokerage Activities
Impact of Broker Suspension or Cessation
Wholesaling
Trust Accounts

The earlier chapters explained who is licensed and what duties a broker owes. This chapter turns to the day-to-day operation of a real estate business and the rules that keep it honest and orderly. Most of these rules are enunciated in Subchapter 9 of the Commission's regulations, titled Broker's Operational Procedures, supplemented by the trust account rules of Subchapter 13 and by several License Code sections. The topics range from how a listing may be advertised, to who may answer the phones, to how a broker must handle other people's money, to what happens when a broker dies, retires, or is disciplined. A new requirement governing wholesalers, effective in late 2025, is included as well. The unifying theme is that the broker is responsible for the conduct of the business, including the people and the money that flow through it.

ADVERTISING REGULATION

What counts as advertising
Core advertising rules
Internet and social media
Broker oversight and approval

What counts as advertising

The Commission defines advertising broadly. It means all forms of representation, promotion, and solicitation disseminated in any manner and by any means of communication, expressly including social networking, for any purpose related to licensed real estate activity (OREC Rule 605:10-1-2). That sweep matters because it means a yard sign, a newspaper ad, a website, a text blast, and a social media post are all advertising and all subject to the same rules. A licensee cannot escape the advertising regulations by moving a promotion onto a personal social media account.

Core advertising rules

The central rules appear in Rule 605:10-9-4. When advertising, a broker must use the registered business trade name or the name under which the broker is licensed, and an advertisement must make clear that the advertiser is a real estate broker and not a private party, using a word such as agency, company, realty, or real estate. The specific requirements include the following:

- a yard sign must include the broker's office telephone number;
- no advertisement may show only a post office box, a telephone number, or a street address;
- a broker operating under a franchise name must reveal the franchise name along with the broker's name or trade name in advertising and office identification;
- a firm may not register or use the trade name of another licensed firm;
- open house and directional signs used with the broker's signs need not carry the associate's broker name and telephone number.

Internet and social media

Because advertising includes social networking by definition, **online promotion is held to the same standards as print**. An associate who posts a listing on a social platform, runs an online ad, or maintains a real estate website is advertising and must identify the broker and comply with the trade name and broker-identification rules. The medium does not lower the bar; an Internet advertisement must satisfy the same disclosure requirements that a print advertisement would.

Broker oversight and approval. Advertising is ultimately the broker's responsibility. Associates advertise under the broker's name and under the broker's oversight, and the broker is accountable for what goes out. Several elements require the broker's approval, such as a team's use of a personal insignia or of a domain registered with the broker. The prudent broker maintains a written advertising policy and reviews associate advertising, because a misleading or noncompliant advertisement exposes the broker, not just the associate, to discipline.

Two small details round out the rules. Legal abbreviations following the trade name or licensed name are acceptable so long as the public can easily identify them, and franchise advertising other than institutional brand promotion must reveal the franchise name together with the broker's name or trade name. The thread running through every requirement is that a consumer reading the advertisement should be able to tell that a licensed broker is behind it and which broker that is. An associate who posts a just-listed photo to social media, for example, cannot leave the brokerage unnamed; the post is advertising and must identify the broker just as a yard sign would.

UNLICENSED ASSISTANTS AND LICENSED ACTIVITY

The line between licensed and unlicensed activity
What unlicensed assistants may and may not do
The broker remains responsible

The line between licensed and unlicensed activity

A real estate office runs on a mix of licensed and unlicensed staff, and the law draws a firm line between them. Any act that the License Code treats as real estate brokerage, such as listing, selling, showing for compensation, soliciting clients, or negotiating terms, requires a license when done for another for a fee (59 O.S. Section 858-301). Knowingly cooperating with an unlicensed person to perform licensed real estate activities is itself a prohibited dealing (OREC Rule 605:10-17-4). The question is therefore not whether a task is helpful, but whether it is a licensed activity.

What unlicensed assistants may and may not do

An unlicensed assistant may perform administrative and clerical support that does not require professional real estate judgment. That typically includes answering the telephone and forwarding calls, scheduling appointments, preparing and distributing marketing materials at the broker's direction, placing and removing signs, and assembling paperwork. What an unlicensed assistant may not do is perform a licensed activity: showing property to prospects, negotiating price or terms, discussing the merits of a property or a contract, or holding himself or herself out as a licensee. When a task crosses into judgment, advice, or negotiation, it requires a license.

The broker remains responsible. The Commission places the burden of getting this right on the broker. A broker is responsible for all real estate related activities of any unlicensed assistant working within the firm (OREC Rule 605:10-9-1). If an unlicensed assistant strays into negotiating a deal or advising a buyer, the broker answers for it. The safest practice is to train unlicensed staff on the boundary, supervise them closely, and make sure that anything resembling a licensed activity is handled by a licensee.

Consider a busy listing office. The unlicensed assistant can schedule showings, order signs, and email a flyer to a prospect, all without a license. But the moment a prospect on the phone asks whether the seller would take less, or asks the assistant to explain a contract term, the assistant must hand the matter to a licensee. The assistant facilitates; the licensee advises and negotiates.

A related boundary among licensees. The same concern about people acting beyond their authority appears one level up. An associate who does not hold a broker or branch broker license but intentionally acts in the capacity of a broker commits a prohibited dealing (OREC Rule 605:10-17-4). The licensing ladder is meant to be respected at every rung: an unlicensed person may not do licensed work, and a licensee may not perform at a level the license does not authorize. Keeping each person within the scope of his or her own authority is a recurring theme of brokerage regulation.

BROKER SUPERVISION

The duty to supervise
Ensuring associates are licensed and supervised
Practical supervision

The duty to supervise

The broker is the responsible head of the firm, and the Commission holds the broker accountable for the actions of every associate assigned to the broker (OREC Rule 605:10-1-2). Supervision is not a courtesy; it is a licensing obligation. A broker who fails to properly supervise associates, or who permits an associate to operate as a broker, or who lends the broker's license to an associate, commits a prohibited dealing (OREC Rule 605:10-17-4). The structure of Oklahoma licensing assumes a real, working chain of responsibility from the broker down to each associate.

Ensuring associates are licensed and supervised

Two rules anchor the supervision duty. A broker must ensure that all persons performing real estate licensed activities under the broker are properly licensed, and an associate may not perform licensed activities outside the broker's supervision (OREC Rule 605:10-17-4). Together these provisions mean a broker cannot look the other way while an unlicensed or improperly supervised person does licensed work, and an associate cannot freelance outside the firm's oversight. The associate's authority to act flows only through the sponsoring broker.

Policy compliance. In practice, supervision means the broker sets policies, reviews contracts and advertising, monitors trust account activity, and stays reachable when associates need guidance. A broker who manages a large firm often designates experienced licensees to help, but the responsibility remains the broker's. If an associate mishandles a transaction, the Commission will look first to whether the broker had reasonable systems in place to supervise the work.

Supervision includes paying associates fairly.. Because associates are paid only through their broker, the License Code makes it a violation for a broker, after receiving a commission, to fail to render an accounting to and pay an associate the associate's earned share of that commission. Supervision is not only about controlling associates; it is also about dealing honestly with them. A broker who collects a commission and then stalls or shortchanges the associate who earned it has breached a duty the Commission will enforce, which is part of why the broker-associate relationship is treated as a regulated one rather than a purely private arrangement.

ENV PLACE OF BUSINESS REQUIREMENTS

Maintaining a place of business
Office identification and the home office
Branch offices
Change of address

Maintaining a place of business

Every broker must maintain a definite place of business (59 O.S. Section 858-310; OREC Rule 605:10-9-1). Associates may not have their own place of business; an associate must be registered with a place of business maintained and registered in the name of the broker. A broker may serve as the broker for more than one firm, but only if the firms are at the same location. Licenses are issued electronically to each licensee through the individual License Portal and are tied to the registered office.

Office identification and the home office

Each place of business must be properly identified to the public (OREC Rule 605:10-9-2). The office may be located in the broker's residence, which Oklahoma expressly permits, so long as it is registered and identified as required. The identification rules exist so that consumers and the Commission can readily tell that a given location is a licensed real estate office and which broker stands behind it.

Branch offices

If a broker maintains more than one place of business and an additional location is an extension of the main office, the broker must obtain a branch office license for each additional location (59 O.S. Section 858-310; OREC Rule 605:10-7-7). Each branch office must be under the direction and supervision of a separate broker, who is considered the managing broker of that branch. A branch office may not be independently owned by anyone other than the firm's broker or entity. The branch structure lets a firm expand to new locations while keeping each one under a qualified, supervising broker.

Change of address. A place of business is a registered fact, so it must be kept current. A broker who changes the office address or office telephone number must notify the Commission of the change (OREC Rule 605:10-9-5). Because associate licenses are tied to the broker's registered place of business, an unreported move can leave the firm's records and the Commission's records out of step, which is why the notice requirement is treated as a compliance matter and not a mere formality.

Branch management. The branch broker requirement deserves emphasis because it shapes how firms grow. A person designated to manage a branch office must be broker-qualified, and a broker activating or reinstating as a branch broker, proprietor broker, or broker manager must document ten real estate transactions within the past five years (OREC Rule 605:10-7-9). A firm cannot simply open a storefront in another town and staff it with associates; it must place a qualified, accountable broker in charge of that location. The one exception to needing a separate branch broker is when the additional location is at the same place as the main office, in which case the main broker may cover both.

TRADE NAMES

What a trade name is
Registering trade names
Name changes

What a trade name is

A trade name is the name a firm is known as, and it uses its advertising to promote and generate publicity for the firm (OREC Rule 605:10-1-2). A firm may do business under the name on its license or under a separate trade name, but either way the public-facing name is regulated. The point of regulating trade names is to prevent confusion about which licensed brokerage a consumer is actually dealing with.

Registering trade names

Every trade name a firm uses must be registered with the Commission (OREC Rule 605:10-9-3). A firm may not register or use a trade name that belongs to another licensed firm, and the advertising rules require that the trade name still make clear the advertiser is a real estate broker rather than a private party. A broker adds, edits, or removes trade names through the License Portal, and using an unregistered trade name in advertising is a compliance problem because the advertising rules are keyed to the registered name.

Name changes

When a licensee or firm changes a name, the change is processed under the Commission's name-change rule (OREC Rule 605:10-7-5). Keeping names accurate matters across the system: the licensed name, the registered trade names, and the names that appear in advertising all need to align so that the public, the broker, and the Commission are working from the same identity for the business.

Suppose a broker licensed as Johnson Realty LLC wants to market under the catchier name Sooner Sky Realty. The broker registers Sooner Sky Realty as a trade name with the Commission and may then advertise under it. The broker may not, however, adopt a trade name already registered to another licensed brokerage, and every advertisement under the trade name must still signal that Sooner Sky Realty is a real estate broker.

One identity, consistently used. Trade name regulation is really about a single, consistent public identity for the brokerage. The name on the license, the registered trade names, the team names, and the words in every advertisement should all point clearly to one licensed broker. When those identifiers drift apart, consumers lose the ability to tell who they are dealing with and the Commission loses the ability to hold the right broker accountable, which is the harm the registration and advertising rules are designed to prevent.

TEAMS

What a team is and why it is registered
Team name standards
Team advertising

What a team is and why it is registered

A team is any two or more licensees who work under the same broker, work together on transactions, and present themselves to the public as a unit under a team name (59 O.S. Section 858-305). The Commission requires every team affiliated under a brokerage to be registered before the team performs any licensed activities, and the broker notifies the Commission when a team name is no longer used (OREC Rule 605:10-9-3.2). Registration lets the Commission track how licensees are grouped and advertised within each firm. A team registration carries a fee.

Team name standards

A team name must be approved by the broker and must be unique. It may not be already registered to another real estate team in Oklahoma, and it may not be identical to any association, corporation, or partnership licensed as a real estate entity by the Commission (OREC Rule 605:10-9-3.2). The Commission reserves the right to deny a team name that is so similar to an existing team name, trade name, or brokerage that approval would likely confuse the public. The standard, as with trade names, is consumer clarity about who is who.

Team advertising

Include the broker's name. Team advertising must keep the broker in front of the public. All team advertising must include the name of the team's broker, or the name under which the broker operates, in a way that is prominent, conspicuous, and easily identifiable, which the rule defines as the broker's reference being at least fifty percent as large as any team reference in the advertisement (OREC Rule 605:10-9-4). With the broker's approval, a team may use its own insignia and a website domain registered with the broker, and within that website the broker's reference must appear on every page.

Imagine an advertisement for The Prairie Group, a team within Sooner Sky Realty. The advertisement may feature the team name, but the broker reference, Sooner Sky Realty, must appear at least half as large as The Prairie Group, so a consumer can plainly see which brokerage stands behind the team. If the team runs its own website, every page must carry the broker reference, not just the home page.

Registration is the broker's job. Team registration is requested through the broker, not the individual associates, and it carries a registration fee. The broker submits the team name for approval, and the broker notifies the Commission when a team name is retired. This keeps accountability where the Code always places it, with the broker, and prevents associates from spinning up public-facing team identities the broker has not vetted. A team is a marketing arrangement within a brokerage, never a substitute for the brokerage itself, and the registration and advertising rules exist to keep that distinction clear to the public.

CESSATION OF BROKERAGE ACTIVITIES

Voluntarily ceasing real estate activities
Death or disability of the broker
Branch office closing

Voluntarily ceasing real estate activities

When a broker decides to stop practicing, the wind-down is regulated so that pending business and other people's money are protected. A broker ceasing real estate activities must notify the Commission in writing of the date of cessation, properly conclude or transfer pending transactions, account for and disburse any trust funds, discontinue advertising and remove signs, and arrange for records to be retained (OREC Rule 605:10-9-7). Real estate transaction and trust account records must be kept for a minimum of five years. The goal is an orderly close that leaves no consumer stranded mid-transaction and no funds unaccounted for.

Death or disability of the broker

If a broker dies or becomes unable to act, the rules set forth a remedial procedure (OREC Rule 605:10-9-6). For a corporation, association, or partnership, the entity-licensing rules govern, to wit, that another qualified broker can step in. For a sole proprietor, all brokerage activity must cease, and a family attorney or representative should notify the Commission in writing of the date of death or disability and advise the Commission where the records are located. All advertising in the firm name must be terminated and offering signs removed within thirty days of the death or disability.

Branch office closing

Closing a branch office follows its own checklist (OREC Rule 605:10-9-8). Unless the Commission approves otherwise, the main office broker closes a branch by notifying the Commission in writing of the closing date and advising where the records will be stored and retained for at least five years, and by returning or destroying the branch office license certificate and pocket identification card along with the associated license certificates.

The Commission must receive the required items when notice of closing is given, although a broker may request additional time. Records retention is the common thread through all of these closures. Whether a broker retires, dies, or closes a branch, real estate transaction and trust account records must be preserved for at least five years, and the Commission must be told where they are kept. This protects consumers and the Commission long after the office doors close, because questions about a past transaction or a past trust deposit can surface years later. A broker who is retiring should treat records retention as seriously as the handoff of pending deals.

A short example ties the cessation rules together. A sole proprietor broker decides to retire at the end of the year. She notifies the Commission in writing of the cessation date, refers her active listings to other brokers with each owner's agreement, disburses or transfers the earnest money she holds, takes down her advertising and signs, and arranges to store her files for five years. If she had died unexpectedly, her family attorney would notify the Commission of the date, identify where the records are kept, and see that all advertising in the firm name ended within thirty days.

IMPACT OF BROKER SUSPENSION OR CESSATION

When a broker can no longer act
Effect on associates and branch offices
Listings, advertising, and funds

When a broker can no longer act

When a broker's authority ends, whether by discipline or by ceasing activity, the consequences ripple through everyone working under that broker. A suspended or revoked licensee must destroy or return the license certificate and pocket identification card to the Commission on or before the effective date, and may not engage in any activity that requires a license (OREC Rule 605:10-17-6). The same protective logic applies when a broker simply ceases operating: the people and transactions under that broker need to be properly dealt with.

Effect on associates and branch offices

The most immediate effect of a work stoppage falls on the associates. When a broker's license is suspended or revoked, the associates under that broker are automatically placed on inactive status for the duration of the broker's inactivity, unless an associate requests a transfer to another broker (OREC Rule 605:10-17-6). If the broker had a branch office, the branch license is placed inactive and its licensees are likewise placed inactive unless the Commission orders otherwise or they transfer. An associate who wants to keep working must move promptly to a new sponsoring broker.

Listings, advertising, and funds

Protecting consumers. Several specific restrictions protect consumers in the interim. A suspended or revoked broker

- may not assign listings to another broker without the written consent of the property owner,
- may not advertise real estate in any manner and must remove all advertising, and
- may not have the office telephone answered in a way suggesting the broker is still active (OREC Rule 605:10-17-6).

Pending contracts, items, and monies placed with the broker must be handled as the Commission directs so that earnest money and transactions in progress are not caught in limbo. Picture a brokerage whose broker is suspended. The associates do not automatically lose their licenses, but each is placed inactive and must transfer to another broker to keep working. The suspended broker cannot quietly hand the firm's listings to a friend down the street; each owner must consent in writing. All of the firm's advertising must come down, and the trust funds and pending deals are handled under the Commission's direction.

Discipline and voluntary cessation converge. Although one situation is involuntary and the other is a choice, a disciplinary suspension and a voluntary cessation raise the same practical problems: associates who need a new broker, listings that need consent to move, advertising that must come down, and trust funds and pending contracts that must be protected. That is why the suspension rules and the cessation rules read so similarly. In either case the Commission's overriding concern is that consumers in the middle of a transaction are not harmed because the broker they were relying on can no longer act.

WHOLESALING

The licensing line for equitable interests
The 2025 wholesaler disclosure law
Consequences of noncompliance

The licensing line for equitable interests

Wholesaling is the practice of putting a property under contract and then selling or assigning that contract, the equitable interest, to another buyer for a profit. Oklahoma defines a wholesaler as a person or entity in the business of securing, negotiating, or facilitating the sale of residential real estate primarily to transfer, assign, or sell an equitable interest for financial profit, including one who contracts to buy with the intent to assign before taking ownership (59 O.S. Section 858-102).

As Chapter 26 noted, publicly marketing for sale an equitable interest in a purchase contract is treated as acting as a real estate licensee, so an unlicensed person who advertises a contract position to the public is engaged in licensed activity (59 O.S. Section 858-301).

The 2025 wholesaler disclosure law

Effective November 1, 2025, Oklahoma imposed specific consumer protections on wholesalers dealing with homeowners (59 O.S. Section 858-314). A wholesaler must do the following:

- disclose in writing to the homeowner, before any contract is signed, the wholesaler's intent to assign or sell the equitable interest for a higher price than is offered to the homeowner;
- include a prominent written disclosure in the contract advising the homeowner to seek legal advice before signing;
- disclose in writing that the homeowner has the right to cancel the contract without penalty within two business days after signing.

Consequences of noncompliance

Failure to include any required disclosure renders the contract invalid and unenforceable by the wholesaler and entitles the homeowner to any earnest money involved. In addition, the homeowner may terminate at any time if the wholesaler fails to comply (59 O.S. Section 858-314). Any earnest money or security deposit taken by a wholesaler must be kept in an escrow account in Oklahoma at a federally insured institution. Finally, the Commission publishes a notice of cancellation form that the wholesaler must include with the contract at no cost to the homeowner. The provisions in the aggregate compel wholesaling to be transparent.

A wholesaler who quietly assigns a contract may be trying avoid the problem that the assignment requires a license. However, one who openly advertises to find a buyer – which is what a wholesaler does -- is engaged in licensed activity and needs a license. Ultimately, the safest course of action for anyone wholesaling residential property is to assume that disclosure duties apply and to be candid with the homeowner from the outset.

A practical illustration helps. Suppose an investor signs a contract to buy a house for two hundred thousand dollars, intending to assign that contract to another buyer for two hundred fifteen thousand. Under the 2025 law, the investor must tell the homeowner in writing, before the homeowner signs, that

- the investor intends to assign the contract for a higher price,
- that the homeowner may want to seek legal advice, and
- the investor must give the homeowner two business days to cancel.

Skipping any of these steps lets the homeowner walk away and keep the earnest money.

TRUST ACCOUNTS

Handling trust funds
Commingling prohibited
Account registration
Earnest money, disbursements, and disputes

Handling trust funds

A broker who holds money belonging to others must keep it in a trust account, separate from the broker's own funds (OREC Rule 605:10-13-1). Trust funds include

- earnest money deposits,
- money received at final settlement,
- rents,
- security deposits, and
- money advanced by a buyer or seller for closing expenses

All such funds must be deposited in a separate account at a financial institution insured by an agency of the federal government, and the broker must be a signer on any account where the funds are held. A landlord's security or damage deposit must be kept in an Oklahoma escrow account in compliance with the residential landlord and tenant law.

Commingling prohibited

Commingling, the mixing of the broker's own money with trust funds, is prohibited. A broker may not keep personal funds in the trust account except amounts sufficient to maintain the integrity of the account and cover the financial institution's service charges (OREC Rule 605:10-13-1).

The broker may place escrow money in an interest-bearing account only after disclosing in writing to all parties that the account bears interest and identifying who will receive that interest. The rule against commingling is one of the most strictly enforced in real estate, because trust money belongs to consumers, not to the broker.

Account registration

Trust accounts are not private arrangements; they are registered with the Commission (OREC Rule 605:10-13-2). A broker registers each trust account, and adds, edits, or removes trust accounts through the License Portal. Registration, combined with the requirement that the broker be a signer and that records be retained, lets the Commission verify that consumer funds are being held properly. Trust account and transaction records must be kept for a minimum of five years.

Accounting and timely payment. Holding the money is only half the duty; accounting for it is the other half. A broker must keep all parties informed of the details relating to the escrow being held, must ensure the timely delivery or return of documents, items, and monies to the parties, and must furnish a signed settlement statement in each transaction at the time it is consummated (OREC Rule 605:10-13-1). After a closing, the broker pays over the funds promptly, and a failure to pay over funds within three days after a closing is prima facie evidence of a violation. These provisions make clear that a broker may not sit on consumer money once the reason for holding it has ended.

Earnest money, disbursements, and disputes

Earnest money is the most common trust deposit, and its handling is closely regulated. A broker must furnish a signed settlement statement at consummation and must distribute funds promptly after closing. Failure to pay over funds within three days after a closing is prima facie evidence of a license law violation (OREC Rule 605:10-13-1). When a transaction does not close, the broker promptly disburses the earnest money to the proper party according to the contract. When a dispute arises before disbursement, the broker may not simply pick a side; the broker must follow the dispute procedure of Rule 605:10-13-3 or file an interpleader action in court so the court can decide who is entitled to the funds.

A familiar scenario shows how these rules fit together. A buyer's earnest money check goes straight into the brokerage trust account, never the broker's operating account. If the sale closes, the broker disburses the money as the contract directs and provides a signed settlement statement. If the sale falls through and the buyer and seller both claim the deposit, the broker holds the money, refuses to release it to either side on demand, and resolves the standoff through the Commission's dispute procedure or by interpleading the funds into court.

The reason the trust account rules are enforced so strictly is that the money in a trust account is never the broker's. A broker who deposits a client's earnest money into the operating account, or who uses trust funds to cover office expenses even briefly, has commingled and likely converted funds that belong to others, which is among the most serious violations a licensee can commit. Treating the trust account as untouchable except for the specific, documented purposes the rules allow is therefore not just good bookkeeping; it is central to keeping a license.

28 Regulation of Brokerage Practices Snapshot Review

ADVERTISING REGULATION

Scope	• advertising means all promotion and solicitation by any means, including social networking (605:10-1-2); online held to same standard as print;
Rules (605:10-9-4)	• use registered trade name or licensed name; indicate broker not private party; yard signs show broker office phone; no PO-box-only ads; disclose franchise name; no use of another firm's trade name;
Oversight	• broker is responsible for and approves associate advertising, team insignia, and domains;

UNLICENSED ASSISTANTS AND LICENSED ACTIVITY

Line	• licensed activity (showing for pay, negotiating, soliciting, advising) needs a license (858-301); cooperating with unlicensed activity is prohibited (605:10-17-4);
Assistants	• may do clerical and administrative support; may not show, negotiate, advise, or hold out as licensed;
Responsibility	• broker is responsible for all real estate activities of unlicensed assistants (605:10-9-1);

BROKER SUPERVISION

Duty	• broker accountable for all associates assigned (605:10-1-2); failure to supervise, lending a license, or letting an associate act as broker is prohibited (605:10-17-4);
Anchors	• broker ensures all performing licensed activities are licensed; associate may not act outside the broker's supervision;

PLACE OF BUSINESS REQUIREMENTS

Office	• broker must maintain a place of business (858-310; 605:10-9-1); associates may not have own office; may be in broker's residence; identified per 605:10-9-2;
Branch	• extra location that is an extension needs a branch office license and a separate managing broker (858-310; 605:10-7-7); not independently owned;
Address	• broker notifies Commission of change of office address or phone (605:10-9-5);

TRADE NAMES

Definition	• name a firm is known as and uses in advertising; all trade names registered with the Commission (605:10-1-2; 605:10-9-3);
Limits	• may not use another licensed firm's trade name; advertising must show broker, not private party; name changes under 605:10-7-5;

TEAMS

Registration
- two or more licensees under one broker holding out as a unit; registered before performing activities; fee applies (858-305; 605:10-9-3.2);

Name
- broker-approved, unique, not identical to a licensed entity; Commission may deny if confusingly similar;

Advertising
- broker reference at least 50% as large as any team reference; broker reference on every page of a team website (605:10-9-4);

CESSATION OF BROKERAGE ACTIVITIES

Ceasing (605:10-9-7)
- notify Commission in writing of date; conclude pending deals; account for trust funds; remove advertising and signs; keep records 5 years;

Death / disability
- entity rules apply for corporation, association, partnership; sole proprietor ceases all activity; representative notifies Commission; advertising and signs removed within 30 days (605:10-9-6);

Branch closing
- main office broker notifies Commission of date and records location; returns or destroys branch certificate and cards; records kept 5 years (605:10-9-8);

IMPACT OF BROKER SUSPENSION OR CESSATION

Broker
- suspended or revoked licensee returns certificate and card by effective date; may not perform licensed activity (605:10-17-6);

Associates
- automatically placed inactive unless they transfer to another broker; branch license and its licensees also inactive;

Listings / funds
- no assigning listings without the owner's written consent; all advertising removed; phone not answered as active; pending contracts and monies handled as directed;

WHOLESALING

Licensing line
- publicly marketing an equitable interest in a purchase contract is licensed activity (858-301); wholesaler defined in 858-102;

Disclosures (858-314)
- before signing, disclose intent to assign for a higher price; advise homeowner to seek legal advice; give a 2-business-day right to cancel; effective Nov 1, 2025;

Noncompliance
- missing disclosures make the contract unenforceable by the wholesaler and let the homeowner keep earnest money; wholesaler deposits held in an Oklahoma escrow account;

TRUST ACCOUNTS

Handling
- others' money held in a separate trust account at a federally insured institution; includes earnest money, settlement funds, rents, security deposits; broker is a signer (605:10-13-1);

Commingling
- no personal funds in the trust account except to maintain integrity or cover bank charges; interest-bearing only with written disclosure identifying who receives interest;

Registration
- trust accounts registered with the Commission (605:10-13-2); records kept 5 years;

Disputes
- pay over promptly after closing (3-day prima facie rule); on non-consummation disburse per contract; on a dispute follow 605:10-13-3 or interplead;

29 Oklahoma Disclosures and Hazards

Agency Residential Property Disclosure Statement
Residential Property Disclaimer Statement
The Licensee's Disclosure Responsibilities
Psychologically Impacted Property
Oklahoma Environmental Hazards

For most of its history, Oklahoma real estate followed the old rule of caveat emptor, meaning let the buyer beware. A seller had no general duty to volunteer the condition of a property, and the burden of discovering defects fell on the purchaser. The Residential Property Condition Disclosure Act (The RPCD Act), found at Title 60, Sections 831 through 839 of the Oklahoma Statutes, changed that for most home sales by requiring the seller to put what the seller actually knows about the property in writing. This chapter explains the two forms the Act uses, the disclosure statement and the disclaimer statement, the transactions that are exempt, and the duties a licensee carries in the process. It then turns to two areas where Oklahoma law deliberately limits what must be disclosed, psychologically impacted property and the presence of registered offenders. Finally, the chapter closes with the environmental hazards a licensee should recognize. The Commission publishes the official forms in the appendix to its rules (OREC Rule 605:10-15-4).

RESIDENTIAL PROPERTY DISCLOSURE STATEMENT

When the Act applies
What the disclosure statement covers
Timing and updates

When the Act applies

The RPCD Act applies to the transfer of improved residential real property with not less than one nor more than two dwelling units, which means single-family homes and duplexes (60 O.S. Section 831 and following). It does not apply to vacant land, to commercial property, or to apartment buildings of three or more units.

The disclosure obligation is triggered in two situations: when the seller is represented by a real estate licensee, the disclosure is required; and when the seller is not represented, it is required only if the purchaser makes a written request for it. The Act is a deliberate modification of caveat emptor, shifting some of the risk of unknown defects from the buyer to a seller who actually knows of them.

What the disclosure statement covers

A seller who has occupied the property, or who otherwise knows its condition, completes a disclosure statement. The statement identifies the items and improvements included in the sale and whether they are in normal working order, and it states whether the seller has actual knowledge of defects in areas such as the following (60 O.S. Section 833):

- water and sewer systems, the water source, drainage and grading, water seepage or leakage, and flood zone status;
- structural systems, including the roof, walls, floors, foundation, and any basement;
- the plumbing, electrical, heating, and air conditioning systems;
- infestation or damage from wood-destroying organisms;
- the existence of hazardous or regulated materials and other conditions having an environmental impact, including any prior manufacture of methamphetamine.

RPCD contains actual knowledge; is not a warranty. The disclosure statement reports the seller's actual knowledge; it is not a warranty of condition and not a substitute for an inspection. A seller is not expected to investigate or to become an expert, only to disclose honestly what the seller in fact knows. A buyer who wants assurance about a system or a hazard must still arrange for a professional inspection.

The Commission supplies the official forms. The Residential Property Condition Disclosure Statement appears in Appendix A of the Commission's rules and the disclaimer statement in Appendix B. The Commission may amend the forms as needed (OREC Rule 605:10-15-4).

For example a seller who has lived in the home completes the disclosure statement and notes a roof leak repaired two winters ago. The leak is a condition within her actual knowledge. She does not have to hire an inspector to find problems she does not know about; she simply reports what she knows.

Timing and updates

The timing for completion and delivery of the property condition disclosure is strict. The seller delivers the statement to the purchaser as soon as practicable, but in any event **before the seller accepts an offer** to purchase. In addition the form must have been completed within one hundred eighty days before delivery (60 O.S. Section 834). If the seller learns of a new defect after delivering the statement but before accepting an offer, the seller must amend the disclosure. Delivering the statement up front, before the contract is signed, is what gives the buyer the information in time to make an informed decision.

.

RESIDENTIAL PROPERTY DISCLAIMER STATEMENT

When a disclaimer may be used
How the disclaimer differs
Exemptions from the Act

When a disclaimer may be used

Not every seller is positioned to describe a property's condition. **A seller who has never occupied the property** and has no actual knowledge of any defects may deliver a disclaimer statement instead of a disclosure statement (60 O.S. Section 833). In the disclaimer statement, the seller states that he or she has never occupied the property, makes no disclosures concerning its condition, and has no actual knowledge of any defects. The disclaimer is the right form for an owner who genuinely knows nothing about the property's condition, such as an investor who bought at auction and never lived there.

How the disclaimer differs

The two forms serve different sellers. The disclosure statement is an affirmative report of what the seller knows; the disclaimer statement is a sworn absence of knowledge by a seller who has never occupied the home. **A seller who has lived in the property, or who knows of defects, may not use the disclaimer** to sidestep the duty to disclose. The disclaimer is narrow on purpose: it is available only when the seller truly has no occupancy and no actual knowledge.

Exemptions from the Act

The Act lists several transactions to which a disclosure simply does not apply, so that neither form is required (60 O.S. Section 838). These principal exemptions include

- transfers ordered by a court, such as those in probate, divorce, or eminent domain;
- transfers by foreclosure or by a deed given in lieu of foreclosure;
- transfers by a fiduciary administering an estate, guardianship, conservatorship, or trust who has not occupied the property;
- transfers between co-owners;
- transfers to a spouse or to a lineal relative; and
- transfers to or from a governmental entity.

In an exempt transaction the seller still may not actively conceal a known defect. Consider an estate being settled. An executor who never lived in the deceased's home is administering the property as a fiduciary, so the transfer is exempt and no form is required. By contrast, an ordinary homeowner selling the house she has lived in for years must complete the disclosure statement, since none of the exemptions fit her situation.

THE LICENSEE'S DISCLOSURE RESPONSIBILITIES

Obtaining and delivering the statement
The limits of the licensee's duty
Property size and square footage

Obtaining and delivering the statement

The licensee has defined duties under the Act (60 O.S. Section 836). A licensee working with the seller must inform the seller of the seller's obligations under the Act, and a licensee representing or assisting a purchaser has the duty to obtain the completed statement and make it available to the purchaser. If a licensee has actual knowledge of a defect that the seller has not disclosed, the licensee must disclose it. A licensee who fails to comply is subject to discipline by the Commission, and violating the Act is itself a prohibited dealing under the License Code.

The limits of the licensee's duty

The Act is careful about what it does not require. A licensee has no duty to the seller or the purchaser to conduct an independent inspection of the property, and no duty to independently verify the accuracy or completeness of anything the seller states in the disclosure or disclaimer (60 O.S. Section 836). The licensee's disclosure duty is limited to actual knowledge of a defect, meaning a condition with a materially adverse effect on the monetary value of the property. The remedy for a violation is also limited: a purchaser's exclusive civil remedy is an action for actual damages, which must be brought within two years after the transfer, rather than rescission of a closed sale (60 O.S. Section 837).

Property size and square footage

A separate statute addresses a frequent source of disputes, the size of the property. A licensee is not required to provide the square footage or area of a property, and if the licensee does provide it, the figure is not a warranty or guarantee of size (59 O.S. Section 858-515.1). When a licensee passes along size information from a third party, such as an appraiser, a survey, or the county assessor, the licensee must identify the source. A licensee who complies has no further duty and no liability for conflicting measurements, which is why prudent licensees cite the source and avoid presenting square footage as their own measurement.

Where complaints go. It is worth knowing which forum hears which dispute. The Commission does not have jurisdiction over the Residential Property Condition Disclosure Act itself; a civil dispute under the Act is decided by a court of proper jurisdiction. The Commission does, however, have jurisdiction over a licensee who fails to comply with the Act, and it develops and maintains the forms. So a buyer who believes a seller hid a known defect pursues that claim in court, while a buyer who believes the licensee mishandled the disclosure duty can also bring the matter to the Commission.

PSYCHOLOGICALLY IMPACTED PROPERTY

What the law treats as not material
The written-inquiry exception
Registered offenders

What the law treats as not material

Oklahoma law deliberately exempts certain emotionally charged facts from mandatory disclosure. Under the psychologically impacted real estate statute, the fact or suspicion that a property was the site of a suicide, homicide, or other felony **is not a material fact that must be disclosed**, and neither is the fact that an occupant was, or was suspected to be, infected with HIV or diagnosed with AIDS, or with any other disease that medical evidence has determined is highly unlikely to be transmitted through occupancy (59 O.S. Section 858-513). No cause of action arises against an owner or a licensee for failing to disclose that a property is psychologically impacted. These facts are treated as **not bearing on the physical condition or value of the home.**

The written-inquiry exception

There is one channel for a buyer to whom such a factor genuinely matters. If a purchaser making a bona fide offer advises the licensee assisting the owner, in writing, that knowledge of such a factor is important to the decision, the licensee must make inquiry of the owner and report any findings to the purchaser, with the owner's consent. (59 O.S. Section 858-513). If the owner refuses to disclose, the licensee must tell the purchaser that the owner has refused. The burden is then on the buyer to raise the concern in writing; absent that written request, there is nothing to disclose.

Registered offenders

A related provision addresses registered offenders. The Sex Offenders Registration Act and the Mary Rippy Violent Crime Offenders Registration Act do not impose a duty on a real estate licensee to disclose any information about an offender required to register under those acts (59 O.S. Section 858-514). A licensee therefore has no obligation to research or report nearby registered offenders. Because the registries are public, a buyer who is concerned can consult them directly, and a licensee can appropriately point a buyer to that public resource rather than undertaking to investigate.

For example, suppose a home was the site of a widely reported suicide. The owner and the listing associate have no duty to volunteer that fact, and no liability for staying silent. But if a buyer tells the associate in writing that the property's history matters to the decision, the associate must ask the owner and report what the owner is willing to share, or report that the owner has declined. The buyer drives the inquiry, and the licensee responds within the limits the statute sets.

OKLAHOMA ENVIRONMENTAL HAZARDS

Hazards within the disclosure framework
Federal lead-based paint disclosure
Recognizing common hazards

Hazards within the disclosure framework

Environmental hazards reach the buyer mainly through the disclosure statement, which asks the seller about hazardous or regulated materials, conditions having an environmental impact, flood zone status, wood-destroying organisms, and any prior manufacture of methamphetamine (60 O.S. Section 833). A property where methamphetamine was once produced can carry serious contamination, which is why Oklahoma singles it out on the form. As with all property condition disclosures, the seller reports actual knowledge, and a buyer who wants certainty about an environmental condition arranges specialized testing.

Federal lead-based paint disclosure

One hazard is governed by federal law that applies in Oklahoma just as it does everywhere. For housing built **before 1978**, federal law requires the seller or landlord to disclose any known lead-based paint and lead hazards, to provide any related records, to give the buyer the federal lead-hazard information pamphlet, and to include a lead warning statement in the contract. A buyer of pre-1978 housing must also be given a ten-day opportunity to conduct a lead-based paint inspection or risk assessment. A licensee involved in such a sale should ensure these federal steps are completed.

Recognizing common hazards. Beyond lead, a competent licensee should recognize the hazards that arise in Oklahoma homes, including radon, a naturally occurring radioactive gas that can accumulate indoors; asbestos and mold in older or damaged structures; underground storage tanks; and contamination from prior methamphetamine production. The licensee's role is to recognize and disclose what is known and to refer the buyer to qualified inspectors and remediation experts, not to test, diagnose, or give expert opinions. Steering a buyer to the right professional is competent practice; pretending to have environmental expertise is not.

Flood risk deserves attention. Flooding is a hazard the disclosure statement addresses directly through its questions about drainage, water seepage, and flood zone status. Oklahoma sees significant flooding, and a property's flood zone designation can drive both insurance costs and the lender's requirements. A licensee should make sure the seller's knowledge of past water intrusion is disclosed and should encourage a buyer to check the flood maps and obtain flood insurance information, while leaving the technical determination of flood risk to the appropriate experts and sources.

A simple example brings the rules together. An associate lists a 1968 home for a seller who mentions that the basement once tested high for radon and that the garage may contain asbestos tiles. The seller discloses both on the disclosure statement, and because the home predates 1978, the federal lead-based paint disclosure and the ten-day inspection opportunity apply as well. The associate makes sure the forms are delivered before the offer is accepted and refers the buyer to qualified inspectors for the radon and asbestos questions rather than offering an opinion.

29 Oklahoma Disclosures and Hazards Snapshot Review

RESIDENTIAL PROPERTY DISCLOSURE STATEMENT

Scope	• Residential Property Condition Disclosure Act (60 O.S. 831-839) covers one- and two-unit homes; not vacant land, commercial, or 3-plus-unit buildings; modifies caveat emptor;
Trigger	• required when the seller is represented by a licensee; if unrepresented, only on the buyer's written request;
Contents	• items and working order plus actual knowledge of defects in water and sewer and flood, structure, mechanical systems, wood-destroying organisms, and environmental and meth conditions (60 O.S. 833);
Timing	• deliver before acceptance of an offer; form completed within 180 days; amend on new knowledge; reports actual knowledge, not a warranty;

RESIDENTIAL PROPERTY DISCLAIMER STATEMENT

Use	• available only to a seller who never occupied the property and has no actual knowledge of defects; states no occupancy, no disclosures, no knowledge;
Exemptions (60 O.S. 838)	• court-ordered, foreclosure or deed in lieu, fiduciary who never occupied, between co-owners, to a spouse or lineal relative, to or from government; no form required, but no active concealment;

THE LICENSEE'S DISCLOSURE RESPONSIBILITIES

Duties (60 O.S. 836)	• inform the seller of the obligation; the buyer's licensee obtains and delivers the statement; disclose any defect actually known; noncompliance is OREC discipline and a prohibited dealing;
Limits	• no duty to inspect or verify the seller's statements; duty limited to actual knowledge of a materially adverse defect; buyer's exclusive remedy is actual damages within 2 years (60 O.S. 837);
Square footage	• licensee need not provide size; if provided it is not a warranty; must identify the source of third-party size data (858-515.1);

PSYCHOLOGICALLY IMPACTED PROPERTY

Not material	• suicide, homicide, or felony on the site, and an occupant with HIV/AIDS or a non-occupancy-transmissible disease, are not material facts; no cause of action for nondisclosure (858-513);
Written inquiry	• if a buyer making a bona fide offer states in writing the factor matters, the licensee inquires of the owner and reports with consent, or advises that the owner refused;
Offenders	• no duty to disclose registered sex or violent crime offenders; registries are public for buyers to check (858-514);

OKLAHOMA ENVIRONMENTAL HAZARDS

Disclosure form

- seller reports known hazardous and regulated materials, environmental conditions, flood status, wood-destroying organisms, and prior meth manufacture (60 O.S. 833);

Lead paint

- pre-1978 housing: federal disclosure of known lead paint and hazards, EPA pamphlet, lead warning statement, and a 10-day inspection opportunity;

Common hazards

- radon, asbestos, mold, underground tanks, meth contamination; licensee discloses what is known and refers to experts rather than testing or opining;

30 Oklahoma Property Management

License Requirements
Broker Relationships Act Requirements
Property Management Agreements
The Landlord and Tenant Act

Property management is a distinct corner of the real estate business, and an Oklahoma property manager wears two hats at once. As a real estate licensee, the manager answers to the Real Estate Commission and to the Broker Relationships Act. As the person standing in for the owner in dealings with tenants, the manager also operates under the **Oklahoma Landlord and Tenant Act** in Title 41 of the statutes. This chapter follows that structure. It begins with citing conditions where a license is generally required to manage property. Subsequently, the chapter explains how the Broker Relationships Act and the property management agreement shape the manager's relationship with the owner. Finally, the narrative reveals how landlord and tenant laws govern the manager's dealings with tenants, including handling security deposits, the respective duties of landlord and tenant, how to deal with abandoned property, lease terms, and eviction.

LICENSE REQUIREMENTS

Managing property is a licensed activity
Exemptions from licensure

Managing property is a licensed activity

Leasing or renting real estate for another person, for a fee or other valuable consideration, is a licensed activity in Oklahoma, just like listing or selling (59 O.S. Section 858-301). A person or company that manages rental property for owners, advertises units, negotiates and signs leases, collects rent, and handles deposits for compensation is performing brokerage services and must be a licensed broker or must work as an associate under a sponsoring broker. The fact that the work is ongoing management rather than a one-time sale does not change the analysis. If the activity is done for another for a fee, it requires a license.

Exemptions from licensure

The License Code exempts several people who might otherwise appear to need a license (59 O.S. Section 858-301). The most important for property management include the following:

- an owner managing, leasing, or renting the owner's own property, and the owner's regular salaried employees acting within that scope;

- a resident manager who lives on the premises and leases units in connection with that employment, whether for the owner or for a licensed broker managing an apartment building, duplex, or complex;
- a resident of an apartment complex who receives a nominal resident referral fee, not to exceed one hundred dollars, for recommending the property to a family member, friend, or coworker;
- a person or entity managing a transient lodging facility, meaning furnished rooms rented on a daily basis for less than thirty days and not as a principal residence;
- employees of a licensed broker who lease residential units only to persons qualifying through a state or federal subsidized housing program in an affordable housing development.

As an example, an owner buys a small house and rents it out herself. This party needs no license, because she is dealing with her own property. A resident who lives in an apartment complex and manages it for the owner is exempt as a resident manager. But a company that manages dozens of homes it does not own and collects a fee from each owner, is performing licensed activity and must operate through a licensed broker.

Public domain rights acquisition exemption . A few narrower exemptions also appear in the Code, such as persons acquiring easements, rights-of-way, or leases for utilities, pipelines, or transportation projects, and for persons acquiring real estate on behalf of a business entity with the power of eminent domain (59 O.S. Section 858-301). Such parties are exempt from licensure.

For ordinary residential and commercial management, however, the rule is simple: managing someone else's property for compensation requires a license.

BROKER RELATIONSHIPS ACT REQUIREMENTS

The management agreement is a brokerage agreement
Duties to the owner and the tenant

The management agreement is a brokerage agreement

A property management agreement is a brokerage service agreement under the Commission's rules, on the same footing as a listing or a buyer agreement (OREC Rule 605:10-15-2). That means the Broker Relationships Act, covered in Chapter 27, applies in full. The manager provides brokerage services to the owner, and the statutory duties of Section 858-353 are incorporated into the agreement as material terms. The manager must disclose the duties and services in writing, just as any broker must, and the agreement must carry a definite termination date.

Duties to the owner and the tenant

The owner is the party the manager serves, so the manager owes the owner the full set of statutory duties:

- **honesty and reasonable skill and care,**
- **accounting** for money and property,
- **keeping the owner informed**,
- **keeping confidential information confidential**, and complying with the Code.

The tenant occupies a different position. When a broker manages property for a landlord under a property management agreement, the services provided to the tenant do not create a broker relationship with the tenant unless the parties agree to that in writing; even so, the manager still owes the tenant the duties of honesty and reasonable skill and care (OREC Rule 605:10-15-2).

The practical upshot is that a property manager works for the owner but cannot mistreat the tenant. A manager may negotiate firmly on the owner's behalf over rent or repairs, which is part of serving the owner, yet must still deal honestly and competently with the tenant. The tenant is not a client, but the tenant is not without protection.

Disclosure still comes first. Because the management agreement is a brokerage service agreement, the same disclosure rules from Chapter 27 apply at the outset. Before the owner signs, the manager **describes and discloses the duties and services in writing**, and the owner confirms the disclosure. If the manager intends to provide fewer than the full range of services, that limitation must be disclosed in writing as well. A manager who, for example, will handle leasing and rent collection but not after-hours maintenance calls should make that scope clear in the agreement so the owner is not surprised later. The relationship with the owner is built on the same statutory duties and disclosures that govern every other brokerage relationship in Oklahoma.

PROPERTY MANAGEMENT AGREEMENTS

What the agreement authorizes
Compensation and trust handling

What the agreement authorizes

The Commission publishes a residential property management agreement, the **Exclusive Right to Lease**, that gives a broker the sole right to lease and manage an owner's property for a stated period. A typical management agreement authorizes the broker to

- advertise and market the property;
- screen and select tenants;
- negotiate and sign leases on the owner's behalf;
- collect rent;

- hold security deposits;
- arrange routine maintenance and repairs up to an agreed limit, and
- account to the owner for the funds

Because it is a brokerage service agreement, it must state a beginning and an ending date, and it should define the scope of the broker's authority clearly. This enables the owner to know what the broker may and may not do without further approval.

Compensation and trust handling

The agreement also sets forth the broker's compensation, which in management practice, commonly combines a recurring management fee, often a percentage of rent collected, with a separate leasing fee for placing a new tenant.

Money the broker handles for the owner and the tenants is trust money. As Chapter 28 explained, rents and security deposits must be held in the brokerage trust account, separate from the broker's own funds, and a tenant's security or damage deposit must be kept in an Oklahoma escrow account at a federally insured institution. The manager accounts to the owner for rent collected and expenses paid, and disburses the owner's share according to the agreement.

To illustrate a management agreement, suppose an owner signs an Exclusive Right to Lease agreement with a brokerage to manage a rental home for one year. The brokerage advertises the home, screens applicants, signs a lease with an approved tenant, deposits the rent and security deposit into its trust account, pays for a plumbing repair within the agreed limit, and sends the owner a monthly statement with the net proceeds. Each of these steps is authorized by the agreement and governed by the trust account rules.

Owner obligations and tenant screening. A good management agreement also spells out what the owner must do, particularly, keeping the property habitable, funding repairs and reserves, and maintaining insurance.

Tenant screening is one of the manager's central tasks, and Oklahoma permits reasonable screening based on factors such as credit, rental history, income, and background. That discretion is not unlimited. A property manager must comply with federal and state fair housing law in advertising, screening, and leasing, and may not make decisions based on a protected class such as race, color, religion, national origin, sex, familial status, or disability. Applying consistent, objective screening standards to every applicant is both good practice and the surest defense against a fair housing complaint.

THE LANDLORD AND TENANT ACT

The Act and the manager's role
Security deposits
Landlord and tenant duties
Disposition of personal property
Lease terms
Eviction and termination

The Act and the manager's role

In dealings with tenants, the property manager stands in the shoes of the landlord and is bound by the **Oklahoma Landlord and Tenant Act**, found in Title 41 of the statutes. Oklahoma has a Residential Landlord and Tenant Act for dwellings and a separate set of provisions for nonresidential, or commercial, tenancies. A landlord and tenant relationship arises whenever rent is paid in exchange for occupying property, even without a written lease, although a clear written lease is strongly advised.

Security deposits

Security deposits are tightly regulated. The deposit is held by the landlord, and for a property manager it must be kept in the brokerage escrow account. Upon termination of the tenancy, the deposit may be applied to unpaid rent and to damages caused by the tenant beyond normal wear and tear, itemized in a written statement (41 O.S. Section 115). Further, the landlord must return the balance, without interest, within forty-five days after the tenancy ends.

Oklahoma does not require interest on deposits, and a tenant who fails to make a written demand within six months after the tenancy ends forfeits the deposit.

Landlord and tenant duties

In residential tenancies, both landlord and tenant owe the other party defined duties. The landlord must

- maintain the premises in compliance with applicable building and housing codes;
- make repairs to keep the unit fit and habitable;
- keep common areas safe; and
- maintain the electrical, plumbing, heating, and cooling systems that the landlord provides (41 O.S. Section 118).

The tenant, in turn, must

- keep the unit clean and safe;
- dispose of trash properly;
- use the facilities reasonably;
- avoid damaging the property; and

- not disturb neighbors (41 O.S. Section 127).

A landlord generally must give at least one day's notice before entering, except in an emergency.

When essential services fail. The Act sets forth tenant remedies whenever the landlord falls short on providing essential services. If the landlord fails to supply heat, running water, for example, the tenant may, after proper notice, take steps such as procuring the service and deducting the cost, recovering damages, or obtaining substitute housing, depending on the circumstances (41 O.S. Section 121).

A property manager who receives a habitability complaint should respond promptly and document the response, both because the law requires it and because a slow response can expose the owner to these tenant remedies.

Disposition of personal property

When a tenant leaves belongings behind after abandoning, surrendering, or being evicted, the Act sets forth the remediation procedure (41 O.S. Section 130). If the property has no ascertainable value, the landlord may dispose of it. If it has value, the landlord must notify the tenant in writing that the property will be treated as abandoned unless the tenant recovers it within thirty days. At this point, the landlord may then sell, dispose of, or destroy such property. A tenant who reclaims the property within the period pays reasonable storage costs. If the property is sold, the proceeds are applied to amounts owed, with any surplus going to the tenant. A separate provision governs the disposition of property when a tenant dies (41 O.S. Section 130.1).

Lease terms

Leases may be written or oral, and they may run for a fixed term or as a periodic tenancy. A month-to-month tenancy may be ended by either the landlord or the tenant with at least thirty days' written notice. A week-to-week tenancy requires at least seven days' notice (41 O.S. Section 111).

Eviction and termination

Oklahoma requires proper notice before a landlord may evict. For nonpayment of rent, the landlord serves a five-day notice to pay or quit; if the tenant pays within the five days, the tenancy continues (41 O.S. Section 131).

For a material breach of the lease or of the tenant's duties, the landlord serves a notice specifying the breach, and the tenancy terminates in not less than fifteen days unless the tenant remedies the breach within ten days (41 O.S. Section 132). A repeat of a similar breach, or conduct that seriously threatens health or safety, can support a faster termination.

Notices must be served in the manner the statute prescribes, beginning with personal delivery to the tenant, then delivery to a resident family member above a set age, and finally posting and mailing if neither can be reached (41 O.S. Section 111).

Eviction goes through the court, not self-help. If a tenant does not comply with a proper notice, the landlord enforces the eviction through a forcible entry and detainer action in district court, after which the sheriff returns possession. A landlord or manager may not resort to self-help by changing the locks, removing the tenant's belongings, or shutting off utilities to force a tenant out. The manager's role is to serve correct notices, document the breach, and let the court process run, which protects both the owner and the manager from liability for an unlawful eviction.

A full example shows the sequence. A tenant stops paying rent in March. The manager serves a five-day notice to pay or quit; the tenant neither pays nor leaves. The manager then files a forcible entry and detainer action, appears in court, and obtains a judgment for possession, and the sheriff carries out the removal. If the tenant leaves furniture behind, the manager follows the abandoned-property procedure, notifying the tenant and holding items of value for thirty days. At no point does the manager change the locks or set the tenant's belongings on the curb, because Oklahoma does not permit self-help eviction.

Residential and commercial tenancies differ. Most property management questions arise under the residential act, but a manager handling commercial space works under the **nonresidential provisions of Title 41**. These provisions give the parties more freedom to set their own terms and follow somewhat different procedures for matters such as abandoned property. A manager should know which act governs a given tenancy and apply the right rules, since the protections built into the residential act for tenants do not all carry over to commercial leases.

30 Oklahoma Property Management Snapshot Review

LICENSE REQUIREMENTS

Licensed activity
- leasing or renting real estate for another for a fee is licensed activity; a property manager must be or work under a licensed broker (858-301);

Exemptions
- owner of own property and salaried employees; resident manager living on site; resident referral fee up to $100; transient lodging under 30 days; subsidized-housing employees;

BROKER RELATIONSHIPS ACT REQUIREMENTS

Brokerage agreement
- a property management agreement is a brokerage service agreement; OBRA applies; 858-353 duties are material terms; written disclosure and a termination date required (605:10-15-2);

Owner vs tenant
- owner is the party served and is owed the full duties; tenant is not a client unless agreed in writing but is owed honesty and reasonable skill and care;

PROPERTY MANAGEMENT AGREEMENTS

Authority
- Exclusive Right to Lease gives the broker sole right to advertise, screen, lease, collect rent, hold deposits, and arrange repairs; states a beginning and ending date;

Compensation and trust
- management fee plus leasing fee; rents and deposits held in the brokerage trust account; security deposits in an Oklahoma escrow account; account to the owner;

THE LANDLORD AND TENANT ACT

Scope
- Title 41 residential and nonresidential acts; relationship arises when rent is paid for occupancy, even without a written lease;

Deposits (41-115)
- held in escrow; applied to unpaid rent and damages, itemized; balance returned without interest within 45 days after termination, possession, and written demand; forfeited if not demanded within 6 months;

Duties
- landlord keeps the unit habitable and maintains systems (118); tenant keeps it clean, avoids damage, does not disturb neighbors (127); 1 day notice to enter;

Abandoned property (41-130)
- no value, dispose; value, written notice and 30 days to recover, then sell or dispose; tenant pays storage; separate rule on tenant death (130.1);

Lease / notice (41-111)
- written or oral; month-to-month ends on 30 days written notice, week-to-week on 7 days;

Eviction
- 5-day pay-or-quit for nonpayment (131); 15-day termination with 10-day cure for breach (132); enforced by forcible entry and detainer in court; no self-help lockouts or utility shutoffs;

31 Other Oklahoma Laws and Practices

Fair Housing and Anti-Discrimination
Antitrust Issues
The Statute of Frauds
Lien Theory and Title Theory
Adverse Possession
Native American Lands
Ownership by Foreign Nationals
The Oklahoma Mineral Estate

This chapter summarizes a set of Oklahoma laws and practices that do not fit neatly into the foregoing licensing and brokerage chapters but that a competent licensee must understand. Some laws, like fair housing and antitrust, define conduct a licensee must never engage in. Others, such as the Statute of Frauds, lien theory, and adverse possession, are foundational principles of property and contract law as Oklahoma applies them. The last three topics, Native American lands, ownership by foreign nationals, and the mineral estate, reflect features that make Oklahoma real estate distinctive. None of these areas is covered exhaustively here; the aim is to give the licensee enough understanding to recognize the issues and to know when to bring in a lawyer, a title professional, or a specialist.

FAIR HOUSING AND ANTI-DISCRIMINATION

Federal and Oklahoma protected classes
Practices the law forbids
The licensee's duty

Federal and Oklahoma protected classes

Two layers of law forbid discrimination in housing. The federal **Fair Housing Act** prohibits discrimination based on race, color, national origin, religion, sex, familial status, and disability. The **Oklahoma Fair Housing Law**, found in Title 25, Sections 1451 through 1453 of the statutes, mirrors the federal protections given in the Fair Housing Act, adding age as a protected class. Thus, **Oklahoma recognizes the seven federal classes plus age**. Oklahoma law is enforced by the Attorney General's Office of Civil Rights Enforcement, alongside the federal Department of Housing and Urban Development. Both layers apply to licensees in every part of a transaction.

Practices the law forbids

Fair housing laws reach far beyond an outright refusal to sell. Notably, fair housing laws make it unlawful to

- refuse to sell or rent;
- to offer different terms or services on the same property;
- to falsely state that a dwelling is unavailable;
- to advertise a preference or limitation; or
- to discriminate in financing or appraisal

when performed because of a protected class.

The same prohibition covers more subtle conduct, including steering, which is guiding prospects toward or away from neighborhoods based on a protected characteristic. Likewise prohibited is blockbusting, which is the practice of inducing owners to sell by suggesting that people of a particular class are moving into the area.

The licensee's duty

A licensee must treat every prospect even-handedly and may not let a protected characteristic shape the service provided. It is critical for licensees to let buyers decide for themselves where they wish to live. A licensee who tells a family that a particular neighborhood would be a better fit for people like them has committed a prohibited act (steering), even if the remark was meant kindly.

The safest practice is to give every client the same full range of choices and the same quality of service.

Limited exemptions, but not for licensees. Federal law contains a few narrow exemptions, such as for an owner who sells his own single-family home without using a broker. A real estate licensee is generally not exempted from anti-discrimination circumstances, and the prohibition on discriminatory advertising applies to everyone with no exemptions at all. A licensee should never rely on an owner's possible exemption as a reason to participate in conduct that the fair housing laws forbid.

ANTITRUST ISSUES

Price fixing and collusion
Market allocation and boycotts
Blockbusting and steering as related wrongs

Price fixing and collusion

Antitrust law protects competition, and real estate is not exempt. The most common violation is price fixing, which occurs **when competing brokers agree on the commission rates or fees they will charge**. Commission rates are always negotiable between a broker and a client, and any agreement among competitors to set or stabilize them is illegal collusion. A broker should set fees independently and should never discuss or coordinate pricing with competitors, since even a casual conversation about rates can be evidence of an unlawful agreement.

Market allocation and boycotts

Two related antitrust violations are market allocation and group boycotts. **Market allocation** occurs when competitors agree to divide territories, customers, or types of property among themselves so as not to compete, such as agreeing that one firm will handle one part of a city and another firm a different part. **A group boycott** occurs when competitors agree to refuse to deal with a particular broker or business, often to punish a discounter. Both are illegal practices because they replace open competition with a private agreement. The remedy for antitrust violations can include severe civil and even criminal penalties.

Blockbusting and steering as related wrongs

Blockbusting and steering, introduced in the fair housing section, are sometimes grouped with antitrust practices as organized behaviors that distort the market. Blockbusting manipulates owners into selling through fear tied to a protected class. Steering channels buyers based on a discriminatory characteristic.

The two are mentioned again because all of these practices, antitrust and fair housing alike, share a common ethic: a licensee must compete and serve clients honestly and may not manipulate the market or a consumer's choices through illegal coordination or discrimination.

Tie-in agreements. Another common antitrust concern is the tie-in arrangement. Here, a party conditions the sale of one product or service on the purchase of another, such as agreeing to list a property only if the seller also uses an affiliated service.

Taken as a whole, price fixing, market allocation, and group boycotts are treated as prohibited antitrust violations, meaning there is no business justification for practicing them. The practical guidance for a licensee is straightforward: set your own fees, make your own business decisions, and avoid any conversation with a competitor that even hints at coordinating prices or carving up the market, because antitrust exposure is one of the most serious risks in the business.

THE STATUTE OF FRAUDS

Contracts that must be written
Why listing agreements must be written

Contracts must be written to be enforceable

The Statute of Frauds requires certain contracts to be in writing and signed, or subscribed, by the party to be charged in order to be enforceable (15 O.S. Section 136). Several categories matter to real estate practice:

- an agreement that by its terms is not to be fully performed within one year;
- an agreement for the sale of real property, or of an interest in real property;
- an agreement to lease real property for a period longer than one year.

The practical lesson is that a purely oral agreement to buy or sell a home, or to lease it for more than a year, generally **cannot be enforced** in court. A handshake is not enough. This is why Oklahoma real estate is conducted through written, signed contracts, and why a buyer or seller who wants to hold the other side to a deal needs that deal in writing.

Why listing agreements must be written

The statute also speaks directly to brokers. When an agreement for the sale or lease of real property is made by an agent or a broker of the party to be charged, it is invalid unless the authority of the agent or broker is itself in writing, subscribed by that party (15 O.S. Section 136). In other words, a broker's authority to bind a seller must be in writing. Although the Broker Relationships Act permits an oral brokerage agreement, a written and signed listing agreement is what gives the broker enforceable authority and protects the broker's right to a commission. The statute expressly ties this requirement to the Broker Relationships Act, linking the two bodies of law.

Memoranda, electronic signatures, and exceptions. The writing required by the statute need not be a single formal document. A sufficient note or memorandum can be assembled from several related writings, and Oklahoma courts have recognized that a name typed at the end of an email or text message can satisfy the subscription requirement, consistent with modern electronic signature law.

Courts also recognize a limited part-performance exception, under which an oral agreement for the sale of land may be enforced in equity when a buyer has taken possession and made improvements or payments in reliance on it. These doctrines soften the statute at the edges, but they are unpredictable, which is why a clear written contract remains far safer than relying on an exception.

LIEN THEORY AND TITLE THEORY

The two theories of mortgages
Oklahoma is a lien theory state

The two theories of mortgages

States divide into two camps over what a mortgage does to title. In a title theory state, the **borrower gives legal title to the lender**, who holds it until the loan is repaid, and the borrower keeps only the right to use the property. In a lien theory state, **the borrower keeps legal title**, and the mortgage simply creates a lien against the property as security for the debt. The distinction matters most at default: a title theory lender already holds legal title, while a lien theory lender must foreclose to fully acquire the property.

Oklahoma is a lien theory state

Oklahoma follows lien theory. A borrower who mortgages a home in Oklahoma retains legal title, and the lender holds a lien rather than ownership. If the borrower defaults, the lender cannot simply take possession; it must foreclose. Foreclosure in Oklahoma is generally a judicial process through the courts, although the state also allows a nonjudicial power of sale foreclosure when the mortgage contains the proper provisions and the borrower does not elect a judicial proceeding. The borrower's retention of title until foreclosure is the defining feature of a lien theory state and explains why the foreclosure process exists.

An example clarifies the point. When a Tulsa homeowner borrows against her house, she remains the titled owner; the bank records a mortgage lien. If she stops paying, the bank does not own the home and cannot lock her out. Instead, the bank files a foreclosure action, obtains a judgment, and the property is sold to satisfy the debt, with the homeowner retaining her rights until that process concludes.

The borrower's equity of redemption. Because the borrower holds legal title in a lien theory state, the borrower also holds an **equity of redemption**, the right to stop a foreclosure by paying the full amount owed before the sale is completed and confirmed. This right flows directly from lien theory: the lender is enforcing a debt secured by a lien, not reclaiming property it already owns, so the borrower can cure the default and keep the home up to the point of sale.

For a licensee, the meaning of lien theory in daily practice is that a seller who still owes on a mortgage remains the owner who can sign a deed, with the lien simply paid off from the sale proceeds at closing.

ADVERSE POSSESSION

What adverse possession is
The Oklahoma elements

What adverse possession is

Adverse possession is a doctrine by which a person who openly occupies and uses land belonging to another for a long enough time can eventually acquire legal title to it. The law favors the productive use of land and penalizes owners who sleep on their rights. In Oklahoma, the required period of adverse possession is **fifteen years** (12 O.S. Section 93). A claimant who satisfies the requirements for the full period may bring a quiet title action and have a court confirm ownership.

Oklahoma adverse possession requirements

To ripen into a successful adverse possession claim for legal title, the possession must meet several elements throughout the fifteen years. It must be

- **actual,** meaning the claimant physically uses the land;
- **open and notorious**, meaning visible enough that an owner would notice;
- **exclusive**, meaning the claimant does not share possession with the true owner or the public;
- **hostile or adverse**, meaning without the owner's permission; and
- **continuous** for the entire statutory period

Successive possessors who are in privity may sometimes tack their periods together to reach fifteen years. Because permission defeats the hostility requirement, a tenant with the owner's consent to occupy can never acquire title by adverse possession.

Adverse possession disputes usually arise quietly between neighbors. Suppose a homeowner builds a fence that, unknown to anyone, sits a few feet onto the adjoining lot, and the family mows and uses that strip openly for more than fifteen years. The neighbor who actually holds title may find that the long, visible, unpermitted use has given the fence builder a claim to the strip, which a court could confirm through a quiet title action.

Prescriptive easements and color of title. Two related ideas round out the adverse possession doctrine. A claimant who possesses under **color of title**, meaning a defective deed or instrument that appears to convey ownership, and who pays the taxes on the land, may have a stronger claim, because these facts reinforce the open and hostile character of the possession.

A separate but parallel doctrine is the prescriptive easement, by which long, open, and adverse use of another's land for access, rather than full possession of it, can ripen **into a right to keep using it**. The same fifteen-year period and the same hostility and continuity ideas apply, but the result is a right to use the land rather than ownership of it.

NATIVE AMERICAN LANDS

Trust, restricted fee, and allotted lands
Why it matters in Oklahoma

Trust, restricted fee, and allotted lands

A significant amount of Oklahoma land exists under a special federal status that ordinary conveyancing rules do not govern. **Trust land** is held in trust by the federal government for a tribe or an individual Indian; Trust land generally cannot be sold or mortgaged without the approval of the Bureau of Indian Affairs, and it is usually not subject to state property taxation. Trust land is **restricted fee land** owned by a tribe or an individual Indian. This land carries federal restrictions on its sale or transfer.

Allotted lands are parcels that were allotted to individual tribal members in the allotment era, many of which remain in trust or have a restricted status and pass under federal rules.

Why it matters in Oklahoma

Oklahoma has one of the largest concentrations of these lands in the country, and the 2020 McGirt decision confirmed that much of eastern Oklahoma remains within tribal reservation boundaries for jurisdictional purposes. A licensee who encounters land that may be trust, restricted, or allotted should recognize that ordinary title work and ordinary closings may not apply, that federal or tribal approval may be required to convey, and that specialized title and legal help is essential. Osage County for example is a special case. In Osage County, mineral estates are reserved for the Osage Nation. Thus, a buyer there may be able to acquire surface usage rights, but not the underlying mineral rights.

PROPERTY OWNERSHIP BY FOREIGN NATIONALS

The restriction and its exceptions
An evolving area of law

The restriction and its exceptions

Oklahoma restricts the ownership of land by certain non-citizens. Under longstanding law, an alien who is not a bona fide resident of the United States generally may not acquire or hold land in Oklahoma (60 O.S. Section 121).

Land ownership exceptions. There are exceptions (60 O.S. Section 122): a bona fide resident alien may acquire and hold land, and a non-resident alien may take land by inheritance or devise, or acquire it in the collection of debts, but in those cases the **law requires the land to be disposed of within five years** (60 O.S. Section 123). Land held in violation of the restriction can be subject to a proceeding to escheat or forced sale.

An evolving area of law

This area of Oklahoma law has been changing. Recent legislation has tightened the rules to address ownership by foreign government adversaries, restricting acquisition of Oklahoma land by certain foreign entities and individuals connected to countries designated as adversaries, and adding disclosure and affidavit requirements in some transactions. Because the statutes here are being actively amended, a licensee who works with a foreign buyer should confirm the current law and direct the buyer to legal counsel rather than assuming a purchase is permitted. The general point for licensees is simply to recognize that some buyers face ownership restrictions that an ordinary buyer does not.

A focus on agricultural land. Much of the recent attention has centered on agricultural land, reflecting a national concern about foreign control of farmland and land near sensitive sites. Oklahoma has long had constitutional and statutory limits on alien land ownership, and the newer measures build on that foundation by requiring affidavits of citizenship or eligibility in some land transfers and by creating mechanisms to investigate and unwind prohibited acquisitions. A licensee does not need to master every detail of these provisions, but should be alert that a transaction involving farmland or a foreign purchaser may trigger requirements that an ordinary residential sale does not, and should bring in counsel early.

THE OKLAHOMA MINERAL ESTATE

Severance and the dominant estate
Minerals and the real estate license

Severance and the dominant estate

In a state defined by oil and gas, the mineral estate is a major feature of Oklahoma real property. The mineral estate can be severed from the surface estate of an Oklahoma parcel of real property, so that one person owns the right to the oil, gas, and other minerals while another owns non-mineral surface rights.

A severancing of rights occurs when an owner conveys the minerals separately or reserves them when selling the surface rights of the property. The mineral estate is the dominant estate, which means the mineral owner has the right to make reasonable use of the surface as necessary to explore for and extract the minerals, even over the surface owner's objection.

Minerals and the real estate license

An important licensing point follows from this. The Real Estate License Code excludes oil, gas, and other mineral interests and leases from the definition of real estate, and provides that the Code does not apply to the sale, purchase, or exchange of those interests (59 O.S. Section 858-102). A real estate license therefore is neither required nor sufficient to broker mineral transactions, which are handled by landmen and others outside the real estate licensing system. A licensee selling a property should know whether the minerals are included or have been severed, because that affects what the buyer is actually getting, but the licensee should leave mineral dealmaking to the mineral specialists.

A common situation makes the distinction concrete. A seller lists a rural tract but reserves the mineral rights, intending to keep any future mineral rights royalties. The buyer purchases the surface, and a mineral company holding a lease may later use part of that surface to drill, because the mineral estate is dominant. The listing licensee must make sure the buyer understands that the minerals are not included, but the licensee does not broker the separate mineral interest, which lies outside the real estate license entirely.

Accommodation and regulation. The dominance of the mineral estate is not unlimited. Under the accommodation doctrine, a mineral owner must make reasonable accommodation of an existing surface use when reasonable alternative methods of extraction are available, and surface-damage rules can require payment to the surface owner for harm caused by operations. Oklahoma oil and gas activity is also heavily regulated by the Oklahoma Corporation Commission, which handles well spacing and pooling, including forced pooling that can bring a reluctant mineral owner into a drilling unit on set terms. A licensee does not administer any of this, but understanding that a severed mineral estate brings its own owners, leases, and regulators helps the licensee explain to a surface buyer what to expect.

31 Other Oklahoma Laws and Practices Snapshot Review

FAIR HOUSING AND ANTI-DISCRIMINATION

Classes	• federal: race, color, national origin, religion, sex, familial status, disability; Oklahoma (Title 25, 1451-1453) adds age;
Forbidden	• refusing to sell or rent, different terms, false unavailability, discriminatory advertising, steering, blockbusting, biased financing or appraisal;
Duty	• give every prospect the same choices and service; follow the client's criteria, not assumptions; enforced by the Attorney General and HUD;

ANTITRUST ISSUES

Price fixing	• competitors agreeing on commissions or fees is illegal; rates are always negotiable and set independently;
Allocation / boycotts	• dividing territories or customers, or agreeing to refuse to deal with a broker, are illegal; penalties can be civil and criminal;
Blockbusting / steering	• manipulating sales through fear of a protected class, or channeling buyers by a protected characteristic; these are fair housing violations;

THE STATUTE OF FRAUDS

Must be written (15-136)	• agreements not performable within a year; sale of real property or an interest; leases longer than one year; signed by the party to be charged;
Broker authority	• a broker's authority to bind a party must be in writing; a written listing agreement gives enforceable authority and protects the commission;

LIEN THEORY AND TITLE THEORY

Theories	• title theory: lender holds title until paid; lien theory: borrower keeps title and the mortgage is a lien;
Oklahoma	• a lien theory state; borrower keeps title; lender must foreclose, generally judicially, with a power-of-sale option;

ADVERSE POSSESSION

Period	• 15 years of qualifying possession in Oklahoma (12-93); confirmed by a quiet title action;
Elements	• actual, open and notorious, exclusive, hostile (without permission), and continuous; permission defeats a claim; periods may be tacked;

NATIVE AMERICAN LANDS

Categories	• trust land (federally held, BIA approval to convey, usually untaxed); restricted fee (Indian-owned with federal restrictions); allotted lands;

Practice
- McGirt confirmed much of eastern Oklahoma as reservation; ordinary closings may not apply; get specialized help; Osage County minerals stay with the Osage Nation;

OWNERSHIP BY FOREIGN NATIONALS

Restriction (60-121)
- a non-resident alien generally may not acquire or hold Oklahoma land; resident aliens may; inheritance or debt collection allowed but must dispose within 5 years;

Evolving
- newer laws restrict foreign government adversaries; confirm current law and refer foreign buyers to counsel;

THE OKLAHOMA MINERAL ESTATE

Severance
- minerals may be severed from the surface by conveyance or reservation; the mineral estate is dominant and may use the surface to extract;

Licensing (858-102)
- mineral interests are excluded from real estate; a real estate license does not cover mineral deals; know whether minerals are included or severed;

CHAPTER TESTS

Answer Key begins after chapter tests

CHAPTER ONE: THE REAL ESTATE BUSINESS

1. Property management and real estate asset management are both real estate management professions. The primary distinction between the two is that

   a. property managers always report to an asset manager.
   b. asset managers have greater knowledge of a property's finances.
   c. property managers handle day-to-day operations while asset managers manage portfolios of properties.
   d. asset managers are primarily responsible for maintenance technicians.

2. People in the real estate business who primarily focus on creating new properties are

   a. brokers.
   b. developers.
   c. zoning administrators.
   d. excavators.

3. The term "commercial property" generally refers to

   a. non-owner-occupied properties.
   b. retail, office and industrial properties.
   c. multi-tenant properties.
   d. retail properties.

4. Which of the following professionals involved in the real estate business are most concerned about procuring buyers and sellers for clients?

   a. Brokers and agents
   b. Property managers
   c. Corporate real estate managers
   d. Appraisers

5. Which of the following ways of specializing is common in the real estate brokerage business?

   a. By type of house
   b. By geography
   c. By financial background of client
   d. By type of mortgage

6. What is an advisory service provider?

   a. A broker of fee simple titles
   b. A corporate real estate broker
   c. A broker performing non-transactional services for a commission
   d. A broker who renders real estate services for a fee

7. The level of government which is most active in regulating real estate licensees is the

   a. federal government.
   b. state government.
   c. county government.
   d. municipal government where the person resides.

CHAPTER TWO: RIGHTS IN REAL ESTATE

1. What guarantees the right of private ownership of real estate in the United States?

   a. Common law
   b. Local statutes
   c. The Napoleonic Code
   d. The Constitution

2. Which of the following is the best definition of real estate?

   a. Land and personal property
   b. Unimproved land
   c. Land and everything permanently attached to it
   d. An ownership interest in land and improvements

3. Which of the following is included in the legal concept of land?

   a. The surface of the earth and all natural things permanently attached to the earth
   b. Only the surface of the earth that is delineated by boundaries
   c. The surface of the earth except for lakes and streams
   d. Everything above, on and below the surface of the earth

4. What are the three unique physical characteristics of land?

   a. Fixed, unchangeable, homogeneous
   b. Immobile, indestructible, heterogeneous
   c. Three-dimensional, buildable, marketable
   d. Natural, measurable, inorganic

5. The primary distinction between the legal concepts of land and real estate is that

   a. real estate includes air above the surface and minerals below the surface.
   b. real estate is indestructible.
   c. land has no defined boundaries.
   d. land does not include man-made structures.

6. The primary distinction between the legal concepts of real estate and real property is that

a. real property includes ownership of a bundle of rights.
b. real property includes improvements.
c. real property is physical, not abstract.
d. real estate can be owned.

7. Which of the following is included in the bundle of rights inherent in ownership?

a. To inherit
b. To tax
c. To transfer
d. To vote

8. Which of the following is an example of intangible property?

a. Real estate
b. Personal property
c. Artwork
d. Stock

9. The right to use real property is limited by

a. the right of others to use and enjoy their property.
b. the police.
c. taxation and subordination.
d. Title 12 of the U.S. Civil Code.

10. Surface rights, air rights and subsurface rights are

a. inviolable.
b. unrelated.
c. separable.
d. not transferrable.

11. Which of the following terms refers to the rights of a property that abuts a stream or river?

a. Allodial
b. Alluvial
c. Littoral
d. Riparian

12. What part of a non-navigable waterway does the owner of an abutting property own?

a. To the low-water mark
b. To the middle of the waterway
c. To the high-water mark
d. None

13. What is the "Doctrine of Prior Appropriation?"

a. A pre-emptive zoning ordinance
b. The right of government to confiscate land and improvements
c. A doctrine that gives the state control of water use and the water supply
d. A real estate tax applied to owners of water rights

14. Which of the following is considered real property?
a. A tree growing on a parcel of land
b. A tree that has been cut down and is lying on a parcel of land
c. A tractor used to mow grass on a parcel of land
d. A prefabricated shed not yet assembled on a parcel of land

15. The overriding test of whether an item is a fixture or personal property is

a. how long it has been attached to the real property.
b. its definition as one or the other in a sale or lease contract.
c. how essential it is to the functioning of the property.
d. how it was treated in previous transactions.

16. What is an emblement?

a. A piece of equipment affixed to the earth
b. A limited right to use personal property
c. A sign indicating a property boundary
d. A plant or crop that is considered personal property

17. An item can be converted from real to personal property and vice versa by means of which processes?

a. Assemblage and plottage
b. Application and dissolution
c. Affixing and severance
d. Personalty and severalty

18. The major sources of real estate law are legislation at federal, state and local level, and

a. court decisions.
b. professional real estate associations.
c. real estate commissions.
d. local practices.

19. What is the primary thrust of federal involvement in real estate law?

a. Taxation
b. Licensing
c. Broad regulation of usage
d. Zoning

20. Which level of government controls zoning laws?

a. State
b. Taxing authorities
c. Federal
d. County and local

21. A grocer temporarily installs special fruit and vegetable coolers in a leased grocery store in order to prevent spoilage. The coolers would be considered which of the following?

    a. Trade fixtures that are real property
    b. Trade fixtures that are personal property
    c. Permanent fixtures that are real property
    d. Permanent fixtures that are personal property

22. Under the doctrine of littoral rights, an owner claims ownership of all of the land underlying a lake where there are three other abutting property owners. Which of the following is true?

    a. The owner's claim is invalid, because the state owns the underlying land.
    b. The owner's claim is invalid, because the underlying land is shared equally with the other owners.
    c. The owner's claim is invalid, because he may only own underlying land to the middle of the lake.
    d. The owner's claim is valid, because the lake is navigable.

CHAPTER THREE: INTERESTS AND ESTATES

1. An interest in real estate is best defined as ownership of

    a. the full bundle of rights to real property.
    b. an estate.
    c. one or more of the bundle of rights to real property.
    d. the right to possession and use of real property.

2. Encumbrances and police powers are

    a. interests that do not include possession.
    b. limited forms of an estate.
    c. unrelated to interests.
    d. types of public interests.

3. What distinguishes a freehold estate from a leasehold estate?

    a. A freehold includes the right to dispose or use.
    b. A leasehold endures only for a specific period of time.
    c. A freehold cannot be defeasible.
    d. A leasehold is subject to government restrictions.

4. The highest form of ownership interest one can acquire in real estate is the

    a. dower and curtesy.
    b. conventional life estate.
    c. defeasible fee simple estate.
    d. absolute fee simple estate.

5. The distinguishing feature of a defeasible fee simple estate is that

    a. it can be passed on to heirs.
    b. it has no restrictions on use.
    c. the estate may revert to a grantor or heirs if the prescribed use changes.
    d. it is of unlimited duration.

6. Upon the death of the owner, a life estate passes to

    a. the original owner or other named person.
    b. the owner's heirs.
    c. the state.
    d. the owner's spouse.

7. How is a conventional life estate created?

    a. It happens automatically when title transfers unless a fee simple is specifically claimed.
    b. A fee simple owner grants the life estate to a life tenant.
    c. It is created by judicial action.
    d. It is created by a statutory period of adverse possession.

8. What distinguishes a pur autre vie life estate from an ordinary life estate?

    a. The pur autre vie estate endures only for the lifetime of the grantor.
    b. The pur autre vie estate endures only for the lifetime of the grantee.
    c. The pur autre vie estate endures only for the lifetime of a person other than the grantee.
    d. The pur autre vie estate cannot revert to the grantor.

9. Which of the following life estates is created by someone other than the owner?

    a. Conventional life estate
    b. Ordinary life estate
    c. Legal life estate
    d. Community property life estate.

10. Which of the following is true of a homestead?

    a. A homestead interest cannot be conveyed by one spouse.
    b. A homestead interest cannot be passed to the children of the head of household.
    c. A homestead interest is a form of conventional life estate.
    d. A homestead is a primary or secondary residence occupied by a family.

11. Dower refers to

    a. joint tenancy of husband and wife.
    b. a wife's life estate interest in her husband's property.
    c. a wife's homestead interest.
    d. a child's life estate interest in his or her parents' homestead.

12. Which of the following is an illustration of the legal concept of elective share?

    a. A surviving spouse places a lien on a debtor's property.
    b. A widow who was excluded from a will makes a claim to a portion of the couple's principal residence.
    c. A spouse who loses her home because of her husband's gambling debt sues in court for exemption from the debt.
    d. A widower whose spouse died without a will sues to change the provisions of the will.

13. A one-year lease on a house has expired, but the tenant continues sending monthly rent checks to the owner, and the owner accepts them. What kind of leasehold estate exists?

    a. Estate for years
    b. Estate from period to period
    c. Estate at will
    d. Estate at sufferance

CHAPTER FOUR: OWNERSHIP

1. When a single individual or entity owns a fee or life estate in a real property, the type of ownership is

    a. tenancy in severalty.
    b. tenancy by the entireties.
    c. absolute fee simple.
    d. legal fee simple.

2. Three people have identical rights but unequal shares in a property, share an indivisible interest, and may sell or transfer their interest without consent of the others. This type of ownership is

    a. joint tenancy.
    b. equal ownership.
    c. tenancy in common.
    d. estate in severalty.

3. The "four unities" required to create a joint tenancy include which of the following conditions?

    a. Parties must acquire respective interests at the same time.
    b. Parties must be legally married at the time of acquiring interest.
    c. Parties must be family members.
    d. Parties must have joint financial resources.

4. Unlike tenants in common, joint tenants

    a. own distinct portions of the physical property.
    b. cannot will their interest to a party outside the tenancy.
    c. may own unequal shares of the property.
    d. cannot sell their interest to outside parties.

5. In a community property state, a basic distinction is made between

    a. property acquired together and property acquired separately over the duration of the marriage.
    b. property owned privately versus property owned by the state.
    c. property acquired during a marriage and property already owned by each party at the time of marriage.
    d. property acquired during the marriage and property acquired after the marriage.

6. Who are the essential parties involved in an estate in trust?

    a. Owner, trustor and lawyer
    b. Owner, trustor and trustee
    c. Trustee, title company, and beneficiary
    d. Trustor, trustee and beneficiary

7. The distinguishing features of a condominium estate are

    a. ownership of a share in an association that owns one's apartment.
    b. tenancy in common interest in airspace and common areas of the property.
    c. fee simple ownership of the airspace in a unit and an undivided share of the entire property's common areas.
    d. fee simple ownership of a pro rata share of the entire property.

8. Who owns the property in a time-share estate?

    a. Ownership is shared by the developer and the broker.
    b. The property is owned by tenants in common or by a freehold owner who leases on a time-share basis.
    c. A real estate investment trust holds a fee simple estate.
    d. A general partner holds a fee simple interest and interval estates are owned by limited partners.

9. Which of the following is true of a cooperative?

    a. A cooperative may hold an owner liable for the unpaid operating expenses of other owners.
    b. The owners have a fee simple interest in the airspace of their respective apartments.
    c. Owners may retain their apartments even if they sell their stock in the cooperative.
    d. The proprietary lease is guaranteed to have a fixed rate of rent over the life of the lease term.

10. One difference between a cooperative estate and a condominium estate is that

    a. a default by a coop owner may cause a foreclosure on the entire property instead of just a single unit, as with a condominium.
    b. the condominium owner must pay expenses as well as rent.
    c. the coop owner owns stock and a freehold real estate interest whereas the condominium owner simply owns real estate.
    d. the condominium owner owns the common elements and the airspace whereas the coop owner only owns the apartment.

11. A unique feature of a land trust is that

    a. the trustee controls both the trustor and the beneficiary.
    b. the trustee takes ownership of both land and improvements.
    c. the identity of the beneficiary may not be identified.
    d. the properties in the trust are probated in the states where the properties are located.

CHAPTER FIVE: ENCUMBRANCES AND LIENS

1. Easements and encroachments are types of

    a. lien.
    b. deed restriction.
    c. encumbrance.
    d. appurtenance.

2. An affirmative easement gives the benefited party

    a. the right to possess a defined portion of another's real property.
    b. the right to prevent the owner of a real property from using it in a defined way.
    c. the right to a defined use of a portion of another's real property.
    d. the right to receive a portion of any income generated by another's real property.

3. There are two adjoining properties. An easement allows property A to use the access road that belongs to property B. In this situation, property A is said to be which of the following in relation to property B?

    a. Subservient estate
    b. Servient estate
    c. Senior tenant
    d. Dominant tenement

4. Which of the following describes a situation in which an easement might be created against the wishes of the property owner?

    a. The property has been continuously used as an easement with the knowledge but without the permission of the owner for a period of time.
    b. The owner of an adjoining property asks the property owner for an easement, is refused, and then uses the property anyway without the knowledge of the owner.
    c. The owner of an adjoining property decides he needs to widen his driveway by sharing his neighbor's driveway and sues in court to create an easement by necessity.
    d. The owner of an adjoining property grants an easement to a third party that includes an easement on the first property.

5. What is the primary danger of allowing an encroachment?

    a. An encroachment automatically grants the benefiting party an easement.
    b. The encroached party may be liable for additional real estate taxes to cover the area being encroached upon by the neighboring property.
    c. Over time, the encroachment may become an easement by prescription that damages the property's market value.
    d. An encroachment creates a lien.

6. A property owner who is selling her land wants to control how it is used in the future. She might accomplish her aim by means of

    a. an injunction.
    b. a deed restriction.
    c. an easement.
    d. a land trust.

7. What distinguishes a lien from other types of encumbrance?

    a. It involves a monetary claim against the value of a property.
    b. It lowers the value of a property.
    c. It is created voluntarily by the property owner.
    d. It attaches to the property rather than to the owner of the property.

8. A certain property has the following liens recorded against it: a mortgage lien dating from three years ago; a mechanic's lien dating from two years ago; a real estate tax lien for the current year; and a second mortgage lien dating from the current year. In case of a foreclosure, which of these liens will be paid first?

    a. First mortgage lien
    b. Mechanic's lien
    c. Real estate tax lien
    d. Second mortgage lien

9. The lien priority of junior liens can be changed by a lienor's agreement to

a. forgive portions of the debt.
b. assign the note.
c. foreclose on the note.
d. subordinate.

10. Among junior liens, the order of priority is generally established according to

a. the date of recordation.
b. the amount.
c. the order of disbursement.
d. special agreement among lienees.

11. What is meant by a "lien-theory" state?

a. A state in which liens are given priority over other encumbrances
b. A state in which a mortgagor retains title to the property when a mortgage lien is created
c. A state in which the holder of a mortgage lien receives title to the mortgaged property until the debt is satisfied
d. A state in which liens exist in theory but not in practice

12. A homeowner has hired a contractor to build a room addition. The work has been completed and the contractor has been paid for all work and materials but fails to pay the lumber yard for a load of lumber. What potential problem may the home owner experience?

a. The contractor may place a mechanic's lien for the amount of the lumber against the homeowner's real property.
b. The lumber yard may place a vendor's lien against the contractor and the homeowner for the amount of the lumber.
c. The lumber yard may place a mechanic's lien for the amount of the lumber against the homeowner's real property.
d. The homeowner has no liability because the contractor was paid for the lumber.

13. The process of enforcing a lien by forcing sale of the lienee's property is called

a. execution.
b. attachment.
c. foreclosure.
d. subordination.

14. An important difference between a judicial foreclosure and a non-judicial foreclosure is

a. there is no right to redeem the property in a non-judicial foreclosure.
b. a judicial foreclosure forces a sale of the property.
c. a non-judicial foreclosure ensures that all liens are paid in order of priority.
d. the lienor receives title directly in a non-judicial foreclosure.

15. A defaulting borrower may avoid foreclosure by giving the mortgagee

a. a promissory note.
b. a deed in lieu of foreclosure.
c. a redemption notice.
d. a lis pendens.

16. A property survey reveals that a new driveway extends one foot onto a neighbor's property. This is an example of

a. an easement appurtenant.
b. an encroachment.
c. an easement by prescription.
d. a party wall easement.

17. A property owner has an easement appurtenant on her property. When the property is sold to another party, the easement

a. terminates.
b. transfers with the property.
c. transfers with the owner to a new property.
d. becomes a lien on the property.

18. A brick fence straddles the property line of two neighbors. The neighbors agree not to damage it in any way. This is an example of

a. a party wall.
b. an encroachment.
c. a trade fixture.
d. a deed restriction.

19. A property owner allows Betty Luanne to cross his property as a shortcut to her kindergarten school bus. One day the property owner dies. What right was Betty given, and what happens to it in the future?

a. A personal easement in gross, which continues after the owner's death
b. An easement by prescription, which continues after the owner's death
c. A license, which continues after the owner's death
d. A license, which terminates at the owner's death

20. A court renders a judgment which authorizes a lien to be placed against the defendant's house, car, and personal belongings. This is an example of a

a. specific judgment lien.
b. general judgment lien.
c. voluntary judgment lien.
d. superior judgment lien.

21. What happens in a short sale?

    a. The transaction is completed before the end of the contingency period.
    b. Buyer and seller complete a transaction without the assistance of a licensed agent.
    c. The proceeds of the sale do not cover the seller's outstanding mortgage loan balance.
    d. The seller agrees to accept less than the listing price.

CHAPTER SIX: TRANSFERRING AND RECORDING TITLE TO REAL ESTATE

1. Which of the following best describes the concept of "legal title" to real estate?"

    a. Ownership of the bundle of rights to real estate
    b. The right of a buyer or lender to obtain ownership under certain circumstances
    c. Possession of a deed
    d. Absolute proof of ownership of real estate

2. A person claims ownership of a parcel of real estate to a prospective buyer, stating that she has lived on the property for five years and nobody has ever bothered her. The claimant also shows the buyer a copy of the deed. The legal basis of this claim is referred to as

    a. prescriptive notice.
    b. constructive notice.
    c. hostile notice.
    d. actual notice.

3. Constructive notice of ownership of a parcel of real estate is primarily demonstrated through

    a. direct inspection to see who is in possession.
    b. title insurance.
    c. title records.
    d. a construction permit.

4. An owner transfers title to a property to a buyer in exchange for a consideration. This is an example of

    a. voluntary alienation.
    b. escheat.
    c. hypothecation.
    d. estoppel.

5. For a deed to convey title, it is necessary for the deed to be

    a. on a standard form.
    b. certified by the grantor.
    c. accepted by the grantee.
    d. signed by the grantee.

6. The only required clause in a deed of conveyance is one that

    a. states restrictions and limitations to the estate being conveyed.
    b. states the parties and the type of estate being conveyed.
    c. states that the grantor has done nothing to impair title to the property being conveyed.
    d. states the grantor's intention, names the parties, describes the property, and indicates a consideration.

7. The purpose of a covenant clause in a deed of conveyance is to

    a. state the grantor's assurance or warrant to the grantee that a certain condition or fact concerning the property is true.
    b. state the grantee's promise to use the property in a prescribed manner.
    c. warrant that the grantor has never encumbered title.
    d. describe the consideration that the grantee promises to give in return for title.

8. The type of statutory deed that contains the most complete protection for the grantee is a

    a. guardian's deed.
    b. special warranty deed.
    c. general warranty deed.
    d. quitclaim deed.

9. A person wishes to convey any and all interests in a property to another without making any assurances as to encumbrances, liens, or any other title defects on the property. This party would most likely use which of the following types of deed?

    a. A sheriff's deed
    b. A special warranty deed
    c. A partition deed
    d. A quitclaim deed

10. A one-time tax levied on a property for purposes of recording a transaction is called

    a. an intangible sales tax.
    b. a documentary stamp tax.
    c. an ad valorem tax.
    d. a franchise tax.

11. If a person dies with no legal heirs or relations and has left no valid will, what happens to real property owned by that person?

a. It is taken by the state according to the process called escheat.
b. It is reconveyed to the previous owner in the chain of title.
c. It is taken by the title insurance company according to the process called involuntary alienation.
d. It is conveyed to the highest bidder at a public auction.

12. Just prior to passing away, a person tells two witnesses that she would like her estate to pass to her husband. One witness records the statement and signs his name. This is an example of

a. an enforceable holographic will.
b. an unenforceable holographic will.
c. an enforceable nuncupative will.
d. an unenforceable nuncupative will.

13. If a person having several heirs dies intestate, the property will

a. pass to heirs by the laws of descent and distribution.
b. escheat to the state.
c. pass to the surviving spouse through elective share.
d. pass to the surviving heirs according to the provisions of the will.

14. A property owner can avert the danger of losing title by adverse possession by

a. recording proof of ownership in county title records.
b. inspecting the property and evicting any trespassers found.
c. claiming hostile and notorious possession.
d. filing a claim of right with the county recorder.

15. A hermit secretly lives in a cave on a 200-acre property. After twenty years, the person makes a claim of ownership to the property. This claim will likely be

a. upheld through adverse possession.
b. upheld because of the length of possession.
c. declined through the doctrine of prior appropriation.
d. declined because possession was secretive.

16. The fundamental purpose of recording instruments that affect real property is to

a. prove ownership of the property.
b. avoid adverse possession.
c. give constructive notice of one's rights and interests in the property.
d. assemble all relevant documents in a single place.

17. What is "chain of title?"

a. The list of all parties who have ever owned real estate.
b. The bundle of rights linked to the recorded title to a parcel.
c. A chronology of successive owners of record of a parcel of real estate.
d. Involuntary conveyance of title by statutory rules of descent.

18. The Torrens System differs from other title recording systems in that

a. title is conveyed only when conveyance is registered on the title certificate.
b. the Torrens System requires prior approval of a transaction before it can be registered.
c. the Torrens System is not recognized by title insurance companies.
d. it allows unrecorded encumbrances to cloud title.

19. To be marketable, title must be

a. registered in Torrens.
b. free of undisclosed defects and encumbrances.
c. abstracted by an attorney.
d. guaranteed by a title certificate.

20. With the exception of a Torrens certificate, the best evidence of marketable title is

a. a signed deed.
b. a title certificate.
c. title insurance.
d. an attorney's opinion.

CHAPTER SEVEN: LEASING ESSENTIALS

1. A lease contract is best described as

a. a temporary transfer of legal title.
b. an instrument of conveyance of limited title.
c. a conveyance of a possessory interest.
d. a title conveyance in exchange for rent.

2. When a tenant acquires a leasehold estate through a lease, what does the property owner acquire?

a. A freehold estate
b. A reduced leasehold estate
c. A leasehold estate
d. A leased fee estate

3. When an owner leases her property, she temporarily relinquishes the right to

a. transfer the property.
b. encumber the property.
c. occupy the property.
d. maintain the property.

4. Which of the following happens when a leased property is sold?

   a. The buyer acquires title subject to the lease.
   b. The lease is cancelled.
   c. The lease expires within thirty days unless renewed.
   d. A new lease is automatically executed.

5. A landlord and tenant complete a one-year lease. The following week, the landlord dies. Which of the following is true?

   a. The lease is cancelled and must be re-written.
   b. The tenant must continue to abide by all lease terms.
   c. The tenant may annul the lease at his or her option.
   d. The landlord's heirs may cancel the lease at their option.

6. If a lease does not state a specific ending date, when does it terminate?

   a. Immediately, since it is an invalid lease
   b. After one year
   c. When either party gives proper notice
   d. Whenever the property is sold

7. In accordance with the Statute of Frauds,

   a. leases in excess of one year must be recorded to be enforceable.
   b. oral leases are not enforceable.
   c. a five-year lease must be in writing to be enforceable.
   d. an unwritten lease is fraudulent.

8. What is one important difference between a sublease and a lease assignment?

   a. In an assignment, responsibility for the original lease is transferred completely to the assignee.
   b. In a sublease, the original tenant retains primary responsibility for performance of the original lease contract.
   c. A sublease does not convey any of the leasehold interest.
   d. A sublease conveys the entire leasehold interest.

9. Which of the following lease types conveys rights other than the rights to exclusive use and occupancy of the entire property?

   a. A rights lease
   b. A percentage lease
   c. A gross lease
   d. A net lease

10. An owner leases a property to a business in exchange for rent. The tenant is required to pay all operating expenses as well. This is an example of a

    a. proprietary lease.
    b. percentage lease.
    c. gross lease.
    d. net lease.

11. The percentage lease is most often used by

    a. industrial landlords.
    b. retail landlords.
    c. residential landlords.
    d. office landlords.

12. Which of the following summarizes the general terms of a ground lease?

    a. The landlord sells the ground to another, then leases it back.
    b. A tenant buys the landlord's ground, then leases the improvements.
    c. The landlord leases the ground floor of the building to a commercial tenant.
    d. The tenant leases the ground from the landlord and owns the improvements.

13. Among the usual remedies available to the injured party if tenant or landlord defaults on the terms of a lease is the right to

    a. sue to compel performance of the contract.
    b. enter a lien against the other's estate.
    c. lock the other party out of the premises.
    d. apply the security deposit to legal expenses.

14. A lease automatically terminates under which of the following circumstances?

    a. The tenant fails to pay rent.
    b. The leased property is foreclosed.
    c. The tenant goes out of business.
    d. The landlord cancels the lease.

15. One of the aims of the Uniform Residential Landlord and Tenant Act is to

    a. create a standard residential lease for use nationwide.
    b. force states to enact tenants' rights laws.
    c. establish uniform rental rates for each type of property.
    d. discourage the use of unfair and overly complex leases.

16. A primary theme of the Uniform Residential Landlord and Tenant Act is that both landlord and tenant

    a. waive their rights to sue for damages.
    b. bargain with each other in good faith.
    c. give sixty days' notice of intent to terminate the lease.
    d. observe the Realtor's Code of Ethics.

CHAPTER EIGHT: LAND USE PLANNING AND CONTROL

11. A central goal of public land use planning is to

    a. balance individual property rights with the community's welfare.
    b. develop an accord between property owners and tenants.
    c. impede development by for-profit developers and construction contractors.
    d. subordinate private interests to the public good.

2. The best definition of a master plan is

    a. an annual review of all land use permits and zones.
    b. a comprehensive analysis of existing land use patterns in a market.
    c. a state or regional land use law requiring compliance on a county-by-county basis.
    d. a fusion of land use laws and local land use objectives and strategies.

3. The principal mechanism for implementing a master plan is

    a. zoning.
    b. referendum.
    c. public elections.
    d. property management.

4. Zoning, building codes, and environmental restrictions are forms of local land use control known as

    a. force majeure.
    b. pre-emption.
    c. police power.
    d. concurrency.

5. If a municipality exerts its power of eminent domain against a certain property owner, what happens?

    a. The owner must pay higher property taxes or give up the property.
    b. The owner must cede an easement without receiving any compensation.
    c. The municipality annexes the property.
    d. The owner must sell the property or grant an easement to the municipality for just compensation.

6. In most jurisdictions, the master plan is managed by

    a. the mayor or county superintendent.
    b. the Board of Equalization.
    c. the planning commission.
    d. the zoning board of adjustment.

7. Counties and municipalities have the legal right to control land use due to

    a. the doctrine of appropriation.
    b. delegation of authority by state-level enabling acts.
    c. custom and tradition.
    d. consensus of the local community through referendum.

8. To be valid, a local zoning ordinance must

    a. reasonably promote community health, safety and welfare.
    b. comply with federal zoning laws.
    c. apply only to unique properties.
    d. be published periodically in the local newspaper.

9. What is the fundamental purpose of a building permit?

    a. To restrict the number of new development projects
    b. To establish the basis for an inspection
    c. To promote certificates of occupancy
    d. To ensure that improvements comply with codes

10. A primary objective of residential zoning is to

    a. control the value ranges of homes in a neighborhood.
    b. regulate density.
    c. ensure that only a limited amount of commercial and industrial activity is permitted in a particular residential zone.
    d. maximize intensity of usage.

11. A non-profit organization wants to erect a much-needed daycare center in a residential zone. Given other favorable circumstances, the local authorities grant permission by allowing

    a. a special exception.
    b. an illegal nonconforming use.
    c. a variance.
    d. a license.

12. A property that conformed with zoning ordinances when it was developed but does not conform to new ordinances is said to be

    a. a special exception.
    b. a variance.
    c. a legal nonconforming use.
    d. an anomaly.

13. One situation in which a zoning board might permit a variance is when

    a. it would cause the property owner unreasonable hardship to bring the property into compliance with zoning ordinances.
    b. the property owner is the one who brings the variance to the attention of the zoning board.
    c. the variance was caused by a contractor rather than by the property owner.
    d. the property is in conflict with no more than one zoning ordinance.

14. The approval process for development of multiple properties in an area includes submission of

    a. a covenant of restriction.
    b. a plat of subdivision.
    c. a court order.
    d. a developer's pro forma.

15. A county or municipal authority usually grants a certificate of occupancy for new construction only after

    a. all contractors have been paid for services.
    b. all work has been completed for at least thirty days.
    c. the construction complies with building codes.
    d. the tax assessor has valued the improvement.

16. In addition to government entities, organizations that may be able to condemn property under the power of eminent domain include

    a. public utilities.
    b. financial institutions.
    c. major employers.
    d. neighborhood associations.

17. A property owner is precluded by deed restriction from developing a thirty foot boat dock. The limitation prompts the owner to sell to another party. The new owner

    a. is free to build the dock since the next door neighbor built a similar dock two weeks later.
    b. takes title subject to the same restriction.
    c. can build the dock with special permission from the zoning board.
    d. may build, since the restriction is extinguished by the sale.

18. A declaration of restriction in a planned unit development is unlike a deed restriction in that

    a. it applies only to aesthetic standards of property use.
    b. it attaches to rights rather than interests.
    c. it cannot be terminated by a single individual.
    d. it takes effect only when approved by a homeowners' association.

19. A deed restriction or declaration of restriction may be enforced by means of a

    a. sheriff's warrant.
    b. zoning commission order.
    c. foreclosure action.
    d. court injunction.

20. A distinguishing feature of a deed condition is that

    a. it gives the grantor the right to re-possess the property if the grantee violates the condition.
    b. it ceases to apply if a violation is allowed to continue for a certain period of time.
    c. it can be filed at any time after title has been transferred.
    d. it restricts who may own the property.

21. Which of the following is a limitation on homeowners' association regulations?

    a. They may not require members to carry insurance.
    b. They may not impose a rule that is illegal.
    c. They may not limit the number of people who can reside in a member's residence.
    d. They may not prohibit certain types of pets on the premises.

CHAPTER NINE: LEGAL DESCRIPTIONS

1. What is the principal purpose underlying legal descriptions of real property?

    a. To create a consistent, unchanging standard for locating the property.
    b. To eliminate all possible boundary disputes.
    c. To comply with federal laws.
    d. To eliminate cumbersome metes and bounds descriptions.

2. Which of the following is a distinctive feature of metes and bounds descriptions?

    a. They use meridians and base lines.
    b. They identify an enclosed area, beginning and ending at the same point.
    c. They use lot and block numbers.as the street address.
    d. They incorporate elevation into the descriptions.

3. A certain legal description contains the phrase "...southeasterly along Happ Road to the stone landmark..." What kind of description is this?

    a. Plat survey plat of survey is
    b. Government grid
    c. Metes and bounds
    d. Rectangular survey

4. The abbreviation POB stands for

   a. perimeter of boundaries.
   b. point of beginning.
   c. point of bounds.
   d. plat of boundary.

5. What are the approximate dimensions of a township in the rectangular survey system?

   a . Thirty-six miles on a side
   b . Twenty-five square miles.
   c . Depends on the state.
   d . Six miles by six miles

6. The area running north and south between meridians is a

   a . range.
   b . township.
   c . strip.
   d . tier.

7. The area running east and west between base lines is a

   a . range.
   b . tier.
   c . parameter.
   d . parallel.

8. How many sections are there in a township?

   a. One
   b. Six
   c. Twelve
   d. Thirty-six

9. A section contains how many acres?

   a. 640
   b. 320
   c. 160
   d. 40

10. How many acres are there in the S 1/2 of the NW ¼ of Section 3?

   a. 20 acres
   b. 40 acres
   c. 80 acres
   d. 160 acres

11. If a parcel does not have a lot and block number and is too irregular to be described as a fraction of a section, the legal description

   a. is the street address.
   b. will include a metes and bounds description.
   c. will use an estimate of the sectional fraction.
   d. will create a special reference number.

12. The legal description of a parcel in a subdivision that has been recorded with lot and block numbers on a plat of survey is

   a. the lot and block number, with section, township and meridian references.
   b. the standard rectangular survey description.
   c. the subdivision plat map.
   d. the lot and block number.

13. A datum is a reference point used for legal descriptions of

   a. agricultural and ranch properties.
   b. properties that straddle state boundaries.
   c. properties located above or below the earth's surface.
   d. irregularly-shaped properties.

CHAPTER TEN: FUNDAMENTALS OF CONTRACT .LAW

1. An important legal feature of a contract is

   a. it represents a "meeting of the minds."
   b. it must use precise wording in a document.
   c. it is not voidable.
   d. it can be created only by an attorney.

2. According to contract law, every valid contract is also

   a. void.
   b. enforceable.
   c. enforceable or unenforceable.
   d. voidable.

3. The guardian for a mentally incompetent party enters into an oral contract with another party to buy a trade fixture. This contract

   a. does not meet validity requirements.
   b. is possibly valid and enforceable.
   c. must be in writing to be valid.
   d. is valid but unenforceable.

4. A prospective homebuyer submits a signed offer to buy a house with the condition that the seller pays financing points at closing. The seller disagrees, crosses out the points clause, then signs and returns the document to the buyer. At this point, assuming all other contract validity items are in order, the status of the offer is

   a. an accepted offer, therefore a valid contract.
   b. an invalid contract.
   c. a counteroffer.
   d. an invalid offer.

5. As part of a construction contract between a contractor and a buyer, the contractor promises to complete construction by November 20. This promise can be construed as

   a. competency on behalf of the contractor.
   b. mutual consent.
   c. good faith.
   d. valuable consideration.

6. An unscrupulous investor completes a contract with a buyer to sell a property the investor does not own. The sale contract for this transaction

   a. is voidable.
   b. must be in writing.
   c. is void.
   d. is illegal yet potentially enforceable.

7. A homeowner encourages an agent to aggressively persuade a buyer to purchase his house by overinflating historical appreciation rates. The agent and the seller agree that 25% annual appreciation would work, even though this figure is four times actual rates. The pitch succeeds, and the seller accepts the buyer's resulting offer. This contract is

   a. enforceable.
   b. voidable.
   c. void.
   d. valid.

8. The statute of limitations requires that parties to a contract who have been damaged or who question the contract's provisions

   a. must act within a statutory period.
   b. must select a specific, limited course of action for recouping their losses.
   c. must arbitrate prior to taking court action.
   d. must wait a statutory period before they may take legal action.

9. The purpose of the Statute of Frauds is to

   a. invalidate certain oral contracts.
   b. require certain conveyance-related contracts to be in writing.
   c. nullify oral leases and listing agreements.
   d. eliminate fraud in real estate contracts.

10. A seller immediately accepts a buyer's offer but waits eight days before returning the accepted document to the buyer. Meanwhile, the offer has expired. Which of the following is true?

   a. The buyer is bound to the contract since it was accepted immediately.
   b. The buyer has no obligations to the seller whatsoever.
   c. The buyer may not rescind the expired offer.
   d. The seller may sue for specific performance.

11. A buyer agrees to all terms of a seller's offer except price. The buyer lowers the price by $1,000, signs the form, and mails it back to the seller. At this point, the seller's offer

   a. is void.
   b. becomes an executory contract.
   c. becomes a counteroffer.
   d. has been accepted.

12. A buyer submits an offer to a seller. Two hours later, the buyer finds a better house, calls the first seller, and withdraws the offer. Which of the following is true?

   a. The buyer may not revoke the offer in such a short period of time.
   b. The first seller may sue the buyer for specific performance.
   c. If the seller accepted the offer, the buyer must perform.
   d. The original offer is legally extinguished.

13. Real estate contracts that are not personal service contracts

   a. may be assigned.
   b. are not assignable.
   c. must be in writing.
   d. are exempt from the statute of frauds.

14. Which of the following contracts must be in writing to be enforceable?

   a. A parol contract.
   b. A six-month lease.
   c. A two-year lease.
   d. An executory contract.

15. A good example of a unilateral contract is

   a. an option to purchase.
   b. a listing agreement.
   c. a personal services agreement.
   d. a sale contract.

16. A contract is discharged whenever

   a. there is a cooling period.
   b. both parties have signed it.
   c. it is performed.
   d. the parties agree to their respective promises.

17. A contract may be defensibly terminated without damages if

   a. it is abandoned by one party.
   b. it is impossible to perform.
   c. it is deemed to be valid.
   d. both parties breach its terms.

18. A landlord suddenly terminates a tenant's lease in violation of the lease terms. The tenant takes action to compel the landlord to comply with the violated terms. This is an example of a suit for

a. rescission.
b. specific performance.
c. damages.
d. forfeiture.

CHAPTER ELEVEN: NATIONAL AGENCY

1. The essence of the agency relationship between an agent and a principal can best be described as a relationship of

a. mutual consent, consideration, and acceptance.
b. diligence, results, and compensation.
c. service, dignity, and respect.
d. trust, confidence, and good faith.

2. In an agency relationship, the principal is required to

a. promote the agent's best interests.
b. accept the advice of the agent.
c. provide sufficient information for the agent to complete the agent's tasks.
d. maintain confidentiality.

3. A principal empowers an agent to conduct the ongoing activities of one of her business enterprises. This is an example of

a. limited agency.
b. general agency.
c. universal agency.
d. special agency.

4. A property seller empowers an agent to market and sell a property on his behalf. This is an example of

a. general agency.
b. special agency.
c. universal agency.
d. no agency.

5. Implied agency arises when

a. an agent accepts an oral listing.
b. a principal accepts an oral listing.
c. a party creates an agency relationship outside of an express agreement.
d. a principal agrees to all terms of a written listing agreement, whether express or implied.

6. An agency relationship may be involuntarily terminated for which of the following reasons?

a. Death or incapacity of the agent
b. Mutual consent
c. Full performance
d. Renewal of the agent's license

7. A principal discloses that she would sell a property for \$375,000. During the listing period, the house is marketed for \$425,000. No offers come in, and the listing expires. Two weeks later, the agent grumbles to a customer that the seller would have sold for less than the listed price. Which of the following is true?

a. The agent has violated the duty of confidentiality.
b. The agent has fulfilled all fiduciary duties, including confidentiality, since the listing had expired.
c. The agent is violating the duties owed this customer.
d. The agent has created a dual agency situation with the customer.

8. A principal instructs an agent to market a property only to families on the north side of town. The agent refuses to comply. In this case,

a. the agent has violated fiduciary duty.
b. the agent has not violated fiduciary duty.
c. the agent is liable for breaching the listing terms.
d. the agent should obey the instruction to salvage the listing.

9. An owner's agent is showing a buyer an apartment building. The buyer notices water stains on the ceiling, and informs the agent. The agent's best course of action is to

a. immediately contract to paint the ceiling.
b. immediately contract to repair the roof.
c. suggest the buyer make a lower-price offer.
d. inform the seller.

10. An agent owes customers several duties. These may be best described as

a. fairness, care, and honesty.
b. obedience, confidentiality, and accounting.
c. diligence, care, and loyalty.
d. honesty, diligence, and skill.

11. An agent fails to discover flood marks on the walls in the basement of a property. The agent sells the property, and the buyer later sues the agent for failing to mention the problem. In this case, the agent

a. may be guilty of intentional misrepresentation.
b. has an exposure to a charge of negligent misrepresentation.
c. has little exposure, since the problem was not mentioned on the signed disclosure form.
d. is not vulnerable, since the problem was not discovered.

12. An agent informs a buyer that a clause in a contract is standard language. After explaining the clause, the agent assures the buyer that the clause does not mean anything significant. If something goes wrong with the transaction, the agent could be liable for

    a. violating duties owed a customer.
    b. misinterpreting the clause.
    c. intentional misrepresentation.
    d. practicing law without a license.

13. An outside broker locates a seller for a buyer representative's client. In this instance, the outside broker is acting as

    a. a single agent.
    b. a dual agent.
    c. a subagent.
    d. a secret agent.

14. Agent Bob, who works for Broker Bill, obtains an owner listing to lease a building. Bill's other agent, Sue, locates a tenant for Bob's listing. In the absence of any arrangement to the contrary, Broker Bill in this instance is

    a. an implied agent.
    b. a dual agent.
    c. a single agent.
    d. a subagent.

15. An agent is operating as a disclosed dual agent on a transaction. In this case, the agent

    a. may not represent one party's interests to the detriment of the other.
    b. must withdraw from the relationships.
    c. must be obedient and loyal to both parties.
    d. must require that the principals share equally in paying the commission.

16. The duties of an agent acting as a facilitator are most similar to those of a

    a. subagent.
    b. single agent.
    c. dual agent.
    d. implied agent.

17. The meaning and import of the agency relationship should be disclosed to the client

    a. prior to completing a listing agreement.
    b. prior to or upon completion of an offer.
    c. upon the initial contact with the person.
    d. whenever a dual agency relationship is indicated.

18. Owner agents must disclose their agency relationship to tenants or buyers

    a. immediately prior to the initial contact.
    b. upon initial contact.
    c. whenever substantive contact is made.
    d. immediately following any offer executed by the customer.

19. A tenant representative should disclose his or her agency relationship to the owner's agent

    a. immediately prior to the initial contact.
    b. upon initial contact.
    c. immediately prior to substantive contact.
    d. immediately following any offer executed by the landlord.

20. A transaction broker should disclose his or her agency relationship to the transaction principals

    a. upon first substantive contact.
    b. upon completion of the listing agreement.
    c. immediately following completion of any offer.
    d. upon initial contact of any kind.

21. Licensee Gretchen of the Jumbo Mountain Agency takes a listing to sell the home of John Hess. Prospective buyer Lucy Bingham asks licensee Calvin Bentley of the same agency to assist her in purchasing the Hess property. What can the broker of the Jumbo agency do to prevent Gretchen and Calvin from creating unwanted dual agency conflicts for Jumbo?

    a. Appoint Gretchen and Calvin as designated agents of the seller and buyer, respectively.
    b. Have Calvin sign an exclusive buyer agency agreement with the buyer.
    c. Have Gretchen sign a non-exclusive subagency agreement with the seller.
    d. Take over Gretchen's listing and act directly as the seller's agent.

CHAPTER TWELVE: LISTING AGREEMENTS: AN OVERVIEW

1. To be valid, a listing agreement

    a. must be in writing.
    b. may be oral or written.
    c. must be an express agreement.
    d. must be enforceable.

2. The type of listing that assures a broker of compensation for procuring a customer, regardless of the procuring party, is a(n)

    a. exclusive right-to sell agreement.
    b. exclusive agency agreement.
    c. open listing.
    d. net listing.

3. An owner agrees to pay a broker for procuring a tenant unless it is the owner who finds the tenant. This is an example of a(n)

    a. exclusive right-to sell agreement.
    b. exclusive agency agreement.
    c. open listing.
    d. net listing.

4. A landlord promises to compensate a broker for procuring a tenant, provided the broker is the procuring cause. This is an example of a(n)

   a. exclusive right-to sell agreement.
   b. exclusive agency agreement.
   c. open listing.
   d. net listing.

5. A property owner agrees to pay a broker a commission, provided the owner receives a minimum amount of proceeds from the sale at closing. This is an example of a(n)

   a. exclusive right-to sell agreement.
   b. exclusive agency agreement.
   c. open listing.
   d. net listing.

6. The most significant difference between an owner representation agreement and a buyer representation agreement is

   a. the client.
   b. the commission amount.
   c. agency law applications.
   d. contract law applications.

7. A multiple listing authorization gives a broker what authority?

   a. To list the owner's property in a multiple listing service
   b. To sell several properties for the owner at once
   c. To sell or lease the property
   d. To delegate the listing responsibilities to other agents

8. A broker is hired to procure a customer for a client. In order to earn compensation, the agent must procure a customer who

   a. has seen the property and reviewed all documents.
   b. is ready, willing, and able to transact.
   c. has completed an acceptable sale or lease contract.
   d. will successfully complete the transaction at closing.

9. One of the most important actions an owner's agent is authorized to perform under an exclusive listing agreement is

   a. showing the property.
   b. assisting the customer in evaluating the relative merits of other properties.
   c. authorizing price adjustments in a timely manner.
   d. executing the sale or lease agreement.

10. An agent's performance of due diligence concerning a listing can best be described as

   a. initiating the marketing plan on or before a deadline.
   b. expending an amount of effort that is commensurate with the nature and size of the transaction.
   c. ascertaining the facts about the client and the property at the onset of the listing period.
   d. helping customers satisfy their needs to the extent they are entitled.

11. The amount of a real estate broker's commission is

   a. established among competing brokers.
   b. established through negotiation with clients.
   c. established by the Board of Realtors.
   d. established by state real estate license law.

12. A client suddenly decides to revoke an exclusive right-to-sell listing midway through the listing term. The reason stated: the client did not like the agent. In this case,

   a. the client is criminally liable for discrimination on the basis of the cause for cancellation.
   b. the client may be liable for a commission and marketing expenses.
   c. the agent can sue the client for specific performance, even if no customer had been located.
   d. the agent has no recourse but to accept the revocation.

13. A "protection period" clause in an exclusive listing provides that

   a. the owner is protected from all liabilities arising from the agent's actions performed within the agent's scope of duties.
   b. the agent has a claim to a commission if the owner sells or leases to a party within a certain time following the listing's expiration.
   c. agents are entitled to extend a listing agreement's term if a transaction is imminent.
   d. an owner is not liable for a commission if a prospective customer delays in completing an acceptable offer.

14. A seller wants a licensee to put her home in the MLS and conduct an open house but do nothing else to sell it for a reduced commission. The kind of listing agreement that would allow this arrangement is a(n)

   a. multiple listing agreement.
   b. transaction broker agreement.
   c. limited services agreement.
   d. open listing agreement.

CHAPTER THIRTEEN: GENERAL BROKERAGE PRACTICES

1. Which of the following represents the core activity of real estate brokerage?

   a. Prospecting for and qualifying potential customers
   b. Buying and selling properties for one's company
   c. Procuring customers for clients and effecting transactions
   d. Negotiating sale or lease terms for a client

2. What is co-brokerage?

   a. An owner agent and a buyer agent combine efforts to complete a sale.
   b. Outside brokers acting as subagents assist a listing agent in procuring a customer.
   c. An owner or buyer lists with several brokers to complete a transaction.
   d. Agents from a single agency cooperate to generate listings for the broker.

3. Which of the following best summarizes the critical skills in real estate brokerage?

   a. Communications, market knowledge, mathematics, and analysis
   b. Selling skills, law, and qualification
   c. Fiduciary duties
   d. Listing, marketing, facilitating transactions, and managing information

4. Which of the following is a valid distinction between a corporation and a proprietorship?

   a. A corporation has perpetual existence; a proprietorship terminates upon the owner's death.
   b. Proprietorships are liable for their actions, while corporations are not.
   c. Proprietorships may broker real estate, while corporations may not.
   d. Corporations are not subject to taxation, while proprietorships are.

5. One similarity between a general partnership and a limited partnership is that

   a. both are subject to double-taxation.
   b. both may broker real estate if properly licensed.
   c. the partners in both organizations take an active role in managing the business.
   d. all partners bear full liability for debts to the extent of the debt.

6. Two real estate companies agree to conjoin their resources for the development and sale of an apartment complex, for which profits will be shared equally. This is an example of

   a. a cooperative association.
   b. a real estate investment trust.
   c. a limited partnership.
   d. a joint venture.

7. Which of the following characterizes a real estate franchisee?

   a. A local brokerage owned and operated by a national franchisor
   b. A locally-owned brokerage affiliated with a national franchisor for purposes of enhanced image and resources
   c. A national brokerage company which charges local brokers fees for membership
   d. A national firm which contracts with local franchisors to promote the national identity

8. The term "Realtor"

   a. is the generic name used by brokers throughout the country as a trade identity.
   b. is the identity for any duly licensed, active agent or broker.
   c. is the trade identity for all members of any properly chartered real estate trade organizations.
   d. may only be used by brokers belonging to the National Association of Realtors®.

9. Real estate sales agents are legally authorized to

   a. represent their employing broker in procuring clients and customers.
   b. act directly on a client's behalf to discharge the broker's listing responsibilities.
   c. negotiate and execute contracts for sale on behalf of the client.
   d. take on the listing responsibilities for other listings in MLS.

10. An important distinction between an independent contractor salesperson (IC) and an employee salesperson is

    a. the IC is responsible for taxes; the broker does not withhold.
    b. the IC must obtain his or her own training; it is not provided by the broker.
    c. the employee is not entitled to company benefits.
    d. the IC must abide by all office policies and meeting schedules.

11. An important commitment employing brokers make to salespeople is

 a. a pledge of continued employment over a predetermined period.
 b. a guarantee of market-based, competitive commission structures.
 c. providing them with all listings in the agency.
 d. producing a sufficient number of customers through advertising to make a reasonable living.

12. A salesperson's commission rate and structure is established by

 a. state regulation.
 b. competitive conditions.
 c. agreement with other brokers in the market.
 d. negotiations with the client.

13. Three of the most important skills involved in the listing process are

 a. persuasion, appraisal, and market analysis.
 b. communicating, co-brokering, and timing.
 c. marketing, advertising, and conducting open houses.
 d. locating clients, pricing property, and making listing presentations.

14. Pricing property correctly is pivotal to marketing listings, because

 a. underpriced properties do not require the broker's services.
 b. overpricing a property will lengthen the time required to receive compensation for services.
 c. underpricing a property does not serve the best interests of a client.
 d. overpricing a property does not serve the best interests of customers.

15. The objective of the listing presentation is to

 a. explain how the agent and the agency enjoy a competitive advantage over other companies.
 b. condition the owner to price the property at the lowest possible level.
 c. provide all information necessary for the owner to execute the listing.
 d. execute the listing agreement, then explain its provisions.

16. In marketing an owner's property, the objective of an agent's marketing plan is to

 a. actively participate in the multiple listing service.
 b. expose the property to the maximum number of prospects in relation to marketing expenses and efforts.
 c. ensure that a transaction occurs that will compensate the agent.
 d. convince prospects of the property's superiority over other properties.

17. In obtaining offers from a buyer, an agent must be careful to

 a. pursue only those offers which are at or near the listing price.
 b. balance the owner's price expectations with the buyer's opinion of value.
 c. avoid disclosing what price the owner will accept
 d. avoid completing offers that are beneath market value.

18. When a property is "under contract,"

 a. the principals have agreed to an option to purchase, provided the buyer can obtain financing.
 b. the buyer and the seller are engaged in negotiations to complete a sale contract.
 c. the principals have entered into a sale contract and must satisfy any contingencies prior to closing.
 d. certain contingencies must be satisfied before the buyer or seller will agree to sign the sale contract.

19. Conversion is the act of

 a. mixing escrow funds with the broker's operating funds.
 b. appropriating client or customer deposits for use in the agency's business.
 c. converting an offer into a binding contract.
 d. converting escrow funds into equity funds in a property at the closing.

20. Commingling is the practice of

 a. blending escrow funds on a number of properties in one escrow account.
 b. mixing socially with prospects at open houses or other marketing functions.
 c. appropriating client or customer deposits for use in the agency's business.
 d. mixing escrow funds with the broker's operating funds.

21. Real estate advertising is a regulated activity. One important restriction in placing ads is

 a. a broker may only place blind ads in approved publications.
 b. a broker must have all advertising approved by the proper state regulatory agency.
 c. the advertising must not be misleading.
 d. sales agents may only advertise in their own name.

22. The three principal brokerage firms in a market agree to pay sales agents 15% more than any other competitor currently in practice. This is an example of

 a. collusion.
 b. price fixing.
 c. allocation of markets.
 d. steering.

23. Two leading agencies jointly agree to raise commissions charged a certain class of client to 8% of the sales price. Which of the following is true?

    a. This is a perfectly legitimate business practice.
    b. The brokers have illegally fixed prices.
    c. The brokers have allocated markets.
    d. The brokers have engaged in legal collusion.

24. A corporation would like an agent to sell its country grocery store. Included in the sale are the inventory, equipment, and real property. The agent locates a full-price buyer who does not want to acquire any of the business's actual or potential liabilities. To do this transaction, the corporation would most likely

    a. propose an asset sale.
    b. undertake a stock sale.
    c. propose an exchange.
    d. enter into a sale-leaseback transaction.

25. A broker is reviewing the balance sheet of her new listing to sell a business. Three of the entries on the books are licenses, trademarks, and goodwill. These would be examples of

    a. tangible assets.
    b. intangible assets.
    c. short-term liabilities.
    d. long-term liabilities.

26. In business brokerage, the notion of goodwill is best defined as

    a. the commitment by the agent to expend maximum effort on the listing.
    b. establishing pricing levels that will generate the good will of prospective customers.
    c. the value or price of the business over and above the value of its other assets.
    d. the portion of the sale price that is depreciable.

27. Which of the following statements about the handling of trust funds is TRUE?

    a. Trust accounts may never contain non-trust funds under any circumstances.
    b. Funds being held for a client must be placed in a trust account within a required number of days after all parties have accepted an offer to purchase.
    c. A salesperson may hold an earnest money deposit until the transaction is completed.
    d. A broker may withdraw funds from a trust account to pay business expenses as long as the funds are replaced before the end of the month.

28. Three brokers from different firms are having lunch together after a downtown business club meeting. In their conversation, a fourth broker from another firm is mentioned. The three brokers agree that they don't like this other broker, and decide they will no longer show her listings to potential buyers. If they act on this decision, they may be guilty of an illegal act of

    a. group boycotting.
    b. market allocation.
    c. violating their business association code.
    d. commingling.

CHAPTER FOURTEEN: OVERVIEW OF CONVEYANCE CONTRACTS

1. Several buyers are competing for the last available home in a desirable new subdivision. One buyer calls the owner-developer directly on the phone and offers $10,000 over and above the listed price. The developer accepts the offer. At this point,

    a. the parties have a valid, enforceable sale contract on the home.
    b. the parties have completed a verbal, executory contract.
    c. the parties may not cancel their contract.
    d. the developer could not entertain other offers on the property.

2. An owner completes a contract to sell her property. Before closing, the seller runs into financial trouble and assigns the contract to her principal creditor. The buyer cries foul, fearing the property will be lost. Which of the following is true?

    a. The buyer can sue the assignee to disallow the illegal assignment.
    b. The buyer can take legal action against the assignor.
    c. The assignor has completed a legal action.
    d. The sale contract is nullified.

3. During the executory period of a sale contract, the buyer acquires an equitable title interest in the property. This means that

    a. the buyer can potentially force the seller to transfer ownership.
    b. both parties own the property equally.
    c. if contract contingencies are not met, the buyer takes legal title.
    d. the buyer owns equity in the subject property to the extent of the funds deposited in escrow.

4. The purpose of an escrow account is to

    a. entrust deposit monies to an impartial fiduciary.
    b. enable the principals to access the funds in escrow without interference from the other party.
    c. ensure that the broker receives her commission.
    d. prevent the buyer from withdrawing the offer.

5. A sale contract contains an open-ended financing contingency: if the buyer cannot obtain financing, the deal is off. Six months later, the buyer still cannot secure financing. Which of the following is true?

   a. The seller may cancel the contract, since it can be ruled invalid.
   b. The buyer can continue indefinitely to seek financing, and the seller's property must remain off the market.
   c. The seller must return the buyer's deposit.
   d. The seller can force a lender to commit to a loan under fair financing laws.

6. In the event of a buyer's default, a provision for liquidated damages in a sale contract enables a seller to

   a. sue the buyer for the anticipated down payment.
   b. force the buyer to quitclaim equitable title.
   c. sue the buyer for all liquid assets lost as a result of the default.
   d. claim the deposit as relief for the buyer's failure to perform.

7. Which of the following best characterizes a conventional sale contract?

   a. Voluntary, unilateral, and executory
   b. Involuntary, bilateral, and contingent
   c. Voluntary, bilateral, and executory
   d. Involuntary, unilateral, and executory

8. A due-on-sale clause in a sale contract puts parties on notice that

   a. the full price of the property is due the seller at closing.
   b. any loans surviving closing become immediately payable.
   c. all of the seller's debts must be retired before or upon closing.
   d. third-party loans surviving closing may be accelerated by the lender.

9. A sale contract may specifically deal with tax withholding responsibility if the seller is a foreigner. What is this responsibility?

   a. The buyer must withhold 15% of the purchase price at closing for the seller's capital gain tax payment.
   b. The buyer must withhold 15% of the purchase price at closing for the buyer's capital gain tax payment.
   c. The seller must withhold 15% of the buyer's funds as a deposit on the buyer's capital gain tax.
   d. The seller must withhold 15% of the sale price to pay the seller's capital gain tax.

10. An important legal characteristic of an option-to-buy agreement is that

   a. the potential buyer, the optionee, is obligated to buy the property once the option agreement is completed.
   b. the optionor must perform if the optionee takes the option, but the optionee is under no obligation to do so.
   c. the contract can be executed at no cost to the optionee.
   d. it is a bilateral agreement.

11. A tenant has an option-to-purchase agreement with the landlord that expires on June 30. On July 1, the tenant frantically calls the landlord to exercise the option, offering the apology that she was busy with a death in the family. Which of the following is true?

   a. Since options contain grace periods, the landlord must sell.
   b. The tenant loses the right to buy, but can claim the money paid for the option from the landlord.
   c. The landlord does not have to sell, but must renew the option.
   d. The option is expired, and the tenant has no rightful claim to money paid for the option.

12. A tenant exercises an option to buy a condominium. The landlord agrees, but raises the agreed price by $3,000, claiming financial distress. The landlord does, however, offer the tenant two months of free rent before closing as an offset. Which of the following is true?

   a. The tenant can force the sale at the original terms.
   b. The landlord has taken a fully legal action which the tenant must abide by.
   c. The option is null, and the optionee may reclaim any option money paid.
   d. The landlord must offer sufficient free rent to equal the $3,000 price increase.

13. Which of the following is true regarding the legal nature of option contracts?

   a. They are not assignable.
   b. They are enforceable, whether written or oral.
   c. They give the optionee an equitable interest in the property.
   d. They must be recorded to be valid.

14. An important distinction between a contract for deed and a contract for sale is

   a. a contract for deed requires no action on the part of the seller.
   b. a contract for deed requires no action on the part of the buyer.
   c. the seller retains legal title in a contract for deed transaction until fully executed.
   d. the buyer acquires legal title in a contract for deed transaction.

15. While a property is under a contract for deed, the seller, or vendor, mortgages her equity in the property, and has a separate judgment lien placed on the property. Faced with financial loss, the vendor assigns the contract to another party, then leaves town. What can the vendee do in this case?

   a. rightfully cancel the agreement and reclaim all deposits.
   b. sue the creditor for removal of the judgment lien.
   c. disclaim the lien and the mortgage due to homestead rights.
   d. comply with the contract and take legal title when its terms are fulfilled.

16. A potential danger involved in a contract for deed is that

    a. the vendor may rightfully sell legal title to another party during the contract period.
    b. the vendor's rights to encumber the property are extinguished.
    c. the vendee may not have a right of redemption.
    d. the vendee must make an inordinately high down payment, which can be lost.

CHAPTER FIFTEEN: REAL ESTATE MARKET ECONOMICS

1. Price is best described as

    a. what suppliers charge for goods and services.
    b. the amount of money consumers are willing to pay for a product or service.
    c. the amount of money a buyer and seller agree to exchange to complete a transaction.
    d. a control placed on prices by the federal government.

2. Four principal determinants of value underlying the price for a product are

    a. durability, quality, scarcity, and materials.
    b. desire, utility, scarcity, and purchasing power.
    c. popularity, utility, quality, and discount.
    d. desire, costs, convenience, and time.

3. A town has a rapidly growing population, but there are no longer any vacant lots around the lake to build more houses. In this case, it is likely that the price of existing homes on the lake

    a. will stabilize, since the population must stabilize.
    b. will increase.
    c. will decline, since no further building can take place.
    d. will not show any predictable movement.

4. If there is a significant undersupply of homes in a market, construction will tend to increase. This is an example of

    a. supply outstripping demand.
    b. overpricing products.
    c. the price mechanism.
    d. the market tending toward equilibrium.

5. If commercial real estate rental prices are falling in a market, it is likely that

    a. demand has outstripped supply of space.
    b. the market is in equilibrium.
    c. the market is over-supplied.
    d. employment is increasing.

6. Which of the following is an important economic characteristic of real estate?

    a. The demand must literally come to the supply.
    b. Real estate is a highly liquid product.
    c. The product is quick to adapt to market changes.
    d. The market is centralized.

7. The foremost factor contributing to commercial and residential demand in a market is

    a. marketing.
    b. base employment.
    c. existing supply of properties.
    d. household income.

8. A construction boom in a market is an indication that prices

    a. have been increasing.
    b. have been declining.
    c. have been in equilibrium.
    d. have exceeded supply.

9. A local government could stimulate the real estate market by

    a. increasing labor costs and curbing the money supply.
    b. increasing taxes and interest rates.
    c. declaring a moratorium on construction.
    d. expanding the sewer system.

10. Two important concerns of retail property users are

    a. trade area population and spending patterns.
    b. quality of life and dwelling amenities.
    c. costs of occupancy and building efficiency.
    d. environmental regulations and access by suppliers.

11. Two important concerns of office property users are

    a. trade area population and visibility.
    b. convenience and neighborhood make-up.
    c. costs of occupancy and building efficiency.
    d. environmental regulations and zoning.

CHAPTER SIXTEEN: APPRAISING AND ESTIMATING MARKET VALUE

1. As a component of real estate value, the principle of substitution suggests that

    a. if two similar properties are for sale, a buyer will purchase the cheaper of the two.
    b. if one of two adjacent homes is more valuable, the price of the other home will tend to rise.
    c. if too many properties are built in a market, the prices will tend to go down.
    d. people will readily move to another home if it is of equal value.

2. Highest and best use of a property is that use which

    a. is physically and financially feasible, legal, and the most productive.
    b. is legal, feasible, and deemed the most appropriate by zoning authorities.
    c. entails the largest building that zoning ordinances will allow developers to erect.
    d. conforms to other properties in the area.

3. The concept of market value is best described as

    a. the price a buyer will pay for a property, assuming other similar properties are within the same price range.
    b. the price an informed, unhurried seller will charge for a property assuming a reasonable period of exposure with other competing properties.
    c. the price a buyer and seller agree upon for a property assuming stable interest rates, appreciation rates, and prices of other similar properties.
    d. the price that a willing, informed, and unpressured seller and buyer agree upon for a property assuming a cash price and the property's reasonable exposure to the market.

4. A significant difference between an appraisal and a broker's opinion of value is

    a. the appraiser tends to use only one or two of the approaches to value.
    b. the broker may not be a disinterested party.
    c. the broker is subject to government regulation in generating the opinion.
    d. the appraiser uses less current market data.

5. A notable weakness of the sales comparison approach to value is that

    a. there may be no recent sale price data in the market.
    b. the approach is not based on the principle of substitution.
    c. the approach is only accurate with unique, special purpose properties.
    d. sale prices cannot be compared, since all real estate is different.

6. The steps in the market data approach are

    a. choose nearby comparables, adjust the subject for differences, estimate the value.
    b. gather relevant price data, apply the data to the subject, estimate the value.
    c. select comparable properties, adjust the comparables, estimate the value.
    d. identify previous price paid, apply an appreciation rate, estimate the value.

7. In the sales comparison approach, an adjustment is warranted if

    a. the buyer obtains conventional financing for the property.
    b. the seller offers below-market seller financing.
    c. a comparable is located in another, albeit similar neighborhood
    d. one property has a hip roof and the other has a gabled roof.

8. To complete the sales comparison approach, the appraiser

    a. averages the adjustments.
    b. weights the comparables.
    c. discards all comparables having a lower value.
    d. identifies the subject's value as that of the nearest comparable.

9. One weakness of the cost approach for appraising market value is that

    a. builders may not pay market value for materials or labor.
    b. market value is not always the same as what the property cost.
    c. comparables used may not have similar quality of construction.
    d. new properties have inestimable costs and rates of depreciation.

10. The cost of constructing a functional equivalent of a subject property is known as

    a. reproduction cost.
    b. replacement cost.
    c. restitution cost.
    d. reconstruction cost.

11. An office building lacks sufficient cooling capability to accommodate modern computer equipment. This is an example of

    a. physical deterioration.
    b. economic obsolescence.
    c. incurable depreciation.
    d. functional obsolescence.

12. A home is located in a neighborhood where homeowners on the block have failed to maintain their properties. This is an example of

    a. curable external obsolescence.
    b. incurable economic obsolescence.
    c. functional obsolescence.
    d. physical deterioration.

13. In appraisal, loss of value in a property from any cause is referred to as

a. deterioration.
b. obsolescence.
c. depreciation.
d. deflation.

14. The first two steps in the cost approach are to estimate the value of the land and the cost of the improvements. The remaining steps are

a. estimate depreciation, subtract depreciation from cost, and add back the land value.
b. subtract deterioration from cost, estimate land depreciation, and total the two values.
c. estimate depreciation of land and improvements, subtract from original cost.
d. estimate obsolescence, subtract from the cost of land and improvements.

15. The roof of a property cost $10,000. The economic life of the roof is 20 years. Assuming the straight-line method of depreciation, what is the depreciated value of the roof after 3 years?

a. $10,000
b. $8,500
c. $7,000
d. $1,500

16. The income capitalization approach to appraising value is most applicable for which of the following property types?

a. Single family homes
b. Apartment buildings
c. Undeveloped land
d. Churches

17. The steps in the income capitalization approach are:

a. estimate gross income, multiply times the gross income multiplier.
b. estimate effective income, subtract tax, apply a capitalization rate.
c. estimate net income, and apply a capitalization rate to it.
d. estimate potential income, apply a capitalization rate to it.

18. Net operating income is equal to

a. gross income minus potential income minus expenses.
b. effective gross income minus debt service.
c. potential gross income minus vacancy and credit loss minus expenses.
d. effective gross income minus vacancy and credit loss.

19. If net income on a property is $20,000 and the cap rate is 5%, the value of the property using the income capitalization method is

a. $100,000.
b. $400,000.
c. $1,000,000.
d. $4,000,000.

20. The principal shortcoming of the gross rent multiplier approach to estimating value is that

a. numerous expenses are not taken into account.
b. the multiplier does not relate to the market.
c. the method is too complex and cumbersome.
d. the method only applies to residential properties.

21. If the monthly rent of a property is $3,000, and the gross rent multiplier (GRM) is 80, what is the value of the property?

a. $45,000
b. $240,000
c. $267,000
d. $288,000

22. A certain house has, in addition to the main house, an unfinished but heated basement where the family's adult son lives; a finished but unheated attic with sloped ceilings are seven feet in height at the ridge, that is used as a child's playroom; a two-car garage that is attached to the main house but not heated; and a large interior central stairwell providing access to the second floor. Which of these spaces would be considered part of Gross Living Area under ANSI and Fannie Mae standards?

a. The basement
b. The garage
c. The attic
d. The stairwell

CHAPTER SEVENTEEN: REAL ESTATE FINANCE

1. A homeowner borrows money from a lender and gives the lender a mortgage on the property as collateral for the loan. The homeowner retains title to the property. This is an example of

a. intermediation.
b. forfeiture.
c. hypothecation.
d. subordination.

2. Which of the following best expresses the mechanics of a mortgage loan transaction?

   a. The borrower gives the lender a note and a mortgage in exchange for loan funds.
   b. The lender gives the borrower a mortgage and receives a note in exchange for loan funds.
   c. The borrower receives a note in exchange for a mortgage from the lender.
   d. The lender gives the borrower a note, loan funds and a mortgage.

3. In a deed of trust transaction, which of the following occurs?

   a. The beneficiary conveys title to a trustee in exchange for loan funds.
   b. The trustee conveys title to a beneficiary in exchange for loan funds.
   c. The trustor conveys title to a trustee in exchange for loan funds from the beneficiary.
   d. The trustee conveys title to a trustor in exchange for loan funds from the beneficiary.

4. A lender lends money to a homeowner and takes legal title to the property as collateral during the payoff period. They are in a

   a. title-theory state.
   b. lien-theory state.
   c. state allowing land trusts.
   d. state where hypothecation is illegal.

5. A lender who charges a rate of interest in excess of legal limits is guilty of

   a. redlining.
   b. usury.
   c. profit-taking.
   d. nothing; there are no legal limits to interest rates.

6. A lender is charging 3 points on a $500,000 loan. The borrower must therefore pay the lender an advance amount of

   a. $1,500.
   b. $3,000.
   c. $15,000.
   d. $30,000.

7. The difference between a balloon loan and an amortized loan is

   a. an amortized loan is paid off over the loan period.
   b. a balloon loan always has a shorter loan term.
   c. an amortized loan requires interest-payments.
   d. a balloon loan must be retired in five years.

8. A distinctive feature of a promissory note is that

   a. it is not assignable.
   b. it must be accompanied by a mortgage.
   c. it is a negotiable instrument.
   d. it may not be prepaid.

9. When the terms of the mortgage loan are satisfied, the mortgagee

   a. may retain any overage in the escrow account.
   b. may inspect the property before returning legal title.
   c. may be entitled to charge the borrower a small fee to close the loan.
   d. may be required to execute a release of mortgage document.

10. In addition to income, credit, and employment data, a mortgage lender requires additional documentation, usually including

    a. an appraisal report.
    b. a criminal record report.
    c. a subordination agreement.
    d. a default recourse waiver.

11. The three overriding considerations of a lender's mortgage loan decision are

    a. points, interest rate, and loan term.
    b. the location of the mortgaged property, the borrower's cash, and the amount of the borrower's equity.
    c. the ability to re-pay, the value of the collateral, and the profitability of the loan.
    d. the amount of the loan, the borrower's income, and the down payment.

12. The loan-to-value ratio is an important underwriting criterion, for the primary reason that

    a. borrowers with no equity will default and abandon the property.
    b. the lender wants to ensure the loan is fully collateralized.
    c. a borrower can only afford to borrow a portion of the entire purchase price.
    d. a fair amount of borrower equity demonstrates good faith.

13. The Equal Credit Opportunity Act (ECOA) requires lenders to

    a. extend equal credit to all prospective borrowers.
    b. consider the income of a spouse in evaluating a family's creditworthiness.
    c. discount the income of a person involved in child-rearing or child-bearing.
    d. specialize lending activity by geographical area for improved customer service.

14. The purpose of an income ratio in qualifying a borrower is to

    a. safeguard against over-indebtedness.
    b. compare one's earnings to one's short-term debt.
    c. identify the highest possible interest rate that the borrower can afford.
    d. quantify the borrower's assets to the fullest extent.

15. A borrower's debt ratio is derived by

    a. dividing one's total debt by one's debt payments.
    b. dividing one's gross income by one's assets.
    c. dividing one's gross income by one's debts.
    d. dividing one's debts by one's gross income.

16. A lender's commitment to lend funds to a borrower in order to retire another outstanding loan is called a

    a. conditional loan commitment.
    b. firm loan commitment.
    c. take-out loan commitment.
    d. lock-in loan commitment.

17. At the closing of a mortgage loan

    a. the borrower pays off the note and receives clear title.
    b. the lender issues a firm loan commitment.
    c. the parties complete all loan origination documents and the loan is funded.
    d. the borrower's loan application is complete and the file closed.

18. Which laws or regulations require mortgage lenders to disclose financing costs and annual percentage rate to a borrower before funding a loan?

    a. The Equal Credit Opportunity Act
    b. Truth-in-Lending laws
    c. The Real Estate Settlement Procedures Act
    d. Federal Fair Housing Laws

19. Which laws or regulations prevent mortgage lenders from discriminating in extending credit to potential borrowers based on race, color, religion, national origin, sex, marital status, age, and dependency on public assistance?

    a. The Equal Credit Opportunity Act
    b. Truth-in-Lending laws
    c. The Real Estate Settlement Procedures Act
    d. Federal Fair Housing Laws

20. Which laws or regulations require mortgage lenders to provide an estimate of closing costs to a borrower and forbid them to pay kickbacks for referrals?

    a. the Equal Credit Opportunity Act.
    b. Truth-in-Lending laws.
    c. the Real Estate Settlement Procedures Act.
    d. Federal Fair Housing Laws.

21. The Federal Reserve System regulates the money supply in which of the following ways?

    a. Selling securities, printing money, and controlling lending underwriting requirements
    b. Buying securities, changing the discount rate, and controlling banking reserves
    c. Printing money, changing interest rates, and selling T-bills
    d. Controlling the prime rate, trading securities, and purchasing loans

22. One of the primary purposes for the secondary mortgage market is to

    a. cycle funds back to primary lenders so they can make more loans.
    b. issue second mortgages and sell them in the home equity market.
    c. lend funds to banks so they can make more loans.
    d. pay off defaulted loans made by primary mortgage lenders.

23. The major players in the secondary mortgage market are

    a. Fannie Mae, Freddie Mac, and Ginnie Mae.
    b. Fannie Mae, GMAC, and MGIC.
    c. Freddie Mac, FHA, and VA.
    d. Fannie Mae, Freddie Mac, and the Federal Reserve.

24. A principal role of FNMA is to

    a. guarantee FHA-backed and VA-backed loans.
    b. insure FHA-backed and VA-backed loans.
    c. purchase FHA-backed and VA-backed loans.
    d. originate FHA-backed and VA-backed loans.

25. The primary role of the Federal Housing Authority in the mortgage lending market is to

    a. guarantee loans made by approved lenders.
    b. insure loans made by approved lenders.
    c. purchase loans made by approved lenders.
    d. originate loans made by approved lenders.

26. The principal role of the Veteran's Administration in the mortgage lending market is to

    a. guarantee loans made by approved lenders.
    b. insure loans made by approved lenders.
    c. purchase loans made by approved lenders.
    d. originate loans made by approved lenders.

27. A graduated payment loan is a mortgage loan where

    a. loan funds are disbursed to the borrower on a graduated basis.
    b. the interest rate periodically increases in graduated phases.
    c. the loan payments gradually increase.
    d. the loan payments gradually increase and the loan term gradually decreases.

28. A buydown is a financing arrangement where

a. the lender lowers the interest rate on a loan in exchange for a prepayment of principal.
b. the borrower pays additional interest at the onset in order to obtain a lower interest rate.
c. the lender requires the borrower to buy down the price of the property by increasing the down payment.
d. the borrower pays the lender additional funds to buy down the term of the loan.

29. The key feature of an adjustable mortgage loan is that

a. the interest rate may vary.
b. the monthly payment increases over the life of the loan.
c. the principal balance does not amortize.
d. the loan term can be shortened or lengthened.

30. One feature of a wraparound mortgage loan is that

a. the loan is a senior loan.
b. the seller offering the buyer a wraparound can profit from a difference in interest rates.
c. the underlying loan must be retired.
d. the second mortgage borrower may make payments directly to the first mortgage lender.

31. A builder is required to secure a loan with mortgages on three properties. This is an example of

a. a participation mortgage loan.
b. a blanket mortgage loan.
c. a permanent mortgage loan.
d. a bridge loan.

32. Which of the following is true of a loan with negative amortization?

a. The loan is an interest-only loan.
b. Payments are not sufficient to retire the loan.
c. The loan balance is diminishing, or going negative.
d. Additional interest is being added to the monthly payment.

33. Hopeful homeowner Henry has an eye on a house valued at $600,000. His lender's LTV is 80%. How much cash will Henry need to put in for a downpayment?

a. $80,000
b. $120,000
c. $360,000
d. $480,000

34. A bank is offering Henry a 30-year loan of $300,000 at a rate of 4.5%. The loan constant for this loan is 5.07. How much will Henry have to pay for monthly principal and interest?

a. 1,251
b. 1,521
c. 1,957
d. 5,917

35. Mary is paying $1,800 per month in principal and interest on a 20-year loan at 4% interest but can't remember how much she originally borrowed. The loan constant is 6.06. Can you help?

a. 284,360
b. 297,030
c. 310,001
d. 376,569

CHAPTER EIGHTEEN: REAL ESTATE INVESTMENT

1. All investors desire their investments to increase in value. However,

a. the degree of return is inversely related to the degree of risk.
b. the more the investor stands to gain, the greater the risk that the investor may lose.
c. investments requiring intense management have lesser returns.
d. the more liquid an investment is, the greater the chances are that the investment will not appreciate.

2. Two of the rewards that investments offer are

a. income and tax benefits.
b. negative leverage and appreciation.
c. appreciation and taxation.
d. positive leverage and prestige.

3. An investor invests in fifteen diversified bond funds. This is an example of an investment in

a. money.
b. equity.
c. debt.
d. real estate.

4. A real estate investment can take a long period of time to sell. For the investor, this means that real estate is

a. management intensive.
b. insensitive to marketing.
c. vulnerable to seller's markets.
d. relatively illiquid.

5. Compared to a stock portfolio, a real estate investment would be considered

a. a riskier investment.
b. a more management-intensive investment.
c. a shorter-term investment.
d. a more leveraged investment.

6. Six investors purchase a shopping center. One investor manages the tenants and another handles the marketing and leasing. Two investors manage accounting and finance, and the remaining two run the management office. This is a possible example of

   a. a general partnership.
   b. a limited partnership.
   c. a real estate investment trust.
   d. an investment conduit.

7. Taxable income produced by an income property is

   a. gross income minus expenses plus land and building depreciation.
   b. gross income minus expenses minus land and building depreciation.
   c. gross income minus building depreciation plus land depreciation.
   d. gross income minus expenses minus building depreciation.

8. As a general rule, in deriving taxable income on an investment property, it is legal to

   a. deduct principal and interest payments from income.
   b. deduct principal payments from income.
   c. deduct interest payments from income.
   d. deduct principal and interest payments from income and capital gain.

9. Which of the following is true of the tax treatment of a principal residence?

   a. The owner may deduct the property's interest and principal from ordinary income.
   b. The owner may depreciate the property and deduct depreciation expenses.
   c. The owner can deduct any capital gain when the property is sold.
   d. The owner may be able to exclude capital gain from taxable income when the property is sold.

10. An investment property seller pays $14,000 in closing costs. These costs

   a. may be deducted from personal income.
   b. may be deducted from the property's income.
   c. may be deducted from the sale price for gains tax purposes.
   d. may be deducted from the adjusted basis for gains tax purposes.

11. Capital gain tax is figured by multiplying one's tax bracket times

   a. the sum of the beginning basis plus gain.
   b. the difference between net sale proceeds and adjusted basis.
   c. the sum of net sale proceeds and capital gain.
   d. the difference between net sale proceeds and capital gain.

12. Cash flow is a measure of how much pre-tax or after-tax cash an investment property generates. To derive cash flow it is therefore necessary to exclude

   a. cost recovery expense.
   b. interest expense.
   c. loan principal payments.
   d. net operating income.

13. One way investors measure the yield of an investment is by

   a. dividing net operating income by cash flow.
   b. multiplying the investor's required yield times after-tax cash flow.
   c. dividing cash flow by the investor's equity.
   d. multiplying cash flow times the price paid for the property.

CHAPTER NINETEEN: REAL ESTATE TAXATION

1. Which of the following is true with respect to real property taxation by the federal government?

   a. It may impose ad valorem property taxes and capital gain tax.
   b. It may not impose property taxes nor tax liens.
   c. There are no federal ad valorem taxes on real property.
   d. It may impose ad valorem tax, but not capital gain tax.

2. According to law, states

   a. may not levy real estate taxes.
   b. may not impose tax liens.
   c. may delegate taxing authority to county governments.
   d. may prevent federal taxation of real estate within their respective jurisdictions, if properly legislated.

3. The role of local tax districts is to

   a. levy income, sales, and property taxes to meet their budget requirements.
   b. manage their budgeted portion of real estate tax revenues levied and distributed by the state.
   c. impose property taxes for specific municipal services.
   d. place tax liens on its facilities.

4. A special tax district might be created to

   a. construct and manage a park district.
   b. create a two-mile extension of county sewer facilities.
   c. establish and maintain a public library.
   d. create a fire department.

5. Ad valorem taxes are based on

   a. the replacement value of property.
   b. the assessed value of property.
   c. the millage value of property.
   d. the broker's estimate of value.

6. The ad valorem tax base of a municipal jurisdiction is equal to

   a. the jurisdiction's annual budget times the tax rate.
   b. the total of all assessed values of properties minus exemptions.
   c. the total amount of ad valorem taxes required by the budget.
   d. the municipality's budget multiplied times the millage rate.

7. As part of the assessment process, many taxing entities utilize equalization boards in order to

   a. adjust millage rates within the district to ensure fairness.
   b. modify the tax rate from one neighborhood to the next.
   c. ensure that property owners have nearly equal tax bills.
   d. smooth out wide discrepancies of assessed values within the district.

8. A homeowner receives a tax bill that she feels is outrageous. This taxpayer may

   a. appeal to adjust the millage rate.
   b. appeal to adjust the district's budget.
   c. appeal to adjust the assessed valuation.
   d. not appeal.

9. The purpose of a homestead tax exemption is

   a. to exempt qualified property owners from ad valorem taxation.
   b. to offer an amount of tax relief on an owner's principal residence.
   c. to encourage multiple property investment.
   d. to exempt owners of principal residences who rent their properties.

10. A millage rate is derived by

   a. dividing the tax requirement by the tax base.
   b. multiplying the tax base times the tax requirement.
   c. adding an inflation factor to the prior year's tax rate.
   d. dividing the tax base by the tax requirement.

11. A homeowner's total tax bill is derived by

   a. dividing the tax requirement by the tax base.
   b. multiplying each district's tax rate times the assessed value of the property.
   c. multiplying each district's tax rate times the taxable value of the property.
   d. averaging the tax rate for each tax district, and multiplying the average tax rate times the assessed value.

12. A unique characteristic of a special assessment tax is that

   a. it only applies to properties which will benefit from the public improvement.
   b. the equalization board discounts levies for properties not affected by the public improvement.
   c. more valuable properties which stand to benefit will pay proportionately more taxes.
   d. it creates an involuntary junior lien on the property.

13. A tax certificate

   a. certifies to tax collectors that a property owner has paid all ad valorem taxes on the property for the calendar year.
   b. entitles its holder to apply for a tax deed after a certain period.
   c. exempts its holder from paying taxes on the particular property referenced by the certificate.
   d. waives a property owner's rights of redemption in a foreclosure.

14. An equitable right of redemption

   a. allows a holder of a tax certificate to redeem it for a tax deed.
   b. gives a delinquent taxpayer a grace period prior to the tax sale to pay property taxes.
   c. gives a holder of a tax deed the right to acquire the property named in the tax certificate.
   d. gives a delinquent taxpayer a grace period after the tax sale to pay property taxes.

CHAPTER TWENTY: PROFESSIONAL PRACTICES

1. The principal theme of federal fair housing laws is to

   a. ensure all Americans a fair chance to own a home.
   b. prohibit discrimination in housing transactions.
   c. ensure that housing transactions are negotiated fairly.
   d. prohibit agents from dealing unfairly with clients and customers.

2. It is illegal to discriminate in selling a house based on race, color, religion, or national origin. This is provided for through

   a. the Civil Rights Act of 1866.
   b. Executive Order 11063.
   c. the Civil Rights Act of 1968.
   d. the Fair Housing Amendments Act of 1988.

3. Which of the following laws or rulings extended discrimination to include gender, handicapped status, and family status?

   a. Executive Order 11063
   b. the Civil Rights Act of 1968
   c. the Fair Housing Amendments Act of 1988
   d. Jones v Mayer

4. An agent informs numerous families in a neighborhood that several minority families are planning to move into the immediate area, and that the trend could have adverse effects on property values. This activity is

   a. blockbusting.
   b. legal but unprofessional redlining.
   c. discriminatory misrepresentation.
   d. negligent misrepresentation.

5. A minority family would like to buy a home in a certain price range. The agent shows the family all available properties in a neighborhood of families with similar backgrounds. The agent did not mention a number of homes in the family's price range in other neighborhoods. This agent could be liable for

   a. blockbusting.
   b. providing unequal services.
   c. steering.
   d. nothing; his services were legal and acceptable.

6. An agent does not like a particular minority buyer, and is very short with the person, refusing to engage in lengthy conversation or show him any properties. A second minority party visits the office the next day. The agent is very forthcoming, and shows the person five prospective properties. This agent could be liable for

   a. providing unequal services.
   b. steering.
   c. misrepresentation.
   d. nothing; both parties were minorities, and therefore no discrimination occurred.

7. Following the client's recommendation, an agent conceals the availability of a property from an employed but pregnant and unmarried minority woman. This agent could be liable for

   a. discriminatory misrepresentation.
   b. steering.
   c. violating fiduciary duty.
   d. nothing: an agent may show or not show any property at his or her discretion.

8. A condominium complex prohibits ownership of any unit by persons under 55 years of age. The association claims it has made the prohibition properly. Which of the following is true?

   a. They are violating the Civil Rights Act of 1866.
   b. They are violating the Fair Housing Amendments Act of 1988.
   c. They are guilty of age discrimination.
   d. The prohibition may be legal.

9. An owner suddenly pulls a property off the market after hearing from the agent on the phone that the agent had received a full-price offer from a minority party. The agent then informs the offeror that the home has been removed from the market and is unavailable. Which party or parties, if any, have violated fair housing laws?

   a. The agent only
   b. The owner only
   c. The agent and the owner
   d. Neither agent nor owner

10. Real estate trade associations promote a code of ethics primarily to establish

    a. minimum standards of practice as imposed by law.
    b. fair housing law.
    c. high standards of practice for all facets of the business.
    d. grounds for license revocation.

11. The parts of the Americans with Disabilities Act that most concern real estate agents are those that deal with

    a. telecommunications and insurance.
    b. public accommodations and employment.
    c. state and local government.
    d. agency and public service.

12. If a licensee knows a negative material fact about a client's property that the client has not disclosed, the licensee must

    a. keep the fact confidential.
    b. report the seller to the local real estate board.
    c. disclose the information to others.
    d. change the seller's disclosure form.

13. How does CERCLA concern real estate agents?

    a. It may cause them to be held liable for improper disclosure of potential violations.
    b. It requires them to conduct Phase II Environmental Site Assessments.
    c. It makes them subject to Environmental Protection Agency orders.
    d. It absolves them of any responsibility for knowing about environmental hazards.

14. Which of the following is a fact about home warranties that an agent should be sure a client knows?

   a. If the homeowner has paid an annual fee for the warranty, there are no additional charges for service.
   b. Conditions that pre-existed the coverage date of the warranty will not be covered.
   c. Any item that is not specifically excluded in the warranty contract may be assumed to be covered.
   d. Warranties are usually purchased to cover the full term of the mortgage loan.
   e.

15. What is an agent's duty regarding inspections?

   a. Personally conduct a detailed inspection of all major structures and systems
   b. Accompany all inspectors as they inspect the agent's listed property
   c. Disclose the result of any inspection, if known to the agent
   d. Interview and hire inspectors for clients.

CHAPTER TWENTY-ONE: CLOSINGS

1. The purpose of the closing event is to

   a. confirm that the buyer has fulfilled all contract requirements prior to title transfer immediately after closing.
   b. ensure that the seller has marketable title before monies are transferred.
   c. conclude the process for loan approval.
   d. exchange legal title for the sale price.

2. A buyer's financing arrangements are often concluded at closing, because

   a. lenders do not fund loans unless title is being transferred.
   b. the lender wants to ensure proper handling of the collateral for the loan.
   c. the loan term must coincide with title transfer.
   d. the deed will be held as collateral for the loan.

3. The Real Estate Settlement Procedures Act prescribes closing procedures that must be followed whenever

   a. a first, second, or third mortgage lien is involved.
   b. the loan is to be sold to the FNMA.
   c. the buyer pays all cash for the property.
   d. the property is a residential complex in excess of four units.

4. A sale contract stipulates that a buyer is to pay the seller's title insurance expenses. This practice is not customary in the area. In this case,

   a. the buyer and seller must amend the contract before closing.
   b. the contract is voidable, since the seller must pay the expense.
   c. the buyer may pay or not pay the expense, at his or her option.
   d. the buyer must pay the expense.

5. A prorated expense on the settlement statement is

   a. a debit to the buyer and seller
   b. a credit to the buyer and seller
   c. a debit and credit to the buyer and seller
   d. a debit to one party and a credit to the other.

6. The amount a buyer owes at closing is equal to

   a. the excess of the buyer's debits over the buyer's credits.
   b. the excess of the buyer's credits over the buyer's debits.
   c. the excess of the seller's debits over the seller's credits
   d. the excess of the seller's credits over the seller's debits.

7. Which of the following are examples of closing items not prorated between buyer and seller?

   a. Taxes and rents
   b. Inspection fees
   c. Utilities and hazard insurance
   d. Condominium assessments and special assessment payments

8. Which of the following items are paid in arrears?

   a. Taxes and insurance
   b. Rents and interest
   c. Taxes and interest
   d. Rents and insurance

9. Which of the following items are paid in advance?

   a. Taxes and insurance
   b. Rents and interest
   c. Insurance and interest
   d. Rents and insurance

10. If a sale contract indicates that the day of closing is "the seller's day," this means that

   a. the seller must pay prorated expenses inclusive of the day of closing.
   b. the seller does not own the property on the day of closing.
   c. the seller may elect the proration method on the day of closing.
   d. the seller must pay the buyer's portion of prorated expenses instead of the seller's portion.

11. Documentary stamps are used to

   a. document the procedures employed to close a transaction.
   b. document the payment of a transfer tax.
   c. certify that a transaction was recorded.
   d. mail closing documents to principal parties after closing.

12. What is the Internal Revenue Service's Form 1099-S?

   a. The buyer's and seller's capital gain form
   b. A form that summarizes and reports transaction data from a closing
   c. A form brokers must submit if the buyer or seller is a foreigner
   d. A lender's tax form showing that a loan was funded for a buyer

13. Assume a seller at closing must pay transfer taxes at the rate of $1.00 for every $500 of purchase price, or fraction thereof. If the sale price is $345,600, how much tax must the seller pay?

   a. $69.12
   b. $70.00
   c. $691
   d. $692

14. If a seller paid $488 for transfer taxes at closing, and the rate was $1.00 for every $400 or fraction thereof of the sale price, what was the sale price?

   a. $195,500
   b. $1,950,000
   c. $195,200
   d. $1,952,000

CHAPTER TWENTY-TWO: RISK MANAGEMENT

1. Of the following risk management strategies, the one that aims at minimizing both the severity and the likelihood of loss is

   a. avoidance.
   b. reduction.
   c. transference.
   d. retention.

2. Insurance is a method of

   a. risk elimination.
   b. risk mitigation.
   c. risk outsourcing.
   d. risk acceptance.

3. How does disclosure manage risk?

   a. It deflects and reduces risk by preventing others from claiming they were misled.
   b. It eliminates the risk of committing an error.
   c. It accepts the risk of revealing confidential information.
   d. It transfers the risk of a code violation to the client.

4. Which of the following statements about a company procedures manual as a risk management device is true?

   a. It places all the responsibility for compliance on the broker.
   b. It relieves the licensee of responsibility for knowing and obeying the law.
   c. It can be a guide to compliance with the law.
   d. It adds to the risk of misleading the public.

5. In what sense is the use of standardized forms a risk management procedure?

   a. It eliminates the risk of being unable to draft a contract correctly.
   b. It reduces the risk of losing a client by having to make a referral to an attorney.
   c. It reduces the risk of committing an unauthorized practice of law.
   d. It eliminates the risk of wasting valuable time in creating custom forms.

6. Keeping thorough records of every transaction is not only a risk management technique, it is

   a. good for company morale.
   b. necessary for obtaining market share.
   c. a technique for discovering market trends.
   d. a legal requirement.

7. Which of the following communication records must (as opposed to should) be kept?

   a. Notes on every conversation.
   b. Copies of required communications to principals.
   c. Notes from company training sessions.
   d. Business cards of licensees one meets at open houses.

8. The standard E & O policy covers damages resulting from

   a. failure to disclose an environmental condition.
   b. antitrust violations.
   c. mishandling of earnest money deposits.
   d. negligence, error or omission in carrying out professional services.

9. Which of the following is a common risk relating to the agency relationship?

   a. Failing to inform and disclose properly.
   b. Failing to take a personal interest in a transaction.
   c. Acting as an exclusive agent without an oral agency agreement.
   d. Forgetting to record the listing agreement.

10. Even after giving buyer and seller the required information about property condition disclosures, the licensee may still be subject to legal action for

   a. failing to detect customer misrepresentations.
   b. failing to disclose known adverse facts.
   c. relying on publicly available market information.
   d. advising the purchaser to exercise due diligence.

11. In performing a comparative market analysis, a licensee must be careful to

    a. use the term "market value" whenever possible in the report.
    b. show a low suggested selling price to avoid a complaint of misrepresenting the value.
    c. include the results of a certified appraisal in the analysis.
    d. avoid creating a false impression that the licensee is a certified appraiser.

12. In fulfilling a listing agreement, one of the major risk areas is

    a. finding a buyer who turns out to be unqualified.
    b. exceeding the authority of the agreement.
    c. showing the property without the presence of the owner.
    d. cooperating with other licensees.

13. A simple way of reducing the risk of committing an error or omission in the contracting process is

    a. use a checklist of all items, contingencies, dates and responsibilities that must be met.
    b. delegate some of your responsibilities to the licensee who represents the other party in the contract.
    c. call the buyer and seller daily to check on progress.
    d. cut the list of necessary tasks down to a few essentials and concentrate on tracking those.

14. Regarding contracts and forms,

    a. once written and signed they cannot be changed except by a lawyer.
    b. real estate licensees may alter forms but not contracts.
    c. whoever originates them can make changes without the risk of unauthorized practice of law.
    d. the principals may make changes as long as they sign or initial each change.

15. The best way to minimize the risk of violating fair housing laws is to

    a. deal only with consumers who do not belong to a protected class.
    b. obtain education in the content and intent of the laws.
    c. make sure there is always a witness present at all meetings with consumers.
    d. stay away from transactions involving public housing.

16. A licensee risks violating antitrust law by

    a. being present at a conversation where the setting of commission rates is discussed.
    b. being present at a discussion of antitrust laws.
    c. charging a commission rate that happens to be the same as that charged by another firm.
    d. cooperating with another firm to do market research.

17. How is an intentional misrepresentation penalized?

    a. License discipline, fines, and possible incarceration.
    b. License discipline and fines, but no incarceration.
    c. License discipline only.
    d. Fines only.

18. All of the following are areas of risk for unintentional misrepresentation EXCEPT

    a. measuring and reporting property dimensions.
    b. describing properties and amenities.
    c. stating that a client should seek legal counsel.
    d. making statements about the presence or absence of hazardous substances.

19. To reduce risks inherent in reporting transaction progress to a client, the licensee should

    a. make reports orally only, never in writing.
    b. leave progress reporting to the inspectors and other experts.
    c. advise the client that it is company policy to make no progress reports until the contingency period is over.
    d. avoid statements of opinion and speculation in all reports.

20. How does sharing the qualifying function with a lender protect a licensee?

    a. It guarantees that a buyer will have a loan.
    b. It reduces the chance of presenting an offer from an unqualified buyer.
    c. It relieves the licensee of his or her due diligence responsibilities.
    d. It allows the licensee to avoid asking embarrassing questions.

CHAPTER TWENTY-THREE: PROPERTY MANAGEMENT

1. Property managers have a _______ relationship with the property owner.

    a. non-binding
    b. partnership
    c. fiduciary
    d. subagency

2. One of the property manager's fundamental responsibilities is

    a. obtaining construction loans for the principal.
    b. financial reporting to the principal.
    c. finding a buyer for the property.
    d. maintaining good standing in a managers' professional association.

3. Effective gross income is defined as

   a. the total of scheduled rents.
   b. the total of all rents and revenues generated by a property.
   c. potential gross income minus debt service and reserves.
   d. revenue from all sources minus losses from uncollected rents, vacancies, and evictions.

4. The efficiency of marketing activities can be measured in terms of

   a. cost per tenant prospect generated per lease.
   b. number of ads produced per marketing dollar.
   c. dollars expended per square foot of vacant space.
   d. percentage of reserves expended on marketing.

5. If a property's vacancy rate is significantly lower than market rates, it may be a sign that the manager needs to

   a. lower rental rates.
   b. raise rental rates.
   c. find better tenants.
   d. improve management quality.

6. Why does a manager need to keep tenants happy?

   a. Happy tenants make fewer demands for services.
   b. Managers are contractually required to please tenants.
   c. Unhappy tenants make the owner look bad.
   d. High tenant turnover increases expenses and reduces profits.

7. What are the three kinds of maintenance a manager has to carry out for a managed property?

   a. Constructive, deconstructive, and reconstructive
   b. Routine, preventive, and corrective
   c. Scheduled, planned, and improvised
   d. Emergency, elective, and optional

8. The Americans with Disabilities Act requires property managers to

   a. ensure that disabled employees have the same level of access to facilities that all employees have.
   b. hire the disabled whenever possible.
   c. remove all existing barriers to the free movement of disabled persons within the property, regardless of the cost.
   d. remodel the ground floor of the property in accordance with ADA standards if it was built before 1978.

9. Which of the following statements about the property manager's responsibility for security and safety is true?

   a. The manager has no responsibilities for building safety beyond ensuring that fire doors and sprinklers are working.
   b. The manager's security responsibilities are limited to the common areas.
   c. A court may hold the manager responsible for the physical safety of tenants, employees, and customers in leased premises.
   d. The manager's security responsibilities are limited to tenants and their employees in their leased premises.

10. Commercial fire and hazard insurance policies usually require coverage to equal at least 80 percent of the property's

    a. replacement value.
    b. reproduction value.
    c. original cost.
    d. depreciated basis.

11. Trust funds to be handled by a property manager are likely to include all of the following except

    a. rents collected from tenants.
    b. cash for the management firm's operating expenses.
    c. security deposits.
    d. capital contributions from the property owner.

12. What kind of agency is commonly created by a management agreement?

    a. Universal
    b. Specific
    c. General
    d. Vicarious

13. The rights, duties, and liabilities of the landlord and manager are

    a. apportioned under the terms of the management contract.
    b. dictated by common law.
    c. identical.
    d. regulated by the Universal Landlord Tenant Relations Act.

14. Which of the following describes a gross lease?

    a. The tenant pays a base rent plus some or all of the operating expenses.
    b. The tenant pays a fixed rent, and the landlord pays all operating expenses.
    c. The tenant pays a base rent plus an amount based on income generated in the leased space.
    d. The tenant pays a rent that increases at specified times over the lease term.

15. If an apartment contains a refrigerator that is not included in the lease,

    a. the lessee is required to buy it from the landlord.
    b. the landlord is required to remove it.
    c. the lease is invalidated because of an incomplete property description.
    d. the property manager does not have to maintain it.

16. A basic responsibility of a landlord is to

    a. provide leased space at market rental rates.
    b. deliver a habitable property.
    c. keep the rental space freshly painted.
    d. refrain from entering the leased space at any time during the lease term.

17. How does a constructive eviction occur?

    a. A landlord obtains a court order to force the tenant to vacate the leased premises.
    b. A court officer forcibly removes the tenant from the premises.
    c. A tenant declares a landlord in default and vacates the leased premises.
    d. A landlord declares a tenant in default and takes possession of the leased premises.

18. Among the essential elements of a management plan is consideration of

    a. the competitive market for the property.
    b. the property manager's career goals.
    c. the property owner's net worth.
    d. the management firm's income goals.

CHAPTER TWENTY-FOUR: REAL ESTATE MATH

(See at end of Chapter 24)

CHAPTER TWENTY-FIVE: THE OKLAHOMA REGULATORY ENVIRONMENT

1. The only governmental body in Oklahoma with authority to issue real estate licenses is

    a. the county clerk's office
    b. the Oklahoma Real Estate Commission
    c. the Oklahoma Tax Commission
    d. the local city council

2. How many members serve on the Oklahoma Real Estate Commission?

    a. Five.
    b. Six.
    c. Seven.
    d. Nine.

3. How many Oklahoma Real Estate Commission members must be licensed real estate brokers having at least five years of experience?

    a. five
    b. four
    c. three
    d. two

4. To be appointed to the Commission, a member must be a United States citizen and must have lived in Oklahoma for at least

    a. one year
    b. two years
    c. three years
    d. five years

5. A homeowner complains to OREC that a licensee advertised a house using a fabricated square footage. Which of the following may the Commission do?

    a. Investigate the complaint and, if it finds a violation, discipline the licensee.
    b. Nothing, because only a court may address the complaint.
    c. Require the homeowner to file a private lawsuit first.
    d. Refer the matter to the city council for a hearing.

6. Under Section 858-208, the Commission's powers include all of the following EXCEPT

    a. issuing and renewing licenses
    b. approving prelicense and continuing education courses
    c. setting the commission rates that brokers must charge
    d. issuing cease and desist orders

7. Members of the Oklahoma Real Estate Commission are appointed by

    a. the State Senate alone
    b. the Oklahoma Association of Realtors
    c. the Governor, with the consent of the Senate
    d. a vote of the state's licensed brokers

8. Grounds for the Commission to discipline a licensee include

    a. negotiating a commission rate with a client
    b. making a substantial misrepresentation in a real estate transaction
    c. advertising under the firm's registered trade name
    d. depositing earnest money into the broker's trust account

9. A licensee is notified in writing that a fine is due but does not pay within thirty days. Under Section 858-402, the fine

   a. is forgiven after a grace period
   b. doubles, and a second thirty-day period begins
   c. is referred to the Recovery Fund
   d. is reduced by half

10. A consumer wins a thirty-thousand-dollar judgment against an agent for a License Code violation, but the agent files for bankruptcy and cannot pay. What is the most the consumer may recover from the Education and Recovery Fund?

    a. The full thirty thousand dollars.
    b. Nothing, because the agent is bankrupt.
    c. Twenty thousand dollars.
    d. Twenty-five thousand dollars.

11. After the Recovery Fund pays a claimant, the licensee's revoked license stays revoked until the licensee

    a. reapplies after one year
    b. completes additional continuing education
    c. passes the licensing examination again
    d. reimburses the Fund the amount paid plus interest

12. A licensee who is convicted of a felony must notify the Commission in writing within

    a. ten days of the plea
    b. thirty days of the plea and again within thirty days of judgment and sentencing
    c. sixty days of the conviction
    d. one year of the conviction

13. An associate receives written notice that OREC is investigating a complaint against him. He must provide an adequate written response within

    a. fifteen days
    b. thirty days
    c. forty-five days
    d. sixty days

14. An unlicensed person earns commissions by selling real estate for others. Under Section 858-401, the Commission may seek a fine of up to five thousand dollars or

    a. the amount of the commissions earned, whichever is greater
    b. the value of the property sold
    c. one year of the person's income
    d. double the standard license fee

15. Money collected from fines for unlicensed activity is deposited in

    a. the state general revenue fund
    b. the broker's trust account
    c. the county treasury
    d. the Oklahoma Real Estate Education and Recovery Fund

CHAPTER TWENTY-SIX: OKLAHOMA LICENSING

1. The entry-level real estate license in Oklahoma is the

   a. sales associate license
   b. provisional sales associate license
   c. broker associate license
   d. broker license

2. Which of the following is a requirement to obtain a provisional sales associate license?

   a. Being at least twenty-one years of age.
   b. Holding a college degree in real estate.
   c. Being at least eighteen years of age and a citizen or lawful permanent resident.
   d. Residing in Oklahoma for at least one year.

3. Before applying for a provisional sales associate license, a candidate must complete approved basic real estate instruction of at least

   a. ninety clock hours
   b. forty-five clock hours
   c. sixty clock hours
   d. one hundred twenty clock hours

4. Completion credit for ninety-hour Basic Course remains valid for

   a. one year
   b. two years
   c. three years
   d. five years

5. How is the Oklahoma licensing examination structured?

   a. As a single combined score.
   b. As an open-book take-home test.
   c. As a national portion only.
   d. As a national portion and an Oklahoma portion that are scored separately.

6. The provisional sales associate license is best described as

   a. non-renewable, requiring a post-license course to advance
   b. renewable every three years like other licenses
   c. valid for life once issued
   d. available only to nonresidents

7. Maria completes her ninety-hour course, passes both exam portions, and pays her fees. Before she may perform licensed activities, she must

   a. complete a college degree
   b. be sponsored by a supervising broker
   c. live in Oklahoma for one year
   d. open her own brokerage

8. To qualify for a broker license, an applicant must document how many completed real estate transactions within the past five years?

   a. three
   b. five
   c. seven
   d. ten

9. The Broker in Charge course required of a broker applicant consists of

   a. ninety hours
   b. forty-five hours
   c. fifteen hours
   d. thirty hours

10. James completes the ninety-hour advanced course and passes the broker examination, but he wants to keep working under his current managing broker. Which license fits his goal?

    a. Broker associate.
    b. Provisional sales associate.
    c. Branch broker.
    d. Nonresident broker.

11. Which requirement applies to a broker applicant but NOT to a broker associate applicant?

    a. Passing the broker examination.
    b. Completing the Broker in Charge course and documenting ten transactions.
    c. Completing the ninety-hour advanced course.
    d. Holding two years of licensure within the previous five.

12. A Texas broker plans to list and sell Oklahoma property regularly. To do so as an Oklahoma nonresident licensee, the broker must

    a. move to Oklahoma within sixty days
    b. give up the Texas license
    c. open an Oklahoma branch office
    d. pass the Oklahoma portion of the examination and appoint the Commission's Secretary-Treasurer as service agent

13. An associate lives in Kansas but is sponsored by a brokerage in Tulsa. For Oklahoma licensing, she is classified as a resident, because residency is determined by

    a. where the licensee lives
    b. where the licensee was first licensed
    c. where the sponsoring brokerage is located
    d. where the property is located

14. An Oklahoma real estate license is issued for a term of

    a. three years
    b. one year
    c. two years
    d. four years

15. A resident sales associate must complete continuing education each renewal term totaling

    a. twenty-one hours
    b. thirty hours
    c. fifteen hours
    d. forty-five hours

16. A resident broker's thirty hours of continuing education must include which of the following?

    a. Thirty hours of electives.
    b. Twenty-one required hours and nine electives.
    c. A college course in finance.
    d. The fifteen-hour Broker in Charge course and six hours of Contracts and Forms.

17. A nonresident licensee affiliated with an out-of-state brokerage must complete continuing education each term totaling
    a. eight hours
    b. thirty hours
    c. thirteen hours
    d. twenty-one hours

18. An associate decides to move to a new sponsoring broker. The change of association must be filed within
    a. two business days
    b. thirty days
    c. ten days
    d. sixty days

19. A broker refuses to release an associate who wants to transfer. After the associate gives the broker and the Commission a final written notice, the Commission releases the associate within

    a. ten days
    b. two business days
    c. thirty days
    d. one year

20. Before his provisional license expires, Daniel must complete a post-license course to earn a renewable sales associate license. That course consists of

    a. ninety hours
    b. fifteen hours
    c. thirty hours
    d. forty-five hours

CHAPTER TWENTY-SEVEN: THE OKLAHOMA BROKER RELATIONSHIPS ACT

1. Under the Oklahoma Broker Relationships Act, a broker is

   a. a fiduciary agent of the client
   b. a subagent of the seller
   c. not an agent, subagent, or dual agent in the absence of an agreement
   d. a dual agent in every transaction

2. The Broker Relationships Act replaced Oklahoma's former system of

   a. common-law agency
   b. statutory warranties
   c. federal licensing
   d. title insurance

3. Under the Act, a person who is a seller, buyer, landlord, or tenant is referred to as

   a. a client
   b. a principal
   c. a fiduciary
   d. a party

4. Which of the following is true of a brokerage service agreement under the Commission's rules?

   a. It must always be in writing to exist.
   b. It may be oral or written.
   c. It is valid only if it omits a termination date.
   d. It applies only to commercial property.

5. A brokerage service agreement includes all of the following EXCEPT

   a. a listing agreement with a seller
   b. a buyer broker agreement with a buyer
   c. a mortgage loan application
   d. a property management agreement with a landlord

6. A listing agreement is signed without stating any termination date. Under Oklahoma rules, this is

   a. a prohibited dealing
   b. perfectly acceptable
   c. required for oral agreements
   d. allowed only for nonresidents

7. A broker manages a rental house for a landlord. What does the broker owe the tenant, who has not signed a brokerage agreement?

   a. The full fiduciary duties of an agent.
   b. Nothing at all.
   c. A duty to represent the tenant as a client.
   d. The baseline duties of honesty and reasonable skill and care.

8. A firm has a house listed and is also working with a buyer who wants to make an offer on it. Before the parties sign, the firm must

   a. withdraw from the transaction
   b. give written notice to both parties that it serves both
   c. choose one party to represent
   d. refund all fees

9. Which duty does a broker owe to all parties in a transaction and may not waive?

   a. Treating all parties with honesty and reasonable skill and care.
   b. Negotiating the best price for the buyer only.
   c. Paying the seller's closing costs.
   d. Guaranteeing the condition of the property.

10. Under the Broker Relationships Act, a broker may provide brokerage services to

    a. only the seller in every transaction
    b. only the buyer in every transaction
    c. one party or both parties in a transaction
    d. neither party to a transaction

11. A seller privately tells her listing associate that the backyard has a chronic drainage problem. Under the Act, the associate

    a. may keep the problem confidential
    b. must disclose the problem, because a material defect is never confidential
    c. must disclose it only to other licensees
    d. owes no duty regarding the problem

12. A seller tells his associate that he will accept ten thousand dollars below the asking price. This information is

    a. a material defect the associate must disclose
    b. public information
    c. something the associate may share with buyers
    d. confidential, and the associate may not reveal it

13. Recent amendments require a broker to disclose, in writing, the compensation and fees to the represented party

    a. before the effective date of the contract for sale or lease
    b. only at closing
    c. within thirty days after closing
    d. only if the buyer asks

14. If a written compensation agreement does not state a time frame, the agreement defaults to

    a. one year
    b. ninety days
    c. sixty days
    d. thirty days

15. The time frame for which a compensation agreement is valid may not exceed

    a. sixty days
    b. one year
    c. two years
    d. ninety days

16. Which duties survive after a brokerage relationship has ended?

a. The duty to negotiate price.
b. The duty to advertise the property.
c. The duty to pay the other broker.
d. Accounting for money and keeping confidential information confidential.

17. The written disclosure of broker duties must be confirmed in writing by each party in a separate provision that is

a. filed with the county clerk
b. posted at the brokerage office
c. incorporated in or attached to the contract
d. published in a newspaper

18. An associate is selling a home to her own brother. Under Oklahoma rules, she must

a. disclose the family relationship in writing to the other side
b. withdraw from the transaction
c. keep the relationship confidential
d. obtain a court order

19. A licensee wants to buy a property that his own firm has listed. Before doing so, he must

a. resign his license
b. make full written disclosure of his interest to all parties
c. pay a transfer fee
d. wait one year

20. Commission rules require a licensee to disclose his or her licensed status

a. only to other licensees
b. only at closing
c. never
d. in advertising

CHAPTER TWENTY-EIGHT: REGULATION OF BROKERAGE PRACTICES

1. Under the Commission's rules, the definition of advertising

a. includes social networking and all forms of solicitation
b. is limited to newspaper ads
c. excludes yard signs
d. applies only to television

2. When advertising, a broker must use

a. any name the broker chooses
b. the registered business trade name or the name under which the broker is licensed
c. only the broker's personal name
d. the name of the listing associate

3. An advertisement for a listing must make clear that the advertiser is

a. a private party
b. a mortgage lender
c. a real estate broker, using a word such as realty or real estate
d. an attorney

4. An unlicensed assistant in a brokerage begins negotiating contract terms with a buyer. Who is responsible for this improper activity?

a. No one, because the assistant is unlicensed.
b. The buyer.
c. The Commission.
d. The broker, who is responsible for the assistant's real estate activities.

5. Which task may an unlicensed assistant lawfully perform?

a. Negotiating the price of a listing.
b. Clerical and administrative support that is not a licensed activity.
c. Showing property for compensation.
d. Soliciting clients for the firm.

6. An associate who does not hold a broker license but intentionally acts in the capacity of a broker

a. commits a prohibited dealing
b. is exempt from discipline
c. may do so with the buyer's consent
d. needs no broker at all

7. Every broker must maintain

a. a separate office in each county
b. an office only in a commercial building
c. a post office box as the sole address
d. a definite place of business

8. May a broker operate a real estate office out of the broker's residence?

a. No, residences are never permitted.
b. Only with a court order.
c. Yes, if it is registered and identified as required.
d. Only for nonresidents.

9. A firm opens an additional office in another town that is an extension of its main office. The firm must

a. obtain a branch office license with a separate managing broker
b. close the main office
c. operate the branch with associates only
d. register the branch as a team

10. Every trade name a firm uses must be

    a. approved by a court
    b. printed on the license only
    c. registered with the Commission
    d. changed every year

11. A team, for registration purposes, is

    a. a single licensee working alone
    b. two or more licensees under the same broker who present themselves as a unit under a team name
    c. two brokers from different firms
    d. an unlicensed marketing group

12. A team wants to begin advertising and taking listings under its team name. Before performing any licensed activities, the team must

    a. open its own office
    b. obtain a separate broker license
    c. file with the county clerk
    d. be registered with the Commission, and a registration fee applies

13. Real estate transaction and trust account records must be retained for a minimum of

    a. one year
    b. three years
    c. five years
    d. ten years

14. A sole proprietor broker dies unexpectedly. All advertising in the firm name must be terminated and offering signs removed within

    a. thirty days of the death
    b. ten days of the death
    c. five days of the death
    d. one year of the death

15. A broker's license is suspended. The associates working under that broker are

    a. automatically licensed as brokers
    b. permitted to keep working under the suspended broker
    c. required to surrender their licenses permanently
    d. automatically placed on inactive status unless they transfer to another broker

16. A suspended broker wants to move the firm's listings to another broker down the street. The suspended broker

    a. may do so freely
    b. may not assign listings without the written consent of each property owner
    c. may assign only commercial listings
    d. must first pay a fine

17. A broker who changes the firm's office address or telephone number must

    a. notify the Commission of the change
    b. apply for a brand-new license
    c. notify only the firm's associates
    d. wait until the next renewal to report it

18. A wholesaler puts a homeowner's property under contract intending to assign it for a higher price. Before any contract is signed, the wholesaler must disclose in writing the intent to assign and

    a. the homeowner's credit score
    b. the wholesaler's license number
    c. the appraised value
    d. the homeowner's right to cancel without penalty within two business days

19. If a wholesaler fails to include a required disclosure, the contract is

    a. fully enforceable
    b. invalid and unenforceable by the wholesaler, and the homeowner is entitled to any earnest money
    c. valid for sixty days
    d. enforceable only against the homeowner

20. A broker who holds money belonging to others must

    a. keep it in the broker's personal account
    b. give it to the listing associate
    c. keep it in a trust account separate from the broker's own funds
    d. deposit it with the county treasurer

21. Trust funds must be deposited in an account at a financial institution that is

    a. located outside Oklahoma
    b. owned by the broker
    c. any institution the broker prefers
    d. insured by an agency of the federal government

22. Mixing client trust funds with the broker's own operating money is known as

    a. commingling, which is prohibited
    b. interpleader, which is required
    c. subrogation, which is allowed
    d. escrow, which is encouraged

23. A buyer and seller dispute who is entitled to the earnest money the broker holds. A proper course for the broker is to

    a. give the money to the seller automatically
    b. keep the money as a fee
    c. hold the funds and, if needed, file an interpleader action so a court can decide
    d. split the money evenly

24. A landlord's security or damage deposit held by a broker must be kept in

    a. the broker's operating account
    b. an Oklahoma escrow account in compliance with the residential landlord and tenant law
    c. a personal savings account
    d. cash in the office safe

CHAPTER TWENTY-NINE: OKLAHOMA DISCLOSURES AND HAZARDS

1. The Residential Property Condition Disclosure Act applies to the transfer of residential property with

    a. three or more dwelling units
    b. not less than one nor more than two dwelling units
    c. only vacant land
    d. only commercial buildings

2. A seller's disclosure statement reports

    a. a full warranty of the property's condition
    b. the results of a required professional inspection
    c. an appraisal of the property
    d. the seller's actual knowledge of the property's condition

3. An owner who has never lived in a property and has no actual knowledge of its condition may instead deliver

    a. a disclaimer statement
    b. a full disclosure statement
    c. a warranty deed
    d. an appraisal report

4. Within how many days before delivery must the disclosure statement have been completed?

    a. Thirty.
    b. Ninety.
    c. One hundred eighty.
    d. Three hundred sixty-five.

5. The seller must deliver the disclosure statement to the buyer

    a. only at closing
    b. within thirty days after closing
    c. only if the buyer sues
    d. before the seller accepts an offer to purchase

6. An estate executor who never lived in the deceased's home is selling it. Regarding the disclosure statement, the transaction is

    a. subject to a double disclosure requirement
    b. exempt, so no disclosure or disclaimer form is required
    c. one that requires an appraisal
    d. one that requires a warranty

7. Which is a duty of a licensee under the Act?

    a. To personally inspect the property for hidden defects.
    b. To guarantee the accuracy of the seller's statement.
    c. To inform the seller of the disclosure obligation and disclose any defect the licensee actually knows.
    d. To complete the disclosure form for the seller.

8. A home was the site of a suicide several years ago. Under Oklahoma law, this fact is

    a. not a material fact that must be disclosed
    b. a material defect that must be disclosed
    c. an environmental hazard
    d. grounds to void the sale

9. Regarding registered sex offenders, an Oklahoma licensee has

    a. a duty to research and report all nearby offenders
    b. no duty to disclose information about registered offenders
    c. a duty to warn only buyers with children
    d. a duty to provide the offender registry at closing

10. A licensee is helping sell a home built in 1968. Because the home predates 1978, federal law requires the seller to disclose known lead-based paint and to give the buyer

    a. a one-year warranty
    b. a radon test
    c. a property survey
    d. a ten-day opportunity to inspect for lead-based paint

CHAPTER THIRTY: OKLAHOMA PROPERTY MANAGEMENT

1. Managing rental property for others for a fee in Oklahoma

    a. is a licensed activity requiring a broker
    b. requires no license at all
    c. requires only a business permit
    d. is handled by the county

2. Which of the following is exempt from the property management license requirement?

    a. A company managing dozens of homes it does not own.
    b. A licensee leasing property for clients.
    c. A resident manager who lives on the premises and manages it for the owner.
    d. A broker collecting management fees from owners.

3. Under the Commission's rules, a property management agreement is

   a. exempt from the Broker Relationships Act
   b. a brokerage service agreement
   c. an appraisal contract
   d. a government lease

4. A broker manages a rental home for an owner. In that arrangement, the tenant

   a. is the broker's client
   b. is owed the full fiduciary duties of an agent
   c. is owed no duties at all
   d. is owed honesty and reasonable skill and care but is not a client unless agreed in writing

5. A landlord must return the balance of a security deposit, without interest, within forty-five days after the tenancy ends, possession is delivered, and

   a. the tenant makes a written demand
   b. the landlord finds a new tenant
   c. the lease is recorded
   d. a court orders it

6. How long does a tenant have to make a written demand for the security deposit before it is forfeited?

   a. Thirty days.
   b. One year.
   c. Six months.
   d. Ninety days.

7. A tenant abandons an apartment, leaving behind furniture that has value. Before disposing of it, the landlord must notify the tenant in writing and allow the tenant to recover it within

   a. thirty days
   b. five days
   c. ninety days
   d. one year

8. A landlord wants to end a month-to-month tenancy. The landlord must give written notice of at least

   a. seven days
   b. ten days
   c. fifteen days
   d. thirty days

9. A tenant fails to pay rent. To resolve the issue, the landlord serves a notice to pay or quit. What amount of time does the tenant have to do this?

   a. ten days
   b. five days
   c. fifteen days
   d. thirty days

10. A tenant refuses to leave after a proper notice expires. To remove the tenant, the landlord must

   a. change the locks
   b. shut off the utilities
   c. file a forcible entry and detainer action in court
   d. remove the tenant's belongings from the premises to the curb

CHAPTER THIRTY-ONE: OTHER OKLAHOMA LAWS AND PRACTICES

1. Beyond the seven federal protected classes, the Oklahoma Fair Housing Law adds which additional class?

   a. Marital status.
   b. Income.
   c. Occupation.
   d. Age.

2. Guiding prospective buyers into or away from neighborhoods based on a protected-class characteristic is

   a. steering, a fair housing violation
   b. a lawful marketing practice
   c. an antitrust violation only
   d. required by federal law

3. Two competing brokerages agree to charge the same commission rate. This agreement is

   a. permitted if put in writing
   b. illegal price fixing
   c. a lawful cooperative agreement
   d. allowed for residential property only

4. Several firms agree to divide a city into territories so they do not overlap with one another. This is
   a. a lawful referral network
   b. blockbusting
   c. illegal market allocation
   d. a fair housing safe harbor

5. Under the Oklahoma Statute of Frauds, which agreement must be in writing to be enforceable?

   a. An agreement for the sale of real property.
   b. A one-week rental of a vacation cabin.
   c. An oral agreement to mow a lawn.
   d. A verbal price quote.

6. Oklahoma is a lien theory state, which means that a borrower who finances a home

   a. gives legal title to the lender until the loan is repaid
   b. holds no interest in the property
   c. must wait five years to take title
   d. keeps legal title, while the lender holds a lien

7. To acquire title by adverse possession in Oklahoma, a person must possess the land for

   a. seven years
   b. fifteen years
   c. five years
   d. twenty-one years

8. A homeowner builds and maintains a fence that openly encroaches a few feet onto a neighbor's lot. The homeowner uses that portion of the property continuously for more than twenty years. At this point, the homeowner may

   a. be fined by the Commission
   b. lose his own property
   c. acquire a claim to the strip through adverse possession
   d. be charged with trespass only

9. A buyer is interested in land held in trust by the federal government for a tribe. Conveying such trust land generally requires

   a. only a standard warranty deed
   b. approval of the city council
   c. nothing beyond a normal closing
   d. approval of the Bureau of Indian Affairs

10. In Osage County, the mineral estate is

    a. reserved to the Osage Nation, so a buyer acquires the surface rights, but not the mineral rights
    b. always included with the surface
    c. owned by the state of Oklahoma
    d. unavailable for development

11. Under longstanding Oklahoma law, a non-resident alien who acquires land by inheritance must generally dispose of it within

    a. one year
    b. five years
    c. ten years
    d. twenty years

12. When the mineral estate is severed from the surface estate, the mineral estate is

    a. the weaker, servient estate
    b. extinguished
    c. the dominant estate, with the right to reasonable use of the surface
    d. owned by the surface owner

13. A licensee is asked to broker the sale of a separate oil and gas mineral interest. Under the License Code, mineral interests are

    a. treated the same as real estate
    b. subject to a special broker endorsement
    c. handled only by the Commission
    d. excluded from the definition of real estate, so a real estate license does not cover them

CHAPTER TESTS ANSWER KEY

CHAPTER ONE: THE REAL ESTATE BUSINESS

1. c. property managers handle day-to-day operations while asset managers manage portfolios of properties. (8)
2. b. developers. (9)
3. b. retail, office and industrial properties. (9)
4. a. Brokers and agents (10)
5. b. By geography (11)
6. d. A broker who renders real estate services for a fee (11)
7. b. state government. (14)

CHAPTER TWO: RIGHTS IN REAL ESTATE

1. d. The Constitution (25)
2. c. Land and everything permanently attached to it (17)
3. a. The surface of the earth and all natural things permanently attached to the earth (16)
4. b. Immobile, indestructible, heterogeneous (17)
5. d. land does not include man-made structures. (18)
6. a. real property includes ownership of a bundle of rights. (19)
7. c. To transfer (18)
8. d. Stock (19)
9. a. the right of others to use and enjoy their property. (19)
10. c. separable. (20)
11. d. Riparian (22)
12. b. To the middle of the waterway (22)
13. c. A doctrine that gives the state control of water use and the water supply (21)
14. a. A tree growing on a parcel of land (23)
15. b. its definition as one or the other in a sale or lease contract. (24)
16. d. A plant or crop that is considered personal property (24)
17. c. Affixing and severance (25)
18. a. court decisions. (26)
19. c. Broad regulation of usage (26)
20. d. County and local (26)
21. b. Trade fixtures that are personal property (24)
22. a. The owner's claim is invalid, because the state owns the underlying land (21)

CHAPTER THREE: INTERESTS AND ESTATES

1. c. one or more of the bundle of rights to real property. (29)
2. a. interests that do not include possession. (30)
3. b. A leasehold endures only for a specific period of time. (31)
4. d. absolute fee simple estate. (32)
5. c. the estate may revert to a grantor or heirs if the prescribed use changes. (33)
6. a. the original owner or other named person. (33)
7. b. A fee simple owner grants the life estate to a life tenant. (34)
8. c. The pur autre vie estate endures only for the lifetime of a person other than the grantee. (35)
9. c. Legal life estate (35)
10. a. A homestead interest cannot be conveyed by one spouse. (35)
11. b. a wife's life estate interest in her husband's property. (36)
12. b. a wife's life estate interest in her husband's property. (36)
13. b. Estate from period to period (36)

CHAPTER FOUR: OWNERSHIP

1. a. tenancy in severalty. (39)
2. c. tenancy in common. (40)
3. a. Parties must acquire respective interests at the same time. (43)
4. b. cannot will their interest to a party outside the tenancy. (42)
5. c. property acquired during a marriage and property already owned by each party at the time of marriage. (44)
6. d. Trustor, trustee and beneficiary. (45)
7. c. fee simple ownership of the airspace in a unit and an undivided share of the entire property's common areas. (48)
8. b. The property is owned by tenants in common or by a freehold owner who leases on a time-share basis. (53)
9. a. A cooperative may hold an owner liable for the unpaid operating expenses of other owners. (52)
10. a. a default by a coop owner may cause a foreclosure on the entire property instead of just a single unit, as with a condominium. (52)
11. c. the identity of the beneficiary may not be identified. (46)

CHAPTER FIVE: ENCUMBRANCES AND LIENS

1. c. encumbrance. (56)
2. c. the right to a defined use of a portion of another's real property. (56)
3. d. Dominant tenement (56)
4. a. The property has been continuously used as an easement with the knowledge but without the permission of the owner for a period of time. (60)
5. c. Over time, the encroachment may become an easement by prescription that damages the property's market value. (61)
6. b. a deed restriction. (62)
7. a. It involves a monetary claim against the value of a property. (62)
8. c. Real estate tax lien (65)
9. d. subordinate. (66)
10. a. the date of recordation. (65)
11. b. A state in which a mortgagor retains title to the property when a mortgage lien is created (67)
12. c. The lumber yard may place a mechanic's lien for the amount of the lumber against the homeowner's real property. (67)
13. c. foreclosure. (68)
14. a. there is no right to redeem the property in a non-judicial foreclosure. (70)
15. b. a deed in lieu of foreclosure. (70)
16. b. an encroachment. (61)
17. b. transfers with the property. (57)
18. a. a party wall. (58)
19. d. A license, which terminates at the owner's death (61)
20. b. general judgment lien. (64)
21. c. The proceeds of the sale do not cover the seller's outstanding mortgage loan balance. (71)

CHAPTER SIX: TRANSFERRING AND RECORDING TITLE TO REAL ESTATE

1. a. Ownership of the bundle of rights to real estate (73)
2. d. actual notice. (74)
3. c. title records. (74)

4. a. voluntary alienation. (75)
5. c. accepted by the grantee. (75)
6. d. states the grantor's intention, names the parties, describes the property, and indicates a consideration. (77)
7. a. state the grantor's assurance or warrant to the grantee that a certain condition or fact concerning the property is true. (77)
8. c. general warranty deed. (78)
9. d. A quitclaim deed (79)
10. b. a documentary stamp tax. (80)
11. a. It is taken by the state according to the process called escheat. (82)
12. d. an unenforceable nuncupative will. (81)
13. a. pass to heirs by the laws of descent and distribution. (82)
14. b. inspecting the property and evicting any trespassers found. (84)
15. d. declined because possession was secretive. (83)
16. c. give constructive notice of one's rights and interests in the property. (85)
17. c. A chronology of successive owners of record of a parcel of real estate. (85)
18. a. title is conveyed only when conveyance is registered on the title certificate. (86)
19. b. free of undisclosed defects and encumbrances. (86)
20. c. title insurance. (86)

CHAPTER SEVEN: LEASING ESSENTIALS

1. c. a conveyance of a possessory interest. (90)
2. d. A leased fee estate (91)
3. c. occupy the property. (91)
4. a. The buyer acquires title subject to the lease. (91)
5. b. The tenant must continue to abide by all lease terms. (91)
6. c. When either party gives proper notice (92)
7. c. a five-year lease must be in writing to be enforceable. (92)
8. b. In a sublease, the original tenant retains primary responsibility for performance of the original lease contract. (93)
9. a. A rights lease (96)
10. d. net lease. (94)
11. b. retail landlords. (94)
12. d. The tenant leases the ground from the landlord and owns the improvements. (95)
13. a. sue to compel performance of the contract. (96)
14. b. The leased property is foreclosed. (97)
15. d. discourage the use of unfair and overly complex leases. (98)
16. b. bargain with each other in good faith. (99)

CHAPTER EIGHT: LAND USE PLANNING AND CONTROL

1. a. balance individual property rights with the community's welfare. (101)
2. d. a fusion of land use laws and local land use objectives and strategies. (102)
3. a. zoning. (102)
4. c. police power. (104)
5. d. The owner must sell the property or grant an easement to the municipality for just compensation. (110)
6. c. the planning commission. (104)
7. b. delegation of authority by state-level enabling acts. (105)
8. a. reasonably promote community health, safety and welfare. (105)
9. d. To ensure that improvements comply with codes (105)
10. b. regulate density. (106)
11. a. a special exception. (108)
12. c. a legal nonconforming use. (107)
13. a. it would cause the property owner unreasonable hardship to bring the property into compliance with zoning ordinances. (108)
14. b. a plat of subdivision. (109)
15. c. the construction complies with building codes. (109)
16. a. public utilities. (110)
17. b. takes title subject to the same restriction. (111)
18. c. it cannot be terminated by a single individual. (111)
19. d. court injunction. (112)
20. a. it gives the grantor the right to re-possess the property if the grantee violates the condition. (112)
21. b. They may not impose a rule that is illegal. (112)

CHAPTER NINE: LEGAL DESCRIPTIONS

1. a. To create a consistent, unchanging standard for locating the property. (120)
2. b. They identify an enclosed area, beginning and ending at the same point. (121)
3. c. Metes and bounds (121)
4. b. point of beginning. (121)
5. d. Six miles by six miles. (124)
6. a. range. (124)
7. b. tier. (124)
8. d. Thirty-six (125)
9. a. 640 (124)
10. c. 80 acres (126)
11. b. will include a metes and bounds description. (124)
12. a. the lot and block number, with section, township and meridian references. (124)
13. c. properties located above or below the earth's surface. (124)

CHAPTER TEN: FUNDAMENTALS OF CONTRACT LAW

1. a. it represents a "meeting of the minds." (130)
2. c. enforceable or unenforceable. (131)
3. b. is possibly valid and enforceable. (132)
4. c. a counteroffer. (136)
5. d. valuable consideration. (133)
6. c. is void. (134)
7. b. voidable. (131)
8. a. must act within a statutory period. (134)
9. b. require certain conveyance-related contracts to be in writing. (134)
10. b. The buyer has no obligations to the seller whatsoever. (137)
11. a. is void. (135)
12. d. The original offer is legally extinguished. (137)
13. a. may be assigned. (137)
14. c. A two-year lease. (138)
15. a. an option to purchase. (138)
16. c. it is performed. (139)
17. b. it is impossible to perform. (139)
18. b. specific performance. (140)

CHAPTER ELEVEN: NATIONAL AGENCY

1. d. trust, confidence, and good faith. (142)
2. c. provide sufficient information for the agent to complete the agent's tasks. (148)
3. b. general agency. (143)
4. b. special agency. (143)
5. c. a party creates an agency relationship outside of an express agreement. (143)
6. a. Death or incapacity of the agent (144)
7. a. The agent has violated the duty of confidentiality. (145)
8. b. the agent has not violated fiduciary duty. (145)
9. d. inform the seller. (146)

10. a. fairness, care, and honesty. (147)
11. b. has an exposure to a charge of negligent misrepresentation. (147)
12. d. practicing law without a license. (147)
13. c. a subagent. (149)
14. b. a dual agent. (150)
15. a. may not represent one party's interests to the detriment of the other. (150)
16. c. dual agent. (152)
17. a. prior to completing a listing agreement. (154)
18. c. whenever substantive contact is made. (154)
19. b. upon initial contact. (154)
20. a. upon first substantive contact. (155)
21. a. Appoint Gretchen and Calvin as designated agents of the seller and buyer, respectively. (151)

CHAPTER TWELVE: LISTING AGREEMENTS: AN OVERVIEW

1. b. may be oral or written. (158)
2. a. exclusive right-to sell agreement. (158)
3. b. exclusive agency agreement. (159)
4. c. open listing. (160)
5. d. net listing. (160)
6. a. the client. (160)
7. a. To list the owner's property in a multiple listing service. (161)
8. b. is ready, willing, and able to transact. (162)
9. a. showing the property. (163)
10. c. ascertaining the facts about the client and the property at the onset of the listing period. (163)
11. b. established through negotiation with clients. (163)
12. b. the client may be liable for a commission and marketing expenses. (163)
13. b. the agent has a claim to a commission if the owner sells or leases to a party within a certain time following the listing's expiration. (165)
14. c. limited services agreement. (162)

CHAPTER THIRTEEN: GENERAL BROKERAGE PRACTICES

1. c. Procuring customers for clients and effecting transactions (175)
2. b. Outside brokers acting as subagents assist a listing agent in procuring a customer. (175)
3. d. Listing, marketing, facilitating transactions, and managing information (175)
4. a. A corporation has perpetual existence; a proprietorship terminates upon the owner's death. (178)
5. b. both may broker real estate if properly licensed. (179)
6. d. a joint venture. (179)
7. b. A locally-owned brokerage affiliated with a national franchisor for purposes of enhanced image and resources (180)
8. d. may only be used by brokers belonging to the National Association of Realtors®. (181)
9. a. represent their employing broker in procuring clients and customers. (181)
10. a. the IC is responsible for taxes; the broker does not withhold. (182)
11. c. providing them with all listings in the agency. (183)
12. b. competitive conditions. (184)
13. d. locating clients, pricing property, and making listing presentations. (185)
14. c. underpricing a property does not serve the best interests of a client. (186)
15. c. provide all information necessary for the owner to execute the listing. (186)
16. b. expose the property to the maximum number of prospects in relation to marketing expenses and efforts. (187)
17. c. avoid disclosing what price the owner will accept. (187)
18. c. the principals have entered into a sale contract and must satisfy any contingencies prior to closing. (187)
19. b. appropriating client or customer deposits for use in the agency's business. (189)
20. d. mixing escrow funds with the broker's operating funds. (188)
21. c. the advertising must not be misleading. (191)
22. a. collusion. (192)
23. b. The brokers have illegally fixed prices. (192)
24. a. propose an asset sale. (194)
25. b. intangible assets. (195)
26. c. the value or price of the business over and above the value of its other assets. (195)
27. b. Funds being held for a client must be placed in a trust account within a required number of days after all parties have accepted an offer to purchase. (189)
28. a. group boycotting. (192)

CHAPTER FOURTEEN: OVERVIEW OF CONVEYANCE CONTRACTS

1. b. the parties have completed a verbal, executory contract. (199)
2. c. The assignor has completed a legal action. (200)
3. a. the buyer can potentially force the seller to transfer ownership. (200)
4. a. entrust deposit monies to an impartial fiduciary. (200)
5. a. The seller may cancel the contract, since it can be ruled invalid. (201)
6. d. claim the deposit as relief for the buyer's failure to perform. (201)
7. c. Voluntary, bilateral, and executory (199)
8. d. third-party loans surviving closing may be accelerated by the lender. (204)
9. a. The buyer must withhold 15% of the purchase price at closing for the seller's capital gain tax payment. (204)
10. b. the optionor must perform if the optionee takes the option, but the optionee is under no obligation to do so. (206)
11. d. The option is expired, and the tenant has no rightful claim to money paid for the option. (206)
12. a. The tenant can force the sale at the original terms. (206)
13. c. They give the optionee an equitable interest in the property. (208)
14. c. the seller retains legal title in a contract for deed transaction until fully executed. (208)
15. d. comply with the contract and take legal title when its terms are fulfilled. (209)
16. c. the vendee may not have a right of redemption. (209)

CHAPTER FIFTEEN: REAL ESTATE MARKET ECONOMICS

1. c. the amount of money a buyer and seller agree to exchange to complete a transaction. (213)
2. b. desire, utility, scarcity, and purchasing power. (214)
3. b. will increase. (214)
4. d. the market tending toward equilibrium. (215)
5. c. the market is over-supplied. (215)
6. a. The demand must literally come to the supply. (217)
7. b. base employment. (219)

8. a. have been increasing. (221)
9. d. expanding the sewer system. (221)
10. a. trade area population and spending patterns. (219)
11. c. costs of occupancy and building efficiency. (219)

CHAPTER SIXTEEN: APPRAISING AND ESTIMATING MARKET VALUE

1. a. if two similar properties are for sale, a buyer will purchase the cheaper of the two. (225)
2. a. is physically and financially feasible, legal, and the most productive. (226)
3. d. the price that a willing, informed, and unpressured seller and buyer agree upon for a property assuming a cash price and the property's reasonable exposure to the market. (228)
4. b. the broker may not be a disinterested party. (228)
5. a. there may be no recent sale price data in the market. (231)
6. c. select comparable properties, adjust the comparables, estimate the value. (232)
7. b. the seller offers below-market seller financing. (233)
8. b. weights the comparables. (234)
9. b. market value is not always the same as what the property cost. (238)
10. b. replacement cost. (239)
11. d. functional obsolescence. (239)
12. b. incurable economic obsolescence. (239)
13. c. depreciation (239)
14. a. estimate depreciation, subtract depreciation from cost, and add back the land value. (240)
15. b. $8,500 (241)
16. b. Apartment buildings (242)
17. c. estimate net income, and apply a capitalization rate to it. (243)
18. c. potential gross income minus vacancy and credit loss minus expenses. (244)
19. b. $400,000 (244)
20. a. numerous expenses are not taken into account. (246)
21. b. $240,000 (246)
22. d. The stairwell (246)

CHAPTER SEVENTEEN: REAL ESTATE FINANCE

1. c. hypothecation. (250)
2. a. The borrower gives the lender a note and a mortgage in exchange for loan funds. (250)
3. c. The trustor conveys title to a trustee in exchange for loan funds from the beneficiary. (251)
4. a. title-theory state. (250)
5. b. usury. (253)
6. c. $15,000. (253)
7. a. an amortized loan is paid off over the loan period. (253)
8. c. it is a negotiable instrument. (254)
9. d. may be required to execute a release of mortgage document. (256)
10. a. an appraisal report. (257)
11. c. the ability to re-pay, the value of the collateral, and the profitability of the loan. (257)
12. b. the lender wants to ensure the loan is fully collateralized. (257)
13. b. consider the income of a spouse in evaluating a family's creditworthiness. (259)
14. a. safeguard against over-indebtedness. (261)
15. d. dividing one's debts by one's gross income. (262)
16. c. take-out loan commitment. (266)
17. c. the parties complete all loan origination documents and the loan is funded. (266)
18. b. Truth-in-Lending laws (266)
19. a. The Equal Credit Opportunity Act (267)
20. c. the Real Estate Settlement Procedures Act. (267)
21. b. Buying securities, changing the discount rate, and controlling banking reserves (269)
22. a. cycle funds back to primary lenders so they can make more loans. (270)
23. a. Fannie Mae, Freddie Mac, and Ginnie Mae. (271)
24. c. purchase FHA-backed and VA-backed loans. (271)
25. b. insure loans made by approved lenders. (273)
26. a. guarantee loans made by approved lenders. (274)
27. c. the loan payments gradually increase. (276)
28. b. the borrower pays additional interest at the onset in order to obtain a lower interest rate. (276)
29. a. the interest rate may vary. (276)
30. b. the seller offering the buyer a wraparound can profit from a difference in interest rates. (277)
31. b. a blanket mortgage loan. (278)
32. b. Payments are not sufficient to retire the loan. (276)
33. b. $120,000 (258)
34. b. 1,521 (263)
35. b. 297,030 (264)

CHAPTER EIGHTEEN: REAL ESTATE INVESTMENT

1. b. the more the investor stands to gain, the greater the risk that the investor may lose. (282)
2. a. income and tax benefits. (283)
3. c. debt. (284)
4. d. relatively illiquid. (286)
5. b. a more management-intensive investment. (286)
6. a. a general partnership. (286)
7. d. gross income minus expenses minus building depreciation. (287)
8. c. deduct interest payments from income. (290)
9. d. The owner may be able to exclude capital gain from taxable income when the property is sold. (291)
10. c. may be deducted from the sale price for gains tax purposes. (290)
11. b. the difference between net sale proceeds and adjusted basis. (291)
12. a. cost recovery expense. (292)
13. c. dividing cash flow by the investor's equity. (294)

CHAPTER NINETEEN: TAXATION

1. c. There are no federal ad valorem taxes. (298)
2. c. may delegate taxing authority to county governments. (298)
3. c. impose property taxes for specific municipal services. (298)
4. b. create a two-mile extension of county sewer facilities. (299)
5. b. the assessed value of property. (299)
6. b. the total of all assessed values of properties minus exemptions. (299)
7. d. smooth out wide discrepancies of assessed values within the district. (300)
8. c. appeal to adjust the assessed valuation. (300)
9. b. to offer an amount of tax relief on an owner's principal residence. (300)
10. a. dividing the tax requirement by the tax base. (301)
11. c. multiplying each district's tax rate times the taxable value of the property. (302)
12. a. it only applies to properties which will benefit from the public improvement. (302)
13. b. entitles its holder to apply for a tax deed after a certain period. (303)
14. b. gives a delinquent taxpayer a grace period prior to the tax sale to pay property taxes. (303)

CHAPTER TWENTY: PROFESSIONAL PRACTICES

1. b. prohibit discrimination in housing transactions. (306)
2. c. the Civil Rights Act of 1968. (307)
3. c. the Fair Housing Amendments Act of 1988 (308)
4. a. blockbusting. (307)
5. c. steering. (307)
6. a. providing unequal services. (307)
7. a. discriminatory misrepresentation. (307)
8. d. The prohibition may be legal. (308)
9. c. The agent and the owner (309)
10. c. high standards of practice for all facets of the business. (324)
11. b. public accommodations and employment. (311)
12. c. disclose the information to others. (313)
13. a. It may cause them to be held liable for improper disclosure of potential violations. (320)
14. b. Conditions that pre-existed the coverage date of the warranty will not be covered. (320)
15. c. Disclose the result of any inspection, if known to the agent (323)

CHAPTER TWENTY-ONE: CLOSINGS

1. d. exchange legal title for the sale price. (330)
2. b. the lender wants to ensure proper handling of the collateral for the loan. (332)
3. b. the loan is to be sold to the FNMA. (333)
4. d. the buyer must pay the expense. (335)
5. d. a debit to one party and a credit to the other. (337)
6. a. the excess of the buyer's debits over the buyer's credits. (336)
7. b. Inspection fees (337)
8. c. Taxes and interest (338)
9. d. Rents and insurance (337)
10. a. the seller must pay prorated expenses inclusive of the day of closing. (339)
11. b. document the payment of a transfer tax. (342)
12. b. A form that summarizes and reports transaction data from a closing (356)
13. d. $692 (342)
14. c. $195,200 (342)

CHAPTER TWENTY-TWO: RISK MANAGEMENT

1. b. reduction. (359)
2. c. risk outsourcing. (361)
3. a. It deflects and reduces risk by preventing others from claiming they were misled. (361)
4. c. It can be a compliance with the law. (362)
5. c. It reduces the risk of committing an unauthorized practice of law. (362)
6. d. a legal requirement. (363)
7. b. Copies of required communications to principals. (363)
8. d. negligence, error or omission in carrying out professional services. (374)
9. a. Failing to inform and disclose properly. (366)
10. b. failing to disclose known adverse facts. (368)
11. d. avoid creating a false impression that the licensee is a certified appraiser. (369)
12. b. exceeding the authority of the agreement. (370)
13. a. use a checklist of all items, contingencies, dates and responsibilities that must be met. (371)
14. d. the principals may make changes as long as they sign or initial each change. (371)
15. b. obtain education in the content and intent of the laws. (372)
16. a. being present at a conversation where the setting of commission rates is discussed. (373)
17. a. License discipline, fines, and possible incarceration. (375)
18. c. stating that a client should seek legal counsel. (375)
19. d. avoid statements of opinion and speculation in all reports. (376)
20. b. It reduces the chance of presenting an offer from an unqualified buyer. (376)

CHAPTER TWENTY-THREE: PROPERTY MANAGEMENT

1. c. fiduciary (381)
2. b. financial reporting to the principal. (382)
3. d. revenue from all sources minus losses from uncollected rents, vacancies, and evictions. (382)
4. a. cost per tenant prospect generated per lease. (383)
5. b. raise rental rates. (384)
6. d. High tenant turnover increases expenses and reduces profits. (384)
7. b. Routine, preventive, and corrective (385)
8. a. ensure that disabled employees have the same level of access to facilities that all employees have. (386)
9. c. A court may hold the manager responsible for the physical safety of tenants in leased premises. (387)
10. a. replacement value. (388)
11. b. cash for the management firm's operating expenses. (388)
12. c. General (389)
13. a. apportioned under the terms of the management contract. (390)
14. b. The tenant pays a fixed rent, and the landlord pays all operating expenses. (393)
15. d. the property manager does not have to maintain it. (394)
16. b. deliver a habitable property. (395)
17. c. A tenant declares a landlord in default and vacates the leased premises. (396)
18. a. the competitive market for the property. (398)

CHAPTER TWENTY-FOUR: REAL ESTATE MATH
(see page 429)

CHAPTER TWENTY-FIVE: THE OKLAHOMA REGULATORY ENVIRONMENT

1. b. the Oklahoma Real Estate Commission. (429)
2. c. Seven. (429)
3. a. five. (429)
4. c. three years. (429)
5. a. Investigate the complaint and, if it finds a violation, discipline the licensee. (430)
6. c. setting the commission rates that brokers must charge. (430)
7. c. the Governor, with the consent of the Senate. (429)
8. b. making a substantial misrepresentation in a real estate transaction. (432)
9. b. doubles, and a second thirty-day period begins.
10. d. Twenty-five thousand dollars. (434)
11. d. reimburses the Fund the amount paid plus interest. (435)
12. b. thirty days of the plea and again within thirty days of judgment and sentencing. (436)
13. a. fifteen days. (436)
14. a. the amount of the commissions earned, whichever is greater. (434)

15. d. the Oklahoma Real Estate Education and Recovery Fund. (434)

CHAPTER TWENTY-SIX: OKLAHOMA LICENSING

1. b. provisional sales associate license. (441)
2. c. Being at least eighteen years of age and a citizen or lawful permanent resident. (441)
3. a. ninety clock hours. (441)
4. c. three years. (441)
5. d. As a national portion and an Oklahoma portion that are scored separately. (441)
6. a. non-renewable, requiring a post-license course to advance. (442)
7. b. be sponsored by a supervising broker.
8. d. ten. (442)
9. c. fifteen hours. (443)
10. a. Broker associate. (443)
11. b. Completing the Broker in Charge course and documenting ten transactions. (447)
12. d. pass the Oklahoma portion of the examination and appoint the Commission's Secretary-Treasurer as service agent. (446)
13. c. where the sponsoring brokerage is located. (441)
14. a. three years. (446)
15. b. thirty hours. (446)
16. d. The fifteen-hour Broker in Charge course and six hours of Contracts and Forms. (446)
17. a. eight hours. (447)
18. c. ten days. (448)
19. b. two business days. (448)
20. d. forty-five hours. (450)

CHAPTER TWENTY-SEVEN: THE OKLAHOMA BROKER RELATIONSHIPS ACT

1. c. not an agent, subagent, or dual agent.in the absence of an agreement (453)
2. a. common-law agency. (453)
3. d. a party. (454)
4. b. It may be oral or written. (454)
5. c. a mortgage loan application. (454)
6. a. a prohibited dealing. (455)
7. d. The baseline duties of honesty and reasonable skill and care. (455)
8. b. give written notice to both parties that it serves both. (456)
9. a. Treating all parties with honesty and reasonable skill and care. (457)
10. c. one party or both parties in a transaction. (456)
11. b. must disclose the problem, because a material defect is never confidential. (458)
12. d. confidential, and the associate may not reveal it. (459)
13. a. before the effective date of the contract for sale or lease. (459)
14. c. sixty days. (459)
15. b. one year. (459)
16. d. Accounting for money and keeping confidential information confidential. (457)
17. c. incorporated in or attached to the contract. (460)
18. a. disclose the family relationship in writing to the other side. (462)
19. b. make full written disclosure of his interest to all parties. (461)
20. d. in advertising. (461)

CHAPTER TWENTY-EIGHT: REGULATION OF BROKERAGE PRACTICES

1. a. includes social networking and all forms of solicitation. (467)
2. b. the registered business trade name or the name under which the broker is licensed. (468)
3. c. a real estate broker, using a word such as realty or real estate. (468)
4. d. The broker, who is responsible for the assistant's real estate activities. (469)
5. b. Clerical and administrative support that is not a licensed activity. (480)
6. a. commits a prohibited dealing. (469)
7. d. a definite place of business. (471)
8. c. Yes, if it is registered and identified as required. (471)
9. a. obtain a branch office license with a separate managing broker. (471)
10. c. registered with the Commission. (472)
11. b. two or more licensees under the same broker who present themselves as a unit under a team name. (444)
12. d. be registered with the Commission, and a registration fee applies. (444)
13. c. five years. (471)
14. a. thirty days of the death. (474)
15. d. automatically placed on inactive status unless they transfer to another broker. (475)
16. b. may not assign listings without the written consent of each property owner. (475)
17. a. notify the Commission of the change. (452)
18. d. the homeowner's right to cancel without penalty within two business days. (476)
19. b. invalid and unenforceable by the wholesaler, and the homeowner is entitled to any earnest money. (476)
20. c. keep it in a trust account separate from the broker's own funds. (477)
21. d. insured by an agency of the federal government. (477)
22. a. commingling, which is prohibited. (478)
23. c. hold the funds and, if needed, file an interpleader action so a court can decide. (478)
24. b. an Oklahoma escrow account in compliance with the residential landlord and tenant law. (477)

CHAPTER TWENTY-NINE: OKLAHOMA DISCLOSURES AND HAZARDS

1. b. not less than one nor more than two dwelling units. (482)
2. d. the seller's actual knowledge of the property's condition. (484)
3. a. a disclaimer statement. (484)
4. c. One hundred eighty. (483)
5. d. before the seller accepts an offer to purchase. (483)
6. b. exempt, so no disclosure or disclaimer form is required. (484)
7. c. To inform the seller of the disclosure obligation and disclose any defect the licensee actually knows. (482)
8. a. not a material fact that must be disclosed. (486)
9. b. no duty to disclose information about registered offenders. (313)

10. d. a ten-day opportunity to inspect for lead-based paint. (487)

CHAPTER THIRTY: OKLAHOMA PROPERTY MANAGEMENT

1. a. is a licensed activity requiring a broker. (491)
2. c. A resident manager who lives on the premises and manages it for the owner. (492)
3. b. a brokerage service agreement. (492)
4. d. is owed honesty and reasonable skill and care but is not a client unless agreed in writing. (493)
5. a. the tenant makes a written demand. (495)
6. c. Six months. (495)
7. a. thirty days. (496)
8. d. thirty days. (496)
9. b. five days. (496)
10. c. file a forcible entry and detainer action in court. (497)

CHAPTER THIRTY-ONE: OTHER OKLAHOMA LAWS AND PRACTICES

1. d. Age. (499)
2. a. steering, a fair housing violation. (500)
3. b. illegal price fixing. (501)
4. c. illegal market allocation. (501)
5. a. An agreement for the sale of real property. (502)
6. d. keeps legal title, while the lender holds a lien. (503)
7. b. fifteen years. (504)
8. c. acquire a claim to the strip through adverse possession. (504)
9. d. approval of the Bureau of Indian Affairs. (505)
10. a. reserved to the Osage Nation, so a buyer acquires the surface rights, but not the mineral rights. (505)
11. b. five years. (505)
12. c. the dominant estate, with the right to reasonable use of the surface. (506)
13. d. excluded from the definition of real estate, so a real estate license does not cover them. (506)

PRACTICE EXAMINATION

Answer Key is on page 569

1. Which of the following professionals involved in the real estate business are most concerned about managing real estate for clients?

   a. Brokers and agents
   b. Property managers
   c. Corporate real estate managers
   d. Appraisers

2. Real estate can be defined as

   a. land and all property contained therein.
   b. unimproved land.
   c. land and everything permanently attached to it.
   d. air, surface, and subsurface rights.

3. Which of the following is included in the bundle of rights inherent in ownership?

   a. To tax
   b. To encroach
   c. To possess
   d. To inherit

4. The overriding test of whether an item is a fixture or personal property is

   a. whether the owner owns the property the item is affixed to.
   b. how it is described in a sale or lease contract.
   c. what the title records on the property indicate.
   d. how the buyer defines the item.

5. An owner of a lakefront property tells a fisherman that he cannot fish in a boat within fifty feet of the owner's shoreline. The fisherman protests that the owner cannot prevent him. Which of the following is true?

   a. The fisherman is correct because the water and the land underlying it are public property.
   b. The owner's prohibition is valid, since the underlying land belongs to abutting properties to the middle of the lake.
   c. The owner can prevent the fisherman from fishing within ten feet, but not beyond.
   d. The owner's prohibition is valid if all lakefront property owners have agreed to it.

6. The distinguishing feature of a defeasible fee simple estate is that

   a. it only endures for the lifetime of the defeasee.
   b. it has no restrictions or conditions on use.
   c. it may revert to a grantor if the prescribed use changes.
   d. it is of limited duration.

7. Dower can best be defined as

   a. a grant of foreclosure immunity extended to a homestead claimant.
   b. a wife's life estate interest in her husband's property.
   c. a husband's homestead exemption.
   d. a grantor who endows property to heirs.

8. A distinct feature of a joint tenancy is that joint tenants

   a. may elect to have any percent of ownership in the property.
   b. cannot will their interest to a party outside the tenancy.
   c. own separate physical portions of the land.
   d. cannot lease the property.

9. Interests in a condominium differ from those in a cooperative, in that

   a. a default by a condominium owner may cause a foreclosure on the entire property instead of just a single unit, as with a cooperative.
   b. the condominium owner owns the common elements and the airspace, whereas the coop owner owns only the apartment.
   c. the coop owner owns stock in the cooperative association, whereas the condominium owner simply owns real estate.
   d. the cooperative owner must pay a pro rata share of the cooperative's expenses as well as rent.

10. There are two adjoining properties. An easement allows property A to use the access road that belongs to property B. In this situation, property B is said to be which of the following in relation to property A?

    a. Dominant tenement
    b. Subordinate tenant
    c. Servient estate
    d. Conditional life tenant

11. Title records of a property reveal several recorded liens: a one-year old judgment lien; a mechanic's lien dating from two years ago; a special assessment tax lien recorded last month; and a first mortgage lien recorded five years ago. In case of a foreclosure, which of these liens will be paid first?

    a. First mortgage lien
    b. Special assessment tax lien
    c. Mechanic's lien
    d. Judgment lien

12. A lender may terminate foreclosure proceedings if the defaulting borrower executes

    a. a wraparound mortgage.
    b. a lis pendens.
    c. a waiver of redemption.
    d. a deed in lieu of foreclosure.

13. A person has occupied a property for seven years, and no one has ever attempted to evict her or co-occupy the parcel. In this case, the person might base a claim of legal ownership on

a. her prescriptive easement.
b. title records.
c. constructive notice of possession.
d. tenancy in severalty.

14. A person wishes to convey any and all interests in a property to another with full assurances against encumbrances, liens, or any other title defects on the property. This party would most likely use which of the following types of deed?

a. A quitclaim deed
b. A general warranty deed
c. A deed in lieu of warrant
d. A guardian's deed

15. The chain of title to a property refers to which of the following?

a. An abstract of the condition and marketability of title
b. The genealogy of successive heirs to a property
c. The list of all current encumbrances and clouds "chained" to title
d. A chronology of successive owners of record

16. A leased property is conveyed to a new owner. What happens to the lease?

a. It remains in effect.
b. It is cancelled.
c. It automatically renews at closing for its original term.
d. It moves with the owner to a new property, if purchased within one year.

17. The Uniform Residential Landlord and Tenant Act fundamentally attempts to

a. promote the rights of tenants, particularly in lease defaults.
b. standardize rental rates.
c. encourage fairness and simplicity in lease forms and provisions.
d. minimize rent escalations in economically depressed zones.

18. A primary objective of residential zoning is

a. regulate rates of appreciation and depreciation of residences.
b. promote the value and planned land use of a neighborhood.
c. eliminate nonconforming uses, variances, and special exceptions.
d. disperse intensity of usage.

19. A shop was originally built in a commercial zone. The zone has since been changed to a residential zone. Zoning authorities permit the use, most likely as

a. a variance.
b. a special exception.
c. an illegal nonconforming use.
d. a legal nonconforming use.

20. Authorities conduct comprehensive land use planning in order to

a. balance public interests with individual property rights.
b. prevent the public from exercising police powers.
c. ensure positive market conditions for development projects.
d. limit growth.

21. The purpose of a formal legal description of a property is to

a. eliminate encroachments.
b. locate and identify the property reliably.
c. eliminate the possibility of surveyor error.
d. qualify for title recordation.

22. A parcel is described as the SW 1/4 of the N 1/2 of the E 1/2 of Section 14. What is its acreage?

a. 160 acres b. 80 acres
c. 40 acres d. 20 acres

23. A suburb has a growing need for single-family housing, but the land available for new construction is running low. In this case, it is likely that the price of existing homes

a. will decline.
b. will increase.
c. will stabilize.
d. will not show any predictable movement.

24. The demand for homes in a market is best expressed in terms of

a. square feet of housing required.
b. number of contracts signed with developers.
c. number of houses listed in the multiple listing service.
d. number of households seeking housing.

25. What is the significance of base employment in a real estate market?

a. It gives the basic number of people who will need housing.
b. It indicates the number of people at the low end of the buying power spectrum.
c. It drives total employment and population growth, which lead to demand for real estate.
d. It indicates the number of people who want to move into the market.

26. The concept known as substitution states that

a. buyers will not substitute the quality of one home for the price of another.
b. the replacement cost of an item cannot be substituted for the item's original value.
c. a new improvement will only increase market value to the extent of the cost of a similar improvement.
d. buyers will not pay more for a certain house than they would for another, similar house.

27. The "price that a willing, informed, and unpressured seller and buyer agree upon for a property, assuming a cash price and reasonable exposure of the property to the market" describes which of the following concepts of value?

a. Highest and best value
b. Substitution value
c. Desirability
d. Market value

28. A warehouse building lacks sufficient ceiling height for the operation of modern forklifts. This is an example of

a. non-conforming use.
b. functional obsolescence.
c. over improvement.
d. economic obsolescence.

29. To derive value using the income capitalization approach, one must

a. divide the capitalization rate by net income.
b. multiply net income times the capitalization rate.
c. divide the capitalization rate into net income.
d. multiply cash flow by the capitalization rate.

30. An office building rents for $600,000, has expenses of $400,000, and a cash flow of $100,000. The prevailing gross rent multiplier is 8. Using the GRM, what is the value of the building?

a. $800,000 b. $1,600,000
c. $3,200,000 d. $4,800,000

31. An owner obtains a loan and gives the mortgagee a mortgage on the property as collateral. The mortgagor/owner retains title to the property, and the mortgagee records a lien. This is an example of

a. intermediation.
b. contracting for deed.
c. subordination.
d. hypothecation.

32. An important characteristic of a promissory note is that

a. it is assignable.
b. it must be secured by collateral.
c. it is not a negotiable instrument.
d. it must be recorded to be enforceable.

33. Disclosure of estimated closing costs is required of a lender in order to comply with

a. the Equal Credit Opportunity Act.
b. Truth-in-Lending laws.
c. Federal Fair Housing Laws.
d. the Real Estate Settlement Procedures Act.

34. The secondary mortgage market organizations do all of the following EXCEPT

a. guarantee performance on mortgages.
b. buy pools of mortgages from primary lenders.
c. sell securities based on pooled mortgages.
d. directly originate loans.

35. Negative amortization of a loan occurs whenever

a. monthly payments are interest-only.
b. a payment does not pay the interest owed.
c. the principal loan balance is diminishing.
d. the interest rate increases on an adjustable rate loan.

36. A borrower earns $3,000/month and makes credit card and car note payments of $500. A conventional lender requires a 27% income ratio. What monthly amount for housing expenses (principal, interest, taxes, insurance) will the lender allow this person to have in order to qualify for a conventional mortgage loan?

a. $810 b. $675
c. $972 d. $1,040

37. A $250,000 interest-only loan carries a 7% rate. Monthly payments are

a. $1,750.
b. $1,458.
c. $17,500.
d. Cannot be determined without loan term data.

38. A lender is charging 2.75 points on a $240,000 loan. How much must the borrower pay for points?

a. $550. b. $5,500.
c. $6,600. d. $660.

39. Which of the following is generally true of a real estate investment?

a. The lower the price, the lower the liquidity
b. The greater the return, the greater the risk
c. The more management, the less return
d. The more liquidity, the greater the return

40. The capital gain on sale of an investment is computed as

a. beginning basis plus gain.
b. sale price minus beginning basis.
c. net sales proceeds minus beginning basis.
d. net sales proceeds minus adjusted basis.

41. The formula for return on equity is

a. cash flow divided by equity.
b. required yield times gross income.
c. net operating income divided by equity.
d. cash flow times the capitalization rate.

42. Mary Bright bought a home for $80,000, paying $10,000 down and taking a mortgage loan of $70,000. The following year she had a new roof put on, at a cost of $2,000. What is Mary's adjusted basis in the house if she now sells the house for $300,000?

a. $12,000 b. $218,000
c. $230,000 d. $82,000

43. An office building has a potential income of $500,000 and vacancy of 10%. Its cash-paid bills total $300,000, and annual depreciation is $5,000. Payments on the loan total $100,000. What is the property's pre-tax cash flow?

a. $45,000 b. $50,000
c. $150,000 d. $155,000

44. A property is purchased for $200,000. Improvements account for 75% of the value. Given a 39-year depreciation term, what is the annual depreciation expense?

a. $3,846 b. $5,128
c. $6,410 d. $8,294

45. An income property is bought for $500,000. Gross income is $100,000, and net operating income is $60,000. Cash flow is $10,000. What is the return on investment (ROI)?

a. 2.00% b. 12%
c. 10.00% d. 60.00%

46. Which of the following is the formula for deriving the tax base of a jurisdiction?

a. The total tax required divided by assessed values
b. The total of all assessed values minus exemptions
c. The annual budget times the tax rate
d. The annual budget divided by the millage rate

47. The purpose of a homestead tax exemption is

a. to exempt owners from ad valorem taxation.
b. to offer tax abatement on a principal residence.
c. to encourage owners to finance their principle residences.
d. to exempt owners of principal residences who rent their properties.

48. A homeowner's tax bill for a taxing district is derived by

a. dividing the tax base by the district's needed revenues.
b. multiplying the tax rate times the assessed value of the property.
c. multiplying the tax rate times the taxable value of the property.
d. multiplying the millage rate times the equalization factor.

49. The village of Parrish has an annual budget requirement of $20,000,000 to be funded by property taxes. Assessed valuations are $400,000,000, and exemptions total $25,000,000. What must the tax rate be to finance the budget?

a. 4.70% b. 5.33%
c. 5.00% d. 11.25%

50. A canal dredging project is to cost $100,000. There are 40 properties along the canal, and 40 others across the street from the canal. The total canal footage to be dredged is 2,500 feet. How much will the assessment be for a 150-foot property on the canal?

a. $1,250 b. $2,500
c. $3,000 d. $6,000

51. A prospective homebuyer offers to buy a house if the seller agrees to pay financing points at closing. The seller gets the offer, signs it, and gives it to his agent to deliver. At this point the status of the offer is

a. a valid contract.
b. an invalid contract.
c. still an offer.
d. an invalid offer.

52. One aim of the statute of frauds is to

a. set time limits for disputing contract provisions.
b. require certain conveyances to be in writing.
c. prevent fraudulent assignments of listing agreements.
d. make all oral agreements unenforceable.

53. A buyer agrees to all terms of a seller's offer and sends notice of acceptance back to the seller. The seller now tells the buyer the deal is off because he has learned that the home was underpriced. Which of the following is true?

a. The buyer must offer the new price to get the property.
b. The seller may counteroffer.
c. The contract is cancelled.
d. The buyer has a binding contract.

54. A principal discloses to the listing agent that she must sell a property within two months to avoid a financial problem. Nearly seven weeks later, a buyer's agent hears of the seller's difficulty from the listing agent and advises his buyer to submit an offer for 80% of the listed price. The buyer complies, and the seller accepts the offer. Which of the following is true?

a. The buyer's agent has violated fiduciary duties owed the customer.
b. The listing agent has violated fiduciary duties owed the customer.
c. The buyer's agent has violated fiduciary duties owed the client.
d. The listing agent has violated fiduciary duties owed the client.

55. An owner's agent is showing a buyer an apartment building. The buyer questions the agent as to whether some cracking paint contains lead. The agent's best course of action is to

a. contract to re-paint the cracked area.
b. assure the buyer the paint is lead-free.
c. suggest the buyer make a lower-price offer to cover the possible problem.
d. inform the seller of the inquiry and test the paint.

56. Agent Jerry, who works for Broker Lucy, obtains an owner listing to lease a building. Lucy's other agent, Linda, a tenant representative, locates a tenant for Lucy's listing. If there is no arrangement to the contrary, Broker Lucy in this instance is

a. an implied agent.
b. a dual agent.
c. a single agent.
d. a cooperating agent.

57. A transaction broker should disclose his or her agency relationship to the transaction principals

a. before receipt of any offer.
b. upon completion of the listing agreement.
c. upon first substantive contact.
d. upon initial contact of any kind with either principal.

58. An agent obtains a listing which ensures compensation for procuring a customer, provided the agent is the procuring cause. This agent has entered into a(n)

a. exclusive right-to sell agreement.
b. exclusive agency agreement.
c. open listing.
d. net listing.

59. A landlord promises to compensate a broker for procuring a tenant, provided the landlord's brother decides not to rent the property within a month. This would be an example of a(n)

a. exclusive right-to-lease agreement.
b. exclusive agency agreement.
c. open listing.
d. net listing.

60. The amount of a real estate brokerage commission is determined by

a. state license law guidelines.
b. negotiation with the client.
c. the Board of Realtors®.
d. agreement among competing brokers.

61. Real estate sales agents are legally authorized to

a. represent buyers on their broker's behalf.
b. enter into approved listing agreements.
c. execute lease contracts for less than one year.
d. transfer listings to other MLS agents.

62. In eliciting an offer from a buyer, an owner's agent must be careful to

a. avoid an overpriced offer that will cause buyer's remorse or lawsuits.
b. complete any offer the buyer might decide to make.
c. disclose what price the owner will accept.
d. avoid completing an offer that contains contingencies.

63. An example of conversion is

a. depositing escrow funds in a business operating account.
b. spending a customer deposit on a surety bond for the agency.
c. spending operating income from an apartment on roof repairs.
d. depositing a commission into an escrow account.

64. Three leading agencies charge identical commission rates for brokering office properties in Phoenix. Which of the following is true?

a. This is a perfectly legitimate business practice.
b. The brokers have engaged in legal collusion.
c. The brokers have allocated the Phoenix market.
d. The brokers have illegally fixed prices.

65. A business owner insists on a price for his enterprise that exceeds the value of the tangible assets, claiming that it is a well-known family business with a loyal clientele. The excess value is known as

a. the buyer's premium.
b. goodwill.
c. the risk factor.
d. the profit margin.

66. An agent informs owners in an area that a decline in property values over the past five years is due to an influx of minority families. He suggests that the trend will continue, and advises them to sell before it is too late. This agent is probably guilty of

a. blockbusting.
b. redlining.
c. discriminatory misrepresentation.
d. negligent misrepresentation.

67. An agent spends two hours with a minority buyer, then shows the buyer five available properties all over town. Later, a similarly qualified minority couple enter the office. The agent spends twenty minutes with the couple, gives them the MLS book to review, and encourages them to drive by the listings on their way home. If they like anything, they should come back the next day to discuss terms. This agent could be liable for

a. misrepresentation.
b. steering.
c. providing unequal services.
d. nothing.

68. An owner suddenly pulls a property off the market after hearing from the agent that a minority party has made a full-price offer. The agent then goes back to the minority party and reports that the seller has decided to wait until next year to sell the home. Who, if anyone, has violated fair housing laws?

a. Both owner and agent.
b. The owner.
c. The agent.
d. No one.

69. An owner completes a contract to sell her property. Before closing, she runs into financial trouble and assigns the contract to her mortgagor. Which of the following is true?

a. The owner has defaulted.
b. The buyer can sue to nullify the mortgage.
c. The assignment can take effect only after the closing.
d. The sale contract remains valid.

70. Buyers and sellers rely on escrow accounts in order to

a. allow a third party fiduciary to handle the funds.
b. have access to the funds without interference from the broker.
c. prevent the broker from receiving a commission until after closing.
d. earn equal interest on their funds.

71. An option-to-purchase expires. The landlord agrees to extend it in exchange for a higher price. The optionee claims he can exercise the option within the redemption period. Which is true?

a. The landlord must honor the option and sell immediately.
b. The landlord can extend the option term, but cannot raise the price.
c. The landlord must extend the option but is allowed to raise the price.
d. The landlord is under no obligation, since options do not have a redemption period.

72. RESPA requires specific closing procedures whenever

a. the loan is to be guaranteed.
b. the loan is to be sold to the FNMA.
c. the commercial property is to be bought by FHLMC.
d. a borrower does not fully understand closing costs.

73. When an item is prorated between buyer and seller on a settlement statement, the closing officer must

a. debit the buyer and seller.
b. credit the buyer and seller.
c. debit and credit both buyer and seller.
d. debit one party and credit the other.

74. Which of the following items are paid in arrears?

a. Taxes and insurance
b. Rents and interest
c. Taxes and interest
d. Rents and insurance

75. A sale transaction on rental property closes on December 16. The landlord received the December rent of $713 on December 1. Assuming the closing day is the seller's, and that the 365-day method is used for prorating, which of the following entries would appear on the settlement statement?

a. Debit seller $345.00
b. Credit seller $713.00
c. Debit buyer $345.00
d. Credit buyer $368.00

76. The most common form of risk transference in brokerage firms is

a. continuing education.
b. errors & omissions insurance.
c. company rules and regulations.
d. self control.

77. Which of the following is a major risk in the fulfilling of listing agreements?

a. Exceeding the limits of the authority granted by the agreement
b. Disclosing a material defect without the seller's permission
c. Failing to receive proper compensation
d. Putting the client's interests above those of the customer

78. In the contracting process, a licensee must be careful to avoid

a. giving the principal any advice about the transaction.
b. describing the normal requirements of a contract to a client.
c. drafting a contract illegally.
d. pointing out to the principals the importance of meeting contingency deadlines.

79. If a licensee is found guilty of obtaining a real estate license under false pretenses, the most likely penalty will be

a. paying a punitive fee.
b. civil suit for damages.
c. extra continuing education.
d. license revocation.

80. A broker responsible for handling a trust account is violating the law by

a. depositing an earnest money check in a personal account.
b. following the seller's instructions to hold an earnest money check uncashed.
c. removing an earned commission from a trust account without permission of the depository institution.
d. opening an account that names the licensee as the trustee of the account.

81. In order to set rents and to estimate the expected return on a managed property, a property manager needs to prepare a(n)

a. cash reserve statement.
b. operating budget.
c. expense report.
d. rent roll.

82. Why is it important for a property manager to maintain good relations with tenants?

a. If tenants like the manager they will like the owner.
b. Happy tenants are easier to work with.
c. The manager owes the landlord the fiduciary duty of pleasing the tenants.
d. Unhappy tenants lead to expensive tenant turnover.

83. While physical maintenance of the property is a primary function of the property manager, the level of maintenance performed must be balanced with

a. the cost of services and the time available.
b. the manager's monetary incentives.
c. owner objectives and tenant demands.
d. the manager's skills and the condition of the property.

84. What kind of insurance would provide coverage for loss of income when a rental property is damaged so badly that it cannot be used?

a. Casualty
b. Consequential loss
c. Fire and hazard
d. Liability

85. Property managers are usually considered to be

a. general agents empowered to perform a wide range of duties for the landlord.
b. special agents empowered to perform a specific task for the landlord.
c. dual agents serving both the landlord and the tenants.
d. employees who have no agency relationship with their employer.

86. The Oklahoma Real Estate Commission operates under the Oklahoma Sunset Law, which means that

a. the Legislature must periodically re-create the agency or let it expire
b. the Commission meets only after sunset
c. licenses expire at sunset each day
d. the Governor may abolish it at will

87. Carlos is seventeen and wants an Oklahoma real estate license. He is not yet eligible, because an applicant for a provisional sales associate license must be at least

a. sixteen years of age
b. eighteen years of age
c. nineteen years of age
d. twenty-one years of age

88. Under the Broker Relationships Act, the duties a broker owes are

a. the fiduciary duties of common-law agency
b. whatever the buyer instructs
c. those set by the local board
d. only those the statute lists, no more and no less

89. An unlicensed receptionist at a brokerage offers to negotiate a price reduction with a caller. This is improper because

a. negotiating contract terms is a licensed activity
b. receptionists may not answer phones
c. only attorneys may negotiate
d. the caller must be licensed

90. The Residential Property Condition Disclosure Act modified Oklahoma's older rule of

a. caveat venditor
b. strict liability
c. eminent domain
d. caveat emptor

91. A property management agreement, under the Commission's rules, is treated as

a. a brokerage service agreement
b. an exempt private contract
c. an appraisal engagement
d. a government lease

92. A licensee tells prospective buyers that a particular neighborhood would suit people like them better. This is

a. lawful advice
b. steering, which violates fair housing law
c. an antitrust violation
d. a required disclosure

93. An administrative fine imposed on a licensee must be paid within

a. ten days of notice
b. fifteen days of notice
c. thirty days of notice
d. sixty days of notice

94. A candidate who completes the ninety-hour Basic Course but waits more than three years to use it must

a. take the ninety hours again
b. pay a late fee only
c. take a fifteen-hour refresher
d. do nothing, because it never expires

95. A buyer's associate plans to be paid for representing a buyer. Under recent amendments, the associate must put the compensation in writing

a. only at closing
b. within thirty days after closing
c. only if the seller objects
d. before the effective date of the contract

96. A broker who holds earnest money and security deposits for others must keep those funds

a. in the broker's personal account
b. in a trust account separate from the broker's own funds
c. with the listing associate
d. in a safe deposit box

97. A seller bought a house at auction, never lived in it, and knows nothing about its condition. The appropriate property condition form for her to deliver is

a. a residential property disclaimer statement
b. a full disclosure statement
c. a warranty deed
d. a lead-based paint report

98. To take title by adverse possession in Oklahoma, possession must be open, notorious, exclusive, hostile, and continuous for

a. seven years
b. ten years
c. twenty-one years
d. fifteen years

99. Rosa, a Tulsa sales associate, wants to move to a different broker. She must file the change of association within

a. two business days
b. ten days
c. thirty days
d. sixty days

100. Which of the following is included in the Commission's broad definition of advertising?

a. A real estate post on a personal social media account.
b. Only printed newspaper ads.
c. Only yard signs.
d. Private conversations between associates.

101. A consumer is defrauded by an agent and wins a court judgment, but the agent cannot pay. The consumer may seek reimbursement from

a. the Oklahoma Real Estate Education and Recovery Fund
b. the county treasurer
c. the Governor's office
d. the brokerage's competitors

102. A seller may designate certain information as confidential in writing, but a known material defect in the property is

a. also confidential
b. never confidential and must be disclosed
c. confidential for sixty days
d. confidential only to buyers

103. Under the Oklahoma Landlord and Tenant Act, a landlord must return a security deposit, less lawful deductions and without interest,

a. within fifteen days of the lease signing
b. within thirty days of any complaint
c. within forty-five days after termination, delivery of possession, and written demand
d. within ninety days of move-in

104. Two competing brokers meet for coffee and agree to stop offering discounts to clients. This agreement is

a. a permitted business courtesy
b. a fair housing matter
c. allowed if disclosed
d. an illegal antitrust violation

105. A broker applicant must document, within the past five years, a number of completed real estate transactions totaling

a. five
b. seven
c. ten
d. fifteen

106. A firm wants to open a second office in a nearby city as an extension of its main office. For that location, the firm must have

a. a separate managing broker and a branch office license
b. only an associate in charge
c. a post office box
d. nothing additional

107. A licensee who has actual knowledge of a defect that the seller failed to disclose must

a. keep it confidential
b. disclose it
c. cancel the listing
d. report it only to the broker

108. A single firm ends up working with both the buyer and the seller in one sale. Before the parties sign, the firm must

a. withdraw from the transaction
b. choose one side to represent
c. refund all fees
d. give written notice to both parties that it serves both

109. When the mineral estate has been severed from the surface estate, the mineral owner

a. has no right to use the surface
b. owns the surface as well
c. may make reasonable use of the surface to extract minerals
d. must buy the surface first

110. A licensee who is convicted of a felony must report it to the Commission in writing within

a. ten days of the conviction
b. sixty days of the conviction
c. thirty days of the plea and again within thirty days of judgment
d. one year of the conviction

111. Whether an Oklahoma licensee is a resident or a nonresident is determined by

a. the licensee's home address
b. the location of the sponsoring brokerage
c. the licensee's birthplace
d. where the licensee took the exam

112. A broker who closes a real estate business must retain transaction and trust account records for at least

a. one year
b. three years
c. five years
d. ten years

113. A tenant stops paying rent. Before filing for eviction, the landlord must serve a notice to pay or quit within

a. three days
b. ten days
c. fifteen days
d. five days

114. How many categories of information does the Broker Relationships Act treat as confidential?

a. Two.
b. Four, defined exhaustively.
c. Eight.
d. An unlimited number.

115. Under longstanding Oklahoma law, a non-resident alien who inherits Oklahoma land generally must dispose of it within

a. one year
b. five years
c. ten years
d. twenty years

116. A broker's license is suspended for a disciplinary violation. The associates working under that broker are

a. promoted to brokers
b. allowed to keep working under the suspended broker
c. permanently barred from practice
d. placed on inactive status unless they transfer to another broker

117. A resident sales associate must complete how many hours of continuing education each renewal term?

a. Fifteen.
b. Twenty-one.
c. Thirty.
d. Forty-five.

118. A buyer is purchasing a home built in 1970. Federal law entitles the buyer to a period to inspect for lead-based paint of

a. three days
b. seven days
c. ten days
d. thirty days

119. The maximum total of administrative fines arising from a single transaction is

a. two thousand dollars
b. ten thousand dollars
c. twenty-five thousand dollars
d. five thousand dollars

120. Even after a brokerage relationship ends, a broker must continue to

a. advertise the property
b. negotiate on the party's behalf
c. account for money and keep confidential information confidential
d. pay the other broker

121. Commingling, which Oklahoma prohibits, means

a. mixing client trust funds with the broker's own operating money
b. filing an interpleader action
c. holding funds in escrow
d. depositing funds in a federally insured bank

122. A resident manager who lives on the premises and manages an apartment complex for the owner

a. must hold a broker license
b. is exempt from the license requirement
c. must register as a team
d. needs a nonresident license

123. A buyer wants to purchase tribal trust land. The transaction generally cannot be completed without

a. a quitclaim deed only
b. city council approval
c. approval of the Bureau of Indian Affairs
d. a standard title policy alone

124. James holds a renewable sales associate license and wants to earn a broker associate license without running an office. Compared with a broker applicant, he does NOT have to

a. pass the broker examination
b. complete the ninety-hour advanced course
c. hold two years of licensure
d. complete the Broker in Charge course or document ten transactions

125. A broker who changes the firm's office address must

a. notify the Commission
b. surrender the license
c. notify only the associates
d. wait until renewal to report it

PRACTICE EXAMINATION ANSWER KEY

1. b. Property managers (8)
2. c. land and everything permanently attached to it. (16)
3. c. To possess (18)
4. b. how it is described in a sale or lease contract. (24)
5. a. The fisherman is correct because the water and the land underlying it are public property. (21)
6. c. it may revert to a grantor if the prescribed use changes. (33)
7. b. a wife's life estate interest in her husband's property. (36)
8. b. cannot will their interest to a party outside the tenancy. (42)
9. c. the coop owner owns stock in the cooperative association, whereas the condominium owner simply owns real estate. (51)
10. c. Servient estate (56)
11. b. Special assessment tax lien (65)
12. d. a deed in lieu of foreclosure. (70)
13. c. constructive notice of possession. (74)
14. b. A general warranty deed (78)
15. d. A chronology of successive owners of record (85)
16. a. It remains in effect. (91)
17. c. encourage fairness and simplicity in lease forms and provisions. (98)
18. b. promote the value and planned land use of a neighborhood. (101)
19. d. a legal nonconforming use. (107)
20. a. balance public interests with individual property rights. (101)
21. b. locate and identify the property reliably. (120)
22. c. 40 acres (126)
23. b. will increase. (215)
24. d. number of households seeking housing. (218)
25. c. It drives total employment and population growth, which lead to demand for real estate. (219)
26. d. buyers will not pay more for a certain house than they would for another, similar house. (225)
27. d. Market value (228)
28. b. functional obsolescence. (239)
29. c. divide the capitalization rate into net income. (244)
30. d. $4,800,000 (246)
31. d. hypothecation. (250)
32. a. it is assignable. (254)
33. d. the Real Estate Settlement Procedures Act. (268)
34. d. directly originate loans. (270)
35. b. a payment does not pay the interest owed. (276)
36. a. $810 (261)
37. b. $1,458. (253)
38. c. $6,600. (253)
39. b. The greater the return, the greater the risk (282)
40. d. net sales proceeds minus adjusted basis. (291)
41. a. cash flow divided by equity. (294)
42. d. $82,000 (291)
43. b. $50,000 (292)
44. a. $3,846 (287)
45. b. 12% (294)
46. b. The total of all assessed values minus exemptions (299)
47. b. to offer tax abatement on a principal residence. (300)
48. c. multiplying the tax rate times the taxable value of the property. (302)
49. b. 5.33% (301)
50. d. $6,000 (302)
51. c. still an offer. (135)
52. b. require certain conveyances to be in writing. (134)
53. d. The buyer has a binding contract. (135)
54. d. The listing agent has violated fiduciary duties owed the client. (145)
55. d. inform the seller of the inquiry and test the paint. (146)
56. b. a dual agent. (150)
57. c. upon first substantive contact. (155)
58. c. open listing. (160)
59. b. exclusive agency agreement. (160)
60. b. negotiation with the client. (163)
61. a. represent buyers on their broker's behalf. (181)
62. b. complete any offer the buyer might decide to make. (187)
63. b. spending a customer deposit on a surety bond for the agency. (188)
64. a. This is a perfectly legitimate business practice. (192)
65. b. goodwill. (195)
66. a. blockbusting. (307)
67. c. providing unequal services. (307)
68. a. Both owner and agent. (309)
69. d. The sale contract remains valid. (200)
70. a. allow a third party fiduciary to handle the funds. (200)
71. d. The landlord is under no obligation, since options do not have a redemption period. (206)
72. b. the loan is to be sold to the FNMA. (333)
73. d. debit one party and credit the other. (336)
74. c. Taxes and interest (338)
75. a. Debit seller $345.00 (341)
76. b. errors & omissions insurance. (364)
77. a. Exceeding the limits of the authority granted by the agreement (372)
78. c. drafting a contract illegally. (371)
79. d. license revocation. (374)
80. a. depositing an earnest money check in a personal account. (378)
81. b. operating budget. (382)
82. d. Unhappy tenants lead to expensive tenant turnover. (384)
83. c. owner objectives and tenant demands. (385)
84. b. Consequential loss (388)
85. a. general agents empowered to perform a wide range of duties for the landlord. (389)
86. a. the Legislature must periodically re-create the agency or let it expire. (429)
87. b. eighteen years of age. (441)
88. d. only those the statute lists, no more and no less. (454)
89. a. negotiating contract terms is a licensed activity. (439)
90. d. caveat emptor. (482)
91. a. a brokerage service agreement. (454)
92. b. steering, which violates fair housing law. (487)
93. c. thirty days of notice. (434)
94. a. take the ninety hours again. (441)
95. d. before the effective date of the contract. (459)
96. b. in a trust account separate from the broker's own funds. (477)
97. a. a residential property disclaimer statement. (484)
98. d. fifteen years. (504)
99. b. ten days. (448)
100. a. A real estate post on a personal social media account. (467)

101. a. the Oklahoma Real Estate Education and Recovery Fund. (434)
102. b. never confidential and must be disclosed. (458)
103. c. within forty-five days after termination, delivery of possession, and written demand. (495)
104. d. an illegal antitrust violation. (501)
105. c. ten. (442)
106. a. a separate managing broker and a branch office license. (480)
107. b. disclose it. (485)
108. d. give written notice to both parties that it serves both. (456)
109. c. may make reasonable use of the surface to extract minerals. (506)
110. c. thirty days of the plea and again within thirty days of judgment. (436)
111. b. the location of the sponsoring brokerage. (441)
112. c. five years. (474)
113. d. five days. (496)
114. b. Four, defined exhaustively. (465)
115. b. five years. (505)
116. d. placed on inactive status unless they transfer to another broker. (475)
117. c. Thirty. (447)
118. c. ten days. (487)
119. d. five thousand dollars. (434)
120. c. account for money and keep confidential information confidential. (457)
121. a. mixing client trust funds with the broker's own operating money. (478)
122. b. is exempt from the license requirement. (492)
123. c. approval of the Bureau of Indian Affairs. (505)
124. d. complete the Broker in Charge course or document ten transactions. (442)
125. a. notify the Commission. (444)

GLOSSARY OF GENERAL REAL ESTATE TERMS

absorption The consumption of available vacant property in a building or market.
abstract of title A written, chronological record of the title records affecting rights and interests in a parcel of real property.
acceleration A right granted through a loan clause enabling the lender to call all sums immediately due and payable on a loan should the borrower violate certain provisions of the loan agreement.
accretion An increase in land caused by natural phenomena, for example a deposit of sand on a beachfront property due to a tropical storm.
actual notice Knowledge given or received directly through demonstrable evidence. Actual notice of ownership: reading a bill of sale, inspecting a deed, searching title records. See also *constructive notice*.
adjustable rate mortgage A mortgage loan having an interest rate that can be periodically raised or lowered in accordance with the movement of a financial index.
adjusted basis The beginning basis, or cost, of a property plus the costs of capital improvements, minus all depreciation expense.
ad valorem tax A real property's annual tax levied by taxing entities according to the property's assessed value.
adverse possession The entry, occupation, and use of another's property without the consent of the owner or where the owner took no action to evict the adverse possessor. May lead to loss of legal title if the adverse possessor fulfills certain requirements.
agency A fiduciary relationship between an agent and a principal where respective rights and duties are prescribed by laws of agency and by the agency agreement executed by the two parties. See *universal agency*, *limited agency*, and *fiduciary*.
agent The party in an agency relationship who is hired by the principal to perform certain duties. In so doing, the agent must also uphold fiduciary duties owed the principal.
air rights Rights in real property as they apply to the property's airspace, or all space above the surface within the parcel's legal boundaries.
air space The air portion of real property. In a condominium unit, the freehold space enclosed by the unit's outer walls, floor, and ceiling.
alienation A transfer of title to real property by voluntary or involuntary means.
allocation of markets An act of collusion where two or more competitors agree to limit competitive activity in portions of the market in exchange for reciprocal restrictions from the others.
amortization A partial or complete reduction of a loan's principal balance over the loan term, achieved by periodic payments which include principal as well as interest. See *negative amortization*.
annual percentage rate (APR) The total cost of credit to a borrower inclusive of finance charges and the stated interest rate, expressed as an annual rate of interest.
antitrust laws Legislation aimed at preventing unfair trade practices and monopoly, including collusion, price fixing, and allocation of markets.
appraisal An opinion of value of a property developed by a professional and disinterested third party and supported by data and evidence.
appraiser A duly trained and licensed professional authorized to perform appraisals for other parties.
appreciation An increase in the value of a property generally owing to economic forces beyond the control of the owner.
appurtenance A right, interest, or improvement that attaches to and transfers with a parcel of real property, such as an easement or a riparian right.
arrears Payment that occurs at the end of a payment term rather than at the beginning. Examples of items paid in arrears include taxes and interest.
assemblage A combining of contiguous parcels of real estate into a single tract, performed with the expectation that increased value will result.
assessed value The value of a property as established by assessors for the purpose of ad valorem taxation.
assessment A periodic charge payable by condominium owners for the maintenance of the property's common elements.
asset A tangible or intangible item of value.
asset sale A sale of a business involving the transfer of assets as opposed to the liabilities or stock.
assignment A transfer of one's entire interest in an item of real or personal property. The assignor transfers the interest to the assignee.
assumption In a sale of real property, the transfer of the seller's mortgage loan obligations to the buyer. Requires, in most cases, the approval of the lender.
balloon payment A lump sum payment on any loan which retires the remaining loan balance in full.
base line An imaginary latitude line within the rectangular survey system that is designated in relation to a principal meridian for purposes of identifying townships.
beginning basis The original cost or market value of an acquired asset.
benchmark A registered marker denoting an official elevation above sea level; used by surveyors to identify other elevations in the area.
beneficiary A party named to benefit from the yield or disposition of an asset identified in a trust, insurance policy, or will.
bilateral contract A contract where both parties promise to perform in exchange for performance by the other party. See *unilateral contract*.
binder A temporary agreement to buy a property evidenced by a valuable deposit. Receipt of the deposit binds a seller to a good-faith agreement to sell a property, provided a complete sale contract is executed within a certain period.
blind ad An advertisement that does not contain the identity of the advertiser.
blockbusting Inducing property owners to sell or rent their holdings due to an impending downturn in their property values, often owing to a change in the area's ethnic or social composition.
broker A direct agent of the principal who is hired for compensation to perform a stated service such as procuring a customer.
broker's opinion of value An estimate of a property's value rendered by a party who is not necessarily licensed, objective, or qualified. The estimate may not be a complete appraisal.
brokerage The business of procuring customers on behalf of clients for the purpose of completing a real estate transaction.
business brokerage The brokerage of a business enterprise in addition to any real property it may own or lease.
building code A specific standard of construction or maintenance of any aspect of an improved property established by local government officials.
bundle of rights A set of rights associated with ownership of property, including the rights to possess, use, transfer, encumber and exclude.

business trust See *syndication.*
buydown A loan arrangement where the borrower pays extra interest in advance for the future benefit of a lower interest rate over the loan term.
buyer representation agreement A broker's listing with a buyer to locate a suitable property for purchase or lease.
buyer's market A market characterized by an excess of sellers over buyers.
capital gain (or loss) The difference between the net sales proceeds of an asset and its adjusted basis.
capital improvement An upgrading of improved property having sufficient magnitude to constitute an addition to the property's basis. Contrasts with repair and maintenance.
capitalization rate The rate of return on capital an investor will demand from the investment property, or the rate of return that the property will actually produce.
cash flow The remaining positive or negative amount of income an investment produces after subtracting all operating expenses and debt service from gross income.
certificate of occupancy A document confirming that a newly constructed or renovated property has fully complied with all building codes and is ready for occupancy and use.
certificate of title A document expressing the opinion of a title officer or attorney that a property seller is in fact the owner of good title based on a review of title records.
chain of title Successive property owners of record dating back to the original grant of title from the state to a private party.
chattel An item of personal property.
closing A meeting of principal parties where a seller transfers title and a buyer pays monies owed the seller and lender.
closing statement A financial summary and settlement of a property transaction indicating sums due and payable by the buyer and seller.
cloud An encumbrance or claim on title to property impeding or diminishing its marketability.
co-brokerage A brokerage practice where agents and brokers outside of the listing broker's agency assist as subagents in procuring a customer in exchange for portions of the commission.
collateral Property liened by a lender as security for a loan.
collusion An unlawful agreement between competitors to monopolize a market, disadvantage other competitors, or otherwise undertake activities in violation of fair trade laws.
color of title A defective title transfer or the transfer of a defective title where the new owner is originally unaware of the defect. Color of title may be used as a grounds for adverse possession, which, if successful, would nullify the original defect.
commingling An unlawful practice of mixing escrow funds with the agency's operating funds.
common elements 1. Portions of a condominium property that are owned by all unit owners, for example the grounds, parking facilities, lobby, and elevators. 2. Portions of a commercial property used by all occupants as well as the public, for which the tenants may have to share in the repair and maintenance costs.
common law A body of law developed by court judgments, decrees, and case decisions.
community property A system of property ownership established by law which generally defines rights of property ownership of spouses; community property is co-owned by spouses, and separate property is owned by a single spouse. Generally, property acquired during the marriage with jointly held funds is community property.
comparable A property having similar characteristics to a subject property in an appraisal. The value or sale price of the comparable is used to estimate the value of the subject.
comparable sales approach See *sales comparison approach.*
comparative market analysis (CMA) A method used by brokers and salespeople for estimating the current value of a property using sale price data from similar properties. Not to be confused with a bona fide appraisal performed by a licensed appraiser.
concurrency A local, county, or regional planning policy that requires developers to correct foreseen negative impacts of a development during the construction period of the project itself rather than afterwards; for example, widening a road during construction to accommodate a future increase in traffic.
condemnation 1. A decree by a court or municipal authority that a parcel of private property is to be taken for public use under the power of eminent domain. 2. A government order that a particular property is no longer fit for use and must be demolished.
condominium estate An estate distinguished by fee simple ownership of the airspace of a unit plus an undivided interest with the other unit owners in the overall property's common elements.
consideration An item of tangible or intangible value, or one's promise to do or not do some act which is used as an inducement to another party to enter into a contract.
constructive notice Knowledge one could or should have, according to the presumption of law; a demonstration to the public of property ownership through title recordation, "for all to see." See *actual notice.*
contingency A condition that must be satisfied for a contract to be binding and enforceable.
contract A potentially enforceable agreement between two or more parties who agree to perform or not perform some act. If valid, the contract is enforceable, with limited exceptions.
contract for deed A financial contract where a seller retains legal title to a property and gives the buyer equitable title and possession over a period of time. During the contract period, the seller finances all or part of the purchase price. If the buyer makes timely payments and abides by all contract provisions, the seller conveys legal title at the end of the contract period.
contribution The increment of market value added to a property through the addition of a component or improvement to the property. Not to be confused with the cost of the component.
conventional loan A permanent long-term loan that is not FHA-insured or VA-guaranteed.
conversion 1. Changing real property to personal property, and vice versa. 2. An illegal act of appropriating escrow funds for payment of an agency's operating expenses.
conveyance A voluntary transfer of real property interests.
cooperative estate Ownership of shares in a cooperative association which acquires a multi-unit dwelling as its primary asset. Shareholders also receive a proprietary lease on a unit for the duration of their share ownership.
cost approach A method for determining value that takes into account the cost of the land and the replacement or reproduction cost of the improvements net of estimated depreciation.
cost recovery See *depreciation.*
counteroffer Any new offer or amended offer made in response to an offer. See *offer.*
covenant A written warrant or promise set forth in a contract or other legal document by one or both of the parties to the contract.
credit 1. An accounting entry on a closing statement indicating an amount a party has paid or is to receive. 2. Loan funds advanced to a borrower.

credit evaluation A lender's opinion of a borrower's ability to repay a loan in view of financial capabilities and past repayment patterns.

curtesy A widower's life estate claim to portions of his deceased spouse's real property. See also *dower*.

customer In agency law, a party outside of the fiduciary relationship of client and agent. If an agent treats a customer as a client, an implied agency may result.

datum A standard elevation reference point used by surveyors to measure elevations of property in an area.

debit An accounting entry on a closing statement indicating an amount a party must pay.

debt coverage ratio An underwriting equation reflecting how much debt service an investment property can reasonably afford to pay out of its net operating income; used to identify how large a loan the property can afford given an interest rate and loan term.

debt ratio An underwriting equation that is used to determine how much debt an individual can reasonably afford in view of the party's or household's income.

debt service Periodic payments of interest and/or principal on a mortgage loan.

deed in lieu of foreclosure An instrument used to convey mortgaged property back to the lender rather than have the lender foreclose on the property.

deed in trust An instrument used to convey real property to the trustee of a land trust. The trustor is also the beneficiary. See *land trust*.

deed of trust An instrument used by a borrower to convey title to mortgaged property to a trustee to be held as security for the lender, who is the beneficiary of the trust.

deed restriction A provision in a deed that limits or places rules on how the deeded property may be used or improved.

defeasible fee A fee estate where ownership is perpetual, provided that usage restrictions or other conditions stated in the deed are upheld. If not, the fee reverts to the grantor either automatically (determinable fee) or by the grantor's actions (condition subsequent).

deficiency judgment A court order enabling a damaged lender to attach a lien on the defaulted borrower's property for an amount equal to the difference between the debt and the proceeds of a foreclosure sale.

demand A quantity of a product or service that is desired for purchase, lease, or trade at any given time.

density A measure of the degree of residential land use within a given area for purposes of residential zoning and land use control.

deposit Valuable consideration accompanying an offer to purchase real estate that signifies the offeror's good faith intention to complete a sale or lease contract.

depreciable basis The portion of a property's total basis that may be depreciated, generally the basis of the improvements, since land cannot be depreciated.

depreciation 1. A non-cash expense taken against the income of investment property that allows the owner to recover the cost of the investment through tax savings. 2. A loss of value to improved property.

descent and distribution, laws of A body of state-level laws that stipulates how an estate will be passed on to heirs in the absence of a valid will.

determinable fee A defeasible fee estate where title automatically reverts to the grantor if usage conditions stated in the deed are violated.

devise A transfer of real or personal property from the devisor to the devisee(s) by means of a will.

discounting A financial practice of reducing the value of dollars received in the future by an amount that reflects the interest that would have been earned if the dollars had been received today. Performed to measure the present value of an investment's future income.

discounted cash flow analysis A financial analysis to identify the discounted value of the cash flow of an investment over a given number of years. See *discounting* and *cash flow*.

discrimination in housing A failure to provide equal opportunity for persons to acquire or finance housing based on race, color, religion, national origin, sex, handicapped status, marital status, or family status.

disintermediation Direct investment without the intermediation of a bank or other depository institution to make loans and other investments.

documentary stamp A tax stamp affixed to a property document or record as evidence that the owner has paid taxes related to the financing or transfer of real property.

dominant tenement The property that benefits from the existence of an easement appurtenant. The holder of the easement is the dominant tenant. See *servient tenement*.

dower A widow's life estate interest in portions of her deceased spouse's real property.

dual agency Representing both principal parties to a transaction.

due on sale A loan provision defining the lender's right to accelerate a note upon the transfer of collateralized property.

earnest money escrow An impound account used for the safekeeping of a buyer's earnest money deposit; accompanied by specific instructions to the escrow agent for holding and disbursing the funds.

easement An interest in real property giving the interest holder the right to use defined portions of another's property. May or may not attach to the estate.

economic life The period during which an improvement is expected to remain useful in its original use. Establishes the improvement's annual depreciation amounts in appraisal. Depreciation in tax accounting is determined by a property's cost recovery class, which is related to economic life.

economic obsolescence A loss of value in a property because of external factors generally beyond the control of the owner, for example, a municipality's lack of funds to improve deteriorated roadways. Also called external obsolescence.

effective gross income The actual income of an investment property before expenses, expressed as total potential income minus vacancy and collection losses.

elective share A right of a surviving spouse to claim a prescribed portion of the decedent's real and personal property in place of the provisions of the decedent's will.

emblements Plants and crops considered personal property, since human labor is required for planting, growing and harvesting.

eminent domain A power of a government entity to force the sale of private property for subsequent public use.

encroachment An unauthorized physical intrusion of one's real property into the real property of another.

encumbrance An interest, right or intrusion that limits the freehold interest of an owner of real property or otherwise adversely effects the marketability of title.

enforceability Legal status of a valid contract or other document that a court of law will force to be performed.

equalization An averaging of assessed valuations in an area to compensate for ad valorem tax inequities.

equilibrium A theoretical market state in which the forces of supply and demand are in balance.

equitable title An interest that gives a lienholder or buyer the right to acquire legal title to a property if certain contractual conditions occur.

equity That portion of a property's value owned by the legal owner, expressed as the difference between the property's market value and all loan balances outstanding on the property.

equity of redemption A mortgagor's right to pay off a defaulted mortgage and reclaim the property, provided the redemption occurs before the completion of the foreclosure sale.

escalator clause A lease clause providing for an increase in rent.

escheat A reversionary transfer of real property to the state or county when the legal owner dies without a will and without heirs.

escrow 1. A trust or impound account used for the proper handling of funds and documents in the closing of a real property transaction. 2. An account that a lender requires a borrower to establish to ensure that adequate funds will be available for payment of taxes and insurance on a mortgaged property.

estate 1. A set of rights to real property that includes the right of possession. 2. The totality of one's personal and real property ownership.

estate in land An estate.

estoppel A legal restraint to prevent a person from claiming a right or interest that is inconsistent with the person's previous statements or acts. An estoppel certificate documents the party's initial position or act, which cannot be contradicted later.

ethics Standards governing proper and professional business practices.

eviction Removal of a tenant from a property because of a lease default.

evidence of title Actual or constructive notice of real property ownership, including opinion of title, certificate of title, and title insurance.

exclusion One of the bundle of legal rights to real property enabling the owner to prevent others from entry or use.

exclusive agency A listing agreement which pays the listing broker a commission if anyone other than the property owner procures a customer..

exclusive right to sell A listing agreement which pays the listing broker a commission if anyone at all procures a customer.

executory contract A completed agreement which enjoins one or both principal parties to perform certain actions in order for the contract to become fully executed.

facilitator A transaction broker who assists principal parties in completing a transaction without acting as a fiduciary agent of either party.

fair financing laws Anti-discrimination legislation designed to ensure that all parties have equal access to mortgage financing.

fair housing laws Anti-discrimination legislation designed to ensure equal opportunity in housing to all home buyers.

Federal Deposit Insurance Corporation A quasi-governmental agency that insures deposits of depository institutions and otherwise develops regulations for the banking industry.

Federal Home Loan Mortgage Corporation (Freddie Mac) A major secondary mortgage market organization which buys conventional, FHA, and VA loans and sells mortgage-backed securities.

Federal Housing Administration An agency of the Department of Housing and Urban Development which insures permanent long-term loans that meet certain qualifications.

Federal National Mortgage Association (Fannie Mae) A government-sponsored agency in the secondary mortgage market which buys conventional, FHA, and VA loans, sells mortgage-backed securities, and guarantees payment of principal and interest on the securities.

Federal Reserve System The principal regulator of the money supply as well as of the American banking system.

fee simple An estate representing the highest form of legal ownership of real property, particularly the fee simple absolute estate.

fiduciary The agent in an agency relationship; receives the trust and confidence of the principal and owes fiduciary duties to the principal.

fiduciary duties Duties of an agent to the principal in an agency relationship, including skill, care, diligence, loyalty, obedience, confidentiality, disclosure, and accounting.

fixture An item permanently attached to land so as to be defined as real property.

foreclosure A procedure for forcing sale of a secured property to satisfy a lienholder's claim.

freehold estate An ownership estate of indeterminable duration; contrasts with a leasehold estate.

full-service lease A lease requiring the landlord to pay all of a property's operating expenses, including those that pertain to an individual tenant.

functional obsolescence A loss of value in an improved property because of design flaws or failure of the property to meet current standards. May be curable or incurable.

general agency A fiduciary relationship which authorizes the agent to conduct a broad range of activities for the principal in a particular business enterprise. May or may not include authority to enter into contracts.

general lien A lien against any and all property owned by a lienee.

general partnership A for-profit business where two or more co-owners agree to share management responsibilities and profits. Does not involve silent partners, as in a limited partnership.

general warranty deed A bargain and sale deed containing the assurance that the grantor will defend against any and all claims to the title.

goodwill An intangible business asset valued at the difference between the sale price and the value of all other assets of the business.

Government National Mortgage Association (Ginnie Mae) A division of HUD which guarantees FNMA mortgages and securities backed by pools of VA-guaranteed and FHA-insured mortgages.

government survey system See *rectangular survey system.*

grantee A party who receives a right, interest, or title to real property from another.

grantor A party who transfers a right, interest, or title to real property to another.

gross easement A personal right to use another's property, granted by the owner; does not attach to the estate, and there are no dominant or servient tenements.

gross income multiplier A shortcut method for estimating the value of an income property. The procedure involves multiplying the property's gross annual income times a multiplier that reflects the ratio between gross annual income and sale price that is typical for similar properties in the area.

gross rent multiplier A shortcut method for estimating the value of an income property. The procedure involves multiplying the property's gross monthly rent times a multiplier that reflects the ratio between gross monthly rent and sale price that is typical for similar properties in the area.

gross lease See *full service lease.*

ground lease A lease of the land-only portion of a parcel of real property

hazard insurance Insurance against loss or damage to real property improvements; required by most mortgage lenders to protect the collateral.

highest and best use A theoretical use of a property that is legally permissible, physically possible, financially feasible, and maximally productive, usually in terms of net income generation.

holographic will A will prepared entirely in the testator's handwriting, complete with date and signature.

home equity loan A junior mortgage loan on a residence, secured by portions of the owner's equity in the home.

homestead laws Laws that protect a homeowner against loss of the homeowner's principle residence to a sale forced by creditors to collect debts. Homestead laws also protect the interests of individual spouses by requiring both spouses to sign any conveyance of the homestead property.

homestead tax exemption An exemption of a portion of the assessed value of a homeowner's principal residence from ad valorem taxation.

hypothecation Use of real property as collateral for a mortgage loan.

implied agency An agency relationship that arises by implication from the actions and representations of either agent or principal.

implied contract An unstated or unintentional agreement that may be deemed to exist by implication because of acts or statements by any of the parties to the agreement.

implied listing See *implied agency*.

improvement Any manmade structure or item affixed to land.

income capitalization A method of appraising the value of a property by applying a rate of return to the property's net income.

income ratio An underwriting ratio that relates a borrower's gross or net income and the debt service of a loan; used to determine how large a loan a borrower can reasonably afford.

independent contractor A sales agent who works for a broker but is not legally an employee. The employer exerts only limited control over the contractor's actions, does not provide employee benefits, and does not withhold taxes from the contractor's pay.

inferior lien A lien whose priority is subordinate to that of a superior (tax) lien. Priority among inferior liens is established according to the time of recordation, with the exception of the mechanic's lien. Also called junior lien.

installment contract See *contract for deed*.

interest 1. A right to real property. 2. A lender's charge for the use of the principal amount of a loan.

interest rate The percentage of a loan amount that a borrower must pay a lender annually as interest on a loan amount.

intermediation Investment by a depository institution on behalf of depositors.

internal rate of return The rate at which inflows from an income property investment must be discounted in order for the total inflows over time to equal the initial outlay, expressed as a percent; may include projected proceeds from the future sale of the property as an inflow.

interval ownership See *time-share*.

intestate Legal condition of a person who dies without leaving a will.

investment Expenditure to purchase an asset with the expectation of deriving a future profit or benefit from the asset.

involuntary alienation A transfer of title to real property without the consent or against the will of the owner, for example, eminent domain, foreclosure, and adverse possession.

involuntary lien A lien imposed by legal process irrespective of the owner's wishes or consent.

joint tenancy A form of real property ownership in which co-owners share all rights and interests equally and indivisibly; entails right of survivorship. Parties must establish tenancy at the same time and with a single deed.

joint venture A partnership created for a specific, pre-determined business endeavor, after which the joint venture is usually dissolved.

judgment A court decision resulting from a lawsuit. If a creditor sues to collect a debt, a favorable ruling is followed by a judgment lien against the defaulting borrower's property.

judicial foreclosure A court proceeding triggered by a foreclosure suit. Involves notice, debt acceleration, the termination of the owner's interests in the property, and a public sale where proceeds are applied to the debt.

junior lien See *inferior lien*.

land The surface area of the earth, all natural things permanently attached to the earth, and everything beneath the surface to the earth's center and above the surface extending upward to infinity.

land contract See *contract for deed*.

land trust A trust in which a trustor conveys a fee estate to a trustee and names himself or herself as beneficiary. The beneficiary in turn controls the property and the actions of the trustee.

land use control Regulation of how individual owners use property in a municipality or planning district. Control patterns are generally in accordance with a master plan.

landlocked A parcel of property lacking legal access to a public thoroughfare; requires a court-ordered easement by necessity to relieve the condition.

law of agency A body of law defining roles, duties and responsibilities of an agent and a principal. Laws also set forth standards of conduct agent and principal owe to a customer.

lease A legal contract and instrument of conveyance which transfers to the tenant, or lessee, a leasehold fee for a certain duration. The lease contract sets forth all tenant and landlord covenants, financial terms, and grounds for default. The landlord is referred to as the lessor.

legal life estate A life estate established by operation of law rather than by the actions or wishes of the property owners. Examples are homestead law, dower, curtesy, and elective share.

legal title Full legal ownership of property and the bundle of rights as they apply to it. Contrasts with equitable title.

leasehold estate An estate that entails temporary rights of use, possession, and to an extent, exclusion, but not legal ownership. Compare *freehold estate*.

legal description A description of a parcel of property which accurately locates and identifies the boundaries of the subject parcel to a degree acceptable by local courts of law.

leverage The relationship between the yield rate of an investment and the interest rate of funds borrowed to finance the investment. If the yield rate is greater than the loan rate, positive leverage results. If the yield rate is less than the loan rate, negative leverage results.

liability 1. An accounting entry representing a claim against the assets of a business by a creditor. 2. A condition of vulnerability to lawsuits seeking redress for potentially wrongful acts or statements.

license 1. Legal authorization to conduct business. 2. An individual's personal right to use the property of another for a specific purpose. Revocable at any time at the owner's discretion. Does not attach to the property and terminates upon the death of either party.

lien A creditor's claim against real or personal property as security for a property owner's debt. A lien enables a creditor to force the sale of the property and collect proceeds as payment toward the debt.

lien priority The order in which liens against a property are satisfied; the highest priority lien receives sale proceeds from a foreclosure before any other lien.

lien theory state A state whose laws give a lender on a mortgaged property equitable title rather than legal title. The mortgagor in a lien theory state retains legal title. See *title theory state*.

life estate A freehold estate that is limited in duration to the life of the owner or other named person. On the death of this person, legal title passes to the grantor or other named party.

limited agency An agency relationship which restricts the agent's authorizations to a specific set of duties. The relationship usually terminates on performance of these duties, as in a real estate broker's listing agreement. Also called special agency.

limited partnership A business enterprise consisting of general and limited partners: general partners manage the affairs of the business while limited partners are silent investors.

liquidated damages In a contract, a clause that expressly provides for compensation a defaulting party owes the damaged party. In the absence of such a clause, a damaged party may sue for unliquidated damages.

liquidity The degree to which an investment is readily marketable, or convertible to another form of asset. If immediately salable, an investment is liquid; the longer it takes to sell, the more illiquid the investment. Real property is relatively illiquid in comparison with other types of investment.

lis pendens A public notice in a foreclosure proceeding that the mortgaged property may soon have a judgment issued against it. Enables other investors to join in the proceeding if they wish to collect their debts.

listing A legal contract that establishes and controls the dynamics of the agency relationship between principal and agent. The principal to the listing may be buyer, seller, landlord, or tenant.

littoral rights A set of water rights defined by state law relating to properties abutting navigable bodies of water such as lakes and bays. Generally, a property owner enjoys usage rights but owns land only to the high water mark. See *riparian rights* and *prior appropriation*.

living trust A trust established during one's lifetime in which the trustor conveys legal title to property to a trustee and names another party as beneficiary. The trustee discharges management duties and the beneficiary receives all profit and gain net of the trustee's fees.

loan commitment A lender's written pledge to lend funds under specific terms. May contain deadlines and conditions.

loan-to-value ratio (LTV) An underwriting ratio that relates the size of a loan to the market value of the collateral. The closer the loan value is to market value, the riskier the loan is for the lender , since the lender is less likely to recover the debt fully from the proceeds of a foreclosure sale.

lot and block system A method for legally describing property in a subdivision where lots are identified by block and number. A recorded metes and bounds or rectangular survey description of the subdivision underlies the lot and block system.

market 1. Buyers and sellers exchanging goods and services through the price mechanism. 2. The totality of interactions between supply and demand for a specific set of products or services in a particular geographic area.

market equilibrium See *equilibrium*.

market value An opinion of the price at which a willing seller and buyer would trade a property at a given time, assuming a cash sale, reasonable exposure to the market, informed parties, marketable title, and no abnormal pressure to transact.

marketable title A condition of title to a property where there are no claims, liens, or encumbrances clouding title or impeding the property's transferability.

marketing plan An agent's design for procuring a customer for a client, including selling and promotional activities.

master deed A deed used to convey land to a condominium developer.

master plan An amalgamated land use plan for a municipality, county, or region which incorporates community opinion, the results of intensive research, and the various land use guidelines and regulations of the state. Acts as a blueprint for subsequent zoning ordinances and rulings.

materialman's lien See *mechanic's lien*

mechanic's lien A junior lien enabling property builders, suppliers, and contractors to secure debt arising from labor and materials expended on a property. Distinguished by its order or priority, which is based on when the work was performed rather than when the lien was recorded.

meridian A north-south line used in the rectangular survey system of legal descriptions.

metes and bounds A method of legally describing property which utilizes physical boundary markers and compass directions for describing the perimeter boundaries of a parcel.

millage rate The ad valorem tax rate of a taxing district, derived by dividing revenues required from taxpayers by the district's tax base. If the millage rate is 30, the tax rate is 3%, or $3.00 per $100 of assessed valuation (net of exemptions).

mill One one-thousandth of a dollar ($.001). Used to quantify the ad valorem tax rate in dollars.

mineral rights Separable subsurface rights to mineral deposits; transferrable by sale or lease to other parties.

misrepresentation A statement or act, or failure to make a statement or act, that misleads a party in a transaction. May be intentional or unintentional. May warrant legal recourse or license revocation.

monument A fixed, artificial or natural landmark used as a reference point in a metes and bounds legal description.

mortgage A legal document wherein a mortgagor pledges ownership interests in a property to a lender, or mortgagee, as collateral against performance of the mortgage debt obligation.

mortgage financing Financing that uses mortgaged real property as security for borrowed funds.

multiple listing service An organization of brokers who agree to cooperate in marketing the pooled listings of all members.

mutual consent Consent by all principals to a contract to all provisions of the contract. A requirement for validity.

negative amortization A situation in which the loan balance of an amortizing loan increases because periodic payments are insufficient to pay all interest owed for the period. Unpaid interest is added to the principal balance.

negotiable instrument A legal instrument that can be sold, traded, assigned, or otherwise transferred to another party, such as a promissory note.

net lease A lease which requires a tenant to pay rent as well as a share of the property's operating expenses to the extent provided for in the lease contract.

net listing A listing which states a minimum sale or lease price the owner will accept, with any excess going to the broker as a commission. Professionally discouraged, if not illegal.

net operating income The amount of pre-tax revenue generated from an income property after accounting for operating expenses and before accounting for any debt service.

non-conforming use A land use that is not consistent with the current zoning ordinance. May be legal or illegal.
non-judicial foreclosure A forced sale of mortgaged property without a formal foreclosure suit or court proceeding. Authorized through a "power of sale" clause in a mortgage or trust deed document.
non-prorated expense An expense incurred by buyer or seller in closing a real estate transaction that is not shared with the other party. Examples include attorney fees, documentary tax stamps, and lender fees.
note An agreement to repay a loan of an indicated amount under certain terms.
notice of title Actual or recorded public evidence of real property ownership. See *actual notice* and *constructive notice*.
null and void Without legal force or effect. See *void*.
obsolescence A loss of property value because of functional or economic (external) factors. See *functional obsolescence* and *economic obsolescence*.
offer A proposal to enter into a binding contract under certain terms, submitted by an offeror to an offeree. If accepted without amendment, an offer becomes a contract.
offer and acceptance A process that creates a contract. Acceptance is the offeree's unequivocal, manifest agreement to the terms of an offer. The offer becomes a contract when the acceptance has been communicated to the offeror.
open listing A non-exclusive listing which pays an agent a commission only if the agent is procuring cause of a ready, willing, and able customer.
operating expense A recurring or periodic expense necessary for the operation of an income property. Examples include utilities, management, and ad valorem tax expenses. Excluded are debt service and the property's income tax liability.
opinion of title An attorney's or title officer's opinion of the condition and marketability of title to a parcel of property based on a recent search of title records by a competent party.
opinion of value See *broker's opinion of value*.
option A unilateral contract in which an owner, or optionor, grants a buyer or tenant, the optionee, a future right to be exercised before a deadline, in exchange for valuable consideration. The terms of the right, such as a right to purchase or lease, must be clearly stated and cannot be changed during the option period.
origination fee A lender's charge for funding a loan.
parallel See *base line*.
parol contract An oral agreement. Potentially enforceable if validly created.
partition suit A lawsuit requesting the court to alter or cancel the interests of a co-owner in a parcel of real property. Initiated when co-owners do not agree to make the change voluntarily.
party wall easement An easement appurtenant where owners of two adjacent properties share an improvement along the property boundary. The parties agree not to perform acts that would adversely affect the other party's interest in the shared improvement.
percentage lease A retail property lease which requires a tenant to pay a minimum amount of rent plus an additional increment that reflects the sales achieved by the tenant.
performance Fulfillment of the terms of a contract.
periodic tenancy A leasehold interest for a lease term where, in the absence of default, the term automatically renews itself until proper notice of termination is provided by either party.
personal property All property that is not considered real property; all property that is not land or permanently attached to land, excepting trade fixtures and emblements.
physical deterioration A loss of value to property because of decay or natural wear and tear. Exacerbated by deferred maintenance, or the failure to repair or maintain property on a regular basis.
planned unit development (PUD) A multi-use development project requiring special zoning and involving deed restrictions.
plat A map of one or more properties indicating each parcel's lot and block number, boundaries, and dimensions.
plottage An increment of value added by the assemblage of contiguous properties.
point One-percent of a loan amount, a lender's finance charge.
point of beginning (POB) The origination and termination point in a metes and bounds legal description.
police power A state's or local government's legal authority to create, regulate, tax, and condemn real property in the interest of the public's health, safety, and welfare.
potential gross income The maximum amount of revenue a property could generate before accounting for vacancy, collection loss, and expenses. Consists of total rent with full occupancy at established rent rates, plus other income from any source.
power of attorney An authorization granting a fiduciary the power to perform specified acts on the principal's behalf. Used to establish a universal agency relationship.
present value The discounted value of an amount of money to be received in the future that accounts for the interest that would have been earned if the money had been received in the present.
price fixing An act of collusion where competitors agree to establish prices at certain levels to the detriment of customers or other competitors.
price mechanism An interaction of supply and demand that determines a price a buyer and seller agree is the value of a good or service to be exchanged. A quantification of value in a transaction.
primary mortgage market Lenders and mortgage brokers who originate mortgage loans directly to borrowers.
principal 1. The employer in an agency relationship, to whom the agent owes fiduciary duties. 2. The loan balance to which interest charges are applied.
principal meridian A designated meridian in the rectangular survey system that is used in conjunction with a base line to identify ranges, tiers, and townships.
prior appropriation A legal doctrine granting a state the power to control and regulate the use of water resources within state boundaries.
priority See *lien priority*.
private grant A voluntary conveyance of property by a private party.
private mortgage insurance (PMI) An insurance policy, purchased by a borrower, that protects a lender against loss of that portion of a mortgage loan which exceeds the acceptable loan-to-value ratio.
probate A court proceeding to validate and distribute a decedent's estate to creditors, tax authorities, and heirs.
procuring cause A party who was first to obtain a ready, willing, and able customer, or a party who expended the effort to induce the customer to complete the transaction.
promissory note See *note*.
property An item that has a legal owner, along with the attendant rights to legal ownership.

property management The business of managing the physical and financial condition of an investment property for an owner.

proprietary lease A cooperative owner's lease on a unit in the cooperative building. The lease runs concurrently with the owner's ownership interest in the cooperative.

proration Apportionment of expense and income items at closing. Examples of items prorated between buyer and seller include interest, insurance, taxes, and rent.

public grant A voluntary conveyance of property by a government entity to a private party.

pur autre vie A life estate where the grantee's interest endures over the lifetime of another party named by the grantor.

purchase money mortgage A mortgage loan where a seller lends a buyer some or all of the purchase price of a property.

qualification 1. A mortgage underwriting procedure to determine the financial capabilities and credit history of a prospective borrower. 2. A listing and marketing procedure to determine the needs and urgency of a client or customer.

quiet enjoyment A right of an owner or tenant to use a property without interference from others.

quiet title suit A court proceeding to clear a property's title of defects, claims, and encumbrances.

quit claim deed A deed which conveys one's possible ownership interests to another party. The grantor does not claim to own any interest and makes no warrants.

range A north-south area bounded by consecutive meridians.

real estate Land and all manmade structures permanently attached to it.

real estate investment trust (REIT) An investment in which owners purchase shares in a trust which owns or acquires real property. Investors receive income and gain on a per-share basis.

real property Real estate and the bundle of rights associated with ownership of real estate.

reconciliation An appraiser's weighted blending of the results of different approaches to value into a final value estimate.

recording An act of entering into public title records any document or transaction affecting title to real estate. Recording gives constructive notice of one's rights and interests in a property and establishes the priority of inferior liens.

rectangular survey system A method of legally describing real property which uses longitude and latitude lines to identify ranges, tiers, and townships. Also called government survey system.

redemption period A statutory period after a foreclosure sale during which the foreclosed owner may buy back the property by paying all sums due the lender. See also *equity of redemption.*

redlining The illegal lending practice of restricting loans by geographical area.

refinancing Obtaining a new loan to replace an existing loan, usually to take advantage of lower interest rates, to obtain a longer-term loan, or to liquidate equity.

Regulation Z A fair financing law applying to residential loans; lenders must disclose financing costs and relevant terms of the loan to the borrower.

remainder A future freehold interest in a life estate held by a third party remainderman named by the grantor. When the life tenant dies, the estate passes to the remainderman. See also *reversion.*

replacement cost The cost of constructing a functional equivalent of a property at current labor and materials costs using current construction methods.

reproduction cost The cost of constructing a precise duplicate of a property, at current labor and materials prices.

reserve allowance An amount of money allocated from a property's income to cover future repair and maintenance costs.

restriction A limitation on the use of a property imposed by deed, zoning, state statute, or public regulation.

reversion 1. A transfer of title from a life estate tenant back to the grantor. 2. Proceeds from the sale of a property at the end of a holding period in a cash flow analysis.

revocation 1. Cancellation of a contract. 2. Cancellation of a real estate license.

right of redemption See *equity of redemption.*

riparian rights Water rights of a property that abuts a watercourse (stream, river).

sale contract A contract for the purchase and sale of real property containing all terms and provisions of the sale and describing the responsibilities of the parties.

sale leaseback A sale of a property executed simultaneously with a lease on the property from the buyer back to the seller as tenant.

sales comparison approach A method of appraising property that relies on the principle that a property is generally worth what other, similar properties are worth. See *substitution.*

salesperson A licensed employee or independent contractor hired by a broker to perform authorized activities on behalf of the broker's client.

scarcity The degree of unavailability of a product or service in relation to demand for the product or service. A critical element of value.

second mortgage A mortgage loan whose lien priority is subordinate to a senior, or first, mortgage.

secondary mortgage market Lenders, investors, and government agencies who buy, sell, insure, or guarantee existing mortgages, mortgage pools, and mortgage-backed securities.

section An area defined by the rectangular survey system and consisting of 1/36th of a township, or one square mile.

securities license An authorization to broker securities. The Series 39 and 22 securities licenses authorize licensees to broker real estate securities.

security 1. Collateral for a loan. 2. A type of personal property investment, for example, bonds, stocks, and mutual funds.

seller financing Any financing arrangement where a seller takes a note and mortgage from the buyer for all or part of the purchase price of the property.

seller's market A market condition characterized by an excess of buyers over sellers.

senior lien See *superior lien.*

servient tenement A property containing an easement that must "serve" the easement use belonging to a dominant tenement.

severalty See *tenancy in severalty.*

severance A conversion of real property to personal property through detachment of the item from the land.

sole proprietorship A business entity with an individual as sole owner. The death of the owner terminates the business.

special agency See *limited agency.*

special assessment lien A lien against property to secure a tax levy for a specific public improvement, such as a new road or sewer. Only properties benefitting from the improvement are taxed and liened.

special exception A land use in conflict with current zoning that is nevertheless authorized because of its perceived benefit to the public welfare.

specific lien A lien placed against a specific item of property rather than against all of an owner's property.

specific performance Forced performance of one's obligations in an agreement, to the letter of the agreement. A legal remedy for a damaged party to take against a defaulting party.

statute of frauds A law requiring certain contracts to be in writing in order to be enforceable. Examples are real property conveyances, listing agreements, and longterm leases.

statute of limitations A law which restricts the period during which a damaged party may seek to rescind or disaffirm a contract or take other legal actions.

steering The prohibited practice of channeling prospective buyers and tenants toward or away from a particular area..

stock sale A conveyance of an incorporated business through the purchase of the stock. Entails the purchase of all liabilities as well as assets. See also *asset sale*.

straight-line cost recovery An accounting method for deducting depreciation expense from income. Periodic cost-recovery charges are made in equal amounts over a depreciation period. For example, the straight-line cost recovery of a $5,000 item over 5 years would be $1,000 per year.

strict foreclosure A court proceeding which gives a creditor legal title to a liened property rather than cash proceeds from a court-ordered sale.

subagency An agency relationship between the client of a listing broker and other brokers and salespeople who have agreed to assist the broker in procuring a customer for the client. The assisting brokers are agents of the listing broker and subagents of the listing broker's client.

sublease A transfer by a tenant of portions of the rights and obligations of a lease to another party, the sublessee. The original tenant, who is sublessor in the sublease, is still lessee in the original lease and remains primarily liable to the landlord for fulfilling lease obligations.

subordination A voluntary or involuntary placing of a lien's priority below that of another. A mortgage lien, for example automatically subordinates to a real estate tax lien.

substantive contact Contact between an agent and others that is deemed relevant to a transaction; used as a benchmark to define when an agent should disclose agency status to a prospective client or customer . If a contact is substantive, the agent must disclose agency status at the time of the contact.

substitution An appraisal principle that holds that a buyer will pay no more for a property than the buyer would pay for an equally desirable and available substitute property. Forms the foundation for the sales comparison approach to value.

subsurface rights Rights and interests to whatever is beneath the surface of one's parcel of real property.

suit for possession A landlord's formal legal avenue for evicting a tenant.

superior lien 1. One of a class of liens that by law have a higher priority than any junior lien; all are tax liens. 2. A junior lien whose priority is higher than that of another lien.

supply The quantity of a product or service available for sale, lease, or trade at any given time.

surface rights Rights to the surface area of a parcel of real estate.

survey A formal measurement of the boundaries, dimensions, and elevations of a parcel of real estate performed by a professional surveyor. Required by lenders to identify possible encroachments, easements, and flood hazards.

survivorship, right of A surviving joint tenant's right to receive all rights and interests in the property enjoyed by another joint tenant in the event of the latter's death.

syndication A real estate investment structure in which investors provide capital and organizers provide management expertise to develop or acquire and manage investment real estate for profit.

tax base The total of the assessed valuations of real properties within a taxing jurisdiction, less the total of exemptions.

tax certificate An instrument that gives the holder the right to apply for a tax deed after paying taxes on a property and after a statutory period.

tax deed A deed used to convey title to property sold in a tax foreclosure.

tax district A local government entity authorized by state, county, or municipality to levy taxes for a particular purpose.

tax rate See *millage rate*.

tax sale A court-ordered sale of a property to satisfy unpaid real estate taxes.

tax shelter An investment that produces depreciation or other non-cash losses that a taxpayer can deduct from other income to reduce tax liability.

taxable gain Capital gain subject to taxation. See *capital gain*.

taxable income Annual income from an investment property that is subject to taxation, generally equal to net operating income plus reserves minus depreciation and interest expense.

taxable value The assessed value of a property net of all exemptions.

tenancy A freehold or leasehold estate held by a tenant.

tenancy in common An estate where each co-owner owns an electable share of the property and can transfer this share to any other party. Does not include right of survivorship; interests of deceased owners pass to heirs.

tenancy in severalty An estate in real property owned by a single party.

testate The legal condition of a person who dies leaving a valid will.

tier An area between consecutive parallels, as defined in the *rectangular survey system*.

time share A fee or leasehold interest in a property that is shared by owners who have use of the property at different times.

title Ownership of real property as well as evidence of such ownership; legal title.

title insurance A policy that protects the holder against loss arising from defects in title or documents conveying title.

title plant A duplicate set of title records copied from public records and maintained by a title company

title records Public records of real property documenting the history of ownership, claims, ownership, conveyances, legal descriptions, and surveys.

title theory state A state whose laws give legal title of a mortgaged property to the mortgagee until the mortgagor satisfies the terms and obligations of the loan. See *lien theory state*.

Torrens System A title recording system that registers title to property, as well as liens and encumbrances, on a title certificate. The certificate is the title and reflects everything there is to be known about the condition of the title.

township An area six miles square, bounded by two consecutive parallels and two consecutive meridians in the rectangular survey system. Contains 36 sections.

trade fixture A fixture necessary for the conduct of a business. Although affixed to the land, it is personal property.

trust A fiduciary relationship between a trustor and trustee. The trustor conveys legal title to property to the trustee, who holds and manages the estate for the benefit of another party, the beneficiary (in a land trust, trustor and beneficiary are the same person).

underwriting 1. A process of investigating the financial capabilities and creditworthiness of a prospective borrower and granting credit to a qualified borrower. 2. The act of insuring or financing a party, business venture, or investment.

unequal services Services that differ in nature or quality from those normally rendered, with the alteration based on race, color, sex, national origin, or religion.

unilateral contract An agreement in which only one party promises to perform, contingent on the other party's performance of an optional action.

universal agency A fiduciary relationship which empowers an agent to perform any and all actions for a principal that may be legally delegated.

usury Excessive or illegal interest charged on a loan.

utility A determinant of the value of an item reflecting the item's ability to perform a desired function.

vacancy A measure of the unoccupied supply of exiting space in a building or market at any point in time. A vacancy rate is the amount of vacant space divided by the total amount of existing space.

validity Legal status of a contract that meets requirements of: competence of parties, mutual consent, valuable consideration, legal purpose, and voluntary good faith. A prerequisite for enforceability.

value In general, the worth of an item as determined by its utility, desirability, scarcity, affordability, and other components and quantified as price.

variance A land use that conflicts with current zoning but is authorized for certain reasons, including undue hardship to comply and minimal negative impact to leave it alone.

void Without legal force or effect; unenforceable and null, such as an illegal contract.

void contract An agreement that is null and cannot be enforced.

voidable contract An agreement that is subject to being nullified because a party to the agreement acted under some legal disability. Only the disadvantaged party can take action to void the contract.

water rights Rights of a property that abuts a body of water to own or use the water. See *littoral rights*, *riparian rights*, and *prior appropriation*.

will Last will and testament; a written or verbal statement by a testator instructing how to distribute the testator's estate to heirs.

yield Investment return expressed as a dollar amount or a percent of the original investment amount

zoning ordinance A municipal land use regulation

INDEX

1031 exchange, 288
abandonment, 83, 97, 140
absorption, 221
abstract of title, 85
acceleration, 256
acceptance, 136
actual notice, 74
ad valorem, 299
adjustable rate mortgage, 276
adjusted basis, 290
adjusted sale price, 290
adverse possession, 83
advertising, 191, 267, 307
advisory services, 176
agency, 142, 148
agency disclosure, 153
agent, 143
agent compensation, 183
air quality, 113
air rights, 20
alienation, 256
Americans with Disabilities Act, 310, 386
amortization, 276
annualized percentage rate, 252
Annualized Percentage Rate, 266
anticipation, 225
anti-trust laws, 192
appraisal, 228
appreciation, 224, 289
appurtenant, 56
APR, 266
ARM, 276
arrears, 338
assemblage, 226
assessed value, 227, 299
assessment, 299
asset management, 398
asset sale, 194
assignment, 93, 137, 194
association management, 398
assumption, 256
bargain and sale deed, 78
base employment, 220
base line, 124
base parallel, 124
beginning basis, 290
benchmark, 128
beneficial interest, 46
beneficiary, 45
beneficiary statement, 332
bilateral contract, 138
blanket mortgage, 278
blockbusting, 307
bridge loan, 278
broker, 10, 142, 175, 177
broker cooperation, 175
Broker in Charge, 443, 447
broker protection, 168
brokerage, 175
brokerage service agreement, 454
Broker's Operational Procedures, 466
broker's opinion of value, 228
Brownfields Law, 319
building code, 109
building permit, 105
Bulk Sales Act, 196
bundle of rights, 18
business assets, 194
business liabilities, 195
business trust, 179
buydown, 276
buyer agency, 149
buyer representation, 161
C.L.U.E. Report, 205
CAN-SPAM Act, 191
capital gain, 288
capital improvement, 290
capitalization rate, 244
cash flow, 292
CERCLA, 320
CERCLA/Superfund, 117
certificate of occupancy, 109
CFPB, 333, 348
chain of title, 85
chattel, 19
Civil Rights Act of 1866, 307
Clean Air Act, 318
Clean Water Act, 318
client, 142
closing, 266, 330
closing costs, 335
Closing Disclosure (H-25), 268, 334
Closing Disclosure form, 348
cloud, 79, 85
code of ethics, 14
coinsurance, 388
collateral, 251
collusion, 192
color of title, 83
commingling, 188
commission, 163
commission splits, 183
common elements, 48
common law, 26
community property, 44
comparable, 232
comparative market analysis, 235
concurrency, 109
condemnation, 110
condominium, 48
conformity, 226
consideration, 133
construction loan, 277
constructive notice, 74
Consumer Financial Protection Bureau, 266, 268, 333, 348
contingency, 201
Continuing education, 446
contract, 91, 130, 199
contract creation, 135, 200
contract for deed, 208
contract termination, 139
contract validity, 132
contribution, 225
conventional loan, 273
conversion, 25, 189
cooperative, 51
cooperative association, 179
co-ownership, 39
corporation, 47
corporation for profit, 178
cost approach, 238
cost recovery, 287
counteroffer, 136
covenant, 62, 77
credit, 335
credit evaluation, 265
credit report, 265
credit scoring, 265
curtesy, 36
customer, 143
datum, 127
debit, 335
debt ratio, 262
debt service, 293
deed, 75
deed condition, 112
deed in lieu of foreclosure, 70
deed in trust, 46, 79
deed of trust, 79, 251
deed restriction, 61, 111
default, 96, 140
defeasance, 256
defeasible fee estate, 33
deficiency judgment, 70
demand, 213
Department of Housing and Urban Development (HUD), 273
Department of Veterans Affairs, 274

depreciable basis, 287
depreciation, 239, 287
designated agent, 151
devisee, 80
devisor, 80
disability, 311
disclosure, 146, 266, 326
Disclosure of Brokerage Duties, Responsibilities and Services form, 460
discount point, 253
discounted cash flow analysis, 295
discrimination, 267, 307
documentary stamp, 342
Dodd-Frank Act, 266, 333
dominant tenement, 56
dower, 36
down payment, 250
dual agency, 150
due diligence, 163
due-on-sale, 256
earnest money, 200
easement, 56
easement appurtenant, 56
easement by necessity, 57
easement by prescription, 59
easement in gross, 58
ECOA, 267, 309
economic life, 241
Education and Recovery Fund, 441
effective gross income, 243
Electronic Signatures in Global and National Commerce Act (E-Sign), 135
emblements, 24
eminent domain, 83, 110
encroachment, 61
encumbrance, 55
enterprise brokerage, 193
environmental controls, 112
environmental legislation, 115, 116
Equal Credit Opportunity Act, 259, 267, 309
Equal Opportunity in Housing poster, 310
equalization, 300
equitable lien, 64
equitable title, 73, 200
equity, 284, 421
Errors & Omissions, 364
errors & omissions insurance, 364
escrow, 200, 255
estate at sufferance, 37
estate at will, 37
estate for years, 36
estate in land, 30
estate in trust, 45
estoppel, 84
ethics, 324
eviction, 96
evictions, 396
exclusive agency, 160
Exclusive Right to Lease,, 492
executor, 80
executory contract, 139
express contract, 138
facilitator, 152
factory-built housing, 24
fair financing laws, 309
Fair Housing Amendments Act of 1988, 308
fair housing laws, 306
FAMC, 271
Fannie Mae, 271
Farmer Mac, 272
Federal Agricultural Mortgage Corporation, 272
Federal Home Loan Mortgage Corporation, 272
Federal Housing Administration, 273
Federal National Mortgage Association, 271
Federal Reserve, 269
fee simple, 32
FHA, 273
FHA-insured loan, 273
FHLMC, 271, 272
fiduciary duties, 144
Financial Institutions Reform, Recovery and Enforcement Act, 247
FIRREA, 247
fixture, 23
flood insurance, 268, 388
FNMA, 271
forbearance, 71
foreclosure, 52, 68, 256
foreign seller withholding, 204
franchise, 180
franchise tax lien, 67
Freddie Mac, 272
freehold estate, 31
full service lease, 94
functional obsolescence, 239
Functional obsolescence, 239
gain on sale, 291
gains tax exclusion, 291
general agency, 143
general lien, 64
general partnership, 47, 178
general warranty deed, 78
Ginnie Mae, 272
GNMA, 271
goodwill, 195
Government National Mortgage Association, 272
government survey, 123
graduated payment mortgage, 276
grantee, 75
granting clause, 77
grantor, 75
gross income multiplier, 245
gross lease, 94
gross living area, 229
gross rent multiplier, 245
ground lease, 95
group boycott, 192
guardian's deed, 79
hazard insurance, 255
heir, 80
high cost loans, 261
highest and best use, 226
holdover tenancy, 36
holographic, 81
home equity loan, 277
homeowners' association, 112, 323
homeowners' insurance, 255
homestead, 35, 300
homestead exemption, 300
Housing and Urban Development, 273
HUD, 273, 309
hypothecation, 250
immune, 300
implied agency, 138
implied contract, 138
inclusions, 394
income capitalization approach, 242
income ratio, 261
income tax lien, 66
independent contractor, 182
inferior lien, 64
insurance, 364
intangible tax lien, 67
intentional misrepresentation, 375
interest, 29, 252
interest-only loan, 276
intermediation, 269
internal rate of return, 295
internet advertising, 369
interval ownership estate, 53
intestate, 81
involuntary alienation, 75
involuntary lien, 63
IRR, 295

joint tenancy, 41
joint venture, 179
Jones v. Mayer, 308
judgment lien, 67
judicial foreclosure, 69
junior lien, 64
kickback, 334
land, 16
land contract, 208
land trust, 46
land use, 101
land use control, 101
landlocked, 57
law of agency, 142
laws of descent, 83
lead-based paint, 115, 117, 317, 319
lease term, 90
leasehold estate, 31
legal description, 120
legal life estate, 35
legal title, 73
lender closing requirements, 332
lessee, 36
lessor, 36
leverage, 283
liability coverage, 364
license, 61, 361
License Code, 468
lien, 55, 62
lien priority, 64
lienee, 63
lienor, 63
lien-theory, 250
life estate, 33
limited agency, 143
limited liability company (LLC), 47
limited partnership, 47, 286
limited services agreement, 162
liquidated damages, 140
liquidity, 282
lis pendens, 69
listing agreement, 157
littoral rights, 21
living area, 229
living trust, 46
loan application, 256
loan commitment, 265
loan constant, 262
Loan Estimate (H-24), 268
loan modification, 71
loan-to-value ratio, 258
lot and block system, 126
love letters, 326
LTV, 258
management agreement, 389
manufactured housing, 24
market allocation, 192
market data approach, 231
market equilibrium, 215
market value, 228
marketable title, 85, 86
marketing listings, 186
marketing plan, 187
Mary Rippy Violent Crime Offenders Registration Act, 485
master deed, 50
master plan, 102
mechanic's lien, 67
Megan's Law, 313
meridian, 124
metes and bounds, 121
mill, 301
millage rate, 299
misrepresentation, 147, 375
mobile home, 24
monument, 121
mortgage, 251
mortgage financing, 250
mortgage insurance, 255
mortgage lien, 63
mortgage market, 268
mortgage underwriting, 257
mortgagee, 251
mortgagor, 251
multiple listing, 162
mutual consent, 133
National Association of Realtors®, 181
National Flood Insurance Act, 268
negotiable instrument, 254
net lease, 94
net listing, 160
net operating income, 244
no-compete agreement, 194
non-agency, 161, 171
nonconforming use, 107
non-judicial foreclosure, 70
non-prorated, 337
nonresidential provisions, 496
note, 250
notice of title, 73
novation, 139
nuncupative, 81
obsolescence, 239
obtaining listings, 185
offer, 136
offer and acceptance, 135
Office of Fair Housing and Equal Opportunity, 309
offset statement, 332
OFHEO, 309
Oklahoma Administrative Code), 439
Oklahoma Broker Relationships Act, 446, 453
Oklahoma Fair Housing Law, 498
Oklahoma Landlord and Tenant Act, 490, 494
Oklahoma Real Estate Commission, 439
Oklahoma Statutes, 439
Oklahoma Sunset Law, 429
Oklahoma Tax Commission, 450
open listing, 160
operating budget, 382
operating expenses, 244
opinion of abstract, 87
opinion of title, 87
opportunity brokerage, 193
option, 206
optionee, 206
optionor, 206
option-to-buy, 206
package loan, 277
parallel, 124
participation loan, 278
partition, 43
party wall, 58
payee, 254
payoff statement, 332
percentage, 94
percentage lease, 94
periodic tenancy, 36
permanent loan, 278
personal property, 19
Planned unit development, 106
planning commission, 104
plat of subdivision, 109
plat of survey, 126
plottage value, 227
PMI, 255, 258
point of beginning, 121
points, 253
police power, 104
policy manual, 362
potential gross income, 243
pre-closing activities, 187
prescriptive easement, 59
price fixing, 192
price mechanism, 213
pricing, 186
primary mortgage market, 269
principal, 142, 252
principal meridian, 124
prior appropriation, 21
private grant, 75
private mortgage insurance, 255, 258

probate, 81
procuring cause, 164
promissory note, 250, 254
property, 18
property condition, 169, 312, 315
property maintenance, 385
property management, 7, 381
property manager, 8
proprietary lease, 52
prorated, 337
proration, 337
protection period, 168
provisional sales associate, 441
public grant, 75
pur autre vie, 35
purchase money mortgage, 277
qualification, 257
qualified mortgage, 260
quiet title suit, 79
quitclaim, 79
radon, 113, 318
range, 124
rate cap, 276
real estate, 17
real estate commission, 14
Real Estate Investment Trust, 287
Real Estate Mortgage Investment Conduit, 287
Real Estate Settlement and Procedures Act, 377
Real Estate Settlement Procedures Act, 267, 333
Realtor®, 181
reconciliation, 231
recording, 84
rectangular survey system, 123
red flag issue, 313
redlining, 308
Regulation Z, 266
REIT, 287
remainder, 33
REMIC, 287
rent setting, 383
replacement cost, 239
reproduction cost, 239
rescission, 139, 267
Rescission, 139
RESPA, 267, 333, 377
reverse annuity, 278
reversion, 33
right of redemption, 70, 303
rights, 19
riparian rights, 22
risk, 283, 359
RPCD Act, 481
Safe Drinking Water Act, 319
sale contract, 199
sales comparison approach, 231
salesperson, 181
scarcity, 214
secondary mortgage market, 270
Secretary-Treasurer of the Commission, 445
section, 124
security deposit, 92, 397
seller financing, 277
separate property, 44
servient tenement, 56
settlement reporting, 356
severalty, 39
severance, 25
Sherman Antitrust Act, 192
short sale, 71
single agency, 149
soil and water, 114
sole proprietorship, 177
special agency, 143
special assessment, 302
special assessment lien, 66
special exception, 108
specific lien, 64
specific performance, 96
Starker exchange, 288
statute of frauds, 134
statute of limitations, 134
statutory lien, 63
steering, 307
stigmatized property, 313
stock sale, 194
straight-line, 241
strict foreclosure, 70
subagency, 149
sublease, 93
subordinate, 65
subordination, 66
substantive contact, 154
substitution, 225
Superfund, 320
superior lien, 64
supply, 212, 217
supply-demand, 217
survey, 123, 332
survivorship, 42
syndicate, 286
take-out loan, 278
tax base, 299
tax certificate, 303
tax deed, 80
tax districts, 298
tax levy, 301
tax lien, 66
tax rate, 299
Tax Reform Act of 1986, 356
tax sale, 303
taxable gain, 291
taxable income, 287
taxable value, 302
taxation, 293, 299
tenancy by the entireties, 44
tenancy in common, 40, 481, 490
tenancy in partnership, 45
tenancy in severalty, 39
tenant, 31, 39, 90
tenant improvements, 386
term, 253
termination, 97, 137, 139
testamentary trust, 46
testate, 81
testator, 80
The Act, 453, 484
the License Code, 439
The License Code, 439
The Residential Property Condition Disclosure Act, 481
The Sex Offenders Registration Act, 485
tie-in agreement, 193
tier, 124
TILA/RESPA Integrated Disclosure Rule, 334
TILA/RESPA Integrated Disclosures Rule, 345
time-share, 53
title certificate, 87
title evidence, 86
title insurance, 86
title plant, 85
title records, 84
title search, 85
Title VIII, 308
title-theory, 250
Torrens, 86
township, 124
trade fixture, 24
transaction broker, 152
transfer tax, 80, 342
TRID, 334, 345
trust account, 188
trust deed, 251
trust fund handling, 188, 378
trustee, 45
trustor, 45
Truth-in-Lending Simplification and Reform Act, 266
unauthorized practice of law, 371
undisclosed dual agency, 150
unequal services, 307
Uniform Commercial Code, 196
Uniform Electronic Transactions Act (UETA), 135
Uniform Partnership Act, 45
Uniform Residential Landlord and Tenant Act, 98

Uniform Residential Landlord-Tenant Act, 397
Uniform Standards of Professional Appraisal Practice, 247
unilateral contract, 138
unintentional misrepresentation, 375
universal agency, 143
Urea formaldehyde foam, 318
urea-formaldehyde foam, 113
URLTA, 98
USPAP, 247
usury, 253
utility, 214
utility lien, 67
VA, 274
vacancy, 221
VA-guaranteed loan, 274
validity, 76
value, 224, 226
variance, 108
vendee, 199
vendor, 199
vendor's lien, 67
voluntary alienation, 75
voluntary lien, 63
warranties, 77, 320
warranty, 78
water rights, 21
wholesaling, 326
will, 80
wraparound, 277
zoning, 105
zoning board of adjustment, 107
zoning ordinance, 105

If you liked Principles of Real Estate Practice in* Oklahoma*, check out the other titles of Performance Programs Company!

Looking for a Oklahoma-specific real estate principles textbook? Get what all the students love -- Principles of Real Estate Practice in Oklahoma!

Principles of Real Estate Practice in Oklahoma is invaluable reference material for real estate professionals. Its 570-pages contain the essentials of real estate law, principles, and practices taught in real estate schools and colleges across Oklahoma.

Where can you buy Principles of Real Estate Practice in Oklahoma?
Principles Real Estate Practice in Oklahoma is available as a printed book or e-book through nearly all online retailers.

Cramming for the Oklahoma real estate exam? You need Oklahoma Real Estate License Exam Prep!

Oklahoma Real Estate License Exam Prep (OK-RELEP) is a 300-page modern learning tool designed to prepare real estate candidates to pass Oklahoma PSI licensing exam. OK-RELEP contains six different sections to provide the knowledge and practice necessary to succeed with both Oklahoma and national questions.

Where can you buy Oklahoma Real Estate License Exam Prep?

Oklahoma Real Estate License Exam Prep is available as a printed book or e-book through nearly all online retailers.

Struggling with real estate math? The solution to that equation is Real Estate Math Express!

Real Estate Math Express is a concise, easy-to-study test preparation guide to help real estate students improve their real estate math scores to pass the state licensing test. The primary feature of Real Estate Math Express is that it contains all necessary formulas and practice questions in 100+ pages.

Where can you buy Real Estate Math Express?
Real Estate Math Express is available as a printed book or e-book through nearly all online retailers.

Publisher Contact
Ryan Mettling
Performance Programs Company
6810 190th Street East, Bradenton, FL 34211
941-677-6043
ryan@performanceprogramscompany.com
www.performanceprogramscompany.com

www.ingramcontent.com/pod-product-compliance
Ingram Content Group UK Ltd.
Pitfield, Milton Keynes, MK11 3LW, UK
UKHW051417290926
15471UKWH00009B/1643

9 781965 482650